NEW SELECTED JOURNALS

1939–1995

also by Stephen Spender

Stephen Spender

NEW SELECTED JOURNALS
1939–1995

Edited by
Lara Feigel *&* John Sutherland
with Natasha Spender

faber and faber

First published in 2012
by Faber and Faber Limited
Bloomsbury House,
74–77 Great Russell Street,
London WC1B 3DA

Typeset by RefineCatch Ltd
Printed and bound by CPI Group (UK) Ltd, Croydon, CRO 4YY

A CIP record for this book
is available from the British Library

ISBN 978-0-571-23757-9

2 4 6 8 10 9 7 5 3 1

Contents

[v]

Plates

All photographs are courtesy of the Estate of Stephen Spender, unless otherwise detailed below.

Stephen Spender, Insel Ruegen, 1931
Isaiah Berlin and Natasha Spender, Geneva, 1946
W. H. Auden, Spender and Christopher Isherwood, Insel Ruegen, 1931
The reunited trio, Fire Island, 1947
Spender, Sonia Brownwell and Cyril Connolly in the offices of *Horizon*, c.1940
Peter Watson, c.1942
Wedding party in the studio of Mamaine Paget, 1941 (© Estate of Cecil Beaton)
Spender in Fire Service uniform, 1941
Post-war German ruins, Cologne, 1945
W. H. Auden, Cecil Day Lewis and Spender, Venice, 1949
Spender teaching in Sarah Lawrence College, New York, 1947
Spender with Jewish children, Israel, 1952
Stephen, Natasha and Matthew Spender, 1946
Matthew and Lizzie Spender with W. H. Auden, late 1960s
Tony Hyndman, Lake Garda, 1934
Reynolds Price, c.1964
Bryan Obst, 1976
Isherwood, Spender and Don Bachardy, 1970 (Photograph Eva Rubinstein)
David Hockney and Matthew Spender, 1979
Spender and Auden, London, early 1960s
The Spenders' golden wedding lunch, Mas de Saint Jerome, 1991

Introduction

Private faces in public places
Are wiser and nicer
Than public faces in private places.

W. H. AUDEN, DEDICATION TO
STEPHEN SPENDER, 1932

The private face of Stephen Spender has been occluded since W. H. Auden's appreciative 1932 dedication to his 'wiser and nicer' friend. Spender is now remembered less as an introspective poet than as a 1930s socialist, a 1950s cold warrior, or a 1970s campaigner for freedom of speech. In the 50 years of his post-war career, Spender acted as a public man of letters who spent more time at conferences, lectures and parties than he spent writing poetry.

This new selection of Spender's journals is intended partly to restore to Spender the private face of the poet, the lover, the husband and the father. For the first time, readers have access to Spender's intimate thoughts about his marriage, his children, his love affairs and his impending death. But even here the private face is seen more often than not in public. In a 1979 article on name-dropping, Spender described his own sense that he was in a double bind when it came to his private and public selves. He was aware that his chief interest lay in the fact that he had 'met the great' (Virginia Woolf, T. S. Eliot). Younger people saw him as 'a kind of satellite dropped from the outer space of death and coded with messages from immortals'. One student at a lecture had turned to him with 'a detached air of blank curiosity' and announced: 'Isn't it extraordinary that I am alive standing beside you who are surviving and who knew all those people. You might so easily be dead, and I would have missed them.' For people like this, Spender himself, in his private capacity, was of little interest. Yet he was aware of the dangers of accepting his public role and dropping the names of the truly great. 'If in company, I mention the name of a famous friend or acquaintance, dead or living, I know that I may be an involuntary player in a game at which someone present is scoring marks against me.'[1]

Here Spender describes a double bind that he is also grappling with in his journals, where he oscillates between his private and his public selves. He is torn between two projected readers: his own later self, who will be interested in his private thoughts and feelings, and the public, who will be interested in the people he knows and has known. For he was writing the journals with an eye to publication. He often rewrote journal entries, and he helped to edit published versions of parts of his journals for his 1978 collection *The Thirties and After* and for a 1985 edition of his selected journals. In a 1975 journal entry, Spender records a conversation with Pauline de Rothschild where she asks him if he is totally candid in his journals and he replies that he does not 'feel impelled to be – or, rather, I felt impelled not to be'. There are, he says, one or two things in his life that he does not write about because he does not understand them himself: 'for instance experiences of falling in love which seemed almost hallucinatory – perhaps a shared hallucination with some other person – and did not seem to touch reality at any point'. This is an oblique answer. The most obvious reason to avoid candour was not the unknowable nature of the self but the danger of public exposure.

In fact, though, the journals do include some candid personal analysis. Spender wrote almost every day for months at a time, so it would be extremely odd if he could have avoided the personal altogether. But he did tend to avoid the privately hallucinatory and focus instead on his public life. He always saw these volumes explicitly as 'journals' rather than diaries. There is little here to rival the intimate, meandering domesticity of the diaries of Virginia Woolf, or the scrupulous sexual honesty of those of Christopher Isherwood. Instead they are journals in the more public sense in which a newspaper can be called a journal. They are a record of Spender's times, written in part for an audience who saw him as a public figure and required him to drop public names. More often than not, the journals reveal Spender in public: attending international political meetings, giving lectures about poetry, or just wining and dining with the great and good of literary London and New York. This is

1 Stephen Spender, 'Drop Me a Name', *Observer*, 25 March 1979, p. 10.

itself fascinating; and it is, as Spender himself realized, what many of his readers will be seeking in the journals.

Spender knew everyone. The journals are revealing documents simply as a roll call of names. W. H. Auden, Isaiah Berlin, Elizabeth Bowen, Cyril Connolly, T. S. Eliot, Christopher Isherwood, Iris Murdoch, Virginia Woolf; Francis Bacon, Henry Moore, Giorgio Morandi; Alfred Brendel, Igor Stravinsky. 'The dead poets', Spender wrote in the name-dropping article, 'disappear into their names, and their names on the lips of those who happened to know them seem winged messengers.' For us, now, when most of the cast of the journals is dead, this is even truer than it was when he was writing. And readers approaching the journals looking for reminiscences of Auden, Isherwood and others should be satisfied with what they find.

So too, Spender was everywhere. As we look back on the dramatic events of the twentieth century, we find that Spender was involved in most of them: the reconstruction of Germany and the construction of Europe (as UNESCO's first Literary Councillor), the development of the cultural Cold War (as editor of *Encounter*), the founding of Israel, the anti-Vietnam movement in America. The journals offer a portrait of a lost age, not least because of the lost public stature of the poet. Spender was one of the last poetic elder statesmen. And because they expose a private face in a public place, they offer a revealing lens through which to view history.

This is an idiosyncratic and partial view of public events which gives us access to history experienced day by day, without hindsight. Except in the sections that have been polished for publication, the musings on contemporary public or political events tend to be transient, private thoughts in process. In October 1979, Spender recorded the 'worst day in history on the American stock market'. But the reader who turns to the history books or stock market charts for evidence finds only a minor blip, now consigned to footnotes by financial historians. For Spender, the alarm bells set off by this financial downturn were personal; he associated 1979 with the more serious crash, fifty years earlier, and conflated the two in his diary entry. The journals provide a personal version of sixty turbulent years of the twentieth century, hovering between diary, autobiography and history.

The best explanation of what Spender is doing in the journals comes from the preface to his own autobiography, *World Within*

World (1951). Here he describes autobiography as 'a story of two lives':[1] the writer who seeks to tell his own story recounts his experience of life 'from behind his eye-sockets' at the same time as he attempts to describe 'his life as it appears from outside in the minds of others'. In this account, autobiography divides into history (the world as seen by the subject) and biography (the subject as a historian of the self). It is just this double vision that we find in the journals. In fact, the journals sometimes feel like notes towards an autobiography; towards a sequel to *World Within World*.

Both the journals and *World Within World* take their place in a tradition of autobiography as history practised by Goethe, a writer greatly admired by Spender. Unlike Rousseau's eighteenth-century *Confessions*, which spawned an autobiographical tradition dedicated to capturing the unique self, Goethe's *Dichtung und Wahrheit* (1811–33) combines the poetry and truth of its title to suggest that the individual's importance lies partly in his historical consciousness. 'The chief goal of biography', Goethe announces in his preface, is 'to present the subject in his temporal circumstances', and to do this the autobiographer must 'know himself and his century'. Here Goethe describes himself in life and art as 'transported out of my narrow private sphere into the wide world', influenced by 'a hundred significant persons' and by 'the general course of the political world'.[2]

Goethe can be seen as the progenitor not just of Spender's autobiographical project but of his whole Germanophile generation. Where Woolf had sought in her impressionistic memoirs to locate the 'moments of being' that constituted the self, Spender, Isherwood and Auden returned from Berlin well versed in the German literary tradition, wanting to map as closely as possible the movements of their fractured political world.[3] The 1930s, the age that both defined and

1 Stephen Spender, *World Within World* (New York: The Modern Library, 2001), p. xxvi.

2 Johann Wolfgang von Goethe, *From My Life, Poetry and Truth*, trans. Robert R. Heitner, ed. Thomas P. Saine and Jeffrey L. Sammons, *Goethe's Collected Works, Volume 4* (Princeton: Princeton University Press, 1994), pp. 16–17.

3 See Virginia Woolf, 'A Sketch of the Past', *Moments of Being* (New York: Harvest Books, 1985), pp. 61–160.

was defined by Spender and his collaborators, was an era of politics, history and, perhaps more surprisingly, autobiography.

When *World Within World* was published, Spender was forty-two, and he joined his contemporaries Henry Green, Christopher Isherwood and Louis MacNeice in writing an autobiography under the age of fifty. For this generation, as for the First World War autobiographers Vera Brittain, Robert Graves and Siegfried Sassoon, the intersection of youth and history made youthful autobiography an urgent task; a vital first step in understanding a world that seemed to be bent on destroying itself.

These were autobiographies in which the self was pinned down by its place in society and politics, written in an era of facts. After the First World War, many writers came to distrust fiction. Facts became a political necessity which would prevent the public from being duped on a grand scale again. In 1937, three left-wing intellectuals formed the people-watching group Mass-Observation with the intention of counteracting the ignorance amongst the public that caused 'mass misery' and 'international shambles'. They were the anthropologist Tom Harrisson, the documentary filmmaker Humphrey Jennings and the surrealist poet Charles Madge (who would run off with Spender's wife Inez Pearn two years later). In their initial publicity, they claimed that they did not set out in quest of truth or facts for their own sake, or for the sake of an intellectual minority, but instead aimed 'at exposing them in simple terms to all observers, so that their environment may be understood and thus constantly transformed'.[1]

It was in this climate that George Orwell wrote his factual analyses of the working-class situation in northern Britain and the Spanish Civil War. And like Spender, Orwell observed himself as a prelude to observing his world. Orwell's Spanish book, *Homage to Catalonia* (1937), is comprised of a personal record of his own experiences in the war, combined with an analysis of the implications of these experiences for communism and twentieth-century history. Like Spender, Orwell took his own sensations seriously here, trying his best to record accurately what he felt, even if it involved extreme pain. When

---

1 Tom Harrisson, Humphrey Jennings and Charles Madge, 'Anthropology at Home', *The New Statesman and Nation*, 30 January 1937, p. 155.

he is shot on the battlefield, he announces that 'the whole experience of being hit by a bullet is very interesting and I think it is worth describing in detail'.[1]

Spender and Orwell's 1930s personal relations were ambivalent, but their artistic projects bear comparison. In 1950, Spender would praise Orwell for turning his life into a 'lived truth', stating that 'Orwell was *really* what hundreds of others only pretend to be': a classless, truthful socialist.[2] The two shared a belief in the value of honesty, about themselves as well as about their world. Spender like Orwell bemoaned the poverty of the unemployed, begging 'In railway halls, on pavements near the traffic', at the same time as he refused 'To make them birds upon my singing-tree'.[3] Spender, too, examined his own motivation as a first step to examining the world. In *September Journal* (1940), he finds that his fear of fascism can approach 'hysteria'. Disliking the obligations caused by the restraints imposed by the government, even in Britain, he dreads 'the idea of being ordered about'. Throughout the journals, he displays a willingness to think against the grain even of his own thought processes in his pursuit of honesty and exact, lived truth.

Occasionally, Spender used his journals to apply this honest analysis to the more intimate details of his life. And the interest of the journals, apart from as a portrait of a lost generation and a public world, lies in their intermittent revelations about Spender's attitude to love and death. In Spender's final two decades in particular, there are moments when the private face in a private place is exposed. In 1976, Spender, then aged sixty-seven, fell in love with a twenty-year-old student called Bryan Obst. For the first time in several hundred pages of journals, Spender broke the taboo he had explained to Pauline de Rothschild, describing that 'hallucinatory' experience of being in love. His times with Bryan were brief, and the affair itself had no future, but the transience itself was part of the joy; denied a future, he could experience happiness in the present tense. Departing from Bryan after three days together, he has the feeling that he 'got

1 George Orwell, *Homage to Catalonia* (London: Penguin, 2000), p. 137.

2 Stephen Spender, *World Review*, June 1950, p 51.

3 Stephen Spender, Poem XXX, *New Collected Poems* (London: Faber and Faber, 2004), p. 22.

out of the plane only to say goodbye', but realizes that 'this very feeling is what gives our meetings their timelessness. Thinking about each other, remembering every little thing, which becomes symbolic, always being happy and in holiday mood when we meet, considering the perfection of our affection for one another the norm – rather than the exception – that is our whole relationship.'

Spender also recorded with scrupulous honesty the effect of the affair on his marriage. Visiting Stephen in Nashville in April 1979, his wife Natasha overheard a telephone conversation between Stephen and Bryan, which was transmitted across the air-conditioning pipe. Tearful, she complained that she had come to America to be with her husband, but that he was engrossed in his own life and in love. Guilty and torn, Spender lamented in his journal that it was 'a relationship of between a week and ten days in a year – that is all I see of B and yet it spoils everything for N and that, I see, is destroying the relationship with B'.

Spender had been married to Natasha for thirty years. It was a loving marriage – loyal on his part, devoted on hers – which provided a warm home for the Spenders' children, Matthew and Lizzie, and continued to provide Stephen Spender with a secure base from which to lead a busy public life. But it did not preclude his falling passionately in love with a series of young men. Out of sensitivity to his family and to the men themselves, as well as out of a sense of his journal as a record of a public life, Spender did not generally mention these relationships in the journals. In the 1950s, Spender was ardently in love with Reynolds Price, but Price appears in the journals only as a neutral friend. Indeed, Spender assured Price in a letter that he was not describing the relationship in his journals. Spender broke his own rule in writing about Obst; the resulting pages of amazed, loving reverie are included in this volume.

Understandably Natasha Spender, who died just before the edition was completed, was reluctant to include some of these passages. The Spenders' was not a publicly open marriage; both Stephen and Natasha worked hard to keep his affairs out of the public eye. Natasha always insisted on the platonic nature of Stephen's friendships with men and on the truth of Spender's declaration in *World Within World* that after his relationship with Tony Hyndman he realized that he did not need male friendship 'on the same terms as before'.[1] Since Natasha Spender's death, we have decided to include these passages because an understanding of Spender's complex sexuality seems essential to an understanding of his public and poetic identity. His attempts to negotiate a compromise between heterosexuality and bisexuality, monogamy and freedom are also fascinating in themselves.

In these passages, Spender's journal seems to be in dialogue with Isherwood's recently published 1960s diaries, which anxiously and honestly interrogate the possibility of a lasting homosexual partnership in which one or both men is promiscuous. Spender is exploring the same problem, but from a position in which the promiscuity has not been accepted from the outset, as it was by Isherwood and his partner Don Bachardy. Where Isherwood was surrounded by bohemian artists in a predominantly gay enclave of Los Angeles, Spender was often to be found in the company of establishment politicians. In 1983, he would be knighted by the Queen. This was not a world in which he could produce a male lover without humiliating his family and damaging his own reputation. So too, Isherwood's or Bachardy's lust for other men need not negate their desire for each other. But for Spender to acknowledge his homosexual desire would be to renege on his shift of allegiance. This would expose Natasha to the possibility that he had never in fact moved from men to women at all, undermining the entire basis of their marriage.

Yet the writer who always considered himself foremost a lyric poet was not prepared to renounce love when it came. Instead, Spender tried to compromise, as he compromised in other areas of his life. He avoided asking too many questions about the funding of *Encounter* because the magazine itself was so clearly worthwhile. He exhausted himself giving lecture tours which left him with no time to write poetry because he accepted the need to support his family. And he compartmentalized some of the most intense experiences of his emotional life into a week or two each year because he did not want to puncture the myth of his conversion to heterosexuality and thereby to humiliate the woman he loved. For there is no doubt that Stephen Spender did continue to love Natasha throughout their marriage. His loyalty to her is evident even in the passage where he describes the

---

1 Spender, *World Within World*, p. 202.

disastrous visit when she overhears his conversation with Bryan. 'I certainly feel the force of N and her sense of a situation,' he writes here, hating the fact that he was making her unhappy 'due to my being what I am'.

Four years earlier, in another intimate passage in the journals, he records his guilt more explicitly in relation to allegations being made about Natasha and Raymond Chandler. In 1975, Natasha was sent an advance copy of Frank MacShane's biography of Raymond Chandler, in which she is described as being Chandler's mistress in the 1950s. Spender recorded in his journal Natasha's outrage and her flustered attempts to clear her name. He himself assured her that she could 'well afford to disdain the charge altogether'; even if it were true, 'it would be completely irrelevant'. For Natasha, always conventional and, in this case, anxious to retain the moral high ground in the marriage, it did matter. 'But I do happen to mind,' she berated him. And Spender acknowledged his own guilt in the situation. 'How awful this is,' he writes. 'My family are made to suffer [. . .] for what is clearly my doing. If I had not neglected Natasha for various young men in whom I was interested, she would never have confided in Chandler.' And now she was reliving her unhappiness about Stephen as well as feeling miserable about her present troubles; suffering again 'situations which are now presented to her as damnations'.

What emerges here is not just Spender's guilt, but his commitment to his marriage. Both Stephen and Natasha had married for life. Natasha was dismissive of a younger generation of women who gave up on their marriages at the first hurdle. She herself did not, as she once announced in an interview, shop for husbands at Selfridges. And in the end they survived. Bryan Obst died of Aids in 1990 (though Spender's first reaction to his death in the journals occurs in 1992). Spender died five years later, and they were years dominated by his gratitude to his family. A few months before his death, comparing himself to his 1930s contemporaries, he found that he had been 'far the luckiest in my personal life, made up by Natasha, Matthew, Lizzie – by all of these'.

In these final years, Spender was as honest and intimate about death as he had been ten years earlier about love. As he was asked more and more to act as spokesman or as medium for his dead friends, he started to feel that they had all 'walked through a door which through some kind of backwardness I have not walked through'. Indeed, it felt like 'belonging to some junior house of a public school, say, in which one will pass on to the upper house'; as always, Auden had got there first.

Spender had first become aware of death as an immediate possibility after a dramatic accident in 1980, when he slipped on a pavement and broke the ligaments in both his knees. At this point, he wrote a series of dislocated musings about the experience. Here he juxtaposed the physical pain with the trivial and morbid thoughts that went through his mind: the need to buy an avocado; the fear that all his assumptions may be misapprehensions. Facing his own death, he surveyed his life and saw only 'a dozen jewels on a refuse dump of failures'. He realized that his death would have no more significance than that of the other inhabitants of his ward, although his name attracted a 'far-flung notoriety' and would be evaluated in obituaries. As Spender balances the consolations of his family against his sense of professional failure, we see how difficult it is to be a posterity-obsessed atheist in the process of dying. He has not done all he hoped he would do, in those heady, promising days of the 1930s. Auden, he thinks, did more: he 'completed his *oeuvre*'. But nonetheless Auden in the end 'seemed far from happy'; 'even if he could think the poems were immortal . . . that was not his immortality'.

By the year of his death, Spender had become used to the sense of himself as an old man and resented the physical indignity it involved. 'One suddenly becomes an object – old – in the minds of friends,' he complained, minding that he now did the things he enjoyed doing 'with ever diminishing faculties'. He was experiencing old age as 'a kind of subjective impotence within the surrounding objective potency' and was sad that he could no longer see himself as a sexual being. 'I do not believe that writing or any other activity I am capable of can exist without sex. Therefore, I am in a state of panic that they no longer exist for me.'

Remorselessly confronting his ageing body, Spender began to face the prospect of his own cadaver, anxious that his death would leave Natasha 'a corpse-laden loner' burdened with disposing of his remains. 'Every death', he observed, 'is a kind of detective story with a corpse.' Imagining Natasha after his death, he seems to have experienced her grief, pre-emptively, as his own. 'I don't mind dying – but on the assumption that I predecease Natasha, some part of my mind is already in mourning for Natasha being left alone.'

In the final months of his life, Spender came to accept his shrunken world peacefully. He could no longer travel to America or Europe; he could no longer lunch and dine. Many of his friends were dead. The circumference of his world moved gradually inwards until it came to include only his home and his family. Death, which in 1980 had signified his lack of a place in the roll call of the truly great, now evoked the image of Natasha, abruptly bereft. The need for posterity dissipated leaving only the private face, 'wiser and nicer', of the private man.

LARA FEIGEL

Note on the Text

Stephen Spender wrote almost a million words of journal entries between his *September Journal* in 1939 and his death in 1995. In choosing only a quarter of these voluminous journals, we have tried to provide a picture of both the lives Spender located in autobiographical writing. The reader encounters both Spender the poet and Spender the biographer, as well as glimpsing Spender the private man. For the first time in a single volume, we see him making major trips to 1940s Germany, 1950s Israel, 1960s Russia and 1980s China. Here, as in Goethe's autobiography, the individual is in contact with important men, influenced by the 'general course of the political world'. In Germany, Israel, America, Russia and China, he met many of the leading political and literary figures of his age. This is a unique picture of the post-war world, presented through snapshots of the countries that shaped it.

On his numerous trips abroad, Spender acted both as a poet and as an official governmental figure. Depending on the occasion, he could be required to pronounce judgements on the imagery of T. S. Eliot or the intricacies of Cold War politics. In his official capacity, the radical poet of the 1930s was now required to conform first in Britain and then, as the poet laureate to the Library of Congress, in 1960s America. Spender was divided between the liberal left and the establishment in both countries. In the 1970s journals, he seems to be venting anger about the Vietnam War that he had to suppress when entertained by American officials in Washington. The world had changed since the 1930s, when radicalism was de rigueur within the intellectual community, and Spender had changed with it. But he was able to square his conscience through his impassioned defence of human rights and specifically the rights of writers in Soviet Russia. Sadly, the founding of the Index on Censorship in 1972 does not get much of a mention in the journals. The writer can become so swept up in the course of the political world that he does not have time to write about it.

In order to provide Spender's habitual readers with new material and to give a sense of the stages of his thought process, where possible we have used the earliest versions of the texts. This is not always an easy task. Although the journal entries themselves were written without hindsight, Spender was constantly revising his own work, including the journals that were not published in his lifetime. There are three versions of a summer holiday in Greece on a yacht with Cyril Connolly and Samuel Barber, which looks as if he was feeling his way towards writing a light-hearted novel about the experience. For five years during the 1950s he recorded onto a dictaphone and this led to more confusion. The dictated version always needed corrections, and sometimes he corrected twice, sometimes not at all.

Where multiple unpublished versions of the journals exist we have tried to use the earliest version, in the belief that it is worth putting up with some clunkier phrasing for the sake of authenticity. Sometimes the original manuscripts have been lost or it is unclear which is the original. The 1939 *September Journal* and the 1945 *Rhineland Journal* in particular have gone through numerous revisions and we have chosen to go with the earliest published versions of these texts. Both first appeared in Spender's own periodical *Horizon* within a few months of the events they describe and so have the immediate feel of a journal entry. The extract from *China Diary* comes from the book published in 1982 shortly after Spender and David Hockney returned from China, as there is no manuscript journal from this trip. A manuscript diary does exist for the trip to Israel which would produce the book *Learning Laughter* (1952) and so we have used this earlier version.

Several of Spender's journals have already been published, in revised versions. Apart from *China Diary* and *Learning Laughter*, the *Rhineland Journal*, with the more controversial remarks about Spender's mentor Ernst Robert Curtius removed, became part of his 1946 book *European Witness*. His travels in America and Paris became the 1969 *The Year of the Young Rebels*. A heavily cut version of *September Journal* appeared in *The Thirties and After* (1978) and a selected version of his journals up to 1983 was published in 1985, edited by John Goldsmith with the selections made by Spender himself. Spender corrected the text for each of these editions, with the benefit of historical and literary hindsight. As a result, except in the case of *China Diary*, the text in the present volume differs from the published books in style as well as content. Readers familiar with the later versions of the texts will find something unexpected here: a less certain tone and a more changeable point of view.

Where we have used unpublished journals, we have tried to keep the formatting and punctuation as close as possible to Spender's original text, adding editorial punctuation only where it is necessary to improve the clarity of the reading experience. This means that the text can have an unfinished or idiosyncratic quality (for example, when Spender misses out commas in lists) and can also be inconsistent (such as in the often rather Germanic capitalization). These journals were written over a fifty-year period and Spender's own style and conventions changed over time, partly in response to changes in the outside world.

The difference in content between this edition and the 1985 edition is pronounced, partly because it includes the final ten years of Spender's life, and partly because the focus of this volume is different. In the earlier volume, Spender chose to privilege his thoughts about poetry – his own and other people's. Here we are able to provide access to the more intimate thoughts and feelings of the private man. We have also chosen to focus on his life as a public intellectual who played a vital part in shaping the European literary and intellectual culture of his age.

Acknowledgements

The editors are grateful to the Stephen Spender Trust for the financial support that made this project possible and to Natasha Spender, whose passionate commitment to the publication of the journals sustained and galvanized the project throughout. It is sad that Natasha did not live to see the volume, which owes much to her tireless research and impressive recollection of the events and people described. We have been lucky to be aided by two extremely helpful research assistants, Miranda Stern and Natasha Periyan; Natasha's ingenuity in solving troubling footnote queries has been especially appreciated. Most of all we owe immense gratitude to Oliver Herford for his meticulous transcribing and proofreading, and to Matthew Spender, who has provided enormous help with the footnoting and has enabled the journals to be a much more interesting and important volume than they might otherwise have been. The warmth and encouragement of both Matthew and Maro Spender has meant a great deal.

NEW SELECTED JOURNALS
1939–1995

The British Prime Minister, Neville Chamberlain, declared war on Germany on 3 September 1939. In mid-July, Spender's wife Inez (née Pearn) had left him to live with the poet and sociologist Charles Madge.

The journal was first published in serialized form in Horizon *in 1940 and the original text is given here.*

SEPTEMBER JOURNAL

3 September 1939, London

I am going to keep a journal because I cannot accept the fact that I feel so shattered that I cannot write at all. Today I read in the paper a story by Seymour Hicks of a request he gave to Wilde after his imprisonment, to write a play.[1] Wilde said: 'I will write a wonderful play with wonderful lines and wonderful dialogue.' As he said this, Hicks realized that he would never write again.

I feel as if I could not write again. Words seem to break in my mind like sticks when I put them down on paper. I cannot see how to spell some of them. Sentences are covered with leaves, and I really cannot see the line of the branch that carries the green meanings.

It so happens that the world has broken just at the moment when my own life has broken. I mean not my life but my relationship with A— — [Inez].[2] Everything I read in the papers about broken faith, broken pledges, disloyalty, etc, seems about her. At the same time, not being a great statesman, I cannot use those words or call down

---

1 Seymour Hicks (1871–1949), British actor and theatrical manager. He was present in court when Wilde was being tried for indecency. Spender had been reading Frank Harris's life of Wilde (*Oscar Wilde, His Life and Confessions*, 1916). *De Profundis*, Wilde's 1901 prison letter to his former lover Alfred Lord Douglas, is clearly a strong influence on *September Journal*.

2 Spender used 'A— —' in his journal to disguise Inez's identity.

[3]

the curses of God on her. For all I know, God may be on the side of the faithless, in private life, at all events. Or rather, I don't mean God, but that the very introduction of moral ideas makes everything, at this stage, meaningless. The moment I start thinking of right and wrong, I think, they may have done me a wrong, but I wonder Are they happy? Perhaps they have the secret of happiness, which I have lost. Perhaps their enjoyment of happiness makes them right and makes everything in my own mind, which is an endless argument, irrelevant.

Anyway, I know that she cannot bear being with me when my forehead is split with anxiety. I drive a wedge through her on those occasions and she makes me feel that I am being cruel to her and almost treating her violently. [. . .]

I must put out my hands and grasp the handfuls of facts. How extraordinary they are! The aluminium balloons seem nailed into the sky like those bolts which hold together the irradiating struts of a biplane between the wings. The streets become more and more deserted and the West End is full of shops to let. Sandbags are laid above the glass pavements over basements along the sidewalk. Last night during the blackout there was a tremendous thunderstorm. We stood at the bottom of Regent Street in the pouring rain, the pitch darkness broken intermittently by flashes of sheet lightning which lit up Piccadilly Circus like broad daylight.

4 September 1939, London

Greenwood and Sinclair were on the wireless last night.[1] They talked about gallant Poland, our liberties, democracy, etc, in a way which raised very grave doubts in my mind. Greenwood even talked about fighting the last war to end war. Personally, I prefer Chamberlain's line to all this sanctimoniousness, which is that he has done his best to give Hitler everything but now feels that he can give nothing more. I dislike all the talk about God defending the right. God has always defended the right, and after such a long experience, he of all people

---

1 Archibald Sinclair (1890–1970), Liberal MP, and Hamar Greenwood (1870–1948), independent conservative MP. Both were staunch supporters of Churchill and anti-Chamberlain.

should realize the utter futility of it. Personally, if I were a close adviser of God, I'd press him to decide the issue one way or the other once and for all and not go on playing this cat and mouse game between right and wrong.

The whole point of being a man is that there is no omnipotence on one's side. One doesn't have to choose between good and evil, right and wrong, but between various kinds of evil. It is not a conflict between God and the Devil, Christ and Judas, but between the systems represented by Hitler and Chamberlain.

With all humility, I am on the side of the Chamberlain system against Fascism. The fundamental reason is that I hate the idea of being regimented and losing my personal freedom of action. I carry this feeling too far, in fact, I must admit I carry it to the point of hysteria – i.e. the point where I would really fight. I dread the idea of being ordered about and being made to do what I don't want to do in a cause I hate. This fear has even forced me into a certain isolation, in which I find that the personalities of my fellow beings often impose a restraint and unwelcome sense of obligation on me. [. . .]

Well then, if war is madness and Hitler is mad, why reply to madness with madness? Why fight? Why not be a pacifist? The answers are (1) That I am not sufficiently a mystic to believe that if Hitler won we would not lose the values which I care about – the possibility of individual development, artistic creation and social change. (2) That in politics, the possibilities of acting effectively are always limited to certain very definite lines. They are not, as some people seem to imagine, extended to every possible idealistic and Utopian attitude. Given a war like the present, a pacifist is simply a person who has put himself politically out of action, and, who in so doing is probably helping the other side. Possibly helping the other side may sometimes further the cause of ultimate peace, but in this war I don't see how it can. Of course, there is a great deal to be got out of refusing to touch evil, in the way of saving one's own soul and being an example to future generations. But actually, personal salvation and getting myself into a morally correct position superior to my contemporaries, don't appeal to me, perhaps because I don't believe in a system of rewards and punishments in an after life. If I ran away it would [be] because I wanted to save my skin or get on with my work, not because I felt that even the world at war was unendurably wicked.

[5]

5 September 1939, London

[. . .] Doubtless my own contempt for my father's recruiting speeches during the War is what undermines my faith in political arguments.[1] When I start a train of argument it is like one of those trains on the Berlin underground which strut confidently above the street on their raised viaducts, surrounded below by the tenements which seem to ask whether after all everything is going quite so well as the passengers, flashing through the slums, seem to think.

I shall try to recollect Germany as it was in 1929–1932 when I lived there for several months of each year. The people I knew there were not like the present rulers of Germany, not like the S.S. men, not like the army, though I think I understand the army. Germans have a greater capacity, I should say, than any other people, of evoking the idea of peace – Ruhe. To us and to the French, peace is a negative state when we are getting on with our business and private lives and are not at war. But to the Germans a state of peace is something positive and breathing and constructive, as opposed to a state of war. The positive idea of peace permeates a great deal of German romantic literature and music. Works like the slow movements of Beethoven's 2nd and 4th Symphonies are hymns to peace. They summon up a vision of a landscape exhaling peace. Dämmerung [twilight] is a peaceful word, and words like Heim, Heimat, Friede, Ruhe, [home, homeland, peace, quiet] are loaded with a greater weight of emotion than the corresponding words in other languages. Other peace-music is Schubert's songs, Beethoven's early piano and piano-and-violin sonatas.

Perhaps it is that the German landscape is particularly peaceful. I think of the Rhine at evening, the Harz mountains, the shores of the Alster at Hamburg with the heavy scent of lime blossom on a summer evening.

I have a German relative who is the wife of a U-Boat Commander. They live in Kiel, which has just been bombed. She plays the piano very well. Recently she came to London and she played an early Beethoven Sonata to us at my grandmother's flat. After she had

---

1 Harold Spender's propaganda work in 1916 was for War Savings, not recruitment. For Spender's father, see biographical appendix.

played the slow movement her face was streaming with tears. 'Excuse me,' she said, 'but this music is so full of peace.'

Ten years after the war, Germany was full of peace, it dripped with peace, we swam in peace, no one knew what to do with all the German peace. They built houses with flat roofs, they sunbathed, they walked with linked hands under the lime trees, they lay together in the pine forest, they talked about French art. Above all, everything was new, and everyone was young. They liked the English very much and they were sorry about the War. They talked about the terrible time they had during the inflation.

This was in Hamburg. I used to bathe, and I went to parties of young people. I had never enjoyed parties before and I never have since, but these were like living in the atmosphere of a Blue Period Picasso. Everyone was beautiful, and gentle, everyone was poor, no one was smart. On summer evenings they danced in the half light, and when they were tired of dancing they lay down in the forest, on the beach, on mattresses, on the bare floor. They laughed a great deal, smiling with their innocent eyes and showing well-shaped, but not very strong, teeth. Sometimes they let one down, sometimes the poorer ones stole, for example, but there was no Sin. I am not being ironic. There really was no sin, like there is in this kind of life in Paris or London.

Of course, it was all very superficial, it has been blown away now. I could not dance. I could not speak German. I stood rather outside it. I think now of the sad refugees who were the exquisite, confident Students of the Weimar Republican days. Perhaps it was all fictitious, but now in letting the mirage fade from the mind, I got very near to the truth, because everything in Germany is inclined to be fictitious. The German tends to think of his life as an operatic cycle emerging from a series of myths. There was the War, then there was the Inflation, then there was the period of Youth and the Weimar Republic, then there was the Crisis, then there was Hitler. Every German can readily explain him- or herself in terms of What We Have Been Through.

This passive attitude to life, the tendency to consider oneself a product of circumstances and environment beyond one's control, gives one the connection between the break-down of external standards and the private standards of people. A young man fighting in the Spanish War wrote a poem to his beloved, beginning:

'Heart of the heartless world.'[1]

He was either optimistic or very lucky. It would have been truer to write:

'Heartless one of the heartless world.'

I was twenty in those days, and I was caught up mostly with the idea of Friendship – Freundschaft, which was a very significant aspect of the life of the Weimar Republic. This, if it was frank, was also idealistic. It was not cynical, shame-faced, smart, snobbish or stodgy, as so often in England. It was more like Walt Whitman's idea of camaraderie.[2] I admit that I do not feel at all easy about this now, but I set it down for what it was. Two friends, young men, faced the world together, they camped, they travelled, they were happy in each other's company. There was usually a certain unpossessiveness about these relationships, a certain casualness, a frank and promiscuous admiration of beauty. The Germans had a reputation at that time of being homosexual, but I think it would be truer to say that they were bisexual, though there were of course a few of those zealots and martyrs who really hate women, whom one finds everywhere. But what the young, free, handsome German looked for in the world was a reflection of his own qualities in either man or woman. It was part of the myth that he should 'travel light' and have no responsibilities.

A life in which people are exercising sexual freedom without, apparently, anyone suffering or paying for it in any way, is attractive. One wonders how it is done. In this case, I think it was done at the price of making everything exist on the same level. The new architecture, the Bauhaus at Dessau, the social equality, the most casual affair, marriage, an abortion, a party, were all just the same. They were a pack of cards all of equal value precariously built up, so that when one fell, the whole house came down.

* * *

---

1 A quotation from Karl Marx and Friedrich Engels, *The Communist Manifesto* (1848). The British poet John Cornford (1915–1936) took it for the first line of his most famous poem, 'Huesca', written shortly before he was killed in action in the Spanish Civil War.

2 The American poet Walt Whitman (1819–1892) extolled universal brotherhood between men.

Again and again I had experience of the German ignorance of Jews. Later, when Christopher Isherwood and I were staying on Insel Rue-gen, and when the Nazis were doing exercises every evening in the woods and the 'movement' had become a serious menace, I got to know one or two of these men.[1] They were not gay, irresponsible, intelligent, like my Hamburg friends. They were heavy, stupid, but friendly and well-meaning. They seemed perfectly content to lounge round all day sun-bathing, listening to the band, going to the dance hall in the evening and having their girls in the pine trees afterwards among the hungry mosquitoes. But actually their fun lacked light-heartedness. For instance, when they sunbathed, they would build little forts for themselves on the beach, set up a flagpost, hoist a Nazi flag on it and gaze upwards in reverence. Whilst they were lounging round listening to the music, they seemed always to be waiting for a patriotic air, and when one was played, they would stand stiffly to attention.[2]

I was with two of them on some such occasion as this when sud-denly I lost my temper and said 'Ich bin ein Jude!'[3] They laughed incredulously: 'You a Jew? Impossible. Why, you're the perfect Nor-dic type,' said one of them. 'You're tall, you have blue eyes, fair hair, Scandinavian features,' said the other, 'that's why we know and like you.' This astonished me. 'Then what do you think when you meet a Jew?' I asked. 'We want to kill and destroy the pest,' they said, 'we want to crush him and knock him down.' 'Then knock me down,' I said. 'Here I am, I'm a Jew, please knock me down.' They looked at me, dazed and injured by the deceptiveness of this wolf in Nordic clothing. I felt quite sorry for them. Then I got angry: 'I don't believe you have any idea what a Jew looks like,' I said. 'You imagine a mon-ster when really you have to deal with a human being. I don't believe you know what you're talking about, and your heads are stuffed with stupid hatred and lies.' Probably I didn't know enough German

---

1 For Christopher Isherwood, see biographical appendix.

2 See Isherwood's 1976 autobiography *Christopher and his Kind* (chapter 5) and 1939 novel *Goodbye to Berlin* (section 3). Spender uses the episode, slightly altered, in his 1930s novel, *The Temple*, first published in 1988 (chapter 4).

3 'I am a Jew.'

to put it quite like that, but I worked myself up into a rage and rushed home to laugh with Christopher about it.

On another occasion someone made friends with me in a train specifically because I was of the Nordic type, and, indeed, now I know exactly the kind of warm response that a Nordic appearance arouses in some Germans. How can one understand the tremendous interest in appearance of a military race? A uniform face, in a uniform physique, dressed in uniform, and marching. In a way my Hamburg friends who wanted girls to be like boys and everyone to have a lovely face on a perfect body, had their craving for uniformity too.

Certainly, 1929 was the beginning of the slump and the end of the efflorescence of the Weimar Republic. [. . .]

6 September 1939, London

I want to go on about Germany, about my landlord in Berlin, about Curtius, but I feel too tired, I can't go on.[1] The first thing about any war is that everyone is tired, countries at war are countries of tiredness, fatigue becomes a spiritual experience. It becomes an illumination, fetters of habit which make one wash and shave every day, which make one preface every contact with one's neighbour with embarrassment, fall away, and one enters into a more easy relationship with one's fellow beings, an exhausted simplified state of being oneself. The wrong words which come into one's mind, which the rigid discipline of wakefulness would reject, are suddenly the right ones, everything flows freely and nervously, one does not even resent the heavy weight on one's eyes, because one sees so much light.

There was an air raid warning last night. A— — [Inez] seems so far away now, I imagine her in her red dressing gown and she looks pale and dazed. I don't imagine her happily. But I imagine her tenderly. Perhaps in a few days I'll be able to think about her without reproach. Perhaps I'll get tired enough during this war to forgive her.

I remember again the water, the flowing line of the hills, the rich harvest quality of Germany. Immediately, of course, I suspect it of a certain falsity, a certain coarseness and thickness and monotony of texture, but still it is there, there like Wordsworth's poem about the

---

1 For Ernst Robert Curtius, see biographical appendix.

peasant girl.[1] E—— took me all over the place.[2] He had a little car, and when he wasn't watching the road, his eyes were on me watching the effect of the storks on the roofs of North German villages, of monkeys playing at the Hagenbeck Zoo, of the Harz mountains. 'If you like music we shall have a great deal in common,' he said when we first met, and if ever I admitted for one moment that I appreciated anything, his eyes were ready to smile: 'Ah, we have a great deal in common.'

So we went to the Harz mountains stopping on our way at Brunswick where we saw in a very dusty and deserted gallery one of the finest Rembrandts I have ever seen. We visited some people called Harman who had a house in the Harz mountains. Like everyone else they had lost their money and all they had was the property itself and, I suppose, the salary of Professor Harman. The whole family, grandmother, son, daughter-in-law, a grandson, two daughters and a brother and sister who were fellow-students of Wolfgang, the son, at —— University, were there.[3] Like nearly everyone I met in Germany at this time, they were obviously living from hand to mouth, they spent what they had, they laughed and talked a great deal, and yet they had an air of having lost everything. Wolfgang had rather pinched, vague features which had a certain pallid, distracted beauty which attracted me at the time.

Several years later, after Hitler's rise to power, Wolfgang came to visit me in London. Earnest, and pale as ever, he had a mission: he wanted to convert me to Naziism. 'Of course, there are things I do not like about the Nazis,' he said. 'I do not agree with their views on literature and art. I do not sympathize with the persecution of the Jews. I do not accept their explanation of the Reichstag fire (though there is more to it than you would think). I do not like Goebbels'

---

1 'The Solitary Reaper' (1805).

2 'E——' is Erich Alport, 'a pale intent young Jew', who – while studying economics in England – invited Spender for his first extended trip to Hamburg in 1929. The event was epochal for Spender and is commemorated at length both in *World Within World* (chapter 3) and *The Temple* ('The Stockman House', chapter 1). It was Alport who introduced Spender to Curtius.

3 Wolfgang Harman is a pseudonym for Wolfgang H. Clemen (1909–1990), who had been a student and protégé of Curtius. After the war, he became a professor of literature at Munich and a distinguished critic of Shakespeare.

propaganda. In fact, I dislike everything nasty about them. But all the same, they have a Faith.' Here his fists clenched and his eyes burned with a dubious mystery. 'They have restored to us our belief in Germany and Life. Some of them are Idealists. There is a good deal of socialism in their economy.' I raged as I had done before. I told him that the most dangerous propagandists of Naziism were people like himself who pretended that they did not approve of its bad qualities and yet had accepted it. I told him he was a dupe, and that the Nazis wouldn't care a damn about his footling little qualifications to satisfy his own conscience, so long as they had got him where they had got him. I said: 'If I were a German, as I well might be, I would by now either be in a Concentration Camp or else deprived of every means of earning my living. You can't expect me to be fair. I don't care about your reasons.' And I am ashamed to say that I kicked him out of the house. [. . .]

But the most remarkable case was that of the young aristocrat I met in Shyah's rooms only a few months ago.[1] He was a Prussian and his name was Jobst. He had the fine looks of all these well-bred Germans, though in his case something seemed to have gone wrong. There were the blonde hair, the blue eyes, the well-defined bones and strong jaw, and yet in spite of its fine structure, his face seemed to have collapsed. Perhaps his mouth when in repose was almost too rich and well-formed, and when he moved it it seemed to become distorted and his lips to disappear inside his mouth. He was tall and strongly built, but his movements were so nervous, and the veins of his hands stood out so much and were yet so fine, that he seemed to be pulled the whole time by hundreds of fine threads. We talked about music, for which he had a passion. I remember that, for some reason, we discussed love in music. But the idea of Germany hung over us, because he was going back there the next morning. His mother who was travelling with him was waiting somewhere a few doors away.

We stayed up till three o'clock, Shyah and Jobst talking without ceasing. I got very sleepy, so sleepy that I lay down on the sofa and attempted to doze off from time to time. But the spirit of Horst, or Werner von L— —, of Wolfgang Harman, of Jowo von M— —, was

---

1 For Isaiah (Shyah) Berlin, see biographical appendix.

pacing the room, and would not let me rest. He did not really attempt to apologize when he said 'Excuse me for keeping you up, but we shall never meet again.' 'Oh, nonsense,' said Shyah. 'No, no. It's not nonsense. I know it. We shall never meet again. This is our last day of peace together.' He did not mention Germany. He only said: 'It is very sad to leave Oxford. I shall never see anything of this again.' Then he started once more on music, illustrating his conversation by singing, and conducting with his hands.

Next morning, he turned up again before breakfast. 'I have not slept,' he said, 'I went to bed at three, lay down for three hours, and got up at six.' 'Why did you get up so early?' 'Because it's my last morning and I shall never see Oxford again.' He held out his long, expressive, conductor's right hand. Other people called, but even when Jobst was silent it was impossible to escape from his drama. He did not rest. When he stopped pacing round the room, he knelt down, with those speaking hands of his touching the carpet. The worst of it was that he was not an actor, he was by nature a quiet, scholarly person, with a rich inner life. Seeing him act was as unexpected and shocking as, say, seeing one's father cry.

8 September 1939, London

When I come to think of it, the trouble with all the nice people I knew in Germany is that they were either tired or weak. The young people in Hamburg were tired, the young Nationalist aristocrats were weak. How are the people of good will today to avoid weakness and fatigue?

9 September 1939, London

Yesterday morning while I was waiting for a bus, some soldiers passed down the road singing 'It's a long way to Tipperary.' An unshaved and very ragged old tramp wearing the ribbons of several medals so loosely attached to his coat that they were almost falling off, said to me: 'They're singing now, but they won't be singing when they come back. Hearing 'em sing reminds me of when I went out to fight in them trenches. We went out singing, but we didn't sing for long.'

In the afternoon I got a taxi to Waterloo before going into the country. We were stopped near Southampton Row by five French-men carrying a flag and singing the Marseillaise. The taximan said to me: 'They won't be doing that for long.'

Peter Watson travelled from Paris to Calais a few days ago in a troop train.[1] The compartment was crowded with soldiers. They sat all the way in absolute silence, no one saying a word.

10 September 1939, London

'The best lack all conviction, while the worst
      Are full of passionate intensity.'[2]

W. B. Yeats, who wrote these lines, himself became a fascist sympa-thizer. He was prepared to accept the worst. He wanted strength at any price.

Why were the gentle and kind people I knew in Germany, tired or weak?

The tiredness of our generation consists in exploring unimportant and superficial aspects of the idea of freedom, without trying to discover the strong basis on which any really free life must be built. Freedom, the young people in Hamburg said, is sexual freedom primarily, then freedom to enjoy yourself, to wander, not to make money, not to have the responsibility of a family, or the duties of a citizen, generally. Freedom is one long holiday. They were tired. What they wanted, in fact, was a holiday.

Beware of people who explain themselves in terms of the difficult childhood they have had, the economic conditions of their country since the war, and everything, in short, that they have been through. Beware of people who say: 'You don't understand me.'

After 1929, it became obvious that the world of these irresponsible Germans was threatened.

      'New styles of architecture, a change of heart.'[3]

---

1 For Peter Watson, see biographical appendix. Watson had left his valuable collection of fine art in Paris.

2 W. B. Yeats, 'The Second Coming' (1920).

3 W. H. Auden, 'Petition' (1929). See also Spender's poem '1929' (1933).

The architecture was mostly swimming baths built with money raised from American loans. The change of heart, sunbathing and sexual freedom, was almost as uneconomical an investment as the new architecture. That's to say, although it produced a charming little shoot, it didn't take root in the stony and barren soil of the difficult post-war years.

I feel uneasy about discussing these things in an airy, Left Book Club manner, suddenly identifying myself with the Workers, in order to sneer at the people with whom I spend my week ends, and dismissing my own promiscuous past as though I have renounced it finally.[1] The fact is that I have just had a first class failure in my personal life, and I am so full of regret and bitterness that I cannot stay in the country because I dream of nothing else. [. . .]

A great cause of weakness today is people putting less important things before those that are more important, for example, personal relationships before work and an objective philosophy of life, sex before love. People who put personal relationships before their work become parasites on each other, form mutual admiration societies, agree to do nothing that may make one jealous of the success in the world of the other. People who put sex before love flee from one marital relationship to another, using love as their excuse; because, for them, sex has become a thing in itself, dissociated from personal relationships. They have an image in their minds of one hundred per cent sexual satisfaction, and when they are in love, they are continually asking themselves 'Am I satisfied?', and they are continually tormented by the thought that perhaps they are not. For them love, at first an opportunity, soon becomes a trap, forcing them to give something instead of taking all the time, and preventing them from grasping at the possibly greater delights they might get elsewhere.

Satisfactory personal relationships exist when the people who enjoy them have a satisfactory relation with society. They exist within society, they are not a conspiracy against society. In the same way,

---

[1] The publisher Victor Gollancz (1893–1967) founded The Left Book Club in the early 1930s to promote socialist opinions. Spender wrote *Forward from Liberalism* (1937) for Gollancz, but the final pages of this book did not meet with the publisher's approval.

satisfactory sex exists within love and can be attained through love, which means patience and loyalty and understanding.

Another cause of weakness is not to admit, but to pursue our failures blindly. There is such a thing as real failure in personal relationships and in sex. How easily then, that which symbolizes failure, the poor substitute improvised for love, becomes the most important thing in life! How people build it up and call the scars of failure their dazzling successes! Masturbation, homosexuality, following people in the streets, breaking up relationships because one has failed in one's own, all these compensatory activities form a circle of Hell in which people can never rest from proving that their failures are the same as love. Yet the lives of countless men and women show that the great compensation lies in accepting failures as failures, and recognizing substitutes as substitutes, and making the most of the rest of one's life. In fact the great artists and poets have almost without exception been failures in life. By this I mean that their relations with their fellow beings were really and truly at some point unsatisfactory, that most of them were fully conscious of this, and that their honesty in admitting a defect restored to their lives a sense of scale which hopelessly neurotic people lack. Baudelaire's relationship with a negress, the breakdown of Gauguin's marriage which led him to go to the South Seas, Van Gogh's failures in love, Rilke's wanderings and sense of being outside love, to mention only a few examples which immediately come to mind, were all real failures in life and to 'the man of genius' the failure to be a complete man must always be a humiliation. The compensations of genius are so dazzling that it is difficult to realize that Beethoven and Balzac paid so great a price, when they yet had the infinite privilege of being Beethoven and Balzac. They suffered as men, they rejoiced as creators.

The creative artist realizes that art is not a complete life, otherwise he would be self-sufficient, he would isolate himself from the world of ordinary living, and there would be happy, unreal artists creating a truly pure art. Some people, who are not artists, or who are bad artists, think that art is like this, a world cut off from the world, where aesthetic experience is everything. These are the virtuosi of art and of appreciation: spirits which have flowed completely into an aesthetic medium, without the friction of living their lives.

Of all the arts, music provides the most self-sufficient alternative world removed from the real world. Painting is the most objective of the arts because visual imagery always has a direct reference to real objects, and in order to get away from the broad day, painters have deliberately to paint visual experiences remembered from sleep – dreams. But music is not a dream that imitates our sleep, it is a world of its own, full of abstract aural patterns, which are not recognizably related to the noises we hear in everyday life. [. . .]

12 September 1939, London

Today I applied for a job as a translator at the War Office. Yesterday I received a printed slip from the Ministry of Information saying that my name was on a list of writers who may be used later. But I don't think I have a chance, as I'm told that they are very overcrowded with applicants. Nor do I think that the War Office will want me, as there must be many translators far better qualified. But as long as I can write and read a good deal each day, I am not really bothering. What I would like most is to complete three books, this Journal, a novel and a book of poems, before I am called up.

I want to remember all I can about Ernst Robert Curtius.

For some reason, E— — [Erich Alport] became very excited at the idea of our meeting. He therefore arranged that I should go specially to Baden-Baden in order to meet Ernst Robert. What I find difficult to explain is my own willingness to fall in with this proposal. It may have been that I had in any case later to meet my grandmother at Hamburg, so that it was quite convenient; or it may have been due to a certain trustfulness and credulity in my nature which I still pay dearly for, and which, in those days led me to fall in with every suggestion that was made to me. I might have been less willing had I reflected that Curtius might not want to see me.

This thought did not trouble me. I simply got out of the train, booked a room in a hotel and, as soon as I had washed, walked straight to the house where Ernst Robert was staying. I do not remember the details, I only remember the feeling of that first meeting. As far as I can recall the house was outside the town and I had to walk some way along a road past various hotels and then along a path through the edge of woods before I came to it. I think that I was shown into a room on the first floor, and perhaps there was a cold meal with fruit and wine laid on a table with a white cloth spread over it. There were bay windows opening out on to a balcony, and a pleasant freshness of the forest at evening filled the room. Everything, I think, gave me an impression of coolness, and for some reason I thought that the host and hostess were ill. The host, whose name I never knew, was dressed in a white suit, and both he and his wife seemed pale.

I did not stay long enough to get to know them, for Curtius immediately stepped forward, grasped my hand firmly and told his friends that he would go to a Bierhalle in Baden with me.

Railway journeys have a disconcerting effect on me. They stimulate me so much that all my usual impressions seem to flow much faster, with the train, like a film that is shown very quickly. I cannot check this. In spite of myself every sort of sensation pours through my mind during a train journey, and when I was younger and played at 'thinking books' a project for some unwritten novel or play would force all its images on to me during a journey. This excess of stimulation leaves me afterwards in a state of drugged tiredness in which I appear stupid to myself and either am able to talk revealingly, or else get confused in every word I say. I was in this mood that first evening, and I talked very freely and indiscreetly to Ernst Robert about my life at Hamburg.

He listened to me with an amusement which slightly yet affectionately was laughing at as well as with me. It forgave a lot. In my deepest friendships, with Auden, with Christopher Isherwood and with Curtius, I have been conscious of being thus 'taken with a pinch of salt'.[1] Sometimes it is disconcerting to be laughed at when one is serious, but as long as it is done affectionately, one is grateful to people who enable one to see oneself a little from the outside. From the first, Ernst Robert's attitude to me was one of gentle raillery; and I think that because he saw so far beyond me and at the same time loved me, I owe more to him than to any other older person.

Being anxious to impress him, I talked about literature, and especially about Dostoyevsky, whom I was reading then. I was interested in madness, partly because at school and Oxford I had been taught to regard myself as mad, and because Auden, who, when he was an

---

1 For W. H. Auden, see biographical appendix.

undergraduate, was anxious to maintain a certain superiority over his contemporaries, always treated me as a lunatic! Experiences like my cerebral excitement during train journeys, my excessive credulity, my lack of a complete understanding with even my best friends, so that I always felt they stood to some extent outside me – bore out the theory of madness. Above all, I was, like everyone, in search of that ecstasy which is so lacking in our civilization that even war and violence are to some people a secret consolation in a world of routine governed by material values; that ecstasy which justifies every kind of unscrupulousness and adventurousness in private life. In Hamburg E— —, with his collector's zeal had discovered an expressionist artist, a woman with a real talent for drawing, recently released from a lunatic asylum where she had done some really terrifying portraits of the lunatics. In Hamburg, she had done a portrait of me making me look wild and mad. I was proud of this, and took Ernst Robert to my hotel bedroom to see it. But, so far from being impressed or interested, he would scarcely even look at it. He said that it was mad and that I did not need to be mad.

During the next few days I walked much with him in the Black Forest, we went swimming together, we drank beer every evening. He criticized Dostoyevsky, he told me to read other books than the Russians, particularly the French. I showed him poems I had written, and, to my surprise, instead of reading them with the superiority which I might have expected from a scholar immersed in the world's greatest literature, he read them with evident delight, and made some translations of them, which were afterwards published in the *Neue Schweizer Rundschau*.[1] He listened to my accounts of my life at Hamburg, and scandalized me by treating this life which I thought of so seriously, simply as pornography in which he was unashamedly interested. But to him it was pornography, it was not, as it then appeared to me, ecstasy.

---

1 Curtius published his translations of poems by Eliot and Spender in the *Neue Schweizer Rundschau*. Founded in 1907, this literary magazine was edited before and after the war by Max Rychner (1922–31), a friend of Curtius. The readership was Swiss-German and scholarly, but it was also a way of publishing articles that might have irritated Nazis had they been published in Germany.

15 September 1939, London

I shall try to make this journal into a book with several levels of time, present and past, which I am able to move in as I choose. During these first days of the war I have tended to live in the past, partly because the present is so painful, partly because it is so fragmentary and undecided. We live in a kind of vacuum now in which the events on which we are waiting have not yet caught up on us, though our hour is very near. We have seen the whirlwind in China, in Central Europe, in Spain, in Poland, and now we ourselves are the next on the list. If I let my mind drift on the present, I have terrible day dreams. Last night, walking the streets in the blackout I had one of an aggressive alliance between Germany and Russia which would not only destroy the whole of the rest of Europe, but divide it utterly on questions of principle.[1] Another of my unpleasant day dreams is a growing fear that this is only the first of a series of wars. This springs from the following reflections. Supposing the Allies win the war, what sort of peace will they make? The answer is that they must either repeat the mistakes of the Treaty of Versailles, or else establish Germany as a strong power under a military dictatorship.

I think that this time they will probably plump for the military dictatorship. What they hope for, I suppose, is a military coup in Germany, whereby the generals will get rid of Hitler, and sue for peace. A smashing victory for the Allies would mean complete internal collapse for Germany, followed perhaps by a Communist Revolution backed by Russia, and probably a war of reactionary intervention which would be boycotted by the workers here and in France. I am sure they do not want that. They are hoping that the military caste in Germany will be pacific and reactionary. But I fear that they are wrong. Hitler has really transformed and stupefied Germany into a military camp, and we must choose between a socialist Germany and a more or less permanent state of war.

Supposing there were an aggressive alliance between Stalin and

---

1 In August 1939, Nazi Germany and Soviet Russia had signed the Ribbentrop–Molotov non-aggression pact, uniting the two totalitarian regimes against France and Britain. Russia's reversal of everything it had promoted hitherto provoked consternation among British intellectuals who had formerly sympathized with communism.

Hitler, on the understanding that Germany is socialized, you would then get a revolution dictated to the rest of Europe by the combined air fleets of Russia and Germany, and including the most rigid tyranny and suppression of personal opinion. In the long run, it might be a good thing, because at any rate it would mean the breakdown of this tragic cycle of rival nationalisms. But it would mean the surrender of everything we call freedom in our lifetime. If such a combination occurred, I think I would become a pacifist, because nothing would then seem to me worth fighting for.

I do not think these speculations are of much value, it is better to go back to the little world I have some concrete understanding of, and the only point in giving rein to the nightmare is to preserve a sense of proportion: to show I am aware of the fact that the life of myself and mine is like Lear's hut on the moor, in the thunderstorm, and filled with madness from within and without. [. . .]

18 September 1939, London

When our existences are threatened, the most sensible thing is to start living as though one could see beyond the darkness of the tunnel to the light outside. However closely one becomes involved in the struggle from day to day, one must have a long term view of the final issues for civilization, and also for reconstructing people's personal lives. Politics alter from day to day and therefore lack continuity: for this reason private life and personal standards become important because they have a continuity which one mustn't allow to be interrupted by outside events.

19 September 1939, London

With Curtius I was in contact with the Germany of Goethe, Hölderlin and Schiller. That is an Apollonian Germany, a Germany of the sun, not the Dionysian Germany of Hitler who rouses himself from a torpid dullness into a frenzy of words and actions. After the war and the blockade, perhaps even the Germans who lay with no clothes on, crucified by the sun, expressed the need for a Germany of 'Light, more Light'. [1]

---

1 'Licht! Mehr Licht!' Goethe's last words.

It was not the madness of Hölderlin that Curtius liked but the peaceful development of a poem such as 'Brot und Wein' in which the sun-steeped and vine-bearing German landscape is lifted at the end of the poem into a unity with the German conception of Greece. We read Hölderlin together, and later on the poems of the Greek Anthology, particularly the erotic ones, because he had a taste for such poetry. [1]

Curtius was an egoist, an egoist of the liberal, Goethe tradition. His life was organized with an enlightened selfishness: he did not take more than he could take, nor give more than he could give. He would not put himself out, even for his best friends, if he thought that his own resilience was going to be depressed by their needs. One could say, perhaps, that he was a fair-weather friend. Once, when I was hard up, I wrote asking him if he could introduce me to people in Berlin to whom I could give English lessons. He wrote back about other things, ending his letter with the curt 'Leider kann ich keiner Verbindungen für Ihnen im Berlin schaffen'.[2] I asked a friend of his about this, and he told me how, at a period of crisis and confusion in his life, Ernst Robert had cut himself off from him completely. I myself have a tendency in my relationships with people never to refuse anything, and often to promise far more than I can undertake. I know how this leads to a feeling of resentment which affects one's relationships with people, and to a fear of making new acquaintances who may plunge one into new commitments. Ernst Robert remained happy and broad and objective. He would not lose this by identifying himself with others in their predicaments.

I do not mean that he was unsympathetic, but that he was un-self-sacrificing because what he had was of too great an objective value to himself and to others to sacrifice. He did not enter into their lives because his generosity lay in the freedom with which they could enter into his.

---

1 One German interpretation of Greek mythology sees Apollo as reason and positive creativity – the sun. Dionysus instead represents something uncontrollable – the dark, demonic creativity of wine and intoxication. In other words, genius pulls in opposite directions. Curtius explains Hölderlin as manifesting both types of creativity; associating Hitler with the Dionysian aspect of the German imagination is Spender's idea.

2 'Unfortunately I cannot make any connections for you in Berlin.'

If one accepted this, he gave a great deal.

Once, when I was staying at Bonn, I went into Cologne for a night and got into an extremely nasty scrape. I liked going to very squalid places and I went to a hotel near the railway station, in the lowest part of the town. When I got into bed I didn't notice that the lock of the door was on the outside instead of the inside, so that the guests in this hotel were like prisoners locked into their rooms, instead of guests who could lock out intruders. In the middle of the night the door was flung open and a man came who put his hands to my throat and threatened to throttle me unless I gave him my money. He was much stronger than I, and I was undressed, so I asked him to pass me my clothes. He did this, and I gave him my money. It amounted to about 60 or 70 marks, which he did not seem to think enough, so he said he would take my coat as well. I protested, but it did not seem much use, so I asked him to leave me a mark at least, to pay my fare back to Bonn. He flung a mark down on the marble-topped table beside my bed, and ran out of the room. I lay in bed staring into the darkness and listening to the noises from outside of whores talking and screaming, and a continuous sound like water running away into the darkness. I felt as though I had reached the goal of something horrible and mysterious in my life, as though it were unfolded from my own flesh and a part of myself. I did not resent the theft, because I thought of it as something I had let myself in for. I did not blame the thief at all, for what had happened seemed an automatic consequence of my choosing this way of life, and, in short, I felt passive, as though a whole process which I had called into being by my own actions were now happening to me, and I knew that I would never escape from this. Because I knew this, it was very difficult for me to resist, but at last I realized that I must do something, so I sat up in bed and shouted for the landlord. A few minutes later, he and two or three other men came into the room, switching on the light, and standing round my bed as though I were an invalid, seriously ill, and they were the specialists whom I had summoned. 'Why are you making such a noise in my respectable hotel?' asked the landlord, in injured tones, 'until you came here, I always had the highest reputation. I shall call the police.' 'For heaven's sake, do call them,' I answered, feeling that I was now prepared for any kind of disgrace, 'I would like to speak to them very much.' This seemed to make him hesitate, and he said quite kindly, 'Why, what do you want then?' 'Someone in your hotel has just stolen all my money,' I said. 'This is a disgrace,' said the landlord, 'I won't have things like this going on in my hotel. Why do you come here and bring this disgrace on me?' 'It isn't my fault,' I answered, 'I am very sorry. I don't mind my money being stolen, but I must have my coat and also an assurance that my trousers won't be stolen, else I won't be able to get home.' 'Nothing else will be stolen,' said the landlord honourably, 'I can assure you of that.' 'Well, might I at least have my coat back?' I asked. He nodded to one of the other men who left the room and returned a few seconds later with my coat on his arm. Then he said 'Good night,' reassuringly, and they left the room.

I felt that nothing else was likely to happen, but I could not sleep, and continued to lie with eyes open in a waking nightmare. At last it was dawn. Then for the first time it occurred to me that when I arrived on the previous night, I had been made to pay my bill before taking a room. Therefore there was not the slightest reason why I should stay any longer. It surprised me to realize that I was free and that nothing final had happened. I quickly put on my clothes and ran downstairs and out of the hotel, without anyone stopping me. I ran until I came to the river. Outside it was cold and raw. In the grey light the cathedral and the bridges and the modern Exhibition Building had a photographic quality. Suddenly I started laughing. I had a gay sensation of release.

After an hour or so of waiting, I went back to Bonn. When I had rested and changed, I called on Ernst Robert, partly to borrow some money from him. When he saw that I was upset he took me for a walk by the Rhine. Full of shame, I told him my story. But to my surprise, instead of being shocked, disappointed or upset, he started laughing, and, putting his arm round me, patted my shoulder.

While I have been writing this last page and a half, I have had the wireless on, performing Hitler's latest speech. His voice varies from a cavernous rumbling to the peaks of an exalted hysteria from which he shrieks like a raucous beast of prey, until the whole chorus of his followers breaks into a stormy night's thunder of triumphant hatred. Undoubtedly there is something disintegrating about that voice, that applause, and everything they stand for. The cities of one's mind seem to be bombarded, as though a threat could make them fall to pieces.

He speaks of a new, terrible, secret weapon, which, if the English oppose him, he will use. When he does this, I feel as though the world could be destroyed by pressing a button, and he were a madman who had access to this button and was about to press it. [. . .]

29 September 1939, London

The probability is that Germany will come more and more under Russian influence, as her militarized state and economy become further socialized. This process will probably absorb all the near Eastern countries. Then our war will develop into a war of intervention against a revolutionary situation in central Europe. At the same time, the war in its early stages will provide the impetus for such a revolution.

The English communists have now twisted again and say that we should make peace on what they call 'the Russian terms'. I think that they are probably insincere in this. What they want is what Russia wants: i.e. to let the war go on, while dissociating themselves from it and using it as a means of getting their own ends. Unfortunately the continuance of the war not only suits the hidden communist aims, it is also essential to the British Empire. If we gave up, Germany and Russia would be able to dictate any terms they like in the East of Europe, France would become a minor power, the British would have lost all prestige, and the Dominions would adopt a policy of sauve qui peut, which would lead to the break up of the Empire. If the war leads to a Revolution under the influence of Russia, involving the whole of central Europe, we shall at least have a breathing space, as the Red Armies will be occupied in regulating this vast new internal situation.

Then what are we fighting for? I think that we ought to be fighting a kind of defensive rearguard action against the development of absolutely chaotic and brutal conditions. In a way, I think the German–Soviet Pact holds out a hope for the future because (a) It may lead to breakdown of the present system of warring nationalisms. (b) The larger the bloc becomes the less important becomes the Prussian element in it. If it extends from Moscow to Berlin, the rights of the Czechs will have to be considered. (c) Communism may, if it expands, recover something of its former liberating zeal. In short, the larger the movement becomes, the more likely it is to overthrow the tyrants who have started it. First Mussolini becomes a cypher, then Hitler, last perhaps Stalin.

In 1929–31, one saw for a short time clearly enough the direction things were taking. Then, for some people, the conditions they were accustomed to re-established themselves, there was 'recovery', and for ten years there was in England and France a precarious state of suspense. Now we see again the plot of our drama. But it may take a longer time than we expect to unfold itself.

* * *

The Blackout time gets a few minutes earlier each evening, so one notices more than ever the drawing in of the autumn evenings. Actually, the weather has been particularly fine lately, the streets glitter a biscuit yellow all day, the crowds waiting at the bus stops for the few buses give the town an air of festivity, the sand bags on the side walks, the strips of paper on the windows, the balloons in the sky, are all sufficiently new in the bright sunlight to be interesting and almost gay.

I went for a few minutes to a party after lunch, then feeling tired, and quite incapable of looking happy and keeping up a conversation, came home and lay down. I couldn't help imagining the comfort of her when her legs are drawn up against her breasts, her hands clasp her ankles, and her head rests on her knees, with the hair falling over them.

I am ashamed of these weak feelings. Weakness isn't going to help anyone today. It is only going to encourage a mood of self-pity which at once isolates people and drains away the energy around them. But after all I can't falsify things here. I am not writing down everything about myself as an example. Nor ought I to condemn myself. The important thing is to criticize and learn. I think that above all people ought to be courageous and strong today. For example, I ought to work all day. There is no excuse for my failure in this respect. What holds me back is of course the fear of writing badly, the fear of not being able to express myself, lack of inspiration and the pain involved when one discovers the failures in oneself. But all that is subjective. What one wants is people who can create more strongly than bombing 'planes can destroy and burn more fiercely with life than incendiary bombs do with death. We want strength, lucidity, a clear line in writing, intellectual conviction, faith in life, a calm indifference to systematized political thought. I ought to be the saint of such a task. [. . .]

The moon shines above the London streets during the blackouts like an island in the sky. The streets become rivers of light. The houses become feathery, soft, undefined, aspiring, so that any part of this town might be the most beautiful city in the world, sleeping amongst silk and water. And the moon takes a farewell look at our civilization everywhere. I have seen it as an omen in Valencia, Barcelona, and Madrid, also. Only the houses were not plumed, feathery, soft, there: the moon was brighter, and they seemed made of white bone. [. . .]

Spender was turned down for active service in the military on medical grounds. After being twice examined he joined the AFS (Auxiliary Fire Service) – later the NFS (National Fire Service) – in September 1941. He would serve until June 1944 as a 'fireman, first class'. His first posting, after training, was at Dyne Road, in North London. A longer retrospective account of his time in the fire service is included in World Within World *(chapter 5).*

28 December 1942, London

Some notes on Dyne Road sub-station of A.F.S.

Dyne Road had, more than any other community I have known, an atmosphere which had the characteristics of a group rather than of any single individual.

No one there was in any way remarkable or outstanding, though in the light of the whole place, the individuality of each person stood out. [. . .] It brought out the warmth, good-nature, humour of all the men. It provided a part, made a 'character' of everyone, to a certain extent a real one. This character which might have seemed unsympathetic in itself was pleasant in the chaff and tolerance of the men. [. . .]

Charlie, the sub-officer[,] is aged 65. He has a nervous flurried look on his fat face, which ought to be smiling and comfortable. He lives in constant terror of getting into trouble with his younger and efficient superiors who are forever introducing new rules into the fire service. He refers to the Divisional officer always as 'Him', with an obvious capital H. 'If He comes along, boys, we'll all be for it,' he says everyday, with regard to something or other.

For thirty years an ordinary fireman, Charlie cannot get used to giving orders and not taking them. He either treats us as though he were a person in an equal position, asking us to do something which he really feels he ought to do himself, or perhaps he grasses at us, or perhaps he invokes ''im'. 'It isn't me who's asking you to do this. I wouldn't write. It's nothing to do with me. It's orders come down from 'Im. If you don't get on with it, it's me what'll get the blame. So 'urry up and get on with it, do.' One day, when we were training, one of the trainees forgot to attend a Roll-call. 'Now one of you fellers didn't report this afternoon. They'll come down on yer for that. Follow my advice, and do what I say, otherwise you'll find yourself on a charge sooner or later. And please to treat me with a little respect when I tells yer to do something. Not so much of the "Charlie" this and "Charlie" that, either. If yer must call me something, call me sub.' 'Not so much of the Charlie,' became a regular joke with us.

The old hands do not altogether trust Charlie. They say that he is two-faced and will do nasty things to you behind your back. He certainly can turn nasty sometimes. But the worst crime they ever suggested he might commit was to put down the bells during the night when we were having supper. 'That's just the sort of thing that old sod would do,' they said.

Sometimes, they are really rude to Charlie. This happened twice in my time, though I was only present on one of the occasions. Charlie swore at old 'Pop' Wakeham for being in the kitchen when he should have been on guard. Instead of going back Pop Wakeham shouted at him: 'I'm not taking orders from you, nor anyone else here, Charlie. I've been on guards in my time which would teach yer something. There isn't any guard here compared with what I'm accustomed to.' Charlie went very red and looked old and helpless. He just made flabby gestures with his hand and could not say anything. [. . .]

Working class people never either exactly listen or not-listen to each other. Their senses seem fairly wide open all round them, and they observe a conversation much as they do the furniture in a room: they are aware of it, without taking much notice. If something strikes them as out of the way in the aural furniture which surrounds them, they pay attention naturally.

When they talk, they do so to please themselves. They don't expect anyone to listen, either, in the ordinary course of events.

If you make a joke and they don't laugh, never mind. What strikes you as funny, may not appeal to someone else. [. . .]

We lived in four army huts. One a recreation room, another a bunkhouse for sleeping in, the third, the kitchen and mess room, the fourth a lavatory.

We got up at 7.30. Breakfast at 8. Clean the place out from 8.30 till 9.45. Parade at 10. Drill 10.15–11. Then more cleaning till 1. After that nothing, apart from 2 hours short leave, unless one had duties of some kind.

Everything very dirty. Mud from the paths and duck-boards got into Rec room and kitchen and Bunkhouse. Cleaning up lavatories, spittle off duckboards.

Often I used to feel humiliated at having to spend my time like this. As I saw it, my humiliation was not personal, it was more a feeling that this was the only use they could put poetry to.

They were all exceedingly considerate to me, in many unexpected and uncalled for ways. They looked after each other. It would be true to say that we were like a family. They had an idea of me that fitted with their drama: that I was helpless, that I never swore, the legend attached to me was that I was 'connected with the B.B.C.' Those disembodied voices and noises talking like a madman to themselves out of the round box shaped like an empty face in one corner of the room, were the voices of Valhalla to the men. They used to say sometimes to me 'This must be giving you plenty to write about. You must write a book about us.' They usually called me 'Mr Spender' half seriously, half facetiously. They often used to refer to each other as Mr; this was also partly ironical, partly an attempt to recreate, or at any rate, parody civilian life, which most of them whole-heartedly longed for.

In their discussion of serious affairs, they were nearly always reasonable and sensible. One day the married ones discussed marriage. They did not think much of Dr Marie Stopes' thesis about periodic intercourse, though of course, they agreed with birth control.[1] Carr

---

1 Marie Stopes (1880–1958), pioneer of birth control and rational sexual relations in Britain; founder of the first birth-control clinic in Britain.

said: 'When you start off, you think that side of marriage matters a lot, but then after you go on you find that the interests you share in common are what really count.' They agreed that it's all a matter of 'considerateness' for each other which makes a marriage a success.

One day Pop Wakeham produced some photographs of Germans, with affectionate inscriptions on the back. He explained that the Germans were amongst the best friends he had. They all agreed that the Germans were 'just like us'. Someone said that when they were in the blitzes with bombs falling all round them, they never thought of the Nazis 'up there' nor wanted reprisals.

The Christmas Party

They spent at least a fortnight preparing the Rec room for this. The leading spirits were Burchfield, Cookey and Smith. Burchfield hung chains of paper across the ceiling meeting in a mass of paper flowers in the centre of the room then he made a trellis work of paper ribbons on all the walls. Then he stuck sheets of dark blue paper on the blackout boards across the windows, and stuck silver stars and a yellow moon on to these. In front of the windows there were orange paper curtains. Then they built a bar, stuck over in front with paper. They moved the stove from the entrance of the room to the back end, and then they painted it over with silver paint. They then constructed a most elaborate lighting system, with dozens of little lights half hidden in the paper decorations. They also had a spotlight at the end of the room near the stove.

This room[,] with its garish yet dingy purple and yellow and blue decorations, was a genuine product of proletarian art. It really expressed what the men whole-heartedly liked. They were all very proud of it and thought it very beautiful. [. . .]

When I was at the Training School we used to have a break every afternoon at 4 o'clock. We ran out of the school buildings down the road to a shop where we could buy cakes and tea.

Dressed in our blue dungarees, outrunning each other, and shouting, we all behaved and looked like rather dingy adolescent schoolboys, with pale complexions and, for the most part, needing a shave.

The blue dungarees smoothed out the excrescences of middle age and reduced our bodies to a teamish, schoolboy uniformity. Above the tunics our heads stuck out, looking prematurely lined with over-large features. Looking at one of us, you might have thought 'That's how he'll look when he's middle-aged': before, an instant later, you recollected that we were middle-aged.

One day, there was such a crowd at the teashop that I gave up the idea of tea and walked over to the pavement opposite the teashop where a few other men, either because they had had their tea, or with the same idea as myself, were standing.

One of these men was looking intently into a shop window. He had a worried, innocent look, with very pale blue eyes which had a fixed expression in his otherwise mobile face, with expressive lips and a creased forehead.

'I wonder 'ow much those cost,' he said, looking through the glass window.

None of his mates replied. The poor have a way of not answering remarks which they do not know how to answer. They don't snub you for them, or express annoyance, they just hand them back to you because they have no use for them.

As I have been taught that it is 'polite' to invent some kind of answer for any remark thrown out by anyone, I followed with my eyes the direction of the man's gaze.

Behind the polished window, which with reflections of the street outside cast an unreal glazed sheen over everything within, there was an array of tombstones lying on green corrugated rubber, evidently meant to insinuate grass. The graves were of the variety that looks like a bath tub filled with gravel, with a cross rising above the drain of the bath, where the taps, or rather, the drain pipe should be. The gravel or the imitation gravel was of an orange-brown colour, and the stone work was imitation stone, looking as if it were made of some kind of coarse rubber, whitened, veined like marble, or rochefort cheese, and stamped out by a machine into the shape of a grave stone.

'I wonder 'ow much one of them would cost,' the trainee said again. I looked at him, wondering also, without saying anything.

'Do you think you could buy one by instalments?' he said to his mates.

One of them said: 'What do you think we'll be having after this. The scaling ladder? Escapes!'

'Taut sheet!' called out another. This was a regular chestnut, referring to the order given when we had to jump off a roof onto a sheet.

'I'd 'ave liked to 'ave bought one of those for my wife,' said the man by the window.

'I 'ope we 'ave a lecture indoors,' said someone, shivering, 'it's bleeding cold.'

'My old lady w'd 'ave liked to be buried in one of those.'

'Time! It's half past four!'

They all started running back towards the school. I was left alone with the man.

'All the same, it doesn't make no difference. We never found the body,' he said, turning away. But he couldn't resist one more look. 'I do wonder 'ow much they cost.'

'We'll be late. We'd better get back,' I said, not so much to him as to explain to myself why I had started running.

After all, what could anyone have said?

In the immediate post-war period, Spender was dispatched on behalf of the Allied Control Commission to the British Zone of Occupied Germany. He made one trip to assist in the denazification of the country's libraries and another to report on the attitudes, during the war and under the Occupation, of German professors and intellectuals. This job was initially made difficult by a decree that there should be no 'fraternization' between occupiers and occupied, English and Germans, but luckily Spender was granted a special dispensation to talk to the Germans, who included his former teacher and mentor Ernst Robert Curtius – here referred to as 'Professor C——'. The Rhineland Journal *was initially published in* Horizon *in December 1945 and the original text is given here.*

RHINELAND JOURNAL

July 1945, Cologne

Cologne
At Hagen I had seen a good deal of damage, and again at Hamm, where most of the centre of the town was destroyed. Also along the route from Oenhausen there were bridges destroyed, detours, temporary wooden bridges touchingly named after some member of the Royal Engineers – McMahon's Bridge, Piper's Bridge, Smith's Bridge, etc; but it was in Cologne that I realized what total destruction meant.

My first impression on passing through was of there not being a single house left. There are plenty of walls, but these are a thin mask in front of the damp, hollow, stinking emptiness of gutted interiors. Whole streets with nothing but the walls left standing are worse than streets flattened. They are more sinister and oppressive.

Actually, there are a few habitable buildings left in Cologne: three hundred in all, I am told. One passes through street after street of houses whose windows look hollow and blackened – like the opened mouth of a charred corpse; behind these windows there is nothing except floors, furniture, bits of rag, books, all dropped to the bottom of the building to form there a sodden mass.

Through the streets of Cologne thousands of people trudge all day long. These are crowds who a few years ago were shop-gazing in their city, or waiting to go to the cinema or to the opera, or stopping taxis. They are the same people who once were the ordinary inhabitants of a great city when by what now seems an unbelievable magical feat of reconstruction in time, this putrescent corpse-city was the hub of the Rhineland, with a great shopping centre, acres of plate glass, restaurants, a massive business street containing the head offices of many banks and firms, an excellent opera, theatres, cinema, lights in the street at night.

Now it requires a real effort of the imagination to think back to that Cologne which I knew well ten years ago. Everything has gone. In this the destruction in Germany is quite different from even the worst that has happened in England (though not different from Poland and from parts of Russia). In England there are holes, gaps and wounds, but the surrounding life of the people themselves has filled them up, creating a scar which will heal. In towns such as Cologne and those of the Ruhr, something quite different has happened. The external destruction is so great that it cannot be healed and the surrounding life of the rest of the country cannot flow into and resuscitate the city, which is not only battered but also dismembered and cut off from the rest of Germany and from Europe. The ruin of the city is reflected in the internal ruin of its inhabitants; instead of being able to form a scar over the city's wounds, they are parasites sucking at a dead carcase, digging among the ruins for hidden food, doing business at their Black Market near the cathedral, which is the commerce of destruction instead of production.

The people who live there seem quite dissociated from Cologne. They resemble rather a tribe of wanderers who have discovered a ruined city in a desert and who are camping there, living in the cellars and hunting amongst the ruins for the booty, relics of a dead civilization.

The great city looks like a corpse and stinks like one also, with all the garbage which has not been cleared away, all the bodies still buried under heaps of stones and iron. Although the streets have been partly cleared, they still have many holes in them, and some of the side streets are impassable. The general impression is that very little has been cleared away. There are landscapes of untouched ruin still left.

The Rhine with the destroyed bridges over it had a frightening grandeur on the day when I crossed over the Engineers' bridge. There were black clouds broken by glass-clear fragments of sky. Gleams of light fell on the cathedral which, being slightly damaged, looks like a worn Gothic tapestry of itself with bare patches in the roof through which one sees the canvas structure. But it is the comparatively undamaged cathedral which gives Cologne what it still retains of character. One sees that this is and was a great city, it is uplifted by the spire of the cathedral from being a mere heap of rubble and a collection of walls, like the towns of the Ruhr. Large buildings round the cathedral have been scratched and torn, and, forming a kind of cliff, they have a certain dignity like the cliffs and rocks under a church close to the sea.

The girders of the Rhine bridges plunged diagonally into the black waters of the Rhine frothing and swirling white around them. They looked like machines of speed diving into the river, their beautiful lines emphasizing the sense of movement. Or where they do not swoop like javelins or speedboats into the river, broken girders hang from piers in ribbons, splinters and shreds, a dance of arrested movement. In the destroyed German towns one often feels haunted by the ghost of a tremendous noise. It is impossible not to imagine the rocking explosions, the hammering of the sky upon the earth, which must have caused all this.

The effect of these corpse-towns is a grave discouragement which influences everyone living and working in Germany, the Occupying Forces as much as the Germans. The destruction is serious in more senses than one. It is a climax of deliberate effort, an achievement of our civilization, the most striking result of co-operation between nations in the twentieth century. It is the shape created by our century as much as the Gothic cathedrals are the shape created by the Middle Ages. Everything has stopped here, that fusion of the past within the present, integrated into architecture, which forms the organic life of a city, a life quite distinct from that of the inhabitants who are after all only using a city as a waiting room on their journey through time: that long, gigantic life of a city has been killed. The city is dead and the inhabitants only haunt the cellars and basements. Without their city they are rats in the cellars, or bats wheeling around the towers of the cathedral. The citizens go on existing with a base mechanical kind of life like that of insects in the crannies of walls who are too creepy and ignoble to be destroyed when the wall is torn down. The destruction of the city itself with all its past as well as its present, is like a reproach to the people who go on living there. The sermons in the stones of Germany preach nihilism.[1]

Professor C— —
As soon as I had arrived in Bonn, I called on Professor C— —. Although half of Bonn is destroyed, his ground-floor flat was in an almost untouched part of the city, and he and his wife were still living there.

I had known C— — very well before 1933. He lectured in modern languages at Heidelberg and then at Bonn. He was one of the foremost exponents of French literature in Germany under the Weimar Republic and had written books on Balzac, the French Symbolists and Proust.

In the summer of 1931 a friend had given me an introduction to C— — in Baden-Baden. At this time he was a man of 45. We went for many walks together in the Black Forest, during which he talked much of literature. He was the only teacher I had (for he was, in effect, my teacher) who never lost sight of the direct connection between literature and living. It is difficult to define this, except to say that he talked about every subject concretely, which made one feel that one could grasp hold of and use it to enable one to live better one's own life. Another of his characteristics as a teacher was his clear grasp of what I could and could not learn. He never gave me the feeling that I ought to be good at things of which I had no understanding. He gave me instead a sense of both my limitations and my potentialities.

Shortly after I had first met him, C— — married. His wife [Ilse Curtius] had formerly been his student. After this I used to go every

---

1 'Sermons in stones', from *As You Like It*, II.i.17.

year or so to visit them, here at Bonn. He had an excellent library and many interesting things. He lived well, liking good company, good food and good wine. He and Frau C— — travelled much, particularly in France, Italy and Spain. He had connections with the outstanding writers and scholars of these countries and he was generally respected.

After Hitler's seizure of power it would have been easy for him to leave Germany and go to Paris, Madrid, Rome, Oxford or Cambridge. His position in Germany was made no easier by the fact that he had, in 1932, published a book in which he violently and even hysterically denounced the activities of the Nazis in the German Universities.[1] This book nevertheless was a defence of the German tradition, written in a nationalist spirit. Besides attacking the Nazis, it attacked the proletarianization of literature and it criticized the influence of Jewish ideas.

Since 1933, I have often wondered why C— — didn't leave Germany. I think really the reason was a passion for continuity, a rootedness in his environment which made him almost immovable. He had modelled his life on the idea of that Goethe who boasted that during the Napoleonic struggle he had been like a mighty cliff towering above and indifferent to the waters raging hundreds of feet beneath him. If he always detested the Nazis he also had little sympathy for the Left, and the movement to leave Germany was for the most part a Leftwards one. Above all, he may have felt that it was his duty, as a non-political figure, to stay in Germany, in order to be an example before the young people of the continuity of a wiser and greater German tradition. In spite of everything, he was very German.

From 1933 to 1939 I saw little of him because I was scarcely ever in Germany, but I remember staying with him for a few days in 1934. At that time he did not concern himself with politics, but his flat had become a centre where every visitor came and upbraided the regime, usually from a Catholic point of view. It so happened that I told him there were a few people in England who thought that although the Nazis stood for many things of which the English should disapprove, nevertheless there was an idealist side to the movement, and that

---

1 *Deutscher Geist in Gefahr* (1932).

Hitler himself was idealist unaware of the evil of some of the men around him.

C— — got up from the chair in his study where he was sitting, when I said this, and said: 'If you think that, come for a walk with me.' We went along the shore of the Rhine. When we had got almost as far as Godesberg, he stopped and pointing with his stick, said: 'Do you see that hotel? Well, that's the hotel where those rascals, Hitler with them, stayed a few weeks ago, and deliberately plotted the murders which took place on June 30th.'[1] (Incidentally, it was the hotel where Chamberlain later visited Hitler.) He looked at me with an expression of finality. Then, surprisingly, he burst out laughing. We walked back to the house.

During the next years I heard from friends that his life became increasingly difficult. At first he seemed indifferent to the Nazis and went on teaching, while refusing to do any of the things which the Nazis required of him. I suppose that later on he must have compromised to some extent, or he would have been imprisoned. Apparently he became more and more unhappy and was driven into greater isolation. Sylvia Beach, who saw him in Paris in 1936 or 1937, told me that then, before he would talk to her, he insisted on taking a taxi to a café in a suburb, and even then he kept on looking round to see if he was observed.[2] He had to stop teaching French and took to Mediaeval Latin. Then, finally, he gave up teaching almost entirely. He and his wife saw almost no one. His reputation became gradually smothered until he was scarcely known amongst the younger Germans. Ten years ago he was well known inside as well as outside Germany. Today, in Germany, he is only known to scholars.

The rooms which had once been well lit, pleasantly furnished, were now bare and dingy. As I came in through the front door, I saw another door on my right with a notice on it: NO ADMITTANCE.

---

1 The so-called Night of the Long Knives, on 30 June 1934, in which the Brownshirts or Sturmabteilung (SA) and its leader Ernst Röhm were liquidated on Hitler's orders.

2 Sylvia Beach (1887–1962), American publisher whose bookshop 'Shakespeare and Company' in Paris published a number of avant-garde books, famously including James Joyce's *Ulysses* (1922). Spender spoke at the bookshop, with Ernest Hemingway, in 1935. Spender recalls this Parisian occasion with Hemingway later in the journals on 20 November 1980.

FOR OFFICERS ONLY. This had been put up by the Americans who had requisitioned part of the flat when they were in Bonn. It was being kept up as a memento.

C— — was moved to see me. He took me into his library, now just a bare empty room with no carpets, very few books on the shelves, and just enough furniture for an alcove to be used as a dining-room whilst the other end of the room was used as a study.

We plunged very quickly into explanations. I said that I had come to inquire into the intellectual life of Bonn. C— — said that there was almost no intellectual life left in the whole of Germany, but that nevertheless it was important that I should talk to people and excellent that a writer like myself should understand what was happening in Germany.

Within quite a few minutes and before any of us had mentioned our personal histories during the past five years, we were talking about the war. C— — wanted me to understand that many students from Bonn had gone into the war not wishing to win, but fighting desperately. They fought for their country, but 'they had that monster on their backs – the Nazi Party. They knew that whether Germany won or lost, they themselves were bound to lose.'

C— — said rather aggressively that anyone outside Germany who maintained that it was possible for the German anti-Nazis to prevent war, should make a serious study of the effects of government by terror, propaganda, lies and perverted psychology in modern scientific conditions. 'You seemed to expect us to stand up or go out into the street and say that we opposed the war and the Party. But what effect could that have had except our own destruction? It certainly would not have stopped the war. It was not we in Germany but you, the democracies, the English, the French and the Americans, who could have stopped the war at the time of the Occupation of the Rhineland. We were all confidently expecting that you would do so at the time. What were we to think when you let Hitler march in?'

'Don't you think, then, that Germany is responsible for this war?'

'Of course,' C— — replied; 'it is absolutely clear that Hitler started the war. There is no doubt about that at all. It is the first fact that every German must realize. In spite of all Goebbels' propaganda, every German who says otherwise is either an ignoramus or a liar. The trouble with the Germans is that they have no experience of political freedom. Right up to the last century they were governed by ridiculous little princelings. Then they came under the Prussian militarists. They have never freed themselves from servile habits of mind. They have never governed themselves.'

I answered: 'I can quite well understand that the general mass of the people were first deceived and then terrorized by the Nazis. What I can't understand, though, is that no section of educated Germans ever put up any united resistance. For example, how is it that the teaching profession, as a whole, taught all the Nazi lies about race and deliberately set about perverting the minds of the young? I can't believe that this would have happened in England. A majority of English teachers would refuse to teach what they considered to be lies about history and biology. Still less would they teach their pupils to lie. And they would have refused to teach hatred.'

C— — shrugged his shoulders and sighed deeply. 'Although some teachers did in fact resist, right up to the end, nevertheless the profession as a whole was swamped by Nazi ideas. Alas, too many German teachers are militarist and nationalist in their minds before they are teachers, and they think of nothing but teaching discipline. Unfortunately this is also true to a great extent of the Universities.'

'If you condemn the whole teaching profession of a nation, surely that is very serious? It implies condemning the whole nation?'

'You cut off the head of a king several hundred years ago. The French also rose against their king and their aristocrats. The basis of freedom in the democracies is the idea that it is always possible to revolt against a tyrant. The Germans have never risen against a tyrant. Even today, it isn't the Germans who have risen against Hitler. The Germans always submit.'[1]

The C—s had many complaints about the Occupation. What struck me in conversation with them and with other intelligent Germans was the undiscriminating nature of these complaints. Some of the things complained about, though distressing, seemed inevitably the result of losing a war. For example, when Bonn University was occupied (Bonn was first occupied by the Americans), an American soldier was observed in the library tearing all those books which had been rescued from the fire, and which were laid on a table, out of

---

1 For Curtis's reaction to this passage see p. 202.

their bindings, and then hacking at them with a bayonet. On being approached by a Professor, he explained his conduct by saying: 'I hate everything German.' This story was circulated in University circles as an example of American barbarity. To my mind, it illustrates nothing except the stupidity inevitably attendant on war. In war, those countries which are invaded suffer from the defects of the invader's civilization. Thus places invaded and occupied by the Americans suffer inversely from the extravagance of American civilization. The Americans, accustomed to a climate of over-production, have been extravagant in their destruction of furniture, grand pianos, books, etc.

Some of the complaints I heard were almost frivolous. For example, in Bonn, people complained that the Americans were far too slow in liberating the Rhineland, and, particularly, Bonn. The story of the townspeople is that in the autumn of 1944 the Nazis were in full flight across the Rhine. Only the frightened S.S. men, out of panic, fired a few shots. At that the Americans made a full-scale retreat of fifteen miles and did not advance again until the spring of 1945. 'We can understand that American civilization is unwarlike and that the Americans do not want to practise military virtues,' a professor said to me, 'but you have no idea how difficult it is being conquered by a people who can't fight. Everything happens so slowly.' This kind of complaint, coming from an intelligent man, illustrates the amazing egotism of the Germans, which has now been accentuated by their having been cut off for so long from the rest of the world.

On two occasions I saw large American trucks (when the Americans were leaving Bonn) drive right over civilian vehicles which were parked against the pavement. In one case a car was transformed in an instant into the shape of a twisted biscuit tin, in another a cart was utterly smashed and the horse thrown wounded on to its back. In neither case did the American truck driver even turn round to see what he had done.

If one measures these things against the monstrous cruelties committed by the Nazis, they are, of course, nothing. I cannot make up my mind whether there is any sense in measuring them in this way. Yet it seems to me that a driver of a truck, when, chewing his gum, he drives over a German horse and cart, may perhaps have an image of Nazi crimes in Holland in his mind. The whole development of our time can, as it were, absorb a good many such small satisfactions in the way of revenge. But one should never lose sight of the fact that the one and only true measure of our actions is not a picture of the past, but one of a future in which it is possible for the peoples of the world to live at peace with one another.

The C—s complained a good deal about non-fraternization. How, they asked, could we influence the Germans if we were not allowed to speak to them nor they to us? Did we realize that Germany had been completely isolated from ideas outside the country for many years, and that now, unless we gave some lead and introduced our own ideas, Germany would be left in a mental vacuum? The Vacuum became quite a key phrase at this time. Finally it even occurred in a directive from Field Marshal Montgomery.[1]

C— — drew my attention to the contrast between our behaviour and our propaganda. Thousands of Germans during the war, especially during the last stages, had listened to the B.B.C. and to American broadcasts promising democracy, freedom, discrimination between our treatment of the good and the bad Germans. Was it in our own interest now to create the impression that our propaganda had simply been empty words and vain promises, like that of Goebbels?

Bonn

I left the C—s and walked back through Bonn towards the Officers' Transit Mess.

A pleasant road, overshadowed with trees, running parallel to the Rhine leads from the end of the road where they live to the centre of Bonn which, from this end of the town, may be said to begin with the University whose entrance bridges the road. On either side of this broad leafy road there were houses and hotels, many of them destroyed. Heaps of rubble often made it impossible to keep to the pavement.

Beyond the University gate everything, including almost the whole of the main old University buildings, the shopping centre and the market-place is destroyed. Over the gate the wall of the University

---

1 The policy of non-fraternization with German civilians was imposed on Allied troops by the US High Command. Initially soldiers were supposed to ignore even German children desperate for food. The policy was abandoned slowly and by degrees, with civilian administrators arguing constantly with the military that the policy did more harm than good.

stood, a yellow colour, surmounted by the gleaming gold statue of St George against the sky among the high boughs of chestnut trees. But there was nothing except charred emptiness behind this outer wall. Between the centre of the town and the Rhine everything had been smashed by shell fire in the last stages of the fighting. Occasionally I saw written on a wall some surviving Nazi slogan – 'VICTORY OR SIBERIA', 'BETTER DEATH THAN SIBERIA', 'WE SHALL WIN – THAT IS CERTAIN', or 'THE DAY OF REVENGE WILL COME'. There was something strangely evangelical about these slogans, and one would not have been surprised to see 'GOD IS LOVE' or 'ABANDON HOPE ALL YE WHO ENTER HERE' among them. Frequently there appeared on the wall a black looming figure with a question mark over his shoulder. At first I thought this might be one of the Nazi leaders, but it turned out to be a warning against spies.

By the banks of the Rhine, the beer gardens, hotels and great houses were all smashed to pieces. In a space amongst the ruins which formed a protected nest, there was a burnt-out German tank. Scattered all round it ammunition lay on the ground – shells the shape of Rhine wine bottles, still partly enclosed in their careful packings of straw and fibre.

The great bridge was down, collapsed into the river. Close to it, by a landing stage, an A.A. gun which had been used as an anti-tank gun, was still pointing with exemplary precision at the end of the bridge on the opposite side of the Rhine.

Bonn stank as much as Cologne or as the towns of the Ruhr. In addition to the persistent smell which never left one alone – like an over-Good Companion – the town was afflicted by a plague of small green midges which bred I suppose in all the rubble and also in rubbish heaps, for no rubbish had been collected for several months and in many streets there were great heaps of waste with grass and even tall potato plants growing out of a mass of grit and stalks and peel.

At night these small flies crowded thick on the walls of the bedrooms. At mealtimes they got into any and every drink. One night I went for a walk along the Rhine. When I returned, the sun had set and the flies lay like a thick bank of London pea-soup fog on either side of the river. They swarmed into my eyes, nostrils and hair, dissolving into a thin green splodge of slime when I tried to brush them off.

* * *

The Rector of Bonn University, Dr Konen, is a vigorous man of seventy.[1] He has a worn, thin narrow face with a refined spiritual expression. He also has a sense of humour. He likes to illustrate what he is saying with metaphors, parables, images, stories. But he does not become garrulous.

Konen lives not far from von Beckenrath in a house on the hills of Godesberg above the Rhine, looking out over the river towards the beautiful Siebensgebirge.[2] His house is old fashioned, crowded with furniture, but at the same time clean and bright.

Konen explained the situation at Bonn University since Hitler came to power during the war. He said that after 1933 the Professors were divided among themselves into several groups. There were those who actively supported the Nazis in trying to introduce a completely nazified education into the Universities; those who were active Nazis but who nevertheless retained a certain respect for objective values and for the tradition of the Universities which they wished should remain independent; those who were non-active Party members; those who were not Party members but who did not oppose the Party; those who remained detached from politics; and, lastly, those who seriously tried to resist the influence of the Nazis. He said that about half the teachers in the University never supported the Nazis, and that there were never more than 45 per cent who were Party members. On the whole, he thought that a high level of teaching was maintained.

I said that most observers in England had the impression that the minds of the young were poisoned by Nazi teaching.

He said that the young were confused, spiritually starved, but not poisoned in the simple and direct way that we imagined. 'Try and imagine what it was like for a young person to be educated in

---

1 Heinrich Konen (1874–1948), anti-Nazi physicist who had been forced out of academic work in 1933.

2 Erwin von Beckenrath (1889–1964), economist, at this date a senior professor at Bonn University.

Germany. If he became whole-heartedly a Nazi, he would be involved in endless duties and fatigues. His time would never be his own. He would be expected to break away from all loyalties to his home and family. His parents, if they wished him to be a Nazi, would have to surrender him body and soul to the Party. In the early days a good many young people were swept completely into the Movement. But later on it was not so. During the war many of my students have visited me. I can assure you that most of them have wanted nothing more from the future than a wife, a home and a job.'

As I was leaving the house, he stopped me at the door and said vigorously: 'I have every confidence that if I am asked to teach my students again, I shall be able to do so. I am not frightened of the students being beyond my control. A University represents a certain benefit to the community, like a farm, and as cows provide milk, so we professors can satisfy an intellectual need.'

Professor Cloos, geologist, whom I met in the classroom of an undamaged building of the University in a suburb, is a small temperamental man with untidy long hair and a sunburnt out-of-door appearance.[1] He has a very emphatic manner. He has thrown himself into the Civil Government, organizing educational activities. He has arranged such concerts and recitals as have recently been given for civilians in Bonn.

Like the other professors whom I had visited, I deliberately selected him for interviewing because he had a reputation for being opposed to the régime. He was emphatic in his defence of his students. 'The brown colour of the Nazis has spread less far than you imagine,' he said. 'In any case, the Rhineland is a part of Germany which has always resisted the Nazis most. I myself have always retained my influence over my pupils because they knew I was no Nazi. It was the Nazi professors who were not respected and who therefore lost their influence. Some of the students passionately desired Germany's defeat. Here in this classroom, there was a reunion of my students to toast the Allied victory when the Americans landed in North Africa.'

He said that several medical students evaded military service, not because they were cowards, but because they were always opposed

---

1 Hans Cloos (1885–1951), German geologist.

to the war. As a geographer he was able to help a few of them to escape into Switzerland by showing them on the map the places where it was easiest to cross the frontier. He said that academic youth had always been a centre of resistance to the Nazis.

Those were the statements of exceptional Germans, and they certainly do not represent the views of the ordinary German. They are the views of the few intellectuals whom Hitler always railed against because they never had faith in German victory and they always stood outside the German community.

Even these men had certain views which, I think, show the influence of ten years of Nazi ideology. For example, they all viewed the outside world entirely in terms of power. They interpreted the Zones of allied occupation strategically. The British zone was to them Die Brücke, the British bridgehead on the Continent. They noted that the decision of the British that they must occupy an area of the Continent from the mouth of the Rhine to the mouth of the Elbe, meant an abandonment of the former British reliance on the bridgehead of France. They did not think that we could afford ever to give up Die Brücke, and they therefore assumed that their fate and future were now cast together with those of Britain. They pointed out that the British, the Rhinelanders and the people of Hamburg had interests and characteristics in common, amongst which was to be counted a hatred of Prussia, and of the centralized government of Germany from Berlin. They regretted very much that we did not firmly and definitely announce our intentions with regard to Germany, so that they could envisage their future as part of the British Empire more clearly. For it was as part of the British Empire that they now were ready to see themselves, and there is nothing very striking about the question of a prominent catholic priest, Father R— — to me: Did I believe that, in ten years, the British Zone might be granted Dominion status?

Another attitude which they shared was a bitter and unconcealed resentment and fear of the French whose occupation of part of the Rhineland they regarded as the greatest of the indignities which they had to endure. The French, they said, were beaten, they were finished as a nation and as an Empire, and the resurrection of the corpse of France by the power of the Allies was intolerable to them.

Until the day of the atom bomb, they shared in common with

nearly all Germans, the view that Russia would eventually either occupy the whole of the European mainland or else be defeated by the Western powers. The habit of envisaging every situation in terms of power, forced their minds to this conclusion. They pointed out that the greater part of the American army soon would have left the Continent and then that the balance of power between Russia and the West would be altered decisively in favour of Russia. To the German mind, the conclusion that Russia will attack the West is inevitable.

Guilt

One morning I called on C— — again. He was sitting at his table which was piled up with many heaps of books. One of these was The Ondt and the Gracehoper, a fragment of *Finnegans Wake*. This contained many marginal notes by C— — explaining the derivations of some of the punning portmanteau inventions of Joyce. The book was inscribed to C— — by James Joyce.

For some time we talked about Joyce. Then he said: 'I want to sell this book, but I don't know how much it is worth.' I said 'I'll try to find out in London. But in any case you couldn't sell it there now, on account of various Exchange regulations.' 'That does not matter. In a year or eighteen months would do.' 'Why do you want to sell your books? Are you hard up?' 'No I'm not. And in any case there is nothing to buy in Germany. I used to like beautiful books and charming things, but now I want to get rid of them all. I have collected bad editions of all the books which I shall want to read during the rest of my life.' He pointed to some drab rows of books on his shelves. I said: 'I shouldn't sell your books, because in five years' time everything will be different, and then you will probably regret not having beautiful things.' 'No,' he said, 'I know it will be impossible for any German to get out of all this – with any dignity or self-respect – for more than five years. We have made ourselves hated all over the world, and now we are condemned to imprisonment in the ruin which is Germany. In five years' or in ten years' time I shall be an old man. I am already sixty.'

Later I discovered that he certainly had another reason for selling his things. He was afraid that during the coming winter his wife might need a store of cash in order to save them from starvation.

We talked of France. I told him that I had seen Sylvia Beach, who was formerly Joyce's publisher. I said that she had been interned during the Occupation of France. I told him that before the war I remembered seeing in her shop a beautiful girl aged 18 or so. This girl was Jewish. The Germans had ordered Sylvia to give her notice. Sylvia explained that she was an American and that as a citizen of the United States, she did not recognize the anti-Jewish laws. The Germans then interned Sylvia. The girl was put on a train for Poland. She was never heard of again.

I spoke also of my friend Gisa Drouin.[1] She also was Jewish and she had, while caring for her family in Paris, been subject to the laws relating to Jews. She had to wear the Star of David, to sit on a special bench in the park, to travel in a special compartment of the Métro, and she was only allowed to shop between certain hours in the morning. In order to keep her family, she had to shop at other hours, knowing all the time that if she was caught she also would be put on a train bound for Poland.

When I was in Paris in May I dined with the Drouins. Gisa sat at one end of the table, her husband at the other end, and opposite me was their little son, Georges, aged 10. Gisa started talking about the Germans when they were in Paris. She told how they made a special choice sometimes of deporting the oldest and the youngest member of a family, a grandmother and a grandchild, for example.

At this, Georges, who had been watching us with large eyes said: 'And they took away one of my comrades from school.'

'Yes,' said Gisa quickly, 'they took away a school friend of his aged 11, together with his grandmother, aged 75.'

'And we never heard of him again,' said Georges. On his mouth there was a strange expression, a frozen mouth of a Greek tragedy mask. We changed the subject and talked of other things.

There was a silence. Then C— — touched my arm and said: 'When you spoke of guilt a few nights ago, I wanted to tell you something. It is that the Germans are guilty of the most terrible crimes, and that they can build nothing new unless they repent of them.

'After the last war, when I was a young man, I was full of hope that we could build a new Germany. But we failed, and during these years

---

1 Gisa Drouin (née Soloweitschik) was the young Jewish girl living in Berlin who provided a model for Natalia Landauer in Christopher Isherwood's *Goodbye to Berlin* (1939). Isherwood met Gisa through Spender in 1930.

I have felt an increasing and indescribable disgust for this people. I have no faith in them at all. And as for myself, I know that I shall be an old man before we have recovered from this.

'What can we hope of a people who accepted as a slogan Goering's "Guns instead of butter", and who yet at the same time were so incapable of drawing conclusions that right up to the outbreak of war they were proclaiming "The Führer is so clever, he will never lead us into war"?'

Poles

Sitting on a bench under some trees, gazing out over the Rhine, with empty expressions on their faces were six men dressed in ragged Reichswehr [Germany Army] uniforms. I thought at first that they were German prisoners, but on talking to them, I found that they were Poles.

They talked very bad German, expressing themselves with uncouth, heavy gestures, rather than with words. Two of them were much younger than the others, and in their grey-blue uniforms, with their thin, pinched faces, looked like Picasso clowns of the Blue Period.

'You English are much too kind to these filthy Germans, much too kind,' one of them said heavily. Another of them took up his meaning: 'Now they all go round here, they all go round, every one of them, saying "I was never a Nazi, no I was never a Nazi."' A third went on: 'They all take off their hats, they all bow. They can't be kind enough to you, not friendly enough.'

'But what were they like before?' This chorus went on, passing from one to another of them, taken up from mouth to mouth, while, when one was speaking, the others relapsed into morose silence: 'We were herded together like cattle. We were made to work like slaves.' 'Nothing was bad enough for us.' 'When we arrived in trucks at railway stations, the children used to gather around us and shout "Dirty Polack!" "Filthy Polack!"' 'We never received a kind word from anyone.' 'We were here for five years, and no one ever looked at us nicely or showed us a kind act. Not one.'

The oldest man said: 'Thirty thousand people were killed in the town where we came from. My son is here with me.' 'Yes,' said his son, 'I am with my father, but we know nothing of my mother and my sister. All the others here have lost all their relatives.'

There was a silence, then one of them said: 'We were paid 20 marks a month for our labour, but most even of that was taken away.' 'Look, two of us were told to unload a whole railway wagon in a morning.' 'If we couldn't do it, we were fined of our wages.'

'We would sooner work twenty years under the Americans or the British than for one year under the Germans.'

Some conclusions
It is surely true that there exists now, in all the world, an international of well-intentioned men and women. If I were to define all their characteristics, I would say that they were not necessarily either democratic or anti-democratic, left or right, or the representatives of any class. On the whole, though, they regard the evils of the democratic systems of government as decisively less than those of the authoritarian ones, their sympathies are more often towards the Left than towards the Right (although not always so), and a proof of their good will is a serious concern with the welfare of ordinary people. Their conscious or unconscious faith is Christianity, and probably the most serious division of opinion between these people of good will is as to whether they regard human nature as more good than bad or more bad than good. But as to aims they would agree that at this stage in the world's history any sacrifice of nationalist or class interest is not only justified but necessary if it is in the interests of establishing peace; that all aggressive nationalist intentions are to be absolutely condemned; that civilization can only be saved if it is founded on a double security of peace and social justice. Above all, these people feel that it is their duty to express and make clear these aims which are already in men's hearts and minds, so that when it becomes clear that they are in fact the deepest wishes of all people in all nations, the doubt and suspicion and self-interest which obstruct their being fulfilled will be the more easily cleared away.

If the previous paragraph sketches a state of mind which is very widespread and which indeed predominates in every international conference which I have ever attended (though it rarely leads to any results), then one can scarcely doubt that there are Germans, living in Germany, who have felt like this. One aspect of the German problem is not that there are no Germans of good will, but simply that there are not enough of them.

The result of this isolation is that the German intellectuals show all the defects of their weakness, sometimes (as in the case of C— —, considering themselves quite outside the German people, by whom C— — is 'disgusted'), and sometimes going over to the cause of the strong, just because they find themselves so weak.

The impression of the Polish prisoners as to the behaviour of the overwhelming majority of Germans whom they encountered in their long wanderings, is undoubtedly a true one. It is a terrible testimony which explains why now in every corner of Germany one stumbles upon some new horror, a mass grave or a prison camp.

At the same time, there were undoubtedly a few Germans who right through the war did not believe in a German victory, and others who feared such a victory almost as much as the enemies of Germany. These were the intellectuals whom Hitler was always railing against, and although one has no sympathy with Hitler's point of view, there was a certain shrewdness in his analysis of these people as being completely cynical, and against everything and everyone. They had lost all faith, because they suffered from a sense of depression the extent of which one can only understand when one has lived for some weeks in Germany.

One great problem is to revive the political life of Germany in a democratic sense. Few people have fully realized the difficulty of this problem, which is that although there are political parties in Germany, there are no real political issues, since neither the fate nor the resources of Germany are in German hands. Political experiments in Germany are rather like political experiments and 'party government' in a progressive school of decrepit boys and girls, living amongst ruins.

Another great problem – which I have never seen discussed – is to create a body of opinion and to present to the German people personalities who are not completely identified with the Occupying Forces, and whom the Germans can respect as being outstanding individuals. It seems to me that this is where the German intelligentsia might play an important rôle. For this is the only section of German society which includes outstanding individuals of good will. Moreover these historians, philosophers, theologians, etc, are not discussing problems which conflict with the interests of the Occupation. At the same time, the need of spiritual leadership in Germany is very great. There is certainly, as Mr Bevin has pointed out, as great a spiritual as a material crisis of starvation in Germany.[1]

From this point of view we can regard Germany as Sodom. If we can find ten good Germans, we can save the spiritual life of Germany. That is to say, if we can put ten Germans who the Germans can respect as being not only Germans, but men accepted and listened to by the outside world, into touch, through every possible means of freedom of movement and publicity, with the German people, and with the outside world, we shall have shown the Germans the path which leads them up from despair and darkness, the path which also leads them into the European community.

There is a great need in Germany to discuss – on the highest intellectual level – not only questions of party, but also questions of religion, questions of German history, the German conception of power, the way of life. In Germany there may be men of exemplary disinterestedness – men who have always been against the Nazis – who can speak to the Germans of these things which concern them more immediately than politics. Such Germans are to be found in the concentration camps, in the Churches and the Universities. Some of them are to be found amongst the refugees. However, the refugees can only influence Germany if they are prepared to give up everything: that is to say, if they are prepared, like Karl Barth who has returned from Switzerland to Bonn University, to go back to their country and live there as Germans.[2] The greatest need of the Germans today is for the

---

1 Ernest Bevin (1881–1951) became Secretary of State for Foreign Affairs after the Labour victory in the general election of July 1945.
Bevin was preoccupied with the political reconstruction of Germany, but the fact that the Four Powers had to agree regarding all directives meant the situation was complex. From the military viewpoint, the immediate problem was to save large numbers of Germans from starvation in the coming winter.

2 Karl Barth (1886–1968), Swiss Protestant theologian. He argued that, since God is unknowable, it is wrong to connect Him with any human activity, whether moral, cultural or social. During the First World War he opposed the idea of associating God's Will with German war aims. For similar reasons in 1934 he opposed aligning the German Protestant Church with the Nazi Party. The following year he lost his post at Bonn University and fled to Switzerland. After the war he was one of the few people willing to discuss the question of German war guilt.

personal example of outstanding people who can teach them how to overcome their despair and how to harness their guilt feelings to an active repentance.

In April and May 1949, Spender went on an extensive lecture tour in the South and Midwest of America, including Lexington (Kentucky), Charlottesville (Virginia), Minneapolis and Chicago. America was in the grip of Cold War hysteria and many of the people Spender met were worrying about the Senator McCarthy's campaign against Communists and other leftists being conducted on the campuses. In the post-war years McCarthy's House Un-American Activities Committee acquired considerable power, resulting in a witch-hunt of supposed communist infiltrators into American institutions. Many careers were wrecked by it.

1 April 1949, New York

Drove in a taxi from La Guardia air field to N.Y. at 6 a.m., noon in London. At dawn the skyscrapers are like proud transparent stones, pillars of agate, huge flint-blocks rising into a pale sky.

In the evening, went to a farewell party for Auden, who was on the point of leaving for Ischia.[1] When I arrived he was playing operatic records of Strauss very loud on a hopelessly out of tune gramophone. The party consisted of young men. Conversation mostly of a facetious kind with an undertone of seriousness about the Church. Also about how Auden would like to be a police chief.

He said to me that I was v. naughty about Xtopher [Christopher Isherwood] in *Partisan Review*.[2] I said that I had shown this to Xtopher who approved of it. Auden said this made no difference. He also

---

1 From 1948 until 1958, W. H. Auden and his partner the American poet Chester Kallman (1921–1975) rented a vacation house at Ischia, an Italian island in the Gulf of Naples.

2 Spender had published five extracts from *World Within World* in *Partisan Review* between November 1948 and September 1949. Auden is objecting to the description of Isherwood in Berlin (*World Within World*, chapter 3).

told me that I was a Protestant, as one might tell someone that he was damned. He said the Bishop of Birmingham should be unfrocked for not believing things which he was paid to believe.[1]

Auden strikes me as being more and more reactionary. I disagree with him entirely now about politics and religion. Also he does not conceal either to me or others his complaints against me. Yet with all this he is still friendly and his hostility is half theoretical half based on genuine fear of what I may write about him. When I am with him my ease overcomes my unease.

2 April 1949, New York

Went to Bronxville. Lunched at college with H[arold] Taylor.[2] After he took me to his study. We had not been alone long before he started explaining to me why he had felt in July that I was making use of him: 'When that evening you said isn't there really a train before 10.30, I began to think "He is only interested in getting me to arrange lectures for him."' Then he went on to expound his myth of my summer that I had got into a state when I thought I had to get lectures everywhere out of everyone etc. Then he added that several of his staff hated me and one or two had asked 'How many more of these god-damn Britishers do we have to have?' Of course, he said, he did not agree with their point of view.

3 April 1949, New York

What is significant about all this is not the accusations which are so trivial as to be not worth answering, but the suspicion and uneasiness of N.Y. intellectual life. For example, tonight I went to a party at Margaret Marshall's when Mary McCarthy's story 'The Oasis' was

---

1 Ernest Barnes, Bishop of Birmingham, had published a controversial book, *The Rise of Christianity* (1947), which prompted a demand for his dismissal as a non-believer.

2 Harold Taylor was President of Sarah Lawrence College, Bronxville, New York, where Spender taught in 1947–8.

discussed.[1] None of her friends speak to Mary. The story is apparently a tissue of revelations about people's most intimate feelings for each other. It is not surprising that people should be annoyed, but the feeling that the story somehow undermines the security of the characters described in it, is rather astonishing.

I note the difference between this terrified insecurity of N.Y. and the fundamental emotion of warmth for one another of my literary friends in London. In England I feel that whatever the things people say, there is a fundamental understanding & appreciation which unites us all. Here connections between people are like ropes which, however strong & tightly tied can easily be severed.

4 April 1949, New York

Lecture at Hunter College[2] [. . .] There is something so extraordinary about the reaction of an American gathering to a successful cultural personality that I must study to see if I can describe it. I am surrounded by people saying: 'How perfectly wonderful.' Whether all mean this, I doubt. But some do experience a transcendental almost mystical illumination which exalts them extraordinarily. Yet this feeling is not unlike that which crowds have for a popular murder, or for a film star. There is an element of depravity about it. The things said are so enthusiastic or flattering that they are outrageous. There is a fragmentariness of response which is frustrating.

5 April 1949, Ithaca, New York

My lecture an enormous success (by this I do not mean it was a good lecture). After the questions an atmosphere of young girls' adulation like champagne. This kind of American flattery & warmth creates an atmosphere which is completely unreal on which everyone seems to float.

---

1 Margaret Marshall was then editor of *The Nation*, a left-wing but anti-Stalinist magazine. For Mary McCarthy, see biographical appendix. Her story 'The Oasis' (1949) satirises left-wing intrigues in New York during the early Cold War. Philip Rahv, editor of *Partisan Review* and a former lover of McCarthy, was upset and tried to block its publication in *Horizon*.

2 Hunter College, on Manhattan's Upper East Side.

Long conversation, mostly about communism with members of the Faculty afterwards – They all seemed v. detached from yet earnestly concerned with communism. Another American sensation: that way of listening which seems as though they're giving you yards & yards of rope with which you may, ultimately, hang yourself, but you have a lovely sense of freedom on the way.

A man at the Century Club pointed out to me that until recently Europe was terribly nervous lest America should not be involved in European security.[1] Now America is very concerned lest Europe will not be involved in the security of America.

7 April 1949, Syracuse, New York

Driven over to Syracuse by Detwold, from Wells [College, Aurora, New York]. This journey took me straight from the atmosphere of a small well-situated women's college on the shores of one of the beautiful Finger lakes [. . .] to that of a campus covered with ugly buildings looking like huge grey boxes distributed untidily on a sloping hill.

The members of the faculty, wearing city suits and felt hats who met me, looked like private detectives.

We had coffee and by then it was time to give my lecture. This was in the Chapel and was crowded with at least 1,500 students. As the car drew up at the chapel, I heard the following dialogue between two students: 'Are you a Spenderite?' 'No, are you?' 'Yeh.' 'What the hell?' 'Kinda feel a gnawing for some Kulter!' 'Huh – ha! ha! ha!'

A member of the Faculty who was there told me she heard the following among some students in the hall. 1st student: 'Say who's the speaker?' Second: 'Edmund Spender.' Third: 'It isn't Edmund Spender, it's Edmund Spenser.' 1st: 'Oh but he died some years ago.' 2nd: 'Oh damn I thought for sure it was him.'

The lecture was well received.

After the lecture a party with some members of the faculty, then dinner with others, then a meeting with students at which I was asked questions, then another faculty party.

---

1 The Century Association, a club for writers and artists on West 43rd Street, New York.

[57]

After the meeting with students, an exceedingly handsome student of the Russian dervish type came up and looking very seriously at me through jet black eyes said: 'Mr Spender, do you think a poet could write a good poem in which he accepted a point of view with which he utterly disagreed?' I was puzzled by this question and said: 'Do you?' 'I do,' he said, and walked away, smiling mysteriously.

Then a young man who looked like Hermes, started talking about some translations he was making. He was intelligent, kind-looking, sensitive. He had that kind of perfection in the American style which is disconcerting. He expressed sensitive opinions, he seemed to have very nice feelings, he smiled at me with beautifully clear eyes and his teeth shone with an astonishing whiteness. Yet his personality seemed to evade me. It was as though he kept shifting from being Hermes to being one of those ads in *Esquire* all the time. His wife, a pleasant looking dumpy girl was with him. When he introduced her he put his arm round her affectionately but also in a way which suggested that their relationship was easy and admirable. I could not imagine him making a mistake. Yet I felt sorry for him because I could imagine him feeling a certain despair for himself.

Everywhere this week when I have been alone with members of the Faculty, they have talked a great deal about communism. As Miss Marshall said: 'One of the things we notice is the great increase of fear amongst ourselves.' The expulsion of the 3 profs from Washington Univ. has made a great impression.

Idealism. Study what Americans mean by idealism. Someone says to me: 'Oh you'll like Mr E. He doesn't care at all about material things.' A moment later she adds that Mr E. is 'on the up and up'.

11 April 1949, New York

Philadelphia Museum of Art. Wonderful Cézannes Renoirs & Courbets. Interesting collection called the Gallatin.[1] A great many rooms arranged as Medieval Cloisters, Moorish interiors, chapels etc, all in suffused lighting. Also drawing rooms of the 18th century French

---

1 Formerly known as 'The Gallery of Living Art', the A. E. Gallatin Collection was loaned to New York University from 1927 to 1943. Later it was moved to Philadelphia.

and English style, and colonial American interiors. Myself I find this kind of museum realism terrifying. A completely dead cloister in suffused light with sham plants or potted ones under a sky made of white paper, with the tramping of a museum guard around the cloister walls, suggests putrefaction to a degree which really frightens me. This realism stops at a post-mortem stage. Curators should go much further if they go in this direction at all & turn museums into human zoos with real monks in the cloisters real houris in the Moorish harem.

18 April 1949, New York

N.Y.C. wonderful this evening like an arrangement of grey blocks of different sizes crowded together in very distinct rows, from the air. What a small island, like Venice of a functional age where every thing is larger scale. The black ships like large toys of wood anchored in the harbour.

19 April 1949, Johnson City, Tennessee

Arrived tired and depressed at Johnson City airport. Met by three ladies of the faculty who conversed with me in strong Southern accents. 'When did you first staht ratting, Mr Spender' I interpreted after a moment as, 'When did you first start writing'.

Country of the foothills of the Smoky Mountains. Emerald green and soft fields and small woods with the flame coloured sandy soil showing through. Occasional stony hills as though within a green cover torn away revealing the osseous strata of rock underneath.

20 April 1949, Johnson City, Tennessee

The students are not much to look at. Too fat or too thin, bony, sometimes cretinous, ill-dressed, they have that air of gormless do nothingness which so avoids the American grace & poise. The Southerners who come North are different. But then they hate the South.

My lecture was full and later I took a class. The students were very polite and probably in a day or two one would get used to their appearance.

Amazing how utterly absorbed the South is in all the old business. Hatred of the Yankees, the negro problem, struggling with poverty, consciousness of the 'hill billy country', the 'Old Kentucky home', etc. It seems a very foreign country. It also has a mysteriousness which seems to me always lacking in the North. And colonial. One of my hostesses said yesterday: 'Of course, they must be making a mess of the German occupation like they made a mess when they occupied us after the war.' She told how the Yankees had put negroes in charge of whites, had sent the 'carpet baggers' etc.

21 April 1949, Charlottesville, Virginia

Fetched by John Kele from the Robt. Lee Hotel at Lexington and driven to Virginia University at Charlottesville.

A marvellous day. We went through the Shenandoah Valley. As we approached Charlottesville, the country became more wooded, and more enclosed. The light through the delicately clothed spring trees and the young grass had a transparency diffused through the whole landscape. Against this filmy silky green the glossy boughs and branches were like the enamelled ribs of a marvellous silk sunshade. We passed an orchard tented with white blossoms held up against the sky by twisting trees. [. . .]

The University is marked by rows of not very high columns along the side of a great carpet of lawn and at the end the colonnaded central building. In the golden light the University seemed a perfect transformation of the grave and expansive ease of the Cambridge Backs into a wonderfully exotic setting which had lost nothing of purity. Like England transformed into New England in the prose of Henry James. The American aristocratic spirit when it appears has immense strength and freshness.

The garden of Mr Milton in the afternoon – the boxwood, the clouds of swallow-tails drifting over the lilac.

24 April 1949, Johnson City, Tennessee

Before going to bed, bought the paper. The news: Chinese Reds race toward Shanghai.[1] Harry Pollitt besieged in Plymouth.[2] The British Editor, Archibald R. Johnstone quits *Britanski Soyuznik* and becomes a Soviet Citizen.[3] My sympathies are with Pollitt who is a brave man. I read with passionate interest about Johnstone. In his statement he says 'the time has come for every person now to decide with whom he stands.' Then there is a lot about Bevin and Morrison and Attlee being tools of America & the Soviet being the cause of peace.[4]

What distresses me is to think that Russia although not the 'cause of peace' is a cause. It has something to offer to millions of people, even if this something might destroy liberty throughout the world for all except the few leading communists in each country. But America is not a cause in the same way. It is just America, with the American way of life and a rooted opposition to unAmerican ways, and tremendous waste, and a radio and a press and a movie industry, not to mention political parties, which advertize a commercialization which is an insult to every race and class of people not directly involved in American ideas and interests. It was scarcely worth discussing outside America, interests almost wholly ruinous and wasteful. There are very few Americans who even realize what torture it is to be asked to choose between loss of liberty according to the communist pattern and American liberty at the American price – a price which few people except Americans can pay. Probably Americans

---

1 The People's Liberation Army under Mao Zedong defeated the nationalist Kuomintang party under Chiang Kai-Shek at Shanghai on 21 April. This marked the final victory of communist forces in China.

2 Harry Pollitt (1890–1960), head of the British Communist Party, was 'besieged' in Plymouth by an angry mob for having published an article defending Chinese communist forces which had shelled a British warship in the Yangtze river.

3 *Britanski Soyuznic* (*British Ally*) was a newspaper that had been published in Moscow since 1942, when Britain and the USSR were allies. Its editor Archibald Johnstone now resigned, publishing a letter in the Soviet newspaper *Pravda* denouncing British 'war-mongering'.

4 Ernest Bevin, Herbert Morrison and Clement Attlee were respectively Foreign Secretary, Home Secretary and Prime Minister of Britain at this time.

are right to see that great virtues accompany great follies within the American system on this continent. But not to see that the Voice of this America can never speak to the world – in fact that it is only by learning the voice of the world of striving peoples that America can ever speak to the world – is a fatality which rots even America itself.

Perhaps this is exaggerated. There is the Marshall Plan, there is American generosity, etc, there are many good Americans.[1] But all this does not make up for the great weakness that America judges others by *her* values and *her* interests which prevents her from either understanding or being understood.

27 April 1949, Terre Haute, Indiana

In the train going to Northfield from Minneapolis, a jolly looking woman accompanied by an older man, who seemed to be her father, got into the compartment talking loudly and laughing. 'So this woman,' she said, 'at the terminus got into the luggage shoot and slid down it out of the station. When she landed on the pavement, she stood up and said: "Well to be sure they have some strange customs in these cities." You see,' she went on 'she'd never been to a big city before & she thought that was the thing to do. Oh I've never laughed so much in my life. I can't stop laughing. Whenever I think of it I laugh till I cry.' She sat down on her seat & laughed till her tears really did roll down her cheeks. Amused and curious someone said 'Where did you see this?' 'In the *Reader's Digest*,' she replied.

12 May 1949, Chicago

May 9, dined with Allen and Mrs Tate.[2] They were extremely friendly and we got on well discussing poetry, criticism etc. Told me that Hart

---

1 The 'Marshall Plan' was a program of massive US subsidies devised by the Secretary of State George Marshall (1880–1959) and intended to 'prime the pump' of post-war economic recovery in Europe.

2 Allen Tate (1899–1979) and his wife the novelist Caroline Gordon (1895–1981) were both writers whose work was firmly linked to the American South.

Crane was consistently drunk during the last 2½ years of his life.[1] He used to sit composing to the music of an old-fashioned horned H.M.V. gramophone. From time to time, he would get up cross the room & put a pinch of salt down the horn of the machine. Told me also that Robert Lowell, who is almost in the position of being their adopted son is pretty well insane.[2] Conflict between Lowell & his parents. When he was 16 or 17 his father found him in his room with a college girl. A row in which Lowell knocked his father down. Now he is looked after by his very silly (according to the Tates) mother. Allen Tate violently against *Partisan Review*.[3] They told me several stories against Wystan [Auden]. Wystan had asked them when they first met him, whether the Tates knew any means by which he could win the Pulitzer Prize. They answered that he could not do so, as it was only available to Americans. Within two years of this conversation, however, Auden was American and had won it.[4] They complained also that Wystan lectured them a great deal on America and the Americans. I said people made rather absurd complaints about Wystan, e.g. that he exploited his situation in America. 'That's exactly what he does do,' said Allen.

He said in a way which was not and yet was serious that the British sent over here writers whom the Americans had to put up with in their helplessness, like Ruthven Todd, with their mistresses or their

---

1 Hart Crane (1899–1932), American poet. A homosexual and an alcoholic, he committed suicide by jumping from a ship as it sailed across the Gulf of Mexico. Tate met Crane in New York in the 1920s when he was working for *The Nation*.

2 Robert Lowell (1917–1977), American poet who wrote about his family and friends in poems which are loosely called 'confessional'. In 1946, Lowell had been appointed the Poet Laureate Consultant to the Library of Congress, a post held previously by Tate (1943) and subsequently by Spender (1965). He suffered from alcoholism and manic depression throughout his life.

3 After the Nazi–Soviet Pact in 1939, left-wingers in New York became bitterly divided for and against Stalin. *Partisan Review*, founded by William Phillips and Philip Rahv in 1934, became the voice of the anti-Stalinist faction. Allen Tate, with other former associates of the magazine such as Mary McCarthy, believed this move to the right in the post-war period meant that the magazine did less than it should have done to defend those who were being persecuted by the House Un-American Activities Committee.

4 Auden became an American citizen in 1946. He won a Pulitzer Prize for *The Age of Anxiety* in 1948.

homosexual friends.[1] 'You have no idea,' he said, quite friendly, 'how we hate you. We hate all the British, but most of all we hate Auden, MacNeice and Spender. You are much cleverer than we and we can't forgive you for it. You come over here and everything is easier for you than it is for us.'

This declaration of hostility was really a declaration of friendship. Allen went on to say how much E. E. Cummings dislikes T. S. Eliot (someone else had told me that E.E.C. calls him Tears Eliot).[2]

All the same, it was a very cordial evening. By being declared, the Anglo-American hatred had receded to a theoretical level.

By the beginning of 1950 Spender was back in England, working as a freelance writer.

10 January 1950, London

Went to movie *The Bicycle Thief* [*sic*].[3] Wonderful child actor with a little man's face with large brown eyes quizzically following the expression on his father's face.

After this tea-ed at my club.[4]

Compton Mackenzie was holding forth about communism, describing a luncheon at Simpsons before the war, with [Harry] Pollitt and Gallacher.[5] Says if the British C.P ever got into power these would be bumped off. Priestley arrived, flanked by his agent A. D. Peters, and another man. They sat down and discussed plans for some movie. From time to time Priestley said: 'There's money in it' or 'that would be wonderful business.' Someone asked him to

---

1 Ruthven Todd (1914–1978), Scottish poet with whom Spender occasionally corresponded.

2 E. E. Cummings (1894–1962), American poet and a contemporary of T. S. Eliot's at Harvard. For T. S. Eliot see biographical appendix.

3 *Ladri di biciclette* (*Bicycle Thieves*) (1948), the classic Italian neo-realist film by Vittorio de Sica. The child actor is Enzo Staiola.

4 Spender was for many years a member of the Garrick Club, most of whose members work in the theatre, journalism or literature.

5 Compton Mackenzie (1883–1972), novelist and founder member of the Scottish Nationalist Party. His *Whisky Galore* (1947) was a bestseller. William Gallacher (1881–1965) was Communist MP for West Fife (1935–1950).

contribute to our discussion and he said: 'I can't enter into all this metaphysics and ethics.'[1]

I forgot to go to be drawn by David Low.[2] Damn.

11 January 1950, London

It is noon and as yet I have done no work.

Went to see George Orwell. He told me he had lost 2½ stone. Looked very thin and sick.[3] Said I was wrong to reply to the Communists. 'There are certain people like communists and vegetarians whom one cannot answer. You just have to keep on saying your say without regard to them, and then the extraordinary thing is they may start listening.'

12 January 1950, London

Bill [Goyen] went this morning to have his knee examined under gas. His dream in which John Lehmann, Elizabeth Bowen, Natasha, Walter [Berns] and I were all pulling at his leg in different directions.[4] He described going under gas as though no-one had ever done so before. Of course, a writer has to regard his experiences as unique, yet such self-centredness is a little trying. Bill's telephone conversation to Miss

---

1 J. B. Priestley (1894–1984) was enjoying great success as a playwright at this time.

2 David Low (1891–1963) was a renowned political cartoonist, inventor of 'Colonel Blimp'.

3 The British writer and essayist George Orwell (1903–1950) had been admitted into University College Hospital, where he died ten days later. The friendship between Spender and Orwell had developed in the 1930s, though both were initially ambivalent about each other, with Orwell dismissing Auden and his comrades for their 'Boy Scout atmosphere of bare knees and community singing'. In 1949, Orwell had married Spender's friend Sonia Brownell (for Sonia Orwell, see biographical appendix).

4 William (Bill) Goyen (1915–1983), American novelist and teacher, appeared in London while he was serving in the US navy during the Second World War. His eight novels were written after 1950. For Natasha Spender (who Spender had married in 1941), John Lehmann and Elizabeth Bowen, see biographical appendix. Walter Berns (b. 1919) was at this point a postdoctoral student at Chicago. Berns and William Goyen shared a house in the 1940s, when Spender met them. Late in life Berns became a leading neo-conservative commentator.

Hulley describing his swollen knee: you would never have guessed from this that Miss Hulley is a cripple.

Dined with Philip, Robert, Freddie Ayer and Janetta.[1] Philip infuriated me. In talking about our respective families and careers, he said, 'You and I are the same kind of failure.' Speaking of religion, Freddie Ayer said, 'If the whole thesis of after-life etc of Christianity were true, it would be just as meaningless as if it is untrue.' He meant that there is no communication between the consciousness of this life and an afterlife.[2]

13 March 1950, Brussels

Went to Brussels to stay with Hansi [Lambert].[3] Hansi met us at the airport. Then to the Avenue Marnix in her American car. En route she explained the great concern of everyone was the Royal question. She was the one person who prophesied that the King would have a 57% majority. Rather to our surprise Hansi spoke very coolly of the King and said he should abdicate in favour of his son Baudouin.[4]

The whole of this stay was dominated by the Royal question.

One day de Wigny, the Minister[,] and the American Ambassador, Murphy[,] came to lunch.[5] De Wigny explained very carefully that the return of the King should depend not on winning an election campaign conducted by his political supporters (who might lose an

---

1 Philip Toynbee (1916–1981), writer and journalist who came to know Spender during the Spanish Civil War. Robert Kee (b. 1919), writer and journalist, at this point literary editor of *The Spectator*. A. J. (Freddie) Ayer (1910–1989), British philosopher whose *Language, Truth and Logic* (1936) introduced Logical Positivism to England, and whom Spender had met before the war, probably through Isaiah Berlin. Spender met Janetta Woolley in the 1930s. She was married at this point to Robert Kee, and was subsequently married to Derek Jackson and later to Jaime Parlade.

2 A. J. Ayer changed his view on death in old age after a near-death experience. Regarding personal survival, he said, 'I'm keeping an open mind.'

3 For Hansi Lambert, see biographical appendix.

4 The conduct of King Leopold III of Belgium (1901–1983) during the German invasion was considered so craven that he was forced to abdicate in 1951 in favour of his son, Baudouin (1930–1993).

5 Pierre de Wigny (1905–1986), Belgian Foreign Minister 1958–61; Robert D. Murphy (1894–1978).

election a few months later), but on the support of a majority of Parties.

'After all,' said Murphy, 'he's got a majority of 57%. That's larger than has ever been obtained by an American President. After all,' he went on, 'his wife hasn't been divorced.'

At this, Madame de Wigny, a large woman looking like an irate bull-frog, exploded. She talked about the bad influence of his wife on the King, her ambition, her origins, the circumstances of the marriage, which took place during the War. At the very moment when the King was 'the Royal prisoner' in the minds of his subjects, he was actually in Vienna, guest of high-up Nazis.

Murphy said to me he thought the King's way of behaving – his failure now simply to get into his car and come to Brussels – showed a lack of sureness. Murphy said to me in an aside that the Americans had no desire to interfere with the Royal question, but they were worried about its effect on the whole Belgian situation.

Murphy was slow and hesitant, rather like a camel. De Wigny is sleek, well-groomed, smiling. He seemed touchy and nervous. He insisted very much that the Belgian crisis was exactly the same as the English Abdication crisis.[1] When I argued a bit about this, he seemed distinctly annoyed.

We had, as usual, a nice though farcical time at the Av. Marnix. Walks in the morning through the park to which we were driven by Gaston – Hansi racing through the avenues, with an intent expression on her face. Then back to lunch, waited on by two or three butlers – delicious though rather over-greasy food – distinguished guests.

Everyone who came to the house seemed caught up in a strange kind of plutocratic egalitarianism, as though shut off from the world by a huge wall of money and talking earnestly about problems which, as a result of the money, existed in a vacuum.

To go out into the street [from] Hansi's house is like descending from the stratosphere into a grey foggy, dirty atmosphere.

Some evenings for painters and art collectors, some for philosophers, some for politicians and economists. Hansi usually says before

---

1 The English abdication crisis of 1936 was caused by the intention of Edward VIII to marry an American divorcée, Wallace Simpson. His open admiration for Hitler is also thought to have compromised his position during this crisis.

luncheon: 'Now I want you to discuss the following problems –' and she tells me what.

Our last evening, Léon [Lambert] returned from Geneva, where he had passed all his examinations brilliantly.[1] After dinner he complained about the journey in his M.G. car and said, 'Maman, je suis très épris par le Jaguar.' [Mother, I am very keen on the Jaguar.] The rest of the evening was spent in selling the idea of a Jaguar to Hansi.

While I was in Brussels I worked on the translations of Hofmannsthal.[2] I read Dostoevsky's stories, 'A Gentle Creature', *Notes from the Underground* and Ernest J. Simmons, *Dostoevsky* – a very dull book.[3]

Dostoevsky suddenly seemed to me a key to how I should write and I regretted the twenty years during which, influenced by a remark of E.R.C., I have read no Dostoevsky.[4]

The central vision of an utterly simple contractual relationship between people, which is betrayed on all sides, but which recurs constantly through certain situations with the force of revelation, is exactly my own.

In 1950, Spender was commissioned by the New York Times *to write a series of articles on European intellectuals who, like himself, had become disillusioned with communism. In this unusual instance of a British intellectual trying to make a bridge with his European colleagues, the Italian writers responded more openly than the French. Although Albert Camus was friendly, he did not give an interview. Nor did Jean-Paul Sartre. They may have felt dubious about the American context of these articles – which in the end were never written.*

---

1 Leon Lambert, Hansi Lambert's son, later worked in the family bank.

2 Hugo von Hofmannsthal (1874–1929), Austrian poet. These translations were eventually completed by Michael Hamburger, who wrote: 'Spender generously passed them over to me when he'd decided his German wasn't up to the very demanding task.'

3 Ernest J. Simmons, *Dostoevsky, the Making of a Novelist* (1940).

4 Curtius recommended French novelists such as Flaubert to the young Spender. He thought Dostoevsky would be a bad influence.

22 March 1950, Rome

Flew over the Alps for the second time this year [. . .] The most wonderful part of the journey then was climbing to a height of 17,500 feet over the Lake of Geneva. The lake changed in a few minutes from looking like a sea to a pool at the feet of melting rocks.

Now the mountains were much more sunny. The snow was plastered and dripping over them, like icing on a cake. Amazing how sharp, like ragged knife blades the mountains look from above. Certain desolate snow fields spread out look like nets in which the aeroplane might be caught if it fell. The high-up villages.

Then the mountains cease to be so serious, and are spaced out as rocks among trees, grass and lakes. As we got to Rome, I was surprised to see how completely on the edge of the city the Vatican is, so that from the air it looks as if there is nothing but country beyond it.

At Rome airport I was met by a man sent from the American Academy. It is still strange driving from a modern airport past walls 2,000 or 3,000 years old.

We went straight to Villa [San] Pancrazio, which is a building like one flat red-coloured plane against a blue sky – a stage scenery building. It has a wonderful ilex tree like a green dome in front of it. Behind is a view of Rome.[1]

Laurence Roberts greeted me. Smiling, boyish, completely unselfimportant. After a day or two we could discuss together what he would do when he left the American Academy, on the assumption that he would have no position whatever.

On Thursday morning I went to see Silone.[2] He lives in a flat in an apartment house on the outskirts of Rome. This is a part of the city which seems quite unconnected with the usual idea of Rome.

---

1 Villa San Pancrazio was the seat of the American Academy in Rome, founded by Congress in 1905 'to sustain artistic pursuits and humanistic studies'. Laurence Roberts was its current director.

2 Ignazio Silone (1900–1978), Italian novelist respected internationally. A communist in the 1920s, he went into exile in Switzerland in the 1930s and took an active part in the Resistance during the war. *Tempo Presente*, the magazine he edited from 1956, tried to steer a course between the Italian Communist Party and the Christian Democrats. This was bitterly opposed by the Communist Party. Silone shared with Spender the conviction that though culture needed defending politically, it should not itself become politicized.

Suburban, industrial, with high white-walled tenements, it is more like Casablanca and belongs to the Rome of the films of Rossellini rather than to that of guide books.[1] Driving to the Campagna through this part of Rome with Bernard Berenson, a year ago, he half-closed his eyes and said: 'Everything they build today is filthy,' as vehemently as if he laid a curse on it: and I had the impression that he wished for human beings to die sooner than build and live in modern houses.[2]

Silone had a rather nice flat which seemed to consist of four, or five rooms divided by partition-like walls. The living room had a dentist's-waiting-room-like air, with magazines laid out on a central table. Mrs Silone [Darina] welcomed me very agreeably, recalling our meetings in Zurich and Venice for PEN Club Congresses.[3] She said, 'He's much better.' She always refers to her husband as 'He' with an Irish mysteriousness which is attractive.

Silone welcomed me in an equally friendly way. They asked me to luncheon but I could not stay. Silone asked me to outline to him my idea for the *New York Times* article, saying that he would then comment on it. I explained to him that I wished to make the point that the European intellectuals who best understood the problems of our time were those who had an experience of communism. I wanted therefore to have the views of himself, Vittorini, Koestler, Malraux and Camus on certain matters: European union; Stalinist communism; the influence of America in European affairs; the English socialist experiment; the attitude of England towards Europe. Finally, I suggested two more general questions: the way out for Europe; and the role of the individual in politics today.[4]

---

1 Roberto Rossellini (1906–1977), neo-realist film director whose works include *Roma, città aperta* (*Rome, Open City*) (1945) and *Stromboli* (1950).

2 Bernard Berenson (1865–1959) was the leading art connoisseur of his time. Initially funded by the Boston collector Isabella Stuart Gardner, he lived a life of immaculate good taste at 'I Tatti', a villa outside Florence.

3 For PEN, see biographical appendix.

4 These intellectuals were trying to cope with the fact that the communist parties of France and Italy were attempting to dominate all cultural activities. Elio Vittorini (1908–1966), Italian writer and novelist, jailed under Mussolini and subsequently a communist partisan, was, like Silone, attempting to find a middle way between the Christian Democrats and the Italian Communist Party.

Silone listened patiently to what I had to say. Then very slowly and carefully, in his French with the faint vibrancy of an Italian accent, answered my questions.

He said that in Italy there was a great deal of interest in European Union. Already in certain quarters there were attempts to formulate the bases of a Pact for a European Federation.[1] On the 2nd April there were to be meetings in several countries to discuss a coalition of democratic parties of the Centre, Catholic and Social Democrats – without either the Communists or the extreme Right to discuss these things. Circumstances were particularly favourable in Italy, where the President is an old Federalist. He was already, in 1917, in favour of a Federal Europe and still very active on its behalf.[2] Officially Christian Democracy was federalist. The Republicans and the Liberals were also in favour of Federation. The Communists were perplexed rather than actively opposed. Silone said: 'I think that in a certain Russian perspective the idea of unifying Europe would even be useful. At all events, it must not be too discredited in the eyes of the workers.'

'The Unity of Europe,' Silone went on, 'must not be a fetish. It cannot solve every problem. Moreover, it would be wrong to accept it at any price or in any form. Hitler and Napoleon both offered it in unacceptable terms. The Soviets today offer an authoritarian union, which is equally unacceptable.

'There is a parallel between the struggle for European Union and that for Italian Union which occurred a hundred years ago. [. . .]

For Arthur Koestler, see biographical appendix. André Malraux (1901–1976), French writer whose youthful adventures in Cambodia provided background for his 1933 *La Condition Humaine (Man's Fate)*. A controversial hero of the Spanish Civil War, during the Second World War he became an ardent Gaullist, and served as Minister of Culture in de Gaulle's last government (1959–69). Albert Camus (1913–1960), French writer of Algerian background, was at this point trying to distance himself from the French Communist Party, a move that brought him into conflict with Jean-Paul Sartre.

1 The Council of Europe, from which the European Union grew, was founded in 1949.

2 Luigi Einaudi (1874–1961), President of Italy from 1948 to 1955, was a supporter of the European Union which he hoped could defuse the rivalry of France and Germany, the cause of three devastating wars in eighty years.

'Unity is desirable for us but only if it is founded on liberty and democracy.

'In a Europe dominated by some general we would be tempted to be separatist.

'There is distrust of encouragement for unity from America. For certain people American support is sufficient reason to be opposed to it. I think, though, that we must not be frightened by such encouragement.

'France, in the past, encouraged Cavour's attempt to unify Italy, for their own reasons – to weaken the Austrian Empire.[1] In reality Italian Unity surpassed what Paris and London wanted. According to this historic example, European unity will surpass the Machiavellianism of diplomacy: and those who want it should not be discouraged by sympathy. It is necessary to make use of help while having confidence in one's own work. One can't say how it will weigh in the total balance of affairs. Europe should have a policy of resolving difficulties by means of examining them one by one and resolving them as they arise – not by making grandiose declarations of unity and peace.

'No European country can make a contribution because separately it has nothing to give: but altogether they would have something to give.

'In the present European situation the worst lacuna is the passivity of the English Socialists. The fact that the Conservatives are the only English who support unity is unfortunate.[2]

'England missed the role she could have had in directing the democratization of Europe after the liberation. The English had an attitude, which remained too mercantile. They thought they could do nothing in Europe on account of their awareness of their own needs. The new Labour leaders concentrated on the interior problems of their country and left foreign policy in the hands of people still inspired by a Nineteenth Century conception of England – with no European plan. What England lacked was the spirit to encourage and

---

1 Camillo Cavour (1810–1861) was a leading figure in the long struggle for Italian unification in the nineteenth century.

2 Clement Attlee's post-war Labour government (1945–51) was concentrating on creating the basis of the Welfare State. Ernest Bevin, Attlee's Foreign Secretary, was sceptical about European unification. This was a disappointment to many European socialists.

direct the depressed Liberal spirit of Europe. It seemed incomprehensible that after the war the English should have been against the Italian people [and] for the monarchy: and that they should have had such a stupid policy in Germany.[1]

'They should have studied the problem of how to coordinate a Federal Europe with the Commonwealth. This remained a problem – but was soluble.

'The weakness of the European movement is the English deficiency.

'For federalists the main question is, "Can we do nothing till the Labour Party is ready for unity?"

'Some people say we can create a nucleus of Federalism. The French are the most timid because they think that without England, Germany will recover as the centre of Europe.

'In the next session at Strasbourg there will be formal proposals for creating a European authority.[2] This will be a critical moment if England sabotages it. The only really effective way of meeting Communism is to examine the objective reasons – economic, social-political and also psychological – which have led important masses of Italian and French workers under Communist influence. The legitimate aspirations of the workers must be satisfied. The future belongs to those countries which have the people on their side. Too many today say what is not true but what America lends itself to – that Russia is the people, America reaction.

'Communism is a much more complicated phenomenon than people realize. The most important problem of today is how to regain in democracy the healthy forces within Communism.'

After my morning with Silone I lunched at the American Academy, where there was a miscellaneous collection of visitors, of whom I

---

1 The reference is to the referendum that abolished the monarchy in Italy in 1947. Clement Attlee supported the monarchy.

2 These proposals were formalized with the Schumann Declaration, proposed by the French Foreign Minister Robert Schumann on 9 May 1950. This was primarily a trade agreement that placed the coal and steel industries of member countries under a higher authority, making war between these states impossible and creating the world's first supranational organization. On 3 June 1950, Germany, Luxembourg, Belgium, France, Italy and the Netherlands signed up to the declaration and between 26 and 28 August the Council of Europe Assembly approved the declaration in Strasbourg.

remember nothing. When they had gone, the Robertses and I had a walk through their garden. Isabel Roberts drove me down to Rome. She told me how they were, in their job, utterly at the mercy of Americans travelling through Rome who expected to be entertained and complained to the Trustees of the Academy in New York if they did not get enough attention. Laurence Roberts also told me how he had been criticized at home for inviting Italian Communists to the Academy. He said that if he didn't do so he had no idea how he would be able to see Italian intellectuals.

25 March 1950, Florence

Went to Florence on the Rapido. Was met by Bill Smith and Barbara.[1] We drove out to their home where I stayed. [. . .] On Sunday had luncheon with Berenson. Raymond Mortimer was there, also Nicky and a woman whom I had met in New York.[2] Impossible to talk to Berenson at luncheon – far away from him and no general conversation. After the meal, he took me aside and talked to me very nicely. He looks extraordinary now, with something of the spirituality of an El Greco, and with a shell-like delicacy of the texture of his face in which every minute line seems expressive [as] in a steel engraving. He said he was sorry I had never stayed with him and asked me to do so if I could while he was still here to receive me. Then he said something about my gifts 'which perhaps I misunderstood' and asked me whether I had ever tried writing a novel.

The Berenson garden was full of most beautiful pale-coloured flowers, purple and red, like anemones. There is a wonderful avenue of dark cypresses leading to the back of the house at one side. Raymond remarked on the fact that Berenson had planted all these trees. Raymond said that Nicky, Berenson's companion, was the nicest woman he had ever known.

---

1 William Jay Smith (b. 1918), American scholar and poet working at the University of Florence. He and his wife Barbara became friends of the Spenders, and later Spender became godfather to their son.

2 Raymond Mortimer (1895–1980), literary critic and lead reviewer for the *Sunday Times*, 1948–52. Elisabetta (Nicky) Mariano (1887–1968) was Bernard Berenson's secretary and companion for forty years.

Eudora Welty, the novelist, came to dinner with Bill and Barbara.[1] Berenson remarked on her great charm. Of her novels, he said they were clearly talented, but 'like all these Americans' when she found one thing she could do she went on doing that and nothing else. 'It's like Walt Disney and all their other discoveries.'

I liked Eudora Welty very much. Tall and dark-eyed, rather craggy yet soft-looking, and with a slight rolling of her eyes which went well with her Southern accent. She was accompanied by a young man called Robinson, stolid but mysterious, and subject of much speculation. She talked about Bill Goyen: said she was greatly impressed when he first sent her *The White Rooster*, but liked less what he sent afterwards.[2] She wrote and criticized the other stories. Six months later she received a letter to the effect that Bill had just recovered from Eudora's letter. 'Now,' she said, 'it struck me that a person who takes criticism in this way cares more for himself than for his writing. Perhaps he regards his writing simply as an extension of himself.'

She told me that she had met Bill in Paris recently. It was in the middle of the road, crossing the boulevard, and he was carrying a bag full of groceries. The first thing Bill explained was that he was engaged to be married. He was, he said, just taking the groceries to his fiancée. This was his last evening in Paris, he went on, his last evening with his fiancée. Nevertheless, if Eudora was free, he would throw up his fiancée and spend it with her. Eudora said she was rather disgusted by the tone of this conversation.

28 March 1950, Florence

Went to the Hotel, where I met Walt, who had just arrived. We spent the afternoon wandering around, getting my air ticket and then, at 6, [Elio] Vittorini arrived at the hotel and asked us both to dine at his home.

We walked a part of the way to his house, Vittorini talking. He said with great frankness that it was not much use my questioning

1 Eudora Welty (1909–2001), writer from the American South, a friend of Bill Goyen.

2 Bill Goyen's short story 'The White Rooster' was published in *Mademoiselle* in 1947.

him for the *New York Times*, if I were also interviewing Silone. For Silone would have far more to say and would say it much better than he could do. He said that now he belonged to no political party, he had no time to reflect on politics. 'All the same,' he added, 'perhaps for a person like myself, not to belong to a party, not even to hold conscious political opinions is the best way of exercising political influence.' To explain his point of view, though, he would tell me of how he had come to break with the Party because that was significant. During the time of the Partisans, he had always worked with the Communists and even considered himself a Communist. However, he had never actually had a Party card. At the time of the Resistance there had never been [a] question of having one. Later, when he had thought about it, he had resisted the idea, because in his mind Fascism was associated with the Party card.

Vittorini, who has black, short-cropped hair, black almost flashing eyes, an expansive mouth which when he smiles reveals broken teeth, talks in illuminated moments of real passion. 'I am against Communism, because it means dictatorship,' he exclaimed violently, as we got into a tram. 'Dictatorship means Fascism and I have fought against that. All the same, I object to a system such as I find in my own village in Sicily, when there are always the same rigid castes, with the landowners at the top, supported by the clergy and always, whatever happened, the peasant at the bottom.'

America obviously did not seem to him to have anything to offer to the peasant. Just as we were going away, Vittorini made a brilliant remark. 'Sometimes, I think,' he said, 'that the choice between capitalism and communism which we are offered, is exaggerated. After some of the monarchs had been deposed, the remaining ones became constitutional monarchs. Perhaps capitalism should abdicate and become constitutional capitalism.'

The poet Eugenio Montale, now literary editor of the *Corriere della Sera* of Milan, was at the Vittorini dinner.[1] I was struck by his extreme irony. He told me that as a poet he could not receive as good pay as the other journalists in the *Corriere*. Being the greatest Italian poet was a disadvantage, which he always had to struggle against.

---

1 Eugenio Montale (1896–1981), Italian poet who won the Nobel Prize for literature in 1975.

There was something very cosy and even affectionate about Montale that evening.

Back in London for a few days, when I revised the last 100 pages of my book [*World Within World*]. Luncheon with Edith Sitwell one day.[1] Saw Catharine Károly, who was very agitated about the trial of Rajk in Hungary.[2] She told me that she was convinced that Rajk was the one honest and good communist in Hungary. His trial was not for what he had done but for what he was capable of doing. Not being Moscow-trained, he was capable of becoming a supporter of Tito.[3] Rákosi's speech in which he had said he could not sleep for many nights on account of the treachery in which he could not believe, had struck her with ironic force: she was sure he did not believe in it. She had evidence about the case of Rajk and wished to publish a pamphlet. Her aim was for this to reach the workers in France and England. She described her difficulties in getting an English or French publisher for this. Catharine Károlyi is one of the most courageous women I know. After years of exile, having fought the Hungarian reactionaries and returned to Budapest for a few months in 1945, now, in exile again, she is willing to fight again for freedom and against an injustice, at greater risk than ever before. She described the methods of extorting confessions, and she said a very profound thing, 'If it is really possible to make a courageous and truthful man denounce himself unjustly, the betrayal of humanity by terror, is even more terrifying than the atom bomb.'

---

1 For Edith Sitwell, see biographical appendix.

2 Catherine Károlyi was the wife of Count Mihály Károlyi, who had been President of Hungary in 1919. He was forced into exile, first to France and then, during the Second World War, to England, where Spender met him. At that time, Károly was Hungarian Ambassador to France, but he resigned in 1949 when László Rajk was tried and executed by Mátyás Rákosi, leader of a Stalin-style dictatorship in Hungary.

3 Josip Broz Tito (1892–1980), leader of Yugoslavia, 1945–80. Tito was a popular figure in Yugoslavia, holding together its constituent socialist states. He balanced successful economic and diplomatic policies and managed a policy of non-alignment during the Cold War by joining forces with other nations that refused to ally themselves too strongly with the Soviet brand of socialism.

13 April 1950, Paris

Returned to Paris to see [Arthur] Koestler and [André] Malraux.

14 April 1950, Paris

Went to Melun on the Seine to lunch with Koestler. He and Mamaine live in a pavilion-like house on the bank of the Seine.[1] The view broad, the country flat but green, and wooded with the forest of Fontainebleau.

Koestler spoke a great deal of the completely 'pourri' [rotten] quality of the French.

He said the most important fact to grasp about the present situation was that Left and Right have lost their meaning. Labour has fallen down on internationalism and Labour England is the main obstacle to European Union.

Every British Government is bound to be isolationist. But the Labour Government is more than this: it is provincial: more so than the Tories. Churchill offered the unification of England with France.

Socialism has broken down on internationalism. Orwell rightly pointed out that [the] Left has never faced the contradiction that if you want internationalism you have to face the sacrifice of a national standard of living which has been at the expense of the rest of the world.

In England nationalism and bureaucratization have reached the point of saturation.

The dilemma of Left and Right has become as false as monarchy versus Republicanism, or Jansenism against the official churches.[2]

Whether you vote Labour in England or S.F.I.O. or M.R.P. or Radical Socialist in France, it all makes no difference.[3] Yet people spend their energies in sterile conflicts. The effect of this in France is that people won't get together to form an anti-totalitarian front.

---

1 For Mamaine Paget, see the entry for Arthur Koestler in the biographical appendix.

2 Jansenism was a rigidly conservative branch of sixteenth-century Catholicism.

3 SFIO, Section Française de l'International Ouvrière, the French section of the Worker's International. MRP, Mouvement Républicain Populaire, a centre-left party of the time.

To be anti-Fascist in 1936 was as honourable as to be For King and Country. [. . .] But today there exists no analogous Front for survival.

Such a Front must be against something – Anti. Its raison d'être must be a menace or a threat.

Nobody in 1936 said, 'I am neither anti-Fascist nor Fascist,' but all the 'clever insiders' now make a point of saying, 'I am neither C.P. nor anti-C.P.'[1]

The appeal of communism is really the appeal of the movement of the workers against traditional oppression.

The basic necessity of thinking is to distinguish between long-term and short-term problems.

Our trouble is that we have so little time. Without Russia we could afford to think in long terms. But, faced with an immediate threat, we are forced to simplify. This doesn't mean we should neglect the long-term view. We have to keep the short- and long-term separate.

Koestler's row with Sartre.[2]
Koestler told me that when he last said 'Goodbye' to Sartre and Simone de Beauvoir outside the Pont Royal, he remarked, 'Let's have luncheon together soon.'[3] There was a pause at the end of which Simone said, 'Koestler, you know that we disagree. There no longer seems any point in our meeting.' She crossed her arms and said, 'We are *croisés comme ça* about everything.'[4] K. said, 'Yes, but surely we

---

1 CP, Communist Party. This is probably a criticism by Koestler of 'fellow travellers', those who were not ostensibly communist but were in effect in its service.

2 Jean-Paul Sartre (1905–1980), the French novelist and philosopher of Existentialism, had a long and tortuous relationship with the French Communist Party, which he considered too powerful to oppose and too compromised to support. Koestler, whose pre-war contacts with the communists had been close and brutal, now split with Sartre over allegiance to Moscow. Koestler, vigorously anti-Soviet, was at this point cultivating connections with the American-sponsored Congress for Cultural Freedom. (For the background of the CCF, see the entry for *Encounter* in the biographical appendix).

3 Simone de Beauvoir (1908–1986) was a French writer and the lifelong companion of Sartre.

4 'We are at cross purposes about everything.'

can be friends just the same. Let's meet soon.' She said, 'As a philosopher you must realize that if each of us looks at a *morceau de sucre* [sugar lump], he sees an entirely different object. Our *morceaux de sucre* are now so different that there is no point in our seeing one another any longer.'

K. has also quarrelled, only this time not so seriously, with Malraux. He was told by Sartre that *Les Temps Modernes* had moved from Gallimard as a result of Malraux's threatening to withdraw his books if they continued to publish it.[1] Koestler reported this charge to Malraux. 'Obviously, I did nothing of the sort,' said Malraux. 'It's gross libel . . . But naturally if published with Gallimard I have the right to withdraw my books if they publish writers whom I detest and who detest me.' 'Then you admit that what Sartre said is true,' said K. 'It is completely untrue, but I have a right to publish with whom I choose,' said Malraux. A certain coldness between them. Koestler said that Malraux's passion was art: his politics were his thyroid gland. Malraux said of Koestler that he was a person perpetually in search of a country. He had sought it in Communism and failed to find it. He thought he would return to the Jews in Israel, but they hated him. He also said something about Koestler which I forget, a sentence beginning, 'comme tous les gens qui boivent trop . . .'.[2]

I arrived chez Malraux at about 8.30, having stayed longer than I should at K.'s (we drank a good deal at luncheon, then siesta-ed, after which I interviewed K.).

Malraux's main room is a large sitting-dining-study-music room. It has a staircase running along one side and a kind of alcove. It is very white. Paintings by Picasso, Buffet and other artists on the wall. Also reproductions done the same size as the original (Malraux has a theory about this). At one end of the room a Pleyel double piano, on

---

1 The magazine *Les Temps Modernes* was founded by Sartre, Simone de Beauvoir and Maurice Merleau-Ponty in 1945. Gallimard ceased publishing it in 1948. Maurice Merleau-Ponty (1908–1961), French phenomenological philosopher. Merleau-Ponty engaged with Marxist thought and empirical psychology to argue for the foundational role of personal perception in human understanding. Spender's unpublished novella *Engaged in Writing* (1956) focused on two French existentialists, Sarret and Marteau, two thinly veiled portraits of Sartre and Merleau-Ponty.

2 'Like all heavy drinkers . . .'

which Natasha [Spender] and Madeleine once played concerti, while Malraux worked, telephoned, received visitors at the other end of the room.[1]

The Malraux were extremely friendly. I thought he looked well and less nervous than usual. Also, I felt more at ease with him than at other times, and immensely drawn to him. Malraux's universalism is very special. It is a series of formulations of topics, each of them completely dealt with and separate from all the others. If there is a theme, it is like hearing a set of very brilliant variations, each complete in itself. If there are different ones, like hearing a succession of brilliant little essays.

Of my themes, Malraux first took up European Union. He said that as it was put before us, it was a 19th-century parliamentarian conception. The idea of Strasbourg was quite inadequate to present circumstances.

England, he said (we must recognize), had interests which put her quite outside the project of a United Europe, if one thought of this in nationalistic European terms.

We should therefore look for a basis for European Union other than that of Europe: 'new enterprise', an event of exploitation into which Europe could enter and reconstruct itself. This was understandably the exploitation of the continent of Africa. [. . .]

Then he passed on to Russia.

The important thing to realize was that Russia was no longer an ethical symbol for the rest of the world. It had become one of two things: firstly an economic structure of Communism; secondly, the police state.

Apart from all arguments about the economic structure, we reject Russia because we reject the police state.

Here we are at once involved with America, because the U.S. is, above all, the country which rejects Russia. We are told that we are as different from America as from Russia and that we are confronted by a choice of American and Russian cultures equally alien to us. But, although the Russia of Tolstoy, Dostoyevsky and Turgenev

---

[1] Madeleine Malraux (b. 1914) is a pianist specialising in the nineteenth- and twentieth-century repertoires. Between 1948 and 1966 she was married to André Malraux.

[81]

turned towards Europe, the Russia of Stalin has definitely turned away from our culture and is in fact completely alien to it. What is America, though, but Europe? America is the development of European culture within American conditions. America has done nothing to shut us out. On the contrary, it is overwhelmed with our production in every art gallery, every concert hall, every library. It is flooded with exactly those manifestations of Europe which Russia does everything possible to exclude and cut out.

We are told that many American things are stupid and dangerous. But when people say this they concentrate on the American form of things which we understand very well because they are also European. Their radio is stupid – well so is ours. Who would want Europe judged just by the radio or the newspapers or the cinema, or any of those things which we choose to label American, though they come from us.

Russia is analogous not to Europe but to Japan at the time when Japan was rejecting everything European. [. . .]

After dinner we moved to another part of the room where we had coffee and cognac. Malraux showed me the proofs of the third volume of his *Psychologie de l'Art*.[1] He showed me enlarged photo proofs of designs on early coins in which every phase of modern art from primitivism through realism to abstractionism had been traversed.

Then he returned to our conversation of the morning and said, 'Of course, there is a great difference between the American and the European concept of individualism. A good deal of misunderstanding is precisely due to this. Americans make individual values too dependent on the possession of personal belongings. Now, although it is nice to enjoy things and possess them, we know very well that we are not dependent on them for being ourselves. In Spain, we were just as much individualists as we are now, though we had nothing then. There are two fundamentals of European individualism. Firstly, the feeling that by virtue of his naked existence, one is both separate and the same as others, e.g. [Jean-Jacques] Rousseau. Secondly, the sense of being great as an objective reality in the sense, that is, of knowing one is a great man. The great man recognizes himself and is

---

1 This work was republished in a single volume as *Les Voix du Silence* (1951), translated as *The Voices of Silence* (1953).

recognized by others as such because he is a meeting place for their aspirations and dreams.'

Malraux gave me a very beautiful reproduction of a painting by Paul Klee, done by a new process.[1]

* * *

On Saturday, April 15th, Koestler was married to Mamaine, both of them having obtained divorces.

I had lunch with Georges and Peggy Bernier and Manolo Jimenez.[2] Peggy very sweet, Georges rather annoyed, I thought, because we left him and had a walk by the Quai alone. He seemed in a bad temper when we rejoined him. We then went to the Café de Flore, where we ran into Koestler and Mamaine. They asked us to join them for drinks.

I had not realized that he was very drunk. He pointed out to us a man whom I have always avoided at the other side of the Café. He is a tall cripple, with a smiling, twisted mouth, which wears a perpetual sardonic smile, and very clear, staring eyes. In addition to a gash on his neck and at the side of his mouth he has only one leg.

'Tell me what do you think of that man?' K. asked us, pointing at this man – whom I knew by the name of Daumaerts. I said I knew him vaguely and did not like him, Peggy and Mamaine both said they disliked the look of him.

At this, Koestler got up, went over to Daumaerts and brought him, grinning, back to our table.

'You see,' said K. pointing at D.'s scars, as though he were a horse dealer examining a horse, 'Hänschen was my comrade in a cell twenty years ago, weren't you, Hänschen.'

'Ja,' said Hänschen.

'This man,' said K., 'was in prison in Columbus house and made to eat shit. Yes, really, shit,' said K. 'They knocked him here and here,' K. went on pointing to dents in his head, 'and cut open a vein here.'

---

1 Paul Klee (1879–1940), Swiss painter influenced by expressionism and surrealism.

2 Georges and Peggy Bernier founded *L'Oeil*, a magazine dedicated to the visual arts, in 1955. Peggy Bernier reappears later in Spender's journals as Rosamond Russell, wife of the art critic John Russell. Manolo Jimenez, a diplomat, was her brother-in-law.

'I wander thou surwivededst,' he said, changing into German.

Daumaerts said, 'I wish you wouldn't' and quite good naturedly pulled K.'s hand away from his wounds.

'Now,' said K., 'this comrade of mine, who has been so horribly beaten up (by the way the leg wasn't lost at the same time but in an incident in the factory where he worked afterwards), this comrade has been through all those horrors, hasn't a penny to live on, and I am a rich man.'

'There is a Marxist explanation for all that,' said Daumaerts.

'You mean I have betrayed?' asked K.

'Your beliefs are perfectly sincere. It isn't a question of sincerity. It is a question of your ideas being the result of your situation,' said D.

At this point K. gave me a kick and asked me to join in the conversation. I said, 'The thing I most dislike about Marxism is the idea that beliefs are the result of historic situations. Such an idea imprisons the present in the present and the past in the past. It prevents the beliefs of the dead having any living validity for us.'

'You are arrogant, Stephen,' said K. 'He is not at all arrogant,' said Mamaine. I didn't reply because I thought K. was referring to the fact that I allowed myself to dislike Daumaerts – and I felt quite horrible about this.

We went to dinner at a rather small restaurant, after some altercation between Mamaine and Koestler. He wanted to drive a long way to some expensive place. Obviously Koestler was extremely agitated by the meeting with Daumaerts. I had the curious feeling that he felt him in some way to be right, and that he, K., would have liked to be back in the C.P. [Communist Party] fold. When we were at table, he said to me: 'There's one thing you shouldn't say in your *New York Times* article. That is, that we're all *dégringolé* [falling to pieces].'

At the same time there was something a bit childish about Koestler as though he were too consciously playing the role of the crusader without a cross. He was very officious about the food and drink in the restaurant and bickered at Peggy (who stood up to him) because she wanted to drink Rosé with lobster. He summoned the waiter and complained about each wine in turn. At the end, he asked for Armagnac, tasted it and said, '*Bon, mais trop jeune*.'[1]

---

1 'Good, but too young.'

Koestler now said he wanted to go to a night club. Celia [Mamaine's sister], his very charming young secretary who was with us, said she had been travelling all night and wished to go to bed. I suggested that perhaps she could rest at the rooms of Henri Louis de la Grange, where I was staying, while the rest of us went to the night club.[1] However, she decided to come with us. We went to one place, which was hot, expensive and incredibly like a bad street singer doing an inferior performance on an off-day to a dejected crowd of jay-walkers.

Koestler suggested we go somewhere else. Celia said that if we stayed on another singer would appear who was more amusing than this one. Koestler got ill-tempered and left the room. Then Mamaine said to me could she and Celia both come and spend the night at my place? I said, 'Yes,' so that is how the Koestlers spent their wedding night.[2] [. . .]

Spent all this week translating Hoffmansthal.

When all has been said, translating is a supreme exercise in tact. What to introduce or omit in order to create rhyme and rhythm, while remaining true to the sense, is simply a question of tact. What has to be avoided is the introduction of tactless pictures, sounds and additions to the sense, which disrupt the intensity of the original inspiration.

8 June 1950, London

Accompanying everything I do there is a voice which says, 'You are wrong.'

If I travel, it says: 'Why are you running away?' If I work, it says: 'Why do you busy yourself with irrelevant actions and fill your mind with clamorous ideas which overreach themselves?'

If I spend money, it says: 'You will never buy anything you want.' If I earn it says, 'You know quite well that you will never earn enough money to be able to put earning aside and think of me.'

---

1 Henry-Louis de La Grange (b. 1924), renowned Mahler scholar and founder of the Bibliothèque Musicale Gustav Mahler. He met Spender after the war and sometimes lent him his flat when Spender visited Paris.

2 According to Natasha Spender, Spender claimed later that he told Mamaine, 'I always wanted to spend the night with you. What a pity it was your wedding night.'

If I sit quite still and do nothing, it says: 'Well, doing nothing has not found the answer.'

Finally I must come to terms with this voice. Firstly, I admit that ninety per cent of what I do is wrong. I am like a plant which is not so much overgrown with weeds as that it becomes a weed. It grows with a quite astonishingly rapid fertility. In fact the consciousness of its vastly assertive growth is one of the distractions, which prevents my being conscious of what I nevertheless feel should be its real shape. It is always growing, all these weeds instead of leaves, which it produces from within itself, cover up that shape which it ought to have which has now become a kind of blank in my mind, the thing which is there but which nevertheless does not exist even as an idea with a defined shape. For these weeds, which it grows, are not only actions and things but they are also thoughts. Any thought, even what I am writing now tends to grow with that disconcerting rapidity and to become a weed – a thought which hides my real thought, a weed substituted for a leaf. Words are very dangerous because they tend just to proliferate themselves, like everything else and to hide me from that which seems wordless, inactive and yet not a vacuum and not the merely egoistic.

In order to discover the real pattern of this plant which grows from itself nothing but weeds, one would have first to take a knife and cut away the false leaves, the weeds. And the first thing to do is therefore to recognize and cut away the wrong ideas, in the hope that underneath them we may find something which if not right at least has the shape of something different from those shapes and thoughts which are entirely false.

Now that I think of it, I see that the weeds vary as it were, in the extent of their weediness. Some leaves are far more completely weed than others. On the other hand, there is no activity I can think of which has the entirely pure shape which contains no element of weed. I might also say, though, that there is no weed which does not contain some element of the true pattern.

Therefore, after all it is not enough to tear away the weeds. I must also classify them and distinguish in them what I consider to be the bad and the good elements. In this way, I may be asked to discover what is common to all the good elements.

This already suggests something to me because I do not believe the bad elements have qualities in common which make up an essential part of the pattern. The leaves become weed, are all weeds of a different kind in their weediness. What they have in common is the element, which is part of the real pattern and therefore not part of their weediness. This is the element, which justifies their existence as part of my existence.

Let me now analyse some of my activities. The voice tells me that all of them are wrong. I can instinctively choose any characteristic activity as a specimen:

Moneymaking. As activity[,] externally irrelevant because it means participating in the machinery of objects for no reason except the making of money itself. In so far as moneymaking is only concerned with making money, it is an arrangement of objects in such a way that according to a system of supply and demand, they automatically produce money. In itself, moneymaking is never a direct form of self-realization. The personality has, though, a relationship to it on two sides: the sides of making and those of spending. One fits one's talents into the machinery of moneymaking. But this does not mean that moneymaking has ever a direct relation to one's talent. There is an intake and an outlet of a machine.

Spending is much nearer to self-expression than making money. An element of the creative in life is the acceptance of necessity: and gaining and spending are necessary. Another element of creativeness is extravagance. It is the nature of extravagance that one cannot calculate it. One cannot speak of a legitimate and an illegitimate extravagance. All the same, there is consciousness of spontaneity and of a point beyond spontaneity.

Fabricating ideas, dealing in words, spending money are all forms of traffic in which there is a continual silent struggle between the person who uses them as a means of self-expression and their own tendency to multiply, to move faster, to carry the personality away on their stream.

Travel, action, politics, the life of the office and the movement.

I participate in movement. I am moved by it and to a small extent I help it to move.

At the same time, I hardly know the direction in which I am going. I forget the purpose of my journey.

And all the time in my consciousness and in my activity I am far from the centre where the wheels turn and, within the wheels themselves, the impulse, which is the critic of movement.

Merely doing nothing. I am aware by empty movement chasing through me. The movement of the world, the movement of ideas and of action all round me.

Not to act, not to move does not create a stillness. It simply leaves me in the dazed condition of not knowing whether it is myself who moves or the rest. As when one sits in a stationary train and another train coming into the station makes one think that one's own train is moving out.

The sun does not really know whether it moves round the world or the world round it.

In all these actions there are elements of the external and of the interior, which create a kind of impurity. The interior is that which corresponds to a real desire to project one's own existence, the pattern of one's own thought into the existence of things. The exterior is that which often has the colour of desire but which is nevertheless the mere gravitation of things towards other things, habit, custom, the movement of the earth through space. At the same time without a certain element of impurity, of mere externality, life would be colourless.

8 March 1951, London

Spent much time interviewing poets for *Picture Post* articles – David Gascoyne[1] – shook so much photographers had difficulty. K. J. Raine[2] gave us tea, remarked: 'When one is above 40 one gets so tired of having to go about all day with oneself.'

---

1 David Gascoyne (1916–2001), British surrealist poet and critic whom Spender had met in pre-war Paris. *Picture Post* magazine, launched in 1938, pioneered British photo-journalism (Stephen's brother Humphrey was one of its photographers). Edited by Tom Hopkinson, it took a firm socialist line.

2 Kathleen Jessie Raine (1908–2003), symbolist poet. She was also the former wife of Charles Madge, with whom Stephen's first wife Inez had eloped in 1939.

1 December 1951, London

'A brutal hurry' occurred to me yesterday as a phrase which adequately describes a good deal of my life.

2 December 1951, London

The Amateurs of Love. Books and writers. Chiefly, 1) Way of All Flesh. 2) Forster. 3) Lawrence. 4) Proust and the Abnormal theme. 5) Politics, Wells and Orwell. 6) Eliot. 7) Auden. 8) Women – V.W., E.B., E.S. [Virginia Woolf, Elizabeth Bowen, Edith Sitwell] 9) Myself.[1]

3 December 1951, London

Juliette Huxley came to lunch. Julian ill, obviously with his kind of partly mental breakdown.[2]

John Craxton came in for coffee.[3] Very excited about having sold 15 paintings at his exhibition. He talked about Lucian Freud saying to him at the party after Noel Coward's play at Warwick House, 'You can home in on the Rothermeres if you like, but you aren't going to do Princess Margaret soon.' He said that Lucian is now going around with a set of people who will not help him at all and will drop him at a moment's notice if he begins to bore them.[4]

4 December 1951, London

Received from the PEN Club, a notice of the following meeting organized by UNESCO:

---

1 Although Spender proposed this book to his publisher, it was never written.

2 For Julian and Juliette Huxley, see biographical appendix.

3 John Craxton (1922–2009) was in his youth connected to a 'neo-romantic' movement in post-war British painting. At this point he was sharing a studio with Lucian Freud, subsidised by Peter Watson, who was also financing *Horizon*.

4 For Lucian Freud, see biographical appendix.

EUROPEAN ASSEMBLY ON POETRY

Poets of fourteen European countries met in Belgium, 7–11 September, and their messages concerned poetry and poets throughout the world. Those who wish to acquaint themselves with the programme and the views expressed on the occasion of this conference should consult the September issue of Le Journal des Poètes (La Maison du Poète, rue de la Lune, 158, Brussels, Belgium).

The conference expressed grave concern over the diminishing appeal of poetry to the contemporary public and challenged poets to confront problems of reality and to apply their genius to the interpretation of the ultimate significance of trends and events. Various speakers dealt with poetry as a spring of humanism, as an expression of human sensibility, aesthetic as well as ethic, and as a force capable of revealing to people of all nations and of different backgrounds the fundamental fellowship of human beings.[1]

This is absolutely damnable and shows the banality of such meetings in which the journalistic spirit always dominates over the spirit of art. In the first place, poets of 14 different countries will not possibly have anything to say to one another since no poet understands 14 languages and poetry is a matter of language. Secondly, the diminishing appeal of poetry to the public is because the concern of poets will justify the public in losing all interest in poetry. Thirdly, a poet's reality is naturally the theme of his poetry and the idea that there is some generalized reality which all poets ought to attend to is absurd. This reality they talk about is only a subject for newspaper editorials. The 'ultimate significance of trends and events' is meaningless abstraction. A poet deals with what is real to him, however large or small this be, and the moment he forsakes his grain of sand for an eternal principle, he is as damned as if he were confined for all eternity to a Congress of poets from 14 nations discussing the obligations of poetry.

---

1 The text comes from a UNESCO flier pasted into the journal at this point. For Spender's involvement with the organization, see UNESCO in the biographical appendix.

[90]

10 December 1951, London

The view of our garden and the surrounding ones is extraordinarily beautiful in this weather. Through a mass of tangled boughs of many trees twining through grey smoke an azure spire points up against a red sunset. Beyond the walls the earth in the gardens seems smouldering, and the green of lawns shine[s] like enamel.

It's 6 days since I wrote this diary. So now it must consist of notes. On December 5, [T. S.] Eliot, William Plomer, Rose Macaulay and Veronica Wedgwood came to dinner.[1]

Eliot came rather late and left rather early also on doctor's orders. He was in a very good humour. The dinner and drink were excellent. But I can remember nothing serious. Rose talked about her early memories. Eliot said he could remember being fed out of a bottle. Rose said, 'In that case you must have been weaned very late.' Eliot said, 'Now, now, Rose, you're making me look ridiculous in public.' Eliot also said at some stage in the evening, quoting the Russian press about him: 'I am a reactionary, anti-semite pornographer.' Everyone was very pleasant.

Another idea [for a book] is, of course, the whole history of Tony Hyndman.[2] I jot down the latest developments:

A few days before I left London, Christopher Isherwood told me that Tony had rung him from Bristol, to say he was in a very bad way.

Before this Tony had, after many adventures, been making a prolonged stay with the Franciscan Brotherhood in the country. They apparently refused to keep him indefinitely, so he had to be rehabilitated. He wrote telling me of this and asking me to pay one or two small debts, which I did.

Now, just after Christopher had left from America, he suddenly appeared in my workroom. He had bloodshot eyes, and a very wooden expression. He held himself as though he were bent with lumbago.

He told me that he didn't want to bother me, but there were just

---

1 William Plomer (1903–1973), London-based South African novelist. Rose Macaulay (1881–1958), novelist and travel writer. C. V. (Cicely Veronica) Wedgwood (1910–1997), British historian and translator.

2 For Tony Hyndman, see biographical appendix.

one or two things he must explain. He had taken a cheque book from the room of one of the Franciscan brothers (who was dead). With this, in Bristol he had signed three cheques, to the value of about £10 – one to Peggy Ashcroft and two to shops (one of them a wine shop).[1] 'This,' he said, almost with a touch of pride, 'is a felony, and now that I've committed a felony, I feel the only decent thing I can do is go to the police and make a clean breast of the whole affair.' I said I thought this was rather absurd. If he went to prison he would have another bad mark against him, and it would be simpler just to get Hugh Ross Williamson or myself to speak to the people to whom the cheques had been paid.[2] 'That's what Hugh said,' he replied. 'But it means telephoning all over the country and is an awful bother.' 'If you go to prison, it will be still more bother, not only for you but for all of us. Your problem is simply to work and be independent.' 'Yes, but that's just what I can't do.' He then explained to me that he could never by work earn as much money as he wanted, because he had got into a habit of taking 10 or 20 benzadrine a day. 'I'm ill,' he said, 'mentally ill. What I want is psychiatric treatment. I'll go to the police and tell them everything and then they can get the court to order me treatment.'

In some extraordinary way he had it all worked out. I got angry and said that he could surely get treatment if he worked, and without having to have a prison sentence. He said: 'No, I'm sick of everything. I hate this world, it's a horrible place.' 'You've done your little bit to make it more horrible for yourself and others,' I said. 'You've been helped more than anyone I can think of. All that's required of you is simply that you should be self-supporting and that you shouldn't add to the burdens of other people.' 'That's just why I'm going to give myself up,' he shouted. 'I don't want your help. The only thing I ask you to do is settle Peggy Ashcroft's account, because it's in your interest to do that,' he added rather spitefully.

We went out into the street. As he went off, he said, 'The person I hate most of all is you, Stephen.'

The next day I rang H. R. Williamson and Tony's other friend,

---

1 For Peggy Ashcroft, see biographical appendix.

2 Hugh Ross Williamson (1901–1978), historian and dramatist. He became an Anglican clergyman in 1943 and converted to Catholicism in 1955.

Bianca. H.R.W. had taken Tony along to Charing Cross Hospital. The psychiatrist had said he would have to wait a month or 8 weeks for treatment. 'You aren't going to kill yourself or anyone else, so you can wait,' he said. 'There are others who may do so, if they aren't treated.'

Tony rang me in the evening, and said he was at the desk of the Hotel where he was staying and that they would not let him out until he paid the bill. I spoke to the manager and said I would settle it by post. He said that was not good enough, he wanted the money before Tony left the Hotel. I arranged that Tony would come along now and get it from me. A few minutes later he rang up and said he could not come all the way to St John's Wood. He had only pretended he was going to see me in order to leave the hotel. I said 'Well anyway you'd better ring them up and tell them that you aren't coming back. They've been quite nice to you.' At that he started talking violently about them. So I rang the hotel and said he wouldn't be back.

H.R.W. rang me the next day to say that Tony had given himself up to the police after leaving the Hotel. The police had been very nice about it. Tony's pockets were full of little bits of paper confessing to things he had purloined and so on.

He came before the magistrate the next day and was bound over for a week with a view to a report being made on the necessity for psychiatric treatment.

Christopher Isherwood was in London all these weeks. We saw a lot of him. He is extraordinarily nice, amusing, kind – better, in many ways than before. Fortunately he is being very successful now with his dramatization of Sally Bowles.[1] But although he looks younger than he ever did, too much of his energy seems now to have gone into acting the role of being himself – which he does ever so attractively and kindly and for the benefit of his friends and perhaps of himself – but perhaps not of his books.

At any rate, the two chapters he read at the I.C.A. of a new novel, seemed [. . .] too Hollywoodish in the way in which the situation of

---

1 The stories in *Goodbye to Berlin* (1939) were eventually dramatized by John van Druten after Isherwood had given up the task himself. The 1951 play *I Am a Camera* and 1972 film *Cabaret* were the most financially successful of all Isherwood's works.

a jealous gay man whose home had been broken up, was dramatized. On the other hand there were wonderful descriptions of California – with a great deal of atmosphere but too black a cynicism perhaps.[1]

In 1952, the Austrian-born British publisher George Weidenfeld (b. 1919), a fervent Zionist, commissioned Spender to write a 'Report on Israel', now four years old, with particular attention to the 'Youth Aliyah' programme. The result was the book Learning Laughter *and in preparing for it Spender, as was his habit, kept a journal.*

'Youth Aliyah' was founded in 1933 to rescue Jewish youth from Nazi Germany. Some 5,000 children were resettled in what was then Palestine, and 15,000 more followed after the war. Many were Holocaust survivors.

12 March 1952, on board ship in the Mediterranean

The ship – the *Artsa* – is absolutely packed with people – Poles, Russians, Germans, French, Moroccans, Spaniards, Italians – and still more packed with their belongings. The cabin I share with a Polish Jew is packed with a wireless set, a box of edibles of various kinds, and two large sacks of onions. My hopes of working during the six days' voyage to Haifa are dashed. Apart from the smell of the onions, I cannot get near the writing table, which is heaped up with parcels. Counting 110 crew – the purser told me – there are altogether 542 people aboard this very small ship.

My first glimpse of the children who are going to Israel was when we drove up the drive of the large transit villa facing the Bay of Marseilles, and saw two leering masks looking at us through the bushes. In front of the house itself, in the driveway children were playing, wearing masks, singing and dancing. Behind them their suitcases, exotically painted with stripes, were laid out.

I had breakfast with Mr Lutz, the head of the house, two girls who look after the children and the brothers Feigenbaum from Poland

---

1 Isherwood read extracts from *The World in the Evening* (1954). The ICA, Institute of Contemporary Arts, was established in 1947 to support a wide range of art forms. Peter Watson, patron of *Horizon*, was involved in its creation.

and France. [. . .] The children – Mr Lutz told me – come from Morocco by applying – or their parents doing so – to an Israeli Bureau of Youth Aliyah, to leave the country. In Morocco they live in a grinding poverty, sometimes in caves, sometimes fourteen or fifteen people in one tiny room. They go out to work at the age of 8, and in the cities they often become corrupted. There are few good homes. They arrive from Morocco equipped with knives which they are ready to use on the least provocation, distrustful, suspicious, and usually suffering from several diseases.

Within three months at a training centre, there is already a wonderful improvement. They have learned politeness, cleanliness and a certain discipline and cooperation. Certainly, to see them in the transition centre, or on this ship, it is wonderful to think they are only three months from the slums of Tangiers or Marrakesh.

Isvi Feigenbaum told me that in Israel they have for a long time a bad inferiority complex, when they are brought into contact with the children from Europe.

On the other hand, they enjoy certain advantages. They have not been spoiled. He told me some of them learned quickly and were glad to do so. Others seemed angry at the idea of knowing the alphabet. One, when he tried to teach him something, attacked him with a knife.

Went on the ship at 3.30. Now, while I write this, we are passing Corsica.

13 March 1952, on board ship in the Mediterranean

Stromboli from the distance, a cone rising isosceles out of the sea. Nearer, with land jutting out from either side at the base of the cone. Under the grey lava-mountain, with fumes of white cloud and dark smoke stuck into its apex, like two feathers into a hat, a village with scattered houses, like dice on a shelf of mossy green above the sea. At one side of the mountain the grey flat wall of slowly sliding larva looks like a chute of slag.

From the distance the straits of Messina were partly hidden by a curtain of rain and shadow under high-massed clouds. Then we approach the rocky coast with lines of strata scratched along its sides, as though a rake had been dragged along it. Palermo looks across the straits at Messina, Messina looks back at Palermo. Ferry boats hover between. The waves of the Straits are tugged back by currents like dogs on a leash, snapping with white-bared teeth at ships. As we move through the straits the day darkens and Messina seems all grey slate with a few sparkling lights under the black mountains which are smudged into the totally black clouds.

18 March 1952, Haifa, Israel

Arrived at Haifa at dawn. Isvi and one or two other Jewish boys and girls stood on the deck looking at the port in the bay with inexpressible pride broken by outbursts of silliness. Seeing a little gun-boat: 'Look, our navy.' A monoplane flies over: 'The Israeli air force!' But, suddenly, in a different tone of voice, Isvi exclaimed: 'C'est tout à nous!'[1] I never understood national pride so well.

Haifa is partly port partly residential town, with boxlike modern apartments struggling up the hillside. It is planted with charming cedars and other beautiful trees, many of them now in flower. Wild orchids, irises, alpine roses, wild cyclamens abound. [. . .]

We met the director who took us to his office and told me about the arrangements for the children. They come to the sorting centre from all parts of the world, at the rate of 350 children a month. They are given a complete medical examination here, and their future is decided on. They go out from here to 200 different places. Children from over thirty different countries have been through the sorting centre. The main groups are: from North Africa 2,000; from Iraq 1,500; from Romania 1,000; from Persia 600.

On an average, children wait at the sorting centre from two to four weeks, but sometimes they are held up for much longer periods.

I saw the Moroccan children, whom I had left on the quayside, arrive. Each was given a piece of soap, a towel, a few clothes, and other essentials, taken to the wash-house and then for a medical examination.

The day after the children arrive at the Sorting Out centre, they are set to do household tasks and simple work in the garden. The grounds bear signs of the things past boatloads of children in their few weeks here have done. Gardens are planted out and there are small

---

1 'It's all ours.'

constructions in them: a fountain, toy houses, etc, made by the children. There were some good mosaics, of a large goose in a manner recalling mosaics at Pompeii, and a sundial with all the signs of the zodiac, done by a boy who passed through.

I also saw soft toys – dogs, kangaroos, etc – handbags, belts and rugs, made by the children.

The Moroccan children had shining faces and looked excited. They greeted me as an old friend in a strange country. They seemed already to have changed in the few hours they had left the ship, and to belong to the life of the camp.

I went into one or two dormitories. In the first were three girls, living in Swedish-built huts, slightly more comfortable than those of the boys. These girls were from Morocco and they had a very playful manner.

In a boys' hut we saw a group of Romanians. A tall, blue-eyed boy, whose name I discovered to be Reuben Butnera, complained to my companion, Dr Melitz that he has been five months in the Bath Sheba with his parents without ever doing or learning to do anything. He now wanted to go to a Kibbutz (a communal settlement) as soon as possible. He wanted to learn a profession as locksmith or carpenter. Melitz said that agronomy was also a profession, but Reuben did not seem enthusiastic about this. He said there was much anti-Semitism in the part of Romania he came from. I asked whether the Communists did not try to stop it. He said it was exactly they who were the anti-Semites.

The whole atmosphere of the camp struck me as something between an English preparatory school and the London Fire Service. Whenever Melitz talked to a boy he started the conversation by taking off the boy's cap, turning it inside out and putting it back on his head like this. This kind of friendliness is of the 'institutional' variety, but it may nonetheless be real. A boy with long black untidy hair, a surly expression, and knife wounds on his body, appeared to have been here for over six months. He could not explain why.

19 March 1952, Jerusalem, Israel

Melitz fetched me at 10 and we drove to Jerusalem. On the way he maintained his role of mentor, contesting my tendency to stare out of the window and go into a kind of green trance. He explained to me the significance of an area of huts, just outside Haifa. The first row of huts we saw were for immigrants, the day after their arrival. Here they are medically examined and questioned. If they are fit and suitable, they are then transferred to a second lot of huts, small houses, or even tents, called a ma'abara. When they leave the first hut they are given a little money, about £10. After this they are expected to make their own way. They work at tree planting, or at any other job in the neighbourhood of the ma'abara. [. . .]

Although it is dominated and given a certain feeling of order by this magnificent skyline, Jerusalem is an untidy, straggling city, spread out round the walled-in Old City, which is now Arab Territory. Right in the centre of the new parts of Jerusalem, there are ungainly bare patches of wasteland of mud, grass, stones, scattered olive trees, and barbed wire from the recent fighting. There is a kind of No-Man's-Land between the buildings, which are officially supposed to be empty. In fact, though[,] they are occupied by the members of the bankrupt ma'abara (immigrant settlement), who simply left their huts and moved in here without asking anyone's leave. These dwellings are in a deplorable condition and create a kind of slum in the middle of Jerusalem. People live in houses one wall of which is missing so that the interior, where they spend their wretched lives, can be seen from the street like the stage of a theatre.

After lunch I went to see one of these harbours where immigrants spend the first year or two of their lives after arriving in Israel. It was not unlike one of those displaced persons' camps in Germany, after the war: acre on acre of dirt and mud, covered with huts a few yards apart, where people seemed to be living lives of organized waiting in miserable circumstances and great poverty. As we walked through the streets or lanes, the stench and wretchedness grew greater towards the centre of the settlement. On the outskirts there was some grass, and in what one might call the suburbs, people had planted little gardens round their huts, which were spaced at wider intervals than those in the centre. In the middle, men and women sat on what served as a pavement outside their huts selling things, and the interiors of some huts had been converted into shops. I noticed that good vegetables, eggs, bread and cakes were being sold. Later I found that people who came from Jerusalem to the ma'abara could buy food there they could get nowhere else.

23 March 1952, Jerusalem, Israel

Went to the Swiss Village, home for mentally disturbed children. A charming place in the hills among larches, pines, olive trees, very green and with the feeling of cool scented breezes moving among leaves. The houses in which the children live seem placed in a delightful garden, surrounded by views of hills and distant villages.

I was shown round by the Educator, a handsome young man like a horseman from the central plain of Hungary, with aquiline nose, strong yet sensitive features, hair falling over his brow in three black waves like plumage.

The children here are nearly all faced by some problem arising from their past. Their parents have died in concentration camps, or they have been lost, or some terrible private or public tragedy has overtaken them. Most have grown up since they were four without parents.

The main symptoms they suffer from are aggressiveness, nervous habits, stammering, and complete inability to cooperate with the other children in the settlements from which they have been taken away.

Only the most difficult cases are given psychoanalytic treatment. The usual treatment is by group analysis. A group of between six and fifteen children is formed and the children are then encouraged to talk about their problems.

The Educator showed us the game the children play in order that they may act out their dreams. They are given a box, which when opened is like a proscenium, formed by the lid, and the auditorium. The proscenium-lid is grooved, and into it a 'scene' can be set, chosen from a number of printed backgrounds portraying a great variety of possible scenes: a forest, a battlefield, a bedroom or other interior, the sea, an island, and so on. There are also a great many cardboard figures representing possible protagonists in the drama of the Ego –

heroes, devils, priests, mothers, fathers, villains, nudes, soldiers, wounded, corpses, etc. The child is invited to choose scenery and 'characters' and then to enact any story he likes.

Here is an example:

A girl from Greece, aged 10½ years[,] has been sent here on account of her habit of bursting into fits of uncontrollable screaming. In the settlement where she was formerly, she was never quiet.

Apart from the fact that she came from Greece, it had proved impossible to get her to relate anything about her past. She seemed to remember nothing before the moment when she arrived in Haifa. Apparently, she knew no Greek: only Hebrew.

She was asked to play the game with the theatre. Immediately she chose a bedroom scene and enacted and told the following story.

There was once a big girl and she wept a lot when she was at home. A man suddenly came into her parents' bedroom, where she was weeping and said, 'Why do you weep, beautiful girl?' She answered, 'I weep because my mother has gone away and never returned.' The man said to her, 'Don't weep. For until your mother returns you can stay with me.' She stayed several days with the man. One day the mother came back and she did not recognize the girl. The mother looked and looked at the girl and yet she could not find her.

(When the girl told this part of the story, she represented the figure who was the mother going round and round the figure who was the girl, but always with her back to her.)

Then the mother went out of the house and sat on a stone and began to weep. Then the girl was glad. She ran out and said to the mother, 'I am your child.' And both went home.

'This was the story,' said the Educator. So I asked her, 'What does the idea of the beautiful girl mean to you?'

She answered, 'It is I. I was always a beautiful girl.' Then I asked her, 'What does the idea of the man who found you weeping alone in the house mean to you?' 'That,' she said, 'was our neighbour.' Then she began suddenly to weep. 'I know now,' she said. 'It was in the night and I screamed. Then our neighbour came to me.' The Educator asked, 'Who is your neighbour?' She avoided the question. 'I was alone all night and the neighbour came only in the morning,' she corrected herself, 'when mother and father had gone away,' and she retold the story in a different form.

'When I was a little child, very small, I woke up one night, and I have never seen my parents since. Then I screamed terribly, till the morning, and a neighbour came, who looked after me for a while and then took me to the Red Cross. Before this, I had thought all men like my father. Now no more.'

'After this,' said the Educator, 'we managed to establish what had really happened. The father had been killed in the Greek fighting and the mother had run away with a Canadian soldier. A neighbour had rescued the girl and taken her to the Red Cross, who got her to Youth Aliyah.'

I write this down because such stories give an idea of the background of torment from which these children who have come to Israel have been saved.

24 March 1952, Jerusalem, Israel

In the afternoon I went to see Recha Freier, the remarkable woman who already in 1932 thought of the idea of saving the Jewish children from Germany.[1]

She is now fairly generally and publicly known as the 'forgotten woman' of the Youth Aliyah movement. (In fact a week after making this entry in my journal, I noticed a letter in the *Jerusalem Post* from Recha Freier recording that she had not been invited to the Jewish Children's Day Celebration at Tel Aviv on March 30th. The letter was headlined: *Forgotten*.)

Probably she is 'forgotten' so deliberately because she is a visionary who had an idea which other people were able to carry out with an organizational ability greater than hers.

There is an almost uncanny quietness about Recha Freier. She looks like some painting, which might be by the Douanier Rousseau, entitled perhaps the Prophetess, of a very ordinary-looking person with something extraordinary about her, obtrusively unobtrusive, a

---

1 Recha Freier (1892–1984), a German Rabbi's wife, founded Youth Aliyah in 1933 with the support of the World Zionist Organization.

kind of excessive, zealous quietness. She is dressed in clothes that look home-made, has uncared-for, brownish hair, and a way of sitting very still, holding her hands together in her lap. During the first few minutes that I was in her room, she said nothing; when she did begin to speak, occasionally she raised her hand, with finger pointed above her head, in an almost apostolic gesture. The stone floor of her room was completely bare, and all the furniture – except the table in a corner – was ranged against the walls, between bookshelves containing books in several languages. [. . .]

I observed that I had heard she was responsible for originating the idea. 'Yes,' she said, 'it was one of those ideas that came to me. I had no experience of social work but in 1932 and 1933 several of the young boys I knew lost their employment and all possibility of any future in Germany on account of their being Jews. So I had the idea of taking them to Israel and training them there to have a future on the land. But at first no one would take it seriously. Even in Germany when the Jews were being persecuted, they laughed at me. They had no idea of what was inevitably bound to happen in Germany. They hoped things would get better, so they thought so. Only the children themselves were on my side,' she said proudly. And I could see very clearly that if she had a tremendous idea, she might inspire children with it, while she might also frighten the parents with her intensity. [. . .]

In 1941 she went to Jugoslavia, to find out whether there might not be some means of smuggling the children to Israel. From Jugoslavia she sent helpers who fetched the children out of Germany. It was still possible for them to leave at this date, provided they signed a document renouncing their German citizenship and saying that they would never return there.

When they had got the children into Jugoslavia, they had to smuggle them to Israel. This was not so difficult as might appear, for a great many people sympathized with these children, including the Jugoslav government of the time and even the British Embassy.

But the whole plan collapsed when a group of girls arrived and were arrested by the Jugoslav police. They were well treated, but their story caused a sensation in the Jugoslav press. The Nazi authorities, fearing the sympathy which the children aroused, forbade any more children to emigrate.

25 March 1952, Jerusalem, Israel

The first *Kibbutz* we visited today was called Buchenwald Netza. It got this name because 60 of the inhabitants originally came from Buchenwald; though later these divided because some were very orthodox religionists, others were agnostic or not devout.

Netza is an old German templar settlement, with a kind of colonial-style architecture of buildings two or three storeys high, with wooden verandas. It is surrounded with eucalyptus trees, beyond which one can see fruit orchards and fields sown with crops – bright green at this time of year. [. . .]

When he [the educator] came here, he said, he didn't know whether to bring children from one country, two or several countries. He decided against one – they would not learn Hebrew – and then against two – they would form rival teams – in favour of as many nationalities as possible. The only means of communication between the children would then be Hebrew. He now has children from sixteen countries, with two or three from each country.

'Look,' he said, pointing down from the veranda where we were standing to a group of children playing ball under the trees, 'Bulgarian, Turk, Egyptian, Moroccan, Belgian, Romanian, Iraqi, Bulgarian again, Persian and German. Could you tell the difference?'

It would not be true to say the children all looked as though they came from the same country, but they didn't look as though they came from many different countries. They looked a rather variegated family, who had something indefinable in common – was it the school? Was it that they were Israelis? Was it that most of them had changed completely from the uncared-for parentless children they had been when they arrived? Was it that they all spoke Hebrew? [. . .]

The director of education who showed us round was a lean-faced, grey-haired, young-looking man with a keen, rather aggressive manner, and mightily receding chin. He looked lithe and intelligent, and was exceedingly dogmatic in all his views. [. . .]

We went to the exemplary dining room and had an orange each. The educator explained to me the life on the kibbutz. The only money anyone receives is £10 a year pocket money for his summer holiday, with an allowance of an extra £1 or £2 each year for each child, graded according to age.

Everything you reasonably require is provided for you. For example if you need a great many cigarettes, you receive more than other people. Clothes are provided according to the need of your occupation. 'For example, as I am a teacher who has to change from his outdoor things to indoor things fairly frequently, I have five pairs of trousers.'

Each married couple has a tiny one-roomed house with simple but bright and adequate furniture provided. No children are allowed to live in the house. They live all day in nurseries or classrooms – according to their age – and sleep at night in communal dormitories. They are visited by or allowed to visit their parents between the hours of 4 and 7 in the afternoon.

'Do you mean to say that babies are taken away from their mothers and made to live in the communal nurseries as soon as they are born?' I asked. 'Of course,' he answered.

He said that the children from the kibbutz studied in the separate children's buildings five hundred yards away from the living places of their parents, and the older ones slept in the four-bed dormitories here. 'They get so attached to being here that many of them do not bother to walk the five hundred yards to see their parents more than once in fourteen days,' he said with pride.

We went to visit the children in their hygienic, white quarters with pleasant, standardized furniture and decorations in the playroom. I must say they looked very clean and spruce and healthy, like children of British army officers living in some colonial settlement together. The educator ragged them a bit and they seemed far less intimidated by him than I was.

'Does any adult sleep in the children's dormitory at night to supervise them?' I asked. 'Of course not.' 'But what happens during the night if some child is frightened or taken ill?' 'It is the task of one girl to be up all night and supervise all the dormitories.'

The educator took us to his comfortable, pure, fresh room and we asked a few more questions. The children, he told us, work all day, six hours at their studies, two hours in the fields (that is, the older ones do) and all their evenings but one are organized for them. 'Tonight chess. Tomorrow discussion group; the night after, some kind of show, and so on.' 'Do they ever get any time alone?' 'Of course not.'

27 March 1952, Jerusalem, Israel

I interviewed Dr Dux at one of the Children's Clinics in Jerusalem. What specially interests me is the differences between the children coming from Europe and those coming from North Africa, so I asked him about this.

Dr Dux said that one of the difficulties the psychologists have in dealing with the Eastern (or North African) children is that the tests which apply to Europeans often do not work in their cases.

If you examine a European child, he has at the back of his mind a certain concept of disciplined knowledge to which he consciously relates the activities of his intelligence. But this relating of himself to a scaffold of intellectual order in his mind does not occur with the Eastern child.

Thus it often happens that Eastern children come to Israel who [have endured severe] shocks, of which we know nothing, earlier on in their lives. These block all their responses far more completely than would happen with Western children. In many cases, when you test such a child, he reveals an I.Q. which turns out to have no relation to the intelligence he subsequently reveals in his lessons.

'The shock he has received affects him and often we find,' said Dr Dux, 'that in the course of treatment his I.Q. increases. This does not mean that his real I.Q. has altered, but that our tests have not succeeded in discovering what it was in the first place.

'Another thing that interests me here is to discover whether the repression of other instincts than sex produces fantasies and obsessions, in the same way that sexual repression does in Europe. It has always seemed to me that Freudian psychology is built on observing the repression of one instinct – which is a typically Western kind of repression – and that, in the East where hunger is above all the instinct repressed, the life of the unconscious mind might turn out to be quite different.'

So I now asked Dr Dux whether the hunger certain children must have endured did not produce a kind of 'hunger neurosis', parallel to the effects of sexual neuroses. He replied,

'We had some Polish children here nine years ago, who made the journey from Poland through Russia until, after terrible adventures, they finally got to Teheran, from where, in 1943, they were conveyed to Palestine.

'These children ate an enormous amount at every meal and, after they had eaten all that they could possibly manage to get down, they would take the bread which remained on the tables and hide it in their rooms in and under their beds.

'When we tried to clean the room of one such child, he began to cry. "Why do you cry?" "Because you've taken my bread." (*My* bread, he said.) "But you can't eat that anyway. It's stale and mouldy." He answered, "You have no idea what bread we used to eat. We ate bread which was months old, years old."

'After that, I told my staff that whenever the children came saying they were hungry, they should give them something to eat at once. In many cases, when a child had eaten enormously, an hour later he tried to eat again. When he could not eat any more and yet still seemed to want to force himself to eat, we said, "Well, take the rest to your room." When they knew that they could always do this, they were released from the compulsion always to seek bread.

'One of them once told me, "I've often stolen ration cards from dead people in Siberia, and in that way I've sometimes been able to get more bread."'

I write down these stories of the children, with the feeling that in some way they justify the existence of the State of Israel more than anything else.

Learning Laughter was published by Weidenfeld and Nicolson in November 1952. In the same month, Spender flew to Brazil to lecture under the auspices of the newly founded Congress for Cultural Freedom, the American-funded, European-based organization that would, the following year, launch the magazine Encounter, of which Spender would be co-editor for fourteen years. He would undertake many such trips over the next few years for the CCF and for the British Council.

29 November 1952, Rio de Janeiro, Brazil

Rio is a dense skirting of skyscrapers and other buildings, edged with an esplanade, along the looped and curling coast. It is a long narrow tapeworm of a city, with great distances from place to place, and it cannot go further inland because of the sugarloaf-type mountains which rise abruptly from the ground only a mile or so from the coast at all points. The city has fine, very wide roads, flanked with the sea along the esplanades, with skyscrapers and high buildings at the several centres of the town. [. . .]

Last night I went to dinner with some Indians at their pleasant apartment on a sixteenth floor. As we had to have the windows open, we could not hear ourselves speak. The Indians were of the intelligent sensitive kind, in need of great conversational attention by the English guests in order to bandage various wounds in their souls. The *Times* correspondent Marshall [who] was there, understood this very well, and even told me in asides from time to time what the wounds were: our host's father had never been allowed to sit down in the presence of an Englishman; but he was also teased by his colleagues at the Embassy (where he is first secretary) because he had not been to an English public school.

Blomfield – the B.B.C. representative – and his dumpy Persian wife, however, without meaning to do so, behaved in such an Anglo-Indian manner that it was embarrassing. The *Times* man and I stayed on an hour after their departure in order to tie up any extra wounds that might have been inflicted. Mrs Blomfield, overtaken by the heat, simply went to sleep, and Mr Blomfield was groaning audibly with boredom, fatigue, Indian curry and the wish that I would exercise the privilege of a tired visitor and leave early. His reaction seemed odd to me as the Indians were charming and this the most delightful evening I have had in Rio.

We had one glimpse of the Indian children, a girl aged 4 and a boy aged 2. They were stretched on their coverless white beds like carved images nailed onto a white board. The boy had the features of a wax-like flower. He did not open his eyes.

1 December 1952, Rio de Janeiro, Brazil

Dined in the evening with Sir Henry King, described to me by someone as 'an intellectual sadist – 99% sadist and 1% intellectual'.[1] He is an elderly, fairly distinguished but slightly flabby-looking businessman,

---

1 Sir Henry King was the Commercial Officer at the British Embassy in Rio.

who lives in a comfortable flat with every up-to-date modern book of any interest, and his Steinway piano. There is a rumour that he had a love affair with Sally Coole, who was at the British Council here (and who seems to have made quite a reputation for herself by pretending that she was the original of Sally Bowles).[1] She drinks like a fish, is immensely gross, though her clothes, except that they are spotted with lipstick and liquor, retain a certain chic – her detractors reluctantly admit. When here, she severed all connections with the British Council – although employed by them as Press Officer – shut herself into a room in the Gloria Hotel where she incurred debts, and only received gentlemen whose social status she would not demean by introducing them to other members of the British Council. In addition to all this, she made a pass at England's most distinguished visitor until I came, John Lehmann, an attempt which will not be lightly forgiven in either Kensington or Rio. At present she has been sent to Ankara, where she is much happier than anyone would wish because the Turks are all sadists, and there is nothing she likes more than a little flogging with scimitars. Sir Henry told me, in his Old World way, that he gets delightful letters from Sally every day and that 'she is blissfully happy', from which one gathers that the British Council authorities were not being very *nuancé* when they tried to demote her. During dinner, Sir Henry began a conversation with me, which commanded the attention of everyone except H[is] Excellency's [the British Ambassador's] Economic Advisor.

He said, 'I hear you are a great friend of my friend, Sally Coole.' I gave them a description of Sally in her thin, innocent, un-snobbish days – thus managing to please Sir Henry, while providing myself with the alibi of 'another Sally' in order not to annoy the others: and if I gave the impression that I had had a love affair with her, this also was with the 'other Sally' – which acquitted me of bad taste, while claiming a privilege which everyone at the table (except H.E.'s

---

1 Sally Coole, whom Spender knew before the war, was in charge of tours on behalf of the British Council. In spite of her claim, she was not the model for Isherwood's Sally Bowles, who was in fact based on Jean Ross, a chorus girl with whom Christopher Isherwood lodged in 1932 whilst staying in Berlin. The surname was taken from the American writer and musician, Paul Bowles (1910–1999), who had visited Berlin in 1931 and crossed paths with Isherwood and Spender.

Economic Advisor) felt he might have shared for the asking. So I thought I was successfully Machiavellian, and had lived up to the account of myself I had just read in the *Times* of Brazil as 'winning all hearts by his modesty and charm'.

After dinner, Sir Henry showed [. . .] me some dirty limericks and also a long even more dirty poem written by himself. This was really almost up to the standard of Norman Douglas's collection, and was very good indeed.[1] Poetry inspired Mr Stephenson, the banker, to recite his own parody of Byron, beginning, 'When the inspector came down, like a wolf on our bank.'[2] After this, there was an embarrassed silence, during which Sir Henry slipped into an alcove with H.E.'s Economic Advisor while the rest of us had drinks on the balcony. Across the other side of the harbour, the Sugarloaf was silhouetted in an agate darkness, like the shape of an immense primitive sculpture of a dog with reclining body but head erect.

8 December 1952, London

On Thursday and Friday, flew back from Rio, via Recife. During this flight, one of the pilots sat himself several times on the seat adjoining mine, and started a conversation by saying that he knew a colleague of mine, Dylan Thomas.[3] He said that in the Thirties he had also been a reader of the Left Book Club books, but had later realized the inadequacy of all that. He now realized that we were living in an extremely late period of the world's history, when we had to discover a kind of intuitive knowledge that had been lost many thousands of years. This knowledge was revealed in the design of the Great Pyramid, which incorporated many of the discoveries of modern science, arrived at without a scientific method. Men had now invented the final scientific machine, which could bring an end to the non-intuitional scientific era. We were living in a period of history which resembled a detective story, where the villain has the power within

---

1 Norman Douglas (1868–1952), author of *South Wind* (1917), a satirical novel set in Capri where he lived. He was well known for his collection of esoteric pornography.

2 The poem parodied is 'The Destruction of Sennacherib' (1815).

3 For Dylan Thomas, see biographical appendix.

his grasp to destroy all the other characters, but the detective – intuition – is about to appear with his clue, which will change everything and take the means away from the murderer.

The pilot, who had the face of a self-educated man – rather soft and flabby, but intelligent – held forth for hours in this way, without changing the subject. It was very tiring, but he knew I suppose that although I thought him rather mad, I sympathized with his kind of madness, and was moved by the feeling or the search for truth which it embodies.

Sunday, the Huxleys came to lunch. Julian seemed better than he has been for years. Monday, lunch party given by us for Janet Adam Smith and Richard Blackmur.[1] Blackmur is on an 'assignment' from the Rockefeller Foundation to inquire into the economic situation of writers in various countries. He seems to me quite dumb, but I dare say he will butt into something in his leaden-headed way. He is a man who should have the innocent outdoor air of a classic American writer, but who actually looks like a chemist. So difficult to conceal one's disappointment.

Sometimes I think that Americans today are the people least like anyone else of any other people in the world. At times I think that Europeans have more in common with savages who worship idols and believe in magic than with these people who approach life as an 'assignment' on which they vent their 'projects'.

In Brazil everyone is a poet, because poets don't have to pay Income Tax. This is an idealization of the European idea of 'enlighted self-interest'. Also sixty percent of Brazilians have syphilis. So they are not difficult for the compatriots of Beethoven or Baudelaire to understand.

But I say to myself that the Americans have lost their European soul in order to find their American culture. Thus their literature is more interesting than that of the million Brazilian poets, even though there may be only twelve good American writers.

---

1 Janet Adam Smith (1905–1999) published many of Spender's early poems when she was literary editor of the *Listener*. Married to Michael Roberts, she was an adviser to Faber and literary editor of the *New Statesman*. R. P. Blackmur (1904–1965), who as an undergraduate was taught by Allen Tate, was at this time a literary critic teaching at Princeton.

Tea with Koteliansky.[1] Lives in his kitchen. Looks pale and haggard, slightly mad[,] with his face which is at once kind and malign. Said, when I arrived, 'First of all, I will have my little grumble. I am not very well, and the fog makes me much worse in my situation. Now let us talk of other things.' So I got him to talk about Frieda Lawrence, whom he described as 'this German animal, slightly civilized by the people whom she met through Lawrence'. 'I am not being malicious,' he said, 'but I knew Lawrence and I wish to tell the truth. Lawrence was a most moral and sensitive man, but this woman opposed all that was best in him.' Brett[2] he seemed to like more than Frieda, but he described her decision to go to Mexico with the Lawrences as totally disgraceful and unforgivable. 'There was her unhappiness, etc, etc, so she attached herself to this extremely sensitive and moral and sick man without the least regard for what she was doing. The point is that he was a real human being. And none of these women were real human beings at all. They only imagined their sufferings.' [. . .] I enjoyed this visit – which I had rather dreaded – as K. has the kind of personality which sometimes gives me a panicky sense of being trapped.

11 December 1952, London

Last night dined at Victor Gollancz's. Pakenhams were there.[3] After dinner Elizabeth and I got together and had a long talk about Oxford days. We talked mostly about the Carritts.[4] She described how, because Auden did not like women, Gabriel introduced him to her by

---

1 Samuel Koteliansky ('Kot') (1882–1955), Russian translator who came to London as an exile in 1911. He became a friend of D. H. Lawrence, Leonard and Virginia Woolf, John Middleton Murry and Katherine Mansfield, and was an editor on *Adelphi* magazine.

2 Dorothy Brett (1883–1977), British born painter of aristocratic background, moved with the Lawrences to Taos in 1924 and remained there with Frieda after Lawrence's death.

3 Frank Pakenham, later Lord Longford (1905–2001), politician and social reformer; married to Elizabeth Harman, a friend of Spender's from Oxford, where they were both members of the Oxford Poetry Society.

4 Gabriel Carritt (1911–1999) was a contemporary of Spender and Elizabeth Harman at Oxford. He later became fiercely communist and broke with most of his Oxford friends, including Spender. He appears in *World Within World* as Tristan.

an elaborate ruse, of arranging that they met by accident in his rooms, where Gabriel had arranged that Auden should wait for him, then arriving deliberately late for the meeting. She said she would never forget the look of horror on Wystan's face when he saw this creature that Gabriel had brought with him. Elizabeth said she was much surprised at those of our contemporaries who had succeeded in being known and those who hadn't.

She also told me that she and Frank were host and hostess to the Anglo-German Club's dinner. The first guest to arrive, while they were waiting to receive, was T. S. Eliot, long before everyone else. They were delighted and said how pleased they were that he had accepted the invitation and come early. Eliot said, 'Well, one could not not come, could one, or could one not do so?' Elizabeth said that they felt so tied up in all the 'coulds' and 'nots' that they stood there quite speechless, and could think of nothing to say.

20 December 1952, London

We gave a dinner for Rosamond [Lehmann], the Connollys and the Redgraves on the 11th.[1] (We are trying to entertain most of our friends before I go to the U.S.) Isaiah [Berlin] was supposed to come too, but he rang up the same morning to ask who the other guests were. When N[atasha] said that the Connollys were coming, he said he couldn't possibly come. Explained he was so shocked by Cyril's articles re. Burgess and Maclean.[2] 'Publishing them an act of pure

---

1 For Rosamond Lehmann and Cyril Connolly, see biographical appendix. Connolly's wife at this point was Barbara Skelton (1916–1996); the marriage ended in 1956. The actor Michael Redgrave (1908–1985), whom Spender knew from Oxford, was currently starring in Shakespeare productions at the Old Vic and at Stratford; Redgrave's wife Rachel Kempson (1910–2003) was also an actress.

2 Guy Burgess (1911–1963) and Donald Maclean (1913–1983) were two senior British diplomats who were also Soviet spies. Burgess knew both Spender and Auden, in fact he tried to contact Auden on the evening before he and Maclean defected to Moscow. Cyril Connolly, fascinated by the case, wrote a short account, called 'The Missing Diplomats'. Connolly took a sympathetic view of the two men; Isaiah Berlin did not. Burgess was also defended by Tom Driberg (1905–1976), MP (1942–55, 1959–74) and Chairman of the Labour Party (1957–8). The controversy persisted for years as it seemed to imply that a connection existed between the Labour Party and the Soviet Union.

cold-bloodedness.' He had already said so much to other people against Connolly that if he met him he would feel obliged to say what he felt. Otherwise, he would never forgive himself. Finally, he said that he would come but 'only as an act of great friendship'. I was out, but when I got home I spent my time trying to get hold of him to stop him coming, which I succeeded in eventually; but not before I had rung everyone else – except the Connollys – and told them not to mention Burgess and Maclean. Cyril, completely innocent, was very disappointed Isaiah had not come as he wanted to praise his lectures.

The next evening Isaiah took me out to dinner at Caprice. He said that he had acted with unmitigated rudeness and was very sorry about it, but had most complicated feelings about Cyril's articles: or, rather, not complicated ones at all, he thought they were only written for money and had caused a lot of pain. He was very nice. We talked about America.[1] He said there were three American political parties: the Democrats, the Republicans and the Radicals. The third party – the Radicals – was not represented and fitted awkwardly into the other two: thus there were Democratic Radicals and Republican Radicals. But the genuine streak of Radicalism (which was not necessarily a proletarian phenomenon, but – rather – an intellectualist one) did not know how to express itself. [. . .]

On the 12th I had dinner at the Huxleys. John Hayward, Jacquetta Hawkes, her husband Professor Hawkes and a man who was head of the British Association was there.[2] Jacquetta Hawkes talked brightly about the plays she was writing and producing with 'Jack' ([J. B.] Priestley) with whom she had just spent some time in America, producing. She told me that Jack had said she had a gift for dialogue. Professor Hawkes glared all the evening and said nothing until quite

---

1 Winston Churchill had appointed Berlin as a special envoy to Washington during the war, where he was well placed to observe the Administration at close quarters.

2 John Hayward (1905–1965), editor and man of letters, with whom after 1949 T. S. Eliot shared a flat in Chelsea. Hayward was disabled and in need of a wheelchair, so the arrangement imposed an emotional strain on both men. It ended in 1957 when Eliot married his former secretary, Valerie Fletcher. Christopher Hawkes (1905–1992), Professor of Prehistory at Oxford, 1946–72. Jacquetta Hawkes (1910–1996), also an archaeologist, married J. B. Priestley later in 1953.

late in the evening, when at some remark of Julian's he suddenly exclaimed, 'That's the first kind thing I've heard anyone say for the last half hour.' This rather froze up the conversation. The Hawkes couple left and we tried to warm up a bit at their expense, but it was rather a deadly evening.

On Saturday, the 13th Natasha did a broadcast. She returned home so tired that she went straight to bed and was not able to move out of bed, even to cross the room. Rather upsetting.

1 January 1953, London

The children saved Christmas from being quite awful. Myself, I find it that part of the year where my vitality is lowest, and I feel most discouraged; corresponding to 3 a.m. in the twenty-four hours. I hate the tawdry excess with which it's overdone: everything you buy [. . .] being wrapped in a Christmas packing, the mails being swamped by a snow of Christmas cards, the choking crowds of people in the shops treating it like a bargain sale. But in the minds of the children it really seems wonderfully pure and free of all this. On the one hand, they look forward to their presents, which are miraculous to them; on the other, they have thoughts about Jesus. I'll never forget Matthew's eyes when he looked at the candles burning on the tree, when he was two or three. Christmas Eve this year, he said to me, 'I wish Jesus was alive today.' 'Why?' I asked. 'Because I'd love him so much.' Then he added a bit later, 'If Jesus was alive, more people would love God.' He was more excited this year about his presents than I've ever seen him about anything. He woke up at 6.30 to look at the pillowcase we'd left outside his door stuffed with parcels. He was really very gentle and sweet helping Lizzie to open hers, and teaching her how to play with her new toys.

The interesting story to write about Christmas would be this birth of something bright and innocent in the lives of the children each year. In the end, I really liked Christmas Day, because they did so much. But it is rather overlaid with memories of that White Christmas seven years ago, when Lolly died.[1]

---

1 Lolly was Humphrey Spender's wife Margaret, who died in 1945. See the Spender family in the biographical appendix.

Our Italian couple of helps, Idelma and Francesca, went to midnight Mass.[1] Just before they went off, Idelma looked distressed, and Francesca explained to me, 'She's upset because she can't think of anything to confess. She hasn't been near a man for two years.' They were very pleased with the rings I brought back from Brazil for them. Granny we gave a wrist watch to, which she liked very much.[2]

In the evening I went to dinner with Julian and Juliette [Huxley]. Natasha did not go because she's saving her strength for the concert at Leeds next week. Julian is certainly rather strange in the way he wants to detach religious experiences from any ritualist or dogmatic context. He was talking about Bach's Mass in B Minor. He argued that the penetration of the music into the divine had nothing to do necessarily with the religion of the Mass. The form was just one which permitted Bach to express a universal experience. I said it was very difficult to imagine Bach doing so, except within the structure of the ritual; and that without such a framework of belief it was difficult for people to express such feeling today. He said, 'Yes, that is exactly the problem.' He thinks the problem is to create a religion of humanity castrated of God. [. . .]

Boxing Day evening, dined with Arthur [Koestler] at his new house in Montpellier Square, furnished, papered and painted with a tasteful kind of tastelessness, a colourful colourlessness. As in most bachelor establishments, one feels the lack of a woman to bring all the disparate elements together. The other guest was a very nice, very Christian young woman secretary to Michael Scott.[3] She and I rather attacked K. for the passage in his autobiography where he says that he sees through women because he can predict all their physical responses to every love situation when he has affairs with them, men because he can do the same thing regarding their intellectual attitudes. He said this applies only (!) to his physical and his intellectual

---

1 Idelma Loncrini and Francesca Ferri came from Torri del Benaco, a village on Lake Garda, where the Spender family had spent summer holidays.

2 'Granny' is Natasha Spender's mother, Rachel Litvin (1890–1977).

3 Michael Scott (1906–1983) was an Anglican cleric who, with Trevor Huddleston, proselytized for African liberation from imperialism. He frequently wrote in David Astor's *Observer*. The secretary mentioned here was perhaps Anne Yates, who wrote Scott's biography.

relations: but, on discussing it afterwards, Miss —— and I agreed that in his book he didn't leave room for much else.

On Saturday the 27th, I worked till 4, when Isaiah Berlin called, bringing with him a student of Russian origin. We had very nice conversation, a renewal of those streams of words from Isaiah in which I have bathed ever since I knew him. Very glad that this relationship has never lost its freshness and affection. [. . .]

Went [. . .] with Natasha to Leeds. Stayed the night of December 30th with a Commander and Mrs Evans. He is Warden of the hall where visiting students stay. Mrs Evans told Natasha she was worried that her daughter, staying in London with Arthur Haskell, might get into 'Jewish circles'. Natasha reassured her by saying that Orthodox Jews are extremely respectable. 'Oh, but these Jews are Christians,' said Mrs E. 'They are Catholic converts.' 'In that case they will combine the Puritanism of the Old Testament with that of English Catholicism,' said Natasha. Afterwards we thought she had not been quite nasty enough.[1] [. . .]

Natasha played – very beautifully on a rather broken down Bluthner Grand. The Harewoods were there for luncheon with the students and were extremely nice. After the concert we drove to Harewood House and spent the rest of the day till we had seen the New Year in, there.[2]

Impressions. The house itself and its grounds, in the grey tangled weather. The large entrance hall, smelling of tennis rackets and outdoor games, with a great many unopened parcels on every table, and even on shelves along the corridors leading from it. Everyone goes for long afternoon walks in the grounds, when the weather permits. My horror when I saw it was three o'clock only (we had lunched at noon) and realized that our hosts had to entertain us for nine hours without relief, as since we were not staying the night we couldn't go to our rooms. George, however, did go and write letters while we were shown some rooms with no light in them by Marion and Mrs

1 The reference is probably to Arnold Haskell (1903–1980), Principal of Sadler's Wells School. Born Jewish, Haskell was a convert to Catholicism.

2 George, 7th Earl of Harewood (1923–2011) was a music lover and musical director of the post-war Edinburgh Festival. His wife Marion Stein was a concert pianist and a contemporary of Natasha Spender. Both had studied with Franz Osborn, a pupil of Artur Schnabel.

Stein [Lady Harewood's mother]. Mrs Stein was too funny, like not so much just a visitor, but like a tourist, saying to Marion as she explained things, 'But how you know that Marion?' 'Well, you know, I've learned a bit since I've been here,' said Marion. Then Mrs Stein to me, pointing to a Sèvres vase, 'You know how much dat cost? How can people have such tings? I'm glad they're not mine. I simply *couldn't* own so much. It vould make me unhappy.'

The room where we had tea (was it the dining room? I forget) had china cups with M and a crown on them, and lots of silver. David [Lascelles] Harewood, aged 2½ and the Princess Royal were there. I sat on the left of the Princess Royal.[1] She was so agitated about tea that it made me nervous. There were about fourteen of us present, and she insisted on pouring out for everyone. There wasn't enough tea or coffee or hot water, and this troubled her greatly. By the time she had finished pouring out, people wanted their cups re-filled. It was difficult to have any conversation, and I was further inhibited by unwillingness to call her 'Ma'am', especially since Ben Britten, sitting on my left, managed to fit in about two Ma'ams to each sentence.[2] I felt like Beethoven refusing to take off his hat to the Duke of Weimar (?), after he had seen Goethe sweep his off and bow to the ground. I was also muddled by the fact that some people were calling her Ma'am, some 'Mum' (Marion and George) and David, for some reason, 'Mummy'. I was afraid I might start calling her 'Mom'. After a bit of practice with questions about her duties as Chancellor of Leeds University, though, I managed to fit in about one 'Ma'am' to every six from Ben Britten.

Princess Mary surprised me by her elegance. She gave an impression all pink, and silver with blue touches of her eyes. She was well-dressed and had her hair perfectly waved. With all those little nervous movements, there was a lot of gaiety at her grandson, the

---

1 Mary, Princess Royal and Countess of Harewood (1897–1965), was their host's mother. She held her title by virtue of being a daughter of George V.

2 Benjamin Britten (1913–1976), composer, was appointed a Companion of Honour in the 1953 Coronation Honours list. His opera *Billy Budd*, with libretto by E. M. Forster, was first produced in 1951. Britten had been a colleague of Auden's at the GPO Film Unit from the autumn 1935 until February 1936. Basil Wright, another colleague, credited Auden with awakening 'Ben's real and imaginative life'.

dogs, etc. Ever since I was a child and we had a photo of Princess Mary as a hospital nurse in our nursery. Then, after reading *War and Peace*, I had thought of her as rather like Tolstoy's Princess Mary, with the beautiful eyes in the plain face and the sweet religious character. In a way my impression at Harewood did not quarrel with this. Princess Mary obviously has a lot of character and feeling concealed under her nervousness, and much simplicity, and goodness. Natasha and I also had the impression that the incursion of the Stein family into her life provided her with a great deal of happiness. The Steins are not at all stuffy, and in a way they must seem a breath of fresh air (if such a simile could possibly be applied to Erwin [Marion's father]!).

This year – 1952 – has been rather better than most for me. That is to say, it's possible to look back and not regard it as entirely wasted. It has had a great disappointment – not getting the Byron Professorship – a blessing hardly disguised as far as all the others are concerned, which hardly consoles me.[1] There was my visit to Israel, of which I kept a complete journal. I spent most of the summer writing this up into *Learning Laughter*, a book of a kind I will never do again – pure reportage – but quite useful, and not in any way a disgrace. During the summer I wrote some poems and they are a beginning for something better, for a new style and a new subject matter. I feel that I have reached a turning point, which I have been waiting for.

3 January 1953, London

On January 2nd, I called on Paul Roche, the young poet whose poem I liked very much in *New Soundings*, and who had written to me some weeks ago. He has very pale blue eyes, an oval face with a pointed nose and pointed mouth in it. The effect is pink and blue and simple, like a Modigliani. He is very naïf, has read almost nothing and surprised me by appearing scarcely to have heard of Auden or Dylan Thomas. He seems to judge poems by what he thinks about them

---

1 After a visit to Athens in 1951, Spender had hoped to be appointed to the Byron Professorship in English at the University of Athens. An unhelpful reference from Harold Nicolson frustrated this move.

when he hears them read on the wireless. He says, for example, that he likes work to be sincere, and if it isn't sincere, he doesn't like it. That is all. I kept wondering whether (when I was 20) I did not make the kind of impression on people who took me out that he – sitting opposite me in the restaurant – made on me. It is difficult to account for the extraordinary charm of unsophistication, a quality which the unsophisticated one himself usually regards as a weakness, but which in fact is more persuasive often than the greatest wit or cleverness.

Duncan Grant has done literally hundreds of drawings of this young man in the nude, all of which he [Roche] showed me.[1] As his room (at Marjorie Strachey's flat) is very small, he made me look at them reflected in a large long upright-looking glass, which he has leaning against the wall, opposite his bed. I could not help wondering what role this looking glass played in his life.[2]

During the meal he told me that if he were rich the thing he would like to do most in the world would be to collect paintings. I agreed that I would like to do this too. Then he said, 'In collecting Duncan Grants I feel that I am beginning in a small way. That's why I get as many out of him as possible.' For the rest, we talked about books, but I was surprised to find how hard it was to hit on anything he had read. He had liked Laurie Lee's poems 'on the wireless'.[3]

I jot down all this, without having any general impression except a sympathetic one. Often at a first meeting, people say things, like his remarks about collecting Duncan Grants, which prove not to be revealing. On the other hand, they may be very revealing. There is a kind of hypothesis which is to be disproved or proved about first meetings.

In his room he had a most elaborate contraption – very ornamental and in shape like an old-fashioned umbrella stand suspended slightly above the floor, in which he kept white mice. He was dressed in corduroy trousers and a sports jacket.

---

1 Paul Roche (1916–2007) met the painter Duncan Grant (1885–1978) in 1946 while working as a Roman Catholic curate. Grant painted him frequently and the relationship lasted until Grant's death in 1978. Roche published two volumes of poetry in the 1960s. Spender was one of the first to encourage his talents.

2 Marjorie Strachey (1882–1962) was Lytton Strachey's sister, also a writer.

3 Laurie Lee (1914–1997), poet and memoirist, famous as the author of the autobiographical novel *Cider with Rosie* (1959).

After lunch we went to the Leicester Galleries, where I saw, for the first time in my life, a [Graham] Sutherland which I really greatly like. I felt a thrill down my spine and I found myself asking Mr Phillips how much it cost. It was £125, and I found I could buy it in easy instalments. I did so, knowing that it was a safe investment, and yet feeling terribly guilty at the same time.[1]

10 January 1953, London

A few things to write about. . . Matthew and I went to Paul Roche's little room. He gave Matthew a dormouse, to which his landlady had taken exception. I noticed in his room that the construction I had described as 'like an umbrella stand' is not at all like one. It's more like a field marshal's baton, fantastically constructed out of crab's claws, escargots, coconuts, and sundry pieces of wood, for mice to live in. He lifts up the cut-out lid of a coconut, as though trepanned, and shows us three mice nested inside. He has a book of photographs with a cover on which there is reproduced the Donatello of a young Medici – which bears a marked resemblance to himself. Is Catholic. The dormouse, by the way, fell down and we had to hunt for it under his bed, which concealed two or three pairs of shoes, some Duncan Grants, and sundry rubbish.

We put the dormouse in a box, and then to the pet shop in Baker Street, where we bought a cage for it. En route, Paul talked with perfect familiarity about dormice, hamsters, mice, hedgehogs, etc. Half the year he goes by himself on the continent with bicycle and kit-bag; last year was robbed of all his money while sleeping with it under his head on the beach at Cannes. [. . .]

Friday. Storm Jameson brought Jeanne Hirsch and Czeslaw Milosz to lunch.[2] Storm was rather self-dramatizing about the trial of having them to stay with her. But, I dare say, we would be if we had to put up

---

1 Graham Sutherland (1903–1980), British artist. Spender owned several of his works.

2 Storm Jameson (1891–1986), British novelist and critic, formerly wartime president of English PEN. Czeslaw Miłosz (1911–2004), Poland's Cultural Attaché in Paris in the post-war period. He defected in 1951 and became a distinguished writer, winning the Nobel Prize for literature in 1980. Jeanne Hirsch was a philosopher who attended the 1946 Rencontre de Genève.

with them. They are both very intense, and also formidably in love. Jeanne Hirsch has a spotty complexion, a long thin nose, a large mouth and black hair pressed very flat against the sides of her head. She looks enormously clever and behind all this there lurks an unawakened animal. I have often wondered whether anyone would dare to waken this, and raise her existentialist ideas to white-hot intensity. Milosz appears to have done so, and I admire this so much that I don't feel as sympathetic as I should for his wife and family in America.

Milosz talks in a soft Slavonic voice, which has a purring quality; but the purr is a tiger purring. He discussed with me the possibility of the Congress [for Cultural Freedom] helping refugees.

17 January 1953, London

On Thursday, I went to the luncheon given in honour of John Lehmann at the Trocadero.¹ Rosamond [Lehmann], Rose Macaulay, T. S. Eliot, E. M. Forster, William Plomer, Cyril Connolly, Joe Ackerley, Laurie Lee, Alan Ross and about twenty other people were there, including Arthur Koestler, whom I was forgetting.² He arrived late and found himself sitting at the end of a table with a group of people, all of whom hated him. The food and drink were inferior and the room very dull and uninteresting. Apparently, it amused Henry Green to have the luncheon here, as all his business entertaining goes on at the Troc. During the meal, Cyril got rather indignant because the

---

1 In December John Lehmann had released a press statement announcing that he had been sacked from his own publishing house, John Lehmann Ltd, 'owing to differences of opinion over future policy'. His principal investors wanted to terminate the company because it was failing to make any clear profit. Lehmann received enormous support from the literary community, with Rose Macaulay writing a letter to *The Times*, which was signed by Spender, Graham Greene, Harold Nicolson and Angus Wilson, amongst others. The lunch at the Trocadero was organized by the novelist Henry Yorke (1905–1973), whose pen name was Henry Green. Yorke was also the managing director of a business firm, which explains the reference to 'business entertaining'.

2 E. M. Forster (1879–1970), author and broadcaster whose six novels, all completed before 1924, have a central place in modernist literature. J. R. (Joe) Ackerley (1896–1967), a friend of Spender's since the 1930s, was literary editor of the *Listener*. Alan Ross (1922–2001) was a poet and editor of the *London Magazine*, in which over the years Spender serialized many instalments of his journals.

waiter – through not having heard what he said – brought him the worst instead of the best wine on the list. After some altercation, I heard Cyril say, 'Well, you can leave it if you like, but I won't drink it!', like a child saying 'So, there!'

Really, it was not at all boring: there were so many interesting and nice people (Louis MacNeice and William Sansom now come to mind) – but everyone behaved as though he was being consciously at once disappointed and a disappointment.[1] The speeches which were made were the culmination of this impression. Henry Green got up and said that, when he thought of having this meal, forty-nine (I think) people were invited and of these, much to his surprise, thirty-seven accepted. If there were only thirty-two present, this was because a lot had suddenly been struck down by flu. He thought it was a jolly good show, and a surprising tribute to John Lehmann. With this, he sat down. Then Eliot got up, looked bowed and old, leaning forward with his hands on the tablecloth and looking down at the table. With infinite gravity, he then said that he shared three occupations – or should he say professions? – with John Lehmann: as poet, business man and publisher. He was quite sure that, whatever had happened – and he didn't have any air of knowing in particular what had happened – that John would carry on with one of these. Then he sat down. John then got up and was more banal than his introducers. He said he didn't know what to say (always a good beginning). He had found himself thrust forth, dismissed, thrown into the world alone, as he thought: and then he had observed that he was surrounded by friends. Support came from (or on) every flank. (At this point the metaphors got very military, and there were references to reinforcements, flak, etc.) He then said that, as an editor, he always had a feeling of being haunted: he was haunted by titles, stories and poems, which came flooding in on him, haunted by ideas for articles and poems suggested to him. He also had to send out a great many rejection slips, by the consciousness of which he was haunted also. (We all shuddered. Cyril putting on an expression as though he were stuffed with John's rejection slips.) Then John said that, when he began editing, he had thought that he was going to be the instigator of a great

1 For Louis MacNeice, see biographical appendix. William Sansom (1912–1976), British novelist and short story writer.

new movement, a new literature, new poetry; that everything would be wonderful. But we had all turned out very differently from what he had expected. He then went on to say that, in the minds of some people, he was thought of as a headmaster who thrashed us all, like Dr Keate of Eton.[1] His speech ended with a peroration in which [he] managed to introduce the titles of most of Henry Green's novels. He didn't want us to think – he said – that he was going to 'pack my bag'. He wanted to assure Mr Green that he intended to go on *living* and that he thanked him for his *loving*, if not his *doting* care. There would be no turning *back*' etc. Embarrassing as this peroration was, it at least spared us to some extent the utter bewilderment caused by John's addressing Eliot, Forster and the rest, as though they were raw young cubs, whose efforts he had rejected.

Cyril cheered up considerably in the course of the meal, and he, Harvey Breit (from the *New York Times*) and I went to Brown's Hotel together, where I stayed till five.[2] Cyril's explanation of John's speech was that it was prepared for another occasion, as a kind of headmaster's oration to a school for writers and potential contributors to one of his organs.

In 1953, Spender was invited to take up the Elliston Chair at the University of Cincinnati, Ohio. The post was specifically endowed for distinguished poets. The appointment was for two academic quarters and the principal duty was a six-lecture course. Spender chose as his subject 'literary modernism' and the lectures formed the nucleus of his book The Creative Element, *published at the end of 1953. Natasha, who had musical engagements, could not join him until April.*

5 February 1953, New York and Cincinnati

I went from Harcourt Brace to Random House [in New York] to try and get one or two volumes of my poems – only to find the American

---

1 Legendary flogging headmaster at Eton College, 1809–34.

2 Harvey Breit (1909–1968), lead reviewer at the *New York Times* from 1940 to 1965. Spender was a regular contributor to the *New York Times* at this period.

editions are all out of print. At Harcourt Brace, Reynal and Robert Giroux are like two abysmally boring, cagily friendly cherubs.[1] They told me Rosamond's book, which they liked very much has not been chosen by the Book Club, which had been getting quite stuffy lately – and this meant dropping 25,000 bucks.[2] They asked me about my lectures in Cincinnati, which I said I wanted to do as a book[,] and listened with a look of 'that won't sell a thousand copies', as I outlined my theme. I wound up rather lamely, 'I suppose my idea that the central impulse of modern literature is an isolated vision, amounts to an attack on Eliot's critical theories.' 'Oh, that's OK with us,' they said, producing the *Collected T. S. Eliot* they've just done – which is the size of a small suitcase, 'Every time anyone attacks Eliot, we just sell another thousand copies of this.'

Random House is a kind of Old World Mansion, with a drive-in like a Tudor Petrol Station surrounded by skyscrapers in the middle of Madison Avenue. Or, perhaps, it is still more like a huge ornamental dog-kennel. You go in and see sitting in the chilling marble entrance hall a girl at a vast rounded desk made of some expensive substance like ebony. She is telephoning to a friend. You sink into one of about six vast leather couches and gaze across the hall at some glass cases in which books published by R.H. are displayed, like expensive ladies' hand bags. Finally, the college girl behind the desk, who has been carrying on her obviously private conversation as though this is but one example of the 'personal touch' of Random House, disengages herself, gives a calculated jump from her chair and says, 'Oh, I say, Mr Spender, but Mr Cummins *will* be dying to see you,' establishes quick contact with Mr Cummins and advises you to walk up to his room – number 333 – on the first floor up those stairs. You get to the top of glorious marble stairs and there you see about six doors all wide open, each leading into a room, richly, thickly carpeted, filled with white light like an ice cube, book-lined with shelves that go up to the ceiling, and with a vast desk and a few more specimens of the same oversize furniture as was in the hall. Seated behind each desk is a Director of Random House. Just as the Directors of H.B. look like cherubs, so

---

1 New York publishers Eugene Reynal of Harcourt Brace, and Robert Giroux of Farrar, Straus and Giroux.

2 Rosamond Lehmann's novel *The Echoing Grove* (1953).

those of R.H. all look like dogs, with gangling loose-limbed bodies, tweedy clothes and features which seem to droop downwards, with great vertical creases like underfed, anxious St Bernards. Mr Cummins, my editor, has a peculiar, whining voice as he welcomes me. His room has a look of unutterable emptiness and the air in it seems to stream through the conditioning machinery with a thin pure sound, such as you hear when you have taken gas at the dentists. After a few moments of conversation with Mr Cummins, you are unconscious of everything but this sound. Mr Cummins said, 'Now do you have a new volume of poems?' 'I shall soon,' I lied, thinking that the very idea of my publishers would purge me of all poetry, if I remembered that I were to send my manuscript to them. 'Well, let me know in plenty of time,' he said, 'so that I can design a beautiful volume. There isn't one of your books we've published that we haven't made a beautiful job of.' This is perfectly true, and I feel less than grateful. Yet I think that really I don't want to run that gauntlet of publishing a volume of poems ever again. Then, I think that this is abysmal cowardice, and I must not think about it at all. I am taken to meet Mr Hass and then someone else – another director – and then I run down the flight of marble stairs into the great pure fresh air of Madison Avenue, which I breathe in like a sea breeze. [. . .]

American professors are an oppressed, overworked, underpaid and now, also, a politically suspect class. Socially, their position is about that of English doctors in my great-grandfather's day, who were expected to call on their rich patients via the back door. This afternoon, I told Clark that I ought to call on Ben Tate.[1] 'Have you any idea what he's like?' 'No,' I answered. 'Well, he doesn't seem to be very like his brother. In fact, I can't imagine two brothers being more different. He's a rich industrialist, only interested in business, and so conservative in his politics that he's regarded as more reactionary than Senator Taft, of whose campaign funds he was the Treasurer.[2] He is a Director of this University, but I don't really know

---

1 William Clark, head of the English Department at the University of Cincinnati. Ben Tate, elder brother of the poet Allen Tate.

2 Senator Robert Taft (1917–1993), though a right-wing Republican, had recently been instrumental in disentangling Spender's visa problems. As an ex-communist, Spender was technically ineligible for admission into the United States.

him as, like most Directors, he has no contact with the Faculty. In fact, the Directors seem to regard the University as like any other great undertaking in which they take only a business interest. I must say, though, that Ben Tate did once give a party for some of the senior members of the Faculty, which is more than most of the Directors have done. The difficulty, though, for us, was to know what to talk about. We seemed to speak entirely different languages.'

At luncheon in the cafeteria, the Dean and Dr Clark told me how it was almost impossible to teach Marxism or anything about it. I said I thought it must be difficult to explain certain American writers – Edmund Wilson, Dos Passos, etc – without any reference to Marx.[1] 'It is,' said Clark. 'And I can only explain this background in a fragmentary or indirect way. Personally, I think the present attitude is a great mistake.' (Clark, by the way, is an ardent Republican.) 'It seems to me that it is necessary to know the ideas of your opponents.' They said there was an almost complete neglect now of Russian language and Russian literary studies, because people were afraid either to teach or to learn them. They told me that in Cincinnati during Henry Wallace's campaigns in the Presidential election of 1948, photographs had been taken of audiences attending Wallace meetings.[2] Subsequently, efforts were made by the anti-Red groups to identify the faces of people in these photographs, in order to persecute them.

7 February 1953, Cincinnati

I opened one of the books I ought to read – Nietzsche's *The Birth of Tragedy*. Instantly, my eye struck phrases like: 'What self-experience, what stress made the Greek think of the Dionysian reveller and primitive man as a satyr?' And I could read no more. An almost intoler-

---

1 Edmund Wilson (1895–1972), American literary critic whose early works were heavily engaged with the writings of Karl Marx. John Dos Passos (1896–1970), American novelist best known for his compendious socialist trilogy, *U.S.A.* (1932–6).

2 Henry Wallace (1888–1965), unsuccessful candidate for the Presidency in the 1948 election. Previously, Wallace had served in the Democrat Party under Roosevelt, but in 1948 he ran on behalf of the newly formed Progressive Party, advocating friendly relations with the Soviet Union and the end of the Cold War.

ably beautiful picture filled my mind, of a little screen of small and delicate cypresses (like those in a drawing of Botticelli), along the roadside leading from the little modern town of Delphi up the mountainside. [. . .]

I must say that I am absolutely torn by the tragedy of Europe. Everything points to it and has always pointed to it, and I wonder whether we have not known about it far longer than we think – longer than my own lifetime. Just as Baudelaire in 1850 writes of the horror of the world being Americanized (which we think of as quite a new conception), so perhaps we were born in this shadow of the decline of Europe. Certainly Nietzsche knew all about it by 1870. The grotesque idea occurs to me that the kindness of Americans to us is like kindness to invalids.

During the summer one thing put to me very forcibly the tragedy of Europe, which has, of course, affected immigrants for hundreds of years, and is really the common human material on which America is built.

It was at Torri [del Benaco]. Idelma and Francesca had invited me to lunch at their house 'in the mountains' – that is five minutes from the village. Matthew took me. When we had gone through the village and turned up the hillside, just across the main road, which bypasses the village we came to the graveyard of Torri. Matthew said he wanted to show me the graves. A little photograph, printed on metal, of the persons buried there. Matthew went to one and said, 'That is Idelma's Zia (aunt). Don't you think she looks like Idelma?' Then he pointed out that some of the graves had little lamps on them. 'They're for the specially good people,' he said. Then, looking all round, 'You see, there aren't many good people at Torri, are there?' We walked up the hillside a little further, then left the road and turned up the path between stone walls, which leads up to the little cluster of houses, where is the Loncrini home. From here, in the cool and shade, you look down at the lake gleaming between the brush-like sky-mirroring leaves of the olives. Here, only five minutes from Torri, there is a little open space in front of the Loncrini house, like a tiny piazza, with a little shrine, opposite the house and beyond that a green slope where Lizzie played. A quite different life was being lived here from that in Torri. For example, I asked Francesca why they hadn't let Matthew go down into the village as much as he wanted, and she said, 'Because it's better and purer up here. Down there, they learn "brutte parole" [bad words].'

10 February 1953, Cincinnati

Two days ago a student came to interview me for the campus *Recorder*, the campus magazine. Although a student affair, the University is so vast and plays such a role in this town, that this is definitely one of the local newspapers and, therefore, has to be treated with caution. The reporter was a freshman, a Jewish boy in some kind of uniform, with a thin, narrow face, big nose, dark eyes, fresh complexion and glossy hair. He reeled off at me the following questions: Where was the first poem you had published, for which you were paid money? This was the only one I could answer. If there was a meeting of your fellow-poets – your colleagues – and they were talking about you, what would they think of your work? What do you consider your greatest accomplishment? Now, when you write a poem what sort of a message do you have in mind that you are trying to convey to your reader? What do you expect to achieve in life by writing poetry? Do you expect to convert people to something? How did you get your appointment to this University? Now, Mr Spender, we've all heard something about your having belonged to the Communist Party, and we would like you to make a statement about this for the *Recorder*. To add to the confusion of these questions, he knew absolutely nothing about poetry or politics, or anything, as far as I could make out. The only one of his questions I might have answered was: What was my greatest accomplishment, because it occurred to me very forcibly, when he asked, that it was being the father of Matthew and Elizabeth. But I did not want to say this, so I simply had to admit that I did not imagine that my fellow poets – if they deigned to discuss me at all – would think much of me, and that I thought nothing about messages, and couldn't express what I thought about achievements. I then told him the old, old story about my Communist affiliation. I always have to remember that this is the recital of a crime, like 'When I was in Sing Sing.' Fortunately, I insisted on seeing the interview before it was published.

Two hours later, the typescript came to me – incredible. It started off about Communism, explaining that I joined the C.P. because the secretary of the British Party had told me that, in exchange for my signing a membership card, he would publish an article by me giving my view on the Spanish War. As Mr Spender was at this time a young writer and lecturer wishing to have his views appear anywhere where they could get published, I accepted this arrangement. The article was terribly ill-written and would have disgraced a boy of ten. I took it to Dr Clark, who showed considerable signs of alarm, as he said he thought it was not only unpleasant for me, but would upset the President if it were published. The next morning he and I went to see Mr Pace, the editor of the *Recorder*. He was a gaunt youth, at once hard as nails and rather amiable. Trying to explain to him why we wanted the article changed was the most exasperating piece of diplomacy – but very revealing – in which Academic Age tries to put its point to Youth with an Eye on the Main Chance. Pace said that Al was a smart lad in his opinion and he'd asked him to go out and get from Mr Spender, just facts, plain facts, because those were what they wanted to plug the *Recorder* with. I pointed out that the facts were all wrong and Mr Pace said that this did not matter, what they wanted were FACTS. Besides, he added, there also had to be a New Angle, different from that of the papers in town. He then revealed that they also wanted a News Sensation and that Al's article was to be the leading news item, with three-inch-deep headlines about the Ex-Communist poet on the campus. Dr Clark pleaded, 'But, surely, the students will have read all this?' To which Mr Pace replied incontrovertibly, 'Our readers never read.'

After a deal of wrangling, there was a victory (we think) of Mr Pace's Better Nature, because he agreed to 'cut the story right out, if you say the facts are wrong – but I don't understand, because I think Al's the smartest guy we've got' – if the other members of his staff agreed.

One of the things that amazed me about this interview was the way in which student and professor negotiated as completely equal powers. Indeed, I had the strong impression that we were throwing ourselves on Mr Pace's mercy. Dr Clark larded his speeches on my behalf with praise for the *Recorder* and its achievements, and he spent over an hour covering and recovering the ground in order that Mr Pace – the student-editor who had just come in from a class – would not feel that he was being asked by a professor to 'climb down' in any way. After we had left Mr Pace, he told me that he had not liked to say to him that the President would be extremely annoyed if the article was published, because this would simply have egged Mr Pace on. And, he added that in the previous year when the President had refused leave to the students to hold a mock election on the campus – which would in fact have been a demonstration for the Democrats – the *Recorder* had come out with an article suggesting that he (the President) was tied up with the Taft organization. I couldn't help comparing in my mind an interview between an Oxford Vice Chancellor and the undergraduate editor of a magazine, under similar circumstances. And the point is that, fundamentally, there would be more feeling of mutual esteem and affection between the Vice Chancellor and the Undergraduate – who would probably be sent down – under such circumstances than there was between Pace and us. The idea that students are the equal of their teachers is simply hypocritical, and results in the genuine dislike and distrust between students and Faculty, which is a striking feature of American universities.

February 1953, Cincinnati

On Friday evening [. . .] I went to dine at the Sagmasters. [. . .] The party was for Jenny Tourel, who is singing with the orchestra this week here.[1] She is very black and white, with thick features, and enormous onyx eyes, frizzy hair and a pale complexion. She must have been rather beautiful when she was young. She had just come from New York, where she said the *Rake's Progress* had been well-received by the public but 'panned' badly by the critics. She told how, when she was in Israel this year, as soon as she got off the aeroplane at Lidda Airport, she was met by three officials who asked her what language she intended to sing the Mahler song cycle in. 'German,' she replied. They explained then that they had been ordered by the Foreign Office to inform her that she could not do this. 'What language do you expect me to sing in?' she asked. 'Hebrew or English,'

---

1 Jennie Tourel (1900–1973), singer at the Metropolitan Opera, New York and teacher at the Juilliard School of Music. She was the first 'Baba the Turk' in *The Rake's Progress*, Stravinsky's opera with a libretto by Auden and Chester Kallman, which premiered in 1951.

they said. She said that maybe she should take the aeroplane away again and not land in Lidda at all. At this, they suggested that she might sing so that the words were unintelligible. She said she would sing in German or not at all.

Just before the concert, as she was standing behind the stage, she heard a member of the orchestra say to another one – in German – that after the concert she was going to be arrested if she sang in German. She went onto the stage very nervously, sang the Mahler, and was given an ovation. After the concert she went to a reception, and a very handsome man came up to her, explained that he was the Chief of Police, and that he had come to arrest her. She laughed and said she would be delighted to be arrested by *him*. Then he explained that he had looked up the law and discovered that as this was a concert and not a theatre or operatic performance, she could sing in German, since the law omitted to cover this point.

On the following evening, I heard her sing the Mahler cycle – the *Song of a Wayfarer* [sic].[1] She sang this much more beautifully than some Rossini which she sang afterwards and which seemed to require a more chiselled type of voice. This work is quite beautiful, but completely backboneless, in the Viennese manner which – like so many other European symptoms of decay – extends so much longer back in time than we think. On the one hand, the music wants to be gay and carefree; on the other hand, it is dominated by an overwhelming sense of defeat and death. These two themes never come to grips with one another, so that you get neither tragedy nor comedy, but pathos. What it does very effectively is simply to represent the mood of the Viennese, who are simply victims.

I was taken to the concert by a lady psychologist called Dr Allen, in the box of friends of hers whose names I forget.[2] Afterwards we went back to the house of these friends, and the dinner which followed did not break up till 3 a.m. Conversation was about Europe – how Americans travelling in France felt themselves hated, the causes of anti-American feeling, etc. They were very interesting about this. Dr Allen had got in touch with me through Sam Barber whom

---

1 *Lieder eines fahrenden Gesellen* (*Songs of a Wayfarer*) (1896).

2 Doris Twitchell Allen (1901–2002), psychologist at Longview State Hospital and Professor at Cincinnati University.

she met in New York.[1] She is interested in arranging international summer camps for children, and Sam had told her about my Israel book. She has quite good ideas – though I can't really see that getting children from twelve or twenty nations together for a month in the year is going to do very much good. But I sympathize. At about 2 a.m. Dr Allen told that, in the Mental Institution where she works in Cincinnati, some of the patients suffering from lack of love were so without confidence that a scheme had been devised to 'pick them up' at the time when they were mentally three months old. This is done by making them lie down and relax completely, while a gramophone disc is played to them which has the necessary reassuring effect. She then said briskly, 'Although this is very successful with real psychotics, it can also be used beneficially by normal people.' Before we knew where we were, we were all being ordered to lie down on the floor and relax completely. Then she put on the record. Crooning music was played and a gentle voice said words to this effect. 'Baby is in the cot . . . Mother loves baby . . . Mother pats baby . . . Mother draws up the blanket over baby and tucks him in . . . Baby feels so calmed and loved . . . Baby is so peaceful . . . Mother loves baby . . . Mother works in the room while baby lies in the cot . . . Mother comes over and feeds baby . . . Mother draws the blanket over baby . . . It is so peaceful . . . Mother loves baby . . .' etc.

This performance slightly shook my confidence in Dr Allen. For one thing, if a gramophone record were a substitute for a mother, life would be much simpler. We were not drunk or anything. The incident was carried out in a perfectly sober, business-like way.

12 March 1953, Cincinnati

I have read an enormous amount since I got here. Probably I ought to write about this in a Journal, but I feel that to write about reading is to make a commentary on thoughts which pour into one, and I feel it more important to write here about external things, people I meet, what they say and so on. Reading this journal through it seems to me gayer and also less spiky about people than I had thought it would be. Of course, doing little vignettes of people you meet right after you

---

1 For Samuel Barber, see biographical appendix.

meet them, it is difficult not to caricature them, and select the things they say which most amuse you. It is difficult to respect their personalities. [. . .]

All the same, things like this do stick in my memory more than others, when I am living so busily. Mrs Wurlitzer asked me to dinner one night with two people called the Fischers, whom everyone speaks of very well.[1] Mrs Fischer, with a very high forehead and the poker features of a man dressed up as a woman, looked to me like the Rake in a Sadler's Wells Ballet of *The Rake's Progress*.[2] Every moment I expected someone to snatch off her wig and reveal a completely bald head of a gentleman in Eighteenth-Century costume. Fischer, at the other side of the table, seemed simply goggle-eyed and myopic, as with his eyes lost behind glasses with very thick lenses, he ate his food, selecting different little bits of each dish with his fork, as a painter dips his paint brush into each of several colours and then putting it into his mouth with an attentive expression on his face as though he were composing in his stomach a culinary painting.

Then, I tend too much to remember single remarks – remarks which I must say have a certain savoury perfection, like that of a Mrs Lazarus I sat next to on a sofa in the Friedlanders' sitting room the other day, who observed to me that in her view the American press had given Stalin far too much publicity for dying. 'I think they should not have drawn attention to Stalin's death,' she said, 'they should have maintained a dignified silence.'[3]

At this party I showed symptoms of saying the kind of things which pop out of a British mouth among Americans after two or three highballs. Sometimes indeed one has the impression of being a batsman in a game surrounded by hands just waiting for one to hit up a nice catch. On this occasion the lob that came curving down was someone's remark that the French had no wish whatever to

---

1 The Wurlitzer musical instrument firm is famous for its electric organ. Mrs Wurlitzer was a leading patron of music in Cincinnati at the time.

2 *The Rake's Progress* (1935), a ballet in one act with choreography by Ninette de Valois and music by Gavin Gordon, was premiered on 20 May 1935 by the Vic–Wells Ballet at Sadler's Wells Theatre. Not to be confused with the Stravinsky–Auden–Kallman opera of the same title.

3 Stalin died on 5 March 1953.

defend themselves from invasion and were a bunch of be-good cowards. I hit up my catch which was, 'They happen to think that buildings are more important than people.' During the rest of the over, I hit up catch after catch and was caught out time after time. I said that if you destroyed Venice and left the Venetians, there would be no Venetians within a few years, whereas if you killed the Venetians and Venice was occupied by the Red Army, within a hundred years there would be Venetians again. 'We don't attach that amount of importance to dead buildings in the U.S.,' someone said. 'We think more about life and defending our ideals.' Some Canadians who took my side said that this was because there were no buildings worth much in the U.S., and, in any case, all the buildings would not be destroyed. 'Then you mean to say that you wouldn't defend yourself,' said Mr Friedlander, my host. 'Oh, yes, I suppose I would or, rather, I suppose the British would,' I said. 'We have a different point of view and we always defend ourselves. But, as a European, and not just a Britisher, although I'm not a neutralist I can see the point of neutralism. After all, if you're likely to be occupied anyway for the third time in less than a hundred years, it is surely reasonable to regard yourself simply as the trustee of buildings which the occupiers are going to occupy. Ultimately, the occupiers may be changed by the buildings. They will only be persuaded by your resistance to destroy the buildings, and no one will be changed, except for the worse, by living among a lot of ruins.' My host was so annoyed that he left the room. 'After all, there are books,' said Mr Wulsin (the son of Baldwin pianos).[1] 'All the books could be taken to the United States and the ideas would go on. In fact, copies of them are there already.' Then he told a story to illustrate the influence of Aristotle emerging in the mouth of a lawyer at court, where he had been that very day. 'Ideas cannot die,' he said. And he added as an afterthought that there were excellent reproductions of paintings. So we were left just with all the buildings of Europe destroyed; no great loss, as long as we had our ideas and had our ideals.

In a way, a conversation like this is utterly unreal, especially as, even if neutralism is right, one cannot admit to being a neutralist

---

1 The Baldwin piano factory was established in Cincinnati in the 1860s. The Wulsin family were also patrons of music.

without inviting the enemy to invade. My point of view was a reasonable though unreal one, but theirs was reasonable but nonexistent. I mean, if you cannot see the necessity of buildings, and if you really think that starving people stumbling about ruins (like those I saw in Germany after the war) are great idealists and living exemplars of democracy, your point of view just doesn't exist. Really, arguments on these lines run rapidly into a vacuum where there is no moral or living air to breathe any more, and both sides are talking dust and ashes. Luckily everyone had a sense of this, so they were not really angry with me. Or, it may be that the Republicans of the Mid-West are, in the long run, more tolerant than the Liberals of New York, because in a smaller New York discussion with people like Diana Trilling, Philip Rahv and William Phillips, by this time they would have been foaming at the mouth and denouncing me as traitor or spy.[1]

I had a nice evening with Mr Samuel and his wife from the Hebrew University. Talk was about Israel, mostly. After dinner a young representative in the local legislature, Senator Gilbert Bettman, and his wife appeared.[2] Senator Bettman looks like a slightly Americanized English school prefect, with high forehead, snub nose, roundish features and a rather pale complexion. He wears spectacles, the glasses of which seem plain glass pressed rather flat against his eyes, and has an appealing, slightly inhibited and uneasy kind of frankness. He said to me, 'Look, you've now been in this country some weeks, do you have the impression that there's a great deal of hysteria and warmongering?' I said no, I didn't think so, but added that the newspapers and radios made me a bit uneasy. He quickly moved into position and began to take both sides at once on various topics. He deplored some of the activities of the Un-American Activities Committee, but not others.[3] He was for complete freedom of education and against

---

1 Diana Trilling (1905–1996), literary critic and wife of Lionel Trilling; both were leading New York intellectuals at the time.

2 Gilbert Bettman, senior figure in the Ohio Republican Party. He and his then wife Liz became great friends of the Spenders.

3 The House Un-American Activities Committee grew out of a pre-war attempt to pinpoint and detach from government anyone whose allegiance to the Constitution could be deemed suspect.

it, etc. He harmonized these seemingly contradictory views with a general line that everything was quite bad but its badness was grossly exaggerated. And he wound up by confidentially and frankly asking our advice. Should he vote for a measure to make being a Communist illegal? He added that he had already made up his mind to vote for it, but he wanted advice, just the same. His wife, who seems to me much cleverer than Bettman kept on challenging him, and would not let him get away with remarks to the effect that, really, the inquiry into the politics of people at universities doesn't amount to anything. She said, 'It all depends on how you define a Communist.' This objection rather surprised me, because I thought that a Communist must mean a Party Member. But no. Bettman said that the definition of a Communist was a person who subscribed to certain organizations. He added that he was going to support the law because he thought it would clear the atmosphere by preventing vague charges, since after this it would be known who were and who were not Communists. No one seemed willing to contradict him about this, though I felt that everyone was rather uneasy.

George Ford told me that Raymond Aron, who has recently been to Washington, went back to France deeply disturbed and published somewhere that, in part, he had to concede the argument he had been having with certain French writers who say there is political persecution in America.[1]

* * *

Dr Staats and his wife still overwhelm me with their generosity. Behind my back Dr S. is negotiating, I believe, with Bill Clark because he still wants to get me a great coat or suit in return for the poem he still wants me to write about Johnnie – or, I am sure, without my writing such a poem. Every other Wednesday, he has a barber come here to give him a hair cut, and he insists on my having my hair cut then, which is very nice. It is also slightly embarrassing though because, while the barber has scissors or razor suspended over me, he

---

1 George Ford, senior member of the English Faculty at Cincinnati, was a scholar specialising in Dickens and D. H. Lawrence. Raymond Aron (1905–1983), leading conservative intellectual, for the most part anti-communist but with misgivings also about the USA. He was editor of *France Libre*, published in London during the war, then for thirty years a columnist at *Le Figaro*.

will come into the room where the operations are proceeding and give him advice, in a rather hearty manner. 'Now, don't cut his hair at the sides. Remember he's a musician or a poet or something. Big Steve, how long before you come here was it that you had your last haircut? Only a week? Well, that's how you want your hair now, isn't it? Plenty long, only tidied up. Now, what the hell do you think you're doing cutting that bit off. You can't put it back now, you fool . . .', etc. The barber whispers to me that the Doc's a great guy, but I'm afraid he'll get nervous and cut off one of my ears.

13 March 1953, Cincinatti

'All things can tempt me from this craft of verse.'[1] [. . .] [Yesterday] a request from the Paris committee of the Congress for Cultural Freedom that I should edit, together with Irving Kristol, a magazine and also take over some of Nicky Nabokov's work while he is in Rome.[2] This is very disturbing because my idea of that Paris office is of a nightmare. The thing to do is to try and think of the alternatives. It is easy to think, 'It will be distracting, I shouldn't do it.' But all work is more or less distracting and if I have been very fortunate here at Cincinnati, I must think of that as an exception. Another job in an American University might not be so agreeable and give me so much time. Allen Tate, for instance, seems to be leading just as distracting a life here as I would in Paris. In addition to which, there are aspects of this kind of life which I hate for my own reasons and which may be bad for my family: being away five or six months in the year, I mean. The editing job would probably mean being half in London, half in Paris, which would be much better. The main thing is that freelance journalism is the most completely distracting thing of all, because it means I have no regular income.

---

1 This line is from Yeats's poem of the same title, in *Responsibilities* (1916).

2 For *Encounter*, Irving Kristol and Nicolas Nabokov, see biographical appendix.

15 March 1953, Cincinnati

America: a country which is entirely different from every other, by dint of being more the same. Existence is reduced to a common denominator. Mystery is stripped from everything. So that all people of all other countries have something in common, which is the sense of mystery. The European, the Latin American, the Asiatic, the African, knows that religion, sex, and poetry are things which cannot be explained. In America, not only is everything explained, but sometimes you get the impression that nothing exists except the explanation. Analyse American existences to the ultimate essence and what you get is an explanation or a fact. This is all contained within the concept 'The American Way of Life' – which is basic to Americans. Dissect an American mind, and finally you arrive at an odourless, transparent concept – the American Way of Life. Sometimes I think that this applies even to nature (for since it applies to the *women* even more than the men, it seems to apply to everything). You drive through the country and the trees say we are American trees. It is true that some of the animals give appalling smells, but this is simply a problem to be solved.

In a way, the whole world is a living conspiracy against America[,] that is, against the American Way of Life. The whole of the rest of the world shares a sense of mystery. At the same time, it sees [that] in The American Way of Life [life] itself [is] robbed of mystery and reduced to a common denominator of life in which everyone is a mechanism, feeding on tasteless foods, with body odours reduced by chlorophyll pills, beauty acquired by another pill (advertised every morning on the radio as 'nature's way') and psychologically complicated only as a machine is complicated: that is to say, capable of being taken down and the tangles sorted out. Hence, the universal horror of what Americans regard as their greatest asset – The American Way of Life.

Sometimes I think there must be an American mystery which the rest of the world doesn't know about, but which is real. Perhaps Faulkner and some of the Southern writers have it. Or Robert Frost. The trouble about this, though, is that even if it were true, it would represent traditions in American life which are fast vanishing. The South is the centre of literary inspiration because it was defeated in the Civil War and has remained an area far less developed than any other part of the country. Even so, inspiration is either decadent and violent, or else scholarly, pedantic and abstract, like the *Kenyon* and *Sewanee Reviews*.[1] With Robert Frost, New England perhaps demonstrates that I am wrong about there being no 'nature' here which is not practising the American Way of Life, and that there is a country tradition of farmers and people living in the country. This is real and will doubtless go on for a long time, but it grows weaker rather than stronger.

* * *

Irving Kristol came here yesterday and I was pleasantly surprised to find he wasn't Elliot Cohen – the other editor of *Commentary* who came to London once to see us and with whom I had confused him.[2] He is a younger, more aware kind of person, with quite a gleam about him. He did not strike me as having any ideas about the magazine which were going to set the Thames on fire. He sees it as a mixture of *Preuves* and *Der Monat*, with articles on United Europe, Toynbee's new book, a review of Martin's life of Harold Laski, [a] chapter from Silone's new novel, a symposium on The Western Mind and 'the mysterious East', etc.[3] We worked out various 'themes', which the magazine should keep going: 1) The Living Past – extracts from unpublished material (like the D. H. Lawrence documents here at Cincinnati, and also from little-known works which have relevance today).[4] 2) Cultural chronicles (music, art, etc.) 3) A documentary section on the background to world events 4) Comments 5) Correspondence which will be in the nature of a discussion Forum 6)

---

1 The *Kenyon Review* was published at Kenyon College, Ohio, and the *Sewanee Review* at the University of the South, Sewanee, Tennessee. Spender contributed to both.

2 Elliot E. Cohen was founder editor of *Commentary* from 1945 until his death in 1959. Irving Kristol had been the magazine's managing editor.

3 The magazines *Preuves* and *Der Monat* were also funded by the Congress for Cultural Freedom. Melvin Lasky (see biographical appendix), who co-edited *Encounter* after Kristol had left, was currently editor of *Der Monat*. Kingsley Martin's memoir of the socialist theoretician Harold Laski was published in 1953. Ignazio Silone's new novel was *A Handful of Blackberries*.

4 Spender had been studying the D. H. Lawrence archive in the University of Cincinnati.

Reviews[:] I suggested that we should have articles by writers like Isaiah Berlin, Arthur Schlesinger, Freddie Ayer, discussing present-day issues in a long-term way and challenging political clichés.[1] E.g., what are the real issues between the Left and the Right today compared with those of twenty years ago? Or: If you strip away the labels, to what degree is America really just as much a socialist country as Great Britain? I add now that similar articles might be by philosophers about the political implications of current bourgeois philosophies, like Existentialism and Logical Positivism.

If we are also able to get good literary material, something very good might be done on these lines. Kristol thought that one advantage of being international is that we shall be able to draw on material from all over the world, which we would not be able to do if we were just English or American.

The name of the magazine stands at present as OUTLOOK. Dull, I think. During the night MARK occurred to me as a possibility. And really, I don't think it's so bad.

5 April 1953, Sewanee, Tennessee

On Saturday, the 27th, I emplaned for Knoxville to meet Natasha and Allen [Tate]. From the plane, most of the country between here and Knoxville looked like crumpled brown paper, splodged over in places by water – broad rivers coiled in loops very close to one another, and sometimes widening as large as lakes. Natasha and Allen met me, and then we drove to Sewanee through old stone gates marked 'The University of the South', through a very large estate of forest, now a cigar-colour brown, just tipped with buds, to the Campus which has something of the atmosphere of a quiet New England village. We went to Allen's cousins, the Myers. Mr Myers is a professor of theology and parson, aged 70, his wife runs the whole house and has had eight children, a few of whom – two boys at all events – were on the premises. The wooden house[,] book-lined, had an air of being lived in by young people, pulled about, liked, tidied and

---

1 Arthur M. Schlesinger (1917–2007), historian and leading liberal intellectual, subsequently advisor to President Kennedy. Author of *A Thousand Days: John F. Kennedy in the White House* (1965).

un-tidied, which was in great contrast to everything at Cincinnati. The thing that most struck me about it was the way in which everything seemed slightly faded. This was not surprising in copies of Holy Paintings and some amateur oil paintings of a dead white river running in what seemed like a deep trench of mud through a perfectly flat green plane, under a whitish sky, but when I saw that even the newest books – Churchill's war volumes, for example – in the Myers' drawing room look as faded as Edwardian novels, I decided it was some quality of the house and the people in it which gave everything this air. The Myers themselves seemed very real people. There was a boy who played the violin and wanted to be a musician, who immediately entered into conversation with Natasha; the other son, Lucas, showed me some of his poems. The boys were excessively polite, saying 'yes sir' and 'no sir' in every other sentence, but like a Frenchman says 'n'est-ce pas' and not in the least ingratiatingly. I had a sense of being suddenly among human beings again.

In June 1953, Spender accompanied T. S. Eliot on a brief lecture trip to the US; the next entry records their return journey to London.

June 1953, London

Tom Eliot in the B.O.A.C. plane from N.Y. June 29.[1] Travelling so incognito, he was given the worst seat in what he called 'the nose' of the plane – I had the best seat so changed with him and was then given a better-than-the-worst-seat, though it wasn't very nice. He was very annoyed with B.O.A.C. because, he said, he had booked his passage 6 months ahead.

At Gander we spent about 3 hours.[2] Here and in the bar of the Stratocruiser, Tom was nice and rather interesting. Told me he had been to Saint Louis [Missouri] and had given a talk at his old University when the temperature was 93° in the shade. He talked about having to publish American lectures and said he had always regretted *The Use of Poetry and the Use of Criticism* and *After Strange Gods*

---

1 BOAC, British Overseas Airways Corporation.

2 Gander, a Canadian town in Newfoundland whose airport is a refuelling point for transatlantic aircraft.

which were originally lectures, and which he could not prevent being published, as Harvard and Princeton (?) owned them. He said that a personal bitterness about his private life had got into both these books and affected his judgement, he felt, though he could never later disentangle this.[1] [. . .]

When we arrived in London there was a great cheering mob, to see the Queen Mother off to Africa in a Comet.[2] As we got out of the plane, Tom murmured to me: 'At first when I saw the crowd I had been afraid it was for us.'

On his return to England in July 1953, after two terms in Cincinnati, Spender took his two children for a seaside outing to Swanage. The trip inspired a long journal meditation on fatherhood.

29 July 1953, Swanage, Dorset

I keep on thinking: the young are idealistic but selfish, the old are corrupt but perhaps less selfish. To the young it seems inexcusable that they – or others – should sacrifice principles to gain: at the same time they are inconsiderate of the fact that their parents have abandoned principles in order to support *them* – their children. As we get old we sadly bury our principles and instead accept the standards of our friends, which we try also to maintain for the sake of our children. Perhaps we also get self-indulgent, but the lack of self-indulgence of the young is not much anyway – it is as much an indulgence to youth, as comfort is late on an indulgence to age.

The really admirable person is he who can nurture the principles of his youth throughout life. But for this not to be just a perpetual adolescence, at some stage his youth has to become a secret life hoarded through his maturity.

The young despise the old for sacrificing principles. But the old

---

1 *After Strange Gods* (1934) contained what critics of Eliot have seen as his anti-Semitism. The book was derived from lectures given at the University of Virginia in 1933 and Eliot later withdrew it from publication.

2 The Queen Mother and Princess Margaret were flying to Rhodesia. The Comet was an English jet built by De Havilland. Metal stress in the bodywork subsequently caused a series of disastrous crashes and the aeroplane was withdrawn from production in 1954.

despise the young for not realizing why we sacrifice principles. To youth age appears negation: but to age youth appears mere negativeness – which is really much more damning.

* * *

In Swanage, I notice how the hills around the bay are very carefully drawn, cautious outlines, just as the horizon is a black bow-string between sea and land. The English landscape is so clean and clear and precise (without being lucid or logical). Every line is carefully drawn, and even our mists and fogs are only veils over the limbs of a virgin. No wonder most painters either make English landscape prim, or reduce it to a formula, and can hardly go beyond attaining taste and charm. Our landscape teaches both, and the gothic Rhineland, Renaissance Italy, the relations of colour which seem to stroke one's eyes in France, or the hide-like, leathery, buskin tragic quality of Spain, are not 'true' here. It is not enough to revolt against the taste this landscape teaches and impose more exotic examples on it. The only thing is to penetrate more deeply into the nature of this virgin herself, without losing her Englishness. This is what only Constable, perhaps, has done. Turner sometimes, Bonington (but he is really Frenchified) and Chris Wood (but he goes to the Breton landscape of Cornwall).[1]

* * *

The English 'occupy' their own landscape. They arrive with deckchairs, Sunday newspapers, tea kettles, and their own native ugliness, relieved occasionally by extraordinary beauty, sit down in front of a mountain or the ocean, stick their legs up in front of them and sit out their holidays. It is their way of pouring their now confident humanity, like tea spilled over a table cloth, over everything which is disconcerting. The French look admiringly, proudly, but reverently at their cathedrals when they pass them in a train. The Germans try to make their sons measure up to the Rhine or the Bavarian Alps. The Americans, with camping laid on amid wild scenery[,] try to go native

---

1 Christopher Wood (1901–1930) belonged to a circle of artists working in Cornwall who attempted to combine synthetic cubism with the English landscape tradition of Samuel Palmer and William Blake.

luxuriously. It's only the English who have this attitude of making the best of the discomfort of a holiday by simply reproducing as nearly as possible the circumstances of 'home' wherever they go. Here at Swanage the beach is a close-packed mass of deck-chairs. These are as it were the front-line trenches beyond which lies the enemy itself, the sea. Reading their papers, and making cups of tea, the front line heroes feel that they are going over the top for the sake of the kiddies, who are supposed to be enjoying themselves. Of course, there are also heroes, V.C.'s in yachts and on mountains, who also really enjoy it, though the old soldier type of holiday maker secretly suspects that they are simply children who haven't grown up [. . .]

3 August 1953, London

Lunched with Isaiah Berlin at the Ivy. It began with an almost philosophic discussion between Isaiah and the waiter about boeuf Stroganoff. Isaiah asked the waiter to describe to him exactly the texture and thickness of the slices of meat in the boeuf Stroganoff, and to offer his opinion as to whether it could be regarded as a dish that came from its country of origin, or whether it should be looked on rather as an English or native product. The waiter replied that he had never had the advantage of being in the country of its origin, so he found it difficult to answer the question. Nevertheless he could assure Isaiah that large quantities of boeuf Stroganoff were sold at the Ivy. 'That is an insufficient reply to my question,' said Isaiah, 'nevertheless I shall try it.' The waiter was fully up to this game, and when Isaiah had finished his meal, he came up to him and asked him whether it tasted foreign. Isaiah said it tasted to him extremely English.

Isaiah was very much against A. J. Ayer's article on Nihilism which I am publishing in *Encounter*.[1] He said that I was quite right to publish it, but nevertheless he thought that it contested points of view which Freddie attributed to the philosophers whom he criticized, which had in fact never been held by nihilists, existentialists or any other kind of philosopher. He said he had a grudge against Freddie ever since the time he had read his essay on existentialism in *Horizon*, which had put him against the existentialists. He said that

---

1 'The Meaning of Nihilism', *Encounter*, October 1954.

Freddie's technique consisted of stating someone's position very clearly and then refuting it. But Freddie was completely naive as regards art and therefore failed to understand what was poetic or artistic behind logical propositions. Isaiah said if one really understood music one understood the wholeness behind other things and that the failure of Freddie was really the failure to understand music.

This I think was the drift of Isaiah's arguments, although there was a good deal that I did not take in. Not taking it in, I was feeling rather stupid. I was slightly humiliated by feeling that I could easily change the subject on to the topic of personalities and that, then, I would have no difficulty at all with this conversation. I was forced back into the position of a person who knows he does not understand intellectual or philosophic ideas; at the same time, I was also in the position of a pupil who does really understand but with part of his mind also refuses to understand. At the same time, I felt that Isaiah knew my feelings about all this. [. . .]

Isaiah told me he was very annoyed because recently on two different occasions, two different people had mistaken him for someone else. He seemed quite anxious that someone in the restaurant should recognize him. When we walked down Charing Cross Road later, and I went into Zwemmer's bookshop to buy a copy of my book to give to him, someone who was standing outside asked him whether I was a relation of Humphrey Spender. He recognized me from the likeness to my brother. This amused Isaiah very much. I said that he had not been recognized by anyone because he did not have a brother.

8 August 1953, London

Try to remember what happened today. I got up just before 7, and found Idelma and Lizzie all ready to go. Lizzie from time to time, with an ecstatic expression, said: 'Matthew seaside Matthew.' Idelma was very gay. Natasha only woke up to come down and say goodbye. When we got to Waterloo the platform was even more crowded than when I took M[atthew] to Swanage two weeks ago. So I took places [in] 1st class. We had to wait nearly an hour in a queue as all trains were made late by a slight accident on the line outside the station. We got into our compartment where there were three other people – two ladies and a sad-looking little boy. Lizzie was extraordinarily gay all the way to Wareham. We stood on the platform there and she looked at a horse across the other side of the track, and said she wanted to take it home, and when she was big, to ride it. After that I very nearly blinded her. She came running up to me while I held a lighted cigarette in my hand and it struck her just below the eye and made a slight burn. As often happens when things are serious, she made less fuss than she often does with less serious things. Also I was surprised by her complete certainty that it was not my fault. She flung herself into my arms and hid her face against my shoulder, and cried very little — all as if to comfort me.

At Swanage there was an appalling crowd — so many people on the station platform, one had to force one's way out. But against the newspapery, vulgar, jostling crowd of holidaymakers, the sea and the shell-pale cliff edge round the bay, and the yachts riding the harbour, looked crisp and fresh as though perpetually renewing themselves.

Matthew pranced out of the hotel and carried Lizzie in his arms all the way to her room. We had lunch in the dining room and then I noticed what an exhibitionistic pleasure I take in our Anglo-Italian conversations. I was wanting everyone in the room to hear our bilingual talk and be impressed.

After lunch Lizzie was extremely untired and we gave up all idea of her having a rest. She ran out onto the beach and without taking any notice of anyone proceeded to dig holes in the sand, which she then filled with water from her bucket. Then Matthew wanted us to go in a motor boat. We did this. Lizzie looked a little pale when we had gone out a little way, at which Granny looked like the wreck of the Hesperus. We landed the females and Matthew and I continued alone. When we returned there was tea in the lounge. Lizzie was tired and we renewed our persuasion that she should go to bed. I said goodnight to her. Then went on the beach and said goodbye to Matthew who was very artistically modelling a turret which surmounted a tower on a sand-castle. He was utterly absorbed and I left about half an hour later than I might have done, feeling strangely sad – as though something immensely important might have happened in that lost half hour.

1953, London

Irving Kristol fascinates me. He looks rather like a caterpillar which has pale bright blue eyes placed rather flatly in his head. He sits at his desk all day long, usually arriving at the office early, but it is very difficult to see what he does. All his friends are called by names like Pfeffernuss or Opalblut. I think he probably writes them long letters about the goddam English.

His occupation, of course, is editing – which, indeed, he is meant to do, but he means something quite different from what we mean by it. He means rewriting, chopping about and tailoring all the articles that come in. He regards a contribution as a chassis to which he then adds the coachwork. He loves doing this. He will arrive at the office saying that he has been up all night 'editing' Nathan Glazer's or Leslie Fiedler's piece.[1] 'Hope he won't mind,' he says. Then adds, reassured, 'Nah, *he* won't. He does the same to mine.'

One day he told me that his real ambition was to be on the editorial staff of *Time* magazine. 'Not the writing staff,' he said, 'I wouldn't do that crap. But the real editing staff which rewrites what the others have written.'

His contempt for writers is absolute. 'You have too much respect for writers,' he's always telling me: 'What they're for[?] They're to fill out the magazine, and it's editorial privilege to do it the way *we* want. It's *our* magazine, isn't? If they have something very important to say which goes twenty lines over a page, just chop off twenty lines, that's all. Nobody'll notice. Readers certainly don't and it's amazing how the writers themselves practically never do. Not as long as you pay them well, that's the advantage of paying them. What they're paid for? So you've got them where you want them, no?'

---

1 Nathan Glazer (b. 1924) and Leslie Fiedler (1917–2003) were both of Russian Jewish origins, both in early life were connected with the Trotsky wing of the American Communist Party, and both were interested in the question of assimilation into American identity, Glazer from the point of view of ethic origins, Fiedler from that of literary archetypes and gender.

29 August 1954, London

Lunched with Koestler who brought Janetta [Kee] with him. We talked for a little – about what? – rather seriously, then Koestler suddenly said, 'Enough of intensity! *Genügend intensität! Basta intensità!*' in several languages, adding, 'I mean *my* intensity!' which made his talk even heavier. What really is annoying with K. in conversation is his effort to manipulate the talk, his unwillingness for it to get out of his hands.

In August 1954, Spender went to Paris on CCF business, specifically looking into the possibility of Dwight MacDonald taking over from Irving Kristol as co-editor of Encounter.

30 August 1954, Paris

Lunch in Paris with Denis [de Rougemont] and François Bondy.[1] 'I have the idea of writing a travel book in the third person.' Denis: 'You will be the first to do that since Julius Caesar.'

In October 1954, Spender undertook a CCF-funded tour to Ceylon (independent since 1948, after 1972 Sri Lanka), the Indian sub-continent and Australia. It was the longest trip of his life hitherto.

29 October 1954, Ceylon

Sir John the Prime Minister of Ceylon.[2] Bristly-haired, strongly built, extremely agitated, throwing out his arms, bursting with laughter, shouting, quite uninhibited.

'From womb to tomb, Mr Spender, from womb to tomb – that's our slogan,' he yelled out as soon as he saw me. Then he started talking about the plans for Ceylon – reforms in rice production etc. 'I've spent 60 million on the University when it was estimated that it would cost 15 million,' he shouted. 'Of course, those fellows in the opposition criticize me a lot for that.'

---

1 Denis de Rougemont (1906–1985), Swiss writer and founder (in 1950) of the Centre Européen de la Culture, which was funded by the Common Market. François Bondy (1915–2003), Swiss writer of German extraction, editor of *Preuves*.

2 John Kotalawela (1897–1980), Prime Minister of Ceylon, 1953–6.

'The trouble is that in our country, the ministers don't administrate. They're treated as worms by their civil servants – just ordered about and told what to do. Now when I was in Whitehall, I was invited to a cocktail party – that's an old tradition that's been handed down in England – cocktail parties – and some sort of soldiers came in bearing glasses on trays – and an officer came up to me and said "Sir John, would you mind introducing me to the minister." "What do you mean?" I asked. "Aren't you here every day with your minister? Don't you tell him where he 'gets off'?" "Not at all," he said, "it's only at a party like this that I have a chance to see the Minister." So, of course, I took him up and said "Minister, here's one of your fellows wants to be introduced to you." Seems that public servants don't order Ministers about here like they do in my country.'

3 November 1954, Trivandrum, India

Arrived here supposedly for one day but found I was completely fixed up with a programme for two days. [. . .]

Often in India, I am left amazed by the complete lack of taste of Indians. Perhaps they have taste in their music but they hardly have any for their own sculpture, murals etc, though they know this ought to be admired. About poetry, they tell you with admiration about 'epics of 30,000 lines', where a Chinese or a Japanese would admire 7 lines. Then their asceticism is surely an exercise in tastelessness. There may be spiritual rules but (to me) it seems there is a poverty of joy in living. Perhaps it just is that I feel (and am) excluded.

Lectures here are absolutely hopeless, since almost no one understands English and far too many people attend.

8 November 1954, Bombay, India

Lunch at Madame Sophia Wadia (of the PEN Club).[1]

At lunch found myself at table with six women, none of them attractive, and two of them immense. They all gulped down quantities

---

1 Shrimati Sophia Wadia (c.1901–1986), wife of B. P. Wadia (1881–1958), the leader of the United Lodge of Theosophists. Both were founder members of the International PEN Club and contributors to the Indian PEN Club magazine.

of vegetarian diet (which included baked eggs), taking up their plates and going to the table where there were dishes, to refuel. The mountainous woman next to me, with pagoda-like earrings and a great belt of flowers in her hair, while devouring rice, told me that she was a film censor. 'They are always trying to get away with things,' she said with a voluptuous shudder. 'I wouldn't like to tell you of the things I have to cut out.' Pressed, she revealed that a film actress had posed as Siva in one film. 'Of course, that had to go.' And so on.

9 November 1954, Bombay

Dom Moraes came to breakfast.[1] He is extremely young and extremely advanced in every way. The awful embarrassment of having a mind of 20 or 30 when you are 16. We went through his poems which are very good. I made one or two suggestions about rhythm and language. He listened attentively but said something which showed he is so much inside his own poems he cannot get outside them.

Very anxious to know – do I really think he is good? etc, do I think he will become a poet?

Talks about stories he wrote when he was 11 or 12, just as an older writer might speak of his work five years ago. At breakfast he said, 'Do you remember coming to my father's house in 1952?' I remembered but did not remember meeting him. 'I asked you for your autograph,' he said. Then he added, 'I sat watching you, leaning forward with my face cupped in my hands, and then I noticed that you were in the same attitude. I thought how curious that the only two people who are poets in this room should sit leaning forward with face cupped in hands.'

Spender wrote the following entry shortly after the first anniversary of the death of Dylan Thomas in November 1953.

December 1954

<u>Dylan Thomas died in New York.</u>

---

1 Dominic Moraes (1938–2004), British-educated writer from Goa, son of the editor of the *Times* of India. Lived in London from the 1960s, making a name for himself as a poet and Soho habitué.

Having written these words I went to bed and dreamed about Dylan Thomas. It was in a large and beautiful chapel, like King's [College, Cambridge], where the choir was singing a Requiem in his memory. The chorale was modern and yet like something of Monteverdi, though not pastiche. Dylan was lying down on the floor beside the place where I was standing, rather pale, but still transparently alive.

I woke up thinking there was something I knew: death was an absurd pretence made by the living that the dead were not here – whereas, in reality, they were alive and omnipresent. As I realized, waking, that my sense of Dylan's physical presence was fading, I was still hammered on, as it were, from *inside* my head, by the realization of how alive the dead are. I felt tired with their always forcing themselves onto life with their persuasion and wholeness which the living lack.

Matthew (aged 9), who was sleeping in the twin bed during my wife's absence had woken me, as usual, with the dawn. We heard a drumming of hooves in the road outside. It was the cavalry on parade from the barracks nearby. Matthew slipped out of bed, drew back the curtains of the window and kneeled on the floor. 'Look! Look! Their heels are on fire!' he said. 'They always do that.' I realized this was the first time he had ever seen so much iron strike sparks from stone. As I knelt beside him, I suddenly saw the sparkling hooves agitating through the darkness against the road surface and breaking into small white flowers of sparks, and the shadowy horses moving through the milky darkness, just as Matthew saw them, for the first time. This first-time-ness also woke me to a sense of how Dylan saw them and how he would describe them, entering into the reality of the scene and singing out of the centre of its existence. At the same time I realized that I myself see things clearly but from the out-side and at a distance through the instrument of my personality, small and clear and upside-down, like on a camera's ground-glass screen.

24 April 1955, London

I have three poetic dramas to review, two of them by minor profes-sional poets, one by Jonathan Griffin, a man who until the age of 50 or so when he wrote this poetic drama, had never written a line of verse.[1] Although Griffin's verse is somewhat improvised in manner, it is much more alive and interesting than that of the two professional poets. Reflecting on this, it struck me that the atmosphere of literary discussion and competition in which modern poetry is written is so dull and analytic, that a modern poet in order to remain alive in his work, has to spend half his time escaping from literary life. One writes a certain amount of poetry, and then tries to escape from the assumptions and criticism and routine which are the background of modern poetry. One escapes, as it were[,] into real life. This theory would explain a good deal about the career of a man like Eliot, who has gone through long periods of writing absolutely nothing, and then for far shorter periods has immersed himself in writing his poetry. One has to escape from one's fellow poets, and of course one's own poems belong to the company of one's fellow poets, so therefore one has even to forget about one's own poems. Certainly, I am now absorbed in business and affairs of editing, and I do not think about my poems except suddenly to realize that I do not think about them. It is at any rate consoling to imagine that I have forgotten my own poetry and even about being a poet for the sake of writing an entirely different kind of poetry, and of getting away from the literary atmosphere.

25 April 1955, London

Natasha has been extremely unwell for several weeks, perspiring all the time and having a slight temperature. She has been preparing a concert for next Saturday, and will have to postpone it. This would be very depressing but that we have found a doctor who has at last made her be thoroughly examined by several specialists. They seem to have diagnosed a condition which has been going on for years, and the doctor is quite sure that he can get rid of the microbes which are poisoning her. The discovery of her illness was made by microscopic tests. It is disturbing to realize that of all the other doctors we have had none thought of making a proper examination during the past two years. I think that one result of psychology is that doctors

---

1 Jonathan Griffin (1906–1990) worked as a diplomat until 1951. His verse play *The Hidden King* was first performed in 1955.

have become rather lazy about making proper laboratory tests. For instance our National Health doctor, whom I have had ever since I was eleven, told me in the spring that he thought the reason why Natasha was ill was because she was upset by the success of my Collected Poems. It seems so easy for doctors to jump to half-baked conclusions of this kind.[1]

1 May 1955, London

I am teaching Matthew Latin, which gives me pleasure partly because it enables me to learn Latin again myself. Yesterday we were studying the past participle, and I could not make him understand that it agreed with the noun to which it was bound. Trying to make him understand this, I suddenly realized that teaching children something they cannot or do not wish to learn is one of the basically sad, melancholic, experiences in life. Somehow one feels that one is violating their ignorance. Also, of course, one is drawing attention to their refusal or inability to learn, and therefore the relationship easily becomes emotional and hurting to both sides.

18 May 1955, London

Went to [Louis] MacNeice party. Then did broadcast for French Service. Coming home found Raymond Chandler carrying on rather drunken conversation with Natasha.[2] His point was that she was a great genius at her music and that I did not drive her enough to perform. I felt there was some truth in this and his drunken way of saying that art was the only thing worth living for seemed to throw some light on what I had been feeling behind all the other things I had done the whole day.

The routine of the day, the routine of all the contributions sent in for me to read, the routine of the paintings I had seen: all this leaves one feeling completely unsatisfied.

---

1 Natasha's illness turned out not to be serious, although she would be diagnosed with breast cancer in 1964.

2 For Raymond Chandler, see biographical appendix.

May 1955, London

I had lunch with a journalist from a Swedish women's newspaper who interviewed me. She asked me questions about Communism, the Labour Party and Religion. I found myself giving quite stupid, irresponsible answers such as that I thought the West had to acquire some of the religion of the East in order that it might win the war against Communism. It is very easy to improvise unreal theories in order to tease people, and thus to find oneself getting more and more cut off from any kind of reality.

Came home, but after a sleepless night due to drinking too much coffee last night, I did not do any work. Went to drink with [the] Glenconners, where I met Ivan Moffat who talked about Christopher Isherwood.[1] The woman journalist, putting questions about religion and politics and doing so in a quite foolish way, nevertheless made me think all the time about something quite different which I felt to be extremely important and which I think about the whole time. In that way she was rather like Raymond Chandler last night when he was drunk and saying rather stupid things in a monomaniac kind of way, he also kept on saying 'Stephen knows quite well what I'm talking about.' Reminds me of a tall young man, an American veteran, in an insane asylum for mental victims of American wars, who came up to me and said, 'We know one another very well. You know you have met me before,' and I felt that I knew exactly what he meant.

The Swedish journalist had pale blue eyes, fair hair and a face which looked like stretched elastic. She wore dressmaker's jewellery in chains round her neck and wrists. She took me to the Czech restaurant in Baker Street which she said was the one place in London where she was sure of getting good food. She asked her questions in a rather inquisitorial manner, cross-examining all my answers.

A disturbing situation has arisen at the office on account of a review of a book about China by an American called Wittvogel. Wittvogel wrote in his review that a Chinese economist called Wei had changed his views from opposing Communism to supporting it,

---

1 Christopher Tennant, Lord Glenconner, (1899–1983) and his wife Elizabeth (b. 1914). Ivan Moffat (1918–2002), the son of the actress Iris Tree, worked after the war as a scriptwriter and producer in Los Angeles, where Isherwood met him.

as a result of a meeting with Chou. Or, rather, he wrote that rumour had this to be true.[1]

While I was in America [William] Empson wrote a letter protesting about this, enclosing another one from someone called Cedric Dover. Irving forwarded this correspondence to Wittvogel recommending him to do nothing about it. When I got home there was an insulting letter from Empson to me, enclosing another one from someone called Joan Robinson. The assumption behind Empson's letter was that we were deliberately distorting facts about Wei, who was not in a position to answer to our assertions.[2]

I have written to Wittvogel, urging him to reply, and as a matter of fact he has already written me a letter saying that he very much wants to do so. But the difficulty is that we are in a situation in which no assertions nor replies nor counter-replies have any authority at all. In China there is a dictatorship, and on our side there is the suspicion that we are trying to do American propaganda. So I am completely between two fires, and this is what I find very distressing.

19 May 1955, London

I went tonight to the Annual Meeting of the I.C.A. Herbert Read, Roland Penrose, Peter Watson and Dorothy Morland, were on the

---

1 Karl Wittvogel (1896–1988), historian of China. 'Chou' refers to Zhou Enlai (1898–1976), Premier of the People's Republic of China from its foundation in 1949 until his death. Teng Wei-Zao (1917–2008), a pioneer of modern Chinese economic study. Between 1950 and 1953 he was Dean of the School of Economics at Nankai University, later serving as the President of Nankai University (1981–86).

2 William Empson (1906–1984), British poet and author of *Seven Types of Ambiguity* (1930). Empson had taught in Peking before the war and had met many leaders of the Chinese Communist Party. His point was that Wei would have made his choices freely, without pressure from Zhou Enlai, but perhaps behind this clash lay the fact that Empson's communist sympathies made him suspicious of the American backing for *Encounter*. Spender was infuriated by Empson's aspersions against the magazine's American backers. The quarrel between the two men escalated over the next few years. Cedric Dover (1904–1961), anthropologist, at this time working in New York. Joan Robinson (1903–1983), economist, leader of the neo-Keynesian Cambridge school.

platform.[1] They asked for criticisms of the I.C.A. and they got them. One after another, members of the organization got up from the floor, and complained. [. . .] The meeting gave me the feeling that the avant garde in England is now an isolated little movement of middle-aged people, with absolutely no support either amongst its contemporaries or amongst the young. [. . .]

This apathy of the I.C.A., is curiously similar to the apathy about the General Election. After attending that meeting last night, this morning I read in the newspapers a report of an article by Aneurin Bevan about the election.[2] Bevan writes: 'There is another influence working against the Labour attack. Spiritual exhaustion, lethargy, of the collective will.' [. . .] Bevan then goes on to complain about the Tories taking advantage of this lethargy. But of course, this is absurd. It would be there, with or without the Tories, just as it was there last night with or without the managing committee of the I.C.A. The lethargy precisely about the ideas which are supposed to be inspiring and positive. The lethargy is really a kind of disillusion in the public mind about the ideas which once were the visionary ones of socialism and of advanced movements in the Arts. Spiritual exhaustion is also only a phrase. It denotes the absence of some quality which ought to be present. It seems far more likely that it is the result of what has happened since the war than of the war. It may even be the result of something profoundly negative about the causes which were once regarded as so positive. It may be that the success of those causes has revealed that what seemed positive in them has turned out to be

---

1 The poet and critic Herbert Read (1893–1968) and the surrealist and patron of the arts Roland Penrose (1900–1984) had founded the ICA in 1947. Dorothy Morland (1903–1999) was the director of the Institute during the 1950s.

2 Aneurin ('Nye') Bevan (1897–1960) had been a moving spirit behind the introduction of the National Health Service in 1946. In 1951, he had resigned from office as Minister of Labour as a protest against Hugh Gaitskell's plans as Chancellor of the Exchequer to introduce charges to the NHS to help finance war with Korea. This undermined Attlee's fading government and Labour lost the 1951 election. In the lead up to the May 1955 election, Bevan was preventing Labour from presenting themselves as a cohesive opposition by splitting the party between the anti-war Bevanites and the right-wing Gaitskellites. Unsurprisingly, the election resulted in an increased majority for the Conservatives.

negative. Thus the things that Bevan stands for, which are Social Welfare, and Security for a great many people, are revealed when they are available, to be after all negative. In the same way advanced movements in the arts have led to abstractions which are negative. So all we are left with is the kind of reaction which is supposed to be positive because it reacts from something which has been revealed to be negative. But this, like anti-Communism, is extremely suspect. Apathy is the result of people seeing that they are poised between the negativism of advanced ideas and the negativism of reaction.

What is positive? A movie I went to this afternoon, called *The Dam Busters* seemed really to be carrying on the conversation started by the I.C.A. meeting and the Bevan article. The raid on the dams which supplied water for the Ruhr was of course a very destructive idea, but it commanded qualities which need not necessarily have been used for destruction. One quality was the absolute devotion of the scientist who invented the bombs for these raids to his own idea and vision. The other was the willingness of the crews to sacrifice themselves and devote themselves absolutely to the pursuit of these ideas, quite regardless, of course, of their welfare.[1]

The tragedy of the war is that such creative qualities should have been devoted to something destructive. But the lesson nevertheless remains true, that they were creative qualities, and one feels that they need not have been devoted to destruction. It also follows that ideas which produce the opposite effects of apathy, are the opposite of the kind of ideas which Mr Bevan stands for. In fact, as long as we are devoted to our own welfare, we probably feel apathetic. When we are devoted to aims which make our welfare seem extremely unimportant to us, then we immediately cease to feel apathetic. Yeats understood this and his last poems are very largely about it. He says in them, again and again, that human welfare is unimportant. What is important is that humanity should sacrifice itself for the purpose of creating objects. Objects, which are pursued with passionate

---

1 *The Dam Busters* (1955) recounts the destruction during the war of two important German hydro-electric dams. The role of Dr Barnes Wallis, the inventor of the 'bouncing bomb', was played by Michael Redgrave, a friend of Spender's.

devotion, for their own sake. Art and religion and science and philosophy offer such pursuits of objects. It is not that welfare and social security are undesirable, but the moment they become the chief aim in life, life itself becomes extremely discouraging. It becomes discouraging in exactly the same way as one would be depressed if, when walking down a street one was forced to be conscious of the state of mind of every unhappy and sick person in that street. So, in the Welfare State, even if we suppress our own grievances, we are forced all the time to be aware of other people's grievances.

Now the only grievance of a person who seriously works in a creative way, is conditions which prevent him from working. On the other hand, the grievance of a worker is the conditions in which he works. It is assumed that he ought to work as little as possible for as high a wage as possible – an assumption which a writer, a poet or a saint would never make. In fact, he would consider it a blasphemy against his art and his calling to think so. The division between two such completely different attitudes towards work, a division which one is constantly made aware of, is itself extremely discouraging.

A film like *The Dam Busters*, suggests that another reason for the English apathy may simply be the awareness that the bluff of the whole of British history has been called by the atom bomb. 1940 was after all a miracle and Britain has existed on a whole series of such miracles throughout its history. The idea that Britain could live by and act on faith and survive all difficulties and all situations, is one which we were all brought up on. That we no longer believe this is as though we have been hustled off the scene of history in which we played a leading part for many hundred years. America has now become the country which believes in its miraculous powers, which are of course connected with its sense of its own historic vocation.

Yet I myself do go on believing, and if I ask what I really believe in it is simply work. As an artist, I believe that somehow people's faith in life could be restored by artistic work. I believe that cities could be transformed, that mediums like the theatre and the wireless could be used in unheard-of ways. I still believe in the idea of the renaissance. But, putting this in a less rhetorical way, all it means is that one goes on believing in the absolute virtue of complete devotion to one's vocation. If one doesn't believe this, there's just apathy and grievances. And ultimately even in politics, the only politicians who will be able to dispel apathy are the ones who while perhaps providing security, can above all restore the faith of people in work.

20 May 1955, London

Yesterday I took the children to tea with John Craxton. They were tremendously excited, and they took their painting things with them in order to paint all the time that they were there with a painter. Lizzie could not even wait to see his studio, but rushed downstairs, spread all her things out on a table and started painting. She even took a glass with her for her water to be in.

After tea, when John Craxton left the room, Elizabeth said to Matthew, 'Johnny Craxton has left the room.' Matthew said, 'Lizzie, I know why you said that. You just said it for the pleasure of saying Johnny Craxton.'

John gave them an enormous number of things: coins, an alabaster vase for holding oil, an image of Osiris from an Egyptian tomb, and some Turkish slippers for Matthew. To Lizzie, he gave a lump of white coral.

25 May 1955, London

Spent last two days in Paris. Meeting of Editors at Congress for Cultural Freedom. In the ferry train, on the way home, Irving [Kristol] mentioned to me that he was no longer to continue editing *Encounter*. He said that he would be going to Milan to prepare the book about the conference there.[1] He told me this without resentment, and with the greatest friendliness and detachment. He did not in any way criticize the decision that had been made about him. He said he thought he would go back to New York, as the one thing he could not bear to do was to go to Paris and work with Nicky [Nabokov] and

---

1 'The Future of Freedom', organized by the Congress of Cultural Freedom in Milan, 12–17 September 1955.

Mike [Josselson].[1] He thought that the choice of Dwight MacDonald to succeed him as my co-Editor, was very rash.[2] He said that one advantage that he had over any other editor, was his experience of the Congress and the fact that he had the cause of the Congress at heart. He thought that Dwight MacDonald was a person who was always flying off at tangents on matters of principle, and that he would never accept the advice or need of cooperating with Nicky and Mike. I was touched by the real goodness of Irving's character when he was discussing this matter. He might well have been annoyed with me for not insisting that he should stay with me, quite apart from the fact that he may well have known that I actually approve of the change that is being made.

31 May 1955, London

On Election Night [27 May], we dined with the Huxleys. Other guests were Lord Horder and two Americans.[3] The Huxleys never seem to have any personal understanding of their guests, which usually makes dinner with them embarrassing, if not boring. At their dinner parties, everyone seems to be there on false pretences. There is no conversation, only interesting moments when someone happens to talk about his particular subject, or to tell a story which is amusing or enlightening. Over brandy, Lord Horder and Julian had a slight tiff. Julian has a theory that certain people die not of any organic illness, but simply of old age, through a kind of shrivelling up of all their faculties. Horder disagreed with this, on the grounds that always some particular organ or function fails. Julian seemed very attached to his theory, I think, because he wants to think that there is something inexplicable about old age and death. Horder, who was

---

1 For Nicholas Nabokov, see biographical appendix; for Mike Josselson, see the note on *Encounter* in the biographical appendix.

2 Editor of *Partisan Review* from 1937 to 1943, and of *Politics* for the rest of the 1940s, Dwight MacDonald (1906–1982) came from the same political background as Nathan Glazer, Leslie Fiedler, Irving Kristol and Melvin Lasky. In the end it was Lasky who took over Kristol's job as co-editor of *Encounter*.

3 Thomas Horder (1871–1955), Lord Horder of Ashford, physician to King George VI and Queen Elizabeth II.

obviously in the right in this argument, simply kept on pointing out to him that he was out of date in his views and quite wrong.

There is something very characteristic about Julian's inability to see the point of view of other people. He fails to see it more or less as a matter of scientific principle.

Juliette told me that when Maria [Huxley, Aldous's wife] was dying, Aldous [Huxley] was the only person able to persuade her to eat. In her advanced condition of cancer, when she went to hospital, all the food that she was given she vomited up. But Aldous was able to hypnotize her, and to get her into a state of body or mind in which she could take nourishment. When one dies, the last faculty which remains is the hearing, and Aldous was able right up to the moment of her death to make Maria, although she could not speak to him, understand what he was saying to her. He reminded her of mystical experiences which they had shared, and was thus able to carry her spirit right through to the moment of her death.

The railway strike is extremely depressing and leads to further thoughts about British apathy.[1] In England, today, there seem to be no margins. We live in a perpetual situation of underlying crisis. This means that a strike like the present one is far too obviously a kind of action which makes the whole of Society, including the strikers themselves, the victims of that action. The expansion and boom which we have recently been enjoying, could obviously be quite removed within a matter of a few weeks of the present strike. A thing like this reminds one that we are just a great crowd of people living on a far too narrow space. The same situation would of course exist even more dramatically if there were a war, when we could be wiped out with a very few bombs. But any kind of activity which is not devoted to improving our situation seems to be a threat at our situation. To have this sense of crowds and no margins of time and space, is fundamentally discouraging. I even wonder whether people might not become so discouraged that they became indifferent to it, and found themselves wanting to do something quite desperate and suicidal like carry on a near civil war, regardless of the fact that it would reduce

---

1 British Rail, the recently nationalized transport service, was crippled from April to June 1955 by a strike over plans for modernization. This did not help the Labour cause.

the whole country to a state of near starvation. Again, the facts that large numbers of people do not see that we are all living in the same boat is also depressing.

Sometimes I think that the basic problem of all government today in every country, is simply how to make people work. Communism makes the workers work by establishing the fiction that it is a workers' government and therefore the workers are not allowed to strike or protest against it. American capitalism does it by turning the trade unions into a huge big business interest, like the big business interests themselves. We in England seem to be divided between envious workers who want complete equality and business men who lose interest in their business because their initiative is always being threatened. We suffer from the disadvantages of both kinds of system – socialist and extreme capitalist.

June 1955, London

Dinner party [. . .] for Lord and Lady Glenconner, the Rosses and Raymond Chandler. Also Kay Cicellis.[1] I do not really enjoy my own dinner parties, as I am much too worried about whether the guests are enjoying themselves. They have a rather nightmarish quality. At dinner, everyone seemed to be shouting and it seemed to me that at other dinner parties conversation proceeds in a much more quiet and leisurely way than this tremendous kind of shouting that was going on in our room. We had hired a refugee cook, who was extremely disagreeable, although she cooks very well. She complained that we had no nutmeg and spices, no sieve, no meat chopper and board, and that the oven door wouldn't fasten properly. She also regarded our own Italian domestic as so incompetent as almost to be an insult to her. Her complaints were not directed so much at us as at the whole of England. For she said that on other nights she always cooked meals for viscounts and viscountesses, and that their kitchens were almost as inadequate as ours. Knowing that all this was going on in the kitchen, made me feel that the whole meal was far from smooth. Raymond Chandler got drunk and insisted on leaving the table with the ladies and not joining the men over coffee and brandy. However,

---

1 Kay Cicellis (1926–2001), Greek-born novelist and translator.

some of the men's conversation was quite interesting. Glenconner talked in a way which I have come to regard as rather characteristic. He began by saying that he sympathized very much with the railway platemen of ASLEF [Associated Society of Locomotive Engineers and Firemen] who are now on strike. He then went on to qualify this by saying that he thought the people who really should be attacked and criticized were not ASLEF but the N.U.R. [National Union of Railwaymen] who had not accepted the rise of pay demanded by ASLEF. He thought the Transport Commission should have accepted ASLEF's demands and then if necessary opposed the strike which would then have been staged by the N.U.R. All this sounded like an extreme Left Wing point of view. But he then went on to say that in spite of his sympathies he thought it was the duty of the government to intervene and that, if the strike went on for a long time, the military would have to run the railways.

10 June 1955, London

Last night had a very serious, rather alarming, conversation with Natasha. She said it is no use dreaming one's way through life. This made me think of the distinction between dream and vision. The condition of dreaming, in which many people must spend their lives, is living almost entirely in a world of reverie and fantasy. You go through the day imagining that things might be otherwise than they are, constructing an unreality of your own, a kind of inner monologue which continues for hours and days on end, and is partly a kind of running commentary on the life around you, partly quite disconnected from life. You make use of dreaming to evade reality. When you are confronted by inescapable facts they either defeat you, or else you sink back into a dream which has now turned to resentment. Such reverie is a decadence of imagination. Vision is an orderly use of the imagination that constructs an ideal world out of bricks made of the real world. It is a discipline whereby whilst one knows the real world, nevertheless one is able to abstract oneself from events to create a different picture which one can then measure against reality. Vision is where creation is also criticism. Dream is desultoriness. Today poetry and the arts are associated with the idea of dreaming, whereas the idea of vision has become archaic and remote.

June 1955, Vienna

On June 12, Cyril Connolly came to stay with us. On the Friday night, Cyril went to hear Wagner, and we went to the Festival Hall to hear Samuel Barber's Songs of Kierkegaard performed. On the evening before Sam's concert, we gave a party at the White Tower Restaurant for Cyril, Barbara [Skelton], Samuel Barber and John Craxton. Afterwards, went to Anne Fleming's where there were Lucian and Caroline Freud.[1] This began a bit stiffly, Lucian obviously being embarrassed by the presence of John Craxton and myself, towards both of whom he has behaved rather badly. He was wearing a bottle green suit, and as Cyril remarked afterwards, one noticed what an extraordinary rise has taken place in his life since we first knew him. Formerly he was bohemian and poor, he now has a car costing £3,000 and is married to an heiress, has danced with Princess Margaret, is always in the gossip columns and is an expensive and fashionable painter. In spite of his large income, he does not seem to trouble to pay debts incurred to his friends before he was so fortunate. He always makes faces, and talks for effect, but on this particular evening he was rather ineffective. It was Cyril who made the party go.

During the past few days with Cyril, I have been trying to discover for myself what are the special qualities of his funniness. To begin with, he is completely uninhibited, and always says exactly what is in his mind. This makes him extremely funny and touching at the same moment; though also sometimes very tiresome. When he is at his most sophisticated he remains an innocent who blurts out the truth. He is moody. When he is not being extremely destructive he can be a most sympathetic critic of, for example, the young. He takes endless trouble to help friends in certain matters of work, such as correcting their style.

At Anne Fleming's party, he started saying how Oxford today was the most impossible place in the world to live in, and he illustrated this thesis by describing his sitting in Maurice Bowra's sitting room and hearing his guests, tuning up their voices like instruments as they

---

1 Anne Fleming (1913–1981), society hostess and wife of the author Ian Fleming. Lucian Freud's then wife Caroline Blackwood (1931–1996) was later married to Robert Lowell.

walked upstairs before dining with Maurice.[1] He is insistently un-ashamedly humanly himself in a way that seems the result of weakness, but which can also turn into a vigorous attack on bureaucracy, respectability and so on. He leads his private life in the public eye of his friends, and yet it remains eccentric peculiar and private. No-one so repeatedly asserts that he is very much in love with his wife, or that his wife is cruel to him and that his life is intolerable. His life seems one long uncomplaining insistence on the right to complain, one long unself-pitying insistence on the right to pity oneself, one long heroic insistence on the right to weep like a child. [. . .]

When we went to Brussels, as soon as he had got on to the aeroplane, Cyril took out a little notebook and scratched out a sentence in it. When the aeroplane was in the air, he explained to me that the sentence contained an unkind remark about a woman we both knew. Characteristically, he added quickly: 'She's not my wife.' He had imagined that perhaps the plane would crash, his diary be recovered, and this unkind remark be taken as his last comment on a friend. For that reason he had altered the evidence with which his death would confront history. He then entered into a lively inquisitive conversation with some racing touts who were on the same table as we were. I gave him a pound and he tried to persuade them to put this sum on a horse at the races that afternoon. (Later in the weekend, he asked to borrow 'the £1 he had offered to put on the horse' because as he explained it made him feel independent to have a little money of his own.) They refused, and immediately he became a tearful schoolboy who had received a snub.

During the Brussels weekend his relations with Barbara steadily deteriorated.[2] Apparently, when they had met that morning on their way to the aeroplane, she had promised to stay several days in Brussels, but as soon as they got to Brussels she started complaining that it was the ugliest city in the world, and she decided she would go home on Tuesday. She even refused to go home by the same

---

1 Maurice Bowra (1898–1971), Classics don and Warden of Wadham College, Oxford, 1938–70. He was said to be the model for Mr Samgrass in Evelyn Waugh's *Brideshead Revisited*.

2 Connolly had invited himself on a holiday the Spenders had planned with Hansi Lambert in Belgium. Connolly's relationship with Barbara Skelton, whom he had married in 1950, was breaking up.

aeroplane as Natasha because she insisted that she must have her hair done early in London, and could not find a friseur in Brussels. (Actually, Cyril learned afterwards the real reason. She did not go to London at all but to Paris.) Cyril told me he had the idea that the only thing that would save their marriage now was to make love a lot and 'prove his magic'. Unfortunately whenever they began to do this, they were interrupted. The telephone would ring and Hansi would ask whether their room was comfortable and warm enough, or a butler would come into the room bearing a suit of clothes which had been pressed, or a servant with one of Barbara's dresses. Finally, when they got to bed after dinner for several guests, they were interrupted by all the clocks striking midnight in their room. Only in extremely rich households do all the clocks in all the bedrooms still strike, Cyril observed resentfully to me. Nevertheless, he acted up wonderfully and was extremely amusing all the weekend.

* * *

I took the plane to Vienna on Monday morning. Arrived there at 8. [. . .] Within twenty minutes of arriving in the Pension Atlanta, I had changed and left again to go to a party given by the City for the PEN Club, at Schönbrunn. I arrived there only half an hour late, but already all the food with which the tables had groaned, had been eaten by the assembled PEN Club. There were all the international writers and intellectuals.

The delegate I most like was [Ignazio] Silone. Silone has an unhappy, clownlike face, with lines round the mouth, and a small Charlie Chaplin moustache, at once solemn and comic. Like Chaplin, when he tells you a story he indulges in frequent gestures – taking his hat suddenly off his head and then putting it on again, shrugging his shoulders, answering a question by simply turning up his eyes, or with a movement of both hands.

20 June 1955, London

More, though, than any gesture one is struck by something unremittingly sad which is the ground bass of his moods, above which a comedy is imposed. The act most characteristic of Silone I can remember is when at a meeting in Paris, he suddenly presented the executive meeting of the Congress for Cultural Freedom with a little clockwork figure of a monkey beating a drum and ringing a bell, and wearing a three-cornered red hat. He said this should be our mascot when we had a Congress meeting in Moscow.

The PEN Club deliberations were not at all exciting. The theme of discussion was the Drama Today. Some good papers were read, but they all consisted of accounts of the situation of drama in various countries. No one got up and said that all contemporary plays ought to be symbolical or social realist, or poetic or political: and that everything which was not whichever one of these he advocated, was trash. We were supposed to have discussions, but hearing a dozen reports, like Budgets, of the way the theatre was going in more countries than anyone could have wished to hear about, there was nothing to discuss. [. . .]

In Vienna I was struck by what is less obvious in England – though certainly noticeable, even there – the tremendous boom taking place everywhere in Europe. I was accustomed to the Vienna of 1934, with unemployment and political agitation. But here was a Vienna of nearly full employment, restorations of old buildings, and new buildings going up everywhere, and a good deal of fairly obvious wealth. [. . .]

In Vienna, I was greatly taken up with meeting and talking to Lucy [Lambert, Hansi's daughter]. She telephoned me the second day after my arrival, and we had coffee and, I think, dinner that evening. Before long, she was telling me exactly what she thought of her mother and the Avenue Marnix. She said quite frankly that she thought there never had been a mother who had made such mistakes as hers. 'Who else,' she asked, 'would have taken her, Lucy, at the age of five, away from the nurse whom she very much had loved' (and whom indeed she still sees), 'and sent her to a very expensive boarding school in Switzerland?' In addition to this, Hansi took Léon and Philippe [her sons] away from the Marie José boarding school, leaving Lucy alone there for months at a time. Hansi thought that if you pay enough money everything will be all right. My mother, Lucy said, is only happy when her children are ill. When her children are surrounded by doctors, and in bed, she at last feels that she has them and can be at peace.

[167]

On Friday Lucy and I had dinner with Count Caruso, the psychologist, and his wife who works in a dress shop.[1] We stayed talking so late – at least Lucy and I did after the Carusos had gone away – that I did not arrive at the Mayor of Vienna's party for the PEN Club until nearly midnight.

Before the Carusos we called at the palace of the old Princess Shönburg. This grey, baroque palace is completely desolate, unrepaired, falling into ruin, in the midst of which all the roses are becoming wild. The grass seems unkempt green hair.

The Princess is an elderly, stalwart, grey-haired and pink-skinned woman, looking strong as a horse. She has lost 6 sons in the war, her husband is dying of cancer in a room of the palace, and she is completely penniless. Lucy said they were so poor that when she went there she was always afraid to eat anything, even a potato. Yet the Princess goes on trying to have parties, recitations and lectures, which no one attends. Lucy told me she was so determined that Count Caruso should give a dissertation there on some psychological subject, that she pursued him for weeks on end. Finally Count Caruso took to his bed when she called one day, pretending that he was ill. She forced her way into his bedroom and demanded that he get up and come and give a lecture to a gathering, which she said was waiting for him at her palace.

23 June 1955, London

Lunch with Edith Sitwell. Sachy [Sacheverell Sitwell], Alberto de Lacerda, John Thompson, Maurice Bowra and a lady called Mrs Black were there.[2] The meal began, as it usually does at Edith's, with

---

1 Igor Caruso (1914–1981), an Italian psychologist residing in Vienna. An 'Existential Freudian', Caruso formed an intellectual friendship at this time with Jacques Lacan.

2 For the Sitwells, see biographical appendix. Alberto de Lacerda (1928–2007), distinguished Portuguese poet, now working for the BBC Portuguese service in London. (Edith Sitwell thought Lacerda the most intelligent man she had ever known.) John Thompson (1906–1965), American-born Canadian neuropathologist, instrumental in introducing the concept of 'medical war crimes' at the Nuremberg Trials. He went on to work for UNESCO, where he promoted the concept of 'informed consent' when using human subjects in medical research.

the Sitwells talking mercilessly about someone who is a particular victim of theirs. They do this out of sheer nervousness, I think, without meaning to be unkind. However it makes everyone feel involved in loyally having to follow the Sitwell line. This may involve one in feeling disloyal to the person discussed. One of the jokes about this particular victim, is to exaggerate her age. Maurice said that according to one calendar it was 106, but according to another it was nearly 100. As we had missed celebrating the 100th birthday according to one system, we must be sure to celebrate it according to the other. And so on. After a bit, one finds oneself racking one's brains to think of something nasty to say about someone. [. . .]

Came back and took Rosamond Lehmann out to dinner. [. . .] After dinner, I took my guests along to Kettner's Restaurant where Lord Pakenham was giving a dinner for some ex-prisoners and people interested in them. The idea was to form a group of ex-prisoners to help one another, and of their friends who may help them. Three of the prisoners were Lord Edward Montagu, Michael Pitt-Rivers, and Peter Wildeblood.[1]

The idea of the proposed organization was Edward Montagu's. No one seemed to have any practical idea how to carry it out. John Thompson, who was there, talked very big about what he was doing with an organization called Feu Vert to help prisoners in France. I was embarrassed, as I believe that John Thompson's imagination sometimes runs away with him. The only thing decided in the evening was that Edward Montagu and Peter Wildeblood should go over and see John Thompson in France. This may be a good thing, but I am not sure.

It struck me that we were all assuming that being sent to prison makes prisoners the same. But this is not so. Those sent for sexual

---

1 In January 1954 Peter Wildeblood (1923–1999), Michael Pitt-Rivers (1917–1999) and Lord Edward Montagu (b. 1926) were charged with inciting acts of 'gross indecency' (i.e. homosexual acts) and sentenced to twelve months imprisonment – eighteen months in the case of Wildeblood, who bravely proclaimed his homosexuality in court. Lord Longford (Frank Pakenham) took an interest in the case and was joined by the Spenders in setting up a lobby to reform the law. This helped bring about first the 1957 Wolfenden Report and, in 1967, the Sexual Offences Act, which decriminalized homosexual acts between adult males.

offences cannot really be compared with those sent for forging cheques or robbing people. This seems a difficulty the organization will have to face.

28 June 1955, London

I shall note down some random impressions of the past few days. Five days ago, on Friday, I lunched with T. S. Eliot and John Hayward. Eliot seemed in better form than I had seen him for a long time. He was smiling and chuckling and really quite gay. John did most of the talking, gossiped, and discussed magazines. They both agreed that *Encounter* had much improved. John said that it certainly contained boring articles, with which I agreed. But Eliot said that he thought that as long as a magazine had one brilliant piece which one had to read in each number, it was doing pretty well. Indeed, he added rather characteristically, it would be a mistake for the reader to feel he had to read everything in each number, because he would have the impression there was too much reading involved. John told me he had quarrelled with [John] Lehmann because he had said at a meeting of the Advisory Board of the *London Magazine*, that *Encounter* was more interesting than *L.M.*[1] Lehmann now refuses to see him. Eliot said that a good editor should not be someone who simply waits and collects the best material that is submitted to him. He has to impose his own personality on the magazine, and he has to have initiative in going out and commissioning stuff.

Last night, we went to the ball given by the Glenconners for their daughter [Emma]'s Coming Out. This was an extremely brilliant affair. It consisted mostly of the aristocratic young, the girls looking incredibly fragile and lovely. The young men mostly a bit goofy and vacuous. It gave me the feeling not as much of a youth I have passed as of a life that I have altogether missed. As someone remarked recently, it was almost unthinkable during the 1930s for us to be attracted by this kind of ball. Yet I realize now how much we missed, how elegant our affairs could have been, instead of being rather sordid and wretched. Even in our loves, we lived then a kind of kitchen sink existence. Last night one certainly did feel that there is a kind of

---

1 The *London Magazine* was edited by John Lehmann at the time.

Restoration going on in England. Perhaps this is because the young feel a need to establish their social identity more than to hold views about society. That Matthew at the age of ten should spend days designing his coat of arms seems in the spirit of the time. If he goes on like this, in ten years' time he will be at a ball like the Glenconners', one of the young men with a beautiful girl in a creamed-fruit-coloured dress crushed against him.

Cyril Connolly was introduced to Princess Margaret. He told me he had expected her to say, 'What! *The* Cyril Connolly!' Instead, she did not even look at him but hurried by, followed by a Lady in Waiting who murmured in an audible whisper: 'Temper! Temper!' [. . .]

Cyril is extremely taken by the Lamberts. The side of him which is partly fun, partly real day-dreaming, was shown by his saying to me late yesterday evening at the Glenconner party, that he already saw himself as Baron Connolly-Lambert. Voyons! Le yacht de Baron Connolly. He thinks half seriously of marrying Hansi, without thinking at all of whether she would wish to marry him. In order to complete the picture, he thinks that I should marry Lucy and that Natasha, having left me, should marry Léon, while Cyril's wife Barbara should marry Philippe. This extravagance gives one a glimpse of the way in which Cyril played with fantasies affecting real issues. He is on the verge of leaving Barbara, as usual.

1 July 1955, London

A strange phenomenon. Reading a great many manuscripts every day, I find it difficult to read anything in the periodicals, or any fiction. At first, I thought this meant that I was getting out of the habit of reading anything. I was very worried at the way my attention tends to wander after reading a few pages. Then I discovered that the difficulty is confined to average contemporary works or contemporary subject matter. For instance, I've read the whole of Steven Runciman's book about the Crusades without difficulty.[1]

And I'm sure I could read any poetry written before this century. It seems really a matter of the contemporary rhythms, and contemporary style of writing, which unless it is quite outstanding I am tired

1 Steven Runciman, *A History of the Crusades*, 3 vols. (1951).

of. It may be though just that what I get to read is inferior, and not being able to take it in, I cannot judge it.

* * *

On Thursday, I lunched with Peter Wildeblood. I had only met him at Lord Pakenham's ex-prisoner meeting. He is quite obviously effeminate, not at all cowardly. He has an open and, I think, courageous attitude about his prison experience. He is very much what he is, unashamedly, and with a curious dignity. If he had not made up his mind to be rather defiant, how embarrassing it would be for him to go into a restaurant or to hear his name mentioned or when he passes someone who recognizes him from the published photographs. He seems though quite to have solved the problems of shame with himself. In conversation, I found him willing to talk about his experiences. I asked him whether to be arrested and tried must not be overwhelmingly shameful, however convinced one might be that the law had no right to judge this offence. He said that at first he felt very shaken, but as soon as he discovered the methods of the police, he was filled with such indignation that he ceased to feel concerned with any moral guilt on his side. I am rather worried about him, because his attitude is almost too straightforward. He is so concerned with seeing other prisoners, some of them now his friends from prison, that I cannot help fearing the police may try to convict him again. I told him my fears, and he replied that he thought that they would not dare pursue a course of such obvious persecution. He said he had no intention of living abroad, as he did not want to take an 'easy way out'. He has written a book about his experiences.[1]

We went to dinner with [George] Weidenfeld. Sonia [Orwell] acted as hostess. Boden and Mary Broadwater were there.[2] Also the Freuds. I sat next to Caroline Freud, whom I found rather charming. She looks at one with large wonderful eyes between reed-like strands of hair falling over her forehead. If one talks at her and cross questions her, she talks rather well, and very pleasantly. She seems never to introduce a topic of conversation on her own initiative. This seems

---

1 Peter Wildeblood, *Against the Law* (1957).

2 For Sonia Orwell, see biographical appendix. Boden Broadwater was Mary MacCarthy's third husband.

characteristic of a whole class of girls whom Lucian, Cyril and their friends fall in love with.

After dinner, many after-coffee guests appeared, among them Peter Wildeblood, John and Rosamond Lehmann and the Gaitskells.[1] I made a point of introducing Peter Wildeblood to everyone I thought might either be helpful to him or should be confronted with him. Hugh Gaitskell seemed a bit embarrassed at first, though a moment later he immediately became very pleasant and friendly. [. . .] The party was rather over-shadowed by people discussing the affairs of Cyril Connolly. At the end of it, Sonia saw Rosamond, Natasha and me off the premises. But she kept us for a long time on the stairs, while I was trying to get a taxi, going on about Cyril's misfortunes. She was quite hysterical in her insistence that Cyril was really utterly miserable. She seemed to feel that everyone except her talked in a frivolous and heartless way. 'But he's really unhappy, he's really unhappy,' she kept on repeating. She was rather drunk, and with her large, collapsed face and untidy hair looked disintegrated, alarmingly so. Diana [Witherby] who accompanied us in the taxi, told us that Sonia has a terrible time, being treated as confidante by all parties in this matter.[2] Everyone tells her how much they are in love, but no one tells her that he loves Sonia.

3 July 1955, London

Ever since I heard [T. S.] Eliot and John Hayward agree, the other day, that Auden was not an intellectual, I have been thinking on and off about this. What they meant, of course, was that although exceptionally brilliant, intelligent and well read, Auden often does not employ the methodical processes of intellectual argument. An example cited was his writing that Tennyson was the stupidest poet in the English language – in his Preface to his Tennyson Selected Poems. It is a provoking remark and one sees what he means, but it is not subject to proof. If he had argued this intellectually, he would

---

1 Hugh Gaitskell (1908–1963) became Leader of the Labour Party in December 1955.

2 Diana Witherby, British poet who met Spender when he was working at *Horizon*.

have had to compare the stupidity of Tennyson with that of one or two other poets. [. . .]

[D. H.] Lawrence also, although extremely intelligent, was not an intellectual. Perhaps, though, the people best equipped to attack and criticize modern life have to be more wasps or destroyers than intellectual whales. The intellectual gets caught up in the methods of research and exposition which are parts of what has to be criticized. Lawrence, Auden, and Kierkegaard have it in common that they treat their time as a gigantic encyclopaedic body of information and behaviour against which they write ferocious comments in the margins. To be an intellectual is to be already partly institutionalized.

Sometimes I am depressed by the thought that today one writes poetry for an audience consisting of a horrible little squabble between swotty students and tramps.

When one is young one wishes to tell everyone the truth[,] and lies to oneself. If one is able to grow old, one lies to everyone, but knows the truth for oneself.

5 July 1955, London

Christopher Levenson came to my office.[1] A fresh-looking open-air countrified Quaker type with a puzzled, frank manner. Deeply concerned with his feeling that he belongs to a generation divided between the prospect of destruction caused by the H Bomb and ever increasing Americanization. He told me that Leavis had questioned him last March as to whether he had ever met me.[2] As a result of his gaffe in inviting me to speak to his College Society, he had had to resign from being its secretary. Seeing me now, he admitted, would be regarded as disloyalty by Leavis, who, he hoped, would not find out. He expressed a wish to write for *Encounter*, but he was extremely

---

1 Christopher Levenson (b. 1934), British poet, naturalized Canadian in 1973, at this point a Cambridge undergraduate. Levenson's poems would be published in *Encounter* later in the decade.

2 F. R. Leavis (1895–1978), influential (and divisive) Cambridge don and literary critic, best known for his remapping of the literary canon in *The Great Tradition* (1948).

frightened evidently of the consequences. It is not only Leavis who intimidates him but perhaps still more his undergraduate followers whom Levenson calls the Levites.

* * *

The whole day over-shadowed by C[yril]'s affairs. He telephoned from Brussels in the morning to ask me whether I could find out from Sonia [Orwell] where B[arbara] is. Whether she left on Friday, as she said she would, whether she is staying with Jean Hugo or Poppet John in the south of France.[1] Then he asked me find out whether (a) she intended marrying W[eidenfeld] and (b) whether W. intended marrying her.

He said he was telephoning me because he could not bear Sonia's sympathetic manner. On no account did he wish to speak to her. Also, I had to find out the answer to the first questions without indicating to Sonia where C. thought B. was, in case, in the event of Sonia's not already knowing, she would inform W., who might then pack his bag and join B. in the south of France. Cyril told me to find out what Sonia truly thought about the question of whether B. was intending to leave him, that he could take it. He added that Sonia would certainly lie if he telephoned her, and not say what she really thought. I made all these inquiries of Sonia and then phoned Cyril again. He did not quite accept 'Yes' as the answer to his last two questions. He said something about B. having said to him that she did not want to go and would not pack her bag etc, and followed this up with the classic question: 'Do you think they would be happy together?' Later in the afternoon he telephoned again, saying he had received a telegram from Joan Rayner saying – 'Return home immediately.'[2] He thought this meant that Joan wanted to advise him to come back to England immediately and arrange matters. He wanted me to find out Joan's telephone number in order that he could get in touch with her.

---

1 Jean Hugo (1894–1984), French artist, the grandson of Victor Hugo. Poppet John (1912–1997), daughter of the artist Augustus John.

2 Joan Rayner (1912–2003), formerly an assistant on *Horizon*, companion and later wife of the writer Patrick Leigh Fermor.

I spent an hour or so working on this. After trying Rex Warner, I got on to Lord Monsell, who was cosy and chatty and said he thought she was abroad, and explained that anyhow he never heard a word from either of his children.[1]

Finally, in despair, I tried Sonia again, knowing that she has the answer to everyone's domestic problems. She at once said she was sure the telegram meant that Joan herself was returning home. I had Christopher Levenson and another visitor in my room during this conversation. I rashly asked Sonia to telephone Brussels herself. She was delighted. And although I felt a little guilty, I reflected that her answer would be such a relief to Cyril that he would be glad to hear her voice.

Of course, what happened I might have anticipated. The first thing Cyril asked Sonia was whether it was true she had told me that the answer to both his questions about Barbara leaving him was Yes. She promptly denied this, and said she had said nothing of the sort. He then told her to tell me that I was a bad friend to have told him something that was not true.

In the evening we went to a party at Jocelyn's.[2] Other guests were A. J. Ayer, the Rosses, an Australian and his wife, whose name I did not catch. The Australians were rather left out of this party, which like the rest of my day was overcast by the shadow of Cyril's problems. It really was a very curious evening, in which all of us were divided between amusement and horror about Cyril. Perhaps on account of this mixture of emotions, Alan [Ross] talked harshly about Sonia. I have never heard him talk like this before. He said Sonia was a tremendous breaker up of marriages and interferer in other people's lives, and gave some really horrifying examples of her interventions.

Jennifer [Ross], hearing Alan talk like this, obviously felt worried about the impression he might be making. She kept on saying nervously that she had never heard Alan talk in this way before, she was

1 Rex Warner (1905–1986), poet and classicist who had met Spender, Cecil Day Lewis and W. H. Auden at Oxford. Viscount Monsell (1881–1961), Conservative politician, father of Joan Rayner.

2 Jocelyn Rickards (1924–2005), film costume designer at this date engaged in a love affair with A. J. Ayer.

sure he did not mean what he was saying, she could not think what had happened to him tonight, and so on. Here was a married couple in momentary disarray, *au fond* perhaps because they were upset by the breakdown of Cyril's marriage, one party wondering whether the other was not giving himself away. I rather admired Alan for being extremely insistent and not withdrawing anything. I am pretty sure he was right about this aspect of Sonia and perhaps this was the occasion to say it. The conversation turned to literature, and Alan said there should be an attack on the young critical Dons. Although I agreed with his general thesis, while he was talking I noticed how very ignorant he is directly he gets off his contemporaries. He belongs to a generation engaged in war at the critical period when they ought to have been reading intensively. In this respect, he is like John Craxton and Lucian Freud, who grew up as young painters at a time when all the galleries were closed.

The whole evening reflected the seismographic disturbance caused by Cyril in Brussels. It was a mixture of chortling amusement – made rather inevitable by Cyril – and real concern about him. At the same time, everyone felt a little ashamed.

I could not help thinking how different our world is from that of Chrisopher Levenson and of the Levites. They accuse us of being a clique. This is wrong, but they would be on surer ground if they reproached us with being worldly, gossipy, too involved in one another's affairs, and too exclusive of everything else.

In July 1955, Spender went to Germany on CCF business.

7 July 1955, Hamburg

Have spent the last two days in Hamburg. What strikes me about this city today, which I had last seen in June 1945, is that it has been almost completely restored to the state in which it was in 1929 when I first went there. In the 1920s, the great passion of the Germans was to build something new. This may have been because the First World War produced poverty and also many signs of spiritual ruin. The Second World War produced material destruction of houses, etc and, within a few years, staggering recovery, unaccompanied by any great spiritual crisis. The Occupation provided an alibi for all moral and spiritual problems.

The Germans, instead of being anxious – as after the first war – to create new things, are simply anxious to use their prosperity to fill the gap in their physical surroundings. They rebuild their bombed cities to look exactly as they did before, in much the same spirit perhaps as one goes to a dentist and asks to have his artificial teeth made an exact replica of the ones they replace. Filling in the gaps is the German passion today.

Here one sees some point in the idea that we are living in a Restoration. Hamburg certainly gives the impression of Germany indulging in a great orgy of bourgeois amenities. Every shop window attempts to mirror what Germans call elegance: German elegance, which is so different from any other kind. Even the parcels in which your purchases are wrapped up all have elegant wrappings, with little tapes glued on to carry them.

Going into a toyshop called *Kinderparadies* [Children's Paradise], I noticed that the paradise of German children is almost entirely mechanical. Practically all the toys were of the constructional engineering kind. The only other well-made things I could find were some neat and pretty architectural models of villages. The bookshops are swamped with books on science and engineering.

I went to the Europa College of the University. This is a nice place, with buildings round a quadrangle, nice rooms for the students, a fountain in the quadrangle, and so on. The students questioned me. One Indian student, who rather monopolized the interview, wanted to prove that he did not like Thomas Mann. There is quite a lot of talk among the German students, whom I met on the following day, about their belonging to a new generation. All the same, they themselves, although they feel a gap between them and the old, complain that they have no idea of a *Neuaufbau* [Reconstruction].

Some of them insisted that their generation did not feel at all represented by a writer like Wolfgang Borchert. (Borchert was an expressionist writer, expressing nihilism and despair very much in the manner of the 1920s, who died in 1945.[1]) Quite evidently his world

---

1 Wolfgang Borchert, born in 1921, in fact died in 1947. After being wounded in active service during the war, he was imprisoned for satirising Joseph Goebbels and never fully recovered.

of chaos had been wiped off the map, and one might say that the main passion of the present Germany is precisely to fill in this chaos.

Everything rebuilt but absolutely no new architecture. There is almost no cinema. Anyway, nothing of the kind which was such a great achievement after the first war. An anthology of poetry of the 1950s which I bought, shows that the most advanced kind of poetry being written resembles the poetry of social conscience written in Paris or London twenty years ago. However, expressionism seems to be rather fashionable, and there has recently been a successful anthology of expressionist poets.

In Germany, Hitlerism seems simply a ghost, a phase recollected beyond a background of ruins. After all, Hitler did not go on long enough! Even Italian Fascism lasted ten years longer, and it is amazing to reflect that Hitler only ruled from 1933 to 1945. A movement has to last at least twenty years to seem more than a phase, however impressive its achievements and catastrophic the results.

An idea that has always haunted me is Hell. I suppose that when I was young I thought of Hell as eternal punishment. Now I think of it as a state of mind in which one is completely conscious of the ill effects which one has inflicted upon the whole existence of humanity of which one is a part. This idea not only haunts me, but I accept it as just. It seems to me, unless the suffering one inflicts on others is ultimately suffering which one inflicts on oneself, then there is no justice. Or to put it in another way, it is even more unbearable to think that people should get away with inflicting suffering on others without their ever realizing what they have done, than that they should be made conscious of it. After all, in every situation what one appeals to is that awareness in another person which makes him realize the consequences of what he has done: and this realization is simply to make the suffering that he has inflicted his own conscious suffering. If one takes extreme instances, it seems wrong that people like Hitler or Stalin should send millions of others to camps or gas chambers: and that this should have no more effect on their own consciousness than that of taking up a pen and writing out an order. I demand a moment in which Hitler realizes the humanity of the action of Hitler upon life – and such a moment would be an eternity. Yet to think of extreme instances is also to remind oneself that the extreme instances may not be the worst just because they are the most evident. In fact the peculiar vice of political theory is to measure one's own political (and external) rightness against the immense quantity of public wrongness which is the other side's. Yet possibly to harm one person deeply is as bad as to harm several thousand or a million. The nature of harm is private because it comes out of one person's individuality – however public its effects. Therefore there is, for the individual, no great difference between private harm done privately and public harm done politically. There are domestic Hitlers. Thus I live in fear of awakening to a final consciousness, a sum total of benefits and injuries done which has boomeranged on myself. And I cannot really say I would wish this otherwise. Eventually one has to accept the idea of complete consciousness of what one has done making one what one is.

I do not mean by this that one should attribute too much importance to guilt. It is quite possible that the things to which one attributes most guilt are those in which one is innocent. For example, people will attach more guilt to any relationship in which there is sex, than to other relationships – such as those with their parents, children and neighbours – in which they may actually do more harm. If one awakens to the real consequences of one's actions, there would be two types of action in which one was guiltless. The first would be those to which one had attached an excessive sense of guilt, and which really did not greatly matter; the second would be those in which the injury was involuntary or ignorant. But there is a third kind of case, in which there is real guilt because one either really knows what one has done or there is a potentiality of knowledge in the act. For this third kind, one would not be acquitted.

11 July 1955, London

Drinks at A. J. Ayer's. People I much wanted to see, Henry Green among others, were there. I had to leave though in order to take the Chair at the I.C.A. discussion on Science and Literature. J. B. Bronowski and K. J. Raine spoke.[1] This was in fact an interesting discussion. Both agreed that modern poetry was too unintellectual,

---

1 Jacob Bronowski (1908–1974), scientist and TV pundit on scientific subjects.

too uncontemporary in terms of modern knowledge. My own feeling is that imagery derived from science has an exactitude of its own, which cannot bear distortion in order to be adapted to the exact statements of poetry. I also feel doubtful of Bronowski's point that the poet should constantly be adapting his picture of the universe to the picture given by science. Bronowski argues that unless he does this he is liable to be intellectually a hundred or a hundred and fifty years behind the times. As Peter Watson pointed out to me afterwards, beauty was not mentioned in this discussion. If it had been, I think it would have been noted that one means something different by scientific beauty and aesthetic beauty. However, when a scientific metaphor in a poem of Empson seems to me to repel the poetic form and content around it, an account of scientific accuracy having an integrity of its own which makes its aesthetic quality irrelevant, this may just mean that I am repelled by a newness of content which will seem assimilated in the poetry to the reader a hundred years from now. [. . .]

After the I.C.A. meeting, went to a party at Lucian Freud. He now lives in Dean Street, where he has taken a whole house. At present the house although painted inside, in shiny white paint, is almost empty of furniture. I noticed that in one room there were nothing but large Chinese looking objects. The main room, in which there was dinner, was L-shaped. Lucian reminisced about the time when we first met, when we kept together a notebook of drawings and poems. He told me that he had given this to Colin Anderson, in return for much financial support from Colin.[1] He surprised me by knowing various poems I had written then, mostly comic ballads, by heart. [. . .]

Some years ago I outlined to myself the idea of an invisible *ménage*. What I meant by this, was that certain people are in a kind of secret relationship to one another which may last throughout life, even if they themselves do not realize it. There are marriages which are not only not recognized by any formality or informality, but which may not even be recognized by the people themselves. Developing this a little, one can see that one is in an invisible relationship with

---

1 Sir Colin Anderson, a director of the P&O Shipping Line, was an early patron of, among others, Lucian Freud and Francis Bacon.

a good many people. There is a bond which nothing can break. I have this feeling of invisible *ménage* with Lucian, and also with Cyril.

13 July 1955, Oxford

Took the 6.50 to Oxford, where I met Mel Lasky and Mike Josselson.

Before dinner I called at the house of the Warners. The door was opened by a beautiful girl with cornflower blue childlike eyes and a pastel complexion, who turned out to be Sarah Rothschild.[1]

I left messages for the Warners, and then walked on a few yards to look at Blenheim Palace. You go through a stone arch at the end of a road just outside the town, and there you suddenly see a view as startling and ornamental as a Bonnard. To the left, the castle partly hidden, so that one side seems obliterated by a frame, to the right a lake reflecting sky, hill, trees, and the arrogantly unnecessary stone bridge across which someone was walking just to prove that it was not pasteboard. Trees like clouds were manipulated across hills like green mirrors by a master's hand. Even picnickers looking like satyrs and nymphs, in a landscape which related everything to its own artifice.

I went back to the hotel and called Mel and Mike to see this spectacle. When we were returning past the Warners, the door was open, and Sarah Rothschild standing there again. She said she had two bottles of wine for us and invited us to come in. We did so. She was sitting with a young man, whom she introduced as Alexander Weymouth.[2] He had cascading hair, a narrow face with curling features that looked as if they had been wrought by some carver of Bamberg Cathedral – except that they lacked austerity. They both entertained us, and he talked as elaborately as he looked. Sarah brought up the subject of Richard Selig and I recollected that I had been told she had pursued him and that he had written her a letter

---

1 For Sarah Rothschild and her parents Victor Rothschild and Barbara Hutchinson, see biographical appendix. At this time Barbara Hutchinson was married to Rex Warner; the marriage dissolved in 1961.

2 Alexander Weymouth (b. 1932), later Marquess of Bath.

saying he would have nothing more to do with her.[1] We drank the velvet claret and it was extremely strange sitting in this room with the two marvellous young people, and ourselves so much in the midst of our publishing and editing business. I asked them to join us for coffee in three quarters of an hour, after we had finished our dinner at the Bear, and they accepted with their smiling, grave politeness, like Martians who have just met visitors blown in from the Earth. But they didn't turn up – to my chagrin, who wanted the vision of their walking across the dining room to our table. I thought there might be some mistake – after all they had been so insistent in inviting *us* – so I went along to their front door and rang the bell, which sounded through the house, three times. There was darkness in the ground floor but lights on in the upper floor rooms.

All this had the surprise of the totally unexpected. Sometimes nothing is more dreamlike than what one is aware will happen.

In the 1930s a Sarah Rothschild would probably have been sitting there with a truck driver.

14 July 1955, London

My life is getting absurdly social, and now it is worse because I am stimulated by curiosity about experiences to put in my Journal.

Today was rather fantastic, owing to two parties.

The first was at Alan Ross's. Alan asked me to bring Matthew, in order to play with his twelve-year-old step-daughter, Victoria. Victoria is a little girl with a wonderful gay luminosity and lightness as though she really treads on air. Matthew first met her two years ago at Torri del Benaco, when they spent a whole day chasing after each other on the lake shore and in the hotel. The next day he refused to go on a trip to Venice with me because he wanted to stay at Torri with her.

What happened at the party was that Victoria and Matthew first of all handed round nuts to the guests, then went into the garden to play quoits, then disappeared into a room by themselves where they were later discovered, smoking. The smoking set me a problem. On our way back home, in the taxi, Matthew produced from his

1 Richard Selig (1929–1975), American poet, formerly a Rhodes Scholar at Oxford.

pocket a cigarette and said he intended to smoke it after dinner. I discouraged this, but seeing that he was very excited, changed my tactics and tried to be a 'modern' parent. I told him that he might smoke, but must promise to finish the entire cigarette. After dinner, he lit up his cigarette, and I watched him, saying rather nastily, the while, 'Go on. Go on. Go on.' Finally, he burst into tears and rushed up to his room. I followed him a little later and found him still crying. 'You don't smoke as fast as you tried to make me. No one's ever smoked as fast as that in all their lives.' I said, 'All right, in that case I'll leave you alone for a quarter of an hour smoking, but you must finish the whole cigarette.' When I came up a quarter of an hour later, he was sitting up, a triumphant smile on his face, and the stub of the cigarette smoked to the end, on the ashtray I had put beside his bed.

* * *

In the evening, went to another party, at MacNeices'. William Empson was there. After rebuking me for not being at the Soho poetry judging meeting (I had judged the poems by mail, and I am going to read at Golden Square on Saturday, but I could not make him understand this), he then started attacking me about the Wittvogel article in *Encounter*. I explained that I was publishing correspondence about this, including his letter. He said: 'It is absurd for Americans to speculate about what Chinese leaders are thinking. They do not go to China but about twenty or thirty of our chaps do each year, and so we know what the Chinese are thinking.' I said that if he wrote about this too, I would be glad to publish his letter.[1]

He drifted away. Later I rejoined him, and I made a little speech to the effect that I admired him immensely as a poet and critic, and that I refused to quarrel with him. He talked about other things.

The Austrian ambassador and ambassadress left. After midnight Empson seemed to get more and more excited. He looks very extraordinary, with his little face like a needling tailor's, hung round with a beard growing under his chin and out of his neck, like a necklace of old brushes. Once he shouted an insulting remark into a conversation in which I was participating.

---

1 For the Wittvogel article see page 155 above.

When there were only a small group of people left, and we were all standing up, Empson started talking about Anthony West with whom – he said – he had stayed in America.[1] 'I like him very much,' he said, 'but, of course, he's a cheat, a dreadful cheat, but not nearly such a cheat as Stephen.' At this, I took up my wine glass and deliberately threw its contents into his face. I thought, and still think, that no other reply was possible, and as a matter of fact, every other person in the room seemed to agree with me that his insult was so gross that he deserved what he got. I thought I should disembarrass the MacNeices by quickly leaving, but the other guests urged me to stay. Laurie Lee said: 'Empson has a radio connected with the strands of that beard, which is tuned in to Peking.' The MacNeices seemed quite pleased, and someone else told Empson that if he could not be witty but must simply deal in insults, he should expect a reply of this kind.

As a matter of fact, I had also been insulted earlier in the evening, at the Rosses by another Communist Drunk – John Davenport – who later rang up to apologize.[2] But there is a mysterious side to all this which puzzles me. Why is a person like Empson, who takes up such an attitude about the Wittvogel article (a great worry to me, anyway), such an anti-social drunk?

19 July 1955, London

I went yesterday to Stratford, to see *Macbeth*.[3] Beyond High Wycombe the train runs through hundreds of miles of densely packed green countryside, which seems completely unspoiled. Through Warwick, near Tewkesbury, all those places that seem nearer to the Elizabethan than any other part of England. Stratford itself is a bit disappointing, except for the stretch of river near the Memorial

---

1 Anthony West (1914–1987), British author living in America, the illegitimate son of Rebecca West and H. G. Wells.

2 John Davenport (1908–1966), writer and critic, friend of Dylan Thomas, with whom he collaborated on *The Death of the King's Canary* (1976).

3 *Macbeth*, directed by Glen Byam Shaw, opened at the Shakespeare Memorial Theatre at Stratford on 7 June.

Theatre. But the swans, the theatre, and the laid out gardens, with Georgian style stone and brickwork, do not altogether escape self-consciously presenting an aspect of England which travel bureaux suppose Americans like.

The play was extremely interesting. It opened effectively with the weird sisters, the picture framed by the stage. There then followed some rather dull pageantry. The Sergeant's speech was effectively done, but there was little excitement. One had the feeling of people trooping back and forth across the stage, and in different directions. [Laurence] Olivier as Macbeth made little impression on me up till later, and one was perhaps too conscious of the special interpretation that he was seeking. He evidently looks on Macbeth as a visionary of a kind, someone who above all sees, a kind of sick poet. He was haggard throughout, and gave no impression of a Macbeth in rude health, of a kind that I have sometimes seen. He hunched, and lunged forward, with his staring eyes, and his idea of Macbeth had a slight suggestion about it of Richard III.

It was not until the lines 'Macbeth shall murder sleep' [*sic*] that the performance seemed to me really to come alive. After this though, one recognized the extraordinary merits of Olivier's performance. The superb part of it was the way in which he made one feel the impact of every single word, without loss of speed or direction. He also had wonderful moments of hectic, violent activity of the kind which makes him one of the great athletes of the theatre. He is the only actor on the English stage who gives the impression of controlled acting with his own body. Magnificent as Gielgud is, he gives too often the impression of acting in spite of his body, nobly rising beyond it.

Vivien Leigh's performance has been criticized, but it seemed to me that it related very well to his. To a great extent, she interpreted Lady Macbeth as a foil. And this is what she imagistically is. When she reads his letter after his meeting with the Weird Sisters, she is a foil to his mind. When she holds out her hands covered with blood, they counterpoise his already covered with blood. She is his fantastically beautiful foil, balancing his wildness with her hysterical calm, in the scene of Banquo's ghost. The sleepwalking scene she did in a sustained, clear way, like the single line of a solo instrument in an adagio. The doctor and the waiting woman muttered behind against her clear tone and beautiful physical outline.

After the performance, I went to the green room and then to supper with the Oliviers.[1] In the green room there were Douglas Fairbanks and his wife, Danny Kaye and his wife, and some French people, Dr and Mme Seidman.[2] Green Room conversation always amuses me. Mrs Fairbanks said that she was so shaken by the performance that she could say absolutely nothing and doubted whether she would recover at all that night. Danny Kaye gave Vivien Leigh a kiss that lasted for at least two minutes.

Dinner was very nice. Vivien Leigh talked about her collection of paintings. She is extremely attractive, in her personality as well as her appearance, and now I come to think of it, I do not believe I really looked at anyone else in the room. Olivier always seems to me a bit like a cricketer who has a sporting attitude towards everything. His utter devotion to his wife is very apparent. In fact it's remarkable how when everyone is acting a role, a strong feeling of this kind can make itself felt. For always with actors and actresses, there is the embarrassment that even if they do feel what they say, they are doing a performance of a person feeling it as though it were written for them by someone else. Danny Kaye seems to have exactly the same charming personality in private life when you meet him as on the stage or screen.

23 July 1955, London

This evening went to the performance of *Much Ado about Nothing* with Peggy Ashcroft and John Gielgud. This is the third time I have seen this same performance, though sometimes with different actors,

---

1 Laurence Olivier (1907–1989) was at that time married to his co-star Vivien Leigh (1913–1967).

2 The actor Douglas Fairbanks, Jr (1909–2000) had spent the war years in England as a US naval officer; his wife was Mary Lee Hartford. Mme Seidman was Ginette Spanier, a director of the Parisian fashion house Balmain; her husband Paul-Emile Seidman was a psychoanalyst friend of Derek Jackson. During the war both Seidmans had worked with the French Resistance. The American actor and comedian Danny Kaye (1913–1987) was married to the lyricist Sylvia Fine (1913–1991).

apart from John who has remained the constant factor in it. I first saw it at Stratford, two or three years ago, then at the Phoenix Theatre, then tonight. Gielgud turns the whole play into a kind of ball in which he and Peggy are the divinely waltzing central couple. There is real gaiety, wit and intellect in the dialogue and also the relationship between Benedick and Beatrice. All the same, after seeing it for the third time, the absurdities of the plot become irritating, and the foolery of the malapropisms of Dogberry tiresome. There is a kind of slum area of stupidity in this play, which destroys its proportions.

John has developed a curious way of creasing his eyes as though they are blinking in a too great light. This gives his face a curious fixity of expression, which is growing on him.

Walking home through the London streets, and seeing people in pubs, and standing in doorways on this hot evening, I was struck again by a terrible thought which always obsesses me – that the world ought to be redeemed by art. This is a stupid thing to think, and yet it so fills my mind that it's like a rock against which I continually break myself, and the real cause of the depression I feel tonight is being aware that the world is a very ugly place, and that I blame myself for doing nothing to transform it, and yet people do not wish to be transformed. They wish perhaps for all sorts of improved facilities, more motor cars, radios, and so on: and I do not blame them for this: but they do not wish to live in a town in which at the turn of the corner one encounters something beautiful, a statue or a fountain. Yet, to anyone who cares about it, ugliness is the most depressing thing in the world and no amount of utilities can redeem cities from ugliness. Also, although people cannot understand this, perhaps their lives are far more depressed by ugliness than they themselves realize. To feel like this is to feel oneself in a prison, to be for ever beating against bars, to long to live in any time or place except that where one does live. Considering how very many people do want to live in some other time, and think nostalgically about the past, probably there are a good many people who do feel in this way without realizing it. John and Peggy are at the centre of a slum which they turn into a dance, and they themselves are the golden waltzing pair who transforms everything round them into light. One goes out of the light theatre into the darkness, and one is immensely grateful to them.

24 July 1955, London

I gave a luncheon party at home for Hugh Gaitskell and his wife [Dora], Sundrin Datta, the great Bengali writer[,] and his wife, and Kay Cicellis, the Greek novelist.[1] It seemed to go very well, as my guests stayed till 4 o'clock, and I think then it was only my signs of impatience that indicated to them they ought to go. I wanted to arrange for the children to go to the cinema.

I asked Hugh Gaitskell about our switchback economy in this country, in which one quarter we are being told that we are doing extraordinarily well, and the next quarter we are being given the impression that the country is on the verge of bankruptcy and complete catastrophe. He said that he thought the heights and depths of the switchback were exaggerated, but that it was impossible for us not to have ups and downs. We must continue to have them until the whole community was equally conscious of the exigencies of the economic situation. On the other hand, he did not think that our bad periods were as bad as we had to make them out to be. In order to prevent over-expenditure, we had to bring a whole mechanism of public warnings to work, which had the effect of rather exaggerating the situation. On the whole, he seemed very optimistic.

I was very impressed by the clear-headedness and also the great calmness of Hugh, which his opponents, I suppose, consider cold-bloodedness. Actually, I find him gay and amusing and friendly, and much easier to get on with than most politicians. If one scratches fairly hard, one comes to a school prefect perhaps, but with most politicians the school prefect or the egotist is completely on the surface. He takes quite an interest in gossip and talk about people, which is always a good sign. He is intelligent, cool, clear and determined. These don't seem very remarkable qualities when one is with him, but if one compares him with his rivals, one sees that they may take him very far indeed. In fact I should say he will be Prime Minister, and I shouldn't be at all surprised if when he gets there people

---

1 Sudhindranath Datta (1901–1989), leading Bengali poet and critic, editor of *Parichay* 1931–42, Professor of literature at Chicago University, 1957–9; had a long association with Jadavpur University in Calcutta. At this point the CCF was considering Datta as editor of *Quest*, the magazine it was about to launch in India. He turned down the offer.

will find him attractive and human. On the whole his opponents in his own party have put across quite a false view of him.

On Tuesday we went to the second meeting of Lord Pakenham's Group, and had some further discussion about the society for helping ex-prisoners. The discussion was on much more practical lines than the previous ones had been. Subjects discussed were whether we should have an office, whether there should be a permanent paid secretary, how to raise money, and so on. John Thompson took the line that the whole thing was becoming too organizational. My own impression is that it does not suffer from this. I may be unfair about John Thompson, but I can never get away from the impression that he is trying to put something across. He may object for quite good reasons against a policy, but I always feel that he is doing so in order to advertise the way in which he does things. He is a man with a very bad conscience, determined to have an extremely good one. This determination probably has the result that he really does good works, but it also has the result that he has to prove his works are good the whole time. Victor Gollancz, who was also there, blows his trumpet more blatantly and crudely than John, but on the whole I find his way of doing it more sympathetic. In fact, if an artist was going to do a biblical portrait of a Pharisee blowing his own trumpet, he would be very well advised to choose as his model Victor Gollancz.

The meeting was divided into three classes of people. One class were those who attended, because they really felt called upon by conscience in order to do so. Amongst these, I include Lord Pakenham himself, Gollancz, and the chairman, a man who writes in the *New Statesman* under the name of C. H. Rolph.[1]

If I did not regard the whole thing so satirically, I would probably put myself into this class. But these people, although supporting the cause and even being at present the chief initiators of it, are when it comes to the point absolutely incapable of giving any time. They are all harassed, busy, tired, and over worked. The next class of people are the social hangers-on, the morbidly or idly curious, and the pretty girls who hope to convert Lord Montagu. I am afraid I belong to the idly curious and amused as well as to the first class. Most of these

---

1 Cecil Rolph Hewitt (1901–1994) worked on the *New Statesman* from 1947 to 1970, where he wrote on legal matters under the name C. H. Rolph.

will probably drop out, and I am not at all sure whether Montagu, Wildeblood etc, will really stick to it. For instance, if they wanted to go abroad, they would leave the whole thing in the lurch.[1]

The third class of people is the humble and devoted people who really are prepared to work. I cannot say whether any members of this class actually exist.

28 July 1955, London

A week ago I lunched with the painter, Matthew Smith, at a Spanish restaurant in Kensington, and afterwards went to his studio.[2] Matthew Smith is now about 70, has an almost retiring air of great timidity, looks out on the world myopically through his glasses. He is extremely mild and gentle yet uncompromising and acute, reminding me a little of E. M. Forster. Over luncheon he talked gently about many things, including painting and France and girls. He said that Morandi must be an interesting man, but he did not really altogether care for his painting, which he found affected.[3] He said he liked some of the paintings of Jack Yeats but he found the large canvases

---

1 The Prison Reform Trust is still active, and recently a Trust dedicated to the memory of Lord Longford was formed to give scholarships to students who have served prison sentences. In a life dedicated to good works, Lord Longford supported some strange causes, such as a campaign against pornography or the release on parole of the murderess Myra Hindley. Peter Wildeblood became a TV producer and campaigner for Gay Rights. Edward Montagu devoted most of his energy to the Motor Museum at Beaulieu, but his autobiography *Wheels Within Wheels* (2000) discusses the trial and its consequences.

2 Matthew Smith (1879–1959) started his career under the influence of Matisse. His best-known works were painted in France, where for a time he occupied Cézanne's old studio in Aix en Provence. His work influenced the next generation of British painters, especially Francis Bacon, who wrote in a rare introduction to a fellow painter's work that he admired Smith for his capacity to attack the canvas directly.

3 Giorgio Morandi (1890–1964), Italian painter living in Bologna. Initially promoted in the 1920s by Margherita Sarfatti, Mussolini's advisor on art, Morandi formed part of a bucolic tendency in fascist art: that of 'Strapaese' (the absolute countryside), as opposed to 'Stracittà' (the absolute town). Mussolini bought several of his works. After the war the tender and anti-rhetorical quality of Morandi's landscapes and still lifes made him appear retrospectively a non-political figure. Spender visited him during a meeting of the CCF in Bologna in 1956 and bought a still life directly from his studio.

which were exhibited at the Tate Gallery some years ago rather empty. He thought that Yeats should have been advised not to show them. He was reserved also about Wyndham Lewis. Obviously, despite his gentle manner, he is not easy to please.[1]

He showed surprising energy in his studio, dragging out dozens of canvases for me to look at. First of all there were two canvases of flowers. He said: 'Nowadays I don't seem able to paint flowers. When I was younger I could do so. I used to get so tremendously excited by flowers I saw that I wanted to take them home at once and start working on them.' His recent paintings have a violence of colour and a freedom of line which astonishes me. I asked him if I might buy a painting, and he just murmured, 'That would be very difficult.' At the end of the afternoon, he suddenly pulled a water colour out of a corner of the room and said: 'Would you like this as a souvenir?' He apologized for the fact that actually there were two water colours, one on each side of the paper. He said: 'I believe this may detract from the value. There was a painting by Gauguin, which had another painting on the reverse of the canvas, and it was supposed to be worth less than the others.' We took the water colour to the framers, and there Matthew Smith looked at an easel with a sketching box attached to it. I pressed him to allow me to buy this for him, but he told me he did not at all wish to have it as he could get the same kind of thing much more cheaply in France. Two days later I learned from Vera Barry[2] that he was quite distressed about this whole incident. He was not certain I would like the water colour, and he was afraid I would be offended by his having refused the easel. I asked Vera Barry whether it would be possible still to buy an oil painting from him. She also said this would be difficult but that I ought to write directly to him and ask him. She said that for some reason he will not show his recent work, which she thinks his best, and only exhibits rather inferior things. Nor will he sell any of his recent work. She did not

---

1 Jack Yeats (1871–1951), Irish artist, brother of the poet W. B. Yeats. Wyndham Lewis (1882–1957), British painter and author best known as the co-founder (with Ezra Pound) of the futurist vorticist movement in 1913.

2 Vera Barry, née Poliakov (1911–1992) was born in Saint Petersburg. At this point married to Basil Burton, she subsequently married the art critic John Russell. In the 1960s she opened a gallery in London, showing younger British artists such as David Hockney.

understand why, as he has no one to leave things or money to, his wife being almost the same age as himself.[1] [. . .]

I have seen quite a lot of Edith Sitwell. First at lunch yesterday with Kenneth and Jane Clark, and today at tea with some young writers.[2] As usual, her conversation was a mixture of intolerance, kindness, silliness, extremely clever anecdote, and real perception. As usual, she humiliated everyone by trying to round them up in her hunts against critics, other poets, poetesses and so on. But yesterday, talking about Osbert [Sitwell], she was suddenly very moving. She said that her life had become almost intolerable because David had come back to live with Osbert.[3] She has an elaborate plot to get David sent to America and then to persuade him, on medical grounds, that he must stay.

In London today it is intolerably hot, almost like New York, airless and stuffy and damp. Today Matthew came back from the party of a school friend, very crestfallen. We had given him money to go out and buy a book to give to his friend. As it was early closing, he was unable to get this present, and so went to the party without a gift. Finally, instead of a present, he offered the money that the book would have cost. The boy's mother was furious and seems practically to have sent Matthew home in disgrace.

I have been having a tiring three days with my colleagues, Melvin Lasky, from Berlin, François Bondy from Paris, Dwight MacDonald, Michael Josselson and, inevitably, Irving Kristol. The faces that Kristol makes whenever any proposal is made to him to improve our magazine, the elaborate bohemian gestures François is always making with his hands, Dwight's ruthless desire almost to scrap our magazine and start all over again under his control, all these things are hard to take in the very hot weather. I expect the others have some similar complaints about me. My colleagues certainly have one

---

1 Matthew Smith was separated from his wife Gwen, who died in 1958. In fact, he left his estate to his muse and lover Mary Keene (1921–1981), who was also formerly the muse of Louis MacNeice and Henry Green.

2 Kenneth Clark (1903–1983) had been the director of the National Gallery (1933–46) and was for many years a key figure in bridging the worlds of art and government in England. In his later years he was a popularizer of art, producing the successful BBC television series *Civilisation* (1969).

3 David Horner, Osbert Sitwell's lover since the 1920s.

characteristic in common. They are all Philistines. They dislike poetry and distrust everything which has high standards. Dwight ought to be an exception to all this, but his knowledge is so patchy, his self-assurance so great, that it amounts to the same thing. He has principles, but they have been undermined by his adopting reactionary views, and he has bright ideas but they let one down by being combined with an almost complete lack of judgement – at all events with bad lapses of judgement. His ignorance is astonishing. For instance, today we were discussing the possibility of having a special supplement about television for *Encounter*. I mentioned that it would be interesting to try to find something out about television in Russia. Dwight said: 'Do you mean to tell me that they have television in Russia?' One is always coming across tremendous pitfalls in his knowledge of current affairs.

29 July 1955, London

Yesterday I lunched with Lord Montagu, his half sister, Lady Elizabeth Scott-Montagu, and Michael Pitt-Rivers. Their determination to make the best of, not complain about, and rise above their situation is quite admirable. With them, one even gets a sense of elation, and excitement which is perhaps a little dangerous. Dangerous especially because they are convinced the police behaved so badly in their cases, but as far as the law is concerned they certainly feel no penitence. Pitt-Rivers said he thought that most people who were members of the group for helping ex-prisoners, unless they had been to prison themselves, would probably expect gratitude or beneficial results at any rate, from anyone they helped. They would not realize that to most ex-prisoners they were simply people who happened to have a little money and who were permitting themselves to be exploited. He said: 'If you or I give each other drinks, we have put one another under some kind of obligation, however slight. But you have to understand that if you give them any kind of help you have put them under no obligation whatever, and you haven't established any basis of confidence with them. That confidence may perhaps come later but it is not in any sense the result of a polite convention of behaviour.'

Montagu said the difference of classes with regard to prisons, was that for the poor there was no absolute division or break between being sent to prison and not being sent. To have been to prison was like having had flu, anyone might have it. Life in and out of prison was one continuous process. For the upper and middle classes, there was a kind of absolute difference between the prisoner and the person who was not a prisoner or who had not been one.

On 4 August, Stephen and Matthew Spender joined the Lamberts on a two-week yachting holiday in the Mediterranean. They visited Auden in Ischia and toured the islands in the Bay of Naples. Other guests included Cyril Connolly and Samuel Barber.

6 August 1955, Forte dei Marmi

I have been reading Wordsworth. The use of 'I' in Wordsworth: 'I' is Wordsworth's whole sentient being, the instrument of self through the sense responds to, and is part of, nature. The sentient I has direct communication with Nature and therefore is not bookish – regards books as dangerous lore or magic, and intellect as only a part of being. Aim of Wordsworth is through being intensely himself in his poetry to be what is beyond himself.

If this attitude is compared with Eliot's elimination of the expression of the self in poetry, one sees that Eliot ends with turning the poet into a machine which records tradition and sensitizes it into poetry. Eliot himself probably aware of this danger – his followers less so.

Keats and Wordsworth's egotistical sublime. Keats and Shakespeare.

But in Wordsworth, the egotistic I is only the door which opens onto the collective I. Hence his great attachment to the period of childhood when the door of egotism has not grown up and the I of the child is perpetually open to the collective I. 'To H.C.' 'Ode on the Intimations of Immortality' etc. His insistence on the spontaneous nature of poetry.

There is also sexual inhibition in Wordsworth which prevents the childish 'I' maturing into an adult 'I' which would not be egotistic. Lawrence insisted on this 'I' which fuses in sex into the 'I' of another person, in phallic consciousness into the 'I' of all nature.

For Wordsworth the 'I' = spontaneous nature = exile from modern cities because civilization has driven out Nature = return to childhood experience.

[195]

At Ischia drove with Hansi and Lucy [Lambert] to Forio to see Auden. When we first called he was not at home and Giocondo[1] told me he was on the beach, so we drove down to the Forio beach and little harbour where all the sand looks grey and the houses seem turned away from the sea. They are not actually with their backs to the sea and they do not gather round in a circle as though hypnotized by the water as in so many other Italian towns. Along the shore beyond the port there is a little sprinkling of white squarish modern villas.

We did not find Auden at the beach so returned to the Via Santa Lucia. Although he is so anti-Indian, in his surroundings Auden always shows an utter indifference to appearance which reminds me of India. The ground floor of the building is like cellars, a disused garage or a bombed-out basement in partial repair partial disrepair. Upstairs there are discoloured damp-looking walls; and – apart from one or two bad paintings by Giocondo hanging skew-ways – nothing exists above the level of the tops of the few chairs. On tables books, magazines, manuscripts, letters lie in disorder. Untidiness, of course, I can well understand, being extremely untidy myself: but what is curious about Wystan's apartments is their air of being the habitation of a mole – some animal that works underground and sees nothing.

Lucy and Hansi stayed only a few moments. They took Wystan's sixteen-year-old nephew Giles – who was with him – to the Port of Ischia and the yacht. Alone with Wystan his dog – Moses – started relentlessly making love with my trouser leg. Wystan told me he was doing – had to have finished by September – a new libretto for the *Magic Flute*. He sang bits of it to me – very beautiful, some of the words, though, necessarily, pastiche, and with many inversions. He said the way he really would like to write was in an idiom in which one would use phrases like 'love's lambent flame'. And he exclaimed rather bitterly that to be a poet now was to attempt to write an inevitable but almost impossible language. He quoted Valéry saying: that if poetry did not exist no one would be able now to invent such a medium.[2]

While we were talking, I smoked. After I had had three or four cigarettes, Wystan said: 'I only have this packet, and you are using up all my cigarettes.' Then he added rather grudgingly: 'Cigarettes are

1 Giocondo Sacchetti, Auden's housekeeper at Forio.
2 Paul Valéry (1871–1945), French poet and philosopher.

very expensive here: almost as much so as in England.' I said: 'Well I would go out and get a packet of my own, but unfortunately I have no *lire*.' He looked as if he regarded this reply as inadequate, so I said, 'All the same I have a pound. If you can give me the *lire* for it then I can buy myself a packet.' 'All right, I'll look in the paper and find out the rate of exchange.' He looked at the paper and said: 'I'm afraid the pound is doing rather badly. I can only give you 1,700 for it.' We exchanged the money and went to buy a packet of Nazionale.

This incident was much more an example of the 'absurd' with Auden than of any meanness. If I had said: 'Now look here Wystan when you stayed with us six weeks ago you drank up all my wine,' we would have started an irrelevant argument in which he could then have pointed out that in 1954, when he left our house he left there 13 bottles of champagne over from a party he had given. Moreover, when I asked him later whether I could not pay him for 4 tickets to *Rigoletto* to which he took Hansi, Lucy and me, he would not hear of it. All the same, not to protest, not to say anything on such an occasion, but just dumbly to go through an absurd farce seemed funny, but vaguely humiliating. It is really an example of Wystan's arbitrariness which comes perhaps partly from a wish to make people submit to rules he invents, partly perhaps out of the need of a symbolic act to assert his independence. When he has fantasies about being Chief of Police at Ischia all the laws he imagines himself intro-ducing have the same quality of 'arbitrariness'; and his need to keep people at a distance is considerable.

Giocondo complained to me that Wystan could not understand that he was not happy to live six months of the year, from September to March, alone in Ischia without ever going on the mainland. He said that Wystan made him get up at 6.30 every morning because Wystan liked to have a cup of coffee punctually at 7 or 7.30. Probably Wystan is so kind-hearted that he can only make people work for him by imposing very strict rules, also probably Giocondo, being a bad artist reduced to cooking for a great poet is self-pitying, bitter, etc. [. . .]

Auden talked about Archie Campbell who is at Ischia.[1] He said

---

1 Archie Campbell (1902–1989), Regius Professor of Public Law at the University of Edinburgh, 1945–72. He was a contemporary of Spender and Auden at Oxford, and introduced them to each other at a lunch party in 1927.

Archie, who is our age, has all the complaints, self-pity, hypochondria, fussiness one might excuse in a man twenty years older. 'After all he has made a great success of his life. He is Professor of Law at Edinburgh University, and a Fellow of All Souls College. He has complete financial security for his whole life, an excellent position and good friends.'

I said that although Archie was exceedingly clever and – much more than this – intelligent and amusing, he was both a physical and moral coward to an extraordinary degree, all the years I had known him. 'Well,' said Auden, 'now he is much less funny. The moment he comes into the room one feels the atmosphere being weighed down. I must say, the one thing I can't stand is people *complaining* unless they have very real reasons to do so.' He said it was true that Archie's mother had died a most frightful death. 'But I don't believe it was just through physical pain. I believe it was the result of deep frustrations coming at last to the surface in her. If, when you come near a person dying, and she screams out: "Don't come near! You'll kill me!" that means the dying person wants to make others as miserable as possible.

'After all,' he said, 'it should be possible to die a good death.'

These remarks about death illustrate the rather tough side of Auden's religiosity. He considers it immoral to give people drugs when they are in great pain on their deathbeds, as this is providing them with an escape from the kind of death which is most suited to them. This seems to connect with the theory Auden held when he was 21, that all illness was the result of psychological tensions.

August 1955, London

At Hydra [Greek island in the Saronic Gulf] Cyril Connolly joined us. [. . .] It was in Athens that Matthew passed the invisible test which Cyril sets everyone. Cyril related how he had been introduced at a party to the Duchess of Kent, and the Duchess had said to him: 'I am so glad to meet you Mr Connolly because I always read *Horizon* – at least that part of it which I could understand.' Irritably, Cyril asked how could one reply to such a remark. What could one say? We each of us made suggestions, and then Matthew piped up. He said: 'I would have said, "We try to make it as clear as possible."'

Cyril was delighted with this reply and ever after this has treated Matthew almost as an equal.

September 1955, London

Cyril came to the office of *Encounter* where was Professor Alan Ross, the writer of an article about U and non-U Language.[1] The Professor is a weedy, tall man with a little beard, a cigarette hanging drably from one side of his mouth. His tweed coat is covered with falling ash. He was at Balliol with my brother [Michael], and he said that even at Balliol there were a group of people who collected upper-class usage, quoting each evening specimens they had encountered that day. Cyril read the proof of his article, and disputed one or two points. The Professor did not seem to mind. Indeed, he seemed very pleased with the fame which has suddenly overtaken him – that will undoubtedly overtake him – when we publish the article. I should not be at all surprised if he makes a coast to coast tour of the United States lecturing about U and non-U. We left the office and walked down into Haymarket, saying goodbye to the Professor at the corner of Panton Street. When he had gone, Cyril said: 'Anyone interested in the habits of the aristocracy always turns out to be a dreary little man, with a cigarette trailing down out of the corner of his mouth.' He started talking about his reconciliation with Barbara. He said: 'I couldn't very well refuse to have her back, when she decided by herself to leave W[eidenfeld], and when she said that she could not sleep at night, and decided to come back on my birthday.' He mentioned that he would probably be able to join me at Brussels in a few days' time, because he had given her leave to go to Copenhagen with J.S. [John Sutro].[2]

---

1 Alan S. C. Ross (1907–1980), Professor of Linguistics at the University of Birmingham, 1951–74, whose academic essay 'Linguistic Class-Indicators in Present-Day English' was criticized by Nancy Mitford in an article for *Encounter*. Her essay 'The English Aristocracy', published in the September 1955 issue, ignited a debate on English usage that drove the circulation of *Encounter* to record heights. Ross was invited to revise and abridge his paper for the November issue, where it appeared under the title 'U and non-U: An Essay in Sociological Linguistics'.

2 John Sutro (1903–1985), British film producer with whom Barbara had an affair.

A very annoying thing happened today. I took the copy of the October *Encounter* to the restaurant where I met Freddie Ayer. I thought he would be pleased as his article is printed in it. He looked at the cover and immediately exploded. The title of his article had been changed without his being consulted by Irving, from 'The Philosophy of Nihilism', to 'Philosophy at Absolute Zero'. I was even more furious about this myself than Freddie was, and the incident has quite spoiled my day. It seems hopelessly gratuitous that at this stage Irving should alter the titles of articles without consulting the authors. However, when I rang him he was extremely contrite and apologetic.

28 September 1955, London

Encounter gave at a private room at Scotts Restaurant, a luncheon for George Kennan the American who was formerly Ambassador at Moscow.[1] The other guests were Isaiah Berlin, Stuart Hampshire, Bill Deakin, W. J. Brogan and Sundrin Datta, the great Bengali writer.[2] Irving and I entertained. It was an extremely successful party, far the best of its kind that we have ever given for *Encounter*.

At coffee, I asked Kennan whether he would answer questions and he agreed to do this. One of the first questions he was asked was what he thought of the Milan Conference. After a few complimentary remarks, he said that the Milan Conference had, amongst a good many other things, almost persuaded him that there was little use Americans attending such conferences where there were Asians. He said that the speeches made at the conference by Minoo [Minocher Rustom] Masani and one or two of the other oriental delegates, showed that whatever the Americans did they were always understood to be acting for a sinister and power lusting and warlike

1 George Kennan (1904–2005) was a Russian specialist at the US Embassy in Moscow in 1946. His reports on Russia's expansionist intentions shaped the post-war American policy of 'Containment', though he subsequently maintained that he intended this policy to be diplomatic and cultural rather than military. Too independent to fit into government service, his proposals concerning international relations were nevertheless read with respect.

2 For Stuart Hampshire, see biographical appendix. William Deakin (1913–2005), Warden of St Anthony's College, ex-British Intelligence officer.

motive.[1] He said that his objection applied not only to the Conference but to American work all over Asia in South America and also in parts of Europe. There were some situations in which it was absolutely impossible for people to get together and it was better for them to part. He explained that he did not mean by this that aid should be abandoned, but the Americans should say quite frankly that when they helped it was simply because they wanted to get 12% profit, and they should not attempt to put any good motives on their actions how ever disinterested in fact their behaviour might be. He said that he thought the work of explaining America to people was absolutely useless, and he felt that the American information bureaus and so on did no good and perhaps a good deal of harm. Asians and other foreigners if they wanted to understand America, should be told that the U.S. was an open country and that they could come over and see it. At the same time they should be warned that they probably would not like it and that they would understand very little about it. He thought that just as there were some situations in which it was no use people going on being married to one another, so this situation of America with the rest of the world. He thought that the British could explain things better in these parts of the world than the Americans. He himself had warned the State Department against trying to do explanation and propaganda of America in South America, and he now thought the same warning applied to Asia and these parts of Europe.

As Isaiah said afterwards, Kennan was an extreme example of an anti-missionary. But Stuart quite rightly added that when he spoke in this way he had an ardent missionary light burning in his eyes. He was an extremely honest, extremely idealistic, extremely sceptical, and at the same time surprisingly amusing man. He has in his utterances a kind of bitterness which is made up for by a note of self mocking. This is very subtle: on the surface he is an idealistic pure American full of goodwill. He gives rather the impression of being a great man and one regrets very much that Kennan seems to have made some blunder in his diplomatic career which perhaps prevents his having a political future. He is certainly a philosopher of modern American politics, and if he is not the only one, one can have a good deal of hope.

---

1 Minocher Rustom Masani (1905–1998), Indian socialist politician.

In October 1955, Spender went to Germany to lecture for the Deutsch-Britische Society in Frankfurt, Dusseldorf, Bonn, Kiel and Berlin. He was lecturing on D. H. Lawrence and George Orwell.

6 October 1955, Berlin

Visit to Ernst Robert Curtius.

As Curtius had declined the dedication to him of my early poems, I felt that perhaps he would not at all wish to see me when I was in Bonn. At first, I thought it might be best not to tell him I was there. But when I got to Bonn, I realized that my reason for asking to go there was because I very much wanted to see him; and that perhaps my visit would, if he found out about it, cause him pain unless I could think of some way of avoiding this.

So I asked Dr Schutz to telephone Ilse [Curtius's wife] and to explain to her that I thought Curtius would probably not wish to see me, but if he did wish to do so, I would like very much to visit him. I thought that telephoning through a third person made it very easy to refuse.

At 9.40 a.m. the telephone rang in my hotel room and I heard Ilse's voice. She asked in German whether it was Herr Spender and when I said yes, asked me whether I would come to tea. I explained that I had to go to Düsseldorf that afternoon, but that I could call immediately. After a moment's hesitation, she said: 'Good. Come now.'

As I walked through the Hofgarten and then along the Coblentzerstrasse, I thought: 'I feel my heart lighten. I feel twenty years younger.' I realized that I had never walked down this street without a feeling of happiness if I was going to see the Curtiuses. I thought that whatever happened I should tell Curtius this. But then again I thought that to say exactly the words which had come into my mind would be like acting lines I had written out for myself. But sometimes there are occasions when such thoughts should be remembered and said. And I felt that this was one of these occasions.

Still walking along the Coblentzerstrasse, my next thought was that Ernst Robert had been ill, and perhaps I should prepare myself to see him changed. But I knew there was no need for such preparation. I knew it was impossible for those whose wisdom and jokes one has shared to be inaccessible. There is no wall which cannot be penetrated by the sense of a seriousness which is also a joke.

When I got to Joachimstrasse – past the other streets I knew so well – I was a little disconcerted by the fact that I was not quite sure of the number of the house. For a long time, between 1939 and 1945 I had always thought of it as number 14. After the war I discovered this to be wrong: now I had it in my mind that the number was 16. But really it turned out to be 18 as I discovered by ringing the door of No. 16 and by seeing the bust of E.R.C.'s grandfather through his library window.

I rang the bell and Ilse opened the door, scarcely greeting me (but she could not really be unfriendly, she can only act the whirlwind from time to time). Inside the house, I saw Ernst Robert waiting for me at the end of the corridor. I have the impression that by the time I had walked to the end of the corridor myself, he was seated at his desk in his room. Here I had a slight shock, although it was the shock of the expected rather than the unexpected. On the desk open in front of him were two books: one was a volume of photographic pictures of Roman busts, the other *The Golden Horizon*.[1]

After his illness Ernst Robert has a certain difficulty in speaking – that is he speaks rather slowly. He seemed simply to be pointing at the page which was open on my *Rhineland Journal*. I explained it was not my fault that this had been republished, as the editor had never sent me proofs of the extract which was printed, and had promised me that he would not put in the parts which were offensive to Curtius.

Curtius said: 'All the same, you could take a *prozess*' [i.e. sue Cyril Connolly]. I explained that this would really have been impossible. I pointed out that I had always said to everyone that I was in the wrong about the printing of the *Rhineland Journal* without Curtius' leave, and that I was extremely sorry for it.

He beckoned me over and pointed out with his finger certain words: 'He was my teacher (for he was really that)'.

I really did not know how he meant me to take this; whether he meant that I had been boasting or lying in saying this, or whether he

---

1 A collection of *Horizon* essays published in 1953, edited by Cyril Connolly and covering the war years. It included a reprint of Spender's 'Rhineland Journal' reporting the views of Curtius on post-war Germany. Curtius had protested at the time, and now protested again at its republication.

realized the sense in which I had meant it as true. I said: 'But you *were* my teacher. I merely meant that you taught me a great deal – more than anyone else.'

Then I said: 'I know I should never have published the Rhineland Journal, but what I do wish you to understand is that what I wrote about you was written with no malice but out of love and respect. I really wrote about you because I wanted to write about you, as I still do. I write about you because you have always preoccupied me, and you will continue to do so.'

He shrugged his shoulders and said: 'This is the barrier between us.' Then, with a movement of his hand, he said, 'Ja . . . Aber . . . .' I had the impression that the whole of our conversation was enclosed in parenthesis between a 'Ja' and an 'Aber'.

I said: 'When Ilse telephoned and said I could come to see you, I felt twenty years younger. I have never walked along this road to your house without a lightening of my heart.'

He said with difficulty: 'I also . . . a lightening of my heart.'

After this, the conversation became much easier. The only trouble was that as he could not speak as rapidly as he thinks, I had to put forward subjects and see whether they were those he wished to hear or talk about. I recalled the very first time we had met in Baden-Baden: I said the people with whom he had then been staying had been a mystery to me. He said they were a professor and his wife from Heidelberg. I reminded him that the first time we had met, he had warned me against my enthusiasm for Dostoevsky and told me to read Stendhal and Flaubert – which I had done. When I said this, I hoped he would realize in what sense he had been my teacher.

I said the impression I had today of Germany was of a bright new glittering haystack in which I looked in vain for a needle of genius. Was there any genius? I asked. None, he said.

But when I asked him about the translator of Chinese poems who was a bank clerk in Cologne, to whom Curtius had given me an introduction at the end of the war, he said: 'He is now a Professor at Munich, and he has done very well.' He added that Professor Franck had been until quite recently at Hong Kong. Then he mentioned one or two other names, and I felt that his sympathy for a few young people was almost the same as optimism about the future of German culture.

We talked a little about France, and he said he saw no-one to take the place of Gide and Claudel.[1] Then he said: 'Yes, there is that art historian . . . .' And he fumbled for his name. 'Malraux,' I suggested. 'Yes, Malraux. He is not a good novelist. But his History of Art is interesting . . . Yes, he was a Communist and then he was . . .' 'A Gaullist,' I suggested. 'Yes, a Gaullist, and now he needs another religion so he makes one from a Pantheon of Art. Aber, aber . . . I don't see it.' He shrugged his shoulders again.

He got up, looked for the poems of Baudelaire and turned up the famous one on great painters.[2] He read out the last stanza very clearly.

'You see, already Baudelaire making a religion of art.'

When he sat down again, there was a pause and I told him that I had gone with Matthew on a yacht with friends in the Mediterranean. 'You were a Communist, and now you go on yachts in the Mediterranean,' he said. 'Ja . . . ja . . . .'

I said that when he first knew me, my life was perhaps better, because I lived always in one room, and had very few needs. But I could not have gone on living like that. I also said that I would tell him what I could not really say in public, because to do so would seem like a renunciation or a denial of my own past, and this was that I had never been in any real sense a Communist. Today I did not dislike and resent the Communists nearly so much as during the few days when I was one. Really only a matter of a few days, because I never joined any Party call or paid any Party dues. In fact I quarrelled with them as soon as I joined.

He annotated, or filled out, as it were our conversation with references. I spoke of Jouhandeau, and he said he had first known his work in the 1920s.[3] ('But when one is old one is uninterested in

---

1 For Curtius, the recent deaths of the French novelist André Gide (1869–1951) and poet Paul Claudel (1868–1955) had signified the end of an era of French literature.

2 'Les Phares' (The Beacons) (1857). The last stanza, in Roy Campbell's 1952 translation, reads: 'And certainly this is the most sublime / Proof of our worth and value, Oh Divinity, / That this great sob rolls on through ageless time / To die upon the shores of your infinity'.

3 Marcel Jouhandeau (1888–1979) was a French writer who was both deeply Catholic and homosexual. His early novels describe the town of Guéret where he was born. Though he married, he continued to write about his homosexual experiences.

anything which is not helpful to one, one throws away what is unnecessary or ballast – so this bores me,' he said.) But he looked Jouhandeau's name up in a reference book and remarked that he was born in 1888. I mentioned the name of Arthur Calder-Marshall who had been with me in Bonn in 1932, and from this we turned to his friend Humphry House and thence to Gerard Manley Hopkins on whom Humphry House had written an introduction to the editions of his Letters.[1] Curtius got up and took down a volume of Valery Larbaud ('a greatly neglected writer') and drew my attention to an essay of Larbaud on Dolben, a young poet who had been a great friend of Bridges and Hopkins.[2]

He gave me a copy of his essays on European literature. I asked him to inscribe it. He took up a pen from a tray of pens and pencils, none of which seemed to work very well, so I gave him my ball pen and he wrote on the fly leaf. I looked at the inscription he had written. It ran:

Für S.S.
Für wie lang!
E.R.C.

I smiled and said: 'This inscription seems to look at me backwards, forwards and sideways.'[3]

Then he said: 'I would like to give you my great book but I cannot find the English edition.'[4]

'Give me the German one. It will be good for my German to read the original.'

So he gave it to me, this time writing on the fly leaf only 'To S.S. from E.R.C.'

---

1 Arthur Calder-Marshall (1908–1992), a contemporary of Spender's at Oxford, later a novelist. Humphry House (1908–1955), also a contemporary at Oxford, later a literary critic.

2 Valery Larbaud (1881–1957), French writer and translator into French of foreign texts. Digby Mackworth Dolben (1848–1867), British poet who drowned tragically young.

3 'For S. S. For how long!' It is uncertain whether this refers to the past (the long period of their separation) or to the future. Curtius was ill, and in fact he died the following year.

4 *European Literature and the Latin Middle Ages* (1948).

I asked him to keep my ball point pen. He handed it back to me saying: 'It is very precious.' I put it down on the tray, and he let it stay there.

He said that shortly they would be going to Rome. 'I cannot bear this darkness. I need light.'

Shortly after this I gently took my leave: saying I must go, staying a few more minutes and then going. At the door, he clapped my arm affectionately.

It was not exactly that I felt I was forgiven, but I felt that that which was unforgiven could not be forgiven and that a great deal else had always been forgiven and could not be unforgiven.

9 October 1955, Berlin

I have spent the whole of the past week in Germany. Lecturing for the Deutsch-Englische Society. I went to Frankfurt, Düsseldorf, Bonn, Kiel and Berlin. [. . .] In Berlin, there is an extraordinary mixture of styles, many of them borrowed from America and owing to American influence, with little that seems either new or to show any awareness of the past of Berlin. The most successful building is perhaps the simple, white stone and glass building of the Freie Universität.

The buildings in the eastern sector have their propaganda purpose. The immense Soviet Embassy recalls the stuffy monumental aims of Exhibition Road in Kensington. It is hideous and stuffy, yet I found the Stalin Allee strangely impressive with its heavy blocked-in masses on either side of the over-wide street. These huge buildings with their windows like cells in a hive and their curious square heaviness, are overpowering and perhaps no one walks down the immense street on account of this. The detail is all hideous, but the masses themselves impressively distributed. They are like great tracks laid down through the decay and chaos and ruin of the rest of the Soviet sector. They brook no contradiction. To translate architecture back into terms of simple propaganda, one may compare the stifling and overwhelming propaganda of the Stalin Allee with the hectic shouting of most of the new buildings in the West.

The Stalin Allee is coated with yellow-coloured tiles like those in a cloakroom. These vast, uncompromising, squat buildings, have the curious fog-absorbent spongy quality of buildings like St Pancras or

Euston station in London, which are so much of their time and purpose that they seem to breathe in the atmosphere of the city, and one accepts them as one accepts spongeous shapes at the bottom of the sea.

The Stalin Allee is a mass of people contained in thousands of small dwellings like warrens – but with almost no one walking in the street. In the West what people seem to want is a glittering street with bright shop fronts to walk up and down endlessly. In Kiel they have built two such wide, illuminated parades, shut out from traffic. People walk up and down all day and nearly all night.

The Western Zone has all the energy, prosperity and success of a tremendously thriving commercial enterprise. The Eastern is just two columns of an army asserting its mass of uniform in a town which consists of nothing but ruins.[1]

The Russian memorials are all uncompromisingly hideous, except perhaps for the statue of a seated, mourning, Russian peasant mother at the base of the burial ground and memorial for the Russian dead in Berlin. All the same, this brutish ugliness is rather impressive. The concrete splayed prongs of a broken arch, or rather, an unfinished arch, which is the American memorial for the pilots of the Air Lift to Berlin, is simply ineffective.[2] It looks like something left over from the building of a world exhibition or fair. Yet the idea of an arch which rises from the ground and then plunges into invisible sky, is a good one. But it is carried out in the wrong material – concrete. And one feels that it is carried out in concrete because of a lack of confidence which could carry out the audacious idea in some transparent material or perhaps in metal lines suggesting at once the air lift itself,

---

1 Post-war Germany was divided into four zones: British, American, French and Russian. The Russian Zone became the DDR, the three western zones became the Federal Republic. Berlin remained behind the frontier of the Russian Zone as an Open City divided into four 'sectors', between which access was supposedly unrestricted.

2 In 1948 the Soviets attempted to force the other three Allies out of Berlin by blocking access by road and rail. The Allies responded by organising an air lift to supply the city with food and fuel. The stand-off lasted ten months. There were about sixty fatal casualties among the Allied personnel, commemorated by a leaning concrete arch with three spikes, symbolising the three air corridors, which bears the names of the pilots who were killed and is situated in the former Tempelhof airport in Berlin.

the rising of machines from the ground, and the vapour trails left by aeroplanes in the sky.

X. is a very prominent and obvious member of the German-Jewish community. He emigrated in March 1933, coming to London where he lived for the next twelve years. With the end of the war, he volunteered for military government, stuffed himself into a civilian military officer uniform and returned to the British Zone as a propagandist for democracy and freedom. He is now frequently to be met in Berlin. To his other accents, he has now added an English one when he speaks German. His conversation consists of saying how he detests the Germans, and how he pines after Maida Vale. He tells stories of villages in the West where Hitler's toast is drunk in Rhine wine, while the band plays the Horst Wessel Lied.[1] Wherever he goes, he encounters anti-Semitism.

Mr X. makes me nervous. I ask myself why did he ever go back to Germany if he so much hates it, and what good he imagines that he is doing by being there. It seems to me that his presence, his attitude, his sayings all breed anti-Semitism. This is still a dangerous and expensive game to play. If he were told this, he would doubtless explain the Germans after their behaviour to the Jews do not demand any consideration. If he is not received, as a friend, he is perfectly prepared to be a scourge. This I understand and can even sympathize with. But it seems surprising to me the Jewish community shows so little concern about its members who go back to Germany detesting and making themselves detested.

* * *

In Berlin, at lunch with Melvin Lasky, I again met George Kennan, whom I think one of the most remarkable men in American public life. Kennan has a high domed forehead, rather bald at the top, and very light blue eyes which look in front of him, creased almost like those of a Chinese. Everything he says nearly, expresses awareness and disquiet; and yet he has a gleam and security about him which are only found in the East, or at any rate more often in the East than

---

1 The battle song of Nazi storm troopers, named after one of their street-fighting 'martyrs'.

the West. He expresses ideas of disillusionment, and yet with an expression that shines with faith and belief.

An Austrian playwright and poet who has just written a play about the Fuchs case which is now being performed in Berlin, was at lunch.[1] He kept on relating every subject of conversation back to the thesis of his play. I mentioned that I had attended the Fuchs case, in order to cover it for the *New York Times* Magazine. I had stood in Court quite near to Fuchs, and when he was sentenced and asked if he had anything to say, I was probably the only person in Court who heard exactly what he did say. This was words to the effect that he thought that his worst crime was not any secret he had betrayed, but the betrayal of his friends.

I said that although there was no doubt a gulf between being a member of the Communist Party and actually betraying some military secret, at the same time from the point of view of some remote future it might seem that we greatly exaggerated the wickedness of giving away some secret to an opponent who'd find that secret in six months' time even if he did not know it already. I could quite understand, from Fuchs' point of view, the information he had given away might not ever have appeared to him a crime, but the realization that he had colleagues in England with whom he worked and who expected a certain loyalty of him, might give him a real sense of guilt. Kennan said: 'Yes. If there is one thing we have learned from these cases, it is that loyalty is perhaps the only absolute value. Thus the real evil done by espionage in cases like the Hiss or the Fuchs case, may turn out to be one that has no apparent connection with the offence committed.[2] With a spy, we know that some definite secret has been given away, but through that spy's disloyalty, there may be some far worse result than betrayal of the secret. For instance, Hiss handed over to the Communists some documents of quite second rate importance. But in doing so, the result of his action was to help McCarthyism in America, more than it was helped by any

---

1 Klaus Fuchs (1911–1988), German scientist convicted in 1950 of passing atom-bomb secrets to the Russians. Released in 1959, he went to live in the DDR.

2 Alger Hiss (1904–1996), a US State Department official, was convicted in 1950 of spying for the Russians. Many assumed he was an innocent victim of the communist witch-hunt then being pursued by Senator Joseph McCarthy. His actual guilt is still controversial.

other single action, and to make it difficult for [Dean] Acheson to remain in office.'[1]

One of the things I like about Kennan is his tolerance and sympathy with other people's points of view, which nonetheless he refuses to be taken in by. This was shown when at Milan [at the 'Future of Freedom' conference] he expressed and obviously felt the greatest sympathy for the delegates from Asian countries, but at the same time quietly decided that the result of their attitude was to prove that it was quite useless for the West to attempt to cooperate with Asia in order to attain any understanding by doing so.

He said that while he was at Berlin he had been to see one or two of the political cabarets performed by young people in the Western Zone. While he sympathized with the political attitudes expressed in these performances, [he] confessed that they made him uneasy. For instance in one cabaret there was a scene of Japanese fishermen who apparently wished only to fish quietly and not to have atomic bombs dropped on them. 'Now, after all,' said Kennan, 'one can wish for Japanese fishermen to be able to fish quietly, but all the same the situation is not quite as simple as that. One cannot forget that the Japanese story began not with the atomic bomb but with Pearl Harbor, and that there is a longer history than this cabaret pretends.'[2]

27 October 1955, London

Recently, meeting at some party a young writer who questioned me very closely about how my contemporaries became successful, I found myself saying some things which seem worth noting down.

---

1 Dean Acheson (1893–1971) as US Secretary of State took up Kennan's policy of 'Containment' and gave it a military bias. This did not save him from attacks from right-wing Republicans who thought his opposition to communism, especially in China, was ineffective. Nevertheless, Acheson did not lose his job because of the Hiss trial and he continued in office until 1953.

2 On 1 March 1954 some Japanese fisherman were exposed to fall-out from an American hydrogen bomb test on the Bikini Atoll. The attack on Pearl Harbor, on 7 December 1941, was a surprise military strike by the Imperial Japanese Navy on a US naval base at Pearl Harbor, Hawaii. Four US Navy battleships were sunk and over two thousand personnel were killed. The next day, America declared war on Japan and entered the Second World War.

What struck me then, and what still seems true now that I think again about it, was that young writers are very much made by their situation, or rather their ability to dramatize their own situation in relation to the history around them. For instance, Eliot and his contemporaries were able to dramatize themselves as the upholders of the values of civilization in the waste land. What is really important here was not their erudition, not their philosophy even, not the fact that they were a school, but [that] they saw themselves against a background of chaos collecting together in their work the fragments of a civilization which was an old bitch gone in the teeth.[1] If one looks back, one sees that the Elizabethans were also able to dramatize themselves, and that the flattery with which they had to surround Queen Elizabeth, false though it may have been, actually helped them in this self-dramatization. So that self-dramatization is even more important than truth. The writers of the 1890s saw themselves as pagans and, when one comes to the 1930s, one sees that my generation thought of themselves as artists to whom a stricken society made a particular kind of appeal that they should unite their artistic conscience with a social conscience. Now one has to admit that today it is extremely difficult for the young writer to dramatize himself. I do not see how he is to relate himself to this background of society.

Another thought, similar to the above. Although it may be important to have self-knowledge, for the purpose of creating anything in the world it is also important to practise a kind of self-deception. One has to have a myth of one's own role, in which one sees oneself as struggling. If instead of seeing oneself as struggling, one sees oneself simply as one is, then one appears unworthy to create anything. If we think of ourselves in terms simply of what we are, we discover that we are too vile to be worthy to do anything. If we think of ourselves in terms of what we ought to do, then we create for ourselves a kind of mask which conceals what we are. Too much analysis and debunking leads to inertia.

---

1 An allusion to Ezra Pound's comment on moving to Paris in 1920 that England had become 'an old bitch, gone in the teeth' ('Hugh Selwyn Mauberley', 1920).

30 November 1955, London

Yesterday I went to speak to the [Lewes] Literary Society at the invitation of Leonard Woolf. Stayed the night with Leonard, at the house where I have stayed before when Virginia was alive.[1] At the age of 70 or more, and living quite alone, Leonard seems exactly the same as I have always known him. Contented, hard-working, amused and amusing, completely independent. He has an almost antique quality which reminds one of the Romanized Jews of many centuries ago. He has added to Jewish intelligence Roman stoicism. He and Virginia were in fact a very Roman pair, her death by drowning herself at a time when she was convinced that she was going to become insane once more, being a very Roman kind of death. Leonard indeed accepted this with the same stoicism as he accepted everything else that came his way. One can very well imagine a sculpture of the two of them as a monument along the Appian Way.

As my Chairman, Leonard made a witty introduction, and he was as interested and curious about all that is going on as he has always been. At breakfast we talked about Rupert Brooke.[2] He told me that Rupert looked like a parody of the most beautiful man one has ever seen. In addition to features which are known from photographs, he had an astonishing colouring and perfect complexion. Leonard said that under a good deal of charm, there was something very hard and ruthless about Rupert Brooke. He said that Brooke was really extremely intelligent and sophisticated, but nevertheless he advertised all the most vulgar qualities of his time. When Rupert Brooke wrote a poem, he would write down the rhymes for each line and then fill up the meanings to suit the rhymes afterwards. We discussed whether Brooke was really a poet or not, and decided that in a sense he must have been because his poems, even if one does not approve of them, nevertheless are extremely memorable and have a quality which one never forgets. Leonard said that Rupert Brooke's poetry always reminded him of the music of Tchaikovsky. One did not necessarily like Tchaikovsky but one could not deny that he was a

---

1 For Leonard and Virginia Woolf, see biographical appendix.

2 Rupert Brooke (1887–1915), British poet killed in the First World War and famously described as 'the handsomest young man in England' by W. B. Yeats.

composer since his music came off, and if one heard it one went on being haunted and irritated by the tunes one had heard for the rest of the day. He said if Brooke had lived he would probably have been a man of action rather than a poet. [. . .]

A famous story about Rupert Brooke and Virginia Woolf is worth recording. Rupert stayed with the Woolves and went for a walk with Virginia discussing a poem that he was writing. Suddenly he said, 'What is the brightest thing in Nature?' Virginia said: 'Sunlight shining on the leaves of trees.' All she did to gain this idea was simply to look up at the trees. Sure enough sunlight on the leaves of trees comes into the poem that Rupert was composing at that moment. I remember Virginia describing herself bathing naked with Rupert. Rupert suddenly said to her 'Let us take off all our clothes.' He was very surprised when she simply did so and swam. What was really most remarkable about this story was the complete detachment with which Virginia told it. Even in her gaiety there was always a kind of dryness and austerity which enabled her to talk about absolutely anything without one feeling that she was personally involved or without embarrassing one. I remember even that she discussed madness as though it was something with which she had no concern.

In March 1956, Spender attended a meeting in Venice between Soviet and Western European intellectuals sponsored by the European Cultural Association. In his 1983 Journals *he described the personnel at the conference: 'The Russians were very weakly represented by the feeble and ineffective Fedin, a dear old museum director from Leningrad called Alpatov, and a third man whom Ignazio Silone immediately denounced as a police agent supervising the other two, and asked that he should leave. The Polish representative was Jaroslav Iwaszkiewicz, an immensely intelligent, profoundly cynical novelist, a kind of Polish André Gide. Two of the French representatives were Jean-Paul Sartre and Maurice Merleau-Ponty. The debates were quickly reduced to absurdity by Jean-Paul Sartre putting forward the view that discussion between the Russians and ourselves was meaningless because we were inhabitants of incommunicable ideological worlds.' Spender wrote a satiric novella about the meeting,* Engaged in Writing *(1958).*

26 March 1956, Venice

The idea of Literature Engagée.

The whole afternoon was devoted to this, as a result of Campagnolo's insistence that any meeting between writers from East and West must discuss the Writer and Society.[1] Sartre and Merleau-Ponty put forward the idea of the writer being *engagé*. I maintained that the only writer who had to be *engagé* was the one whose social conscience could be realized in the results of his imagination. A writer who wrote poems about bees did not have to be told to write them about factories.

The reaction to this example shows the degree of subtlety and crudeness of the idea of 'engagement'. With Merleau-Ponty the idea is subtle because by engagement he means that everything one writes reflects a social choice. One's way of describing the bees, the metre one chooses, all reflect one's attitude to society, one's environment. However, this (with which I would agree) means that there is no difference between engaged and disengaged literature. Sartre makes a difference by insisting on the importance of consciousness. One should be fully aware of which side one is on and consciously direct one's writing towards it. An example he gave seemed a bit crude but had the advantage of being very concrete. When he was in China Chinese writers were called upon to write children's stories. Should they or shouldn't they do so? He emphasized that there were very few writers in China and a great many children. What he didn't seem to take into account (nor did anyone else) was that the stories would have to please not only the Chinese children but also the Chinese government. Merleau-Ponty said he would be glad to write a children's story. I said that if I were a Chinese child I was not sure that I would be delighted by the story of a Chinese Merleau-Ponty.

J. D. Bernal brought up the subject discussed by Shelley in 'A Defence of Poetry' (not that he mentioned Shelley or any writer) that 'we should imagine that which we know'.[2] He said that we

---

1 Umberto Campagnolo (1904–1976), philosopher of Jurisprudence involved in the discussions regarding European unification after the war.

2 J. D. Bernal (1901–1971) was a distinguished scientist who joined the British Communist Party at the age of twenty-two. He remained a Marxist all his life. At this period he was interested in the cause of intellectual liberty, and from 1959 to 1965 he was President of the World Peace Council, a communist front organization directed towards disarmament.

were on the threshold of a future of enormous scientific development and control of resources, which would transform life. For the first time, he said, we lived in a history in which immense changes benefiting everyone could be achieved simply through knowledge and without a revolution. (Will the Communists perhaps become Godwinians?)[1] He reproached the writers for not writing works that revealed any awareness of this future. He said there had never been such a gap – not even in the 1890s – between the littleness of literature and the greatness of man's powers and knowledge.

I must say I am Shelleyan enough to feel the force of Bernal's reproach. All the same he was discussing in terms of knowledge what would only be real if discussed in terms of imagination. I pointed this out and after the meeting he said, 'You have me there.' But nonetheless, he said, there were non-literary writers despised by critics, who did try to grapple with this future.

Vercors put the case for *engagé* writing in what seemed to me the most journalistic way: he said, 'If I am confronted by a great injustice, I feel called upon to set aside my own preoccupations and interests and write about that.'[2]

The Russians, who had brought their interpreters[,] were so badly served by these that they obviously could not understand what was being said. However, they improvised for the time being, and said that tomorrow – when they had studied the translated material – they would speak. Meanwhile, Fedin said that he thought the first demand on a writer was to be sincere with himself, the second to be responsible towards society. It was out of the tension between these two sometimes opposed loyalties that literature was made.[3] Polevoy

---

1 In 'A Defence of Poetry' (1821) P. B. Shelley argues that poets are 'the unacknowledged legislators of the world' because they are masters of words, which frame ideas. William Godwin (1756–1836) was Shelley's father-in-law, and an influence on his unusual brand of anarchic radicalism.

2 Vercors was the pen name of Jean Bruller (1902–1991), a French writer who began his career as an electrician and a pacifist. During the war he joined the Resistance and co-founded Les Éditions de Minuit, an important French publishing house.

3 Konstantin Aleksandrovitch Fedin (1892–1977) was head of the Soviet Writers' Union from 1959 to 1971, during which period he denied Solzhenitsyn

whenever he speaks always says the same thing: 'Let's not talk about politics, dear colleagues, because if we do that we'll find we disagree. Let's just stick to culture.'[1] To illustrate this line, which he is evidently very determined on, he told me that when he accompanied Molotov in America and there was much political discussion it was impossible to come to any understanding with anyone.[2] But as soon as he travelled around alone disembarrassed of Molotov, he found himself getting on excellently with 'ordinary Americans'. 'Ordinary Americans', he discovered, loved Russians, and wanted peace.

Iwaszkiewicz, whilst explaining that he was not a Marxist, adopted very much the social realist line.[3] However, Jelenski, who sees him in private tells me that he detests Poland, says things are worse there than any of us who are outside realize, and is extremely pessimistic about Khrushchev's declaration.[4] He cannot bring himself to believe in the possibility of any real change. Jelenski says that altogether the intellectuals behind the Iron Curtain seem quite stunned by recent developments, cannot believe the evidence of their own ears and eyes, and are wildly indiscreet in their bewilderment.[5]

the right to publish *Cancer Ward*. His novel *Cities and Years* describes the difficulties of a mediocre bourgeois in joining the Revolution. A satirical account of him appears in Spender's *Engaged in Writing* (1958).

1 Boris Nikolaevich Kampov (1908–1981), whose pen name was Polevoy, achieved a reputation for his reports from the Front during the war. His 1947 novel *Story of a Real Man*, describing the experiences of a Soviet war hero, was immensely popular.

2 Vyacheslav Molotov (1890–1986), hard-line Soviet politician, a protégé of Stalin. He helped shape the Molotov–Ribbentrop Non-Aggression Pact which freed Germany for a campaign in the west at the outbreak of war. He was placed in retirement after Stalin's death.

3 Jarosław Iwaszkiewicz (1894–1980), who wrote under the name of Eleuter, Polish poet and essayist. He was President of the Polish PEN Club.

4 Constantin ('Kot') Jelenski (1922–1987), Polish émigré intellectual and, like Spender, a CCF employee.

5 The speech given by Nikita Khrushchev (1894–1971) to the 20th Party Congress on 25 February 1956, in which he denounced the crimes of Stalin, had a devastating effect on communists worldwide. Coming as it did from the Party Secretary, it destroyed the possibility of nursing any illusions about Russian communism.

Campagnolo insists on dominating the discussions, is very opinionated, and extremely obtuse. The thesis he wants to thrust on us all is that the writer must not only be *engagé* but must enter completely into politics. All he omits to say is *what* and *whose* politics. At the same time in an effort to avoid disagreement he is capable of saying things like: 'No one here is a Marxist or anti-Marxist, Communist or anti-Communist. We are all completely objective.'

28 March 1956, Venice

Last night at la Columba [restaurant near St Mark's Square], I sat with the Russian (Polevoy) who looks like Malenkov and the mysterious official (whom Silone calls the Fourth Man) who supervises the Russians. Polevoy was very friendly, inviting me to stay with him in Russia. The Fourth Man, who always overdoes things rather, told me that when I was in Russia they would be glad to hear my criticisms because although they were proud of their achievements in some ways, they were always grateful for criticism. The daughter of Iwaszkiewicz told me she had walked through Venice that morning and made friends with a young Venetian 'très beau et très jeune' [very beautiful and very young], aged 20, called Marius.

The previous evening I had sat next to Carlo Levi.[1] He is cheerful looking with a curly head of hair and a profile in which the forehead forms a continuous curve from the base of the hair to the tip of the nose, and the neck starts off just below the chin: like a stoutish tortoise. Disregarding the menu fixed for us all, he had made friends with the waiter and ordered on his own, an *hors d'oeuvre* of *calamoretti* and *scampi* which he followed up with a course of razor shell fish, that looked like long white worms in their long knife-blade shells. He told me that you could attract these animals by sprinkling salt over the small holes they leave in the wet sand. Sensing the salt they think the tide has come in and come out of their holes. He talked with vital charming vanity about the immense popularity of his own work – answering a question of mine, whether it was true, as I'd

---

1 Carlo Levi (1902–1975), Italian writer and activist best known for *Christ Stopped at Eboli*, his 1945 memoir of his time spent in exile after being arrested for anti-fascist activism.

heard, that Italians don't read many books. He said that where he lived there were peasants who knew pages of his works by heart, and that it was the custom there for someone who could read to read a page a day to the other villagers. Thus – allowing for harvest and holidays – they read 300 pages of Carlo Levi per year.

30 March 1956, Venice

We went to see the film of a story by Pratolini called *Poveri amanti* (I think).[1] It counter-pointed the lives of Florentines living in a rabbit warren of workers' flats with the brutal events of the rise of Fascism. Anti-Fascists spent their time being shot up by Fascists. I thought it must be curious for the Soviet guests – fresh from revelations about Beria, Stalin etc – to observe the stone-age methods of repression of the Fascists; and that it was still more curious to offer this film to our mostly Leftist Conference as a tribute to our Russian Friends' hatred of oppression.[2] Thinking these thoughts, I was curious to see how Bernal sitting on my left was reacting. So while an anti-Fascist was being shot several times in the back and then thrown by Fascists into the flames of his motorcycle (which they had set alight by firing a few shots through the petrol tank) I stole a few glances at my colleague. His mouth hung open, he was breathing heavily and perspiring, from time to time he passed his hand over his forehead, at moments he shut his eyes unable to bear the sight of the pain on the screen. This, I thought, from a man who is so intent on the vision of socialist construction that he considers the deaths of thousands of people, slave labour etc, as quite irrelevant. [. . .]

After the meeting to discuss the text of the communiqué and the programme for the Congress, I got hold of Sartre alone and asked

---

1 Vasco Pratolini (1913–1991), Italian anti-Fascist writer and friend of Elio Vittorini. In the post-war period he was a scriptwriter for leading neo-realist filmmakers. His novel *Cronache di poveri amanti* (1947), filmed in 1954, won an award at the Cannes Film Festival but ran into censorship problems back in Italy.

2 Lavrenty Beria (1899–1953), Georgian soviet politician, Head of the People's Commissariat for Internal Affairs (NKVD) (1938–46), appointed General Commissar of State Security (1941). Beria enjoyed considerable influence under Stalin's reign, becoming the head of Stalin's secret police. In 1945, Stalin placed him in charge of the Soviet atomic bomb project. After Stalin's death in March 1953, Beria was arrested in a coup headed by Nikita Khrushchev and later shot dead in December 1953.

him: 'What would you say if in certain circumstances you were imprisoned in a city where there was a communist government, and I, knowing you were innocent, started a campaign against the communists on your account?' 'Ah,' said Sartre, 'that is an extremely difficult question. It all depends. But it is just possible that I in my prison, though innocent, and even hating my oppressors, might nevertheless think it better that I should be condemned than that my case should be made the occasion for an accusation against the cause which in the long run is that of the proletariat.' 'It seems to me that the only good cause has always been that of one person unjustly imprisoned – whether this has resulted in Habeas Corpus or a furious campaign conducted by Voltaire in pamphlets.' 'That's the whole drama. That perhaps we live in a situation in which the injustice against one person no longer seems to apply.'

* * *

Conversation with Bernal.
On the way to Torcello, in the motor-boat, one of the lady interpreters asked: 'How is it that Mr Bernal who is so logical in every way, so objective, and who also has a sense of humour, can be so completely illogical and unobjective whenever the discussion comes round to Communism?'

At Torcello I was asked to sit next to Karl Barth. Beyond him, was Bernal. Somehow, I managed the conversation so that I could make Bernal himself answer the interpreter's question. I asked him again what he thought about Stalin, and he said: 'We seem to have made some very serious mistakes. I don't know how it happened, but it is bad.' I asked him whether he did not think such mistakes were inevitable with a communist system. He said: 'There is not just one system in the world. There are two to choose from. And, of the two, I prefer the communist.' 'What makes you prefer it?' 'You have to think of the utter unnecessary misery and waste and lack of opportunity that exist in the world as it is at present. What people fail to realize is that things don't have to be as they are.' 'Then what prevents them being better?' 'Well, for one thing people themselves. Human beings are the trouble. One person who is greedy and dishonest who gets into a strong position can undo the good done by hundreds.'

I told Barth and Bernal about the question I had put to Sartre. 'Ah,' said Barth, 'but you assume Sartre to have been innocent. How can you invent a hypothesis of such a society in which people who are political prisoners are innocent?' 'Well, for one thing, they might not have committed the acts for which they are condemned.' 'Still, in the circumstances of that kind of society, they might have been out of step. It might be enough for them to be guilty in the minds of the rulers.' I said: 'All the same the people who were condemned by Stalin are now rehabilitated.' 'It may be a matter of time. In 1956 they may be innocent. In 1937 they may have been guilty.' I looked astonished, and he said: 'All the same, I don't approve of such a society.'

There is a kind of *Schadenfreude* among theologians who are delighted to prove that without their absolute values, all justice is completely relative.

5 May 1956, London

Yesterday, John Hall came into my office, and with a grin asked: 'Do you know this fellow Peter Watson who has been found dead in his bath?[1] It was announced in the stop press of the *News Chronicle* this morning.' Thus I heard of the death of one of my greatest friends. I can hardly imagine any death that could leave his friends sadder. In the first place, Peter really lived for other people, and for that reason other people are bound to feel that something of their lives has gone out. That which Peter was in their lives, in spite of faults, was generous, disinterested and good. He gave to everyone who asked him and to a good many who did not ask. If he sometimes neglected one, this simply was the result of a kind of fatigue, of his not being able to do everything. In my own friendship with him, which is an example of the course of many of his friendships, there seems absolutely no cloud, though perhaps a certain fading out. I think in our thoughts about each other we were the same as we had always been. One felt that one understood Peter and that he understood one. This was on account of the qualities I have mentioned: his essential goodness, his disinterestedness.

Secondly, he really had a burning and passionate love of the arts.

---

1 John Hall was an assistant editor on *Encounter*.

His judgement was good, though perhaps slightly modish, but what is more important than his judgement is the fact that for him the pursuit of art was a quest. So that even his exclusiveness was an aspect of a choice which was really spiritual and creative in him. I remember his saying to me once about Paul Klee, that there was something painters like Klee did which had never been done before, and this was to paint interior light shining outwards. He was therefore searching for certain qualities in painters. He found it difficult to count those who did not have these qualities as worthwhile. Pavel Tchelitechew painted him as a young man in armour and that he was a kind of knight is true.[1] He was permanently in the service of his cause, which was the modern, and which yet was somehow undermined by modern life: so that he was at once believing in genius and disappointed. He did not look forward to a better future. [. . .]

Talking about Peter again with Cyril today, Cyril said that Peter liked people to be unsuccessful. At any rate it is true that he regarded success as suspect. He could tolerate the second-rate when it was unsuccessful and perhaps he even felt that he could aid it: but when it became successful it was out of reach of possible help. All this meant that he was not at all a snob. And yet, especially when he was young, he had more real elegance than anyone I have ever known. He was also in those days much courted by people in society.

What made him really so exceptional was that although he believed in the highest standards, he did not think of himself as an example of them. He had nothing about him of the intolerant critic, someone like F. R. Leavis, whose standards seem inextricably identified with his own ego. One cannot even say that he was modest because it would not have occurred to him that he had anything to be modest about. He had a certain vanity or pride about his own expertise which made him sometimes rather contemptuous of the opinions of other people who talked about painting without, in his view, their knowing about it. There was perhaps an element of vanity in this, but this is different from immodesty or egotism.

I think he was one of the most consistently good people, in the part that he played in other people's lives, that I have known. His faults

1 Pavel Tchelitechew (1898–1957), Russian surrealist painter admired and protected by the Sitwells. He moved to the United States in the mid-1930s.

can all be put down either to the fact that he was self-educated, so that he had the self-educated person's mistrust of other people's knowledge, or simply that he tired easily, was not very strong, and had many people making more demands on him than he could possibly fulfil. Sometimes he was depressing company, because his perfectionist's view that everything was getting worse and worse became insistent, almost obsessive. He did not wish to be cheered up, and all one could really do was sympathize with his gloom. But this produced a negative effect. Being absorbed in my own work, and thinking that one just has to work according to one's lights without asking too closely whether one's best is of the very best, I found his insistence on a best which was rapidly giving place in our civilization to the worst, somewhat discouraging. He pursued the kind of logic which brings creative effort to a stop.

I first met him in 1934 or 1935, when he was living in Paris. He was living at that time with Denham Fouts, whose life forms a separate history.[1] Peter was too perfectionist to be an easy person to live with, and he seems to have driven those who were close to him into a kind of empathetic despair. He was, as it were, essentially made for honeymoons and not for marriages. I mean that the best possible relationship to have with Peter was to be taken up by him very intensely for a few weeks, and then simply to remain on his visiting list for the rest of one's time. By this I mean that Peter dropped people. Myself I believe that everyone is not made for continued intense relations with one or more friends. I think that for some people the honeymoon is an ideal kind of relationship. All that matters is that it should end with understanding and mutual respect. With Peter's friends, who were more or less his equals, this happened. What was really unfortunate was when, as in the case of Denham Fouts, a friend really fell in love with him or became completely dependent on him. Then the fact that he suffered from other people not having the same perfectionist standards as him became evident.

His despair, his cynicism, which went with his idealism, was gay and laughing, if rather bitter.

---

1 Denham Fouts (1914–1949), a famously dissolute American artist, was Watson's lover before dying suddenly in his mid-thirties.

I stayed with Peter in Paris, and in the spring of 1939 he took me for a trip through Switzerland, where we stayed at various places and visited people who had private collections of modern painting. We also visited the painter Paul Klee who was then dying of cancer. He received us with the utmost kindness, and showed us the gouaches.

At this time Peter was one of those rich people who without seeming at all dependent on his wealth, and without having many standards, yet manages to get the utmost in the way of pleasure and beauty out of riches. When I think of him then, I think of his clothes which were beautiful, his general neatness and cleanness which seemed almost like those of a handsome young Bostonian, his Bentley and his chauffeur who had formerly been the chauffeur of the Prince of Wales, one wonderful meal we had in some village of the Savoie, his knowing that the best food in Switzerland is often to be obtained at the buffets of railway stations. Of course his most wonderful quality as a companion was his complete frankness, that of someone who tells you everything he admires, and who in his private life has no respect for conventions and therefore nothing to hide. He was not uncritical of people's morals, but to him genius and intelligence were far more important than morals, and when they were combined with immoral behaviour he regarded this simply as tiresome and tried to ignore it. He was always very intelligent about other people, and for that reason to be alone with him among a lot of other people was always amusing.

After all, he was a person who enjoyed things. During the past two days, I have repeatedly thought when I saw the trees in flower in London, how this would have delighted him; when I went and looked at German Expressionist paintings in the Tate gallery this morning, how interested and intelligent his comments would have been. It seems strange that only when people are dead one fully realizes the kind of communion which knowing them really means. What is this? One meets people, eats with them, talks with them, travels with them, and even the greatest intimacy is either fragmentary, like crumbs that have fallen to the floor from a table, or hallucinatory like most love affairs. Then suddenly one has the impression that one has completely entered into another person's being, that his being is a part of one's own. It seems a mockery that one never fully realized this. For instance, it seems to me now that if I had understood the extent of the communion I now feel with Peter, when he spoke to me about the discouragement he felt with modern life, I would really have tried to encourage him. I would have pointed out to him how much achievement in modern art there had been, and that he himself really appreciated modern art more than any achievement of the past, and that all this great work had been produced in conditions which at any given moment seemed unfavourable. I did not point this out, because I thought of us as two people sitting on either side of the table one yapping at the other. It seemed more important to agree with him than to argue with him because agreement showed one's sympathy. I see now that disagreement might really have been more valuable. This feeling of communion may also be an illusion but it seems very real. The fact [is] that the crumbs and the fragments and the division add up to something in common which is spiritual communion, which makes [it] at moments difficult not to believe in a separate life where friendship and love and so on are real. I think of Peter, partly because it is him thinking in me. These thoughts are in some sense an endeavour to express his thoughts. It is difficult not to think things such as: 'Now he has joined Denham, and their misunderstandings are removed.' Still it is better not to speculate further than the reality of the feeling, which exists, like the truth of what is imagined in poetry. It is certainly very real.

* * *

On Wednesday last we gave a dinner party for Clarissa Eden, Charlie Chaplin and his wife, Harold Nicolson, James Pope-Hennessy and Jane Howard.[1] We took a great deal of trouble about this, and even went so far as to buy a long overdue new dining room table. The evening went very well. Charlie Chaplin is always amusing and extremely interesting when he talks about his youth, which I always try to get him to do. He said that when he was first in films, out at

---

1 Clarissa Eden (b. 1920), wife of Sir Anthony Eden, Conservative Prime Minister from 1955 to 1957. The British filmmaker Charlie Chaplin (1889–1977) was then married to Oona O'Neill (1925–1991). Harold Nicolson (1886–1968), diplomat, author and publisher, husband of Vita Sackville-West. James Pope-Hennessy (1916–1974), biographer and travel writer. Elizabeth Jane Howard (b. 1923), formerly an actress, at this point a well-regarded novelist.

Hollywood, he intended, like all the other movie actors, to return to the stage and regarded the movies as a craze which might not last and which anyhow had not very great importance. Then one day he was in New York, when he went to a cinema to see one of the movies in which he appeared. Surrounded by the public, for the first time he realized, that he himself and the little group of people with whom he worked, who acted almost in barns, and who in the evenings used to go to the drugstore or stand at the street corner, that these people were part of an enormous development which would become the great amusement of the future. He talked about meeting Bulganin and Khrushchev.[1] He said that he did not like Bulganin who struck him as being a stuffed shirt, but he found Khrushchev very sympathetic. Obviously Chaplin sympathizes with people like himself whom he feels to be little men who have become enormously powerful big men but who still retain their interest in the little man and the poor. I am sure that the basis for his sympathy for communism is that he feels the communists to be an enormously large version of a poor little man's success story, the Cinderella of Asia.

Our evening started off with [. . .] James and Harold asking Clarissa about the sable which she had been presented with by the Russians. They asked her why she was not wearing this. She laughed and said it was quite useless, being simply a lump of fur still attached to the skin of the animal – or something of the sort. Harold then described the present given by Stalin to Sir Archibald Clark Kerr when he was Ambassador for Moscow. This was given him at the airport in a parcel and without opening it he put it on the rack of the aeroplane. He was very curious what was in the flat long-shaped parcel. Finally he could not resist opening it. It contained the entire skin of a baby bear. Harold obviously told this story to follow up neatly Clarissa's story, by giving another example of an inept Russian present. But Clarissa said: 'How delightful! I can't imagine a nicer

---

1 Charlie Chaplin met the Soviet Prime Minister, Nikolai Bulganin (1895–1975) and First Secretary of the Communist Party, Nikita Khrushchev, during their visit to London in April 1956. At this point, the Soviet leaders were in search of trade contracts and Chaplin was in self-imposed exile from the United States. According to *Time* magazine, Bulganin said to Chaplin, 'They repudiate you, but we recognize you. You have been a big help.' (*Time*, 7 May 1956).

present to receive than a baby bearskin.' She did not say this to crush Harold, I really cannot think why she said it except that it was the sort of thing that Clarissa always does say. She sat on my right, and we talked about Isaiah Berlin. She said she was worried about him, or had been worried about him, because he led such an extremely social life. She said this disappointed her very much. I said: 'But what do you mean by society? I never quite understand what society is in England. You must know. Please tell me about it.' She said: 'Oh, but I know nothing about it. We never see anybody. It is you who lead a social life.' This conversation was rather absurd. I felt like saying that I could not really discuss it with her, as the very fact of being with her proved that I must be a very social person. Therefore I could hardly explain to her that I was not, since her presence in the conversation proved the contrary. Every conversation with her has this strange, rather edgy quality. As James pointed out to me afterwards, Charlie Chaplin seemed distinctly damped down as long as Clarissa was there. When the ladies left the room he brightened up considerably and chatted away a great deal about the film he is making, which is about the visit of a king who has lost his throne to New York.[1]

Here are a few notes about things happening this year which I have not noted in this diary.

Christopher Isherwood spent several weeks in London. He was accompanied by his friend Don.[2] Don is very young, bright and attractive, with eyes that follow Christopher's expression with a filial admiration. He accompanied Christopher on visits mostly to actors and film stars. He was less interested in Christopher's older friends, but maybe this lack of interest was partly discretion. He felt that Christopher's older friends would like to be alone with Christopher.

Christopher seemed exactly as he always has been when he is on his best behaviour. He was bright, alluring, charming and smiling. He sympathized with everyone, and the only thing that seemed new was his almost excessive self-effacingness. On his last evening, he gave a party at a restaurant which turned out to be very extraordinary

---

1 *A King in New York* was released in 1957.

2 Don Bachardy (b. 1934), painter and since 1953 the companion of Christopher Isherwood.

indeed. His mother, who is aged 85, and his younger brother, who is almost an idiot, Don, Peter Watson, Natasha were all there. Christopher was exceedingly drunk and kept on saying the same things very slowly, clearly and distinctly. From time to time, he said: 'I'm terribly afraid we have offended John Lehmann. Won't someone telephone John Lehmann and tell him to come along?' Accordingly, each of us in turn telephoned John. This was extremely badly received by John. He said that he could not come as his sister was dining later, and he would not invite us as his sister had to be quiet. Christopher's mother smiled all through this with a brilliance and complete refusal to give away what she was thinking which put one extremely in mind of Christopher. Even Richard, his brother, gave nothing of his feelings away, but simply chuckled to himself from time to time.

6 May 1956, London

Today we drove down to the country with the children, to visit Henry Moore and his wife and their daughter Mary, who is Lizzie's age.[1] There were some Americans from St Louis, called Weil, who were there to buy sculptures. It was a beautiful day and the children played in the garden very happily. Henry showed us his work in his studio attached to his house, and also in a large new studio built in his garden. Beyond this large studio there is a field and a small wood, in which he has placed some large pieces of sculpture in order to see how they look in the open air. One of the pieces was a very large statue of the torso of a warrior with shield upraised, which is going to the memorial for the British paratroopers who fell at Arnhem.[2] Another is a very long attenuated, skeletal statue which Henry said was suggested

---

1 For Henry Moore and family, see biographical appendix.

2 The Second World War Battle of Arnhem, also known as Operation Market Garden (17–26 September 1944). This famous military engagement was conceived by General Bernard Montgomery and involved a land- and air-based attack of the area around Arnhem, on the Denmark–Germany border. Montgomery's aim was to capture the network of canals and bridges in this region and hasten an end to the war. The attack failed due to strong German resistance, resulting in Britain's decision to withdraw troops on 25 September. There are several memorials in Arnhem and the surrounding area, commemorating troops who died in the offensive. Henry Moore's 1954 *Warrior with Shield* depicts a wounded warrior, missing a leg and an arm.

to him by the bird men in Africa of whom he had seen photographs a long time ago. This figure had two heads, almost identical, and simplified as the points of large pins. He said he had done this in order to make this open figure expand at the top as though it was taking off [from] the earth in flight with wings. He talked about Giacometti.[1]

Henry Moore said that he admired the sculpture of Giacometti very much, but that people did not like it who looked to sculpture for bulk and solidity. He said that Giacometti was doing in sculpture something which was complementary to what other sculpture did. Instead of bulk he produced lightness and thinness. It was the sculpture of the shadow cast by the rotundity of sculpture. He spoke very sympathetically of Peter Watson, and said how many people now whom he had helped would be without assistance. I said that the very personal way in which he helped people, helping them first because he thought they had talent, and afterwards because he remembered that they were human beings who simply needed help, was different from the way in which people like the Clarks patronized artists. Henry said, Yes, being helped by the Clarks was rather like being helped by the Ford Foundation.

9 May 1956, London

Yesterday morning Sonia Orwell telephoned from Paris that all his friends in France were saying that Peter Watson had committed suicide. They had got this impression from Tony del Renzio. Since I knew that Norman and Tony would be the only people apart from his brother going to the inquest, I decided to go.[2] The small court in Horseferry Road had only about a dozen people apart from the police and the Coroner. The first person I noticed, wearing a pin-striped business suit, was Peter's brother, Sir Norman Watson. He had Peter's slightly forward bending stoop, the little wrinkles at the back of the jaw and across the neck, his rather protruding eyes. But he was not in any way Peter. I remembered how when we went to

---

1 Alberto Giacometti (1901–1966), sculptor and painter whose sculptures are distinctive for their elongated, waif-like appearance.

2 Tony del Renzio (1915–2007), surrealist artist, resident in Paris. Norman Fowler, Peter Watson's lover.

Switzerland, Peter had been annoyed with me for having a pin-striped suit which I had bought with money he had given me to buy something suitable for visiting rich Swiss art patrons. I was never able to wear it.

Before the proceedings began, loudly whispered conversations were held between Sir Norman, and Peter's doctor, and Norman Fowler. From these conversations, I learned that the doctor thought Peter could easily have died by simply falling asleep in his bath, since he was a very deep sleeper. It seemed rather curious that Sir Norman had not met any of the important key witnesses before.

The Coroner had bright eyes, a pink face and ears that stuck out. He had the manner of someone who comes to mend something that has gone wrong with the house. It was a very friendly and kind manner. He elicited from the doctor and the police most of the facts I had already heard. Then Norman Fowler was put in the witness box. His story was that Peter had come home after a weekend with people whose names Norman did not know. Norman attempted to find out from him where he had been. This evidently annoyed Peter very much and they had a very bad row. Norman said that he seemed extremely agitated. Norman asked him whether he would like some wine, and he said: 'In my present state, that is exactly what I need.' Normally he did not drink at all. Finally, he ordered Norman to go off to bed. When Norman was settled down, he came into Norman's room and emptied a suitcase of some clothes. He then said he was going to take a bath, and disappeared into the bathroom. Norman went to sleep. He woke up in the middle of the night, feeling extremely worried. He started looking around the flat for Peter. He found the bathroom door locked. He called to Peter and got no answer. Finally, terrified, he went into the street and summoned a policeman. The policeman broke the door open and found Peter's body. Next the doctor was cross-examined before Norman and established that Peter had died from drowning in his bath. He had evidently intended to take a bath in a perfectly normal way, and had even soaped himself in the bath because there was soap found in the stomach.

Both Sir Norman and the doctor witnessed that he was an extremely heavy sleeper and often very difficult to wake up. Norman Fowler, however, mentioned in his evidence that Peter had not been sleeping at all well lately.

The verdict was Accidental Death, and the Coroner was extremely emphatic that any possibility of suicide was quite ruled out.

Today Tony del Renzio came to tell me that Norman was very annoyed that I had attended the inquest. He said that no friend of Peter except himself had the right to attend. Tony pointed out to him that this was quite unreasonable, and that I had known Peter for twenty-five years, but this did not satisfy him.

The fact probably is that Norman felt frustrated in his relationship with Peter, was so little involved in his life, that he is determined to be involved in his death. There is something in his attitude of: 'At least this belongs to me and to no-one else.' When people are terribly shocked, their behaviour sometimes comes straight out of their unconscious wishes, and they certainly ought not to be blamed for it. Shock is one of those acid tests which show us what we really are.

10 May 1956, London

Last night I went to a party at Anne Fleming's. Cecil Beaton was there and he talked very sympathetically about Peter.[1] He said he was always elusive, and there was nothing that pleased him more than to make an appointment when one was travelling with him at a certain time, and then not to appear, and later to appear to be very annoyed when one asked him where he had been. He said he had a great many drawings of Peter, and one painting, which he had done at various times.

This afternoon had lunch with Joan Rayner, Cyril [Connolly] and Natasha, and then drove out to the crematorium at Golders Green. The brief, dreary little service, intoned by a parson who has a quarter of an hour for each such ceremony, throughout the day. As Joan remarked, if we had appeared a quarter of an hour later, we would have attended the wrong person's funeral, perhaps without our realizing it. The pale wood coffin of Peter on rollers like a boat which one puts on rollers and drags across them to avoid a weir. The whole service was waiting for the moment when the doors open and the coffin slides through them into the furnace. After this had been done

---

1 Cecil Beaton (1904–1980), society photographer, diarist and costume designer.

– the whole thing took about a quarter of an hour – we went out and looked at the wreaths and flowers. Graham Sutherland, Cecil Beaton, Norman Fowler [. . .] and a few other people were there. Cecil looked as if he did not want anyone to speak to him. Cyril and I talked a little to Sir Norman, who seemed very nice to us. Then we drove back in the car, and Cyril remarked what an inhuman service it was. How it was dominated by the idea of the cremation itself, which seemed so unnatural compared with just lowering the coffin into the earth. Then he said: 'This shows how strange life is. Two weeks ago, and none of us would have realized that Peter Watson, this elegant and intelligent young man, was going to be drowned within a few days and then burned. It is the tragedy of man that he knows he is going to die. The animals are much luckier because they don't know.'

Of course, every time someone dies, the whole light in which the universe has all met at one's point of consciousness, is put out. People never seem conscious enough of the fact that if the human race disappeared, the universe would have no centre. We went home and had tea; then I took Joan in my car to Knightsbridge.

Natasha and I gave a farewell dinner party for Raymond Chandler. He behaved extremely well, and was extremely friendly with everybody. He left presents for the children and Francesca and Dmitri [Francesca's son]. This was really very thoughtful of him. One of the guests was Theodora Benson.[1] I happened to talk about editing, and she said she had no idea I was an editor and asked me what was the name of the magazine that I edited. When I said it was *Encounter* she said she had never heard of it. I could not make out whether this was a studied insult or whether she simply prided herself on being ignorant. I gave her two copies to take away at the end of the evening. Still thinking about Peter. [. . .]

Cyril also said that during the last two days, or for two days after Peter's death, he found himself all the time thinking very sweetly of Peter, as though all the affection that Peter felt for his friends was present in his mind and he was haunted by it. He said this gave him the feeling of Peter being near to him, and one could not at all explain it. There is certainly no rational explanation for this, but it strikes me that we are denied knowing what we feel about certain of our friends

---

1 Theodora Benson (1906–1968), short-story and travel writer.

until they are dead. Human relations are so intermittent, and also so self-interested, that one sees them from day to day, and, unless they are forgotten about, they are always attached to a future in which one expects them to arrive at some kind of climax. Death cuts them off at an instant from this idea of the future, relieves them of the element of self-interest, and thus we are able to enter into them as it were outside the stream of our personal history, and to experience them for a few days of intense feeling as though they are entirely in a present which has neither past nor future. One suddenly enters into what is really one of the most transitory of feelings, the feeling of timelessness: really the feeling of being outside time for a few minutes or hours. All this is tinged with regret, because one cannot help feeling bitter that one never really knew the true nature of one's feelings when the dead person was alive. One feels that one ought to have valued much more every moment in the past much more [*sic*]. But though this may be true, the more important truth is that during life one could not really ever have understood this. There are too many barriers, too many things came between, and one could not have a relationship with the dead person in the light of his death. Cyril said that after a time one became hostile to the dead, as though one resented their being outside our time and our lives. I am not sure if I have ever experienced this feeling, though of course I know what it is to forget the dead, or rather not be able to recapture them. As one has to go on living, the dead too inevitably get, as it were, out of date. They become like faded photographs, associated only with the particular style of dress that they wore on a past day. One just has to accept all this. One can learn very little. For example, although I think that if I had known all this, about Peter, I would have made much more effort to see him, I cannot think of anyone around me, now living, who, as a result of this I will alter my attitude towards. In the case of the few people whom one really loves, one knows exactly where one is, so there is no need to make any alteration. But in the case of the borderline cases of people for whom one feels a far greater attachment than one realizes at the time, one simply cannot realize at the time. Some deaths, which one ought to feel a great deal, one does not feel at all; and other deaths which might leave one almost indifferent, one feels acutely. In life, there is very little possibility of discovering the values that are made very apparent by death.

[233]

15 May 1956, London

Two nights ago I had a very curious hallucination, or fancy, not exactly a dream. I lay in bed and I thought, supposing that I had had an accident, that I had been unconscious and then that I had half awoken, and was either imprisoned in my car, or else in bed in hospital, quite out of my mind, and that I imagined I was in my bed at home lying awake. This image became so intense that I could not see the slightest reason why it was not the reality: for supposing that I had had such an accident, and was in such a situation, the only thing that might make me suspect the truth about what had happened, would be the faint suspicion that I was lying in bed at home imagining that I had had an accident. So the fantasy became a vicious circle. In some way, this kind of hallucination is characteristic. Ever since I was quite young, I have been so conscious of time rushing past and of death approaching, that often I have seemed to be living not so much in the present as in a future out of which I was looking back on myself in the present. It is as though what I was living was a memory of my own life after it was over. Another very uncomfortable feeling of the same kind arises often when I am in art galleries or reading about people who have lived in the past. Suddenly I think 'these people are all dead, their portraits, their history, the stories they told, the songs they sung, the pictures they painted, are all a kind of mockery. The fact is that they are all under the ground, and everything they have left behind them only lingers on like a smell.' People often talk about what is meant by history, why it has to be studied, and so on. I think it was in the National Gallery that the idea occurred to me very vividly, that history is simply our way of getting to know the dead as though they were our contemporaries, and of forgetting how dead they really are. That we should read about Charles James Fox[,] that we should follow his aspirations, his ups and downs in his career, is a game which we play with ourselves even more extraordinary than any fiction.[1] Because fiction is concerned with what has never existed. But history is concerned with that which is finished and done with. And the most important fact about all the real people whom we

---

1 Charles James Fox (1749–1806), charismatic but unsuccessful Whig politician, an early promoter of parliamentary reform.

read about is the bare reality[,] is death. I marvel at the historic imagination much more than at the novelist's or the poet's fictions.

At present, my life seems to me to be very wasted. This simply means that I am not writing and that I am even beginning to think of my writing as a kind of withered up faculty, a muscle which has become atrophied. This is made worse by the fact that I am perfectly aware that the muscle was never in the first place fully developed. But other things I do than writing, seem to take up a larger and larger place in my life. It is this happening which suddenly makes one feel that one is being reduced to the status of an amateur. Of course, it is rather difficult for very active people however devoted they are to their poetry, to write poetry all their lives, and for that reason their lives get filled up with other things. Writing poetry is to spend three-quarters of one's time in a kind of masterly inactivity. It is this which makes me feel it would be much easier to be a painter or a composer than a poet, because all problems are settled for painters, at all events, because they can paint almost the whole time. The lives I most envy are those of people who have spent all their time doing their best.

* * *

For a good many months now, I have tried to interest myself in a writer left over from the 1930s, called Phil O'Connor.[1] O'Connor is an alcoholic, and probably a lunatic. During the 1930s, he wrote with great rapidity several surrealist poems which are extremely alive and amusing. What interests me about him is that he is, as a matter of fact, very alive, and intensely concerned with living. He also has the kind of moral superiority and contempt for other people which goes with this total concern with living values. However, I have noticed that this kind of contempt for other people often goes with madness. Nevertheless, Phil O'Connor is a real anti-bourgeois, and I think that twenty or thirty years ago people would have tried to take a more sustained interest in him. He wrote an autobiography, part of which we published in *Encounter*, called *Memoirs of a Public Baby*.

---

1 Philip O'Connor (1916–1998), bohemian writer, habitué of London's Fitzrovia, many times married. Spender wrote an introduction for his best-known work, *Memoirs of a Public Baby* (1958) on its republication in 1989 and was generally helpful in O'Connor's erratic career.

This was an extremely lively, perceptive, shrewd, account of his childhood. Unfortunately directly it got beyond his childhood it tailed off into moralizing. Philip O'Connor does not write well. It was rather difficult for me to arrive at this conclusion, as he can write at times brilliantly, and at other times with tremendous concentration and perception. But these qualities simply arise out of the life and out of his personality, without his exercising any kind of literary skill.

Philip realizes that I am a kind of sucker for him, and that we are in some peculiar kind of moral relationship. He probably thinks that I have a vocation to be mad which I have not fulfilled. This gives him a kind of power over me. At the same time, I have never admitted this, and I treat him with great reserve. I play with him my role of being a respectable bourgeois, successful literary figure. I play it rather sardonically. Yet underneath in some way we know one another very well. What we are probably both looking for in one another, in the elaborate kind of moral game we play, is for some real betrayal, something that we can really condemn in the other's character. I am not sure whether I have found this in him, but today I did at all events discover something in which he had gone altogether too far. Miss [Maureen] Kilroe of the Pen Club, came to tell me that O'Connor while getting money from *Encounter* every week was allowing his wife and child to starve almost.[1] He gave them no money at all. Ten minutes after Miss Kilroe had left me the telephone went and it was Philip O'Connor to ask me whether I would send him money per Poste Restante somewhere as he was tramping round. He was worried that he would not be able to get this money on Whit Monday. With a feeling of secret triumph, I put down the receiver. A few minutes later he rang up again and said we had been cut off. This gave me a certain satisfaction, because it showed that his intuition, which is very considerable, had failed. Except that perhaps he did not really believe we had been cut off. I explained to him that I put down the receiver on purpose, because I had just heard he did not help his wife and child, and therefore I did not wish to help him. This was really playing the role of a kind of father figure, or a bourgeois, but with a deep moral

---

1 An extract from *Memoirs of a Public Baby* was published in the July 1955 issue of *Encounter*. O'Connor had not written for *Encounter* since then.

justification which perhaps even had some roots in bohemia. I expect Phil really understands that I was simply exercising my right to be as whimsical as he can be pestering and tiresome. All the same, I don't see how we can go on supporting him indefinitely. But, like a great many other helpless people, he goes on living, and will probably continue to do so for a very long time. The relationship of people who support other people although they consider them to be practically hopeless, is one of conspiracy. In a world in which personal values are disappearing, this kind of conspiracy is disappearing also.

26 May 1956, London

I took the children, Natasha and Granny to Funtington to spend a weekend with the Booths.[1] Myself, I left on Saturday to go to Vienna. The children were wildly excited about the weekend. On Saturday they got up at 6 and came into my room at 7:30 each with a little bouquet of what they said were 'wild' flowers. They put their tent up in the garden. Lizzie kept asking the Booths whether they had any animals.

After breakfast, we took them to Bosham to look at the sea. We stopped at a shop where they wanted to spend their pocket money. ('What do you want to buy?' we asked Lizzie. 'Anything,' she replied.) Matthew got out of the car. Standing in the road, he said in a strained voice, 'Quick. Open the door. My finger is caught in it.'

He was so calm, at first I thought he was pretending. He sat in the back of the car, blood streaming from his finger and tears from his eyes. 'Oh, God, how it hurts. Oh, damn, oh damn, oh damn,' he kept exclaiming. We got him to the District Nurse. She bound it up and said he must go to the hospital. On the way, he started singing hymns to forget the pain. Lizzie was very calm, obviously paying attention to Matthew at some level of her mind, and tactfully serious but getting on with her own interests. I did drawings with her in the garden of the hospital, while Matthew had his hand examined, was given a local anaesthetic, and part of the nail removed and X-rayed. Luckily nothing was broken.

When I got home I discovered another shock for Matthew. His tropical fish were scarcely moving through the water as though it had

---

1 The Charles Booth family had helped bring up Natasha Litvin as a child.

turned to jelly. One angel fish was flattened against the surface, another was only just moving its fins, like a sea anemone's tendrils – where it lay at the bottom of the sand. Erika had accidentally disconnected the electric plant and the water had got cold. Looking at the fish was like looking at Matthew's damaged finger – brought to mind so many past episodes – his dog being run over, his canary being eaten by the cat in front of his eyes.

He was getting on quite bravely with his Latin. He sits on a sofa with me as he does it – having put his arm right round my neck, as a precaution that I won't bark at him.

28 May 1956, London

I had a letter from the solicitors of Peter Watson, asking for the addresses of Cyril [Connolly] and Sonia Orwell. I telephoned the solicitor and this confirmed what I had thought, that Peter has made bequests to Cyril and Sonia, but not to me. The last few months have been my first experience of living in a world in which wills suddenly count, and it is a very strange experience. Peter's is the only one I mind about, and all day I had a quite childish feeling of being very hurt, and feeling left out. This was exaggerated by the impossibility of one's being able to do what a child always can do, namely effect a reconciliation. It was rather like not receiving a letter from Peter and now knowing that I could not ever receive one. I was left feeling that I did not want a bequest at all, but would just like to have a line in his will mentioning my name.

As a matter of fact, here is a very good subject for a short story. The ideas of the dead conducting a kind of campaign through their voices beyond the grave, letters left, remarks in wills, etc. Obviously people have some consciousness of this, when they announce to you that they are going to leave you something, thus preparing a kind of posthumous revenge.

Oddly enough, again we have had this experience lately. For instance, Raymond Chandler was always telling Natasha he was going to leave her money, and Edith Sitwell, looking at her a few days ago, said that she was sure that her (that is, Edith's) jade beads would suit her very well and therefore she, Edith, intended to leave them to Natasha. I have also received two small legacies this year, one from a great aunt whom I scarcely knew, another from Winifred Paine.[1] Both of these were useful, but neither of them meant anything emotionally to me. So here, one has an interesting mixture of things: legacies which are just windfalls, messages or silences from the dead, and promises or threats from the living about the course of action they may or may not adopt when they are dead. All these three situations have arisen in my own experience within a matter of a few days. So here there is quite an amusing and at the same time disturbing idea for a plot.

9 June 1956, London

Auden stayed with us for three days from the end of May till June 2nd. The effects of coming back to England to take up his professorship of poetry at Oxford, is to make him revert to something like his undergraduate style of behaviour.[2] He was entirely absorbed in his hopes and fears about Oxford. His conversation was mostly of the Senior Common Room at Christ Church, the problem caused by his not being allowed as an American citizen to take a job in England, and his financial difficulties. One notices how he becomes completely absorbed in his own preoccupations, and hardly gets outside them. For example, previously when he had been here he has been very nice to the children. This time they might just as well not have been there for all the notice he took of them. When he is nervous like this, conversation consists largely in his waiting for an opening for a lecture on some topic. On the other hand, when he is on a congenial subject, or when he needs some other point of view than his own, he becomes his old self. But one does have to lead him round to things that concern him, or which have been his interest for a long time. He was very helpful about the Profile I wrote about him for the *New Statesman* while at the same time preserving an almost supercilious

---

1 Winifred Paine was the young Spenders' housekeeper after their parents' death in the 1920s. She is depicted as 'Caroline' in *World Within World*, and is the subject of *Miss Pangbourne*, the novel on which Spender was working at the time of his death.

2 Auden was elected Professor of Poetry in 1956 and held the post, which required residence and lectures, for the statutory five years.

attitude about it.[1] This is a little hypocritical, since I am rather sure that he takes a great deal of interest in his publicity and in how he affects other people. To see Auden read something like this Profile or any passage of a book one shows him, is rather disconcerting. It illustrates his manner of taking in everything around. He reads at an enormous pace, grunting from time to time approval or disapproval. He appears to take in from the page the general line of argument, then to glance over it, looking out for points that he agrees with or disagrees with. In this procedure, there seems no room for his taking in any shade or nuance that he has not already expected from the writer, or which he does not regard as challenging to his own ideas.

We gave a dinner party for him at which there were Elizabeth Glenconner, David Jones, Francis Bacon and Sonia Orwell.[2] I forgot that there was also Osbert Sitwell, whose illness is by now so far advanced that it is extremely upsetting. He shakes so much that one cannot avoid noticing it all the time. When Osbert had gone (he left early), Auden remarked that the thing he hoped most for Osbert was that he should die very soon before his illness got worse. This is understandable, yet like a lot of things Auden wishes for other people, it seems a little too sensible and reasonable. There is no gap left in his ideas for the possibility that Osbert may want to go on living under worsening circumstances even. During dinner, Auden annoyed Francis greatly by declaring that Lucian Freud was a crook. 'He just isn't straight about money, and I don't approve of it.' Here again he was right, but his dogmatic manner showed no realization of the feelings of Francis, who happens to be very fond of Lucian. Afterwards, when they had argued about it, he admitted that Lucian was very nice and he liked him very much, etc, but the admission had the same

---

1 Spender published no 'Profile' of Auden in the *New Statesman*, though he did review Auden's *Collected Shorter Poems 1930–1944* for that magazine on 18 March 1950. His reference here is probably to the article 'W. H. Auden and His Poetry', which appeared in the *Atlantic Monthly* in July 1953 (vol. 192, no. 1, pp. 74–9).

2 David Jones (1895–1974), Welsh artist and author of two books that Spender much admired: *In Parenthesis* and *The Anathemata*. Traumatized by his experiences in the trenches in the First World War, Jones turned to mysticism and mythology. Spender owned several of his watercolours and inscriptions. For Francis Bacon, see biographical appendix.

kind of rigid quality of distinctions as the criticism. Francis was utterly repelled by Auden's manner and declared afterwards that he detested his priggishness, that he was sure Auden was extremely ambitious and self-seeking, and that he could not bear him. This may partly be because Francis has an extremely bad record about money matters himself. It was really one of those strangely unsatisfactory controversies between the prigs and the anti-prigs, in which both sides are really in the wrong, one through failure of human sympathy, the other through failure to appreciate moral feelings.

We gave a luncheon for Auden and the Austrian Ambassador and his wife [. . .]¹ Auden and I were due to leave for Oxford after this luncheon. For some reason, he was absolutely determined that we should leave precisely at three. This was quite unnecessary as we did not have to be at Oxford until six. However, at about a quarter to three, he started looking very demonstratively at his watch. At the same time, he took no more interest in the conversation, evidently feeling that as far as he was concerned, the hospitality was at an end. Princess Schwarzenberg said to me: 'I think we shall have to go, as evidently you have to be off.' In her letter afterwards, thanking us, she said something with hardly veiled irony, to the effect that she hoped they had not stayed too long.

Driving to Oxford, Auden was very pleasant again. He told me he loved driving, but it also made him very irritable, as he secretly felt that when he drove the roads ought to be cleared of all other traffic. He said that he associated driving in a car with being an engine driver, so he passionately wanted to have a completely clear run from start to finish. We talked about Christopher Isherwood. I asked him whether he thought that Christopher had any sense of having failed in his vocation as a writer, or any bad conscience about having abandoned it. We speculated then how Christopher would answer such a question. He would say that of course it was exactly the question that troubled him most, that he never thought of anything else, that he lay awake at night aware that he was wasting his talents, etc, etc. But at the end of all these explanations, one would feel that he had somehow evaded the question. Auden said: 'After all, perhaps the

1 The Austrian ambassador was Johannes von Schwarzenberg. In October 1957, Auden bought a house at Kirchstetten, Austria.

truth of the matter is that what Christopher likes is lying in the sun in California and being surrounded by boys who are also lying in the sun. Maybe this is all he really wants from life.' He said he had never known anyone who had less grown out of his past interests than Christopher. He said that Christopher often hurt his older friends deeply by his lack of interest and his neglect of them.

When we got to Oxford, Auden seemed quite unwilling that I should leave him, and was anxious that we should breakfast together the next morning. This we did. He has a room in Christ Church, belonging to an elderly Don, whose walls are covered with photographs and reproductions of the world's masterpieces: the Parthenon, the Venus of Milo, Renaissance pictures, and so on. The rooms are very depressing. I think that Auden has a hard time in the Common Room at Christ Church, where several of the dons twit him about America, and where he is half-fascinated, half-bored by the endlessly cliquey Oxford donnish conversation. He was due to have dinner that night with Sir Maurice Bowra, who was the chief supporter of his opponent, Harold Nicolson, for the poetry Chair. Maurice, as it turned out, did not give a party for him but simply invited him to the High Table. This seems to me a rather studied insult.

I was at Oxford because I had undertaken to speak to the Spanish Club. They had persuaded me that I had something interesting about Spain to say to them, but an hour before speaking I remembered that my impressions of Spain from over twenty years ago were extremely vague. I thought that I would be able to speak about the Spanish Civil War, however. This hope was somewhat damped by having dinner with the Secretary of the Club, and a girl: I forget both their names. The Secretary explained to me that most of the officers of the Club were supporters of General Franco. After all these years, this confession still has the power to bore and disgust me. The Secretary had a conventional fascist-type face: a thin nose, a lip that seemed waiting for a small bristly moustache, a small mouth, and ears protruding from each side of his head like the handles of a Woolworth china cup. The girl was very pretty in a Germanic way. Dinner was a tiresome business, as I found it very difficult to make conversation, and these two officers of the Society also had little enough to say. In my speech, I explained that I only knew the Spanish Republican part of Spain from the time when this was a geographical unit. I talked about the Spanish poets I had met, and about translating Lorca. In fact, the talk went rather well. When I had finished, a Spanish don from Queens College called, I think, Mr Chaplin or Chapman, got up and said that if I assumed that all the members of the society were pro-Franco, I was wrong. Most of the members of the Society were agreed with the views of Spain that I had expressed. This was very nice. [. . .]

I went from Monday till Friday to Rome for a meeting of editors. Mel Lasky, François Bondy and Irving Kristol were present, to meet Nicola Chiaromonte and [Ignazio] Silone.[1] Chiaromonte and Silone were not altogether pleased with the meeting, as they have only just started their Italian magazine, *Tempo Presente*, and they thought that we were coming to criticize them and not leave them alone. We had however some quite useful discussions. We decided to have articles about 'Tourism', television all over the world, and events in Budapest, Prague and Warsaw, since the death of Stalin. Mel Lasky also made a very useful suggestion about a survey of the situation of publishing and writing in different countries. We shall be able to commission these articles for four magazines at once, and thus pay writers much better than they would be paid for a single article. I went twice to lunch with the Robertses [Laurence and Isabel] at the American Academy. On Friday evening, *Tempo Presente* gave a large cocktail party for us, and after that we went to dinner with Luigi Barzini. One of the things that annoyed Chiaromonte and Silone was the enthusiasm of Irving and Mel and François for Barzini, whom they regard as a hack journalist.[2]

On Wednesday evening I went to a party with Jenny Nicholson

---

1 Nicola Chiaromonte (1905–1972), anti-Fascist Italian intellectual who fought in Malraux's air squadron during the Spanish Civil War. In New York after 1941, he wrote for *The Nation* and *Partisan Review* and became a close friend of Mary McCarthy. Like Silone, he was attempting to find a position independent from the Christian Democrats and the Italian communists. For *Tempo Presente* see note 2, p. 69.

2 Luigi Barzini (1908–1974), Italian journalist with a good understanding of America. *The Italians* (1964), written for an American audience, was influential at the time. Chiaromonte and Silone, in their desire for independence, had no wish to appear as spokesmen for the United States.

(whose married name is now Cross). Iris Tree was there.[1] She was very drunk and talked a great deal about Christopher Isherwood. She said that he was now completely absorbed in his friend Don [Bachardy], and that Don although devoted to him obviously wanted more freedom. For this reason, she felt it was impossible for Christopher to do any serious work. She thought that Christopher had made a kind of life which was exciting and perhaps even beautiful up till the age of thirty-five, but that after this age, it became fruitless and tragic.

I saw Mary McCarthy several times in Rome. She had a nice idea that the story of Irving editing *Encounter* with me was like Henry James's novel *The Ambassadors*. Irving was Strether, the hero, who is sent by interested people in America to save Chad, the young man, from ruin in Europe. We embroidered this a good deal.[2] I noticed that Irving in conversation with other Americans talks almost as if he is British. He had a violent argument with Chiaromonte in which he defended the British position in Cyprus.[3] Just as Irving and I were leaving from the B.E.A. office in Rome, an Italian came up to us and tried to sell us some cameos. Irving said: 'Why do you come to the British? The British are poor. You should try the Americans at T.W.A.'[4]

At first I was rather disgusted at the idea of coming to Rome and having to attend committee meetings. But somehow the impression of Rome permeated through the routine of meetings. One cannot take the smallest walk or taxi ride across the city without coming to something – a church, a fountain, statues – which seem pivots on

---

1 Jenny Cross (1919–1964), daughter of poet Robert Graves and his wife Nancy Nicholson. Iris Tree (1897–1968), actress, poet and bohemian, daughter of the actor-manager Herbert Beerbohm Tree, mother of Ivan Moffat.

2 The plot of Henry James's *The Ambassadors* (1903) centres around the trip to Europe of the protagonist, Lewis Lambert Strether, who goes in search of Chad, his widowed fiancée's wayward son. During his time with Chad in Paris, Strether falls in love with the city and with Marie De Vionnet, a friend of Chad's who is estranged from her unpleasant husband. Strether's fiancée, impatient for the return of both Strether and her son, sends forth new 'ambassadors' to bring the pair home.

3 The Greek-Cypriot Enosis movement and its military arm EOKA fought against the British Protectorate in order to gain union with Greece. The war dragged on until 1960, when the island achieved independence.

4 BEA, British European Airways; TWA, Trans World Airlines.

which the whole of Rome turns. It is perhaps the Piranesi engravings which make me feel that every monument in Rome is one picture in a unique gallery, which reflects and includes all the other pictures.[1] I have only visited Rome for a very few days at a time, and only a few times, across a number of years, but unlike other places, one does not forget it. One takes up each visit, across years perhaps, at exactly the point where one left off the last, and gradually constructs a complete picture of Rome in one's own mind. [. . .]

Irving had bad hay fever most of the time and, although his natural amiability always charms me, his efforts to get over this by drinking a great deal at the Barzinis and again one evening when we were out with Mary McCarthy, were rather tiresome. Suddenly at a certain moment, he begins to look like a little fat parakeet, he gesticulates a great deal with his hands in a manner which I imagine him to think is continental, his eyes start bulging out, and he talks in a loud aggressive voice. He also has the air of one who imagines that he wins all hearts. Some people in conversation give away the fact that they think they can get away with saying or doing anything, and one sees that they believe themselves to be in the minds of others so spontaneous and natural that everything is forgivable in the light of their bare charms. However, with Irving I only felt that he was irritating as I must also be irritating – the kind of annoyance one feels when one sees people behaving humanly, with a humanity that one also feels oneself to have.

16 June 1956, London

My interest in different views of different people about one person – for example, Auden to Stuart Hampshire or Lucian Freud – comes from my not believing anyone ever understands the real person. All each sees is facets. The different views project transverse lines at right angles from the planes, which might reach the centre.

Behind every explanation of a person's conduct there is always a 'Why?' Behind the fact that Auden sees everything in categories is a reason that lies at the centre of his invisible existence.

---

1 Giovanni Battista Piranesi (1720–1778), Italian architect and artist, most famous for his intricate engravings of Roman ruins.

I myself often behave weakly. But I am weak because I am not strong. And I am not strong because there is a reason for avoiding strength. Therefore anyone who described me in terms of examples of weakness of behaviour would produce a convincing portrait but he would leave out the essential fact that I might have been strong and might therefore have acted in a dozen ways different from the particular ones held to be characteristic of me.

When a novelist gives an extraordinarily exact portrayal of the external behaviour of a person whom one happens to know – like Angus Wilson's portrayal of Sonia – I feel that he sees Sonia as the role she has cast for herself, or which has been cast for her by her conditions.[1] Real curiosity about life always leads to a sense of mystery. Sometimes I doubt even whether any such thing as character exists. Everyone is, as it were, amorphous potentiality that chooses at different moments to assume such or such a form. Every time a miser is mean he knows that he is choosing to be mean. He also knows that he could be generous, or he knows that this person [who] would be generous can only choose to be mean. There is in his circumstances and in his conditioning something that perhaps makes it impossible for him in fact to stop being mean. Nevertheless, he is perfectly aware of a choice to be what he is, and the consciousness which is aware of choosing is the real miser. This is something that a writer like Angus fails to see.

12 July 1956, London

Went yesterday to Oxford, at the invitation of a club called the Mermaid Club. The guests were Auden and myself and our hosts were six or eight undergraduates. We first of all had drinks at New College in the rooms of an undergraduate who had also invited Jean Cocteau who was coming to Oxford to get his degree.[2] We then went to a cellar-like room in Christ Church, where we dined. The dinner was

---

1 The novelist Angus Wilson (1913–1991) was supposed to have depicted Sonia Orwell as 'Elvira Portway' in his 1956 novel *Anglo-Saxon Attitudes*.

2 Jean Cocteau (1889–1963), French poet, painter, designer, filmmaker and boxing manager. On 12 June 1956 he was made Doctor Honoris Causa of Oxford University.

rather late, and Auden as usual complained rather bitterly that he was getting hungry. I sat next to a tiresomely effeminate young undergraduate who wore a cloak lined with red satin and carried a cane, and who talked in a somewhat camp way about his fiancée. There was a young Welsh instructor called Jimmie Thore who made a set first at Auden and afterwards at me in a very intense Welsh kind of way. The effeminate undergraduate, who talked as though he had modelled himself on Shakespeare's Osric [in *Hamlet*], said in a weary voice that the trouble about Jimmie Thore was that he was always intelligent. Auden observed dryly that if this were so it would not be a fault. Thore was not intelligent, and he was not stupid either; he merely tried to involve one in himself. One or two of the other undergraduates seemed much nicer than these two. We drank a good deal and, adjourning afterwards to one of the undergraduates' rooms in the houses, the evening got noisier and noisier. At dinner, Auden was complaining about the extremely officious way the British Authorities behaved to him with regard to his having permission to do work here. He talked in his usual categorical way, which is sometimes agreeable, sometimes illuminating, sometimes brilliant, sometimes funny, sometimes irritating or even disagreeable. We talked about the question of whether or not, morally-speaking, Dylan Thomas had committed suicide, Auden saying that he had done so. He then made the curious assertion that he had been able to tell exactly which of his preparatory school pupils would be killed in the war.[1] He even went so far as to say that in the case of two sets of twins, he knew which twin of each set was doomed to die. Another odd thing he said was that Americans in their approach to biography demanded, and were right to demand, to know exactly what happened to people. As Auden hates people to write about his life, I found this puzzling. He said the English pretend everything happened in a mist.

Before going to Oxford, I had lunch with Dom Moraes, who was shy, concerned with whether or not I liked his poetry or thought he was a good poet, and as preoccupied with his own problems as ever. His mother has been released from an asylum and his father wants him to return to India. Myself I think this would be a mistake, but as

---

1 In the 1930s Auden taught English at two boys' preparatory schools: Helensburgh from 1930 to 1932 and the Downs School from 1932 to 1935.

I do not know the circumstances, I was extremely reluctant to tell him what I thought, very anxious as he was to have my opinion. While we were lunching, Lucian Freud arrived in the restaurant, The Perroquet, with his friend Charlie. They were both dressed like workmen, Charlie almost in rags, without neckties. The restaurant was appropriately shocked. Waiters served us trying not to look at our two guests. I thought this is part of the war of the bohemians against the bureaucrats. Lucian is trying to demonstrate that I, in my dark suit, am a bureaucrat. However, he was very amiable and gave me an article by Augustus John to publish in *Encounter*. He spoke unhappily about Auden, said Auden did not approve of him, but was in no position to judge about his affairs, that he does not want to have to justify himself to him. He told me that Auden complained about him, Lucian, now, but that after the war when he came back to London he had complained always to Lucian about me, and had said there was no one in England he wished to see except Lucian. Lucian told me a long involved story about how Lincoln Kirstein commissioned a portrait from Lucian, which Lucian had half finished, and Lincoln had half paid for.[1] After this, Lucian had a breakdown. In the course of the next year, Lucian wrote to him several times, asking him what he should do with the portrait. As he received no reply from Lincoln, finally Lucian sold it. Obviously he felt uneasy about this, but was also convinced that, as Lincoln had expressed extreme dislike of the portrait, he was not interested in having it. Lucian regarded the small payment he had already received as compensation for his loss of time and he imagined Lincoln thought this also. It may well be that Auden knows this story and has formed his own judgement of it. [. . .]

Dreamed all night about Peter [Watson]: conscious of wanting to go on dreaming in order to have more time with him. Part of the dream was being in his flat. He said he had wanted to give me something, and he gave me what was an oil painting by Jean Cocteau. The painting was inscribed by Jean to Peter and it bore a quotation from Keats. In the dream, I remember thinking that Jean did not paint oil

---

1 Lincoln Kirstein (1907–1996), impresario. While still at Harvard, Kirstein edited *Hound and Horn*, a literary magazine to which Spender contributed articles. He went on to found the New York City Ballet. He was also a patron of the arts, promoting the work of the painter Paul Cadmus (1904–1999), who was his brother-in-law, and the sculptor Elie Nadelman (1882–1946).

paintings, and also the quotation from Keats showed a French lack of understanding of Keats.

How everything connects! On Sunday on the *Brains Trust* programme of the TV there had been a discussion of Keats' lines: 'Beauty is truth, truth beauty.' Yesterday, George Harris came into my office and said, 'Peter, I just can't get over Peter.' Harris is the little man who goes from stall to stall promoting the sales of *Encounter*. We had him for *Horizon* and he became part of the life there. Harris told me Peter had invited him only a day before he read about his death, up to his flat to hear his new gramophone. No one except Peter, or at any rate no one else, would have dreamed of inviting Harris to his home. How discomfiting the memory of Peter is, something like a reproach. Partly, no doubt, because he was like that: quite un-snobbish, completely generous, quite unvulgar.

July 1956, Bologna

Here are some notes that I should have written in London. [. . .]

I talked at a branch of London University called Queen Mary's College in the East End. The discussion that followed afterwards was mainly around one thing: which is more beautiful – a statue of Michelangelo or an aeroplane? Hence, of course – is our civilization more or less creative than theirs?

I was amazed how many of them seemed to think a jet bomber quite as beautiful as a cathedral. They were obviously unimpressed by arguments that machinery does not last, is as subject to changes of fashion as women's hats. The argument that modern industrialism produces a hideous environment did not interest them either. Someone advanced the view that what has been done in the past has been done and we should not judge our own achievement or even our existence by the past at all.

* * *

Edward Upward wrote me a letter saying he now realized he had been wrong and I right about Russia.[1] He said he hoped in future to be a rationalist and not believe in anything. My first reaction was

---

1 For Edward Upward, see biographical appendix.

surprise that he had ever believed in the Moscow Trials, etc.[1] I thought he had some complex almost metaphysical reason for his Communism. Already, one forgets that many people did believe in Stalin's propaganda.

We say now they were dupes, but dupe is a comparative term. In public matters, subject to emotion fortified by propaganda, we are all dupes – dupes and counter-dupes. The dupes believed Stalin, the counter-dupes believe Khrushchev.

A measure of dupery is provided by the subject of German atrocities. In 1914, thousands of people believed in German atrocities in the First World War. By 1920 many of the same people believed that German atrocities were propaganda. They became counter-dupes and believed there had been no German atrocities. In 1933, with Hitler in power, it became credible again that Germans could commit atrocities. At the same time, it was not until the occupation of Buchenwald and Belsen, that anything was proved.

The point is that most of us cannot and do not *know* what goes on in British colonies, Nazi Germany, Stalinist Russia. All we can do is read what is put before us and then judge as best we can. But to the non-expert his judgement is a matter of belief – belief tempered perhaps by common sense. One should not blame people for being dupes or for ignorance; one should perhaps blame them for lack of common sense.

Where there is much propaganda, however, it is very difficult to judge. Where there is propaganda and counter-propaganda there is the devil. And one might say that in the game of propaganda, the winning card is the adroit use of counter-counter-propaganda.

'Sincere' communists who believed in Stalin were not, I think convinced by the direct propaganda of the Comintern or Cominform. What really convinced them was the argument that everything said in the Capitalist press or by anyone with a foot in the Capitalist camp was 'objectively' bound to denigrate and lie about the Soviet Union.

---

1 The Moscow Trials were a series of trials conducted between August 1936 and March 1938. Stalin instigated the trials as part of his Great Purge to rid the Soviet Communist Party of dissidents, but most of the evidence against defendants was fabricated and the verdicts predetermined. For most British intellectuals, including Spender, the trials undermined Stalin's credibility, but some such as Upward continued to defend the Soviet regime.

Since this includes everyone not a communist, then the communist became the only source of truth. The most powerful argument in the Soviet armoury was then counter-counter-propaganda.

In July 1956, Spender went to Bologna for a meeting of the European Cultural Association.

July 1956, Bologna

[Giorgio] Morandi – his look of a Roman senator. White curls round his gaunt head, tall and holding himself straight, as if by a certain effort, a grave yet smiling manner – the courtesy of painters. A bit like Jamini Roy, Jack Yeats, Paul Klee.[1]

'Shall we talk here or shall I take you to my studio and show you the few things – the very, very few – that I have in my studio?'

His reception room simply that of a family who have lived like this a hundred years. I think how impossible it is for an American – perhaps even for an English – painter to live like this, in transmitted surroundings.

We go along a passage through a bedroom in which there are, wide apart, two iron beds, covered with white bedspreads. On the walls large Victorian engravings of holy subjects, one or two tiny paintings by Morandi himself, in an earlier manner.

We go through to the studio, which is an ordinary room, bare of furniture except for a divan and a chair, with a long tall window opening onto a view of the backs of brown-coloured houses which are partly blocked out by the luxuriant green of trees with foliage like rockets at the end of a garden.

In the centre of the studio, an easel. The rack was thickly covered with a heap of what looked like petrified dust – really, I suppose, paint mixed with dust or sand. Round the room, various Still Lifes were arranged – one on a flat table, another on what looked like a revolving table, a stage set on a miniature cyclorama. These exhibits had the air of having been there, in exactly the same position, for

---

1 Jamini Roy (1887–1972), Bengali painter based in Calcutta, whom Spender had visited during his 1955 trip to India.

years. The tops of bottles and objects like cans were covered with that dust which was perhaps deliberate, 'part of the picture'.

There were three such arranged Still Lifes. One with cubes like a child's blocks which had been painted, yellow, grey, salmon pink, for the purpose of painting them in the picture. Under the tables there were innumerable objects – jugs, jars, cans, bottles, tins, canisters – some of them painted white, all of them covered with dust. One jug – of the kind used to fill a washbasin – was filled with dust right up to the brim.

On the walls, about half a dozen paintings of the still life with coloured cubes. The one on the table in front of the easel. This was exceptional for Morandi because it contained a bottle with a convoluted embossed pattern. The last painting was of the curious arrangements of objects on the round table – a flat, round tin, like a biscuit tin, two or three objects like canisters, above the oval top of the tin (seen sideways), a bottle like a watch-tower.

What surprised me was the extreme exactitude of the paintings. The one of the objects on the oblong table was exactly the same proportions on the canvas. The shadows were painted with particular care. Evidently, the foundation of the picture is very exactly laid down for Morandi by the arrangements of objects. He will even paint the objects on the table before painting the picture. His painting is a profound analysis of a prepared experiment with real objects.

Alfredo Rizzardi, who had taken me to see Morandi, said that he prepared all his own painting materials, was particularly concerned with ways of priming canvases, and that he scarcely ever repainted.[1] If he made a mistake or produced an effect that dissatisfied him, he took a new canvas and started a new picture, simply.

I told Morandi that sometimes his Still Lifes seemed to me to resemble landscapes, villages in which objects were walls and towers. He seemed pleased at this idea and said he thought the reason lay in the construction of his pictures, which was architectural.

Of the picture of the round tin and the tower-like bottle rising above its circular lid, he said he did not see how it was going to develop. I asked him what were the problems. He said there weren't

---

1 Alfredo Rizzardi, Professor of American Literature at the University of Bologna, later a translator of Spender's poetry.

problems – everything in painting was a matter of space and light. By this I took him to mean that difficulties were resolved within the relations of the objects themselves, and he discovered the development of the picture through study of these relations.

He was very interested in a brochure advertising a new type of white paint, sent him from America. He got Rizzardi to translate this for him. 'This paint contains a considerable quantity of white lead, but the colour has exceptionable durability.' 'Ah, white lead goes black.' He was sceptical about the claim that any mixture containing white lead would not blacken.

'Ah this time, this time,' he said. He thought that in the past art had had a certain kind of social efficacity [*sic*], but now perhaps if it had a social task, this was different. Obviously he had no sympathy with social realism and spoke of Guttuso as a young painter who had once had talent.[1] For his own part, he did not have a very great productivity – but Vermeer – we only knew for certain of perhaps 36 Vermeers, add to them twice as many lost and we still only have a hundred odd of paintings.

When I looked out of the window again at his garden, I saw that a strange thing had happened. The constructions, the insights of light and shadow in his very quiet still lives had imposed themselves – I saw the simplified forms of houses and trees, shadows were like lines that underlined.

July 1956, Bologna

The meeting of the executive of the European Cultural Association was held in the Centro Commerciale at Bologna, in a kind of court room. M. Babel from Geneva and [Umberto] Campagnolo sat on a magisterial bench, the rest of them sat in rows in the body of the court opposite.[2] The room was fake Gothic. Its acoustics were so bad it was almost impossible to hear anything said from the bench. In

---

1 Renato Guttuso (1911–1987), Italian painter whose early work showed strong social commitment. Although he started his career with the support of the Fascist Party, after the war he became the semi-official artist of the Italian Communist Party.

2 Antony Babel (1888–1979), Swiss historian.

two days I only heard one remark of Campagnolo. Maurice Cranston had complained he was illogical about something.[1] Campagnolo retorted: 'You have your logic, I have mine.'

Campagnolo hates anyone to make distinctions of any kind, adores terms like 'universalisme de culture', hates art and artists, detests people who make distinctions between one idea and another.

Mayou, who is *communisant* [a communist sympathizer], made a long and curious speech.[2] He said that he and a group of his friends (among them, Claude Roy and Amrouche) were making a study of relations between Asia and the West.[3] Their thought was that the Westerners had won a great victory through being driven out of Asia. So long as we were occupiers we were detested. But now that we had left and come back, on equal terms, as cultural emissaries, etc, we were welcomed everywhere. It was possible for there to be a meeting on the basis of 'the universalism of culture'.

I got up and pointed out that to talk of a 'victory' was absurd if meant literally, and if intended in any other way, was simply a reversion to some idea of winning the East through culture as the East Indian Company had won it through commerce. I said that I thought universalism of culture a dangerous phrase, if not meaningless. The fact is that our culture is different from theirs, and since every contemporary idea is imported into their tradition from the West, it is extremely dangerous to them. They were also in some ways a danger to us. Each side ought to realize that it had values to defend, and meet perhaps with the idea of exchanging ideas, but not with any ideas about universalism or victories.

---

1 Maurice Cranston (1920–1993), British political philosopher, at this date a Professor at the London School of Economics.

2 Mayou remains to be identified. It could be a *nom de guerre.*

3 Claude Roy (1915–1997), French writer. Associated with the extreme right before the war, Roy subsequently joined the resistance and became a communist. Active as a commentator, poet and novelist, he broke with the French Communist Party after the invasion of Hungary in 1956. Jean Amrouche (1906–1962), French Algerian poet and director of radio programmes, mainly with Radio France Paris, where he interviewed many leading French intellectuals.

19 July 1956, London

I returned on July 9th to London, as I had to take part in the PEN Club Conference this week. Our activities were partly to organize a poetry reading conducted at the I.M.A. by the MacNeices, Hedli and Louis, Laurie Lee and myself.¹ This went off quite well. [. . .]

On Wednesday evening I went to dinner at Claridges with Jack Beddington, who had invited various guests chiefly with the idea that they should become interested in *Encounter*.² It was an exceedingly good meal, and Jack was an excellent host. Apart from Bill Coldstream, Michael Ayrton, and Christiansen, the editor of the *Daily Express*, I am a bit vague about who was there.³ In fact I wrote to Jack today to ask him to send me a list of the other guests. One of them, however, appeared to be the head of Shell Mex. Knowing that Michael Ayrton is a great enemy of *Encounter*, I tried to buy him off by telling him the moment I arrived that I liked very much a piece of sculpture by him which I had seen in the Leicester Galleries. He was quite pleased and I then got him on to various subjects that we could more or less agree about, such as the painting of Wyndham Lewis exhibited at the Tate Gallery. However, at a certain point in the meal he started telling me how much he had disliked the first number of *Encounter*, and saying that he had scarcely ready a copy since then, though he did occasionally pick one up. I found it impossible not to adopt a sarcastic tone with him, telling him it was very kind of him to have read *Encounter* at all. The dispute was stopped by guests changing places at the table. After the brandy, Michael Ayrton apologized for having been hostile to me, and I said that I had to admit that if there was an objective observer he would probably say that I had been just as hostile. However, I did not find that I could feel at all warmly to Michael. He seems to me quite clever, extremely

---

1 Louis MacNeice had married the singer Hedli Anderson in 1942.

2 Jack Beddington (1893–1959), businessman (a director of Shell Mex), patron of the arts and friend of John Betjeman.

3 William Coldstream (1907–1987), painter and founder of the Euston Road School of Art, where Spender once studied. At this date, head of the Slade School of Art. Michael Ayrton (1921–1975), artist and novelist. Arthur Christiansen (1904–1963), editor of the *Daily Express* since 1936.

competent, but somehow coarse-grained and obtuse in everything. One thing he said was that all political issues today were as simple as they had been in 1930. One would either have to be extremely perceptive and analytic to say this, or else extremely stupid. Politically speaking, Michael Ayrton is simply a reader of newspapers, some of which he likes, others which he dislikes. He sides with *Tribune* and gives himself credit for doing so.[1] The thing that really annoyed me was his saying that the Spanish war was a perfectly simple affair despite the reporting by someone whom he called 'Gloomy George'. I said angrily that George Orwell was able to judge matters by the standards of his own life which in politics were as exacting as those of a saint, and I did not see that Michael Ayrton showed in his life any observation or practice of any standards of a kind that would justify him to criticize Orwell.

At about 2 a.m., Christiansen, Michael Ayrton, Beddington and I adjourned to Jack's offices in Brooke Street. I had drunk very little, as I am extremely careful about drinking when I have to drive. But I thought I should stay as the party was being given for me. Ayrton now told Christiansen that the *Daily Express* was an altogether disgusting and filthy paper from beginning to end. He said this was his opinion and, if called upon to do so, he would substantiate it: however he thought it would be boring for the company if he did so there and then, and accordingly he would be willing to invite Christiansen to luncheon any day of the following week should Christiansen wish to know why the *Daily Express* was despised by Michael Ayrton. Part of the stupidity of Michael Ayrton was that he did not realize how incensed Christiansen was by this kind of boorishness. For a moment, Christiansen did lose his temper, but immediately controlled himself. I said that I could not agree with Ayrton, although as a matter of fact I did have a genuine grievance against the *Daily Express*. I told Christiansen how a *Daily Express* correspondent had extracted from me a letter from John Lehmann about Burgess, at the time of the Burgess–MacLean scandal, and had printed a Photostat picture of this letter. Jack said: 'I see, Stephen, that you are still as sensitive as you always have been.' Christiansen said: 'No, as a

---

1 The *Tribune* was the official newspaper of the British Labour Party.

matter of fact he is quite right. We behaved quite improperly about this, and I would like to apologize.'¹

I liked Christiansen, though I suppose that ultimately I would agree with Ayrton's view of the *Daily Express*. On the other hand, Ayrton's extreme self-righteousness, with that kind of self-assured attack on anything which he considers a bad cause in the name of a good one, repels me today. He kept on dragging public issues into a personal meeting, or a meeting of persons, and bludgeoning the persons with them. What I really felt was that if the *Daily Express* was going to be criticized it should be done as between persons; to treat Christiansen simply as if he were the *Daily Express*, was offensive, unjustified, and uncharitable. In fact, Ayrton did his best to ruin the evening.

In August 1956, the Spenders went to Le Zoute, Belgium, and then to Gstaad, Switzerland, as the guests of Hansi Lambert.

14 August 1956, Gstaad, Switzerland

We spent a very pleasant week at Zoute in the house on the disused golf links, with the sea beyond the dunes. [. . .]

Nicolas Nabokov (who came for two days) and I went over to Rotterdam to see the Rembrandt exhibition. No other exhibition of an 'old master' has ever seemed to me to throw such a critical light on modern painting. Just to go from this exhibition to the other rooms in the Boymans Museum, where there are impressionist and more recent paintings is to receive a shock. Suddenly these seem thin, light, empty. Even Courbet seems pale.

No Exhibition of an Italian master would produce the same disconcerting effect. I can only think it is because Rembrandt has some of the problems which are peculiarly modern, and answers them in a

---

1 On 15 June, Spender had innocently shown *Express* reporter Owen Seaman a letter from John Lehmann, where Lehmann warned his friend that he should stop defending Guy Burgess's good name, as he had recently learnt that he was in fact a spy. Spender hoped to demonstrate his own ignorance of Burgess's activities and Seaman asked to show the letter to his editor, promising that he would return it. But much to the chagrin of both Spender and Lehmann himself, the *Express* printed Lehmann's letter the following day.

way which makes later attempts seem scattered and evasive – gestures, expressions, flights, virtuosities, instead of penetrations of a centre.

Rembrandt's self-portraits are like a steel thread driving through all his other work. They portray a figure that might well be likened to a ship. In the earliest portraits it is a figure in full sail, pennons flying, triumphantly scudding through sunlit, choppy waters, acclaiming the toast of the voyage to happiness. At the end, the ship is a hulk, with the noble battered look of awaiting the breakers.

Meanwhile the paint has got thicker, not just opaquely, but transparently thick, as though the layers of colour provided a chord whose lowest note touches the canvas itself. What does one look through to in the last self-portrait in the National Gallery, where Rembrandt looking out of the canvas seems to be slowly moving forward towards the spectator? If one could see an exhibition consisting entirely of Rembrandt self-portraits, one would have, I think, a sense of superimposition, as though the increasing thickness of the paint in the later work was caused by the painting of the older painter over successive layers ever younger Rembrandts.

And of course, the density of the superimposed layers of paint in those pictures which are not self-portraits, has the same preoccupation with his own identity. In some works the painting of the subject itself is not nearly as moving as the painting of some part of the work which is not the face of the sitter. (For this reason, reproductions always do Rembrandt a disservice, since they inevitable concentrate on the subject and not on the actual paint.) In the portrait of Titus seated at his desk, more impressive than the face of the boy (which, in photographs looks a bit like a Greuze) is the density, colour and brush strokes of the wooden front of the desk. In the wonderful family group at Brunswick it is in the texture of the mother's and child's skirts that is as moving as the painting of the skin in Rembrandt's own late self-portraits.

Why then, after the Rembrandt exhibition, if one wanders through the galleries of modern painting, does so much of what one sees seem superficial? The reason I think is that Rembrandt's preoccupation in his painting was the search for his own image or identity towards which his religion was an aid. The impression made by the exhibition is that he solved his problems, which are those that are still with us, by this single-minded pursuit of his own identity. That is why this exhibition makes later painting seem specialized (the Impressionists) or centrifugal (Picasso). Cézanne seems the one great modern example of singleness of purpose. And remembering Rembrandt's self-portrait one sees Cézanne's images of himself looking through the transparency of his landscapes.

Of course, this is only a mood, and very soon the relations which catch one in the net of Impressionism re-establish themselves, and one is involved again in the inventions and discoveries of modern art.

20 August 1956, Gstaad, Switzerland

Cyril [Connolly] in very good form. He was very funny last night describing Sonia Orwell to the Lamberts. He said that Sonia's affair with Merleau-Ponty was based on a complete misunderstanding. It took place at a time when Madame M.-P. was having an affair with Raymond Queneau.[1] Sonia therefore thought that she would be the philosophical companion of M.-P. who could understand why M.-P. objected to Sartre saying that while being a non-Communist, he was still more anti-bourgeois than anti-Communist, etc, etc. She looked forward to all this hair splitting and was surprised when M.-P. showed no interest in her philosophical ideas. To him she was simply 'ma belle anglaise' ['my beautiful Englishwoman'] – a role she did not comprehend at all. To her amazement, Merleau-Ponty being free of his wife, instead of marrying Sonia, announced that he must go away and live with his mother.

He said Sonia was a girl married to her telephone.

In November 1956, Britain was embroiled in the Suez Canal Crisis, which came to signal the decline of Britain's role as a world power. The Suez Canal had historically provided a vital trading route for Mediterranean powers to the Red Sea, Africa and Asia. By 1955, approximately two thirds of Europe's oil trade was carried along this route. In 1956, Gamal Abdel Nasser, Egypt's president, nationalized the canal, prompting the invasion of Egypt by British and French troops. On 31 October, British troops bombed Cairo and Cairo

---

1 Raymond Queneau (1903–1976), French poet and novelist.

International Airport; by 7 November, the British and French claimed to have occupied most of the canal as far as Ismailia. The international intervention of the United Nations called a halt to this invasion, with the first UN troops landing on 21 November at Port Said. By Christmas 1956, British and French troops had withdrawn from the area. The fiasco would contribute to Anthony Eden's resignation as Prime Minister on 10 January 1957.

14 November 1956, New York

Two days ago, at Princeton, I saw George Kennan. He entertained the Buttingers and myself at his pleasant, frame-built house.[1] With his very bright eyes, blue in slits, he looks like some very tall fair oriental, who has learned philosophy and football in America. He carried on with our conversation broken off in Milan over a year ago. He spoke in that manner where bitterness seems to contradict a faith that shines through his expression. He was extremely disappointed and disgusted even by the election of Eisenhower [in 1953]. He said he felt that now it was time for people like himself to step off. [. . .] Kennan said that when he turned on the television, and saw the American delegation being supported by all the riff-raff of the Middle East in its denunciation of British policy [in the Suez crisis], he felt that this was where he got off. People like himself no longer had anything to say in American affairs. He recalled how, at Milan, he had felt that if Asians regarded the West as to blame for everything, then it would be best for us to have nothing to do with them. His own impression was that during the past few years, the West had been more abused and perhaps ill-treated by the East, than the other way round. Jo Buttinger mentioned Africa and Kennan said: 'There's only one solution for Africa. That is for all the white settlers to be removed. This would be a major operation, involving shifting about two million people, but if we in this country had the will and the good sense, we could do it.'

The day before this, with the Buttingers, I went to lunch with

---

1 For Muriel Gardiner and her husband Joseph Buttinger, see biographical appendix.

Robert Oppenheimer.[1] Oppenheimer lives in a very beautiful house, the interior of which is painted almost entirely white, where he has beautiful paintings. As soon as we came in, he said: 'Now is the time to look at the Van Gogh.' We went into his sitting room and looked at a very fine Van Gogh of a sun above a field, which is almost entirely enclosed in olive shadow.

Oppenheimer himself is one of the most extraordinary looking men I have ever seen. He has a head like that of a very small intelligent boy, with a long back to it, reminding one perhaps of those skulls which were specially elongated by the Egyptians. His skull gives a peculiar impression of fragility, and is supported by a very thin neck. His expression is bright and ascetic. Natasha, who was there with us, said that he gave a great impression of moderation combined with steady, strong feeling. He told us his wife was ill upstairs and added: 'Who could be well this week anyway?' Unlike Kennan, he did not approve the English action, but he regarded it as a mistake rather than detestable. He said: 'For someone who is writing an essay on "The Future Force" his ideas have undergone a lot of alteration in the past week.' We talked about Nehru's reluctance to comment on the Hungarian situation. I remarked that Nehru was extremely vain, and that one had more confidence in his sister and his daughter than in his own judgment. Oppenheimer agreed about the women surrounding Nehru, but not quite about the vanity. He said: 'Perhaps he is not so much vain as something deeper and worse. At the end, what he may be judged for is not vanity but pride, which is something much more serious.' As when he corrected me about Nehru, I often had the feeling that he examined something which was said to him, and marked it as being too superficial.

We talked about Blackett, and I raised the question of Blackett's political past and present.[2] I was very interested to know what

---

1 Robert Oppenheimer (1904–1967), Director of the Manhattan Project during the war and thus popularly known as the 'Father of the Atom Bomb'. In 1954, he was prosecuted for allegedly having protected a communist sympathiser on his team. His security clearance was revoked, thereby blocking any further participation in atomic research. At this date, he was a director of the Institute for Advanced Studies at Princeton University.

2 Patrick Blackett (1897–1974), eminent British physicist. Radically left-wing in his early years, he was sympathetic to Oppenheimer's situation.

Oppenheimer thought about this, on account of a curious remark Blackett made to me at the time of the Oppenheimer case: he had said that one should not altogether defend Oppenheimer. I could not at the time, nor can I now, make out from what point of view Blackett was talking. Oppenheimer seemed to indicate that he did not think Blackett had the same political affiliations today as he might have had previously, and he added: 'In the case of people's political pasts, the quality with which one should judge is charity.' He seemed to think there was too little of this quality in American life.

December 1956, London

Nicolas Nabokov told me two days ago that Stravinsky said he would very much like me to bring T. S. Eliot to see him.[1] Yesterday he said that Stravinsky had had a very bad night. He seemed to think he may have had a minor stroke again, but he said nevertheless he was still very anxious to see Eliot even if he had to do so lying in bed. I arranged with Eliot to fetch him from his flat at Carlyle Mansions at 3.30, and take him to the Savoy Hotel for tea with the Stravinskys. When I arrived I found Tom in very good humour, and I drove him to the Savoy. We waited downstairs, and then Mrs Stravinsky came with Robert Craft the young American musician who conducts Stravinsky's work and who is a kind of companion, and perhaps a Boswell, for the maestro.[2] We went in to tea in the restaurant, while waiting for Stravinsky to join us. He soon did. He looked older and a little bowed, but not ill. He is very small, or anyway small, and has a conductor's way of holding his hands forwards and outwards, rather like a crab its claws. Although so short, he gives the impression of stooping over one. His face is that of a very intelligent tortoise, extremely clever, yet with surprisingly little back to his head which has the hair plastered close to the skull. He has the slightly old-fashioned appearance of a pedantic character in a play of Chekhov who wears pince-nez.

---

1 For Igor and Vera Stravinsky and Robert Craft, all mentioned in this entry, see biographical appendix.

2 James Boswell (1740–1795) was the constant companion, observer and biographer of the writer Samuel Johnson (1709–1784).

Robert Craft told us that the doctor had allowed Stravinsky to conduct in Berlin (?) in order to demonstrate to him both that he could conduct and could not do so: that he was well enough to conduct, but not well enough to do so with ease and facility.

The conversation was carried on mostly in English, though with quite a lot of conscientiously accentuated French from Tom. Stravinsky started talking about his health. He complained that all the doctors told him to do different, sometimes quite opposite things. He suffered from an excessive thickening of his blood, and at present the London doctors were trying to cure this by bleeding him every day. They also encouraged him to drink beer. Eliot said that he always drank beer, and that a pint of beer did him less harm in the middle of the day than even two glasses of red wine.[1] Stravinsky went on a good deal about his health, and I began to fear we were going to hear about nothing else. However tea went on for nearly an hour and a half, and a good many subjects were touched on. He asked me about the libretto I am doing with Nicolas, and then I asked him about working with Auden.[2] He said this went marvellously. Auden arrived at Hollywood, ate an enormous dinner and drank a great deal, went to bed early, and then was up at 9 o'clock the next morning ready to listen to Stravinsky's ideas. No sooner were these explained to him than he started composing the libretto. He would think of some idea, and then ask himself where it should be fitted in, pulling out lines and saying that they should be inserted in such and such a place, as though (Stravinsky said) he were fitting the pieces into a puzzle. Then Auden went back to New York, and within a few days had sent the libretto all typed out. Only quite minor alterations had to be made, and Stravinsky had only to make a suggestion and the solution came back by return of post. He said a second libretto which Auden had sent to him did not appeal to him as an idea.

I asked him whether he had heard the programme of his symphony and his canticle of psalms [*Symphony of Psalms*] from the B.B.C. the

---

1 It became one of Spender's favourite stories, and it improved with the telling. Thus Stravinsky told Eliot that his blood was 'immensely rich', cupping his hands as if holding a precious liquid. To which Eliot replied that his doctor had told him, 'Mr Eliot, your blood is the thinnest I have ever tested.'

2 Spender was writing the libretto for Nicolas Nabokov's opera *Rasputin's End*, which was performed in 1958.

[263]

night before. He said he had not heard it and had no intention of doing so, because he did not think the conductor, Sir Malcolm Sargent was qualified to conduct any modern work.[1] Mrs Stravinsky said that the newspapers had rung her up to ask her whether Stravinsky was going to listen to this broadcast and she had tried to put them off by saying that they had no wireless. Then a woman reporter had rung up, suggesting that she bring a wireless set and that she herself come taking notes on the reactions of Stravinsky. Mrs Stravinsky had replied that she had no intention of listening to any radio programmes.

This got Stravinsky talking about his publicity. Eliot asked him what he did when people wrote requesting photographs. Stravinsky said that he did not send them because they cost money. He said this in a way which called to mind his whole reputation of being extremely careful and even grasping about money. He said that when he was in Venice where especially choral work was performed in the St Mark's Cathedral, *Time* magazine had created a link between him and T. S. Eliot, by captioning the review they published: 'Murder in the Cathedral'.[2] He said that after this performance, he waited 25 minutes so that the crowds might disperse, and then accompanied by friends, walked out into the piazza. There were very few people by that time, but as he walked across the square, a few people seated at tables saw him and started clapping all round the square. He said he was extremely touched. The performance had been broadcast through amplifiers into the square, and these people, most of them young, had waited in order to applaud.

I asked Eliot how it felt for him to address 14,000 people in Louisville [in 1950].[3] He said: 'Not 14,000, 13,523. As I walked into the arena, which was of the largest sports stadium there, I felt like a very small bull walking into an enormous arena. As soon as I had started talking, I discovered that it is much easier to address several thou-

---

1 Malcolm Sargent (1895–1967), at this date director of the Promenade Concerts. (When Natasha Spender later performed Stravinsky's *Capriccio* for piano and orchestra under Sargent, the conductor told the orchestra to cut out the rests in the first twenty bars, as listeners might think their radios were not tuned.)

2 The caption alluded to Eliot's play *Murder in the Cathedral* (1935).

3 In the autumn of 1950, Eliot had given a major lecture tour in America, addressing vast audiences of his former countrymen.

sand people than a very small audience. One has not the slightest idea what they are thinking, one sees no features of any face, and one feels exactly as if one is speaking to an anonymous unseen audience through a broadcasting system. They all seemed very quiet, but I could not tell how they reacted.'

Stravinsky seemed thoroughly at home in this kind of café conversation consisting partly of reminiscences. He talked about Marcel Proust whom he met quite often in Paris before the war. He said that Proust was not an exciting or vital man to meet, but nevertheless he impressed one as being someone. He looked extremely ill, and he talked about music in a way that annoyed Stravinsky. Proust would keep on talking about Beethoven's last quartets, which, Stravinsky agreed, were admirable music, but at that time in his career he would have liked to hear about something rather more new. There also seemed to be some difficulty because Stravinsky was not (just then, he said) homosexual. Proust used to arrange meetings at the most extraordinary hours usually after 1 a.m., often at 3 a.m., which were the times when he felt that he could face the world outside his sickroom.

The Stravinskys said they hated Hollywood now. Fifteen years ago when they had bought their house, the climate had been delightful, it was now foggy and most unpleasant.

I asked Stravinsky whether Proust had talked about César Franck.[1] Stravinsky said luckily he had not done so, as he considered this the most horrible music ever written. Altogether he did not have a good word to say about any other composer. I had the impression this was not so much through jealousy as because he has created a world so entirely his own in his music, that other music – or at any rate, other modern music – does not impinge on it. His is a music in which every note in every chord counts to the utmost possible degree, and all the music that depends on melody and development must seem to him a kind of journalism.

When Stravinsky talked about his music one did have a very extraordinary sense of his commitment to his world of music.

1 The composer Vinteuil's 'little phrase' in Proust's *Du côté de chez Swann* (1913) is thought by some to be a tune by the Belgian composer César Franck (1822–1890), which is perhaps why Spender mentions him here.

Although he conducts rather badly, he hates anyone else to conduct his work, because he is so infinitely aware of all its shades which he does not believe anyone can interpret.

He talked about the new opera of Henze – which he had heard in Berlin.[1] He summed it up in a phrase: 'Too much water.' He said he thought the opera called *Boulevard Solitude* which we heard in Rome was better, although even there the second act repeated the material of the first act.[2]

He told us that he had a correspondent in Brazil, who wrote to him not because he was in the least interested in Stravinsky, but because he was interested in Rimsky-Korsakov. He thought Stravinsky, being Russian must have some connection with Rimsky, and perhaps possess some of his manuscripts. He was always writing to Stravinsky asking for a few sheets of Rimsky's music. 'However, recently he has improved,' said Stravinsky. 'He wrote to me the other day to ask me whether I would send him a few sheets of my own music.'

In February 1960, Spender visited the USSR as the guest and travelling companion of Muriel Gardiner, who was visiting her artist friend Sergey Konenkov and wished to make sure he was thriving after his unexpected return from America (his home of many years) to the USSR. The Cambridge spy Guy Burgess, resident in Moscow, made a surprise telephone call to Spender at his hotel at 1 a.m. and visited him there the following morning. Spender was later requested by the British Foreign Office to write a confidential report of this encounter.

1 Hans Werner Henze (b. 1926), German composer. His new opera *König Hirsch* (*The Stag King*) premiered in Berlin in September 1956.

2 *Boulevard Solitude*, which opened in Hanover in 1952, is Henze's one-act version of *Manon Lescaut* (1731) by Antoine François Prévost. Three full-length operas on the same story exist, by Auber (1856), Massenet (1884) and Puccini (1893).

4 February 1960, Moscow

Met our Intourist Guide who looks rather like the Queen when she was princess.[1] She took us a tour of Moscow – housing settlements, the outside of the University, the view of the city, Bolshoi theatre, Mayakovsky's statue, sports palladium, etc. New buildings nearly all resemble those of the Stalin era.

With help of [Angus] Rae [from the British Embassy], I tried to contact Soviet Writers' Union and finally was asked to go to their headquarters at four. There I met two very friendly ladies. They asked me who I would like to see. Lily Brik unwell, Akhmatova in Leningrad, Fedin away in the south, Ehrenburg in London, Nekrasov unobtainable for some reason, Duvetsov – well they would see what they could do.[2] They were very smiling and friendly and explained that there were very few specialists who would know anything about my work, but they would see if it were not possible to arrange a small gathering on Tuesday.

5 February 1960, Moscow

Guy Burgess telephoned me at 1.15 a.m. one evening. He called on me at 10 the next morning. As soon as he arrived and I had asked how he was, he said 'I love living in this country. It's solid and expanding like England in 1860, my favourite time in history, and no one feels frightened.' But a few minutes later while we were talking he waved in the direction of the wall and said, 'I suppose they're listening to everything we're saying.' He seemed oddly changed – looked at full-face, he seemed quite like he was before: a bit florid, the same bright eyes and full mouth. Side-face he seemed very altered indeed – almost unrecognizable – thick and receding chin, eyebrows

---

1 Intourist, founded by Stalin in 1929 and staffed by Communist Party officials, was the official state travel agency of the Soviet Union.

2 Lily Brik (1891–1978), writer and sculptor, 'muse of the Russian avant-garde', mistress of the poet Vladimir Mayakovsky whose statue Spender had seen, and sister-in-law of Louis Aragon. Anna Akhmatova (1889–1966), poet, critical of Stalin and consequently banned from publication 1925–40, visited by Isaiah Berlin in Moscow in 1946. Ilya Ehrenburg (1891–1967), Soviet writer best known for his controversial 1954 novel *The Thaw*. Viktor Nekrasov (1911–1987), critical writer, editor, journalist.

with tufts of hair that shoot out and overhang. Sometimes looking at him I got the full-face and side-face impressions disconcertingly together. A person I knew who had added on an unrecognizable frame to his familiar features. I was puzzled whether this was just the effect of jumping the span of years (as he might be getting from me) or due to all that had happened to him. He had a seedy, slightly shame-faced air, and shambling walk: like some ex-consular official you meet in a bar at Singapore and who puzzles you by his references to the days when he knew the great, and helped determine policy.

He said: 'I have a black mark against you' and cited a letter I had written to *The Observer* about him.[1] I said I didn't remember very distinctly what it was and he said: 'Never mind, only a tease,' quite affectionately. Later, I did remember and said: 'Well when I wrote in that letter that Auden (whom you failed to contact at my house, just before you left) even if you had not done so [i.e. failed to contact him] might have refused to see you, I was not attacking you, I was meaning to protect Auden.' 'In that case it's perfectly all right. I understand completely,' and added rather wistfully: 'There's probably some quite reasonable explanation of Goronwy [Rees]'s article about me – in which case I would forget everything.'[2]

He told me he was advising for a publishing house. We discussed books they might translate. They have never done Jane Austen. He was trying to persuade them to do Trollope (incidentally, I heard an instruction went out early this year that current English books should be translated – so there is a gap of a generation between the early 1930s in modern English literature and today when they suddenly

---

1 The *Observer* article, published on 10 June 1951, which was quoted extensively after Burgess and Maclean decamped, voiced Spender's (then premature) belief that they were probably not spies, and that the phone calls made to Auden before Burgess's flight, when the poet was staying at Spender's house in Loudoun Road, were entirely innocent.

2 The British journalist Goronwy Rees (1909–1979) was another member of the Cambridge Five spy ring. On five consecutive Sundays between 11 March and 8 April 1956 articles on Guy Burgess were published in a Sunday newspaper, the *People*, written anonymously by 'his most intimate friend – a man in high academic position'. The source of the information was soon identified in the *Daily Telegraph* in March 1956 as Principal Goronwy Rees of Aberystwyth University.

have books by John Wain and John Braine, and performances of John Osborne).[1]

He was also he said working with a branch of the government which spread peace: 'Although he won't be aware of this, I was able to be a good deal of help to Macmillan during his visit.[2] I wrote a report that he was in favour of friendship and should be trusted whereas all the others wrote that he was a dangerous reactionary. I got a note thanking me afterwards. So I am present. I am in good order.'

He wanted chiefly to have gossip from me about the old days and about our friends. The person he spoke of most affectionately was Rosamond Lehmann. I was astonished at the extent to which he had woven most detailed legends around every day belonging to the past. For instance although he and I were never at all close, he remembered, it seemed, every occasion on which we had met – when in Paris I told him at lunch about being psychoanalysed – when I had lent him my flat in London – all things I had completely forgotten. But he talked about all his friends in the same way. I asked him whether he had friends in Moscow. He said yes. 'Like your friends in England?' 'No one has friends anywhere like they have in England. That's the thing about England.' [. . .]

I recalled Cyril telling me of a conversation he had with Maclean in which Maclean had said we were wrong about the Korean War in taking the side of Syngman Rhee.[3] Burgess said no, the turning point wasn't for him the Korean War but Greece – the surrendering of

1 John Wain (1925–1994), British poet and critic, close friend of the 'Movement' writers Kingsley Amis and Philip Larkin. Wain was sometimes seen as part of the group of 'Angry Young Men' centred around the playwright John Osborne (1929–1994) and including the novelist John Braine (1922–1986).

2 The Prime Minister of Britain, Harold Macmillan (1894–1986), led a high-profile delegation to Moscow in 1959.

3 Syngman Rhee (1875–1965), the first president of South Korea, 1948–60. He was supported by America because of his hard-line approach to opposing communism. However, he alienated many of his supporters by assuming dictatorial powers and allowing internal security forces to detail and torture suspected communists.

Greece to 'the Fascists'.[1] He added – 'Of course, you won't agree about this' and indicated that he recognized friendlily my position as an American agent. (Whenever I took the trouble to repudiate this idea of me, he laughed – 'only a tease'.) I told him I wasn't at all enthusiastic about the Greek regime. I remembered dining once at a restaurant on the top of a hill overlooking Corfu. As it darkened the whole landscape became filled with shouting and clanking noises. I asked an elegant Greek lady – daughter of an ex-premier – who was at the dinner party what the noise was. 'Oh,' she said, 'it's the political prisoners. Tonight is Saturday and they always make this noise because it's the only night they have enough food to be strong enough to protest against not having more.' But, I said, I supposed that if *his* side had won the same scene might have taken place – if, indeed, the prisoners would have been in the position to protest at all. He did not say anything to this.

He invited me to lunch at his apartment, and telephoned through to his cook to say we would be there. 'We shall lunch off grouse.' We waited for a taxi and he asked a policeman how to get one not pre-empted by Intourist ('Moscow policemen are sweeties,' he said.) The apartment house where he lives – one of the ugliest – is near a beautiful monastery. 'I chose it to be near here.' He seemed a bit nervous about the impression his apartment would make on me. 'I was offered something very grand, but I insisted living in this place for very Spenderish reasons. I thought I couldn't live in five or six rooms, when people were living [. . .] a family to a room.' [. . .]

He apologized a lot for his flat. It seemed to me small but very nice, neatly and sympathetically arranged – lots of books, a small upright piano with a Bach or Mozart volume of Sonatas open upon it; a Chagall reproduction, one or two paintings by gifted amateurs,

1 In November 1935, King George II of Greece (1890–1947) was reinstated as monarch after political upheaval and unrest since his exile in 1924. In August 1936, the Greek prime minister Ionnis Metaxas (1871–1941) exploited labour unrest to dissolve Parliament and rule as a fascist dictator, although he did introduce several social and economic reforms. In 1938, Metaxas was elected head of the government for life, and in 1940 he led the Greek victory against Italian invaders, following conflict with Mussolini who had demanded occupation rights in Greece. Metaxas died in 1941, with George II, politically enfeebled by the Metaxas regime, driven into exile in April 1941 following Hitler's invasion of Greece.

modest furniture. The elaborately carved back of a bed – Guy explained – had belonged to the bed of Stendhal. I had said earlier that I would not publish in the press any account of our meeting. He pulled from the bookshelf a volume of Winston Churchill and opened it at the flyleaf with the inscription to this effect: 'To Guy Burgess in agreement with his views. Winston S. Churchill.' Under this was written in pencil: 'and we *were* right. Anthony Eden.' 'If you like, you can reproduce that in *Encounter*.'[1] [. . .]

My own feeling for Guy, which is shared I think by several of the British in Moscow, is to be sorry for him – and, as someone said, to wish that he would go back to England, the whole thing be forgotten and that he would have some kind of a new start.

10 February 1960, Moscow

The same evening as I arrived I went to dine at the flat of the R[ae]s, of the British Embassy. [Angus Rae] asked me about my plans. When, among other things, I mentioned my hope that I might meet Pasternak, he put up his hand and indicated that we should stop talking.[2] We continued the conversation on one of those contraptions for writing on a tracing paper placed against a sheet of carbon paper with a wire between the sheets that you pull out on a tag in order to obliterate what you have written. He made it clear that the one matter in which the Embassy could not help me was this. But, he said, they had approached the Writers' Union and hoped that they would arrange for me to meet some writers. They told me there were microphones in the rooms of all the Embassy staff, and that their servants spy on them.

For our general impressions of Moscow my two companions and I were rather in the hands of Intourist Guides and Black Marketeers (who might be looked upon as the antidote to Intourist just as the Writers' Union might be a kind of superior Intourist, I suppose).

---

1 Before the war, Guy Burgess had joined Winston Churchill and Anthony Eden in criticising Neville Chamberlain's policy of appeasing Hitler. The volume in question would have been Winston Churchill's *The Gathering Storm* (1948), the first volume of his history of the Second World War.

2 Boris Pasternak (1890–1960), Nobel Prize-winning Russian poet and writer, best known in the West for *Doctor Zhivago* (1957). It later emerged that one of the poems Pasternak most admired was Spender's '1929'.

Our Intourist Guide, called Lydia, wore always exactly the same fur coat and green beret. [. . .] Neither W[eissenberg], an American architect of Austrian origin, nor I could resist pressing her to produce the kind of information which provides much more a guide to the manners of Intourism than to Russia.

The slightest inquiry revealed embarrassing gaps between her information and that of informants not so primed. On our tour of Moscow University she took us up to the 14th floor and showed us a room which was, she said, typical of 14,000 in each of which one student lived. It was like diminutive quarters in a modern modest hotel: in one room, a bed, a table, useful cupboards, a radio; adjoining this room, separate lavatory and shower. One or two other people I asked thought that perhaps 5,000 students had such rooms. The day we left, at the airport there were some Indonesian students from the University. I asked them how they lived and they said there were three of them to a room.

One day I told Lydia I had been a Communist for a short time. 'Why aren't you one now?' 'Because much as I admire the achievements of the Soviet Union, I still think that the most important thing – from my point of view – is freedom to say and write what I think.' 'Oh, but there is more freedom in Russia than in any country of the world.' 'In that case, why is there no press which represents a point of view criticizing the government?' 'Oh, there could be!' she smiled. 'Nothing would be easier. But, you see, no one would read it. No one at all. One of the things that distinguish our kind of society from the West is that in the Communist world there are no contradictions. They have disappeared and everyone agrees about everything.'

* * *

Jean Pierre Wigny – son of the Belgian Foreign Minister – is at Moscow University studying Russian foreign economic relations.[1] He is intelligent, serious, Catholic and full of good will. He came to dinner with me at the National Hotel. He said that the University was very good for his purposes; he could get the books he wanted (or he thought that he would be able to do so) and there didn't seem to be propaganda in their approach to his subject. All the same the

---

1 Spender had met the Belgian Foreign Minister Pierre de Wigny in Brussels in 1950. See entry for 13 March 1950.

atmosphere at the University was, officially, and on the surface, oppressively conformist. It reminded him of his Jesuit upbringing. 'Sometimes we children complained to the Father that after all we had no freedom. He replied: "You have the only freedom worth having: freedom to be good."' This was very much the attitude of Moscow University. All the same, a few, just a few, students would say to him suddenly, when he was alone with one, 'You think we agree with all this, but we detest it.' (I did not ask how many he meant by a few: but if it were more than two who said this, it would seem to me quite a lot.) He said he did not think that the students were greatly spied on. The whole place was too noisy and crowded for there to be microphones, he thought. All the same, when I asked him whether he had any friends at the University he said he did have one who was always coming to see him, more than Wigny wished perhaps – a young man, very well dressed, with suede shoes, a nice suit. Other students had warned him that this friend was a police agent. Wigny said occasionally there were rumours: for example, recently there had been one that a Russian student had gone to the embassy of a small country (perhaps Holland) and asked for protection. The Ambassador explained that he could not smuggle him out and could not keep him on the (Dutch) soil of the Embassy in Moscow. He told him that he would have to go back to the University. But in order that he might do so unobserved, it was arranged that he should leave by a back door just at the moment when the Ambassador himself left with as much fuss as possible at the front. But when, with his suitcase, he went out of the back door, he was seized by two men who put him in a car and drove away. 'End of story,' shrugged Wigny.

I told him my experiences – such as they were – and he asked: 'Are you disappointed?' I said I wasn't, as all this seemed so much of a pattern that it had a certain formal quality which didn't really seem quite real. I was too impressed, for example, by the tremendous evidence of building in Moscow to be disappointed by the unreality of the figures which might be supplied by our Intourist Guide. Wigny seemed rather pleased, as though he did not want me to be disappointed, and found much to admire in Russia himself.

* * *

I was taken by R[ae] to meet an art collector, G— —, whose name I was supposed to forget.¹ He evidently belongs to what Raymond Aron calls 'official clandestinity' but he supports the unofficial kind. He is a Russian Greek, living with his wife and children in a nice apartment with three rooms, two of which are hung with his collection. This is fantastic. In a back room he has many icons, which I cannot judge, but that seemed to me marvellous. The living room is hung with Kandinskys, Chagalls and the most impressive Malevich I have seen, belonging to what I learn is called the Constructivists' Cubist–Futurist period. This large canvas is the fragmented portrait of a pianist done in the blown-to-bits style. G— — also has a great many things that are not on his walls: for instance, a marvellous early sketch book of Kandinsky, and nearly a hundred quite uninhibited drawings by a young Soviet artist Z— — (of whom more) illustrating *The Golden Ass* of Apuleius.²

When we arrived there were three other visitors: a painter, a poet-and-painter, and a poet from Leningrad. They were figures out of the Marx Brothers. The painter like Chagall, the other like a modest sensitive young bricklayer, the poet small, white, with thick spectacles and fair hair untidy on top, and bristling from his unshaved chin. The poet spoke a little English, and knew about the English poets of the Thirties. It was rather comforting to know there was a Spender 'specialist' around. He asked me questions about T. S. Eliot, the young English writers and so on. They were all three Bohemian – looking as if they might lie down and go to sleep in the snow without a murmur – and two of them were about to catch a train. [. . .]

G— — then showed us his collection. The most interesting part of this was more than a hundred works by a young Russian painter Z— — [i.e. Zverev]. Z— — has no official existence, and only at certain points does he seem to attain even to semi-official clandestinity.

---

1 'G— —' is George Costakis (1913–1990), Russian art collector with an extensive collection of Russian avant-garde art. In 1946 Costakis came across three paintings by Olga Rozanova and rediscovered constructivist art in Russia. Spender was one of many Western tourists to visit his collection, which constituted a kind of unofficial national museum.

2 'Z— —' is Anatoly Zverev (1931–1986), founder of 1960s Russian expressionism.

His paintings are very varied, but they have in common the quality of being done with great rapidity and with the idea of conveying a single hallucinated *coup d'oeil* in each picture.[1] Most of them were gouaches and had something suggestive of Soutine and Chagall: but that is only my attempt to say the 'kind of thing' they were. They did not strike me as imitative and, indeed, G— — said that Z— — was scarcely interested in the works of other painters. 'I show him books of reproductions I have here, but he scarcely looks at them. He will rush through a gallery, occasionally pausing to examine minutely some small section of a painting and to say, "I like the way that is done."' G— — kept on telling anecdotes to demonstrate his belief that Z— — was better than any other of the modern painters in his collection. 'I told Eva Chagall that I would like him to show some of these to her father. Eva said, "You seem to forget that my father is an old man. It would depress him too much."' G— — had a book in which various visitors, including Alfred Barr and d'Harnoncourt of the Museum of Modern Art had written their impressions of Z— —'s art. D'Harnoncourt's was cautious.[2]

If you are shown over a hundred specimens of one painter's work in the course of an hour, you are overwhelmed by his idiom, and it is rather difficult to form an idea of his merits. But I do think Z— — is probably a very remarkable painter, immensely varied and energetic, an extremely sure draughtsman, and a visionary. His work has the absolute indifference to everything except expression and the criteria of his art, his attitudes movingly recall Gaudier-Brzeska: whom, indeed – to judge from the photographs I was shown of a serious, smiling, ardent young man with his arm round a girl who was his first, second, or third wife, or mistress – he seems temperamentally and touchingly to resemble.[3] 'I told Z— —,' said G— — 'that if he spat on the ground and trampled the spit onto a sheet of paper I

---

1 Literally 'stroke of the eye', used to mean glance.

2 Alfred Barr (1902–1981) and René d'Harnoncourt (1901–1968) were successive directors of the Museum of Modern Art, New York.

3 Henri Gaudier-Brzeska (1891–1915), French sculptor whose short career took place in England. His drawings are influenced by Chinese 'immediacy' and his sculptures refer to Jacob Epstein, tribal art and cubism. Ezra Pound knew Gaudier-Brzeska and wrote a posthumous memoir of him. Spender owned several of Gaudier-Brzeska's drawings.

would take it from him. He is an inspired, completely devoted and convinced artist.'

The arrangement G— — has with Z— — is (I gathered) that he gives him 200 or 300 roubles a time according to his needs, and holds back his paintings until a time when they will be marketable. 'People come here asking for a Z— — offering 2,000, 3,000 roubles, but I do not want to sell. I do not myself know what they are worth until there is an exhibition.' He seemed confident that there would eventually be one, and he was interesting about his conversation with one of the high officials of the Artists' Union, who said: 'Look here, we might sometime exhibit one or two of Z— —'s paintings in a mixed show; but if we gave him an exhibition to himself, then there would be a revolution in the style of all Soviet artists. We must introduce his work step by step, gradually.' To this, G— — replied: 'You are quite wrong. I have drawings of Malevich in my possession which embody the architectural ideas that could have been the basis for building the new Moscow. But Malevich, of course, you have banned. With the result that now you are having to look abroad to get Danish architects to design better buildings than the terrible apartment houses you put up all over Moscow. You ought to give an entire exhibition to Z— —.'

Meanwhile, however, they won't, and it seems unlikely that they could have an exhibition giving the idea of Z— —'s range: which is from glittering landscapes in oils, in which he usually chooses a Church as the central object of attention, to drawings uninhibitedly obscene.

I finally dared ask whether I might buy a gouache of Z— — to show friends in England so as to give them an idea of subterranean Soviet art. G— — hesitated. He said that he had given one or two paintings abroad – with results dangerous to Z— —. For instance, a Scandinavian critic had written an ironic account of the May day celebrations in Red Square combining this with ecstatic praise of Z— —'s paintings. He ended with the apostrophe: 'Billions of roubles on arms and flags and parades – while the greatest painter in Russia is officially without any existence!' (Something of this kind, I forget exactly how it went and I have paraphrased the argument.)

G— — agreed though to give me a painting, and would not accept my suggestion that I make a nominal gift to the artist. 'I know what they are going to say: that I have kept Z— — hidden and collected all his works for myself, in order that I may make a fortune later from them.' The disadvantage of his generosity was that I could not choose for myself, and therefore I have a picture which would only be a good example in the context of a good many more paintings.

I asked him what the work of the other painters I had seen was like. He said that he could not make up his mind. 'One of them seems rather gifted, but his work is almost indistinguishable from that of Jackson Pollock.'

* * *

M— — [Muriel Buttinger] took me to the studio of K— —, the most honoured Soviet sculptor.[1] Aged 85, and with a straggling white beard, he is a very extraordinary man. M— — knew him years ago in Vienna and New York. K— — is profoundly religious, to the point of having delusions of prophecy about the future of the world. He returned to Russia in the middle of the war, after one of his prophecies had been fulfilled: that he would receive a letter from Stalin inviting him back as honoured 'artist of the people'.

At this advanced age, K— —'s studio is crammed with works in progress: marble statues of Ulanova, and approved dead poets and other dead artists, in the approved manner.[2] A man of great originality and independence he has the good fortune, in his best work even, to practise a style which has never offended a dictatorship: the universally accepted peasant style. Far and away his best things are his grotesques in wood. One of these was of the figure of a demonic worker riding a horse and holding in his upraised waving hand a rake. The horse's hooves were being assailed by four serpents, which represented capitalism in various countries, 'one of them,' said K— —, 'I am afraid, America.'

It would be a mistake though to think that K— — is a lackey of the

---

1 'K— —' is Sergey Konenkov (1874–1971). In 1923, he moved from Russia to America, where he was befriended by Muriel Buttinger. In 1945, Stalin sent a ship to New York to bring back Konenkov to the USSR, where he spent the rest of his life and was honoured with the title People's Artist of the USSR.

2 Galina Ulanova (1910–1998), Russian ballerina.

regime. Basically his imaginative idea is apocalyptic not social realist. This leads him to have to alter the titles of his more prophetic efforts. For instance he spent many years doing a study of Samson breaking his chains. When he offered this for exhibition he was told that the title was too biblical and that he would have to change it. It was moved into the exhibition hall, and he was then told that workers did not trail dangling locks of hair and he would have to shave his Samson. He protested very strongly, but finally he was persuaded to do this. Just before opening day of the Exhibition, Khrushchev paid an unofficial visit to see how art was going, and discovered K— — chipping the hair off his 'Worker tearing apart his Chains'. He inquired what the artist of the people was doing, and on being informed said grandly: 'Leave the hair on. The artist must be free.'

At one end of the studio there was a large curtain in front of a tall carving in progress. K— — pulled the curtain away and said: 'This cannot be shown until after a Catastrophe.' It was a figure of Christ. K— —'s present belief is that there will be a world disaster after which the world will return to a kind of Christian communism in which Russia will take the lead. At the same time, he is very much the artist of material triumphs; and the Sputnik plays [a] big role in the symbolism of his recent work.[1] He showed us a grandiose plan for a vast memorial to the Revolution (or to Lenin?) with at least seventy enormous figures, and with astral shapes supported above them on wires.

The K—s remain very nervous about their situation. Mme K— — sent messages through M— — to all their American friends not to write and not to expect any communication from them. They said that things were far better now, but they were by no means recovered from the terror of the past years of Stalin. Mme K— — had frequently been examined by the police. Among other things she had to do was write letters, which were dictated to her, to [Albert] Einstein (of whom she was a great friend), asking him to visit the Soviet Union.

---

1 In 1957 the Russians had launched a series of robotic spacecraft missions known as the Sputniks. The word 'sputnik' means 'travelling companion' or 'satellite' in Russian.

This is a postscript to our visit to Moscow. Soon after my return, I happened to go to a party where the Home Secretary R. A. Butler was a fellow guest.[1] He at once came up to me and said in a friendly way: 'I hear you've been seeing Guy Burgess in Moscow. Does he want to come home?' I said that I thought he wanted to see his mother who could not travel. R.A.B. said: 'Well, if you write, please tell him that as far as I'm concerned, he's perfectly free to come and go as he chooses.' He went on, with a rather noble air. 'Of course, if he comes back and the Home Office takes no action, I'll be attacked, the press will be after me. But I'm prepared to face the music.' After a pause, he added, 'Of course, the boys at M.I.5. may take a different view of the matter. That's nothing to do with me though. As far as I'm concerned, there's absolutely nothing against him.'

Shortly after this, Tom Driberg who had never arranged any kind of meeting with me before, suddenly wanted to lunch with me. Soon after we sat down his reason for wanting to see me so pressingly became clear. He had heard about my conversation with R. A. Butler, and he was in a state of considerable alarm at the prospect of Guy Burgess coming to England. 'Whatever you do,' he said, 'don't encourage him' and he made it clear that his return would be extremely upsetting to a number of people.[2]

I did not write to Burgess encouraging him because it was clear that what the Home Secretary had said to me did not provide the slightest guarantee of his safety. In any case, he had not said that he was considering coming to England. He had only expressed a vague desire to see his mother.

The other consequence of my Russian visit was that a few months later, as soon as Tvardovsky, the courageous editor of *Novy Mir* and publisher of the works of Solzhenitsyn, together with the

---

1 Richard Austen (Rab) Butler (1902–1962), Conservative politician, author of the 1944 Butler Education Act, appointed by Harold Macmillan as Conservative Home Secretary in 1957 after the two had competed to succeed Anthony Eden as Prime Minister.

2 Tom Driberg (1905–1976), Labour politician and journalist, an old friend of Burgess, of whom he wrote a memoir, *Guy Burgess: A Portrait with Background* (1956). Driberg had some private contacts within the Russian elite. Presumably he had no desire to see these revealed by Burgess if he ever came back to London.

novelist Fedin (whom I had met in Venice) arrived in London they informed their hosts at the British Council that they wished to see me.[1] The only reason I can think of for their doing this is that, thinking it would amuse him, I had told Yevtushenko about the way in which I had been received by the ladies at the Soviet Writers' Union, and instead of finding this funny, he had been furiously angry.[2] I surmised that he had communicated his feelings to Tvardovsky and that they were trying to make up for the discourtesy.

Whatever the reason our meeting was cordial. At the end of their visit, Natasha and I gave a dinner for them at Loudoun Road. Before doing so, I showed Tvardovsky the guest list. He seemed perfectly happy until he came to the name of Hugh Gaitskell upon which he reacted strongly, saying he had no wish to meet him. I asked him why, and he said: 'Because he is a politician.' Evidently he regarded every politician as a bureaucrat and lackey of the government. I managed to persuade him that Hugh was leader of the opposition and a cultivated man with independent views.

31 March 1960, London

I took Fedin and Tvardovsky to luncheon at the Garrick yesterday. They were accompanied by a young British Council interpreter, Mr [Peter] Norman, who was excellent, and whom they obviously liked, and who contributed a lot to the party. Fedin talked pleasantly about our meeting in Venice. I asked Mr Tvardovsky whether [. . .] I could translate one of his poems and publish it in *Encounter*. He seemed very pleased at this suggestion, and said that he would like to translate one of my poems and publish it in *Novy Mir*. He also said that he was very willing to enter into an exchange arrangement of articles between *Encounter* and *Novy Mir*. I mentioned that I would be glad to have non-political articles on Soviet literature. I suggested that

---

1 Aleksandr Tvardovsky (1910–1971), Russian poet, chief editor of the Russian literary magazine *Novy Mir*, 1950–54, 1958–70.

2 Yevgeny Yevtushenko (b. 1933), Russian poet, vociferous critic of Stalin's regime.

such an article might be an attempt to answer the question in the minds of some English readers – 'How does Soviet literature compare with Nineteenth Century Russian literature? Are there Soviet writers who should have the same impact on the writers of Europe as Tolstoy, Dostoevsky, etc?' I said I thought that this question is buried in the minds of most readers here, and it would be a good idea to try to bring it out in the open. They thought this was a real question and discussed it at some length, saying that although today no one would dare to assert the greatness of twentieth-century Russian literature, also in the nineteenth century it had not been realized how great it was. Mr Tvardovsky brought up the question of my asking for a non-political article, and smilingly asked why we always seemed to assume that they were concerned with politics.

(While I was talking with them, I had an impression rather different from the one I got in Venice. In Venice, I thought the Russians were being rather cunningly political, in avoiding politics. But yesterday, I had the impression that they really wanted to be considered as writers, and they did not want to be implicated in our political thinking about them, nor did they want to implicate us in their political thinking about us. If we insist on talking about politics, they are embarrassed because it is not an area in which they can express themselves very freely. So they really have a quite sincere reason for wishing to avoid the topic.)

Then I told them I had been to Moscow four weeks ago. They explained that they had not been there at the time. I said I thought that there had been some coldness towards me by the Writers' Union, and I said I quite understood this, and had no grievance on that account, but I wanted them to understand that basically, we were very well disposed to them, and that we thought that cultural relations between Russians and English were of the greatest importance.

They said that perhaps it was a mistake of mine to have gone Intourist. I mentioned that [Victor] Ehrenberg had said, in an interview in Rome that Silone and Spender would not be at all welcome in Russia. They pooh-poohed Ehrenberg's remark, and Fedin added, rather oddly, 'In any case, we do not consider you at all like Silone.' I said that Silone was a friend of mine, and that I agreed with him about a good many things.

None of this conversation was at all sharp or disagreeable. Although we mentioned these things, we did so in a friendly way. I then developed a bit my own ideas about cultural exchange. I said that I thought that if one could arrange an exchange between writers which had very little publicity and which was as little official as possible, and which would involve their studying together in some quiet place for some little time, this might be a very good idea. I added that I thought that a meeting of eight Russian and English writers for about a month of this kind might be very useful. Mr Tvardovsky said, 'Not eight, sixteen.' He took up the idea enthusiastically, and said that he knew exactly where it should be in Russia.

We then left this subject for a bit and talked about literature. They seemed to know almost nothing about T. S. Eliot and asked me to explain what kind of a poem was *The Waste Land*. I said that it was essentially a poem about the decline of Western civilization, with an idea that Christianity still offered hope of salvation. I compared it with Alexander Blok's *The Twelve* (which I had read in a German translation) and which also contains the idea of the complete breakdown of everything, and the idea that salvation might be achieved by the Red Army soldier, who is identified with Christ.[1] They indicated that perhaps the difference between Eliot and Blok is that Eliot is an extremely intellectual writer, writing for an intellectually privileged public, whilst Blok was a popular writer whose poetry was taken to the hearts of the whole Soviet people. This interested me because it seems that in their thinking they have come to attach much more importance to the idea of the popular base of Soviet writing than they do to its ideology. They asked me whether Eliot's style was based on popular ballads, and I explained that it was based on Shakespearean blank verse. (It was explained to me that 'blank verse' means 'free verse' in Russia, but Fedin then recited to me some pentameters of Pushkin. I asked him how much he thought Pushkin was influenced by Byron.)

---

1 Alexander Blok (1880–1921), Russian lyric poet whose 1918 long poem *The Twelve* narrates the march of twelve Bolshevik soldiers through revolutionary Petrograd. They are explicitly likened to the twelve Apostles, and the poem ends with the appearance of Christ.

April 1960, London

We went to see Henry Moore. He showed us the new large room which he has built on to his house, where they have only been living for the past two or three days. I explained to him my plan for *Encounter*, namely that we should ask artists for illustrations, pen and ink drawings, demonstrating different aspects of their work. I told him that I would like very much to know what were the differences of his aims when he did an abstract drawing, or a representational one, or a portrait. He told me that there were at least five or six different kinds of drawing.

1. The kind of drawing he made when he was trying to study the organic form or nature of an object. This was the kind of drawing which consisted of trying to find something out. He said in this connection that it was impossible for anyone to do drawings without making a discovery about the structure of objects.
2. Trying to describe the objects, for example, when he did a drawing of his daughter or some other life figure, or perhaps even of a bone.
3. The kind of drawing he did when he was trying to clear his mind of an idea for a piece of sculpture: to plan it out, to see it from different angles and so on, to get an idea of what it would be like.
4. Drawings which he would call exploratory. He would start simply perhaps by scribbling a few lines and then discovering from them a shape which led on to something else. These are the kind of drawings which arise from doodling.
5. Drawings in which he attempted to explore the metamorphosis of objects. He would draw something realistically and then try to discover how it could take some other shape. He would turn realistic subjects into an abstraction through drawing it first realistically and then abstracting from it.
6. What he called 'imaginative' drawings in order to create an atmosphere of drama. In this category, he would draw figures standing against a background. [. . .]

[283]

We went back to the house, and he showed me various drawings which I might choose from for *Encounter*. I selected eight of these. I also chose three drawings which I might choose for Jim Hart and myself. [. . .]

I forgot to say that when we were in the studio we saw a study for a head, and I asked him how he arrived at these heads with great clefts down the whole of the centre. He explained that when he was a boy in his Yorkshire mining village, he used to go with two or three other boys to a slaughter house and see animals being killed. The men who killed them used to do this by hitting them with a mallet in the centre of the forehead. If they hit in exactly the right spot the animal died at once, but if they didn't succeed in doing this they had to hit two or three times more. There was one man of whom the others said that he was a wonderful slaughterer because he never had to hit an animal twice. Henry said that he had only been two or three times to the slaughter house, that it was a terrible experience that had haunted him all his life.

When he did his statue of the warrior he wanted to suggest a stricken dehumanized head, and he found himself, without first realizing that he was doing so, influenced by his memories of the axed animals in the slaughterhouse. Of a piece of sculpture of a pregnant woman, he said that he had tried to alter it because it seemed too descriptive. When we got back to the house I asked him what he meant by 'descriptive'. He explained that sometimes when he was working he found that he was becoming too influenced by his feelings or memories about real things. For instance, when he was doing the pregnant woman he found himself thinking of his mother and her pregnancies and somehow he was describing his feelings about them. So he tried to alter the work.

5 April 1960, London

We had dinner with T. S. Eliot and his wife Valerie. We arrived a little late and found that the other guests were already there. They were the poet Ted Hughes, and his wife Sylvia Plath, who is also a poet and short story writer.[1] They were a good-looking pair, Ted Hughes

---

1 For Ted Hughes and Sylvia Plath, see biographical appendix.

having a craggy Yorkshire handsomeness combined with a certain elongated refinement, very sensitive drooping hands in contrast to his ruggedness, rather soft toned and not saying very much.

His wife, who talked more, was a very pretty, intelligent girl from Boston.

Cyril Connolly had given me an early edition of a book by Eliot called *Ara Vos Prec* [1920] which he asked me to get Eliot to inscribe. So I quickly asked him to do this, in order to get that business over, and at the same time he signed my edition of *The Waste Land* printed by the *Dial* magazine. He said that the title of the book was misprinted as it had 'Vus' for 'Vos', and he corrected this. He said that Ezra Pound had been very shocked by the misprint and had given him a wigging for it. [. . .]

We went into the dining room and ate roast chicken served by Mrs Eliot. Eliot seemed relaxed, talked about Virginia Woolf and Wyndham Lewis. Mr and Mrs Hughes said very little. Whenever there was a pause in the conversation, Mrs Eliot gave her husband an encouraging look across the table which positively radiated help. This made me nervous and I talked too much to keep the conversation going.

Spender went on holiday with the Lamberts. Cyril Connolly accompanied him.

11 April 1960, Paris

Arrived in Paris for lunch at Hotel Meurice with Hansi [Lambert], [Czeslaw] Milosz, [Constantin] Jelenski and Mme Philippe de Rothschild.[1] [. . .]

Cyril arrived in time for wine. Lucy [Lambert], he and I went to see *L'Oeuf*, by Gabriel Marceau, a play about a young man who does not feel he belongs to 'the system' (which is bourgeois society) and who then joins it so effectively that he marries a bourgeois wife, who betrays him with a soldier returned from Indonesia, on whom he then fixes the penalty for his own murder of his wife. At first quite

---

1 For Philippe and Pauline de Rothschild, see biographical appendix.

amusing and likeable, Marceau's hero becomes too mad and too incredible by the end of the play.[1]

Cyril in his bath – to me: 'You may look at me in my bath. Hot stuff, don't you think?'

Talking to me about the trip: 'Everything depends on us. We must act as nurses, take turns in keeping up the morale of the Lamberts –' etc.

12 April 1960, Madrid

Got into a frightful plane called an Armagnac, which flew us to Madrid. It must have contained over 100 passengers, had an interior like a vast hall. Spent the night in Madrid.

13 April 1960, Santa Cruz, Tenerife

Flew from Madrid to Santa Cruz in Tenerife. This took about 8 hours, and was really very exhausting. To get through the customs at Madrid, Hansi had given Cyril and me each 10,000 pesetas. Cyril told me he had an awful nightmare which was that he would go out with a tart who would steal his 10,000 pesetas and give him clap. Then he would spend the whole of the time in Tenerife trying to explain away the fact that he did not have the money and taking a secret cure for clap.

The only pressure on either of us is to be ourselves.

This might mean just that we expect one another to be very 'good' in our writing. But it is also a test of our faith that we should recognize the goodness even if it's not recognized. Beyond this, even writing is not the authentic thing, which is something religious.

31 December 1961, New York

Went to the *New Yorker* office and talked with Dwight MacDonald. The nice thing about this bearded opinionated public-minded man is that he adores gossip above all else. His first remark when I entered

---

1 Felicien (not, as Spender writes here, Gabriel) Marceau (b. 1913). His two-part play *L'Oeuf* was first performed in 1955.

his office was, 'Heard the New York News?? Norman Mailer's on the wagon.' I feel that he was all set to be a sociologist when at some moment in his life Mary McCarthy – or someone – torpedoed the armour-plated public man he might have been and left him interested in persons and personalities.

After seeing Dwight I went to dinner with Auden and Chester Kallman. Other guests were Mr and Mrs Louis Kronenberger.[1] Auden's news was that the Hamburg Opera are doing his *Magic Flute* libretto translated from his English into German. Also he is adding a room on to his house in Austria. While I was looking at a water colour sketch of this house (which I have not seen) he said: 'I can stand in the garden and cry with gratitude that I have it.' Chester cooked dinner which consisted of a very Oriental chicken.

At about ten, the K[ronberger]s left. Then a friend of Chester's – John Button, the painter, arrived.[2] I thought I should stay on a bit longer and not leave the moment he arrived. Wystan took no part in the conversation but started moaning gently in his chair. So, at 11, I said that it was really, by English time, 6 a.m. for me so I must go. Auden said, 'Yes, do, my dear. I don't know how it is you've managed to stay up so late. In your place, I would have gone to bed *hours* ago.'

3 January 1962, New York

Tea with Isaiah Berlin at the Carlyle Hotel to meet Marianne Moore.[3] Her conversation consists of a stream of minute observations about her recent journeys to Rome, Athens, Mycenae, etc. She is almost flatteringly (ironically?) courteous: 'Well, Mr Spender, I count it a very great honour that Mr Berlin should have invited me to join you, when the two of you could have been alone.' She has considerable acerbity: 'Now I don't think Mr Auden is always quite discriminating with his praise. I asked him how it was he could find so much to admire in the poetry of Mr W. If Mr W. had written anything really

---

1 Louis Kronenberger (1904–1980), American critic and writer.

2 John Button (1929–1982), American artist.

3 Marianne Moore (1887–1972), American poet, editor of the *Dial* in the 1920s, patron of poets such as John Ashbery and Allen Ginsberg.

good, it must be his most recent work, which I haven't yet seen.' In the taxi on the way to her home (she dropped me off at my hotel), she explained to me how her black woman servant cleans up for her twice a week, how from her wages she supports her husband who fell off a water tower and is incapacitated but cannot get insurance, how every Christmas Mrs Murray Crane gives a lavish gift to her (Marianne Moore's) servant who then says to her: 'Miss Moore, I know that Mrs Crane wouldn't give this just to me – it's for you that she's giving it', etc.

She told us at tea about a TV programme she was on. 'I insisted on its not being shown till I'd seen it. My skirt was rather short and I thought it showed coming up above my knees, and – well, I'm extremely proper about such things. But they assured me that there was no impropriety of a kind which would upset anyone, so I allowed myself to be persuaded . . . .'

29 March 1962, London

London. We went to *Figaro* with the Berlins. The Stravinskys were invited. They came to the first act then went on to the performance of *Sacre du Printemps* at the Albert Hall, conducted by Monteux, in order that composer and conductor might receive an ovation.[1] They insisted that they did not want to go, only went to please Monteux, etc. Stravinsky sat without emotion through the first act of *Figaro* which was conducted by Solti.[2] It was a gala performance, honoured by the presence of the Queen Mother. Next day he said the best thing about last night's *Figaro* was the Queen Mother.

12 May 1962, London

Lunched with Matthew – or didn't, rather – because he had only ¼ hour as he has to go in a fencing match this afternoon. He showed me the Picasso drawing he bought for £30. Told me all his friends at

---

1 Pierre Monteux (1875–1964), French conductor, at this date principal conductor of the London Symphony Orchestra.

2 Georg Solti (1912–1997), Hungarian-British conductor, at this date musical director at the Royal Opera House in London.

school suffer terribly from not having girlfriends: at the Slade, the models look like elephants. 'I might study better if Maro wasn't there. I always end up drawing Maro.' He has two Gorkys in his room, one of which Maro has seized from her mother and given him.

Dinner at William Sansom's for Yevtushenko, the John Russells, Peter Norman and another interpreter.[1] Some conversation about poetry with Y. who wanted to know why English poets never seemed to know their poems by heart. His concept of poetry very public. Peter Norman, who has spent several days with him, describes him as insincere: an actor who is playing a role but whom he thinks profoundly political. He looks and is charming. His wife seems altogether a nicer character. When he danced, we saw the jitterbug night-club side of him.

13 May 1962, London

Lizzie returned home and seemed very much grown up in the four months I was away.

14 May 1962, London

Got up at 6:30. Took children to their schools. Matthew said last night: 'Dad, if I get a scholarship to Oxford will you promise to leave *Encounter* and do nothing but write poetry?'

16 May 1962, Paris

Paris, for Stravinsky 80th birthday celebrations. Lunched with Nicolas N[abokov], Mike Josselson and [Melvin] Lasky. Slept. Called on Jean Cocteau to give him back his *Encounter* drawing but he was away and I was told to return tomorrow.[2] At six went to Stravinsky's hotel and found Boulez, Bob Craft and others

---

1 John Russell (1919–2008), British art critic, at this time writing for the *Sunday Times*; a neighbour of the Spenders in St John's Wood.

2 Cocteau's sketch of a three-faced King Oedipus was on the cover of the June 1962 edition of *Encounter*.

surrounding him.[1] Stravinsky very cordial. They go to South Africa tomorrow. Dinner at Chez Laurent. About a dozen people there, including Simone Signoret and husband, and various other prominent people.[2] I sat next to Kot Jelenski and talked to him almost the whole evening. Was far away from Stravinsky. When the party broke up, I[gor] was still very lively, violently denouncing to the head of French Radio the attitude of the critics to him in 1922.

Yevtushenko spoke to us on the plane before we got out at Paris and was charming and friendly, saying, 'We meet next in Moscow.'

17 May 1962, London

Called at Berkeley Hotel to say goodbye to Stravinskys and Bob Craft. Stravinsky was sitting up in his chair with bright eyes like in a Beatrix Potter. He was excited about going to Africa and showed me Alan Moorehead's books, especially a photo of a rhino.[3] 'I want to see that animal,' he said. 'It's like this.' Suddenly he was on all fours, his stick with hook turned up like a horn, his eyes glazed, a rhinoceros.

Bob asked me, 'Have you any Cocteau drawings for me?' On reflection I took the hint, and gave him the drawing Cocteau had done for *Encounter*, saying, 'If I give you a note to Cocteau, he will probably give this to you.'

18 May 1962, Bruern, Oxfordshire

Went to office. Dispatched reviews to *Sunday Times*. Lunched with Reynolds, who goes to U.S. this evening.[4] Both of us 'a bit distrait' – he through packing and getting ready to leave, I through just coming back. We lunched at Asiatique, then went to Marlborough Galleries and looked at van Gogh exhibition, then at I.C.A. at the

---

1 Pierre Boulez (b. 1925), French composer and conductor.

2 Simone Signoret (1921–1985), French film actress.

3 The Australian-born British war correspondent Alan Moorehead (1910–1983) was the author of *The White Nile* (1960) and *The Blue Nile* (1962).

4 For Reynolds Price, see biographical appendix.

[Sidney] Nolans.[1] R. thought only 2 or 3 of the Nolans were any good. We both felt oppressed by its being a farewell. He's also nervous about the business of having a film made of his novel.

Drove Lizzie and Anjelica Huston to Bruern. Dined with Michael and Pandora [Astor].[2] Michael very interested about Yevtushenko and rather inclined to the view that I was antipathetic to him and he to me. So I misjudged him because he did not like me.

23 May 1962, London

Saw Francis Bacon's exhibition at Tate. The paintings make horrifying statements with very great force. They are by an observer so profoundly affected by the kind of life he observes that, although protesting, they seem corrupted by the corruption. After Bacon most other contemporary painting seems decoration, doodling, aestheticism, or stupidity. His work extremely devoid of pleasure. Perhaps this is partly due to the life of disillusionment he leads, which he faces in its implications; perhaps it is the old English puritanism and dislike of pleasure cropping up again.

25 May 1962, London

Fetched Stuart [Hampshire] from 19 Gordon Square and drove to see [William] Coldstream exhibition in South London. We were kept waiting outside the gallery because the BBC was filming. When we went in, Tom Driberg was there. While I stood transfixed in front of Bill's portrait of Inez [Pearn], Tom Driberg made a speech to the cameras about the Arts Council – which was responsible for this exhibition and others like it. Then he came over urbanely and said this was a partly political broadcast because support for the Arts Council was one of the few things the Labour Party agreed about. He asked us if we would be interviewed and we said no.

---

1 Sidney Nolan (1917–1992), Australian painter, moved to London in 1950.

2 For Bruern and the Astors, see Michael Astor in the biographical appendix. The actress Anjelica Huston (b. 1951), daughter of the film director John Huston, was at this time a school-friend of Lizzie Spender.

28 May 1962, London

Ray Gosling lunched with me.[1] Teddy-boy appearance, with lock of hair shooting horizontally over forehead. Pale blue eyes. Rather weak features. Exaggerated gestures. Personable smile. Lively and observant. Told me how he upset man at newspaper stall in Birmingham buying copy of *The Queen* and then *The Daily Worker* to read in train. He arrived at 12.30 and waited for me at pub while I went to see Chuck and Natasha.[2] When I returned he was already quite drunk and went on drinking throughout meal. Wanted advance on article. Mel [Lasky] told me he had already had £10 – which he, Gosling, didn't tell me.

He was genuinely moved by reading the very interesting poems we have had sent in by a juvenile delinquent. On the whole, I didn't feel too optimistic about Ray G.

We gave dinner party for Jimmy and Tania Stern. Angus Wilson, Sidney Nolan, Sonia Orwell. It went on a long time, everyone talking at once.[3] [. . .]

This afternoon heard Isaiah give lecture on Russian attitude to painting, at Slade. [. . .] Coldstream said that when he gave a lecture or made a speech, he was unutterably bored listening to the sound of his own voice coming out of his head as though out of a wooden box. Isaiah said that he was nervous before a lecture: during the lecture he fixed an eye on the right hand corner of the ceiling and heard a torrent of meaningless words coming out: after the lecture he felt – shame. No one could ever persuade him that the lecture was good, after he had made it, he simply was incapable of believing it.

I have the experience of boredom with what I am saying. As Angus Wilson also said this evening, when one states ideas one is bored because one knows what they are and one is preoccupied with nothing but the effort of stating for others what one has thought out already. When one is writing a story or a poem, one really does not

---

1 Ray Gosling (b. 1939), journalist and later TV documentary maker. At this date part of the New Wave provincialism, and neo-realist movements in 1960s culture.

2 Chuck Turner, friend of Samuel Barber and Gian Carlo Menotti.

3 James Stern (1904–1993), Anglo-Irish novelist and short-story writer.

know how it is going to develop, whether one can do it – so one is fascinated to see *what will happen.*

29 May 1962, London

Dined with Magouche Phillips.[1] [. . .] Francis Bacon. Various people came in afternoon. Francis told me his oldest friend Paul Latham had died suddenly in Tangiers a week ago. He seemed interested in reaction of Ghika, [Sidney] Nolan etc to his exhibition, which was one of feeling challenged and horrified.[2] I said that Ghika had said a) the paintings were true and one could not get away from this, b) they were not transcendental, by which he meant they did not discover and exploit qualities of beauty and texture discoverable within, but apart from, the subject matter, c) that he [i.e. Bacon] only really painted a section of the picture (the image) not the background. It should be possible Ghika said to cut out a section of any picture and make a separate picture of it. Francis said he understood this criticism very well, and he remarked that all the critics said his paintings were full of hatred and expressed no love. He had spoken very movingly about his dead friend and I said it did strike me that he didn't express in his paintings what he must have felt about Paul Latham and also Paul Danquah.[3] He said he was not able to do this at present: that Paul Danquah was far too beautiful for him to be able to distort and he had always distorted. I said Picasso had painted pictures of Dora Maar as well as his fishwomen, and that there seemed no Dora Maar side of Francis' painting.[4] He said: 'The paintings of Dora

---

1 The Spenders had met Magouche Phillips (formerly Gorky) two years previously through Barbara Hutchison. Meanwhile Matthew Spender had met her eldest daughter Maro Gorky in Greece. They would marry in 1967. (See Matthew Spender in biographical appendix).

2 Nicolas ('Niko') Ghika (1906–1994), Greek artist. Spender admired his work and wrote an appreciative study co-authored with Patrick Leigh Fermor (*Ghika. Paintings, drawings, sculpture,* 1964)

3 Paul Danquah (b. 1925), film actor. He was one of first black actors to star in a major film, Tony Richardson's 1961 adaptation of Shelagh Delaney's play *A Taste of Honey.*

4 Dora Maar (1907–1997) was Picasso's lover and muse in the 1930s and 1940s.

Maar *are* distorted.' I said: 'That's what I mean. You can also distort to do a beautiful painting.'

30 May 1962, London

Finished reading Upward's novel on the Thirties, which is a masterpiece – or the trilogy of which it is part one should be – I think.[1] Will review it for *Encounter*.

1 June 1962, London

On reflection, I think that Edward Upward is the best of all the generation of the Thirties, better than [Lawrence] Durrell even, and that his novel will be in more ways than one the justification of that time.[2]

2 June 1962, Bruern

Vita Nicolson died. She was very kind to me when I was twenty and when my left-wing politics greatly alarmed her.[3]

3 June 1962, London

Half in sleep last night thinking again about Edward Upward's career of school-mastering – thirty years which seemed to me finished almost before begun. Then thinking about the children and how although I realize they are older they nevertheless do seem to me at the same time 12 and 17 and as they were at 4 or 5. And I realize that I am both still 30 and 70, writing this at the age of 53. Time really is the greatest illusion. One believes in a future when one is young, and when one is older we no longer believe in it, and this is the greatest disillusionment.

---

1 Upward's trilogy *The Spiral Ascent* incorporated *In the Thirties* (1962), *The Rotten Elements* (1969) and *No Home but the Struggle* (1977).

2 Lawrence Durrell (1912–1990), expatriate British writer best known for *The Alexandria Quartet* (1957–60).

3 Vita Nicolson, née Sackville-West (1892–1962), British writer and gardener, friend of Virginia Woolf.

4 June 1962, London

Letters and telegrams re. my C.B.E.[1] The nicest was from John Hayward who almost justified the existence of honours. The nastiest from John Lehmann who reproached me for 'a crushing snub' in not attending the lunch in his honour.

5 June 1962, London

Joined Natasha and Matthew at Edith Sitwell's flat in Hampstead. She seemed better than we had seen her for several years. Her secretary told us that a previous nurse had put her on tranquillizers and this had been bad. She now has much better nurse. Talked maliciously about [T. S.] Eliot, who is in disgrace because he wrote to *Observer* protesting against the memoir she had written about Wyndham Lewis.[2] Told how when she was four she was madly in love with a peacock which was slightly larger than her – then it fell in love with a peahen. She was nasty about D.H.L[awrence]. Said '*Lady Chatterley* is all about the Sitwell family.' When D.H.L. visited them he spent the whole afternoon explaining to them their relationship with their parents, and their parents' with one another!

10 June 1962, Bruern

Drove over to Fawley Bottom farm to lunch with the John Pipers.[3] Saw his new studio with model of the window in Coventry Cathedral which, he said, he had made there, over 2 years. He took the view that Francis Bacon's paintings were only about 5% of life. Said how fond he was of Bacon as a man, and that he was almost a saint, unlike Graham S[utherland], who was not very nice.

---

1 Spender received a CBE in the 1962 Queen's Birthday Honours.

2 In November 1960 Sitwell had written about Wyndham Lewis in an *Observer* article entitled 'Hazards of Sitting for My Portrait'; Eliot wrote an article in Lewis's defence.

3 John Piper (1903–1992), British artist who worked as an official war artist during the Second World War; and his wife Myfanwy Piper (1911–1997), art critic and librettist who collaborated with Benjamin Britten on *The Turn of the Screw* (1954), *Owen Wingrave* (1971) and *Death in Venice* (1973).

After lunch we went into the wood near the farm where the Pipers have put up a slender monument surmounted by a ball, and made of broken flints, and an arch made from two classical seventeenth-century figures bought from an antique dealer's. I asked John during our walk whether, when he went to Venice or Rome, he had some idea in his head of what the relationship of a painter today was to the work of previous artists who had worked in those places. John said he had given a great deal of thought to this and that what interested him when painting Rome or Venice was to maintain the tension between modern abstraction and topographical art. He thought that English artists had a topographical tradition and that they still had a contribution to make in relating the past to the modern.

14 June 1962, London

Afternoon gave my dreadful lecture to the dreadful Gresham College.[1] Went at 6 to a party given by Lys Koch's sister.[2] This was appalling, full of people who hadn't met for 35 years and were trying to be cheerful about it. A frightful Mansions type flat. Then we went on to dinner with the Glenconners. The Kochs arrived later. Robin Ironside was there, quite brisk and cheerful.[3] Dr Koch is bearded, has a carved-wooden semitic profile, a smirking expression, and a very loud voice.[4] He called everyone 'old boy' which he seems to think the right therapeutic approach to the English. As he got drunk, he started doing imitations of English speech in which he delivered attacks on the English food etc. I congratulated him on being so brave as to imitate the English in front of them and said I never dared do this to Americans. He was pleased at the compliment. Lys who was just as silly as 25 years ago tried to cover all their life in protective myths,

---

1 Gresham College is an independent college founded in the sixteenth century to give free public lectures in the City of London.

2 Rosemary Lys Koch, née Dunlap, later Lubbock (1918–1989), was an academic editor in London and New York, and a collaborator on *Horizon* in its early days with Spender and Connolly. It was through her that Natasha Litvin met Spender in 1940.

3 Robin Ironside (1912–1965), British artist.

4 Sigmund Koch (1917–1996), American psychologist, second husband of Lys Koch.

telling me they never went out at Duke [University, North Carolina] because Sigmund Koch shut himself up to write his six great volumes on psychology, how they had refused to let Basic Books publish them as B.B. were not good enough, but now rather wished they had been more generous to B.B. Lys told interminable stories at dinner about uncles and aunts all of which were to illustrate her new attitude to England derived from Sigmund K. He was quite brusque with her. Lys telling her stories made me want to pee so much I had to leave the room.

In 1962, Spender went to Germany on CCF business.

16 June 1962, Hamburg

Met at airport by a young jurist Dietrich Bernecker, who is considerate to us. Arrived at Hotel 4 Jahreseitzen to find Stravinskys don't arrive till tomorrow. N[atasha] rested. I went for walk along the Alster, which was beautiful, reminiscent of when I was 20 and first came here, and walked each day whole length of lake from [Erich Alport]'s house at far end, to meet H. List for lunch at the vegetarian restaurant.[1] Conscious of being old. Young lovers walking along bank hand in hand. Not at all my contemporaries! Possible to think of them, on a spring day near the wisteria, as being inwardly as sunlit, as responsive to one another, as oblivious of everything, as 'sincere' as the light shining on surfaces makes them appear. But inside he is already thinking of sums; there is a question mark inside her – can she cook, make both ends meet? Baited traps. When you are young your beauty is quite sufficient to decorate the barest bed-sitting room, your laughter almost warm enough to keep it heated. Then you start accumulating the externals to surround your walls which have left your physical sides. The only compensation for being old is to be spiritually and intellectually very alive, to be several astonishing stages beyond the young, to make them seem geese. The old need a certain public life even to keep alive privately, perhaps.

---

1 Herbert List (1903–1975), photographer, a pre-war friend of Spender's in Germany. Spender wrote an introduction to a collection of List's work, *Junge Männer* (1988).

[297]

17 June 1962, Hamburg

Got up 8.30. Went with Bernecker[,] and a student who drove, to Lübeck and beyond to be shown the Grenzschütz.[1] A 2,000 kilometre border from here to Czechoslovakia with a ribbon of 50 kilometres all along it made of scorched earth. Watchtowers, machine guns, a smaller strip ploughed every day so as to show footsteps of anyone escaping from East. Guards and tourists look at one another through field glasses. No other contact now (since the Wall) between East German and West German police. We had lunch at picturesque old sailors' restaurant in Lübeck. Saw the 14th-Century Old Mens' Home and the Marienkirche. I asked political questions and there was obviously tension between Bernecker and the student driver in giving the answers. Bernecker argued that West Germany could never come to understanding with Communists because Poland and Czechoslovakia had been so ill-treated by Germany that the Russians could not come to an understanding without alienating the satellites.

Went with Rolf Liebermann and his wife to meet Stravinskys at airport.[2] Many photographers. Stravinsky very charming with them, smiled held out his arms kissed us all, etc. What is nice is he does this not out of vanity but genuine sympathy with the people, including the photographers, who come to meet him. I asked him whether he was tired. He said 'Not tired, just drunk.' Bob Craft said later, *en passant*, 'The last time he was sober was in Paris on March 19th.' Went to hotel. Had drinks with Stravinskys, Liebermanns, Bob Craft and Balanchine till nearly midnight.[3] We gave S. for his birthday *A Latin Portrait* with inscription:

Spenders, simple spondees, offer this Latin gift to
Stravinsky, making a dactyl, to honour his eightieth birthday.[4]

---

1 Literally 'border protection'; the 'iron curtain' surrounding East Germany.

2 Rolf Liebermann (1910–1999), Swiss composer, currently director of the Hamburg Opera House. On 24 June 1964 there was a Hamburg Stravinsky festival in honour of Stravinsky's 80th birthday. Stravinsky had been invited by Liebermann to present a Stravinsky ballet programme, which included performances of *Agon*, *Orpheus* and *Apollon Musagète*.

3 George Balanchine (1904–1983), Georgian-American choreographer, co-founder of the New York City Ballet. He worked extensively with Stravinsky.

4 *The Latin Portrait*, an anthology by G. R. Hamilton (1929).

18 June 1962, Hamburg

Sketched, fairly completely, three poems. In the morning went to rehearsal by Balanchine but this failed to materialize. Lunched with von Buton and another at Anglo-German Club. Read, and rested. We called on Willy Haas who was lively and amusing.[1] While we talked he drank ¼ bottle of brandy and a lot of gin. Dined with Herr Schnorr and Dieter Bernecker at a restaurant overlooking harbour. The division between zones is much more a living tragedy and problem than I'd realized. This at all events [the] lesson of dinner: of lunch, the still surviving guilt among older Germans about Nazis.

19 June 1962, Hamburg

Stravinsky said last night and again this morning, so I feel he must have meant it: 'I can see you are a composer. I don't mean by that music – but as a poet: you like syllables. I like them too.'

Went to rehearsal of *Agon*. Bob conducting. It was very good. Stravinsky whispered to me, about the orchestra. 'It is a Wagner orchestra, a Strauss orchestra . . . emmerdant [shitty].'

21 June 1962, Berlin

Visited Academy of Arts. Saw exhibition of Gilles which is about to be hung – a decorative Mediterranean-scenic painter with no real force.[2] Conversation over coffee at Academy with Wolfdietrich Schnurre and his attractive wife [and] Friedrich Luft [. . .].[3] This was mostly about the Wall, whether Schnurre was right to have refused to have his works published in East Germany etc. He said that as long as they refused to publish Faulkner, he didn't want to be published. Conversations of this kind are often so theoretical (at the PEN Club

---

1 Willy Haas (1891–1973), German film critic and screenwriter.

2 Werner Gilles (1894–1961), German painter who spent much of his life in Italy.

3 Wolfdietrich Schnurre (1920–1989), German writer, a member of the postwar group of left-wing German writers Gruppe 47. He protested against the building of the Berlin Wall in 1961. Friedrich Luft (1911–1990), German theatre critic.

for example) and the positions taken up so schematic, that it was quite hard to realize that the situation they were talking about was real and only five miles away.

22 June 1962, Berlin

Had lunch with Sebastian Haffner.[1] Talked politics. He said we are entering now an interregnum in international politics, about common market, with future of Germany, post-war economic system (which shows slight cracks in Germany as in other countries etc). I asked what he thought about future of Berlin and he mentioned possibility of an agreement between Khrushchev and Adenauer over the head of Ulbricht.[2] I said I had already discussed this with several people and they all seemed agreed that such an agreement would create too great difficulties for Russia in East Europe. S.H.: 'East Europe is not really a single concept. It consists of Poland, Czechoslovakia, Hungary, Romania, and East Germany – all quite different.' He discussed possibility of a European bloc which consisted of France, Poland and Germany, and seemed to think this would be a more realistic third force in Europe than the sterilized centre of a neutralized Germany and surrounding countries of the Rapacki Plan.[3] (A sterilized area would be far too open to influences outside that area, whereas the Gaullist alliance would be a vigorous, yet dealable-with organism.)

Haffner said he was against disarmament, abandoning tests, and even allowing any country that wanted them to have atomic weapons. His grounds were that to stop the tests [would be] to halt the development of knowledge at its present stage which was no less dangerous than any later stage would be, and was anyway unrealistic

---

1 Sebastian Haffner (1907–1999), German journalist. In 1938, he emigrated to England where he wrote for the *Observer*, and returned to Berlin as the newspaper's German correspondent in 1954.

2 Konrad Adenauer (1876–1967), premier of the West German Bundesrepublik; Walter Ulbricht (1893–1973), premier of the GDR (1960–73) The GDR had declared Berlin to be its capital in 1949 (illegitimately, since the city was still under four-power administration).

3 The 'Rapacki Plan' was a scheme to de-nuclearise Western Europe, named after the Polish politician Adam Rapacki and presented at the UN in 1957.

because, fortunately or unfortunately, you cannot halt knowledge. Disarmament would increase [the] danger of one power thinking that it would attack another either because it was disarmed, or because there was no longer the danger of universal destruction by war. Everything showed that to have the H bomb had a remarkably sobering effect on those countries that had it.

I did not like this point of view but it made me reflect on the gulf there is today between morals and the actual realities of politics. Morally the bomb is abominable, but it is more important to stop war than to base a political attitude on moral outrage. The essential tragedy is that morality cannot stop knowledge, and we have in the modern world knowledge of a kind that cannot be dealt with simply by moral forces just because it cannot be stopped. [. . .] The Immorality of course arises again among those – if there are such – who really want war. But those who are agreed that their aim is to prevent war, should be able to dismiss means as realities, and among one another as equals, without one group claiming moral superiority over others . . . . Perhaps . . . . Perhaps though the C.N.D.-ers do have an advantage in that they have invented a technique for caring a great deal of the time.[1] Whether they are right or wrong the most important thing is that people should care and be able therefore to make the sacrifices necessary in order to carry through the best agreed policies.

In the evening walked down Kurfürstendamm which was crowded as in old times, the Film Festival more than the warm fine evening bringing out the crowds. There is more feeling of commonality, of belonging to one another, in Berlin than in other cities, because, I think, there are shared points of view here, beginning with a general tolerance of nightlife, vulgarity and entertainment, and rising to respect for individuality and for culture. The Film Festival is of course the highest common factor of Berlin culture. Hotted up photographs of cultural heroes, their features made shiny with oil before the camera clicks, have always been Berlin fetishes.

Went to a bar just off the Kurfürstendamm which was almost empty, because all the habitual visitors were walking up and down looking for film stars. The waiter had nothing to do and sat next [to]

---

1 CND, the British-based Campaign for Nuclear Disarmament, set up in 1958.

me at the bar grumbling cheerfully. Would only drink 'Sanft' [a soft drink] because if he drank anything else he 'ärgert sich' [lost his temper] and might knock someone down. He told me about ships he had been a sailor on until he had found this bar where everyone was like one family. Started doing his sums and said on all the money he had taken he had earned nothing, so I said I would give him 20% on my bill, so he said: 'Ich sage nie nein.'[1] Quite felt I belonged in Berlin again.

23 June 1962, Munich

Met [. . .] by Dr Jering, referred to in my typewritten programme as my Betreuer [tutor, supervisor]. This is a use of the word *Betreuung* which would be objected to by Sternberger–Storz–Süskind, authors of *Aus dem Wörterbuch des Unmenschen*, a very interesting study of the dehumanization of the German language by officialdom.[2] Or perhaps they wouldn't object because they write: 'treu sein und bleiben ist eben, wie man daran leicht sieht, nichts weiteres als ein menschliches Verhalten und Verhältnis.'[3] So Dr Jering and I are certainly menschlich. But when introducing himself he said 'I bring you the greetings of the Bavarian government,' he risked crossing a border line into officialdom, not crossed on account of his ironic smile. In fact he is violently anti-bureaucratic (almost too much so perhaps) and as soon as we had got into the car was inveighing against the hideous bureaucracy of Bonn (which he had come from an hour previously) and pointing out to me which were the bureaucratic quarters of Munich. At dinner the following points emerged: that he regards the Adenauer government as the most reactionary in Europe except Franco; that he thinks the Americans and British who support the idea of arming 700,000 Germans haven't given thought to the people whom they will rearm; that the British, in particular, by whom he

---

1 'I never say no.'

2 Dolf Sternberger, Gerhard Storz and Wilhelm E. Süskind, *Aus dem Wörterbuch des Unmenschen* (1957). This 'dictionary of inhumanity' sought to expose the residual effects of the Nazis on the German language.

3 'Being and remaining loyal is, patently, nothing more than a human behaviour and way of being.'

partly meant people with a 1930s public record like myself hadn't given any lead in the present situation.[1] [. . .] I mentioned Sebastian Haffner's ideas but he evidently thought the idea that we were now entering a period of interregnum was superficial; and he objected strongly to Haffner's favouring rearmament. He said that Haffner was very conservative. He also talked a lot about the younger generation and seemed disappointed with his son (aged 16) though when he went on telling how he knew all about painting and music, disappointment seemed very comparative. The point is however that the young are what he calls the 'pragmatic generation', entirely practical in outlook. When they went to Italy Dr J.'s son could manage everything they needed (buying at the market) on fifteen words of Italian, and since these were adequate, showed no desire to learn more. At home too Dr J.'s children are completely self-sufficient, and he seemed a bit surprised when I said my wife was not here because she was looking after our twelve-year-old daughter in London. His twelve-year-old daughter needed no looking after and could be left alone for weeks on end, it seemed. I did not like to say that my son is impractical enough to atone for a whole pragmatic generation.

25 June 1962, Berlin

Went to *Salome* [by Richard Strauss]. Dr Jering lectured me a lot about music, his Hausquartet in which he plays the cello, etc. He makes a very odd impression. Talked ecstatically yesterday about the marvellous time he had in France during the Occupation, how much he appreciated French culture, how he formed a library and collected all the vols of the Pléiade edition etc. When he sees pictures his idea is always to say they are like other pictures 'almost a Tintoretto, almost a Caravaggio, etc.' He likes pictures to be very crowded with 'realistic' life, e.g. prefers the most crowded scenes of Breughel to the simple ones. On the other hand in music he likes Mozart above all else, with real understanding and passion. His politics are like a violently wavering needle, but on the whole directed against the powers that be and to the left. He said that what is left over most from

---

1 The Western Powers' policy of rearming Germany started during the Korean War in 1950 and was a fiercely debated topic throughout the decade.

Nazism in Germany, is love of power and bureaucracy, wanting to touch the hem of the garment of whoever is important. This seems true. But my general impression is that this older generation of Germans is slightly crazy, sometimes sympathetically so – as Wolfgang Clemen – sometimes a bit sinisterly, with a dangerous hostility to almost everything covered over by superior seeming enlightened points of view. I could imagine Dr J. with his pointed features, sticking out ears, currant eyes, and Baltic look, very well in Nazi uniform. He spoke very toughly about the children and abruptly to the driver and to waiters, though making an effort to restrain himself. Throughout *Salome*, sitting next to me, he whistled perhaps asthmatically. I had to keep on getting up to stretch my leg, which was agonizing, so we were both odd.

26 June 1962, London

Got up at 6. Flew home via Frankfurt. [. . .] Dinner for eleven owing to the fact that I had forgotten that I had invited Mr and Mrs Wheelock, as well as Allen and Isabella Tate, Rosamond Lehmann, Mr and Mrs Seferiadis and Freddie and Dee Ayer.[1] Evening was characterized by the utter inaninity of Mrs Wheelock, who turned all the conversation to nonsense. Ros and Isabel in their different ways turned it all to themselves. E.g. Ros said she thought there was something demonic and destructive about Francis's painting, that he deliberately chose the dark side of life etc. I said this was perhaps true and that he had told me he could not paint Paul D[anquah] because Paul was too beautiful and too nice. Ros said: 'That's exactly what he said about me – you're too beautiful to paint.' I thanked Isabella for her hospitality in Minnesota and she replied: 'And I'm so grateful you're going to publish my sestina in *Encounter*.' [. . .]

In the morning light I've decided that on the whole Mrs Wheelock must have been drunk when she arrived. For she seized on a book of Augustus John drawings, started leafing through it furiously, explaining that each of the subjects was a character in whichever novel it is

---

1 John Hall Wheelock (1886–1978), American poet. George Seferis [Seferiadis] (1900–1971), Greek poet and diplomat; Spender translated some of his poetry.

of Aldous Huxley that has John portrayed in it.[1] She also told me she admired John's early drawings; so I said, 'Would you like to see a John?' 'No, I don't need to,' she answered, 'I'm all fixed up.' 'I didn't mean that, I meant an Augustus John' 'No, thank you, I went before we came out.' It was impossible to clarify the position although as she was actually holding the volume of John in her hands during the conversation, she should have been able to bisect the ambiguity. Towards the end of dinner, I somehow got with Isabella on to the subject of dying, and I said that I knew one or two people who because they had had strokes were confronted with death at every moment (like Ivan Ilyich in Tolstoy's story) and this gave them a very haunted appearance. Isabella took this up in a competitive way, as a challenge to her. 'Oh, that's like me,' she cried, 'ever since I was eight I've been haunted by death, every day of my life.' Seeing her florid page-boy face, I suddenly felt very irritated and said, looking at Freddie: 'You're talking absolute nonsense.' 'Why are you telling Freddie he's talking nonsense?' someone asked. 'He's looking at me out of politeness but he's addressing himself to his neighbour,' Freddie said. 'And is he right?' Allen asked. 'He's perfectly correct,' said Freddie.

6 July 1962, London

Got home to find Wystan there and that he couldn't come to the country, because he has to go to the Sterns [James and Tania] on Sunday. He gives the impression of being somehow sated: fairly contented, but self-sufficient and not wanting to see anyone; only interested in what already interests him. He has an odd way of hardly looking at one while he makes himself comfortable, putting on his carpet slippers and settling down to his own thoughts, or a book. I don't think there is anyone from whom he gets anything new, unless perhaps a theologian. However, when he gets in to his subjects he is more interesting than any other writer I know and he has a lot to say. We listened to the new recording of [Wagner's] *Rheingold*, which warmed him up a lot. At dinner, discussed Desert Island Discs, the kind of conversation he enjoys because it is a game. He says he would

---

1 The British artist Augustus John (1878–1961) appears in *Point Counterpoint* (1928) as John Bidlake.

take no Mozart or Bach or Beethoven – but mostly the first act of *Tristan*, and some Strauss: 'just to annoy Stravinsky'.

After dinner he talked about form and surprised me greatly by saying he thinks endlessly about what form would best suit his subjects. Explained he wants now in his poetry to write something which seems to the reader almost like prose but in which he is playing an elaborate formal game, e.g. *Encomium Balnei* is written in lines each of which has 13 feet or 8 feet and then that are broken up into what look like separate lines

It is odd that the English   13
      a rather dirty people
8   should have invented the slogan
<u>Cleanliness is next to godliness</u>   13
         meaning by that

Etc etc.[1]

In 'the English', 'the' and 'Eng' elides and in one foot the English.

He said that for him poetry now meant 1) having something truthful to say, 2) exploring the possibilities of the English language.

Dislike of Yeats because Y. takes himself so seriously in his rhetoric and has the air of revealing important truths when he is really telling lies: –

'Once out of nature I shall never take
My bodily form of any natural thing. . .' etc.[2]

All lies.

Lycidas [by John Milton] all right because it is the greatest museum poem in the English language.

Discussed how what we hated about writing was the whole business of the literary life. We talked about Alvarez, etc.[3] Auden said he

---

1 Spender would print Auden's April 1962 'Encomium Balnei' in *Encounter* in August 1962.

2 Spender quotes from Yeats's 'Sailing to Byzantium' (1928): 'Once out of nature I shall never take / My bodily form from any natural thing'.

3 Al Alvarez (b. 1929), British critic and poet. Alvarez's much discussed anthology *The New Poetry* (1962) pointedly excluded Auden and Spender in favour of such new writers as Plath, Hughes and Lowell, who defied what Alvarez called the crippling British 'gentility principle'.

was very glad he had always kept clear of the lit. life. He said he thought I did very well with *Encounter* and that I had to deal with this awful literary world.

William Faulkner died.

7 July 1962, Bruern

At breakfast, Wystan said he had been told by Lincoln Kirstein, that [E. M.] Forster had written to Christopher, 'Don't send me any more of that autobiographical Mr Ishervoo stuff.' Lincoln not reliable but it seems quite likely Forster did something of the kind. [1]

We came down to Bruern. Last night W. and I drank 1½ bottles each of Pouilly Fuissé, and I have had quite a hangover all day.

10 July 1962, London

Evening dinner for Wystan with I. A. Richards, Erich Heller.[2] Richards talked about [F. R.] Leavis. Discussed how when after World War I he first lectured at Cambridge, Leavis attended his lectures, assiduously noting down all he said. Later Leavis turned against him with extreme violence. He dated this revulsion to the time when returning from China he (Richards) gave a lecture on India in which he said among other things that we could be grateful to the public school system that British officials didn't take bribes. He thought that Leavis's distrust of everyone was due to a social inferiority complex – his father sold prams. Leavis, Richards said, was friendly with C. P. Snow at Cambridge.[3] Wystan and Richards agreed

---

1 Isherwood is known by his German landlady as 'Herr Issyvoo' in his Berlin novels.

2 I. A. Richards (1893–1979), British literary critic, a guiding force behind the New Criticism movement in the 1930s and an important influence on critics such as Allen Tate, William Empson and F. R. Leavis. Erich Heller (1911–1990), German-British academic. Heller was currently resident at Northwestern University in Chicago, where Spender was a visiting Professor in the 1960s and 1970s.

3 C. P. Snow (1905–1980), British physicist and novelist. Leavis subsequently denounced Snow and his 'two cultures' thesis in an article in *The Spectator*, 'The Significance of C. P. Snow' (9 March 1962).

that fundamentally L. was a non-conformist who left no room in his criticism for the *enjoyment* of literature as language. I said that he had written good criticism of Hardy's poetry. Richards said: 'He has never criticized a single poem of Hardy that I did not discuss in those early lectures L. attended.'

Wystan was grumpy about the Richardses coming to dinner. 'So serious, so Cambridge.' I reminded him that last time he was in London we dined at [the] Garrick Club, and he insisted on bringing Mrs Gardiner and her Indian sister-in-law, and that he himself then left at 10.30. He agreed: 'Yes, that was Hell.'[1]

11 July 1962, London

After breakfast Wystan questioned me about biographical facts for my obituary, which he is writing for *The Times*. Asked me whether I would like anything special said. [. . .] Later I thought I would like him to say somewhere that my life was in some ways very ambiguous, like one of those arranged photographs which, if you look at it from one direction has a different face from that which you see from another. A feeling always of a different life at a different time and place. It's this which makes me, like others, emplane for Rome, Athens, Asia, South America. Yet when you get there you see a museum, scenery – and you have the same conversation. This not quite true – there are moments, for instance, when I first went to Florence when I was young, and saw the things in the Bargello, the Medici Tombs – and heard at Settignano the nightingales. Even two months ago, at the Sistine Chapel – on a day when there was a different light and the sky in the background of Adam and God etc shone like a silver shield.

Moreover there's always been a fringe of friendship with people who were outside the set pattern of this routine and life, above all not to do with literature.

Looking at our generation – Wystan, Christopher, Cyril – it seems to me this generation had in our minds when we were young the

---

1 Margaret Gardiner (1904–2005), educationist, patron of the arts and partner of J. D. Bernal, by whom she had a child.

image of a man or woman of 40 who had become completely stuck in a job, a family, and ideas: we were very determined not to be like this, to remain fresh, changing, on the move, and the people whom we admired – mostly artists and writers – were those who had not got stuck – e.g. Samuel Butler, Lytton Strachey, V. Woolf, Lawrence. [. . .] Whatever our defects we move[;] if Wystan, for example, seems a bit fixed, it is in a fixed direction, not that he is stuck. He does realize, of course, that you have to be yourself.

12 July 1962, London

Office. Lunch with Dom Moraes. He took me to a Chinese club near South Kensington. He was nice. Showed me a long poem, very gifted, but too facile; his inability to work into the detail. Told me he had been hired by the *Daily Express* for a month to be their guest writer at £100 a weekly article. The articles under his name which appeared were not only completely altered but about completely different books. I said if this is so he should write us an *Encounter* article describing his Beaverbrook press experience. He looked a bit dashed at this suggestion and said he had to consider whether doing such a thing would damage his earning capacity. He gossiped amusingly about George Barker, Paul Potts and other figures in lit. life.[1] All lies. The impression of a life of people entirely concerned with one another's affairs, getting money by any means, smiles with knives, verbal in a personal or perhaps a critical-scholarly way, but with no taste for anything but their own words, each other's personalities, sex, money, drinks, living in stuffy rooms, drinking rather than eating, no pictures, no music.

Went to see Magouche [Phillips], to discuss Matthew & Maro's financing of their summer holiday. Magouche was very cheerful in her light airy house, and despite everything her relation with Maro seemed gay and pleasant. Johnny Craxton was there, and I suddenly felt very happy. We all went then to tea with Sonia, Cyril, Deirdre

---

1 George Barker (1913–1991), bohemian British poet who was helped by Spender at various points. Paul Potts (1911–1990), anarchist British poet, like George Barker and Don Moraes a Soho bohemian, and friend of Peter O'Toole.

[Connolly], Anthony Hobson, Wystan.[1] Started talking with Cyril about Elizabeth Jane [Howard]'s husband.[2] I said he was like a male pick-up and her attitude to him was like this and she practically said to me: 'Look at his thighs.' I said he looked as if he was made of rope all over, thick rope. Cyril started giggling [. . .]

I went alone to Anne Fleming's after dinner as I had promised to take Elizabeth Glenconner there. Peter Quennell, Hugh and Dora Gaitskell, Tom Driberg, Diana Cooper, John Bayley and Iris Murdoch, Iris Tree.[3] Iris M. told me she knew a lot about politics. Said I realized I knew nothing. I hate women knowing about politics, and it put me off her. She talked a lot to Hugh, I suppose trying to convert him to C.N.D.

Iris Tree talked about Christopher's novel.[4] Reminds me that Wystan talked a lot about Christopher. He said that he felt Christopher never wanted to have anything to do with people who were his equals, and indicated that this had spoiled his own relations with Christopher. 'His books are about Mr Norris, Sally Bowles, Denham Fouts, people to whom he feels, and is, superior.'

13 July 1962, London

After the office I went to Hecht and collected Matthew Smith and [David] Bomberg paintings which had been reframed. Also, got the small [Graham] Sutherland from Marlborough Fine Arts. Then rearranged paintings at home. Was too tired to do anything else. All the same I think I spend far too much time doing this sort of thing. Surround myself with art instead of writing my own art.

Met Francis Bacon on the street and had a drink with him. He said he liked the two little poems I sent him and wondered why I did not

---

1 In 1959 Cyril Connolly had married Deirdre Craven, his third wife.

2 Elizabeth Jane Howard's second husband was the Australian journalist Jim Douglas-Henry. By this point, the marriage was in difficulties and she would shortly leave him for Kingsley Amis.

3 Peter Quennell (1905–1993), British biographer and literary historian. Diana Cooper (1893–1986), British actress. For Iris Murdoch and John Bayley, see biographical appendix.

4 *Down There on a Visit* (1962).

think they were good. I said maybe I was predisposed towards the poems I had been working at a great deal. He said he thought sometimes it was a good thing to take a very long time over things and he was thinking he should do just this.

17 July 1962, London

Lunch with Julian Huxleys who were very pleasant. Dinner with Mary Hutchinson.[1] Other guests a publisher John Calder who is also organiser of literary conference at Edinburgh Festival, and Michael Hamburger.[2] John Calder extremely anti-German, feels that Germans will not alter their nature for 100 years, that the West provoked the situation which produced the Wall, that if the Nagy regime had been more sensible Hungary would now be as Poland is, that the West is aggressive, etc.[3] Michael and I argued against most of these views. Whether right or wrong, the idea of 'the German character' which makes it impossible to hope anything of the Germans, Western aggressiveness which produces Russian policy, the activities of the C.I.A. in East Germany etc, are conventions of argument which also presuppose that but for Western provocation everything would be peaceful now.

---

1 Mary Hutchinson (1889–1977), Bloomsbury writer, cousin of Lytton Strachey and the mother of the Spenders' close friends Barbara and Jeremy Hutchinson.

2 John Calder (b. 1927), Canadian-Scottish publisher, founded Calder Publishing in 1949 and published much of the work of Samuel Beckett as well as early translations of Chekhov and Dostoevsky. Michael Hamburger (1924–2007), British translator and academic, known for translations of German writers including Paul Celan, Bertolt Brecht and W. G. Sebald.

3 The reformist Imre Nagy (1896–1958) had replaced the more hard-line Mátyás Rákosi as Prime Minister of Hungary in 1953, during a period of liberalization following Stalin's death. However, in his continued role as Party Secretary, Rákosi was able to undermine and discredit Nagy who was quickly removed from office.

19 July 1962, London

Lunched with Stephen Lushington and Alasdair Clayre at the Garrick.[1] [. . .] A. Clayre is a young Fellow of All Souls [Oxford], vague, talented, gently rebellious, who has written a novel and is now working at poems. He said he hardly goes to All Souls because it is not conducive to work. Talked about the anti-creativeness of Oxford Senior Common Rooms, where every impulse dissolves in talk which surrounds the unreasonable compulsive fantasizing effort which is creative. Oxford is too sceptical, asks too many questions, is too superior. The attitude of Oxford when I was there – 'an Oxford aesthete', 'an Oxford poet', 'an Oxford undergraduate in love' – in every case the epithet Oxford implied consciousness that this situation had arisen before, that Oxford has seen through it, ignored it, survived it, tolerated it, laughed at it, known better than it. When I was at Univ. [University College, Oxford] the thing that really brought Sir Michael Sadler into contempt with his Senior Common Room was not that he was an old fuddy-duddy who waffled on about education, but that he had the most wonderful flair for modern painting, and had Gauguins, van Goghs etc at the Master's Lodgings.[2] As the son of the tutor who was Professor of Aesthetics said to me knowingly, 'the other dons simply pee on Sadler because he has those crazy paintings.'[3]

To write a poem or novel is to a Senior Common Room a way of giving yourself away, showing that you are unhappy or obsessed or in love, that there is something in you which has been held back and is not resolvable into the Oxford culture – which is one of shared conversation. If you write a poem or novel, or paint a picture, it is about something – and this means it is about a situation which has already arisen and been made a subject of knowledgeable discussion

---

1 Stephen Lushington was an English master at Westminster School and Matthew Spender's housemaster.

2 Michael Ernest Sadler (1861–1943), British educationalist and champion of the public school system. Master of University College during Spender's years there, and a friend of Stephen's father. He is described in *World Within World*: 'a famous educationist whose interest in education seemed to stop or to be arrested when it came to governing his own college' (chapter 2).

3 The son was Gabriel Carritt, who appears as 'Tristan' in *World Within World*.

– and it has probably already been written and painted better than you are likely to do it. Therefore to create anything reveals your ignorance of what has been done already. Moreover, if you do it you do it in one way rather than another, which indicates ignorance of the many alternative ways in which it might have been done, probably better.

In the evening we dined at Anne Fleming's: Sir Edward Boyle, Stuart Hampshire, Maurice Bowra and the Glenconners were there.[1] Sir E.B., who has just been made Minister of Education, gives a curious Pickwickian impression, like a Victorian or Edwardian who wears his modern clothes as though they were fancy dress. He looks flushed, with a delicate pink skin, an intelligent and extremely interested baby. He seemed very eager to learn everything possible about education, and Bowra seemed very eager to tell him. In fact Bowra did not stop talking for a minute and then at the end of dinner bounced out into the street to catch his train back to Oxford, without saying good-bye. Bowra not only holds forth, but if interrupted emits loud 'ohs, ahs, quite so, not at all, no no you're wrong there' – like a radio station's continual signal sounding through other broadcasts.

31 July 1962, London

Went to Sonia's after dinner. Rosamond [Lehmann], Frances Partridge, two American friends of Wystan and Ron [Clairemont] an American friend of J. Craxton.[2] Sonia rather drunk. Conversation about Wilde's Letters.[3] I said Wilde was passionately nostalgic for the Renaissance, and considered himself without self-questioning a Renaissance genius. And I added that this kind of historic nostalgia was characteristic of several modern writers. It was an illness of our time for artists to believe passionately that they spiritually lived in the past: this tendency began in the 19th century with Ruskin,

---

1 Edward Boyle (1923–1981), British Conservative politician, Minister of Education, 1962–4.

2 Frances Partridge (1900–2004), writer whose diaries recording her life in Bloomsbury, published late in life, were widely read.

3 Rupert Hart-Davis's edition of the letters of Oscar Wilde was published in 1962.

Carlyle, Morris etc. Really the great effectiveness of Eliot and Pound in English letters was not due to their being Americans but to the fact that, as American travellers in Europe, they reinforced European nostalgia.

1 August 1962, London

I read Wilde's *Letters* [. . .] The extraordinary thing about Wilde is his complete confidence not just in his genius but in his seriousness as an artist. He doubted everything else about himself except that he was a marvellous poet and genius who turned philosophy into myth etc. Yet I feel that the significance of his imprisonment and *De Profundis* is that it made him get beyond his superficiality as a person: he accuses [Lord Alfred] Douglas again and again: 'the greatest crime is to be superficial,' and yet though he could see through his own behaviour he couldn't see through himself as an artist. He couldn't even see that it is serious to be a comedian. He regarded his epigrams, etc as sugaring the pills of a profound philosophy, and when – as in *The Importance of Being Earnest* – he was free of this pretence and therefore his realest Self as an artist, he regarded this as mere *jeu d'esprit*.

Part of his fatal lack of seriousness was his inability to have a relationship with any one else which was of an unquestioning, mutually respecting kind as between equals. Friendship should be based on two people being able to meet seeing in each other the fundamental situation of being alive and having to die, and disregarding who is more successful or more beautiful or more gifted than the other since, as regards each other, they are *dans le vrai* [in the right]. Intelligence and sensibility and imagination are necessary only to the extent that without them there cannot be understanding. But given such understanding when two people are friends, then the qualities in which one may excel the other are evident to the world, but do not count within their friendship. The greatest defect of Wilde's letters is that one feels that he scarcely ever ceased to be in competition or to feel competed with by his friends.

2 August 1962, London

Office. Lunch with Antony (?) Costa and Francis Hope.[1] Costa is a supporter of the Centre 42, Arnold Wesker, Osborne, Pinter, etc.[2] He considers John Arden the great poetic dramatist of the time.[3] He is also very interested in the 19th-century German theatre: not only Büchner, Kleist, Schiller's *Wallenstein*, etc, but also Lenz and one or two writers I have not read. Very apprehensive about the National Theatre which he seems to think will become the bulwark of academicism.[4]

The English theatre is now divided into two groups or gangs, the academics and the *nouvelle vague* [new wave], as they might be called. The entirely new style of actors and acting has emerged at the same time as the entirely new plays of a young generation. The new playwrights seem to have coincided with the right producers and actors for them almost providentially. The characteristic quality of the academics is that they are 'stars'. Whenever they act a role they duplicate with it their own acting personalities, which the public somehow separates from the role being played and which it really prefers to the role. An Olivier or a Michael Redgrave should never obliterate this acting personality in his role. He should be recognizable not just as the name of the role he is playing but as his own name printed in the programme. Redgrave or Gielgud plays Hamlet: but equally Hamlet plays Redgrave or Gielgud.

At present the new actors are excellent because they seem anonymous. They just seem the soldiers, tramps, clerks, beatniks which are the kind of roles the new playwrights invent for them. 'At present' because their faces and style are of course recognizable to an

---

1 Both Antony Costa and Francis Hope were assistant editors on *Encounter*.

2 The 'Centre 42' was established at the Round House in Camden by the British playwright Arnold Wesker (b. 1932) in 1961 with the aim of finding a popular audience for the arts and was supported by the Trades Union Congress.

3 John Arden (b. 1930) was, like Osborne and Wesker, a British social dramatist.

4 Although planned in 1951, the board of the new National Theatre had been set up only in July 1962, and the new theatre would open in October 1963 with a production of *Hamlet*.

audience of actor-connoisseurs, who very soon recognize in each of them the qualities carried over from play to play named by their own names, and not obliterated in the role. It will be just as difficult for them to avoid this happening as for the working class playwrights to save themselves from writing like the rich playwrights, directors of several tax-evading companies, which they have inevitable become.

4 August 1962, London

Whenever I try to write down my views about art, literature etc, I find I am quickly bored, or suddenly I feel unserious. Today I was typing out my book [*The Struggle of the Modern*] and I discovered that my damned typewriter – the instrument of my mocking subconscious – had typed out as one word: 'visualfart' instead of 'visual art'. How can one go on after that?

Modern Christian writers like [T. S.] Eliot, [Allen] Tate etc are ironic in their poetry and evidently consider irony a necessary 'modern' attitude. But Christianity is entirely without irony and does not even contain the potentiality of such an attitude.

5 August 1962, London

Natasha and I alone at Loudoun Road. Everything extremely quiet without the children.

Worked all the morning. At six we went for drinks to Edith Sitwell whom we found in bed. I did not realize for some time that she had had a kind of relapse – a return of symptoms she got from a fall a year ago, when as she explained to me she 'dislocated several vertebrae'. She described the original fall vividly, how she got up in the night to open a window, could not find it and then missed her way back to bed, fell over a chair and was not found till the next morning. She said she was accident-prone as a result of having been kept in iron braces by her parents when she was a child – 'they finally even tried to put my nose in irons'.

The present accident causing the dislocation to recur so that she had been 'screaming with pain' was the result of the chauffeur braking too suddenly. Edith, who was standing up to get out of the motor, was flung down. It is quite difficult to believe that Edith is in great pain and ill a lot of the time, though it is equally obvious that she really is. But everything she says seems to be on the same plane of unreality and almost all of it is said in exactly the same voice. Thus when we arrived she said she had had one of the most terrible weeks of her life because the *Sunday Times* had sent round an interviewer who asked her whether she liked being 75, was afraid of dying etc. Another thing – the papers had announced that the sale at Christie's of her manuscripts had brought in £3,000 when really it was £15,000. This she considered libellous. Finally Marilyn Monroe has died today and the papers keep ringing Edith up about this.[1] Another reason it is extremely difficult to take Sitwell illnesses as seriously as they really are is that the whole ménage is given to falling down on a scale that seems grotesque. Osbert (who is better, she said) falls a great deal as the result of his [Parkinson's] disease. David Horner – Osbert's friend, companion, and heir-presumptive – fell down a flight of stairs, also at Montegufoni, has not recovered and cannot speak yet, Edith said, rather hopefully.[2] 'It was a sacrifice to Bacchus,' she said and added: 'The Horners have a fantastic power of recovery. Nothing seems to kill them.'

One never knows who is in favour[,] who out, with Edith. It is safe to assume that all catty remarks about women writers will be well received. But, knowing she greatly liked Alberto de Lacerda who – I read – has been imprisoned in Portugal, I asked tenderly after him.[3] She said he had a terribly swollen head before he went and she hoped that prison would deflate it a bit. There were a lot of grim truths about Alberto – she indicated – that she would not tell me. Arthur Waley had sent her a postcard saying that Alberto was released, so she assumed he was all right.[4]

She was genuinely upset by a paragraph in the *Sunday Express*

---

1 Sitwell met and was photographed with Monroe during the shooting in England of the film *The Prince and the Showgirl* (1957). The two women got on well. Monroe died on 5 August 1962.

2 Montegufoni was the name of the Sitwells' property in Tuscany.

3 The Portuguese poet Alberto de Lacerda was briefly imprisoned under the authoritarian, right-wing regime in Portugal controlled by António de Oliveira Salazar. Lacerda had translated some of Spender's poems into Portuguese.

4 Arthur Waley (1889–1962), British Orientalist.

about two boys who had tortured a cat and gouged out its eyes. All that had happened was they were fined £5. She said she wanted to write to the *Sunday Express* suggesting that people who were cruel to animals should be pilloried, the police seeing that people did not attack them. It was Osbert's idea – Osbert is a magistrate – that this would be a suitable punishment. N[atasha] said she thought that the onlookers would take no notice of those put in the stocks. I tried to discourage her from writing such a letter.

11 August 1962, London

Last night we dined with Paddy Leigh Fermor and Joan Rayner.[1] The other guests were Peter Mayne (from Tangiers), Eddy Gathorne Hardy (whom I had not seen since Athens two or three years ago) and Francis Bacon.[2] It was a marvellous evening, an exquisite dinner, and everything as nice as only Joan can make it. Paddy seemed a bit subdued, perhaps because Francis talked so fantastically well about painting which Paddy knows little about.

16 August 1962, London

The last few days entirely taken up with finishing my book [*The Struggle of the Modern*]. Stayed up till 2 a.m. last night writing it, and went in at 6.30 a.m. Delivered it complete all but the last 5 or 6 pages.

Last Sunday we called on Henry Moore. He was in very good form. He likes to receive on Sunday afternoons, he told us, because when he was a boy he was so miserable on Sundays, that now he wants to be distracted and cannot work. There were an Indian and two Americans being shown round. With them we went in his garden and field. The field now with hedges along the side, an irregular

---

1 Patrick Leigh Fermor (1915–2011), British travel writer. He and Joan Rayner would marry in 1968.

2 Peter Mayne (1908–1979), British writer of travel books principally set in North Africa. Eddy Gathorne Hardy (1901–1978) was a 'bright young thing' satirized by Evelyn Waugh as Miles Malpractice in *Vile Bodies* (1930).

rectangle narrowing at the far end, almost to a triangle, looks very theatre-like.

He is experimenting with breaking up the theme of the reclining figure into two or three portions. In the most recent, the two separate pieces are almost at right angles and the knife-blade half figures look almost like the turning of a corner.

Henry said almost any two pieces of anything laid horizontally or with one vertical, look to him like a reclining or seated figure.

In 1962, Spender took part in a five-day International Writers Conference held at the Edinburgh Festival between 20 August and 24 August. The Conference was chaired by Malcolm Muggeridge and the theme was 'How does the novel form stand today in this country, in the continent of Europe and in America?' There were furious arguments about nationalism and internationalism in literature, with Angus Wilson arguing in favour of nationalism and writers such as Mary McCarthy, Hugh McDiarmid, and Alexander Trocchi taking the wider view.

21 August 1962, Edinburgh

Very rainy. We drove into Edinburgh. Lunched with the writers. At 2.30 there was the first meeting of the conference about the novel. The hall was packed. Angus Wilson and Mary McCarthy spoke first.

Angus said that he was going to talk about the serious novel in England which corresponded to the art novel in America. The English novel began by being a middle class expression. On the whole it was a conservative force, protecting a given way of life and behaviour. [. . .] It was not metaphysical or particularly interested in ideas. [. . .] It was the novel of manners and concerned with right and wrong manners not with good and evil.

The English novel was weak then in philosophy and had its limitations. But it also derived from them its strength. It provided a coherent way of looking at things. It was concrete and not rhetorical or empty. [. . .]

The world of the right and wrong protected English values has broken up, and for this reason Angus distrusted all the more English novelists who don't realize it has done so [. . .] Mary McCarthy said the one thing with which she agreed with Angus in all this was that the national novel was dying in England. [. . .] She thought that the English novel had shrunk. What English novels had today in common was a kind of smallness, an extreme carefulness, a pretty smallness like that of many English handwritings. [. . .]

These two introductions seemed immensely promising but after this there was the usual collapse into back-scratching, sly self-felicitation, over-modest disclaimers, special pleading of special groups which is inevitable in writers' conferences.

What was very noticeable was that the writers of countries outside America and England simply made no attempt to grasp the theses of Angus and Mary, which they regarded evidently as strange exotic utterances of people living in worlds utterly removed from theirs. [. . .]

Lawrence Durrell was grand and simple and unhelpful. 'The only yardstick is to ask yourself three questions of a novel – Has it made me care? Has it brought me joy? Has it changed me at all?'

Later, Muriel Spark got up and waxed indignant about the question, 'has it changed your life?'[1] She said the last thing a novelist should do was attempt to change anyone's life. 'Don't let us forget the dignity of our profession which is not to change the public but to serve it.' She also claimed to know nothing about novels because she wrote them. 'I couldn't write them if I knew anything about them.' [. . .]

Rebecca West said it would have been no loss to the world if most of the critics now writing had been strangled at birth.[2] She seemed to attribute to T. S. Eliot the view that the novel should not be about character. Her general grudge was that, if you wrote novels with characters in them they got bad reviews whereas if you wrote the novel of sensibility or about states of consciousness below the level of conscious character, you got praised. Perhaps the person who should really have been strangled at birth – to satisfy Dame Rebecca – is Freud. Anyway, it was not Eliot, but a novelist, D. H. Lawrence, who wrote to Edward Garnett in 1914 that he was sick of the novel of

---

1 Muriel Spark (1918–2006), Scottish novelist best known for *The Prime of Miss Jean Brodie* (1961).

2 Rebecca West (1892–1983), British novelist and journalist.

character and interested in forces moving through life which were below the level of character.[1] And another novelist, Virginia Woolf, attacked the 'characters' in Arnold Bennett's novels and suggested that they disguised the real nature of people.[2] A character after all is a lived fiction, a person's self-myth, and the whole development of the modern novel has been to plant an isotype [*sic*] into human behaviour which gets below the level of the dramatized consciousness.

In October 1962, Spender visited Argentina, under the auspices of PEN and the CCF.

8 October 1962, Buenos Aires

Talk by Robbe-Grillet at PEN [Congress].[3] He said that he began his adult life as an engineer and research worker. When he was in a laboratory no one wanted to know his views about society. But the moment he published his first novel – which was a *roman policier* – he was transported into the role of being an intellectual. He was asked to state his views on Budapest, Algeria, etc, to sign manifestoes.

He did have views about these things, though he felt some astonishment that while he was working in a laboratory no one had asked him his views.

He was then asked why he didn't express the views he held in his books. His reason for not doing so was that he believed that social problems could be solved by values which exist in society already. If the role of the novelist is to illustrate these values, then the novel has no role. The function of the novel, as of poetry, is not to illustrate given social theses, but to bring into the world new meanings. The novelist writes to discover himself.

---

1 Edward Garnett (1868–1937), British writer and editor, instrumental in obtaining a publisher for D. H. Lawrence's *Sons and Lovers* (1913).

2 Virginia Woolf dismissed Arnold Bennett's brand of realism in her 1923 essay 'Mr Bennett and Mrs Brown'.

3 Alain Robbe-Grillet (1922–2008), French writer and filmmaker.

12 October 1962, Buenos Aires

The Pen Club Congress went on in much the same way as before. On the last day [Ignazio] Silone, Don Salvador and I spoke.[1]

I went to three evening parties [. . .] I saw Borges on several of these occasions.[2] Borges has a young-old face with an alert, eager, *listening* expression of the blind. One thinks of the strained shining eyes, the mouth about to speak. He mentions his own shyness often. He speaks excellent English, but a bit like someone deaf rather than blind. His subjects are Anglo-Saxon and Icelandic literature, and etymologies. He has the questioning speculating way of talking rather reminiscent of Walter de la Mare. 'Do you know, that one word in one language is the same as another word in another,' he asks, in a speculative voice as though he didn't quite believe it himself but were trying out an idea. The last evening I saw him – at the house of V. O'Campo's sister – he was accompanied by an extremely pretty young lady who, he said, was a Superstar and 'my best pupil at Anglo-Saxon'. He likes greatly to have a following of devoted lady admirers. He's not married, lives with his mother, aged 86. Apparently at one time there was the idea he might marry the philosopher-lady, who is not attractive.

3 December 1962, Bruern

In the past few days, though, we have done such things as go to Henry Moore's with Léon and Phillippe Lambert and Phillippe's American wife. Gave a dinner party for the Lamberts at which there were the Ayers and Mary McCarthy. Phillippe's wife trying to hold her own was rude to Freddie [Ayer], who told her stiffly he was not used to being spoken to in that way. After the Lamberts had gone, Mary, Freddie and I had an interesting and perhaps important conversation about whether if one was a writer or artist it was better or worse to live today than two hundred years ago. Freddie cited [James] Boswell going with his friends to see the lunatics at Bedlam, people

---

1 Don Salvador de Madariaga (1886–1978), Spanish diplomat and writer.

2 Jorge Luis Borges (1899–1986), renowned Argentine writer who was now completely blind.

going to public hangings, etc. He insisted that he could not see any reason why there should not be a Shakespeare or a Tolstoy living today. He said that complaints about the industrial age were disproved by the fact that the nineteenth century was a great age of literature, although being the industrial age. [. . .]

This weekend I went with Matthew, Lizzie and Mercia to Bruern. We left Matthew at Merton College where he had the guest room.[1] I took Lizzie and Mercia to Bruern, then came back to Oxford and took Matthew out to a buffet party mostly of dons at John Bayley and Iris Murdoch's. Iris told me she was very dissatisfied with her life: too much work that took her away from her real work. I asked her what her ideal of life would be. She said: 'Something much more ascetic.' Raymond Carr and John Bayley were there.[2] Raymond said that Christ Church (where Matthew had his viva Saturday) was sure to snatch him up. I did not feel certain about this. A don from Ch.Ch. who was to sit in Matthew's examining board was there. He asked me what the external view of Ch.Ch. was and I told him it was thought of as a College of baying bloods. He said this wasn't quite so: though last term the worst rag ever had taken place – all the windows in Peck Quad broken and two or three undergraduates thrown in the fountain of Mercury in Tom Quad. I began to feel glad Matthew had not asked for a place at Ch.Ch.

Went back to Bruern. Came to Oxford Saturday. [. . .] After lunch we went to a café opposite Ch.Ch. Conrad Asquith was there.[3] Then Matthew left and walked across to his viva. After about twenty minutes Conrad and I went to the Common Room which was full of trembling boys from Westminster and from Charterhouse. There was one amusing one doing imitations of the examining dons, which made us all nervous. Matthew emerged and said it had been terrible – there were 25 dons, all dressed up in academic robes and staring at him. They had asked him 1) why he had not applied for a place at

---

1 Matthew Spender was being interviewed to read History at Oxford. At the time, each College set its own exam. He failed to get into Christ Church and Merton and was finally accepted at New College.

2 Raymond Carr (b. 1919), historian, fellow of New College, Oxford.

3 Conrad Asquith (b. 1944), grandson of the prime minister Herbert Henry Asquith (1852–1928) and friend of Matthew's at Westminster.

Ch.Ch. if he didn't get a scholarship, 2) whether he wrote poetry, 3) whether he played an instrument like his mother. He felt he had done badly but so did all the other Westminster boys who had been interviewed.

I drove him back to Bruern and later on we discovered that Watson, Conrad Asquith and another boy had got a scholarship and exhibitions, Matthew nothing and of course not a place either. He was quite dejected. Suddenly I realized that I wanted him very much to go to Oxford, that it is an élite, that his friends Conrad Asquith and Phillip Watson are going there, and that if he doesn't he will be left behind by the best members of his own generation. I felt this specially driving into Chipping Norton to get the Sunday papers. It is a thought that runs contrary to my principles and even my sympathies, but I realized that I thought of my Oxford contemporaries as in some way superior beings. Going there makes one enjoy such conversation and exchange of ideas in circumstances of easy companionship and comparative leisure with the best contemporaries of one's generation, during their most formative years. For M. not to continue there with the very nice friends he has at Westminster is like a relationship being cut off just when it is maturing and may be most valuable.

I thought how little Oxford had done for a good many of my friends, how it made people in some way unreal, how as a community it isolated us for the rest of our lives, how the most energetic tough and creative talents will probably now not come from Oxford. But I still wanted him to go.

18 December 1962, London

Drinks with Edith Sitwell. There were about five people there. Edith sat in her wheel chair looking very pale and tired and ill and really doing all the talking because when she is with a group of people she can only listen and talk on her own wavelength. There was a humiliating atmosphere of everyone being sycophantic, like courtiers, feeding her with titbits of gossip and malice which would amuse her or draw her out. Whenever there was a silence it was appalling, as though boredom and sterility might seep like dense fog through a chink in a door or window. Anecdotes were dragged out of the past and held up for inspection. No one was quite successful in living up to Edith's own tone, and as a matter of fact she was rather brilliant, although this gave one the feeling that she had to make all the effort and added to the sense of humiliation. She gave one or two amusing examples of her replies to foolish letters. She had a letter from some silly woman saying Dear Dame Edith, As an admirer of your poems I am nevertheless greatly disturbed by a poem containing a line about the mating of tigers. I have a daughter of 14 – at that age where the brook runs into the river – and a son aged 10, who is very restless. I wish to entreat you, dear Dame Edith, when you write your poetry to consider the disturbing effect that lines like those about the mating of tigers may have on the young. Edith wrote back, 'Tell your dirty-minded little brats to read *King Lear.*' This seemed superb, though she embroidered it a bit unnecessarily with explanations that the mating of tigers could not be compared with th[at] of human beings because their paws were not suitable for wedding rings.

In September 1964, Spender went to Budapest on CCF business. From 1945 to 1956, Hungary had been ruled by the Stalinist dictator Mátyás Rákosi. In February 1956, Khrushchev had denounced Stalin and his disciples in a 'secret speech' and in June, Mátyás Rákosi was deposed as General Secretary of the Hungarian Communist Party and forced to move to the USSR. Encouraged by these developments, 23,000 protestors convened in Budapest on 23 October 1956. The next day, the protestors were attacked by Soviet tanks and fighting between the protestors and army continued until 27 October, when Nagy expressed his support for the rebels and formed a temporary democratic government with some non-communist ministers. The government was initially sanctioned by the Soviet regime, who arranged a ceasefire with the rebels. However, on 30 October armed protestors attacked the officials guarding the Budapest Hungarian Workers Party headquarters and the Soviet leaders reversed their decision, crushing the Nagy government in an act of violence that lost the communists many of their surviving supporters in the West. Khrushchev instated János Kádár as the new leader of Hungary.

12 September 1964, Budapest

Drove with the PEN Club secretary Laszlo Kery, and my guide Tamas Ungurari along the Danube loop to Szentendre and Esztergon. At Szentendre called at the villa of István Vas and his wife Piroska Szanto a painter. Vas is a translator and poet, a very nice man.[1] All these people talk frankly about their difficulties ('I have to do a great deal of translating' etc). [. . .]

We went to the Catholic museum at Esztergon. Here, there are the marvellous Grünewald-like paintings of the unknown 15th (?) century master M.S. A tormented crucifixion. We also visited a literary shrine – the house of the poet Babits.[2] This is on a hill with a marvellous view of the Danube. Babits was a greatly admired poet also the editor of a literary review and distributor of the benefits of something called the Baumgarten fund. He was a kingmaker among poets, and caused much bitterness by not extending his favour to Attila Jozsef.[3]

In the evening I was by myself so climbed through the park [to] the Gellert hill and looked down over Budapest. The park was full of lovers. The walk was much longer than I thought and there was no restaurant on top, so finally I dined at the Gellert [hotel].

14 September 1964, Budapest

Ungurari called for me at 11 and took me 'sight-seeing'. [. . .] [He] had brought with him István Örkény a short story writer aged about 50 and his much younger girlfriend (an actress).[4] We went to Ungurari's house where his wife (the foremost Hungarian actress) served us coffee. Conversation was very frank, beginning with talk about Rákosi whom everyone can be frank about. Ungurari said that Rákosi was not dead but in a Russian nursing home. A rumour of his death had been spread by Rákosi himself in order to test the reaction in Hungary, or to obtain an official *démenti* [denial] of it. He said that after Rákosi's disappearance his house was looted by his guards

---

1 István Vas (1910–1991).

2 Mihály Babits (1883–1941).

3 Attila József (1905–1937).

4 István Örkény (1912–1979).

who could not agree on a sensible division and therefore divided a tapestry into nine separate pieces[,] took each of them home one white telephone apparatus etc. When Rákosi got to Moscow he went every day to the Hungarian Embassy and telephoned to the Cabinet in Budapest. This became a great nuisance and finally they asked the Russians to remove him from Moscow.

István Örkény talked of his own position. He is a short story writer who in some way has fallen into disgrace and cannot get published. While he was driving me to the British Embassy (where I had lunch) Ungurari told me that Örkény was by origin a man of independent means who in his youth had travelled all over the world. In 1948 he became 'perhaps quite authentically (I myself have never been a party member)' a communist. But he was never trusted by true communists, and whereas other writers who had been in disgrace had got into good positions, he could not get his stories published. The feeling that there was something against him depressed Örkény and perhaps even prevented him doing his best work. All the same he had not experienced further persecution. He was allowed to keep his house and his 2 cars.

Ungurari told me he was very sorry I had not time to stay at his house so he could show me his property and 1,800 acres.

In Hungary you are allowed to have property and even to leave it, so long as you are not an exploiter. [. . .]

In the evening was taken to Kodály's very boring operetta, by Lili Halapy, the guide who was attached to David Carver for two weeks.[1] Middle-aged, schoolmistressy, very preoccupied with her health, official but so anxious to put herself out and be friendly that she says what she thinks – perhaps even more than the others, who act a bit saying what they think.

(Tito, Kádár and the president were sitting in the royal box at the opera.[2] Tito I am told dyes his hair and wears high heels. He looks like a resigned old governess.)

---

1 Zoltán Kodály (1882–1967), Hungarian composer, friend and champion of Béla Bartók who shared his interest in collecting Hungarian folk music. Both were leading figures in the Budapest Sunday Circle which also included the writers Georg Lukács and Béla Balázs.

2 Tito was instrumental in persuading Khrushchev to choose János Kádár as the new leader of Hungary in 1956.

After 2 acts of the opera I persuaded Mrs Halapy to eat at the Royal Hotel restaurant. She started talking about Kodály, said his best works were his chorales. He had written a magnificent chorale on the theme of a 16th century poem, 'Do not hurt Hungary', which had been played all the time in 1956 at the time of the rising. Since then it had not been played. She was greatly embarrassed at having said this. 'Please forget I ever said it. Don't on any account tell anyone I told you that.' Then she started saying how everything was much better in Hungary than it had been before 1956. For example, her washerwoman was now on a state pension, had been sent by the government on a free holiday etc. Mrs Halapy herself, not feeling well, had applied to the Writers' Union for a room at a hotel in the mountains which was kept available for sick writers, had obtained this and was off on a two weeks holiday at only 40 [forints] a day.

I said that it was very difficult to weigh the freedom of artists and writers against the pension of a charwoman and I could understand that the government might feel that complete freedom of expression would lead to a revival of reaction. 'I don't think that's necessarily true at all,' she said, 'I don't see why they shouldn't be free.' Then she explained that the real cause for lack of freedom was that publication was always in the control of the same people, the directors of the state publishing houses, just as the galleries were in the hands of those who were resolved against exhibiting abstract art. She went on like this and then said: 'I myself – I translate and do other things, and I try to keep myself in a situation in which I dare look at my own face in the mirror in the morning. I mean I try to keep my integrity.' She then said she thought she had drunk too much – which she hadn't as we only had a small carafe of wine between us.

15 September 1964, Budapest

Luncheon alone at the Hotel Royal. Then at 5 gave my talk on the '30s at the Hungarian Writers' Association. Was extremely nervous about this, thinking that it was the worst possible subject to talk about. Also I had to give the lecture sentence by sentence each one being translated by poor Mrs Halapy who often got very confused. In fact, the talk seemed to go well. It was in a large club sitting room with comfortable chairs, coffee and a liqueur were served and the atmosphere was relaxed. The writers followed attentively and when there were difficulties in translating a phrase they helped Mrs Halapy out.

Afterwards there were questions concerning *Encounter* and not referring to the rather risky issues raised by my lecture. I was asked by one writer (who, as I was later told, had spent fifteen years in Russian concentration camps) why *Encounter* had published two articles (one by Dwight MacDonald, the other by Robie Macaulay) hostile to Ernest Hemingway.[1] I explained it was no part of editorial policy to attack Hemingway. Another writer raised the matter of our articles about life behind the Iron Curtain. He said, 'from what we have seen of you, it seems that you believe in coexistence, but *Encounter* in its attitude towards the East pursues a Cold War policy.' I said that I myself did not feel happy about everything we had published about life in the people's democracies, but that I was quite sure we had no cold war policy. In fact we had tried to arrange exchanges of articles with *Novy Mir*. I added that one way of correcting the impression produced by an article they disagreed with would be to write to *Encounter* protesting about it. Ivan Boldizsar said that if they did this *Encounter* readers would assume that it was an official protest.[2] I said this was a difficulty but I didn't think all readers would have this reaction. Anyway that he should think this demonstrated the difficulty on both sides: for whatever we published was taken by them (and also by Western readers) to be Cold War propaganda, and any protest published from their side was regarded as official démenti [denial].

A point I had made in my talk was that in Hungary, Poland and other central European countries, anti-Nazism was an extension of the politics of the intelligentsia which had been directed against dictators in those countries long before Hitler; whereas in England the writers who became anti-Nazi in the '30s had previously paid little attention to politics, their literary attitudes deriving from Eliot, Joyce,

---

1 Dwight MacDonald dismissed the Hemingway of the 1930s as a big man who 'drank a great deal' and 'wrote very little' ('Ernest Hemingway', *Encounter*, January 1962). For Robie Macaulay, Hemingway 'lacked the X-ray vision of a true parodist' ('A Moveable Myth', *Encounter*, September 1964).

2 Ivan Boldizsar (1912–1978), Hungarian writer and President of the Hungarian PEN club.

Lawrence and so on. An expert on Joyce asked me what I thought the attitude of people to Joyce was. I pointed out that Joyce spoke of himself as a socialist.

After this pleasant meeting I went with István Vas, Ungurari and a few others to dinner at a journalist's club.

This morning (Sept 15) I was taken to the offices of *Nagy Vilag*, a magazine devoted exclusively to translation. The editors showed me numbers of their magazine which contained poems by Kingsley Amis, Donald Davie, D. J. Enright, Philip Larkin, Thom Gunn and prose by Rhys Davis and Irwin Shaw. Another number had J. D. Salinger, Günter Grass, [Hans Magnus] Enzensberger among Western writers. We discussed the situation of the intellectuals and they said they thought there was very little Marxist dogmatism. I brought up the subject of abstract art, and they agreed, yes, that exhibitions of work which was officially disapproved of could not be held. They said they had to admit that the government was 'rather conservative' about this. But they pointed out that in Poland, for example, abstract art is officially allowed, and they said that even in the realms of ideology, there was a great deal of debate going on now in the People's Republics, and they hoped there would be a broadening of official attitudes here in Hungary. One often has the feeling talking to intellectuals here that there is no real disagreement between us, simply that they feel they have to defend certain positions. They talked a lot about the great advances in education in Hungary. They said that although all curricula and even hours of schedules in schools were the same at the same levels, nevertheless that the standard of teaching differed according to the quality of the teachers.

István Vas said: 'Between 1984 and 1956 – Oh, excuse my mistake' and 'Our revolution – I mean our counter-revolution.' There seems real embarrassment which to call it. Mrs Halapy, I suppose, put the official version as it has been made acceptable for intellectuals when she said that the 1956 uprising began by being a good thing but after the first days it became evident that reactionaries were gaining control of it. At any rate everything has turned out comparatively – and surprisingly comparatively, for the best. Someone else told me that during the revolution-counter-revolution there was a surprising proliferation of opposition groups[,] 'about ten parties all quarrelling among themselves – and we didn't know who all these people were.'

Again someone else said talking about the émigrés 'about two thirds of those who left did so because, being cut off from the West, they thought it was the land which would fulfil all their dreams. What a disappointment. To be an émigré is to arouse first a little sympathy then to be a bore.'

We discussed the émigrés a great deal. Not altogether unsympathetically but with a rather complicated resentment. The resentment is partly, of course, the not convincing sense that the émigrés have betrayed their country. It is more deeply I think that the émigrés put those who have stayed into the position of being accused of having betrayed their ideals by not going away. The existence of émigrés creates a situation of mutual recrimination, and I found one or two people defending themselves for staying.

Attitudes towards other Iron Curtain countries. Romania despised: a foreign policy which is of the 1960s, a policy at home which is Stalinist. Barani (?) the 22 year old student who gave an interview saying everything [was the] fault of the older generation who accepted Stalinism.

16 September 1964, Budapest

This morning spent an hour with Georg Lukács.[1] I walked up the stairs to his small flat on the fifth storey of an apartment house (the interior well of the courtyard is pocked with gunfire). I rang the bell and was shown into his study. The professor was telephoning so I had a moment to look at the booklined shelves, the small bronze bust of Goethe, and a few bronze plaques lying on his desk. His study that of a *Gelehrter* [savant] crammed with learning, but in this fine September day light and airy. Lukács came in we shook hands and he sat at his desk. He is short with a large head on a small body, and a somewhat emaciated face which emphasizes the high forehead, the pronounced nose, the rather sticking-out ears, the bright eyes in their sockets that look tireder than their expression. While we talked I was

---

1 Georg Lukács (1885–1971), Hungarian Marxist philosopher and literary critic. In 1956, he was appointed Minister of Culture by Nagy's revolutionary government, and in the hard-line backlash following the revolution he was then deported to Romania. He was able to return to Budapest a year later and regained political favour in the mid-1960s.

as it were anxiously taking account of the balance between his sustained powers of expression in the foreign English language, and his frail appearance. He looks a bit worn but quite ageless, one does not think of his being 80 though he referred several times to his age.

His manner was extremely courteous and on the one occasion when he disputed opinions in *Encounter* he did so firmly but apologetically. With the little bust of Goethe in front of him, the *Collected Works* behind him, his side of the conversation was Olympian and I had a feeling of great privilege – almost of exultation – in being in the same room with him. If it had not been that Ungurari was going to fetch me I would have left far earlier. As it is I am grateful that we talked for an hour. [. . .]

To start the conversation we recollected that we had met at the *Rencontres de Genève* in 1946. We talked of the death of Merleau-Ponty.[1] He said that at the time of this conference he had admired the liveliness and interest of Merleau's mind and had formed the impression that he was a man of more advanced views than Sartre. That subsequently M.-P. had become academic a 'bit of the university Prof.', whereas it was immensely to the credit of Sartre that he had developed so that his most recent works – whether or not one agreed with them – were the most interesting.

He said that now he had given up making conferences attending meetings etc. It was time that he sat down and tried to sum up the conclusion of a lifetime spent in thinking about certain things. His case was the exact opposite of that of his colleague Bertrand Russell, who had written his philosophical conclusions at a fairly early age and was now free to make pronouncements and participate in the world. [. . .]

He asked me what I was writing, so I said that what he had said interested me, because I was devoting several years to writing a poem exploring one's experience of the action upon one's self of relations symbolized by personal pronouns – I, thou, he, she, we, they, etc. For example, it seemed to me that in one's relations with society one

---

1 Maurice Merleau-Ponty had died in May 1961. Spender recalls meeting Merleau-Ponty at the first of the Rencontres de Genève in 1946, when intellectuals from throughout Europe were brought together to discuss questions of reconstruction, civilization and post-war guilt.

passed through an early phase of consciousness of oneself as 'I', then a consciousness that everyone else was 'I'. There was also a phase of thinking of oneself as 'we', and this was stressed in some situations in opposition to 'they'. For example, the 'comrades' in revolution were 'we', pitting themselves against a ruling class who were 'they'. From the point of view of such a 'we', it is significant that 'they' is masculine, feminine and neuter: so that they are not only people to who 'we' are opposed, 'they' also tends to merge into the property and things which belong to them.

Lukács said that nevertheless everything social had a subjective basis. It was an illusion to suppose that a governing class was not subjective. I said that all the same people did think of themselves as living in an impersonal history, amid historic forces. To think oneself into the history of our time so that the 'I' thinking identified with the 'I' which set up concentration camps, and the 'I' of the victims of concentration camps, was the aim of my poem. [. . .]

Lukács said that he thought that perhaps the art from 1914 to the 1950s was the reflection of a period when for many people in Europe the problem of living was the question of mere survival. He thought that in spite of everything we were moving out of a period of dark into one – comparatively – of light. He said: 'I think that's true of all parts of the world[,] of this as well as the other. After Stalinism there really has been a great change. If you don't mind my saying so, what I'd reproach *Encounter* for is that you don't see this. You are very conservative in this respect and you go on writing about the countries of the People's Democracies as though we were living still in the Stalinist era, and you still had to promote the views which were those of Koestler and Orwell a generation ago.'

He said he was very glad that his life happened to have coincided with 80 years of great historic change. He had been in Mittelschuler when *Buddenbrooks* had been published.[1] He had lived through the pre–1914 years which now seemed an almost unthinkable period. The period 1914–1956 now began to take its place in history as a continuous darkness – war, revolution, unemployment, hunger, fascism, concentration camps, and then after the second war the dark years of Stalinism. He thought that we were now for the first time

---

1 Thomas Mann's *Buddenbrooks* had been published in 1901.

moving into a completely new period and this would affect people's views about everything – including literature and art.

In 1965, Spender received the highest honour hitherto of his literary career with his appointment to the Consultant's position at the Library of Congress (the American equivalent of the Poet Laureate). He was the first, and still the only, British poet to be so honoured. Meanwhile, the Vietnam War was wreaking havoc between the generations in the US. The Democrat president, Lyndon B. Johnson (1908–1973) had succeeded to the presidency following John F. Kennedy's assassination in 1963 and then secured a victory in his own right in the 1964 election. During his term he conducted a 'War on Poverty' improving healthcare for the old and poor at the same time as escalating the American involvement in Vietnam.

24 September 1965, New York

We went Wednesday to New York. [. . .] Dined with the Stravinskys and Bob Craft. Stravinsky seemed in very good form, talking a great deal about the Soviet edition of Chekhov. He said how stupidly this was edited e.g. in a stage direction it says that a character wears *pince-nez*. A note states 'pince-nez, a French word'. As I.S. said, anyone could tell it was a French word, but if a note were required, it could only be of use to say what a *pince-nez* is – as they are unknown in the Soviet Union. He said that the Soviets dealt with a very selected and edited picture of Chekhov.

At dinner I.S. said to N[atasha] concerning [Pierre] Boulez, 'An important figure and very French: more French than important.' Talk about English critics who had given poor Bob Craft a terrific going over at their recent London concert.

I had had vodkas at the McGraths [Earl and Camilla] before going to the S[travinsky]s. These were followed by more vodkas with the Stravinskys and wine at dinner (Igor was very happy going to and fro among his guests passing caviar sandwiches).

At dinner we got very drunk – especially me, so much so that I can't remember anything, except that towards the end of dinner S. started talking (I think!) about Poles and young Russians, and I was suddenly seized with an idea of transcendental importance – which I repeated several times – that he must write a message to the young musicians and artists of that part of [the] world. I remember tactfully avoiding saying that it should be a posthumous testament. Every time I said this Vera said in her patient tolerant smiling way, 'But you know my husband never writes letters.'

26 September 1965, New York

[On Friday] evening we took Isaiah and Aline Berlin, Robert (Cal) Lowell and Bob Silvers to dinner at the Coffee Club.[1] Cal brought with him a friend, Mr Parker. Cal talked a lot and made some rather strange though not unexpected pronouncements: that Ezra Pound is the greatest translator of the 20th century; that the poems of Wordsworth's last ten years have – some of them – rhythmic qualities as good as the Prelude. He is very taken up with translation and asked 'Would you rather have an exact rendering of a masterpiece or a poem which was equally a masterpiece in English?' – which seems a loaded way of putting the problem. [. . .] [Saturday] evening we dined, at the Stanhope Hotel with Henry Moore and Harry Fischer.[2] After attending the unveiling of his large bronze at the Lincoln Center, and having a very rackety two days of TV etc in New York, they had gone to Chicago, which they said they preferred to New York. [. . .]

Henry was more revealing than any time I've been with him, I think. During dinner he talked about Mary [his daughter] and said that what worried him a bit was that she had experienced things too easily – going to Italy, for example, and seeing pictures, when she was sixteen – when these things had been perhaps a greater experience for him in his youth because he had attained them with much effort and difficulty. He talked also about Giacometti, saying that G. was someone who wanted to arrive at a final statement through art, rather than to produce solid objects, and this did not have good results in sculpture, it led to thinness and repetition. Nor did he think

---

1 Robert Silvers (b. 1930), co-editor of the *New York Review of Books*.

2 Harry Fischer and Frank Lloyd were co-founders of the Marlborough Gallery in Bond Street, which for many years represented among others Francis Bacon, Frank Auerbach, Henry Moore and Lucian Freud.

Giacometti nearly such a good painter as his father.[1] He thought that where he was really best was in his drawings because in them he tried to describe objects and his concerned and worried way of doing so was very complex. After dinner when we were having drinks in the bar the discussion got round to values in art. I had said that I found I was less interested in Klee now than I had been when I was twenty-five. Henry said he felt the same way and it was because Klee was not an important artist. This annoyed Harry Fischer who argued that Klee was just as good, in his way, as Picasso. Henry said that nevertheless Picasso was much greater and this was what mattered. [. . .]

What stood out in this was Henry's very individualistic Renaissance idea of a hierarchy of the great and the less great. He sees a line of important figures – Masaccio, Michelangelo, Rembrandt etc – who matter, and compared with them Vermeer, Chardin, the painters of purity and taste do not matter. He likes great figures that produce great works.

He said that it was nonsense to be taken into a current exhibition of Pop Art and be told that this is the latest and greatest development in painting. Without there being great painters, whom one knows to be great and who are painting in a certain way[,] movements mean nothing. Cubism was the only recent movement which was great because it had three great painters attached to it – Picasso, Braque and, to a lesser degree Juan Gris.

29 September 1965, Washington DC

Went to the White House for the signing by the President of the Arts and Humanities Bill. Arrived at 9.30[,] waited for quarter-hour at North West Gate while everyone's invitations were scrupulously examined. Then went into a lobby where there were many official looking dark-suited people, including Johnny Walker and excepting Morris [Graves], then into another waiting room, then along a corridor into a courtyard with colonnade of the White House at the

---

1 The father of Alberto Giacometti was the painter Giovanni Giacometti (1868–1933).

end, and chairs in the courtyard where everyone sat down.[1] After a time the President appeared, at first unnoticed among several people standing on a platform, then he moved over to a rostrum which had in front of it the enlarged insignia seal of the President of the U.S., and he made a speech. His face looked as usual so lined and corrugated that only two expressions are possible: one, even more corrugated, in a smile; one less so, despondent. After this the President signed the document using a battery of pens in front of him to do so. He seemed to write part of one letter with each pen. Then we filed past him and were given a pen in a box with his signature and the Presidential seal stamped on it.

During the wait, I had some conversation with Paul Engle who was there – looking very pinched and wizened like an engraving of a shoemaker in an illustration to Grimm's Fairy Tales.[2] He asked me whether I was enjoying myself and I said that my job was very good as regards shutting myself in a room where I had to work but I found Washington a bit depressing. I added that I had a similar sabbatical in what Edmund Wilson had described to me as extremely uncongenial circumstances, in view next year at Wesleyan [University, Connecticut]. Paul Engle said, 'I refuse to shed tears over S.S.'s enforced leisure.' I said I hadn't asked him to do so but had only attempted to answer his question truthfully. Later, Engle told me that someone from a new English university had written to him about a project there for a creative writing course – did I think this a good idea? I said I didn't know what to think but on the whole such courses seemed more justified in America because they substituted for meetings in cafés or journeys to the great centres which were easier arranged in England than in America. This annoyed Paul because it sounded like criticism of America from a Limey. Later he asked whether I would recommend young English writers to come to Iowa. Thinking of Harry Fainlight [I] said I could think of one who would

---

1 Johnny Walker (b. 1939), British abstract painter. Morris Graves (1910–2001), American expressionist painter. Walker and Graves were also being honoured by the President.

2 Paul Engle (1908–1991), American writer and editor, director of the University of Iowa's celebrated creative writing programme, the Iowa Writers' Workshop, 1941–65.

not undermine his institution.[1] He said: 'We've put up with a great many oddballs, without disastrous results. We're not so easily upset as that.' We parted coolly. Karl and I went to a coffee and juice bar. He asked me what I thought of my early poetry and of writing in poetic form. He said he had grown so disgusted with poetic form he had given up writing poetry. I told him how I had said to Auden in Berlin in the winter that the thing that made me most doubt whether I was a poet was my complete uncertainty about forms in which to write. Auden said: 'What obsesses me is form. So I put poems into them arbitrarily and make them as abstruse as possible. What I like is writing in very strict forms but breaking them up on the page so the reader won't recognize them as such.'

30 September 1965, Washington DC

Yesterday after the Pen-giving ceremony, we went to a luncheon [. . .] Then, rather tired, worked at the library and wrote a few letters. At six we went to the Smithsonian Institute [of] Technology, for a party given by Roger Stevens.[2] Nothing happened for about two hours then Vice President Hubert Humphrey appeared.[3] We were taken downstairs to a panelled room to meet him. Bill [Robert] Rauschenberg who looks attractive, rather a dandy, was there and I was delighted to meet him[,] feeling such awe of painters.[4] H. Humphrey came in and shook hands with us and others with a great deal more friendliness than President J. He has a really benevolent manner as though he were humming with good will. We went upstairs and he made a speech not remarkable but spontaneous.

---

1 Harry Fainlight (1935–1982), British surrealist poet who suffered from psychological mood swings aggravated by drugs. He was much helped by Spender over the years.

2 Roger Stevens (1906–1980), British academic and civil servant, at this date Vice Chancellor of the University of Leeds and advisor to the first Secretary of State on central Africa.

3 Hubert Humphrey (1911–1978), Vice President of America under President Johnson, 1965–9.

4 Robert Rauschenberg (1925–2008), American artist most famous for his 1950s 'Combines', which integrated painting and sculpture and included discarded objects found in the street.

13 October 1965, Washington DC

Had dinner with Arthur and Marion Schlesinger at Rive Gauche in Georgetown. Arthur has openness friendliness intelligence and understanding. He also knows a great deal and is a modern historian whose interest in history is interest in the world: not just the world of power but also of gossip, anecdote, and the arts. [. . .]

Conversation about President Johnson. Arthur describes him as an egomaniac whose conversation is a monologue and who requires only complete obsequiousness from those around him. When one of his aides, Valenti – whom Arthur likes – made a speech – quickly notorious and cruelly attacked – saying that he slept better at night for reflecting that Johnson was on watch at the White House a cartoon was published depicting Johnson as a slave driver with a leather thong whipping slaves who were kneeling before him in an adulatory fashion.[1] The caption was from Valenti's speech. Arthur rang Valenti thinking that attacked on all sides – from the public and also by the President whom he exposed to such ridicule – he must be in need of sympathy. To his surprise Valenti seemed highly satisfied. The President was delighted with the cartoon, which reflected his own view of his relations to his aides. Arthur said it was quite untrue to say that J. F. Kennedy had snubbed L.B.J. On the contrary he had done everything to encourage him and keep him in the picture. But [despite] Johnson's repellent personality Arthur said it was difficult to fault his policy in any way. He had been excellent about Civil Rights, Arthur saw no alternative to his Vietnam policy, he had largely retrieved the gaffe about the Dominican Republic.[2] The Johnsons had

---

1 Jack Valenti (1921–2007), Press Officer to the Kennedy administration and then special assistant to Johnson, for whom he had a life-long fidelity. He informed an audience in Boston in 1965 that he slept 'each night a little better, a little more confidently because Lyndon Johnson is my president'. In 1966, he would resign from the White House and become President of the Motion Picture Association of America.

2 In April 1965, US troops invaded the Dominican Republic, intervening in a civil war between Loyalists and Constitutionalists. President Johnson sanctioned a US invasion ostensibly to 'protect American interests', preventing harm to foreigners, none of whom had been killed or injured. Johnson's true motive for American involvement was fear of 'a second Cuba' on his doorstep, and part of a wider impulse to prevent a communist threat to American interests, despite the fact that there was no clear evidence that the Dominican Republic's civil war was a struggle for communism.

extensively taken over the Kennedys' concern with the arts. He said he thought Johnson had admired Kennedy.

16 October 1965, Washington DC

Yesterday morning Natasha left for the airport. She seemed very tearful at going. Having got to the airport she discovered she had left her fur coat so took the taxi straight back in order to get it. I thought she was really too miserable, and that perhaps I had not seemed concerned enough about her leaving, so I arranged to go to Boston on Sunday to join her at the Bruners.[1] If she is depressed, she may find New York and Boston just sad. I rang her in New York. I got onto Cal Lowell who was very upset about the death of Randall Jarrell.[2] Randall has been ill – nervously ill – for several months; seemed to be better, went home, started teaching again, had returned to the hospital for some kind of treatment. He walked out of the hospital and threw himself against a passing car.

Everyone concerned at the Library of Congress was upset. They asked me into a room, where we listened to Mr Mumford's remarks about Jarrell, which were being broadcast.[3]

The thought that Jarrell had perhaps become disillusioned with poetry occurred to me. This arose from a curious conversation I had with a marine (Peter John Leacacos) who brought me his poems to read at the Library of Congress (they are interesting). He said he had stopped writing six months ago because he had become disillusioned with poetry. I asked why and he said because he had decided that all poetry was rhetoric and he didn't see how rhetoric could cope with our world. To go on with this – he told me he'd decided now to be detached about going to Vietnam, to regard it as an experience. I said

---

1 Jerome Bruner (b. 1915), American psychologist specialising in cognitive psychology and the use of learning theory in educational psychology. Following an operation for cancer, Natasha Spender was beginning a new career of research into the psychology of music and Bruner had become a colleague.

2 Randall Jarrell (1914–1965), American poet, was run over and killed by a car on 14 October. The coroner declared the death to be accidental at the inquest.

3 L. Quincy Mumford (1903–1982), Librarian of the United States Congress, 1954–74.

he ought to take a lot of notes and if he didn't do poetry then write a journal about it. [. . .]

In the evening, went alone to the Circle Cinema, got fed up with an Italian film, then tried *Call me Pussycat* [i.e. *What's New Pussycat*], got fed up with that too. Sometimes, I can't work yet am too preoccupied with thoughts about work to do anything else. The films just seemed celluloid pictures, faint, unreal. Illusion failed to project. One thing that had put other things out of my mind was that Charles Frankel, who was at the Federal City Club and whom I spoke to for a few minutes before [Henry] Brandon arrived, told me I was going to be asked to write a poem, to be read before the assembled guests, at the International Cooperation meeting on November 28. I was thinking that I would not write the soupy poem they want, but a fierce one on the idea that international cooperation means the idea of love being armed as strongly as the idea of hate.

18 October 1965, Washington DC

Spent Sunday with the Jerome S. Bruners at Harvard. He is a psychologist very interested in the arts. Very helpful to N[atasha] about her research into aural perception. A serious intelligent and very friendly couple. They took us in a motorboat on the ocean at Manchester, near Boston. Saw an island called Misery Island. A very beautiful fall day of golds and crimsons with underneath whip-like branches and trunks of trees. Sea like a field with metallic brown waves shining turned sideways by the breeze as by a plough. A Monet day. The yachts somehow very American in their cleanness, their cared-for look, and their many shining gadgets.

22 October 1965, Dayton, Ohio

Spent two days at University of Dayton, Dayton, Ohio. In the aeroplane on the way there, I was thinking of quite other things, so obsessively that I got into a panic wondering whether I would be able to pay any attention to Dayton University at all. Sometimes on these flying visits there is a feeling of complete unreality as though an old film is being run through for the thousandth time: one gets out of the plane walks into the airport lobby. There is a wild feeling of hope for a few moments that no one is there to meet the plane. One is still free, perhaps one can take a taxi to the hotel, lie down on the bed, read a book, write notes, look at TV (occasionally this has happened and I've been left alone for hours). But no, a pallid young instructor, or two or three embarrassed giggling students come from nowhere say: 'Are you Mr S.? We weren't sure we'd recognize you,' and one is taken off to the car. If it is the young instructor, then there is nearly always evidence in the car that he has a young planned family – a baby's basket in the back seat, a miniature child's toy driving wheel by the wheel. During the drive to the 'school' which usually lasts half an hour frantic efforts are made to 'communicate'. Plans for the day are broken to one: the coffee hour with the students, the lunch in the cafeteria, then a question hour, then the lecture, then an hour or so to 'limber up'[,] then a select dinner at the 'only good restaurant down town' with a few of the faculty, then – very sorry for you at this point – a party for graduate students and faculty. They are frightfully apologetic about this, as though they have no idea one is being paid as much for a few hours as they are for two weeks.

At Dayton during the question hour, a girl with a fringe and pale eyes and a voice like a mosquito said: 'Please Mr S., will you read this poem and then explain what it means?' and she held in front of me a poem called 'The Drowned'. Then there are the questions: 'Why do you write?' 'How do you think of a poem?' 'When did you start writing?'

Owing to the fact that I had endless time at Dayton some of these questions began to get near the bone and became 'Why are you here with us and not sitting at home writing?' Then one explains that 'the poet' is not paid for writing poetry, but only for talking about writing (or not writing) poetry – and so generous are these Americans that one becomes at once a kind of multiple object of sympathy – for being there at all and for being paid exorbitantly by them to be there and not to stay at home. They begin to suspect that one hates them and – about time too – they begin to hate one (ever so slightly) also.

The possibility looms that all the veils might be torn down and there be total war.

As I was leaving, the little girl with the voice like a mosquito suddenly appeared and got into the back seat of the car and opening my *Collected Poems* again said: 'But Mr Spender, you didn't quite explain this line . . . .'

Reading one's own poems in front of an audience is very strange. I begin with a big resolution to concentrate on what I am reading by paying attention to the visual line. 'After the first powerful plain manifesto,' I begin and feel hopeful. I'm really going to get through the ride this time without getting off that express till it explodes into a branch of honeysuckle with the last line. It is like a film, a late 1920s film – Russian – called *Turk Sib*.[1] But I am already thinking these thoughts and I am not yet at the third line which is 'But gliding like a queen she leaves the station.'[2] This line always embarrasses me slightly and I begin visualizing not the express at all but an Oxford queen called Molesworth gliding down the High when I was an undergraduate. I was rather willowy myself and am still outsize, I wonder whether anyone has the sense to think it absurd – a six-foot-three poet with a limey accent and sibilant voice saying 'gliding like a queen she leaves the station'. However now we are off, although it is a bit like Robert Louis Stevenson's 'The Child's Garden of Verses'

> She passes the houses which humbly crowd outside
> The gasworks, and at last the heavy page of death

Printed by graveyards in the cemetery.

I succeed in seeing the gasworks and the heavy page of death. But, of course, I reflect, they have nothing to do with the Trans-Siberian Railway or the 'further than Edinburgh or Rome', they are what one sees on the railway travelling from London when one approaches

---

1 *Turk Sib* (1929), a silent film directed by V. A. Turin, about the Turkish-Siberian railroad.

2 Spender is quoting from his 1933 poem 'The Express', which opens:

> After the first powerful plain manifesto
> The black statement of pistons, without more fuss
> But gliding like a queen, she leaves the station.
> Without bowing and with restrained unconcern
> She passes the houses which humbly crowd outside,
> The gasworks and at last the heavy page
> Of death, printed by gravestones in the cemetery.
> Beyond the town there lies the open country
> Where, gathering speed, she acquires mystery,
> The luminous self-possession of ships on ocean.

Oxford. And that is what I am in fact seeing now – visualizing hard – the gasworks shutting out everything then as the window of the compartment slides past them – the tombstones like white sugar loafs and beyond them the vertical spires. Often there are grey and white clouds in the sky, their turrets and scallop shell curves repeating the rhythms of the grey and white architecture below. When I was an undergraduate there was a famous Oxford poets' walk by the gasworks, what Auden called 'the most beautiful walk in Oxford'.

25 October 1965, Washington DC

On Friday afternoon I went to Philadelphia, heard the orchestra play Sam Barber's piano concerto. John Browning was the soloist.[1] Extremely brilliant both the work and the performance. [. . .] John Browning was friendly but has a very conscious manner, like an East End cockney tailor; smiling, very watchful, defensive, not tactful.

Sam Barber said afterwards to me that he had known J.B. for eight years, during which his manners had scarcely improved. He thought J.B. ought to go for six months to a girls' finishing school. [. . .]

[On Sunday there was] a lunch party given by Chuck [Turner] and Steve [. . .] [A] composer called Martin Levy whose opera is going to be put on at the Met was there – discussion of Ben Britten. There was an off-Broadway playwright called Bill Hoffmann, who told in very lively fashion how he had been attacked in Greenwich Village by three thugs: how he had completely lost his temper and wrenched off the TV [*sic*] aerial from a nearby car, lashed out blindly at them (it was one of those telescopic aerials) extended it and started using it as a sword, nearly killing one of his assailants. They ran away.[2] Lunch lasted till about 6 pm.

Sunday evening went to the Lowells where there was Stuart Hampshire. Cal, Stuart and I had dinner at The Russian Tea Room. Cal seemed a bit tired and defeated. I was myself exhausted after the

---

1 John Browning (1933–2003), American pianist. He premiered Barber's Piano Concerto at the inaugural concert of the Lincoln Center and made it his signature piece, later recording Barber's solo piano works.

2 William Hoffman (b. 1939), American playwright whose work became well known in 1985 with his play *As Is*.

long lunch. He talked about Eliot, John Crowe Ransom, Allen Tate a bit. We discussed the fact that poets have far fewer readers for their poems than they have for their reviews. I told how I had published in seven sections a long poem in Shenandoah and received almost no reaction to it. He said he got five letters for an article or review where he got one for a poem. At this moment, I remembered I'd never told him how I admired his poem about Central Park in the *New York Review* [. . .][1]

We went back to his apartment for a bit, where there was his wife, Elizabeth Hardwick.[2] Talk about Vietnam. Although in his public utterances Cal seems so specific in his condemnation of the government, in private he is more likely to say that what is happening is 'tragic' than that it's 'wrong'. Both the Lowells did seem convinced though that the South Vietnamese do not support the Americans and that their leaders are quislings. Conversely, that the Viet Cong would not fight as they do unless they were immensely convinced. Cal asked me: 'Don't you have the feeling that something is going terribly wrong now in this country?' By this he meant a return of a situation like McCarthyism.

26 October 1965, Washington DC

Most of yesterday devoted by the Poetry Office [of the Library of Congress] to Kenneth Rexroth: lunch for him in the Whittall Pavilion.[3] He has got very paunchy with a big pot belly almost a shelf on which he occasionally rests his hands. He has a rather distinguished almost Scottish appearance, like a gillie with literary leanings, a notched, Nordic nose, grey hair, bristly grey moustache, and tired eyes under drooping pouched lids. In fact, he seemed tired, and kept on forgetting people's names. He wore a countryman's suit, with

---

1 The first version of 'Central Park' was first published in the *New York Review of Books*, 31 March 1966.

2 Elizabeth Hardwick (1916–2007), American literary critic and novelist, co-founded *The New York Review of Books*; married to Robert Lowell, 1949–72.

3 Kenneth Rexroth (1905–1982), American poet who supported the Beat poets, compèring the 1955 reading in the Six Gallery and serving as a defence witness at Ginsberg's subsequent trial for obscenity.

waistcoat and many pockets, of green tweed – designed by himself according to the *Washington Post* – a fob in waistcoat pocket. He talked about travels, France, Italy etc, about finding rare material in print and bookshops, translating from the Chinese. The egotism of the autodidact, I thought, or if he isn't [an] autodidact he shows off like one. In the evening he read his poems which are Beatnik in their exhibitionism, effusive, and full not only of cliché words like 'wonderful' but of cliché thoughts:

> Longing to kiss the corners of your smile
> Your special, simple ironic. . .
> perfume of your flesh.[1]

I always feel 'perfume of your flesh' would be a more effective phrase if women didn't use perfume. How do you distinguish between Chanel No. 5, deodorant, sun-tan ointment and the real flesh scent? He read his poems, partly gobbling them, partly in a subdued booming, like a sick trombone. [. . .]

Party afterwards at Margaret Hayford's apartment. Incident characteristic of my being at Washington. A small intense man who runs an art gallery cornered me, and started asking in an accusing voice whether I still cared in my writing about politics. I said I never had wanted to write about them very much, but I was interested, I saw political people in Washington. 'Do you see Trades Unionists?' he asked. 'Why if Walter Reuther was told you wanted to see him and discuss what use poetry could be to the Unions, he'd fall down

---

1 Spender is slightly misquoting Rexroth's poem 'An Easy Song', part of a sequence entitled 'Air and Angels' (1964):

> It's rained every day since you
> Went away. I've been lonely.
> Lonely, empty, tenderness –
> Longing to kiss the corners
> Of your mouth as you smile
> Your special, inward, sensual
> And ironic smile [. . .]
> Because I can call to mind
> Your body in a warm room [. . .]
> A rose cloud standing naked,
> In the perfume of your flesh.
> Moi aussi, je suis content.

flat.'¹ 'Well, I saw a Trades Unionist who was a head of the Long-shoremen at San Francisco,' I countered. 'Harry Bridges?'² 'No not Harry Bridges. But someone almost as far left. My friends at Berkeley told me to keep it quiet.' The little man eyed me suspiciously, so I said (always assuming he was anti-State Department), 'I see Robert Lowell.' 'His statements show he has no political grasp of the situation.'

9 November 1965, Washington DC

The poet James Dickey reading at the Library of Congress.³ [. . .] His reading was odd. He is a large man, with a cylindrical body and a face with a squashed Greek nose. He must have been handsome when young. He had an elaborate anecdote or series of anecdotes tagged on to each poem, often more interesting – entertaining at any rate – than the poem itself. All the anecdotes were autobiographical and the poems seemed to be straight autobiography. One of them was called 'Adultery' and was also tagged on to some anecdote identifying the reader, the poet, with the act. I felt a bit embarrassed for Mrs Dickey who was sitting next to me. But she did not seem at all concerned. American poets reading their poems seem to take it for granted that their lives are the *matière* [subject] of their poetry, and if they say 'I wrote this after a three-day binge' or 'this is about when I was sent up in the insane asylum,' or (as Kenneth Rexroth said in his reading) 'the girl I fucked in this poem is now about forty-five. I look her up sometimes,' no one is any more surprised than if a scientist in giving a general lecture refers to the procedures of a laboratory experiment.

10 November 1965, Washington DC

Read Louis MacNeice's *The Strings are False*, memoirs of Ireland, school, Oxford etc. Very clear and lively, sharply remembered. Very

---

1 Walter Reuther (1907–1970), American labour union leader.

2 Harry Bridges (1901–1990), American labour union leader, prosecuted by the American government in the 1930s, 1940s and 1950s.

3 James Dickey (1923–1997), American poet. He would succeed Spender as Poetry Consultant to the Library of Congress, 1966–8.

decent and warm and courageous his attitude to politics in the Thirties, his going at the last moment, after the honeymoon, to Spain in autumn 1938. His limitation is his excessively well-trained mind and imagination – no weeds, no ragged borders: or if by free associating words from time to time, he allows himself some freedoms, the effect is of someone who has gone into the woods, uprooted some primroses and ferns, and planted them in his own garden. Something that seems to throw light on his curious aloofness – to judge from his recollections, he always seems to have been fully conscious, at the time of the relationship, of his own dispassionate regard of people. E.g. in the account of his first marriage he had from first meeting her almost a completely detached view of Mary. He certainly did seem to 'cast a cold eye' and perhaps this explains why when one was with him one was so aware of him leaning back, regarding one with amused detachment through drooping eyelids. In fact, his memoir shows he did regard me in this way. But I can't quite believe he was so completely bifocal about his first wife all through their honeymoon and marriage. Why did he drink so much? To transcend this detachment, even though he was as little successful in this, as in his attempts to be wild through free association. There is also certain lethargy beneath his energy and brilliance: at his very best, excellent as this is, he never seems to be going quite all out but that may be the result of the remarkable inhibitions of his classical education combining with his temperamental nonchalance.

11 November 1965, Washington DC

Yesterday attended a small luncheon party given by Mr and Mrs Wilkinson for the Menuhins.[1] When I arrived Yehudi kissed me on both checks which rather surprised me. Although he said 'Stephen' I think really he was acting by association from my white hair and general largeness, with Nicolas Nabokov. I have thought since yesterday about Yehudi with his extended hands and manner as though he were lifting something, his wide-open bright slit eyes – he is an archaic sculpture of an Indo-Hellenic Apollo. He is in fact a god and

---

1 Yehudi Menuhin (1916–1999), American violinist, established the Menuhin School in Cobham, Surrey in 1963.

he could tame the beasts with his music, which is done for its own sake and for its beauty and because it belongs to the pantheon of divine composers, and not for career and money, but out of radiance and benevolence, a wish to give to the world.

At lunch, sat next to his wife who talked nicely about children, told endless stories, rattled on about how her brother-in-law Louis Kentner had only made $5,000 from an American tour.[1] She has a somewhat strangled-looking neck like a half-wrung chicken.

18 November 1965, Washington DC

Friday went to New York. Party given by the McGraths. [. . .] Monday I gave lunch for Cal Lowell, Wystan, E[arl] McGrath and R[eynolds] P[rice] at the Algonquin. L[owell] frowned in Earl's direction when he came in and said, 'Who's that?' He barely looked at all at R.P. and concentrated on Wystan – which was a good thing. I spent Monday evening with R.P. We met at the Algonquin before dinner where I had joined Jason Epstein for a drink.[2] Jason asked R.P. to join us and R.P. said, abruptly: 'Stephen, I think we ought to go if we're to get to our movie.' Outside he told me that he detested J.E. who had behaved worse to him than anyone in his life. His novel had been accepted by Random House and he had been paid an advance. Then J.E. had read it, had said it was the worst novel etc etc he had ever read, refused to let Random House publish it and asked for the advance back, which R.P. refused to return. Having told me all this R.P. was a bit apologetic for his unsociability, said though that meeting Earl McGrath, S.B., etc made him realize how little he cared for New York society, that he was a recluse etc. On reflection, I realize, a bit surprised that this is true. Proof is, that all the time I've known him, he has never as a result of meeting people become involved in social or amorous success which must in some way have altered our relationship. This, though less intense, remains curiously intact. He invited me to dine as his guest and we went to the Plaza. I

---

1 Louis Kentner (1905–1987), Hungarian-British pianist. Kentner's wife was Yehudi Menuhin's sister-in-law.

2 Jason Epstein (b. 1928), American publisher and editor, co-founded the *New York Review of Books* in 1963.

said: 'I cast my bread upon the waters and it is come back as roast duck.' [. . .]

Sunday, I went to Princeton, stayed with Isaiah and Aline [Berlin]. Conversation with Stuart [Hampshire] and Isaiah about Vietnam. S. believes 'they' could make a truce; Isaiah does not. [. . .]

Sunday afternoon Renée [Hampshire], Stuart and I went to Buttingers for drinks.[1] More talk about Vietnam. Jo supports the idea that there *can* be a truce though ultimately whatever happens the Communists are bound to win. What should be aimed at is a three year stalemate with negotiations so that things can cool off to the extent that there will not be reprisals and massacres. Then elections at the end of three years.

Monday as above, except that in the afternoon I called on little David Rieff.[2]

Tuesday [. . .] cocktail party at British Embassy for Snowdons.[3] So exhausted standing two hours I have hardly recovered. Sharman Douglas asked me to dine with someone called Charles Willis and the 'head of a small airline' called McLeod.[4] Charles Willis who entertained the Snowdons at Georgetown and who is presumably rich took us to a miserable restaurant called Tivoli. Charles Willis was either drunk and quite incoherent or he is a moron. He kept on assuring me (he called me 'Mr Spen') that the chicken I was eating was the best in town, and the operatic music being sung in the restaurant unique. I went home[,] changed and then went to the select Katzenbach after dinner party for the Snowdons. This was very boring and stiff. Michael Straight was there and left the table where he was sitting with Binny [Straight] and me, went over to Princess Margaret's table, and asked her to dance with him, which she declined. He was very abashed, his evening ruined. It seemed to me to show a

---

1 At this date Muriel and Joseph Buttinger were living on their estate at Pennington, near Princeton. Muriel practised psychiatry at local hospitals.

2 David Rieff (b. 1952), the son of Susan Sontag, would become a publisher, writer and policy analyst focusing on international and humanitarian issues.

3 Princess Margaret (1930–2002) and her husband Lord Snowdon, the former Tony Armstrong-Jones (b. 1930).

4 Sharman Douglas (1928–1966), American socialite, friend of Princess Margaret.

surprising side of him. Why also are the Straights so smart? It hardly fits with our picture of them.[1] The Snowdons made great efforts and never stopped smiling and asking people questions about their jobs, like elementary examination papers, or the questions on forms for people applying for visas. 'What do you do?' 'Where do you do it?' 'Do you have a house in the country as well as in Washington?' etc. They certainly got A+ for Effort. A Mrs Ginsberg, who is French, sat down beside me and told me she thought they were common and uninteresting, etc. Princess M. does have a very clear skin and sparkling eyes. She wears hideous British export clothing.

Parties where there are royalties show up a curious streak in people. Once again everyone becomes the child wondering whether he or she will catch the captain of the hockey team's eye. Nothing whatever can be said that isn't sucking up. The Snowdons, being small and square, almost never sit down which is the pigmies' revenge on people over six feet tall who are made to stand up interminably with their varicose veins spreading like ivy over the skin under their dress suits.

19 November 1965, Washington DC

Dinner at Henry Brandon's. The Joseph Krafts, the James Restons and the New Zealand Ambassador and his wife were there.[2]

The most interesting part of the evening was the men's conversations after dinner. Reston talked about [Lyndon B.] Johnson and America in a somewhat idealistic but very interesting way. He said the great aim of America after 1945 was not to repeat the mistake which she was reproached with after the First War of dissociating herself from the rest of the world. At Yalta Churchill and Stalin had asked Roosevelt how long the Americans intended to stay in Europe and he had answered 'two years'. Already now they had stayed twenty. Reston said that even in Vietnam America was observing the

---

1 Michael Straight (1916–2004), American man of letters. The 'smartness' of Michael Straight presumably stood in contrast with his left-wing views.

2 Joseph Kraft (1924–1986), American journalist, speech-writer for John F. Kennedy. James Reston (1909–1995), American political journalist, sometimes seen to be an apologist for American foreign policy.

principle that wherever there was aggression she would intervene and stop aggression. Joe Kraft, Brandon and I demurred at this point and said that America's aim in Vietnam was to stop China. We discussed Imperialism and I argued that America was filling the vacuum left by the European Empires in Asia, etc. Also America was concerned, as England had been in the past, with the Balance of Power. Reston said this might be true but all the same America was concerned with more far-reaching aims than Wilson, Heath, Shastri etc and if she was not supported in these would probably withdraw into some new form of isolation.[1] [. . .] He kept repeating the word 'greatness', and he quoted Walt Whitman's 'O Pioneers!' Whereas in the past Americans had thought that perhaps Europeans were tired, and that she must turn away and discover her own goals, since the war she had been turning to the rest of the world for an affirmation of the 'American dream' of having aims which lay beyond Empire and the use of power. 'When we expected some response from England,' Joe Kraft said, 'all that happened was that [Harold] Macmillan came to Washington to beg for some Polaris submarines.'[2]

The conversation turned to Johnson and all three said from their experience, how different Johnson was when he talked in private, to when he used his public voice. In private he was full of ideas, pithy, using brilliant metaphors and anecdotes. In public he failed to communicate. 'Compared with Kennedy, he is like a man who has the words but can supply no melody,' said Reston. He recalled how at the White House once he had seen Johnson being followed round by his photographer trying to record his best image, and he had said to

---

1 Edward Heath (1916–2005), leader of the Conservative Party, 1965–75; served as Prime Minister, 1970–74. Harold Wilson (1916–1995), leader of the Labour Party 1963–76, served as Prime Minister twice (1964–70 and 1974–6). Lal Bahadur Shastri (1904–1966), a significant figure in the Indian Independence Movement and the second Prime Minister of India (1964–6).

2 In November 1962, Britain cancelled the development of Skybolt, its air-launched ballistic missile programme designed to carry nuclear weapons. In December 1962, Harold Macmillan successfully negotiated with President Kennedy for the use of the more effective Polaris submarines in the Nassau Agreement. The missiles were to be used for international defence of NATO countries against the Eastern bloc, except when, as Macmillan noted, 'Britain's supreme national interests' were at stake. This theoretically allowed Britain to retain some degree of nuclear independence.

the President, 'You are using the wrong instruments. What you should have is a tape recorder to take down the things you say when you are grappling with your ideas among a few friends.'

21 November 1965, Washington DC

On Friday I went to Princeton to give my first of two Gauss Seminars about the Romantic idea of imagination and Modern Poetry. [. . .] The lecture was given in a classroom, with a noise of a heater or aerator in that fashion which forms a background to so much American life, like a subdued nightmare. The audience consisted of Prof. Robert Oppenheimer, the Berlins, a Russian priest aged 85, a German professor of comparative languages aged 80, Nicolas Nabokov, two Japanese students of I don't know what who had come hoping to be kept au fait with Allen Ginsberg, one or two mad-looking old ladies, Ed Cohen and Mr Borgerhof.[1] This was about all. The first half of the lecture which was mildly entertaining seemed to go quite well, though no one except Isaiah followed my remarks about Matthew Arnold's scholar gipsy being identical with Keats' nightingale.[2] After about half an hour (I was supposed to speak an hour) I was glad I had brought a text to read, though of course I began also to think this boring. And at my back I always heard a remark I'd read in the train on my way to Princeton in an article of Malcolm Muggeridge in the *New York Review* about members of the 'consciously cultivated classes' 'drivelling away their lives in university lecture halls or the editorial offices of high brow journals.'[3]

As we walked back to the Berlins' house, Shyah said to me that I had not disgraced myself – meant – as between us understanding one

---

1 Allen Ginsberg (1926–1997), American poet and leading figure of the Beat Generation.

2 Matthew Arnold's 'The Scholar Gypsy' (1853) and John Keats's 'Ode to a Nightingale' (1819).

3 Malcolm Muggeridge (1903–1990), British journalist, author and satirist. Spender alludes to Andrew Marvell's 'To His Coy Mistress' (1681) ('But at my back I always hear / Time's winged chariot hurrying near') via T. S. Eliot's *The Waste Land* (1922) Part III 'The Fire Sermon' ('Sweet Thames, run softly, for I speak not loud or long. / But at my back in a cold blast I hear / The rattle of the bones, and chuckle spread from ear to ear').

another – not as negatively as it sounds. All the same, there was something flat and disappointing about the occasion – as I suppose there will be when I read my poem at the International Cooperation meeting. We all went to bed early. [. . .] Conversation with Isaiah about the Romantics. He said they were all haunted by the fear that the Universe might be a perfectly regulated totally unalterable machine which man stood outside and could not influence in any way or enter into at any point. He said also that they wanted in their works not just to stand outside nature, but to enter into it with their own feelings, so that a tree or landscape became a vital animistic situation felt as forces of life and energy responding to the feelings of the poet.

Lunch with Stuart and Renée. We talked about what we would secretly like to be. Stuart said his secret image of himself was as a power behind the scenes, the man who influenced policy and changed governments, not in the full light of publicity, but recognized by historians and scholars as an *eminence grise*. I said that I wanted to live a good, very simple life with no thought of money but just devoted to work. On the other hand I also wanted to be generous, extravagant, travelling first class, giving people delicious meals, etc. These two images were hard to reconcile.

Returned to Washington after lunch. Went to the enormous party given by Kay Graham to Truman Capote, the Alvin Deweys and Mrs Roland Tate – these three being people involved in catching and sentencing Dick and Perry the killers about whom Truman Capote has written his best-selling book.[1] After the Snowdons, Washington is entertaining this extraordinary troupe – the Joe Alsops have given a

---

1 Kay Graham (1917–2001), American publisher who oversaw her family's newspaper the *Washington Post* during the Watergate coverage that eventually led to the resignation of Nixon. Truman Capote (1924–1984), American writer best known for *Breakfast at Tiffany's* (1958); his 'non-fiction novel' *In Cold Blood* was published in 1965. Capote called his novel 'immaculately factual' and it was based on the real-life murder of the Clutter family in Garden City, Kansas, as reported in the *New York Times* on 16 November 1959. Capote afterwards went to the town with Nelle Harper Lee, a childhood friend, to produce a piece on the murders for the paper. It was while Capote and Lee were in town interviewing the town's inhabitants about the victims that the police arrested Dick Hicock and Perry Smith for the murders. Keen to redress the balance of his narrative, and offer a perspective on the killers as much as on the victims, Capote interviewed the suspects whilst they were under arrest and then on Death Row.

huge party for them and Johnny Walker a luncheon at the National Gallery.¹ It seems macabre and strange and a bit tasteless. Nonetheless perhaps what is really being celebrated is Truman's kindness and imaginativeness in giving a big treat to these people, one of whom, at least, has never been East of Kansas City. The evening was made pleasant for me by my sitting between Mrs Joe Kraft and Mrs Paul Mellon.² I like the Krafts very much and Mrs Mellon talked with interest about her collection, etc. She is rather a grand lady. At the end of the evening had some conversation with Truman. He said that within a few weeks of arriving at the small mid-western town, scene of the murder, he had got more fond of some people in this town than of any people he'd ever met. I asked him if it was true – as someone had told me – that after studying Dick and Perry, he was in favour of capital punishment. He said this wasn't what he thought at all – he was against it – but he did think that real killers just went on killing. He said they had to be put away and put away for good. They were dangerous not only to society but even to their fellow prisoners. In one prison twenty-four prisoners had – over a number of years – been killed, in the prison yard, by fellow prisoners. Talking about his book he said he had a theory that a new type of literature could be based on reportage. He had arrived at this idea before writing this particular case history. In fact he had spent weeks scanning the newspapers before discovering the brief report which sent him to Kansas. He had spent six years writing his book, two and a half of them on the scene of the crime. He had cut his book down from 4,000 pages to its present length.

29 November 1965, Washington DC

A party in New York Wednesday night given by [Mervyn] Levy.³ Practically all the guests in this party were young men in TV. [. . .]

---

1 Joseph Alsop (1910–1989), American journalist.

2 Paul Mellon (1907–1999), American racehorse breeder and philanthropist. He commissioned Louis Kahn to build the Paul Mellon Center for Studies in British Art at Yale University, which was completed in 1970 and housed the extensive collection of British art that Mellon had donated to Yale.

3 Mervyn Levy (b. 1915), Welsh artist and critic.

These people are so totally interested in career one wonders whether they can take their minds off it when they are writing their poetry. I had a letter from Anne Moynihan saying that John Ashbery in his mania to ingratiate and promote himself in New York had accepted the work of 35 poets.[1]

At this party there was W[ystan]'s doctor who told me he thought W. would die quite soon of premature old age. He said W. was convinced he'd live till 80 because his father had done so, but he refused to lead the controlled life of his father. He drank far too much. I said this was terrible and I suggested he should really frighten W. Tell him unless he drank less, he would certainly die. He said he'd try this.

8 December 1965, Brookdale Farm, Pennington, New Jersey

A week ago I took the Conrad Aikens out to lunch, calling for them at their rooms for a drink before doing so.[2] They had two martinis before lunch (and were drinking already when I arrived) and went on with martinis during lunch and ordered more martinis after lunch. How is it possible they can drink so much? Aiken has a staring exposed look from wide blue eyes though an inflamed complexion. *Inflamed* would really be the word to characterize him. Mary Aiken is cosy, intelligent, a bit disinterested but very friendly and reassuring – as indeed they both are. Took them to lunch at a place on Pennsylvania Avenue which they frequented when he was Poetry Consultant. Talked about the early days of Eliot. He remarked that a young man had recently written a thesis on the Influence of Santayana on Eliot

---

1 For Anne Moynihan, see biographical appendix. John Ashbery (b. 1927) was part of the New York School of Poets which included Frank O'Hara, Kenneth Koch, James Schuyler, Barbara Guest, and Bernadette Mayers. After working as a freelance art writer in Paris from 1955 to 1965 he had returned to New York, his home city, where he had taken on the role of arts advisor for Anne Moynihan's *Art and Literature*, hence accepting the work of poets.

2 Conrad Aiken (1899–1973), American novelist and poet. Aiken was Poetry Consultant at the National Library of Congress from 1950 to 1952. He and T. S. Eliot were old friends and professional rivals. They had met during Aiken's freshman year at a dinner in 1911 and both worked on the Harvard *Advocate*, a student journal. They later both lived in London at the same time after Aiken moved there in 1921.

[. . .] at Harvard.¹ He had sent this to Eliot and received a very categorical letter in his own hand from T.S.E. telling him that Santayana had never had the slightest influence on him at H[arvard], indeed T. had thought him rather a charlatan. Aiken thought this an example of Eliot's trying to cover his tracks, because nothing could be less true, he averred.

Aiken said he remembered very well Eliot writing to him when he first met Ezra Pound that E.P.'s poetry was 'pathetically incompetent'. There was a great change in his attitude three years later when he wrote the essay on Pound's metrics.²

We talked about [Robert] Frost.³ I said that everyone seemed agreed that Frost was very designing, but I did not suppose this could have been the case when he was a young man. 'Oh no,' said Aiken, 'he was always the same.' When he returned from England to America, he gave Aiken advice about whom to meet there. The name of J. C. Squire came up and he said: 'Greet him from me, but in an off-hand way.'⁴

Aiken's conversation is full of these anecdotes – messages really, pellets hurled very effectively at reputations. He said that Eliot was extremely adroit at handling his own literary career. His real ambition was the drama, and in fact his poetry was always dramatic. When Aiken went to visit him at Faber's once in the Thirties, he found Eliot holding a book which had just arrived. As soon as Aiken came into the room E. got up from his chair pressed the volume into A.'s hands and said: 'I've done it again.' It was *The Cocktail Party*.

---

1 George Santayana (1863–1952), Spanish-born philosopher and poet, who taught at Harvard (1889–1912) and whose students included T. S. Eliot, Conrad Aiken and Robert Frost.

2 T. S. Eliot's essay 'Ezra Pound: His Metric and Poetry' was initially published anonymously in 1917.

3 Robert Frost (1874–1963), American poet best known for his depictions of rural life in New England. Frost lived in England between 1912 and 1915, getting to know the poets of Ezra Pound's circle.

4 For Spender and the Edwardian poet, J. C. Squire (1884–1958) see *World Within World* chapters 2 and 5. The young Spender, as secretary of Oxford's University English Club, had an encounter with J. C. Squire in which he informed him, 'When you are my age, you will look back and think: Well, perhaps after all, to have married that girl and had those children is worth more than to have written four hundred sonnets.'

Something of Aiken's own sad character comes out in this – his role as Greek chorus to E's success. The Greek chorus is capable of coarse and acid comments. [. . .]

On Wednesday (Dec 8) Jim West telephoned me that he was in Washington.[1] So after I had given a lecture to the English teachers of North Virginia, I went round to his hotel room. He was very agreeable as usual, but seemed rather worried under the blandness. He said that there were rumours that Mary and he were separating. Kind friends, like Sonia [Orwell], rang anxiously, curiously, to inquire: 'Are you all right? Do you need help?' He dismissed all this in his bitter-mild way, but left a doubt in my mind. He said they had taken the Nabokovs' country house at Verderonne. 'How beautiful,' I said. 'Yes I suppose it will be like the other house we had. With luck we'll go there two days in two months.' He said that though their previous country house had been lacking in amenities, he much preferred it to Verderonne. Mary was not getting much writing done. She had now quite a social life in Paris and was more and more caught up in TV interviews etc on the B.B.C. 'The B.B.C. act as though they own Mary,' he remarked drily. 'One night in Paris recently they rang her three times at dinner.'

'Now I have a difficult job in front of me,' he said. 'Cal Lowell is sick again, and I suppose I'll have to ring his wife. The trouble is that if there's one person I hate from the bottom of my heart, it's Liz Hardwick. It's not so much that she wrote that parody of *The Group* which appeared in the *N.Y. Book Review* as that, after, she went on proclaiming that she was Mary's friend.'[2]

I said that just possibly, living under the burden of Cal's breakdown, Liz occasionally became exacerbated and lashed out at her friends.

He disregarded this and described a 36 minute telephone call from New York to Paris that Cal Lowell had made to him. After a time he protested to Cal, 'This call is awfully expensive.' Cal said: 'I can well

---

1 James West, husband of Mary McCarthy since 1961.

2 In November 1963 Elizabeth Hardwick published a parody of Mary McCarthy's 1962 novel *The Group* in the *New York Review of Books*, under the pen name Xavier Prynne.

afford it. I've just turned down a teaching offer from Dallas at $30,000 a year.'

In the course of the conversation, Cal said he'd approached Dean Rusk to ask him whether he would be permitted to join the Viet Cong.[1] Dean Rusk had explained that this would not be possible. He had then asked Rusk whether it was possible for him to mail a bomb through the post to the White House. Dean Rusk had said that also would be difficult as there were rules against sending live arms through the mail.

The strange thing was Jim West's smiling blandness about this conversation, which he said had been very pleasant.

[undated] New York

Sam [Barber] played the tape of his [opera] *Antony and Cleopatra* which I liked a lot.[2] I worked on the poem, wrote a review of T.S.E., *The Critic on the Critic*[,] and notes for my Princeton Seminar.[3]

On Saturday had dinner with the Lowells. Fred Dupee was there, on the 'wagon' as he'd been ill.[4] Cal Lowell was strange, as Dupee said when we left together afterwards, 'on the edge of something'. Cal began making an awful lot of Wystan having said that [Lyndon] Johnson should send 20,000 Queens to Vietnam, as they'd certainly win the war. He was very amused by this, but later he spoke rather resentfully of Auden, saying he was always trying to put everyone right, that his most frequent way of talking was to say 'You ought to do so and so'. He said that showed Auden was the one person, apart from [the Apostle] Paul and Jesus Christ who believed intensely in Original Sin. I disagreed[:] said that right or wrong were moves in a game of chess for Auden, being on the white or the black square. He didn't really care which you were on. Later Cal said the theme of all

---

1 Dean Rusk (1909–1994), US Secretary of State, 1961–9, serving under both Kennedy and Johnson.

2 Barber's *Antony and Cleopatra* opened the new Metropolitan Opera House at the Lincoln Center in 1966.

3 Spender refers to T. S. Eliot, *To Criticise the Critic* (1961).

4 F. W. Dupee (1904–1979), American editor, academic and critic, notably of Henry James. Bisexual, close friend of Gore Vidal.

English novels was a man sacrificing his wife his children and all that was closest to him for the sake of vocation. He said all Shakespeare's plays were about failed marriages. He also said Shakespeare was completely homosexual. He talked quite a lot about homosexuality and guilt, as he had once before, saying that Housman's best poems were about guilt on account of homosexuality.[1] He said that when he (Cal) went crazy he was not violent to anyone else, but he beat his wives up. He'd turned all his wives from being literary critics into story writers.

At dinner Elizabeth said she was distressed when Cal and she went to dine with the Stravinskys, because most of the conversation by-passed Stravinsky, and because Bob Craft kept on talking in front of Stravinsky about him in the third person or as 'Mr S.' I said, pretty well this always happened. Cal said: 'It wouldn't have happened if my wife hadn't insisted on talking all the time about . . .' (I've forgotten what but which could not have concerned S.).

After dinner Cal said 'Let's read poetry' and read his own poems for an hour or so. In the course of the evening he also said that all that mattered in life was one's closest relationships, one's wife and one's friends. He said to me: 'You see, I'm a Christian agnostic.'

Once or twice in the course of the evening Elizabeth buried her face in her hands. Cal also said – a bit resentfully to me – that the only friend who had written to him about his new book (of those to whom he'd sent it) was Jacqueline Kennedy (I have not written [. . .] for lack of time).

There was an undercurrent of 'I am the greatest poet' about his conversation. Thinking about all this afterwards, I thought it would be irrelevant to say of Cal (or of Wystan) that he is an egotist. The point is that he is absorbed into[,] overwhelmed by[,] his own world and he talks out of this.

---

1 A. E. Housman (1859–1936), poet and classical scholar whose hugely popular collection of lyric poems *A Shropshire Lad* (1896) made him synonymous with the innocence of pre-war rural England. While studying Classics at Oxford, Housman fell unrequitedly in love with a contemporary male student. Housman prefaced his edition of the first book of Manilius's *Astronomica* (1903) with an elegiac poem, written in Latin, and addressed to 'to my comrade, Moses Jackson, scorner of these studies'. The poem is influenced by Ovid's *Amores* and contains a homoerotic subtext.

Stephen Spender, Insel Ruegen, 1931

Isaiah Berlin and Natasha Spender, Geneva, 1946

W. H. Auden, Spender and Christopher Isherwood, Insel Ruegen, 1931

The reunited trio, Fire Island (off Long Island, New York), 1947

Spender, Sonia Brownwell and Cyril Connolly in the offices of *Horizon*, c.1940

Peter Watson, c.1942

Wedding party in the studio of Mamaine Paget, 1941. Guests included Cyril Connolly, Lys Lubbock, Sonia Orwell, A. J. Ayer (in uniform), Guy Burgess, Louis MacNeice and Ernö Goldfinger

Spender in Fire Service uniform with Arthur Bliss, Wittersham, 1941

Photograph of post-war German ruins in Cologne, 1945, taken by Spender while writing the *Rhineland Journal*

W. H. Auden, Cecil Day Lewis and Spender, Venice, 1949, photographed by Natasha Spender

Spender teaching in
Sarah Lawrence
College, New York, 1947

Spender with rescued Jewish children in Israel, where he spent most of 1952 researching
and writing *Learning Laughter*

Stephen, Natasha
and Matthew Spender,
Loudoun Road,
London, 1946

Matthew and Lizzie Spender with W. H. Auden, late 1960s

(top left) Tony Hyndman, Malcesine, Lake Garda, 1934

(top right) Reynolds Price, c.1964

(left) Bryan Obst, 1976

Isherwood, Spender and Don Bachardy, New York, 1975

David Hockney and
Matthew Spender,
London, 1979

Spender and Auden,
Loudoun Road, London,
early 1960s

The Spenders' golden wedding lunch, Mas de Saint Jerome, France, 1991

In the 1960s and early 1970s, the Spenders bought a ruined farm-house near Maussane in Provence, and renovated it. It was re-named 'Mas St Jerome', and over the years they would spend summers and olive-picking seasons there, often entertaining friends. Natasha created an 'English garden' (see An English Garden in Provence, *2002)*

20 June 1972, Mas St Jerome, Maussane, Provence

Joseph Brodsky came to stay.[1] Pale intense, very unhappy, bitter. I took him to the TV where he was interviewed and gave uncompromising answers to questions he was asked on the ITV *Midweek* programme. 'Did the fuss made in England and outside Russia on behalf of Russian intellectuals help them?' Not at all. It wasn't the slightest use.[2]

Cecil Day Lewis, then Poet Laureate, died on 22 May 1972. He had married the actress Jill Balcon, his second wife, in 1951 (see biographical appendix).

30 June 1972, St Jerome

Jill Day Lewis and Jane Howard came.[3] Jill alternately quite cheerful and shuddering with grief. Not able to sleep, suddenly abstracted etc. She puts up a tremendously good show however and chatters away [. . .] The Amises behaved wonderfully – better than any people I can think of – in inviting C[ecil] & J[ill] to their house, and letting C. die there without being taken to hospital.[4]

---

1 For Joseph Brodsky, see biographical appendix.

2 In 1968, in response to Soviet persecution of Russian intellectuals, the Spenders had organized a protest which resulted in the founding of the journal *Index on Censorship* (see biographical appendix). The persecution continued with such high profile cases as that of Brodsky (expelled in 1972) and Solzhenitsyn (expelled in 1974).

3 Elizabeth Jane Howard was at this date married to the novelist Kingsley Amis (1922–1995).

4 The Amises' house, Lemmons, was in North London. In her autobiography *Slipstream* (2002) Howard records a brief affair, earlier in life, with Day Lewis.

16 August 1972, St Jerome

Met David [Plante] and Nikos [Stangos] at Avignon – nearly missed them because I had said meet me at café outside station and there was none.¹ Found them in café in the main street – we bought squids at St. Remy which Nikos cooked.

18 August 1972, St Jerome

Went to Ardèche. A beautiful day. We went down to the river at the bottom of the gorge, very transparent so that we could see every crevice of every stone below the stream. We had to climb down a narrow path through many shrubs and trees. Butterflies. There were a few not too many people about. Quite gay and charming. We had our picnic on the flat rocks at the edge of the stream. There were canoers and one big boat with 20 or 30 people in it. Suddenly 3 hippy-like Germans strode out of the water and stood in front of the people on the shore, stark naked. It was like some painting of a pagan scene en plein air.

19 August 1972, St Jerome

David came down to breakfast saying he'd thought all night who were those three Germans and found the answer. They were the Rhine Maidens. I took D. and Nikos to Les Baux which was very beautiful in a high wind. Then drove them to Avignon where they got their train for Italy.

13 September 1972, Château Mouton Rothschild, Pauillac, Médoc

Went to Mouton for the vendange [grape harvest]. [. . .] Other guests were delightful. Raymond [Mortimer], Monroe Wheeler, George Rylands.²

---

1 For David Plante and Nikos Stangos, see biographical appendix.

2 Monroe Wheeler (1899–1988), American art gallery curator. George (Dadie) Rylands (1902–1999), British theatre director and Shakespearean scholar, fellow of King's College, Cambridge.

There were also Beatrice and Robert de Rothschild who came over from Lafitte two or three times and were glamorously fed and wined.[1] On the first of the occasions Philippe [de Rothschild] was a bit drunk and attacked the Lafitte contingent for their lack of cooperation with his plans. Beatrice was beautiful and much more open and friendly than before – really delicious.

17 September 1972, Mouton

We had pleasant meetings at tea time in Pauline's room. Dadie Rylands read *Lycidas* and poems by Donne chiefly. Dadie added enormously to the pleasure of the whole stay.

At the end of their stay in France, the Spenders accompanied Philippe and Pauline de Rothschild to Mende, on the edge of the Cevennne National Park, so that Natasha could read the original English version of a collection of Elizabethan poems translated into French by Philippe de Rothschild for a French television programme.

27 September 1972, Mende, France

We left Saint Jerome early. Natasha in very great pain [having strained her back while packing], so I drove. Went the very long journey past Nîmes through the Massif Central to Mende, where Philippe and Pauline had a room for us at Hotel Lion d'Or.

28 September 1972, Mende

Went to rehearsal of the reading of Philippe's translation of Elizabethan poems in the synagogue at Mende. A medieval (?) building with tiers of seats at several levels round a platform and opening above between roofs into the sky. Natasha was heroic. She found that if she remained more or less in one position she had controllable pain.

---

1 Beatrice and Robert de Rothschild were the children of Philippe's brother, Alain. Eric de Rothschild, their brother, was in charge of nearby Lafitte Rothschild and a certain rivalry existed between the two distinguished wine growers.

Lunch with Philippe and Pauline both at their most pleasant. Philippe tremendously baronial as he shouts across the dining room of the hotel and even runs across it to wheel the hors d'oeuvres to his table when he wants it. Evening, the recording of the TV programme made, with totally inadequate preparation, dresses, scenery and even cameras. The French actress reciting forgot her words. Natasha did extremely well and we were glad we came all the way.

11 October 1972, London

Meeting of editorial committee of *Index* [*on Censorship*] at 35 Bow Street. Not at dinner because Victoria B[rittain] finds combination of eating and meeting frivolous.[1] She was there looking very charming in her smiling sea-urchin way. Stuart [Hampshire] and I dined at Savile Club later. [. . .] Henry Reed who drunkenly embraced me, there with attractive youthful boy friend, an actor.[2]

14 October 1972, London

Buffet dinner at the Stokes, for a lot of their friends, a kind of farewell party for Adrian who will soon die of cancer.[3] He knows this. Either because of drugs or because he feels burdens suddenly lifted he is elated, gay. He was very pleased at a letter I had written him about a picture of bottles he gave us and handed me a letter in which he had written: Stephen, it's very kind reading and gives me the calm and pleasure and fullness of help. Yes I'm calm but perhaps its doltishness. Too late of course but I shall hope to do things more.

15 October 1972, London

Worked desperately finishing the Orwell article for *N.Y. Review*. I mailed [it] at 6 p.m. [. . .] Dined with Vera Stravinsky and Bob Craft at the Savoy. They are entangled in frightful involvements: the

---

1 Victoria Brittain, foreign affairs journalist principally on the *Guardian* during this period.

2 Henry Reed (1914–1986), British poet and journalist.

3 Adrian Stokes (1902–1972), British art critic, artist and poet.

Libman book, about Stravinsky and bitterly attacking Bob; the will disputed by the Stravinsky children etc.[1] Vera also still shaken at the death of S. Their journey to Venice to see the Manzu plaque which had not arrived being still in Rome.[2] Bob said N[icolas] Nabokov was completely generous unacquisitive brilliant but not able to get his genius into his music. Also incapable of being discreet and unmalicious. Story of farewell party to Wystan in N.Y. President of Random House began nervously : 'I do not know what is meant by a genius – but [–]' Wystan, drunk, interrupted – 'Who does?' [. . .]

At the Savoy we had asparagus. Vera leaned over to me, and said 'When Bob first came to live with us, he knew so little about life. One day we ate asparagus and after the meal he took me into the bathroom and said "I think I have an illness." He had not pulled the plug and in the bowl his urine smelt – like it does after you eat asparagus.' The remark of someone in love, I thought.

20 October 1972, London

Moved my things to Natasha's room in view of Wystan's imminent arrival. Agitation (which I felt rather ashamed of) about decision not to buy the Sickert. [. . .] Wystan arrived. Coffee – lunch. He told us four anecdotes (Jesus Christ and who will cast the first stone O mother etc) for 10th time. [. . .] Went to reading by Wystan at Poetry Soc. He hesitated, forgot, didn't seem to care. Kept saying to photographers 'Please stop' – yet somehow the reading involved one.

21 October 1972, London

Apart from a bit repetitive, Wystan seems much calmer more considerate happier than a year ago. Took him to Paddington at 9.15. At breakfast he talked about Pope and Dryden. Said Pope thought in couplets, Dryden in paragraphs. Was funny about [A. E.] Housman,

---

1 Stravinsky had died in April 1971, leaving four children from his first marriage. Lilian Libman's *And Music at the Close: Stravinsky's Last Years: A Personal Memoir* had appeared in 1972.

2 Stravinsky was buried in Venice, alongside Diaghilev. A plaque was commissioned from the Italian sculptor, Giacomo Manzu (1908–1991).

said he was a passive anal type who wanted to be had by young men and this must have depressed him as the classic Greek and Latin orators despised it, but approved of pederasty. After he had gone I worked. Natasha upset by Lizzie telling her how unhappy she was when we went away in her childhood (it all seems so near).

22 October 1972, London

Wrote review of New O[xford] U[niversity] Book of English Verse in the morning and mailed it to *Guardian*.[1] By the time I'd finished our luncheon guests were arriving – Derry Moore, Brian Patten and Mary Moore.[2] It was a pleasant uneventful meal. Again I felt rather doubtful about Brian who seems nice, sensitive, poetic but always acting his Liverpudlian role. He told me he got an income tax allowance for 'clothes to wear at poetry readings'. Said he disliked [Percy Bysshe] Shelley which may or may not be a good sign. He writes children's stories. I told him I was going to Arundel to do a reading for Peter Porter.[3] Said Peter Porter had insulted him when he asked for a match to light a cigarette by saying 'Can't you afford to buy one of your own?' The monkey house of little poets. Neither Natasha nor I slept much through thinking about Lizzie's revelation of her far from happy childhood. I slept after lunch. The party was nice but ruined the day for work. Woke up this morning thinking that I was wakened by N calling out in her sleep 'Oh Lizzie'. Couldn't at all make out whether this was real or I had dreamt it.

Following his resignation from Encounter *in 1967, Spender was offered a chair at University College London. He taught at UCL from 1970 to 1975 and set up an extra-curricular workshop on writing for undergraduates, nominally to assist with tutorial essays. In*

---

1 *The New Oxford Book of English Verse, 1250–1950*, chosen and edited by Helen Gardner (1972).

2 Derry Moore (b. 1937), British photographer who would photograph Spender in 1992. Brian Patten (b. 1946), British poet. He, Roger McGough and Adrian Henri were collectively known in the 1960s as the Liverpool Poets.

3 Peter Porter (1929–2010), Australian-British poet.

October 1972, Spender joined the annual English department trip to Cumberland Lodge, in Windsor Great Park.

24 October 1972, Cumberland Lodge, Windsor Great Park

Tutorial with Jackie Garrett who wrote interesting paper about Eliot. Writing workshop which becomes more and more like a creative writing course. Then lunch at the Empress Restaurant with Valerie Eliot and Mary Lascelles a rather sweet sad distinguished poetic lady who talked about Australia where she had taught for a term and said she was withdrawn from everything at Oxford where she now lives.[1] Conversation about Bob Craft. Clear that Valerie dislikes him because he describes wrongly things in her flat in his diaries published by Faber.[2] N[atasha] defended Bob rather vigorously. V. said that Tom detested Bob when he came to dinner with them with the Stravinskys. Also mentioned that Tom took no interest in and had no time for Cecil [Day Lewis], though she never understood why. Afternoon Eliot seminar which Lizzie and her Argentine friend Maxy attended. Then drove Keith, Patrick Roberts and Frank K. to Cumberland Lodge in Windsor Park (where I'm writing this) for an overnight outing of faculty and students.[3] Quiz after dinner from which one quote was from *World Within World*.

25 October 1972, London

Got up at 8 at Cumberland Lodge. Found Frank already pacing the grounds. He said he never slept more than 7 hours. Directly after breakfast drove to London. Appalling traffic great solid blocks of frustrating metal and smelling fumes all the way. Thought how hatred of traffic (traffic to which I was contributing) one of the constant under

---

1 Mary Lascelles (1900–1995), British scholar, teacher and poet. Tutor in English at Somerville College, Oxford, 1931–60, and Honorary Fellow, 1967–95.

2 Robert Craft's *Dialogues and a Diary* had been published by Faber in 1968.

3 Keith Walker, Patrick Roberts and Frank Kermode were all colleagues in the English department at UCL. For Frank Kermode, see biographical appendix.

surface emotions of modern life. People are already beginning to leave the cities in a kind of panic before their own mess – only to foul up the country. [. . .] Arrived at St Martin in the Fields for Cecil [Day Lewis]'s memorial service. Jill sitting in front row next to aisle greeting people with her effusiveness but that agonizing expression on her face. Rex Warner. John Betjeman there looking very absorbed: thought his thoughts: it might be me: I'm going to die: terror: church: the architecture.[1] Not much of his poetry left. I spent much time having unholy thoughts about Wystan. Remembering our wind-blown youth, the school of three that people made us, however absurdly; remembering how Cecil addressed him as 'Wystan my bully boy': wrote an elegy for his 21st birthday (to which I was not invited) containing the line 'Who has not lain with Wystan in the shade?' how unfeeling, how disregarding of his own past, how blank to memory – not to put finis to this trio by quietly turning up! [. . .] Afternoon came home, slept, worked. Dinner at Boulestin with Jill, Jane Howard, Kingsley Amis, Austen Williams.[2] Talked a lot with Kingsley whom I like despite his views.[3]

26 October 1972, London

Lunch Cyril [Connolly] at Whites. He was very anxious to know what I thought about Bob Craft and Stravinsky. I was not so pro-Bob as perhaps I should have been – or as V[era] and B. would have

---

1 John Betjeman (1906–1984), British poet and broadcaster who was a passionate defender of Victorian architecture and committed to keeping old churches in use. He had succeeded Cecil Day Lewis as Poet Laureate in 1972.

2 The Revd Austen Williams (1912–2001), at this time Vicar of St Martin-in-the-Fields, 1956–84, and Chaplain to the Queen's Household; he would soon become Prebendary of St Paul's Cathedral, 1973–2001. He was a friend of Cecil Day Lewis and had conducted his memorial service.

3 Amis's views on higher education had become increasingly right wing. He expressed his 'more means worse' thesis in the so-called 'Black Paper' on education in 1969, which denounced the expansion in Higher Education in Britain's universities and the increased intake of students. The Black Papers were named in contrast to government's parliamentary White Papers and were issued by the poet and educationist Brian Cox (1928–2008) and the homosexual rights campaigner and educationist A. E. Dyson (1928–2002).

expected me to be. But I did say that I thought that it was really a love affair – Bob and Vera and Strav: that Bob had renounced his relations with Lucie Lambert as a result of the Stravs' insisting. C. told me when he went on holiday from *Sunday Times* first week he thought 'I have lost all my identity. Connolly no longer exists. He is not in *S.T.*' Second week he thought: In spite of his not appearing in *S.T.* Connolly just continues to exist. Third week he thought Connolly going strong although not appearing in *S.T.* 4th week he thought 'What's the *S.T.* anyway?'[1]

29 October 1972, London

Did not go out [. . .] After dinner Lizzie and I watched *Some Like It Hot* on T.V. which L. thinks is the greatest movie ever made (anyway her favourite since she first saw it in California, when she was 9). She still laughs from beginning to end and it really cheered us up after a dreary day.

31 October 1972, London

Lunch at *Spectator* with Christopher Hudson. The young playwright Christopher Hampton (author of *Philanthropist*) was there. Talked about a play he's writing about the Indians of the Amazon in Brazil – a dying culture completely ignored by Brazilian Govt.[2] We talked about playwrights. How they become successful and move completely out of the world of their own early experiences and even of other writers. John Osborne. Hampton talked about the attack in John Osborne's house, by someone who was the lover of his (cook? butler?) who was in drag when attacked.[3] I liked Hampton.

---

1 At this date Connolly was chief literary critic on the *Sunday Times*.

2 Christopher Hampton (b. 1946), British playwright whose play *The Philanthropist* had been performed in 1969 and who would shoot to fame in 1985 with his adaptation of *Les Liaisons Dangereuses*, which became the film *Dangerous Liaisons* in 1988. Spender refers to Hampton's new play *Savages*, which would premiere at the Royal Court in 1973.

3 On 29 September 1972 an intruder had broken into Osborne's house and threatened to kill him, claiming that he had sold out from the working class. The intruder fled after Osborne's wife, Jill Bennett, retorted with 'Go away. I will not be late for the ballet.'

18 November 1972, London

Finished reading *The Good Soldier* [by Ford Madox Ford]. Went to the conference for tutors on *The Waste Land* at which I had to give the introductory address. Christopher Ricks and several people from UCL were there, rather to my horror.[1] Questions for the most part stupid. [. . .]

Writing this diary I feel that if it were complete it would include memories of the past which are so much part of my day. E.g. today I thought about how when I was first married to Inez I came home to our high-up flat at Brook Green and found Inez and Denis Campkin weeping – especially Denis.[2] Afterwards he went out into the night alone. I often remember this scene and think why didn't I ask him to stay the night. My thoughts are always about the past or the future e.g. Matthew arriving next week. Could one not write a story in which the present is almost submerged by ghosts of past and future.

19 November 1972, London

I thought of writing a story on three floors. Scene a house where the husband has had 2 marriages. His thoughts are of the first marriage while he is living the second one. The children's childhood in between multiple time-strands. I've always wanted to do this. Story about Dick Crossman.[3] Read interesting article in Sunday supplement about Tolstoy. Rewrote 6 pages of lecture for Edinburgh University.

---

1 Christopher Ricks (b. 1933), British literary critic.

2 Denis Campkin had been a rival, along with many others at Oxford University, for the hand of Spender's first wife, Inez Pearn. Campkin and Spender spent time together in Spain, during the Civil War. Spender and Inez lived in Queens Mansions, Brook Green, Hammersmith.

3 Dick Crossman (1907–1974), British Labour Party politician, editor of the *New Statesman* 1970–72. Crossman had been a contemporary of Spender at Oxford and edited *The God that Failed* in 1949, a collection of essays to which Spender contributed.

21 November 1972, London

Waiting for Matthew. Morning. Writing seminar. Work. [. . .]
I took Pauline and Philippe [de Rothschild], Cyril Connolly, Wystan, Nikos (his birthday) out to lunch at the Neal Street Restaurant. Very good. Thought that people would get on badly but in fact they got on well. Cyril ordered teal (two birds) which looked very nice, then found them undercooked, had them cooked again, then they were burnt and hard. Obviously his lunch was ruined. W complained at the service being slow. In fact everyone was in character. Wystan said he was against Libman's book on Stravinsky but for Bob's, Cyril said Bob hated writers and did W. have any idea what Bob had written about him – for example that in Venice he had burst into tears because he could not have a hotel bedroom with bathroom.[1] Various other examples. Wystan ignored all this just as he had ignored the book itself. Went to reading by Wystan and Peter Porter of Dryden and Pope. Wystan and [Peter] Porter at the National Book League. Very good. Went home to dinner, prepared by Lizzie (who is at various parties). Granny sitting on stairs, waiting for Matthew. W. talked about poetry and was very interesting.
Matthew breezed in at about 11 p.m. He looked very well but was very unforthcoming [. . .] I had a sense of anti-climax. He was very helpful washing up dishes however.

22 November 1972, London

Went to British Museum exhibition of drawings with Matthew. On the way talked about his exhibition. I said that I thought it suggested about 6 lines of development none of which he had really explored. He said that was how a first exhibition should be. He had a lot of ideas now for Still Lifes he wanted to paint. I said his pictures could do with more observation and that in the drawings Saskia [Matthew's daughter] was his best invention and a sign which also contained observation. He agreed with this. After the British Museum we went to Anne Moynihan's show at the Redfern then the [Auguste] Rodins at Delbanco. Matthew had a long conversation

---

1 Robert Craft, *Stravinsky: Chronicle of a Friendship* (1972).

with Delbanco who asked to see his things (he will take them tomorrow).[1] Lunch at home at 1.30 (by Wystan's special leave). Lizzie's Argentinian friend came. I asked him about Argentina. While he answered Wystan looked frightfully bored made extraordinary noises like a prolonged – a-aaaaaah – like a telephone bell which requires answering. Then he broke in producing one of his anecdotes. Evening took Mateo [Matthew] to dine with the Wollheims who had asked a rare book producer called (Ensa?).[2] A middle aged man of bristling energy and vital speech. He looked at M.'s engravings and drawings. He said to me 'One cannot advise Matthew or attempt to break into his isolation. He is a horse that I should back, that is all.'

26 November 1972, London

Worked at the V. Woolf review for *L.M.* [*London Magazine*] and a bit at my book. Dined with the Bruces at Albany.[3] John Wells, Pauline de R[othschild] and two other people there.[4] Virginia Cowles arrived afterwards.[5] Evangeline [Bruce] is a very nice woman beautiful and intelligent but got up to look like a Reynolds or Gainsborough portrait. Her flat gives the impression of tall satin hangings. The large pictures seem tied to the walls with ribbons. Talked a bit about politics with David Bruce who is extremely courteous like a character in a Henry James novel. Found myself extremely embarrassed inhibited trying to talk to Evangeline. It was really like an illness. At dinner J. Wells was entertaining and kept things going. But the evening gave

---

1 Gustav Delbanco (1903–1997), proprietor of an art gallery in Cork Street.

2 Richard Wollheim (1923–2003), British philosopher specialising in the mind and emotions and visual art; as Grote Professor of Mind and Logic at UCL he was a colleague of Spenders in the 1970s. In 1967, he had married the ceramicist Mary Day Lanier.

3 David K. E. Bruce (1898–1977) had been US Ambassador to the United Kingdom, 1961–9.

4 John Wells (1936–1998), satirist appearing in *Private Eye* and on the television programme *That Was The Week That Was*. Spender knew him through the 'German club', a private dining club which they both, as German speakers, attended.

5 Virginia Cowles (1910–1983), journalist who wrote under the pen name 'Nancy Swift'.

me that feeling social occasions often do that the people who have money and means to meet have nothing to say to one another. John Wells and I went to E.'s bedroom and watched TV performance of him in *That Was The Week That Was*.

Récapitulation de Novembre 1972

This month and the first week in December seem to me a turning point in English bankruptcy and self-disgust. Two by-elections in one of which disillusioned Conservative voters just win over the even more disillusioned Labour ones.[1] A play by John Osborne written to express disgust with theatre with playwrights with the audience with everything. The 'strike' of John Arden and his wife against the direction of their play by the R.S.C. because, as they say, their revolutionary message is twisted to make it look 'imperialist'.[2] A letter to the *Times* from the director of the company to say the company is leftist and puts on plays propagandizing left wing views. The failure of Peter Hall's 'Space Age' musical on Broadway.[3]

8 December 1972, London

Natasha woke up with bad flu. I telegraphed Wystan cancelling his Monday stay here.

---

1 Spender refers to the Uxbridge and Sutton and Cheam by-elections, which took place on 7 December 1972. In fact, the Sutton and Cheam seat went from Conservative to Liberal, while the Uxbridge seat remained Conservative.

2 John Osborne's satire of the theatre world *A Sense of Detachment* premiered in 1972. The playwright John Arden and his wife Margaretta D'Arcy (b. 1934) decided to strike when they were denied a company meeting by the Royal Shakespeare Company to discuss disagreements over the interpretation of their play *The Island of the Mighty*. During a preview performance, the playwrights came on stage and attempted to hold the meeting in front of the audience.

3 *Via Galactica*, a space-age rock musical by Peter Hall (b. 1930), lost a million dollars on Broadway after opening and closing in November 1972.

11 December 1972, London

N. still not well but perhaps a bit better. Went to U.C.L. where one of my students had flu, another came to see me but was very unwell – neurotically, I think. I called Nikos [Stangos] and we lunched at the Tavola Calda. Told him how Wystan who was supposed to stay with us today had never – after the telegram I sent telling him N. had flu – telephoned to ask how she was. Nikos said: 'Well all *he* will have thought when he got the telegram will have been – "What a nuisance for me."' He told me how Vera Russell had taken W. to the country to see H[enry] Moore on account of an illustrated volume of some poems by W. which Henry is doing. How Wystan didn't at all discuss the poems and illustrations but said when he entered the room – 'You must be a millionaire.' Then asked why it was that painters were often millionaires – poets never – but reflected that when painters slumped then they never recovered. They had ribs of beef to eat which W. devoured ravenously – then remarked – 'Well after all I prefer Mutton.' The rest of five hours he spent talking about himself and telling his anecdotes.

12 December 1972, London

Lunched Garrick Club with Philip Spender, John Wain, Karl Miller.[1] John Wain was very disillusioned about the state of England. Told us how he had decided not to have a car etc. Recently he had two accidents. 1) when while he was bicycling, a van with mirrors on the left hand side had hit him on the back of the head. He woke in the stretcher taking him to hospital. 2) when he was driving along Banbury Road a motorcyclist dived through his windscreen. A terrible shock for J.W. who was he admitted perhaps technically in the wrong. Karl and I started laughing almost uncontrollably at Wain's total assured egoism. A rather Dickensian day, really because Michael Peak came to the seminar on *What Maisie Knew* [by Henry James] in a coat with metal buttons. With his terrific Cockney accent, his

---

1 For Philip Spender, see biographical appendix. John Wain would run against, and beat, Spender for the Oxford Professorship of Poetry a few months later. Karl Miller (b. 1931), British literary editor and writer, editor of the *Listener*, 1967–73.

perkiness, his wit and sharp features, he is very Dickensian. Peggy Ashcroft [. . .] came to dinner. P[eggy] [. . .] talked about the members of the Angry Brigade who were friends of Nicky Hutchinson.[1] The girl who worked in aid of delinquents and then became so despairing of the whole system which produced delinquency that she supported violent revolution. Corin Redgrave who advocates at meetings demands which he thinks should never be negotiated at all but simply presented to employers.[2]

13 December 1972, London

We dined with Richard and Mary Day Wollheim. Isaiah and Aline Berlin there, also R[ichard]'s son Rupert and Barbara Epstein.[3] Isaiah told me he had a 2-page letter from Wystan about Isaiah's Turgenev lecture.[4] I said I'd sent a wire to W. saying Natasha had flu so could he stay with his brother [John Auden] and had never had any enquiry from him about Natasha's health – not a word. Isaiah said 'Of course not. If you get a letter from a hotel saying your booking is cancelled because the hotel manager has flu, you don't telephone anxiously enquiring after his health.'

16 December 1972, London

Went to John Osborne play *A Sense of Detachment* at Royal Court. Met David P[lante] there.[5] A group of actors appear on the stage and discuss with the director what they are going to do. They insult one another[,] members of the audience insult them. Nasty remarks are

---

1 Nicholas Hutchinson (b. 1945), son of Jeremy Hutchinson and Peggy Ashcroft. The 'Angry Brigade' was an anarchist-terrorist underground organization, responsible for a number of bomb attacks in London in the early 1970s. Members of the group were currently under trial.

2 Corin Redgrave (1939– 2010), British actor, son of Michael Redgrave and Rachel Kempson, founder of the Workers Revolutionary Party.

3 Barbara Epstein (1928–2006), founder and editor, with Robert Silvers, of the *New York Review of Books*.

4 Berlin had given his Romanes lecture on Turgenev's *Fathers and Sons* in 1970. Auden refers to the printed version.

5 For David Plante see biographical appendix.

made about Queers, TV, Harold Pinter, critics etc. The possibility that the audience might find this very boring is covered by the actors themselves saying it is boring. [. . .]

David told me that Adrian Stokes died yesterday. Jonathan Miller, Nikos [Stangos] and he were all there.[1] For some hours before dying Adrian breathed so heavily that his breathing could be heard by the guests visiting the show of pottery made by Ann Stokes in the next room.[2] The day before he died, Adrian finished his last picture which David said was his most beautiful one.

17 December 1972, London

Had a bad cold. Went to tea with Peggy Ashcroft. After that, called on Ann Stokes. She was highly excited bright-eyed, talking about the pots we had bought from her sale etc. Showed us the pictures Adrian had done in the weeks before he died. They were mostly still lifes, but the image dissolved more and more into the light in the flaky paint. Sometimes the paint had a lumpier texture in places than in his earlier work. Probably these are his most beautiful paintings.

In the autumn of 1972, US President Nixon's National Security Advisor, Henry Kissinger, was conducting a series of peace talks with North and South Vietnam, hoping to end the war before the November presidential election. Peace seemed to be in sight but a week after Nixon had won the election on 7 November he pledged his support for the South Vietnamese President Thieu, which in turn led Thieu to increase his demands on North Vietnam. On 13 December, Kissinger presented the North Vietnamese President Le Duc Tho with a list of changes to the settlement demanded by Thieu. Nixon issued an ultimatum to North Vietnam, stating that serious negotiations must resume within 82 hours. When Hanoi failed to respond, Nixon ordered what would be Operation Linebacker II, eleven days and

---

1 Jonathan Miller (b. 1934), British theatre and opera director and broadcaster who originally trained as a doctor and at this date held a research fellowship in the history of medicine at UCL.

2 Adrian Stokes's widow Ann Stokes (b. 1922) is a ceramicist and potter, whose work often features birds and trees.

nights of maximum-force bombing, ending on 26 December. The so-called 'Christmas bombings' were widely denounced by American politicians, the media and various world leaders, including the Pope.

18 December 1972, London

After lunch read poems about Vietnam and worked. News that the Americans are starting again full scale bombing of Vietnam. Dined at the Stafford Hotel with Bob Silvers; other guests, Francis Wyndham, Hugh Frasers, Naipaul.[1] Talked with Antonia Fraser who is writing a life of Cromwell. She was really very nice, modest. Hugh Fraser talked about Christianity. It was difficult to have any word with Bob which was disappointing. We left at 11.30 and went to Ben Nicolson's party at the Elysée restaurant. Had a long conversation with Nigel Nicolson who seemed rather out of it and alone – about the book he is doing, a third of which is his mother's very scrupulous detailed scientific account of her love affair with Violet Trefusis. He is supplementing this with relevant documents. Also an account of his parents' marriage which he said, despite their both being homosexual, was among the happiest he had ever known.[2] Told me he was worried about how the book would be received. I said he should expect – hope even – that someone would stick up for the horrid V. Trefusis, but apart from that he should take the position that the book was a contribution to

---

1 Francis Wyndham (b. 1924), British novelist, journalist and editor, currently with the *New Statesman*. Hugh Fraser (1918–1984), British Conservative politician who was at this time married (until 1977) to the British biographer and novelist Antonia Fraser (b. 1932), daughter of Spender's friend Frank Pakenham. V. S. Naipaul (b. 1932), Trinidadian-born British writer.

2 Ben and Nigel Nicolson were the sons of Sir Harold Nicolson and Vita Sackville-West. Nigel (1917–2004) was a biographer, publisher and Conservative politician and Ben (1914–1978) an art historian and editor of the *Burlington Magazine*, 1947–78. Nigel's biography of his parents, *Portrait of a Marriage*, was published in 1973. He describes his mother's affair with the British socialite Violet Trefusis (1894–1972), which also featured in Virginia Woolf's 1928 novel *Orlando*.

scientific knowledge of human understanding. We talked of death of
H. Nicolson.[1]

19 December 1972, London

Rang U.C.L. and discovered that I was to lunch at the Hungarian
Embassy which I did do. [. . .] There were only four other guests one
of them George Steiner.[2] Conversation amiable but wary. Steiner
described his meetings with Georg Lukács. Steiner looks like the
murderer in *M* played by Peter Lorre.[3] A bit Japanese too. Like an
oriental doll made of pieces fitting into one another. The lunch was
for a very top professor who (G.S. told me afterwards) is also a top
member of the central Committee of the Communist Party.[4] Certainly the Party was mentioned several times during luncheon with a
reverence I had not remembered since the Thirties. The Ambassador
or the Professor (we were all professors) said that Lukács had made
a 'profound' remark in 1968 at the time of the invasion of Czechoslovakia to the effect that in the short run the Party committed errors
but in the long run it was great. 'How long a run?' I asked and a sudden sharp smile passed over the face of one Hungarian. We were also
told that the trouble with the intellectuals was that they had no sense
of the responsibilities of power. I said that if as a person with values
one respected power too much and left no margin for criticizing it,
one made one's life a function of power. Steiner supported me in this.
But he also discussed his plans for going on an official visit to Hungary in June, gave instructions to the Cultural Attaché about visas
etc. He told me afterwards that our luncheon meeting would certainly be used in Budapest to indicate our sympathy with the regime.
Damn!

---

1 Harold Nicolson had died in 1968. He had been badly affected by the death
of his wife in 1962, suffering a series of strokes the following year.

2 George Steiner (b. 1929), Austrian-American literary critic and philosopher.

3 Spender had seen Fritz Lang's film *M*, which stars Peter Lorre (1904–1964)
as a sinister serial killer, in Berlin when it was released in 1931.

4 Arnold Kettle (1916–1986), professor of literature at the Open University.

20 December 1972, London

Day dominated by rage and disgust about the bombing of N. Vietnam. Spent the morning trying to write an article about this. Wrote only a draft. Went to the passport office and fetched passport. Then to Hayward Gallery and saw French Paintings of London. Came out onto Waterloo Bridge at dusk and the scene was all mauve buildings and dark blue chimneys, golden lights in windows. The House of Commons like profiled feathers of a hat silhouetted beyond the harsh lines of Charing Cross Bridge.

Matthew and Maro Spender had settled in Tuscany, in their house Avane, near Lecchi-in-Chianti, where both followed their respective artistic careers while bringing up their daughters, Saskia and Cosima.

21 December 1972, Avane, Lecchi-in-Chianti

Woke at 4.30 with thoughts about Vietnam. I see that morose louring face of Nixon with the obligatory smile and all these B-52 bombers proceeding from his mouth. Wrote to Isaiah and to several other people (though not about Vietnam). Slept a bit and got up at 8.30. Bought papers etc. Decided that Lizzie should not drive us to airport. Ordered hired car. We left at 10.15 arrived London Airport. Plane delayed an hour owing to pressure of Xmas traffic. Terribly crowded plane rather agonizing. Matthew met us at Milan. We rather lost our way driving to San Sano and did not get to Avane till 6. Maro welcomed us, as did Saskia. Saw Cosima. Had dinner. Maro very funny about Trevor who plays his flute almost unceasingly, scarcely eating any meal except breakfast, and who says he is searching for the 'ideal tone'.[1]

22 December 1972, Avane

A day has gone by very quickly. [. . .] Read in *Nazione* about Nixon's ultimatum to both sides in Vietnam war. It is a kind of schoolboy

---

1 Trevor D. W. Jones was the French-Canadian boyfriend of Maro's half-sister, Antonia Phillips. (He played an old Haines flute which he refused to have serviced, so the ideal tone he was looking for was unattainable.)

gamble to tell N. Vietnam that he will continue bombing until they come to agreement and S. Vietnamese that he will withdraw aid if *they* do not do so (bombing N. Vietnam *is* aid to S. Vietnam). After lunch, M. and I called on Tim Behrens who was not at home.[1] His wife looked harassed. M gave us copies of his prints of the birth of Cosima etc, which are very beautiful. I started on Monet article for *New Statesman* – Natasha made a dress for Saskia's doll. I wrote a poem ('To My Daughter') which Maro is going to do a decoration for, as a Christmas card. Restful day.

24 December 1972, Avane

At Avane all day. Matthew and Maro did etchings for my poem To My Daughter. Maro's was printed. Matthew framed the original of his which is figurative, with him and Saskia (very beautiful) for Stucchi family. [. . .] Went to midnight mass – or, rather, two midnight masses, – one at Baptistry the other at the Cathedral of Siena. With the service in Italian the whole service has become like a series of announcements of arrivals of trains in a railway station. The congregation and priests seemed equally perfunctory. People stood around like waiting for a train. Such music as there was was muzak quality and out of tune. The lit up interior of the cathedral however looked very beautiful as did the town itself – the piazza by moonlight with the very tall dramatic façades of the buildings – a stage set with the piazza itself like a great oval shaped sunk floor with shafts of passageways leading down to it from the sides.

25 December 1972, Avane

A very nice and rather crazy day. We decided to go for a walk, at 11. Maro said 'A long walk or a short one?' Thinking of all we had to digest we said a long one. We set out, M, M, N, Saskia, Cosima and I. Then Maro said: 'We have forgotten the goat. She loves walks.' So M went for the goat which trotted along after us. We went down a path through a long valley and then came to a stream. We crossed

---

1 Tim Behrens (b. 1937), British artist and writer, former friend of Lucian Freud, now living in a village near Matthew and Maro.

this by M putting stepping stones in it and carrying Saskia and the baby over. Then we couldn't get the goat to cross. Finally Maro had to go back and carry the goat. We walked to a group of ruins called San Paulo, which Natasha immediately started planning to live in. We then went a circuitous way along a dirt road back to Avane. But Saskia had dropped her new woollen cap so Mateo had to go back and fetch it. Then the baby started crying and wanting to be fed which Maro did. N wanted to walk on to look at another house. I trailed behind her with Saskia who wanted to be carried. We did however eventually all catch up with one another, but Saskia got tired and screamed a bit. Home, N, M and M made Christmas lunch which we had at about 5.

Earlier we opened presents all of which were nice. Matthew gave us an ink drawing, Maro a pencil drawing of Matthew. Natasha gave dress jewellery and material to M. I gave Paul Klee books to Matthew and Maro (one each). I rewrote Monet essay.

27 December 1972, Avane

I read newspapers all day about Vietnam. Am more enraged with Nixon than about any public figure since Hitler. The Americans have got into a position in which the rest of the world has to permit them to give way to neurotic fears and to express these with a hideous violence which – if any other country indulged in – would provoke complete incredulousness and also a world war. Imagine Russia behaving like this in the Middle East, for example.

On 29 September 1973, W. H. Auden died in Vienna.

1 November 1974, London

Suddenly, it seems, several of my generation – which seemed so enduring – have died, or been stricken with illness. The strangest thing is this feeling of being an unchanging consciousness sitting in a scratched vehicle. My friends' dying makes my legs ache.

3 November 1974, London

Saw the second half of the programme about Harold Macmillan on TV last night. He was talking about various scandals in his government, those connected with Vassall, Profumo etc.[1] His explanation of his attitude to these was that he believed what he was told. He regarded 'sexual immorality' as a matter of fashions in manners (in a world where respectability is not the characteristic of 'society' and at parties everyone calls everyone else 'darling'). He could not cope though with a colleague who told his colleague lies about sexual lapses (rocks which could be struck but then floated off from again).

Macmillan has some quality of being thoroughly concerned with politics but at the same time retaining above that concern a more elevated civilized humorous super-consciousness which is always about six feet above it, shining, smiling. That is the reality hinted at in the phrases 'unflappability', 'Super-Mac'. He is very consciously a gentleman of an old school: at the same time sympathetic to the difficulties of the young. He ended with a wonderful, acted-out, totally sincere yet sophisticatedly corny peroration about the need of something to believe in which otherwise-catastrophic wars had provided, the opportunities offered by Europe, the great adventure etc.

I was not able to get to Paris for the opening so saw only the catalogue of David Hockney's exhibition. Hockney is one of those artists who turns everything he sees into himself which he then transforms into drawings and paintings. The unanswerability of such art is that one has only to see a line by him to say 'That is Hockney.' We think of this as a literary quality because it is what we find supremely in literature. A line of Keats gives the feeling of putting one's hand on the poet's wrist and touching his pulse.

Hockney is not a 'modern' artist at all except in so far as Hockney himself is very much a modern man.

---

1 Macmillan's ministry had fallen in 1963 amidst scandals generated by the Vassall spy case and the defence minister John Profumo's resignation, having lied to Parliament about his relationship with the call girl Christine Keeler.

4 November 1974, London

One of my students not turning up, I walked along to the Harley
Street Clinic at 10.30 a.m. to see Cyril. He was asleep when I entered
the room so I sat down beside him. He opened his eyes and said:
'Stephen . . . I'm terribly tired.' I said 'I'll go away and come back.'
He said: 'Yes, come back again. I'm dead to the world.'

11 November 1974, London

Dreamt of Wystan. He was very worried, he said because he had no
pension. I said 'But you must have at least $100,000' and he said
'Yes, well I must,' and cheered up.

12 November 1974, London

I woke at 5.30 and read *Between the Acts* [by Virginia Woolf] for my
seminar – with eyes that had to struggle to see, I read: 'Why judge
each other? Do we know each other? Not here, not now. But somewhere, this cloud, this crust, this doubt, this dust – She waited for a
rhyme, it failed her; but somewhere surely one sun would shine and
all, without a doubt, would be clear.'

I find it more and more difficult to believe in personal immortality.
Considering how often we are unconscious, what is the difficulty of
being unconscious forever? The far side of sleep is stonier sleep. Yet
the blinding clarity of these lines suddenly made me feel that the idea
that human consciousness could be meaningless within the eternity
of all futures, was also incredible. The only point at which the universe says I could blow out and there be not a thought in eternity.

Cyril: 'I do not recommend dying.' 'I'm dead to the world.'
He must have tasted dying very fully. Subsided into the submerged
diving-bell Cyril.[1]

*In November 1974, UNESCO adopted a resolution at its 18th
General Conference excluding Israel from any regional grouping and*

---

1 Spender would elaborate the idea of Connolly and the diving bell – an image
of his ego-centred isolation from the world – in his funeral eulogy for his
friend.

[383]

from eligibility for appropriations, following what was seen as Israel's illegal occupation of the West Bank and the Gaza strip in the 1967 Six-Day War. European anxiety about the situation in the Middle East was high following the 1973 so-called Yom Kippur War, staged by Syria and Egypt in an attempt to regain Arab losses in 1967. This conflict had quickly escalated into an indirect confrontation between Israel's and Egypt's supporters, the USA and the USSR, and there was widespread fear that the Arab–Israeli conflict could result in worldwide nuclear war.

Meanwhile on 20 October 1973, as a result of the 1973 Arab–Israeli war, Arab oil-producing countries (OPEC) imposed a ban on oil exports to America which had global effects, including an increase in the price of coal in Britain. This weakened the already fragile British economy. An increase in inflation had contributed to government-enforced pay restraints and price increases which had already resulted in trade union industrial action, particularly amongst the National Union of Mineworkers (NUM). With coal now at a premium due to the oil restrictions, the NUM was in a position of strength and pushed for higher pay. The Conservative government refused, and instituted the three-day working week from January to March 1974, in a bid to preserve fuel resources. In February, the NUM unanimously rejected an offer of increased pay and the government called a snap election, which eventually resulted in a Liberal–Labour coalition government as Labour was a minority government. The Labour Prime Minister, Harold Wilson, managed to stabilize the position with the miners and in October a re-election was called, with Labour securing a tiny, but sufficient, majority of three seats.

17 November 1974, London

We have reached a stage where those who are not responsible for the consequences of their actions (oil producers, trades unionists) always win, because the consequences of confrontation are so dreadful that those who are responsible give in. This would have been called loss of nerve but in fact it is sense of reality. It has become realistic to abandon Western civilization. For there can be no civilization which is dominated by rational ignominy.

[384]

John Gross told me that UNESCO is going to expel Israel.[1]

20 November 1974, London

Meeting with about seven publicists, including the Israeli ambassador and Alan Sillitoe [. . .] to discuss public relations with Israel.[2] The Ambassador drew a picture which was terribly depressing. He said the policy of the Arab powers was now the total destruction of Israel. Meanwhile the inclination of other powers to come to the rescue was diminishing every day. Important sections of the English press were in bad financial straits and therefore becoming dependent on Arab money (e.g. the *Times*, with its supplements).

Meanwhile I am involved in sending a letter to the said *Times* to protest against Israel being boycotted by UNESCO.

24 November 1974, London

Writing for the sixth time my memoir of Cyril. Rang his home and learned from his stepdaughter that there is some hope. Heart and liver improved. He has rallied. Will be moved to another nursing home. [. . .] May linger. May recover.

25 November 1974, London

Lunch with Diana Cooke [née Witherby]. Talked about Cyril. She was very loving about him but told me it was true he was cruel – punishing – to women. She said that the worst thing she found when she had her affair with him was that he not only deceived her, but that he liked doing so – took pleasure in telling lies. She thought my idea was right that being left by his mother midway between South Africa and England – at Corsica – when his mother (whom he thought was going with him to England) left him, and returned to South Africa to join his father – was a traumatic experience that put him in the

---

1 John Gross (b. 1935), author and literary critic, who had resigned with Spender from *Encounter* in 1967 following the revelations of CIA funding and was currently editor of the *Times Literary Supplement*, 1974–81.

2 Alan Sillitoe (1928–2010), British novelist.

position of being the child of promise to whom the implied promise made by his mother was broken so that in later life he punished others and himself by not fulfilling his promise or doing what was expected of him.[1] She was extremely upset because Sonia [Orwell] had told Cyril very recently, since his illness, that she[,] Diana, had said he was a bad father. If Sonia said this she must be a bit mad. Diana has always said (which is true) that he is a very good father. I telephoned Barbara Ghika who told me that on Sunday, Cyril had been moved (without Deirdre being consulted) from the Harley St Clinic to a nursing home kept by nuns in Ladbroke Grove: that when he arrived there the nuns had made a great scene: said they could not keep him, he was dying, and they had no equipment to deal with his kind of case . . .[2] Also she said the doctor said he would not recover but might linger on in the same condition for weeks or months: and if by chance he did recover he would suffer from the effects of anaemia of the brain. There is general dread that he will go on, a ghost of himself.

On 26 November 1974, Cyril Connolly died. In his eulogy, Spender wrote that 'Cyril's death marked the end of the Horizon *era, identified with his pleasure-loving personality, overflowing witticisms, aesthetic perceptions expressed in a prose like silver Latin: an era, overlapping with, and in many respects the opposite of that of the thirties' political conscience, transformed into theology in later Auden. There was so wide a gulf between the two – reflecting that between two Oxford generations of the aesthetic twenties and the political thirties – as to make it seem strange that Auden and Connolly died within a year of each other'.*

---

1 The phrase 'child of promise' is an allusion to Connolly's best-known work, *Enemies of Promise* (1938). Connolly's mother left her husband for another man shortly after her son's birth; Connolly's father, a soldier, had been posted to South Africa.

2 Barbara Ghika, née Hutchinson was now the wife of Nicolas Ghika; she had formerly been married to Victor Rothschild and to Rex Warner.

29 November 1974, London

Cyril died on Tuesday a day after he had been moved. Deirdre (accompanied by Peter Levi) had gone to see him on Monday and he had been conscious and lucid.[1] Deirdre seemed happy about the visit [. . .] The whole week is vague to me, dominated by thinking about Cyril and writing the reminiscent article for the *T.L.S.*[2] [. . .]

Rang John Gross who said he liked the piece. I wish I had the chance to read it two weeks hence. I keep on remembering things I'd intended to put in, but haven't e.g. I mention Cyril's love for a semi-identification with animals – (lemurs, passage about in *Palinurus*).[3] I meant to go on to say that though not a visionary he had a vision of the world of fauna and flora which made them the Paradisal realization of his idea of a passive state of ecstasy which is creative. Among the animals it does not create an artefact, it is a condition of being. But his idea of poetry and art is that they should arise out of such a condition of the creature amid the creation producing his song. [. . .]

I think that in my article I was also very hurried in what I said about *Horizon*, what I meant to say was that editing at the outbreak of war provided Cyril with a situation, partly passive and receptive (reading manuscripts) which also released an almost effortless flow of energy in the *Comments* which are his most vital writing.[4] *Horizon* in the early part of the war, when England suddenly became one beleaguered family, also put him into a harmonious relationship with a significant, though limited, public he would address as individuals, some of whom appreciated him, others of whom scoffed at him and his hedonism (but he took the scoffing with great good humour). The result was that he wrote commentaries in which he was really able to relate his great awareness of the sensuous particularities of living to politics. Not just democracy, and the present and all possible future English forms of society were threatened – also the civilization was

---

1 Connolly's third wife Deirdre (née Craven) would marry the poet and Oxford academic Peter Levi (1931–2000) a few months later.

2 'Cyril Connolly. Connolly's "millstone of promise"', *Times Literary Supplement*, 6 December 1974.

3 *The Unquiet Grave: A Word Cycle* (1944), written by Connolly under the pseudonym 'Palinurus'.

4 Spender refers to Connolly's editorial comments at the opening of *Horizon*.

threatened: and to get the full sense of this the political system had to be seen as intrinsic with the civilization. He made implicit claims that *Horizon* ought to be supported by the Ministry of Information – and looking back on its role in the war, he was justified in doing so.

A joke about Cyril was his love of eating lobsters.¹ But since he was so much a person with a romantic idea of the things he loved, I wonder whether he did not love lobsters because of some deep affinity with them as that part of his feeling of unity with the animal world which descended to the depths of the sea. His imagination was like a diving bell.

2 December 1974, London

Cyril's funeral. Went from Victoria to Eastbourne by train with Sonia Orwell, Jack Lambert, Noel Blakiston, Diana Cooke.² Met by a cortège of Daimlers which took us (I went in car with a Mr and Mrs Hamburg relations of Deirdre Connolly) to Berwick Church. Very pretty interior further prettified by decorative paintings of Duncan Grant and Vanessa Bell.³ Duncan was seated there at back of church, with his daughter.

Anthony Hobson read lesson.⁴ Lesson and Psalm all about resurrection of the body – seemed unsuitable to Cyril. The vicar who has a stick without which he can't stand up, talked very briefly and understandingly about Cyril and his work. We stood around the flower-covered grave, in the wet and windy cold weather, just a

---

1 Rose Macaulay quipped of Connolly 'Lobsters he loved, and next to lobsters, sex' (*pace* Walter Savage Landor's 'Nature I loved, and next to Nature, Art').

2 Jack Lambert (1917–1986), literary editor of the *Sunday Times*, where Connolly was chief book reviewer. Hugh Noel Blakiston (1929–1984), writer who would publish a volume of his and Connolly's letters in 1975 under the title *A Romantic Friendship*.

3 Vanessa Bell (1879–1961), painter sister of Virginia Woolf and the lover of Duncan Grant. In 1941, they were commissioned by Bishop Bell of Chichester to decorate Berwick Church, which was a few miles from their home at Charleston in Sussex.

4 Anthony Hobson (b. 1921), scholar, bibliophile, and head of Sotheby's books division.

tarpaulin of some kind over the coffin. The person who seems most stricken is Joan Leigh Fermor. I held her arm a moment but didn't dare speak to her. She looks 20 years older.

I drove in Alan and Jennifer Ross's car to the party at Deirdre's afterwards. All the guests including Peter Levi were there. Lots of champagne. Cressida [Connolly] took me aside and said in a very solemn stage whisper that I must promise to speak at the memorial service because if I didn't someone else whom she didn't like at all (meaning Peter Levi) would do so. Matthew Connolly was brought in and sat very docilely on people's knees – blond and quiet almost like our Matthew once.[1]

At the end of 1974, the Spenders spent a month in Israel with Noel and Gabrielle Annan and their children, the Berlins and Stuart Hampshire. They had each received an invitation from the mayor of Jerusalem, Teddy Kollek, to stay at Mishkenot Sha'ananim, the first area of Jewish settlement in Jerusalem outside the walls of the Old City. Spender would write up his impressions for the New York Review of Books.

21 December 1974, Jerusalem

Flight to Jerusalem with four Noel Annans, Aline and Isaiah Berlin, Stuart Hampshire.[2] Plane late. Arrived midnight.

22 December 1974, Jerusalem

Went to old town with Aline. Bought a rug. Shopped at supermarket and stocked up our kitchen. [. . .]

Reading, to review for *Spectator*, Joe Ackerley's letters, which brings back a lot about him.[3] Gerald Heard who was extremely acute once said that Joe and I were very alike (when I was 25, Joe, I

---

1 Cressida (b. 1960) and Matthew Connolly (b. 1970) are the children of Cyril and Deirdre Connolly.

2 For Noel Annan, see biographical appendix.

3 Ackerley had died in 1967 and his letters were published in 1975 (ed. Neville Braybrooke).

suppose, 40).[1] (Gerald also said that Wystan was essentially a monkish scholar who had the handwriting of a monk who writes comments in the margin of a text that runs down the centre of the page.) Walking down Regent St in the early Thirties – William [Plomer], Joe [Ackerley], Tony Hyndman and I – Joe and T. walked ahead, William and I behind, and William remarked 'I had never noticed before how revealing Joe's walk is from behind' – There was a slight S-like sinuosity. Joe was elegant but never in the least dressy. I never saw him wear any overcoat but a trench-coat. He lived apparently alone but always had relatives in his hair – his mother, his sister, his aunt. A young Apollo for celibacy, he was pursued by Bacchantae who were close blood-relatives more than anyone I have known, and across the years they tore him limb from limb, though he kept them at a distance with his Alsatian, Queenie. He was a man of great gentillesse [kindness], literary, a stylist, but with no pretensions as a Critic or a Creator who lay down rules about the Tradition or discussed the Novel as if it were an abstraction. He made an excellent editor, very interested in his contributors, independent, direct, friendly. He also had a sceptical attitude to *The Listener* and the BBC (which later he came to refer to as slavery but which in fact was probably good for him).[2] When he left the BBC his character changed considerably. He had almost no money and drew his old age pension after having failed to get on the dole. He was still burdened with his female relations. The main interest in his life was his Alsatian bitch Queenie. His novel *We Think the World of You* shows that the Alsatian whom a working class family asked Frank (the hero) to look after while her owner a young man with whom the hero is in love is doing a term in prison, became a substitute in the hero's mind for the animal beauty and high spirits, innocence and natural affection, which Frank had looked for in the young man. This youth had a beautiful body, but his character was degraded his mind corrupt. Queenie was not only beautiful but also in affection, fidelity, joie de vivre, uncorrupted.

Although Joe had discovered the ideal friendship he wished for among the animals, the result of this was to increase his contempt for human beings who did not live up to the animals, whom moreover

---

1 Gerald Heard (1889–1971), historian and philosopher.
2 Ackerley was literary editor of the BBC magazine the *Listener*, 1935–59.

they slaughtered and treated with the utmost cruelty. Nevertheless, Joe denied that he was misanthropic, and pointed out in his letters that he loved his friends (as, indeed, he did). Merely, he would like to see ⅔ of the human race eliminated by some form of 'Spanish flu'.

After Queenie's death he became ever more solicitous about animals, nursing a hurt seagull, taking home a sparrow which had fallen out of its nest, and actually keeping it until it had learned to fly, going long journeys to keep company with the domestic pets of friends who were abroad. His attitude had truth in it as well as sentimentality (indeed the sentimentality only emerges when he turns his love of animals against human beings). We human beings incurred great responsibilities towards the animals on some of whom we feed, and who share with us the air and earth and oceans which we have polluted. To take one example only: keeping battery hens lambs and calves in an environment designed with no aim except to make them food for human consumption compounds the original crime of humanity against the animals we eat – (a crime which probably affects us unconsciously even though it is made excusable by the fact that we ourselves are conditioned to live on other life): with a new and modern crime of our scientific world which renders our inhuman attitude towards the animals doubly inhuman. Joe had insight into this and the nature passages in which he pleads the case of the animals are genuinely moving. They are made less though by the fact that he does not believe that any but a few of his friends will listen to his plea.

23 December 1974, Jerusalem

Whole day trip with Aline Berlin, Peter Halban and the Annans along the Dead Sea coastal road, from Qu'mran to Eilat and then inland to Dimma and thence to Kibbutz Revivion.[1]

The desert is a landscape of clouds made of rock and sand, the sculpting of dunes by wind, rains and erosion. It acts as a much-embossed reflector to the woods and the sky. [. . .]

We drove past Sodom (difficult to think of anyone ever getting any

---

[1] Peter Halban (b. 1948), Israeli publisher and son of Aline (née Halban), who married Isaiah Berlin in 1956.

enjoyment out of what's geographically if not morally the lowest spot of the world) and then up to Damona. Here we had lunch. Damona is a 'new town' in the Negev desert, like a frontier town, a cut-rate version of many rigged up towns in the Californian desert, an affair of concrete shacks, trestled concrete platforms like rough overways, along whose sides there are rows of little shops and eating places, miniscule shopping centre with chairs outside a café on its piazza – a mockery of American and European centres, which hideous though it is, will perhaps be the site of a flourishing city. Beersheba since I was last here, when it was a sprawling brave frontier town, is now a second-class city with buildings that seem buds that will burgeon into skyscrapers – a Middle East version of São Paolo.

Unless indeed all this development which seems here an irresistible natural force is held back by world economic crisis, or blasted out of memory by a third Israeli–Arab war. Meanwhile a hitch-hiking soldier to whom we gave an illegal lift (soldiers are not supposed to thumb foreign cars) told us that London had more bomb explosions today than Israel. True. But that we do is a small part of the calamity that threatens Israel.

25 December 1974, Jerusalem

The Annans, the Berlins, Stuart Hampshire, the Spenders – we all went to Cohen's restaurant, where the dinner consisted of six varieties of meat-balls stuffed into six varieties of vegetables. Teddy Kollek drove four of us there.[1] On the way he reverted to the theme of the new buildings in Jerusalem. He said that Jerusalem was the only city in the world where in addition to putting up new buildings they were clearing spaces within the city itself, to make it more beautiful. He drove by a part of the wall where two buildings had been torn down to reveal a most beautiful part of it. 'What city in the world of comparable size has 60,000 acres of public gardens?' he asked. He then

---

1 Teddy Kollek (1911–2007), Hungarian-born Israeli politician. He emigrated to Palestine 1935 and was Mayor of Jerusalem, 1965–93. Although Kollek was a Zionist who openly admitted that he would 'love the city to be empty of Arabs' he was pragmatic in his attitude towards the Arabs, attempting to treat them well so as not to alienate them, and he advocated and nurtured religious tolerance throughout his time in office.

took us on a little tour to show us the effects of flood-lighting, done in slightly varied colours, on the wall and many buildings including the Russian monastery where, he mentioned, a Russian princess descendant of the Romanovs and now aged 92, is a nun. He said that there was practically no night life in Jerusalem, and that is why they had decided to light up a good part of the city at night – to provide some effect of beauty and pleasure. We passed a place which, he said, 'almost proved my undoing'. 'Why was that?' I asked. 'Because against the wishes of my council I had a memorial put up here for the Arab dead in the Arab–Israeli wars. Speeches and articles were made asking "Where in England was there a memorial commemorating the German dead?"' Isaiah said that as a matter of fact there was one in some Oxford or Cambridge College. Teddy said he regretted he hadn't known this. We drove on a bit further and then suddenly stopped the car driving it across the verge of the road. 'Get out,' he said 'and walk to the edge of the gully.' We did so and saw almost immediately below us the old first-century Jewish Cemetery, with the tomb which is called Absolom's – a dazzling white pyramid, and to the left of it another cone-shaped white tomb. These shone out of the down-sloping darkness through which one could see many other tombs. Above there was the Russian monastery, living tomb of the Russian Princess who had now become a romantic figure to me.

26 December 1974, Jerusalem

I talked with Joshua Palmon who is an expert on Jewish–Arab relations, having worked among Arabs since his youth (he is now middle aged) and who is an adviser to the government in these matters.[1] He said that there was no difference between Arabs in Jerusalem and those on the Western Bank of the Jordan. They are all Jordanians. [. . .]

Joshua Palmon said that the feeling of the Arabs for the family was stronger even than that for the nation. The family was identified with the place where its members lived. The refugees do not want to leave the camps in which they live [with] their families round them.

It was difficult for the Palestinians to come to an understanding

---

1 Joshua Palmon (1913–1994), Israeli politician.

with Hussein because he had killed 1,000 of them.[1] To live with Israel meant approving the borders of '67. But to have bad relations with Israel cuts them off from their communications which pass through Israel. It is also impossible for Israel to accept the idea of a Palestinian state when the P.L.O. remains a terroristic organization which refuses to recognize the existence of Israel and is indeed dedicated to its destruction.[2]

I asked him what solution was possible in Israeli–Arab relations. He said that there were two. One must be done immediately. An agreement must be reached which provided security for Israel and hope for the Palestinians. War must be held off by maintaining a situation of semi-peace and semi-good relations. The other solution – the real one – was to promote and encourage certain developments. King Hussein has to retreat from his position of absolute power and gradually become a constitutional monarch. He has to become more democratic – and in the meantime a solution has to be found for the refugees, who have no citizenship and are living on the Western bank in camps.

One of the things that makes it difficult to find a solution is that the evident fear of the Western World of being cut off from its petrol supplies and having to reduce its standard of living is producing a feeling among the Arabs of Mohammedan expansionism. Events such as the appearance of Arafat at the United Nations create

---

1 Hussein bin Talal (1935–1999), King Hussein of Jordan, 1952–99. Following the end of the British Mandate for Palestine and the foundation of the state of Israel in 1948, Palestinian territories were absorbed into the borders of Jordan, creating a Jordanian population that was over 60 per cent Palestinian in ethnic origin. On 16 September 1970, King Hussein of Jordan ordered his forces to drive the Palestinian movement from his country, claiming that Palestine had become a 'state within a state' and represented a threat to his power. This resulted in the deaths of thousands of Palestinians and the devastation of the PLO infrastructure. King Hussein of Jordan reluctantly agreed to end the assault at an Arab League meeting on 27 September 1970.

2 PLO, the Palestinian Liberation Organization, a political and paramilitary organization founded in 1964 to promote the reinstatement of the borders of Palestine, as agreed in the British Mandate for Palestine in 1922, and fight against Zionism. In the 1970s, the PLO was increasingly seen as a legitimate political organization and the official representative of the Palestinian cause.

immense excitement in the Arab world.[1] At present the Russians help the Arabs. But quite possibly they will have second or third thoughts.

He went on to say that the Arabs do not hate the Israelis so much because they are Jews as because they are not-Muslims. The rest of the world is mistaken in thinking that the Arabs are simply motivated by their economic interests. What they really want is for other people to admit the superiority of the Muslim faith.

Nor do the Jews want to rule the Arabs. Most Jews would be delighted to be rid of the responsibility for the 6,000,000 Arabs on the Western bank of the Jordan, if they could exchange not having to rule them for their security. They spend more energy and money on the Western bank than they get out of it.

28 December 1974, Jerusalem

Israel seems a democratic, socialistic society – much more so than England, unless we are to think of the England of 1940. The army is extremely democratic as we found 3 years ago when we were touring the neighbourhood of Jericho with a general and we gave a lift to a soldier who immediately recognized him and settled down to a friendly conversation with him and then invited us all to a cup of tea at his barracks where all the soldiers treated him in the same way. Members of the government are extremely accessible just as were members of the Spanish Republican government during the Spanish Civil War. They are looked on as 'ours'.

29 December 1974, Jerusalem

Luncheon with Clara Malraux.[2] C.M. asked me immediately what I thought about this country. While I was hesitating before replying,

---

1 On 13 November 1974, Yassir (Yasser) Arafat (1929–2004), leader of the PLO, was allowed to address the United Nations. The PLO was granted 'observer status'. Arafat provocatively carried a pistol, visible during his address. The speech was hugely controversial and outraged Jewish groups. For Palestinians it provided official recognition of their struggle for political independence.

2 Clara Malraux (1897–1982), writer and divorced wife of André Malraux, who had spent time on a kibbutz in 1948 and was involved in the fight for Israel, campaigning on its behalf, especially after the Six Day War (1967) and the Yom Kippur War (1973).

[395]

my other guest Charles Taylor appeared so I did not have to answer.[1] Then after trivial conversation I asked her what *she* thought about it. She said 'Well I have the impression that the Arabs can do anything they like.' She added: 'After all, the Israelis made great mistakes after the '67 war.' 'What mistakes' asked C.T. rather sharply. 'Well they should have announced immediately after their victory that they renounced all claim to the territories they occupied.' '*All* the territories? Would that have been advantageous supposing the Arabs had not taken it in the spirit in which it was meant, and had started another attack?' 'Well, at any rate they should have announced what they were going to keep and what they were not going to keep, and given their reasons for doing this, and done something about setting up a Palestinian State.'

C.T. agreed that, with hindsight and at any rate with a view to getting world opinion behind them that might have been wise.

I said that if Israel was all that was concerned, perhaps C.M.'s pessimism was justified. But after all Israel did represent multiple interests. The interest of America in seeing that Israel did not disappear off the face of the earth was considerable. (C.T. added that it was difficult to think of an American administration surviving the reaction that such a catastrophe would produce among Americans.) I said there was a certain interest of conscience. I did not really believe that after the holocaust of 1945 the conscience of Europe would permit another holocaust to take place in the Middle East. C.M. said: 'Well, it is because I am French that I am what you call pessimistic. I can assure you that the French have completely forgotten about Israel. They could not care less. If Israel disappeared the French would not give it a thought.'

30 December 1974, Jerusalem

[I visited] the apartment of M[enahem] Milson a senior lecturer in Hebrew literature at the Hebrew University. We talked first about modern Arabic literature, and he said that though there were some good poets and writers of stories, when it came to translating them

---

[1] Charles Margrave Taylor (b. 1931), Canadian philosopher, student and friend of Isaiah Berlin.

into French or English, they appeared out of date and not to fit into modern literature as we understood it in the West.

Milson and his wife live in a pleasant apartment, simple, in the Israeli style. He told me that he was a fifth generation 'sabra' [Jew born in Israeli territory] and had no idea that he could possibly live anywhere else but Israel. He looks Grecian with black curly hair a short straight nose eyes and eyelids and mouth that look as if they were chiselled, they are so clearly defined and a clear skin and pale complexion. He seemed perfectly assured and at ease in everything he said, and not in the least excited about or dramatizing of the situation. I asked him whether he knew many Arabs, and he told me he had very close friends who were Arabs. I asked him what they felt about unification. He said that he did not know a single Arab who accepted the idea even of there being a sovereign Jewish nation in this part of the world. He told me anecdotes to illustrate this. One was about a friend of his a great scholar with whom he was able to talk quite freely about every subject. An American producer had been sent to this area to make a film for TV etc about the Middle East. Part of the very expensive exposition was a conversation between M[ilson]'s friend and an Israeli who was his counterpart. The conversation was extremely friendly and showed great understanding on both sides. At the end of it, the interlocutor – chairman – asked the Arab in what circumstances he would wish the Arab states to be related to Israel. The answer said with restraint and dignity 'I do not recognize the existence of the Jewish state.' The American producer cut this part of the conversation of the film, M. asked him why he had done so and he said: 'it did not fit into the picture of Arab–Israeli reconciliation which I wished to give in my film.'

The attitude of enlightened Arabs to Israel was that they were prepared to tolerate Jews living in this part of the world and even to have friendly relations with them as individuals and people – but they could not accept the idea of Israeli sovereignty. He thought that the idea of some people that Israel could be part of a democratic Middle East – one democracy among Arab democracies – was nonsense because the Arab countries did not have the concept of democracy. Another story illustrated this. He met a Lebanese Muslim at some meeting in Beirut with whom he had a candid conversation, at the end of which the Lebanese said: 'You and I understand each other perfectly. Apart from the question of the Jewish state, it is nevertheless people like us who ought to be running this part of the world. In my opinion there are three types of Jews: firstly the sabras who have been long established there; secondly the immigrants from the West; and thirdly the Orientals. The first two are very good: but the third lot, the orientals are fellaheen [farmers].' M[ilson] explained to him that he thought quite the opposite of this: that the two supposedly superior classes should get together to improve the status of the third class.

He said that he thought the Middle East experts had made a mistake when they wrote that what the Arabs wanted was that their honour should be satisfied. Honour was not their chief motivation in the history of Islam. True, to the outer world, they spoke of honour but to their own people, they talked of 'rights'. By 'rights' they mean that they recognize the personal rights of the Jews but not their national rights. National rights are the rights of the Arabs. The Jews are a minority community to be tolerated but for them to set up as a sovereign nation is presumptuous.

I said that to an outsider the realism of the Israelis about war, combined with their confidence, was very striking. I asked him how he felt about being in Israel in the presence of such appalling risks. He said 'I realize there were threats of terrible weapons which may be used, but I could not live anywhere else. Besides we've built here something which is very precious. Another reason for being here is that this is the place where Hebrew is spoken. There is the unique phenomenon here of a cultural unity – and that will disappear if Israel is destroyed. After all, quite apart from the state of Israel, there is a healthy core of Jews living here. They are more rooted in this place than the Arabs, who are rooted in the Arab world.

'All the same I can understand the Arab point of view. In the Islamic world Jerusalem is just a provincial town. It was never a great capital for the Muslims. To them we are a pain in the neck which they would like to get rid of. There is a type of Jew who has eliminated certain characteristics from his cultural heritage. What I reproach even the most intelligent Arabs I know for is that they have not made a similar effort. If only modern Arabs would eliminate from their heritage that part of the Koran which prophesies that the Jews and others who are not of the Muslim faith are destined to humiliation and misery!'

[398]

9 January 1975, London

Lunch party at the Stafford Hotel given by K[enneth] Clark on the occasion of his coming to London en route to Cairo where he is making a film. Other guests – John Pipers, Henry Moores, Freddy Ashton, Jock Murrays.[1]

Jane Clark was wheeled in, looking magnificently made-up, round and waxen like a large pink puppet.[2] Henry M. sat on her right, I on her left. Henry seemed very cheerful, said his ankle which he had broken was now mended and he was modelling again. He arrived and left in a chauffeur-driven car ('Oh they're all so rich,' sighed Freddy). Henry and I had to make heroic efforts to hear what Jane was saying. She talked to me a bit about her nurse and a bit about the etching of sheep which Henry had given her. She said Philip Hendy had had a much worse stroke than she.[3] Henry and I took turns lifting her plate up close to her, so she could lift food to her mouth with her right hand, her left being paralysed. She said once or twice that she was very unhappy. But Henry said she had never looked better, braving untruth. Mrs, or Lady, Jock Murray told me it had always been Jock's ambition to atone for the House of Murray having burned Byron's memoirs, by publishing a complete edition of his letters.[4]

At the end of lunch Jane was wheeled out and there was some general conversation about Abstract art, particularly in relation to Victor Pasmore.[5] Kenneth said what a wonderful painter Victor had been and that he had now reduced abstraction to a kind of solipsistic

---

1 Frederick Ashton (1904–1988), ballet choreographer. Jock Murray (1909–1993), head of the John Murray publishing house and publisher of the best-selling book of Kenneth Clark's television series *Civilisation* (1969).

2 Jane Clark had been bedridden since 1973 and she would die in 1976.

3 Philip Hendy (1900–1980), art historian who succeeded Clark as Director of the National Gallery, 1946–67. He suffered a severe stroke in 1975 but lived for five more years.

4 Famously, the first John Murray decided to burn Byron's posthumous memoirs, to protect the poet's reputation. The complete letters, and surviving journals, of Byron were published by the firm between 1973 and 1984 under the editorship of Leslie Marchand.

5 Victor Pasmore (1908–1998), British artist, one of the Euston Road School with whom Spender had once studied.

art which related to no-one outside himself. Henry got rather excited and talked about the time when Ben Nicolson, Barbara Hepworth and he had done abstractions in the early Thirties. John Piper and Ivy Hendy joined in. All the artists felt that a long discussion was going to ensue. But the waiter announced a telephone call from Jane to K[enneth] who left the room, saying 'This sounds serious'. He came back a few minutes later saying it wasn't serious, but all the same the mood had been broken. We realized we were all expected to go. Henry said: 'Jane looks very well.' K. said rather stiffly 'That's completely wrong. Things are very bad.'

14 January 1975, London

The usual rush in which days go by scarcely noticed. Friday, lunch with Karl Miller who discussing his own gloom, said 'Why do you always seem so serene and happy?'[1] I found it difficult to answer this question. Possibly on some kind of Goethean philosophic principle that one ought to [be] positive, count one's blessings and – also – avoid being got down either by one's own imaginary or even other people's real misery. Partly because I live too much in the day and therefore on the surface. Lack of self-pity combined with selfishness. Also gratitude, for my family, Natasha and my children. Yet it rather surprises me people see me as happy. Whenever I see myself (as in photos) I look miserable. We saw on Saturday evening the T. S. Eliot TV programme on which I looked miserable.

22 January 1975, London

Chester Kallman died in Athens. I don't know anything about this except that Charles Monteith rang me on Saturday to say he had died that morning.[2] Sense of the inevitability of his death. Nikos [Stangos] had told me that when he was in Athens a month ago he rang C[hester] who seemed delighted to hear from him and arranged that they should meet at a bar and then go to lunch. At the bar Chester was surrounded by American Queens and very tough Greek boys,

---

1 Karl Miller was now head of the English department at UCL.

2 Charles Monteith (1921–1995), senior editor at Faber, Auden's publisher.

including Chester's own (ephezone? Greek soldier) whom Nikos said was very tough but very beautiful. They stayed drinking at the bar from one to five during which time, Nikos said, C. drank four bottles of ouzo. (He had been told six months ago when he was sent to hospital that he must stop drinking completely, which he did for a time.) N. felt horrified and amused about the boys who, he said, were like 'alley cats'. He said the Americans showed deep concern for Chester (he also added that C. said he had no money and N. was left to pay the bill).

Chester was warm, witty, genuine, but completely a 'slob', with his endless 'camp'[,] his hopeless self-indulgence. A scene that stays in my mind is being in (1950?) Venice, having drinks in Florian's on the piazza. Chester, Wystan, Cecil Day Lewis (I think) and I were there. In the middle of the conversation Chester got up and followed a sailor out of the square. Wystan went on talking but all the time his eyes were following Chester, and tears were trickling down his cheeks.

Chester and Wystan certainly adored and understood one another and were not even incompatible, but nevertheless it was impossible for them to live except intermittently together. Although Wystan enjoyed campy conversation and was completely tolerant of promiscuity and every kind of sexual irregularity, he could not tolerate infidelity, unpunctuality, late hours. It was as though there was a structure of sexual morality in his head and also a set of rules related to timetables and rituals. He was quite open-minded about sexual morals but completely closed about the timetables and rituals. Thus he did not at all disapprove of Chester's *moeurs* except in so far as they broke the rule of fidelity and upset the timetables and rituals of meals and games and going to bed early. And, of course, they made him suffer.

Bob Silvers rang from N.Y. and told me among other things that Chester had died intestate. He has a very ancient father, and a brother who has a very active wife who is set on getting Wystan's inheritance. I felt v. resentful for the fifth or sixth time at the memory of Chester's slobbishness. The end of the Auden–Chester relationship – that Auden's estate goes to his [Chester's] brother and sister-in-law (a very active lady, Bob Silvers said) seemed altogether depressing.

23 January 1975, London

Memories about Wystan: 1) that he would have liked to give evidence at the *Lady Chatterley* trial supporting the prosecution, stating that it *was* pornographic; 2) his very reserved attitude about love at the end of his life.[1] He once noted to me an Elizabethan poem (possibly by Shakespeare) about this, which he had put in the Viking Anthology he edited with N. Holmes – must look this up.[2]

29 January 1975, London

Lunch yesterday with Harry Fainlight who is extremely paranoid. As we walked along Tottenham Court Road, I asked him what he was doing. He said, 'Mostly street fighting.' 'Street fighting, what do you mean?' 'It's got to the stage now where they are murdering poets.' He explained that in the streets there was running war between 'revolutionaries' and others. As I understand it, the revolutionaries ought to be on the side of the poets but weren't. There is also a lot of telepathy, inter-comm of auras, and extra-sensory perception. So far it all sounds convincingly mad, and of course Harry is mad and has been institutionalized (the mad are now let out in society as the result of the insanity of the people who look after the mad and who have decided simply to let most of them out. Or perhaps this just reflects the idea that our society with its pop groups its hippies its pornography – and Mrs Whitehouse – is a madhouse anyway – which may not be an altogether a bad thing for it to be).[3] But with a mad poet one may suddenly get the impression that he is simply living out

---

1 In 1959 Penguin had published the uncensored version of D. H. Lawrence's 1928 novel *Lady Chatterley's Lover* following the introduction of the 1959 Obscene Publications Act, which made it possible to publish so-called obscene texts on the grounds that they were of sufficient literary merit. Various prominent writers and critics testified on the novel's behalf at the trial in November 1960 with the result that Penguin was found 'not guilty'.

2 *Poets of the English Language* (1950), ed. W. H. Auden and Norman Holmes Pearson.

3 Mary Whitehouse (1910–2001), anti-pornography crusader. A main sponsor of the Christian mass rallies known as the 'Festival of Light', aimed to uphold moral decency, in 1971.

metaphors which would not seem mad at all if they were confined to his poetry. Thus the idea of a life going on today in the streets in which there are different sides who are, indeed, dressed for their roles – some in business attire, some in leather jackets, some with hair flowing down the shoulders of men and wearing necklaces and bracelets, and that the relation between these teams is one of running hostilities – this is a metaphor that would appear 'respectable' in a poem. To say this is to distinguish between poets who live their metaphors and are 'mad' in their poetry and out of it – and those who keep that part of their life which is metaphorical thinking, feeling, and creating below a kind of plimsoll line which itself is respectably visible on their sides as being 'well above water'. (Funny, that metaphor of the plimsoll line has been in my unconscious ever since I first saw a ship with one, when I was ten, on holiday in Cornwall, and my father explained it to me. And I don't think I've ever used it before. I can see an old cargo-ship with a plimsoll line on its side sailing before me, as I write this.)

7 February 1975, London

Thoughts while shaving. Things I am most ashamed of: 1) the fact that I find exaggerated confirmation of my 'identity' by reading my name in the newspapers. My heart does really do something – stop a beat – give a jump – something *journalistic* – if my eye hooks onto the printed word 'Spender' or even – now I am getting a bit astigmatic – any conformation of letters like it.

I really admire people who regard any publicity attached to them as vulgar and odious. I think of them in their cottage gardens which have old-fashioned overwhelming-smelling red and white roses and are enclosed by thick hedges. Nothing they do is to the slightest degree influenced by any publicity. For them to think that a television crew might arrive one day and do a film of their utterly pure life would be a terrible betrayal.

11 February 1975, London

Monday, lunch with Elstob, Secretary of the PEN Club.[1] Asked me whether I would be president in 1976 of the English branch. Said I would agree in principle. Tuesday rang V. S. Pritchett who said it would give him much pleasure if I'd accept.[2]

16 February 1975, London

Sunday. Roy and Jennifer Jenkins and Paul Channon and his wife came to lunch.[3] Talk about Mrs Thatcher being Shadow Conservative Leader. Also about Dick Crossman's journal. I told malicious stories about Dick at Oxford, remembering all the time that I was doing so a reading tour at Crackington Haven when there were H.W.B. Joseph as tutor, Crossman, Jay, Herbert Hart, Pilkington – and where at the suggestion of, I think, Jay, I had taken a room in the village, though not being part of the reading tour but going with them on outings and walks.[4] One day I had a slight 'affair' with Dick which was compounded of passion and lust on both sides, and was not in the least serious. It was part of Dick's wilfulness, contempt and perversity into whose focus I came at one moment – for a half hour, let's say. What I said now was how from Winchester on, Jay had a passion, active all the time he was at Oxford, for unmasking Dick. He told some story of a Winchester–Eton match at Winchester at which, at the touchline, [a] Wykehamist had said to an Etonian who was with the visiting team: 'Do look at that boy' (referring to Dick) – 'He plays against his own side.'

---

1 Peter Elstob (1915–2002), writer and activist, General Secretary of International PEN, 1974–81. Spender became President of English PEN for 1976–7.

2 V. S. Pritchett (1900–1997), British writer, President of English PEN, 1971–5.

3 Roy Jenkins (1920–2003), British Labour politician who was currently Home Secretary in Callaghan's Labour government and would become the first British President of the European Commission, 1977–81. Paul Channon (1935–2007), British Conservative MP for Southend West, 1959–97.

4 Douglas Jay (1907–1996), Labour MP, fervently anti-Common Market, for which he lost his senior cabinet post. Herbert Hart (1907–1992), legal philosopher. Richard Pilkington (1907–1976), Conservative politician. All three were contemporaries of Spender's at Oxford.

All these memories are now overweighed though by the news on the wireless that Dick's only son Patrick, aged 17, has hanged himself. In the announcement this was connected with some remarks in the extracts from Crossman's Journals published in the *Sunday Times* last week with reflections on his reasons for giving his son public education at a 'comprehensive' rather than the private education at the Dragon School and Winchester which he himself had.[1]

I don't know whether this suicide was connected with the publication of Dick's Journals but if it is, this is the third or fourth recent example of the influence of the actions of the dead on the living. One, Cyril's debts which both leave his family in great difficulties and make claims on his friends, beyond the grave; second, Chester's dying intestate with the result that all Wystan's money, royalties etc will go to an eighty-three-year-old dentist – Chester's father – whose young girl friend, as a result of the bequest, married him two weeks ago. Thirdly, the suicide of the Crossman boy in the same week as pages of Dick's Journal are published, which include a remark by Dick that whatever happens to him, his wife will be kept loved and happy by their two children Patrick and Anne. I don't see the trite and common sense morals to be drawn from these things. Only a Hardyesque irony especially evident in what happened about Auden's money which he strove so hard to make Chester's.

21 February 1975, London

Yesterday, cursing myself for my extravagance took Robert Conquest and a post-grad student called Morrison to lunch at Bianchi.[2] M.'s thesis is about the 'Movement' so I thought he should meet Conquest who seems to have originated it with a preface in *New Lines*. Of course, what emerged was that there was no such thing as a seriously planned 'movement' with manifesto, members, etc, simply a grouping of friends of the same generation who were reacting (not very

---

1 The Callaghan government vainly tried to prevent the serialization and publication of Crossman's cabinet diaries in 1975. Crossman himself had died in 1974.

2 Robert Conquest (b. 1917), British historian of the Soviet Union. Blake Morrison (b. 1950), later a British poet and author, was at this date writing a PhD on 'The Movement' at UCL, supervised by Karl Miller.

whole-heartedly) against the work of a previous generation (the so-called 'Apocalyptics').[1] Such positive ideas as Conquest etc have are to do with groupings rather than poetry – and the real poet among them, Philip Larkin, quite escapes their definings.[2]

Evening, we went to fetch Juliette Huxley from her house now towered-over by the new hospital, to take her to dine with the Julian Trevelyans.[3] She looks pale and miserable, a week after Julian (Huxley's) death.[4] In the car she talked of the cremation service which she said had been very beautiful – how helpful her sons Antony and Francis had been – of plans for internment of ashes in Surrey, a memorial service in London, etc. She seemed wretchedly aware that the mourners for Julian are unlikely to fill St Martin-in-the-Fields (where Julian and she were married). [. . .]

But at the Trevelyans' party (where there was also my brother [Humphrey] and Pauline [his wife]), Juliette entertained us all with her spirited defence of Ottoline Morrell whom she said had been greatly abused by all the *literati* who enjoyed her hospitality, particularly D.H.L[awrence]. and Frieda.[5] She said O.M. wanted nothing except to help other people, that she existed for the sake of some idea of Beauty which was real to her and which she hoped to find realized in the lives of those poets (who then turned round and sneered at her). Juliette said that D.H.L. had always been extremely kind to her. She agreed with me that Philip Morrell was a meaningless person – a handsome dummy and seducer of chambermaids.[6] I asked her about

---

1 The 'Apocalyptics' was a school of poetry which bloomed during the Second World War, whose acknowledged leader was Dylan Thomas. Spender was always dubious about their poetic worth and what he saw as their lack of discipline.

2 'The Movement,' whose principal luminary was Philip Larkin, was launched with Robert Conquest's *New Lines* anthology in 1956. Spender was sympathetic to their controlled, cooled-down style.

3 Julian Trevelyan (1910–1988), British artist married to the painter Mary Fedden. In the 1930s, Trevelyan was part of Mass-Observation and of the English Surrealist Group.

4 Julian Huxley had died on 14 February 1975.

5 Ottoline Morrell (1873–1938), aristocrat and Bloomsbury hostess who was the friend of Virginia Woolf and the lover of Bertrand Russell and Dora Carrington.

6 Philip Morrell (1870–1943) was Ottoline's husband.

T. S. Eliot at Garsington and she said 'Oh, he floated in and out.'[1] Juliette besides being intelligent and witty is an utterly truthful and fearless person. The only thing that narrows her is the Swiss protestant Puritanism which makes her disapproving (it makes her hate *Lady Chatterley's Lover*, for example) and causes her to torment herself about any failings: as it torments her now about Julian being sent to hospital, for example (tho' I understand that the image of his misery in the ward is imprinted on her eyes).

26 February 1975, London

Yesterday lunched with Karl Miller in the college refectory (or one of those horrible places). Bill Coldstream joined us. Rather red in the face, he was perhaps a bit drunk, but he was extremely funny. He started talking about Wystan. He said he had first met him when he (Bill) was seventeen. They had both been taken to see a play called *White Cargo* by a journalist who was queer called Michael Davidson. After this he had met Wystan frequently and they had gone to films the theatre etc. His pockets were really always stuffed with papers on which there were poems. He remembered a line from one – 'The midwife seen against the curtain' (?). Bill also went to Wystan's home. His father was a very nice rather subdued man with the kind of voice which is like someone talking behind a hedge. But his mother was upright and downright, the kind of High Church which goes with near-upperclassness. Bill who was sceptical about Wystan's religiousness said that it was simply a return to his life with mother. Mrs Auden had an immense influence on Wystan. On one occasion Wystan asked Bill to bed with him 'in the nicest way possible, so that it was easy to refuse'. Bill became elated about his and other people's sexuality. I said I thought Wystan's attachment to his mother was the cause of Wystan's being queer. He said: 'Nonsense. What you are sexually is simply innate. All men have something feminine about them, some more than others. I have very little myself. I was in love with a boy when I was very young. He had blond hair and I liked looking at the back of his head. I thought he was extremely beautiful. But it was a

---

1 Garsington Manor in Oxfordshire was the Morrells' country house and the seat of an artistic salon during and after the First World War.

spiritual reaction. When I was young (you wouldn't believe it now) I was very attractive to men. Many were always making propositions to me, on Hampstead Heath, and everywhere. But I was only interested in women. I had lots of affairs and they were always most unfortunate. Brought me nothing but unhappiness.' He described his life with his sister-in-law Nancy, who had a real temperament, was a remarkable woman, and now quietened down and very nice, but had been impossible to live with – always hitting one on the head.

His early friendship with Wystan must have been in about 1925. Then they had met again in the early Thirties, when they worked together with John Grierson on the P.O. Film Unit.[1] J.G. was a tremendous admirer of the proletariat and used to do films in which workers appeared undressed to the waist, covered in sweat, while the voice of a background narrator described in heroic tones what they were doing. The best effect was produced if an enormous white-hot steel girder was shedding its strip of light on their upturned faces. Auden and Bill were very irreverent about the pieties of Grierson and used to leave their office and go to the pub saying how much they hated the British worker. In a run-through of one film about a factory, they heard the voice of the narrator say: 'Ever on the alert, this worker lubricates his tool with soap.' Grierson was furious when they told him he ought to cut this line. Bill said it was a pity it had not been left in. It would have been much appreciated in the North of England.

Recollections: Auden saying to me late in life, 'I'm glad you've become a gourmet.'

After an act he walked out of the dramatization by Nevill Coghill of *The Canterbury Tales*, objecting to the coarse humour.[2] He said it showed the difference between action and the written or spoken word without the action. Reading or listening to it read you would

---

1 John Grierson (1898–1972) was a socialist film-maker who founded the General Post Office Film Unit in 1933, initiating a golden age of British documentary film. Auden worked with Grierson in the mid-1930s, making his most notable contributions to *Night Mail* (1936) and *Coal Face* (1936).

2 Nevill Coghill (1899–1980), a medieval scholar, had been Auden's tutor, and close friend, at Oxford. Coghill's 'modernized' version of Chaucer's *Canterbury Tales* was a perennial bestseller in Penguin Classics paperback. A musical version, adapted by Coghill and Martin Starkie, was produced on the London and New York stage, 1968–9.

find it funny because you were not confronted by the brutal fact but to see enacted someone having a poker shoved up his arse or being thrown down a latrine was merely nauseating.

2 March 1975, Yester, East Lothian

This house, Yester.[1] 18th-century, looks like a large reddish-brown casket, settled among its hills and woods. Grounds with a stream running through. Kitchen garden. Walks all round the house. Huge long dining room, with fireplaces each side – both lit, but still cold. [. . .]

Gian Carlo told me about meeting Wystan soon after the war when there was an idea (suggested by Lincoln Kirstein) that Wystan should write a libretto for G.-C. G.-C. abandoned the idea when he was invited to dinner by Wystan and confronted by Chester [Kallman] who, Wystan explained, would be his co-librettist. [. . .]

Gian-Carlo said that he had bought Yester for Chip [Phelan], Menotti's lover, and since 1974 his adopted son[,] whose dream it had always been to possess an 18th-century house.[2] There is something magnificently crazy about this. G.-C. belongs much more to the 19th than the 20th century. He is one of those artists obsessed in his life by the dreams and rhetoric that go into his work, but haunted by the fact that the work has to be made to pay for the work. On the hilly inclines of his woody park, he has I thought the look of a noble stag, his head always raised, the image of it which most strikes the spectator being when it is almost in profile, with the brown Italian eyes, the thin and bony, rather craggy nose, the expressive mouth. Although anchored here, everything seems precarious, and he is at the age (the same as mine) when he thinks a lot about death. 'This is my final folly. After this I shall die,' he says. Last night after dinner he said that he never took any thought for the morrow. He just lived his life like a story about someone else. What happened, happened. He often thought about possible situations in which this person – himself – might be found. For instance he had thought a lot about

---

1 Gian Carlo Menotti's Adam-style country house near Gifford in East Lothian, Scotland. For Gian Carlo Menotti, see biographical appendix.
2 Menotti adopted Chip Phelan for inheritance purposes.

being sent to prison. If he were, who of his friends would visit him? Not many, he thought.

12 March 1975, London

F[rancis] B[acon] writes about the 'frustration and despair' he feels when painting. I think that for him there is no exaggeration here. The feelings must be real. His whole account of his way of painting is that of an artist who sets up for himself a situation of despair and then creates his images out of, and overcoming, it. The situation is that of having no blueprint (in the form of a sketch or already determined mental image) of the final painting. Although he does not put it quite like this, everything is in the moment's inspiration or chance. In fact, his account of the art of painting is not dissimilar from that of an artist for whom he has little respect, Jackson Pollock. What makes him different from J.P. is that J.P. was concerned with nothing but the behaviour of the paint. Bacon despite his respect for paint is concerned with human behaviour. His concern is not just the medium itself but human behaviour as Bacon sees it realized through the medium, as interpreted by B. in *the image*.

15 March 1975, Paris

Paris. Rain. Taxi to Hilton Hotel. Left my things there. Then took taxi to Danton's statue, Boulevard St. Germain, direction given me by Lizzie for finding David Hockney's studio. This is in a little courtyard called Cour du Rohan where Balthus lived (David told me, pointing out as we left a view of the courtyard exactly as it is in a Balthus painting).[1] Stumbling on the dark stairs to find my way to D.'s door, I was supported by a rather oriental-looking Swede, whose name I learned later was Ben Sederowsky – half Swedish, half Polish. D.'s studio – a large room not looking like a studio except for a certain bareness, – not many chairs. Paintings by D. on the walls. Two of a girl walking in the rain on a sea front. Still lives. Nothing very striking, though all of them pretty. The most beautiful not on the wall but leaning against a chair a rather faint but quite large and wonderfully clear

---

1 Balthasar Klossowski ('Balthus') (1908–2001), Polish-French painter whose classical style incorporates surrealist elements.

and pure nude in coloured pencils of a boy called Gregory – frontal. Gregory, who was seated on the sofa, though not in the nude, and very stoned, had the look of a Dürer woodcut of Adam. David's friend Yves was there, and also Kasmin.[1] I had the impression that David's life in Paris is not so very different from his life in London. We arranged to dine at Coupole. David, Ben and I walked there, the others went by taxi. En route David said he greatly preferred Paris to London, that London was dull and lifeless, nothing was open after midnight, in order to enjoy yourself there you had to spend a great deal of money at expensive night clubs – there were no cafés etc. And the worst of London was that no one protested about it. If he came back he would protest. All this in his attractive Yorkshire accent. He also talked rather angrily about the state of art in England. And about Art Schools. He said he now dared to say he hated modern art. At some art school he had visited, whoever showed him round said 'In this room the students do whatever they want' as though it were a Kindergarten.

16 March 1975, Paris

A whole day of meetings about the UNESCO discrimination against Israel.[2] Lots of speeches. Finally quite a good resolution, drafted

---

1 Yves St Laurent (1936–2008), French fashion designer. John Kasmin (b. 1934), British art dealer who showed David Hockney and other British and American Pop artists at his London gallery in the 1960s.

2 In the early 1970s, the Arab-led bloc in UNESCO voted a variety of sanctions against Israel which resulted in the suspension of some of Israel's rights of membership. It was widely felt that such actions went against UNESCO's code of practice which subordinated political conflict to wider aims of educational, scientific and cultural advancement. In 1974, the tension reached its height with a series of actions against Israel that made its place in UNESCO untenable. In October 1974, the Director General withdrew support to Israel in education, science and culture following a longstanding dispute over the archaeological work Israel wanted to take in the disputed area of Jerusalem. UNESCO claimed that these contravened the Hague Convention of 1954 (Convention for the Protection of Cultural Property in the Event of Armed Conflict), but Israel disputed this, claiming that UNESCO had no legal standing. In the same year, Israel was disallowed from the European member state group, the most obvious place for the nation within UNESCO and the PLO was granted Observer Status of the UN, making it eligible to receive aid and empowering the organization to take part in UNESCO meetings.

mostly by Raymond Aron. I sat next to Aron at lunch. He seemed less gloomy about Israel than I thought he might be. Believes Sadat really does not want war and wants to come to an understanding with Israel.[1] There is something very trying about the state of excitement some people get into at conferences. Isaac Stern got into a terrific state of excitement about the protest artists should be making.[2] He got covered in perspiration and kept on dashing up to his room for aspirin.

17 March 1975, London

Flew back from Paris. The 'Metropolis' architecture of de Gaulle Airport which carries people on moving platforms along tubes crisscrossing to what are called their 'satellites' (gates for boarding planes). Hysteria of customs, waiting for planes, tickets, boarding passes, etc. Got home for lunch. Juliette Huxley and Veronica Wedgwood came to dinner. J. looked ill but on the surface is very self-possessed. Talked about the UNESCO meeting and various UNESCO characters. Reminiscences of our time at UNESCO. She said a great mass of arrangements and the horrible last weeks of Julian's illness had formed a barrier between her and her life with Julian. She did not even understand any more who this man was she had married. She wished she could meet a 'guru' who would tell her what to think. Juliette's two ideas 1) a book of essays about Julian 2) a bourse or scholarship based on sale of his books.

23 March 1975, Oxford

Went to Oxford for the St Cuthbert's dinner at Univ[ersity College]. Was supposed to have drinks with John Sparrow – but he was all dressed up receiving distinguished guests for his own college festivity

---

1 Anwar El Sadat (1918–1981), Egyptian President 1970–81. Sadat led the 1973 Yom Kippur war against Israel, making him a hero in the Arab world. He later became instrumental in securing Arab–Israeli peace, signing a peace treaty with the Prime Minister of Israel, Menachem Begin, in 1979, which lead to both politicians being awarded the Nobel Peace Prize.

2 Isaac Stern (1920–2001), American violinist of Ukrainian origin.

– so I did not stay long and went to Univ – for which I was early.[1] The Chaplain took me to his rooms. Everyone was in a state of excitement (but not too much) because Harold Wilson was coming to dinner (he was changing into his dress suit in the Master's Lodgings). I talked with the Chaplain, who is delicate and distinguished looking. He had been to London, seeing *A Bigger Splash* and *Wozzeck*.[2] He had taken an undergraduate and some girl to see *A Bigger Splash*. I thought how different from when I was at Univ, when we used to read *Ulysses* surreptitiously and even the most broad-minded dons would argue that *Ulysses* was pornographic because it was about sex whereas Rabelais was OK because it was 'lavatory humour'. I tried to draw the Chaplain on whether he really thought it was all right to take a student to see two handsome gay men making love. He said the undergraduate had taken the scene 'thoughtfully and seriously'. We weren't really candid with one another I thought.

The difference between the Univ of my time and today came up again when two dons lamented that Michael Sadler had not given one of his post-impressionist paintings (Van Gogh's *Sunflowers* or Gauguin's *Self-Portrait as Artist* [*sic*]) to the college because every member of the Common Room so disliked them. Certainly when I was at Univ they were vocal about this. Gabriel Carritt said that the thing that made all the SCR pee on Michael Sadler was his collection of paintings.

As we were waiting to go in to dinner, John Maud suddenly seized my arm and said 'Come and talk to the P.M.'[3] So I went over to him and could think of nothing much to say so I asked him how he had managed the economics of the College when he was Bursar. He told me he had done wonderfully and at once started producing examples of his aptitude. But I could hardly hear what he said in the din – and his confidential way of talking makes it rather difficult to hear him

1 John Sparrow (1906–1992), Warden of All Souls, Oxford, was a near-contemporary of Spender's at Oxford in the 1920s.

2 *A Bigger Splash* (1974), Jack Hazan's documentary film about David Hockney. *Wozzeck* (1925), opera by Alban Berg.

3 John Maud was the Oxford tutor who helped the undergraduate Spender during his infatuation with 'Marston', i.e. John Freeman (see the opening section of *The Temple* ('English Prelude') and chapter two of *World Within World*).

anyway. He looks very pleased with himself but his manner is not offensively public. Later in the evening I asked him whether he had read Frank Longford's Essay on [Richard] Crossman in the New College annual and whether it was true as F.L. had written that Dick's political career had been ruined by Bevin's disagreeing with him about Israel.[1] Wilson said: 'That seems remarkably perceptive of Frank Longford. It's more than I would have expected of him. Bevin and also that gentleman over there' – pointing to the portrait of Attlee on the wall [–] 'were determined to keep Dick out of office. So he didn't have a job in the Cabinet till I gave him one.' (Wilson had made Dick Minister of Housing.) Wilson reeled off several examples of gross inaccuracy – if not pure invention – in Dick's diary. He also said that Dick seemed to have an idea that politics was a matter of deep intrigue in which people were subtly plotting against one another. 'But they aren't subtle at all. If they are plotting against you they turn up with a large label attached to them on which is written "I'm plotting against you".'

In March 1975, Spender went to America to catch up with friends in New York, lecture in various universities and prepare a biography of W. H. Auden, which he was planning to write with Edward Mendelson.

28 March 1975, New York

Got up at five – apart from anxiety about taxis the journey went quite smoothly to N.Y. Took a taxi to 166 East 68th Street. Put down my things and then went straight to the Metropolitan Museum to see the Francis Bacon show.[2] It is immensely authoritative with lasso-like

---

1 Ernest Bevin, Foreign Secretary in the post-war Attlee Government, was fiercely anti-Zionist, believing that the militant Zionist Irgun and Stern Gangs (the National Military Organization in the Land of Israel and the Fighters for the Freedom of Israel), which aimed to evict the British authorities from Palestine to allow for the formation of a Jewish state, were criminals. It was widely believed that there was a plot by Jewish extremists to assassinate him in 1949. Richard Crossman was pro-Zionist and a founder member of the 'Labour Friends of Israel' group.

2 Metropolitan Museum of Art, 20 March–29 June. This exhibition, for which Bacon came to New York, together with David Sylvester's 'interviews' with Bacon, published in 1975, promoted the artist to worldwide fame.

rhythm of line lashing round those forms of violent copulations, photographers, people vomiting, bulls etc. There is perfect control and precision of violence.

29 March 1975, New York

Lunch with Ed Mendelson.[1] We talked about the Wystan biography. Dinner with Harold Taylor and his girl, an actress called Vellacott, I think – Liz Lowell [Elizabeth Hardwick] and a caricaturist and his wife, whose names I didn't get, Kurt Vonnegut and his wife [the] photographer.[2] I told Liz we were thinking of writing Wystan's biography and she said: 'Oh but that's just what he didn't want isn't it?' We discussed Wystan quite a bit. She said she thought Cal [Robert Lowell] was isolated and unhappy in England rather like Wystan had been. As we left after dinner I said H. Taylor was such a strange mixture of sincerity and bogusness – about 50% of each. She said: 'Oh, but the question is whether anything goes on inside him at all.' She was very sympathetic to Vellacott and said she was an excellent actress, but had never had any success. I thought V. looked very ill.

During the night I had further thoughts about the Auden book taking into account fact that a) he expressed wishes no biography should be written b) that nevertheless I believe he did really want to be written about – but without gossip and exposure of his private life. Anyway with respect for the privacy of the private and the separation of public from private worlds. c) that an authoritative book should be written.

---

1 Edward Mendelson (b. 1946), American academic and the literary executor of the Estate of W. H. Auden. Spender and Mendelson abandoned their plans to collaborate on a biography of Auden, but the first volume of Mendelson's biography would be published in 1981 as *Early Auden* and was to be followed by *Later Auden* (1999). Spender himself had put together a collection of essays by people who had known the poet (*W. H. Auden: A Tribute*, Weidenfeld and Nicolson, 1975).

2 Elizabeth Hardwick was currently a consultant editor on the *New York Review of Books*; her marriage to Robert Lowell had ended in 1972. The caricaturist is David Levine (b. 1926), resident caricaturist at the *New York Review of Books*. Kurt Vonnegut (1922–2007), American novelist best known for his satirical science fictions *Cat's Cradle* (1963) and *Slaughterhouse-Five* (1969); his soon-to-be wife is Jill Krementz (b. 1940).

Lunch yesterday at the spacious apartment of Earl and Camilla McGrath. Sam Barber also came. Earl looked as young as when I first met him, having been through a phase of ten years or more of drugs etc, when he looked terrible. The kind of Earl retort I like – I said to Sam that he had done very well in that the critics had attacked the Juilliard performance of his rewritten *Antony and Cleopatra* but the public had gone to it.[1] That put him in an invulnerable position. Sam demurred and I said perhaps invulnerable was wrong. 'Not so much wrong as simply naïve,' said Earl. He has a way of saying things which draws attention to his character as a comedian. But he can also be boorish as when over lunch he said to me in front of Camilla that he hated Italy and never wanted to go there for the rest of his life. Camilla, the very rich Italian princess, dotes on Earl of whom Auden used to say: 'He is the one person I know who is an old-fashioned adventurer.'

The McGraths took us to lunch at The Russian Tea Room, where Natasha and I used often to eat blinsky [*sic*] and sour cream with the Stravinskys.

I looked at Sam, a bald, fat, puffy, solemn-seeming old gent, shuffling rather as we walked later along Central Park West and remembered the slender almost matinee idol young man who had visited me in 1939 in London and played to me the record of his setting of 'Dover Beach'. Now he talked to me about Gian Carlo, saying how crazy it was of him to buy Yester how he was always getting into financial straits sending telegrams asking to borrow $5,000, etc. He said the Met would never put on anything by Gian Carlo. That G.-C. had lost the realization that to write a serious work you had to put aside three years of your time. And so on. I felt désolé [sorry] for G.-C. and also for Sam.

---

1 Samuel Barber's *Antony and Cleopatra* premiered at the Metropolitan Opera House on 16 September 1966. This production by Franco Zefferelli was panned by the press for its gaudy costumes and overcrowded set-piece scenes. (At one point there were 165 people, three horses, two camels and an elephant on stage.) Barber spent the next decade revising the opera and produced a new version in collaboration with Gian Carlo Menotti at the Juilliard School in 1975.

1 April 1975, Dartmouth College, New Hampshire

In the morning an appalling radio interview with a man I was supposed to address as 'Chuck' who asked me about my life and work, preceding his questions by apologizing because he knew nothing about either. And wasn't interested so why bother him or me? This pretence of interest in order to 'sell' one like a commercial product, is one of the real tortures of modern life. Being alone with him in a room where there were at least six old-style microphones and being asked stupid questions which I then answered in a stilted voice, to break off and hear him say: 'Well that's an extremely profound remark – a statement that our listeners will cherish for its extraordinary profundity' is worse than open mockery, because it's the deceptive mockery of Public Relations – the thick gluey oil put between cogs of different teeth to make them somehow mesh without tearing one another apart.

2 April 1975, Conway, Arkansas

Memphis: Stayed with the head of the English Department, Dr William Osborne, who met me at the airport with three other members of the English Department. They were amusing and civilized and talked about literature a bit – showing an interest one can't take for granted at ex-teachers' Colleges. I stayed with the Osbornes in their house, which was absolutely predictable. Wall-to-wall carpeting of some synthetic plastic material. Large sofas and chairs of the kind one sees advertised on TV. A large bright yellow picture in thick paint put on with the palette knife and suggestions of domes, towers, sea dominates the room and becomes a discussion point. Is it Venice? Osborne does not know much about it – such as who is it by. In a corner of the room some stiff bull-rush coloured leaves in a vase. Everything in the house reflects the same processed conformity. I go to the University and talk to some students, who ask questions. Return to the Osborne residence and 'rest up'. Then supper which consists of cold cuts and some coffee, though Mrs O. confesses she doesn't know how to make coffee. (It is quite good.) She is a tall thin wax-complexioned woman with a pronounced stare from behind her imitation tortoise-shell-frame glasses. She explains she has been 'teaching school' all day and describes her class of twelve-year-old near-illiterate and not-wishing-to-learn racially mixed children. From the way she talks one suddenly realizes she is conscientious, brave, intelligent, overworked, liberal and good. Something happens as so often happens I find in America which is like the change when water reaches the freezing point or boiling point – and there is a rearrangement of patterns of atomic structure – and I suddenly see these people in a warm and sympathetic light, which makes their furnishing of their house and all the rest of their conformism by which one might so easily judge them, irrelevant. If they are unimaginatively conventional in one respect[,] in their sympathies they are conventionally American in quite another respect. Mr Osborne appears to be witty and informed. Twenty-four hours later I hear on TV about the thousands of Americans pleading to adopt Vietnamese war orphans and one sees this creative, conscientious side of the country again – as though people had stopped reckoning the gain or loss of Southeast Asia and were concentrating entirely on a salvaging operation which would do practical good and in doing so to some extent atone for the price to the Vietnamese themselves of American failure in Vietnam. When America was bombing the North on such an unprecedented scale one heard very little of the Vietnamese (except from those who opposed the war). Now all Americans are united in wanting to help the victims, and to commit themselves to doing so for as long as it takes to bring up and educate a Vietnamese child.

18 April 1975, New York

Went with Ed Mendelson to see Peter Matson and discuss arrangements about the Auden book.[1] P.M. rather surprised me. Instead of the businessman type, he was amused and amusing, easy. We discussed the form the book should take. He first of all seemed to think the publishers would want their money's worth in the form of scandal, gossip etc. But we said we were not going to [do] this and I think I convinced him of our idea [that] we should write a book about the life leading into the poetry, not the poetry into the life, and that we need not discuss facts simply on the basis of their being facts if they were not relevant to the work and the intellectual and moral development of Auden. [. . .]

On Thursday afternoon I went to the Met and bought presents of

---

1 Peter Matson, American literary agent.

replica jewellery for Natasha and Lizzie. Later, walking down Madison Avenue I saw a woebegone man with a look on his face that combined suffering with gentleness and sympathy, sitting on a trashcan at the edge of the sidewalk. The bright sun made a halo of his white hair, his head was bent sideways, I was reminded of some self-portrait of the artist's face combining anguish and wry humour, by Goya. This was Robert Lowell. For a moment I thought I'd pass him by but something sweet and touching about his appearance made me decide I would risk talking to him (I had been told by Bob Silvers the previous Wednesday evening that he'd had a breakdown). So I went up and said, 'I hear you've taken an overdose of your pills and that you are in hospital.' He smiled affectionately and said, 'Yes, I'm better now. I'll be out in a few days.' We talked a bit and he was very easy to converse with, didn't seem to be under any strain, and put me at ease. I was just thinking we looked like two down-and-outs in some black-and-white sidewalk photo by [Alfred] Stieglitz, when some quite smartly-dressed women started staring at us with a look of recognition. 'They're my nurses,' said Cal. 'I'll have to rejoin them,' and he walked along a few paces behind them as they crossed the street. I accompanied him to make sure he did not get run over.

19 April 1975, Boston

Tea and dinner with Pauline de Rothschild. She seemed to have dropped all her old affectations and to be calm and clear and sensible. Talked about my TV and radio advertising the Auden book and she said: 'It's wholly discouraging, isn't it? One has the feeling that no one any longer reads books because they want to do so. They buy certain ones because they think some virtue attaches to them, like in the Middle Ages they used to buy indulgences. The only books they really read are all those "How to express yourself" ones.' I agreed with this because it reaffirmed the view I've already been forming, that even the young at the Universities take it for granted that they read in time paid for by their parents and/or the Universities to do so. They press to read very modern literature because without being paid, it is doubtful whether they would even read what strikes them as being of their generation. Several times on this trip I've said to students who say they ought to have courses including writers who've produced books within the last year or two, 'But surely you'd read those anyway, quite apart from your courses – and besides why should your teachers be qualified to instruct you about things that are nearer to you than to them –' and they look at me in [an] astonished way as though it was the most elementary misunderstanding on my part to assume that they do any reading 'out of school'. One wonders what would happen to literature without this immense underpinning of it in its emanation as paperbacks at University Book Stores and its promotion by the 'media' as certificates or medallions to lie around on tables in sitting rooms.

Pauline also talked about Glenway [Wescott] telling her that his Journal was the first completely candid one ever written about the life and loves of a homosexual.[1] 'He keeps on saying this, but I can hardly think it isn't a gross exaggeration.' I agreed it must be. There was [André] Gide's journal for example. She asked me whether I was totally candid in my Journal and I said I did not feel impelled to be – or, rather, I felt impelled not to be (for that is what I meant). I told her about one or two things in my life I would not write about because I did not understand them myself: for instance experiences of falling in love which seemed almost hallucinatory – perhaps a shared hallucination with some other person – and did not seem to touch reality at any point. I said I sometimes had the experience of loving someone as though we shared one another's dreams, and she said 'Oh but that's exactly what I think love is or can be, that you understand something about someone else which does not belong to their everyday lives and which you go on sharing with them.' She said this did not have to be a continuous relationship, you could let it lapse for years and then meet the person with whom you share the dream as though there had been no interval in time. [. . .]

People I meet sometimes say 'I've read your books.' Secretly I do not believe that anyone has read anything (apart from a few anthologized poems) I have written. When I was young I was so convinced of this that I used to write unkind things thinking they would never

---

1 Glenway Wescott (1901–1987), American novelist prominent in the expatriate literary community in Paris during the 1920s. The journals were published posthumously as *Continual Lessons: The Journals of Glenway Wescott, 1937–1955*, ed. Robert Phelps with Jerry Rosco (1990).

be read. I do now realize that arrows, if they are tipped with poison, always reach their target.

The noises of America: the curdling shrill telephone bell, the assertive, melodramatic, almost triumphant shriek of the police cars, fire engines, ambulances, the romantic at-the-centre-of-the-night clang of bells of trains, seem to dramatize their situation.

When Wystan was young he was totally uninhibited when he was old he became stratified.

In the 1970s and 1980s, Stephen and Matthew Spender undertook a number of vacational 'honeymoons' (as the son called them) together in Italy, indulging their mutual love of art and architecture. It was instigated by Natasha and taken up by Matthew as part of his 'tackle your father complex' policy.

28 June 1975, Venice

I got a taxi to the Venice terminus, then took a vaporetto [water-bus] to the Accademia (the taxi driver had told me to do this) from where I had a considerably long walk carrying my suitcase. When I had got to my room Matthew emerged from a bath, looking extremely elongated, and smiling. We decided to have a fairly extravagant evening. This was easily achieved by going to the restaurant near the Fenice Theatre, where we had a moderate meal and a bottle of Soave. M. produced a list of things we were to see which he had copied out from a guide book which was the property of the Pension. We were both very tired and went to bed at about ten – at any rate by the London time on my watch which I had not changed, not realizing there was an hour's difference between here and London. Matthew has no watch, only a very approximate idea of the time, and not the faintest interest in it. [. . .]

We decided to use some of our letters to hostesses and spent most of the afternoon trying to convey letters to the Countess Brandolini and the Countess Cicogna.[1] M. had found on the map of Venice a

---

1 Countess Cristiana Brandolini and Countess Anna Maria Cicogna were influential Venetian hostesses. Spender had written the letters of introduction himself.

Brandolini house which was near the Rialto bridge, and it was impossible for me to persuade him that the Palazzo Brandolini was at the other end of the Grand Canal. We were more successful in finding the Cicogna palace, but it was completely shut up. Finally we established contact by shouting to some domestics who were sitting in a second floor room above the Canal Grande. I gave them a letter, but as soon as we had gone, realized that accidentally I had given them that meant for the Contessa Brandolini. We had dinner at another restaurant much recommended to us – the Madonna, near the Rialto bridge. It was good and half the price of our first meal (still, 20,000 lire).

30 June 1975, Venice

A.M. Went to the Correr museum. Lunch at the hotel with wife of William Jay Smith, a French lady.[1] In the afternoon we went to the Guggenheim Museum, which was crowded with American tourists. Suddenly someone said, 'Hello, Stephen' and it was Peggy.[2] She seemed very content with the success of her museum. Asked us to cocktails on Wednesday.

2 July 1975, Venice

It was raining. Venice looked like the interior of a dim theatre where no one has turned up the stage lighting on the scenery. One notices only how squalid and tatty these sets are. They consist of course of street scenes, with very flat frontages facing the water. Without colour and lighting one notices the texture of these. How worn and cracked and decaying most of them are, how much in need of repair. Windows of whole palaces appear like patches covering over interior darkness. One has again and again the impression that nothing is going on inside all these drab, rusted, often boarded up exteriors.

---

1 William Jay Smith had married Sonja Haussmann.

2 Peggy Guggenheim (1898–1979), American art collector and philanthropist. The current Peggy Guggenheim Collection is located in her former home, Palazzo Venier dei Leoni on the Grand Canal in Venice and was inaugurated after her death in 1980.

One longs for someone to switch on the lighting and produce an illusion which comes largely from the water and wavelets reflected on marble and a great expanse of blue sky behind domes and campaniles. Matthew brought one of those cheap plastic macintoshes which you get in a packet about the size of a tobacco pouch and which expand to the proportions of a human being, like those Japanese nodules of compressed paper which when put in water expand to water lilies or some other flower. It was purple, and clothed in this semi-transparent shining envelope, with his nose the main feature visible above it and body, legs and arms swathed in its light, he looked very like one of those figures, in Tintoretto's Transportation of the Bones of St Mark, painted with a brush dipped in some transparent colour predominantly white, who rush away from the storm under the arches of the piazza.

7 July 1975, Avane

On the Tuesday we went to a party given by Peggy Guggenheim. Peggy, aged 81, is now a dignified rather withdrawn figure, looked after by her secretary John and by a male black servant. Her mind and memory are completely unimpaired, and she talked to me with her usual zest about mutual friends, most of them dead: about some woman Herbert Read had been terribly in love with – she expressed total incredulity when I said that Herbert had been rejuvenated and transformed through love of his first wife.[1] 'Oh she was some sort of a musician wasn't she?' she murmured. But the charms of Ludo playing the viola awoke no echo of the past in her warm vague mind.[2] She said she thought there were no good young painters now. She was fascinated by the idea of Matthew having married 'Miss Gorky'.

Matthew pointed out to me that her [Joan] Mirós in her museum

---

1 Spender had been on friendly terms with the art historian and critic Herbert Read since Read's perceptive review of *Poems 1933*. Spender regarded him as the most useful of his critics. Peggy Guggenheim became friends with Read in the 1930s when he was editing the *Burlington Magazine* and the two planned to found a Museum of Modern Art in London but were thwarted by the outbreak of the Second World War.

2 'Ludo' refers to Margaret Ludwig, the second wife of Herbert Read and a professional viola-player.

were in a very bad state, but I thought it would be as well not to mention this to Peggy. As M. and I were leaving, a fellow guest said to me that all the restaurants in Venice were on strike, so that if Matthew and I wanted to dine, we'd better join him and his wife and have dinner at Harry's Bar. We accepted gratefully, but he kept on apologizing about the invitation. He was a kind, serious-looking man; his wife was a middle-aged blonde who had been having a long conversation with Matthew at the party, apparently about the role of sadomasochism in marriage. When we left Peggy's house (which is guarded in the front overlooking the canal by the Marino Marini bronze rider with his erection, like a banner raised in perpetual salute of Peggy's defiantly Surrealist past) – Matthew admitted to being rather 'sloshed' as he had drunk four whiskeys at the party. Our host and his wife decided not to wait for the 'traghetto' [ferry] but to take a gondola the few yards to Harry's Bar. It cost them 5,000 lira. We waited a few minutes for our table, in the crowded Bar/Restaurant. I talked a bit to our host who told me that the great hotels of Venice were ruined as there were very few people left who could pay 150,000 lira a night for a suite at the Gritti Palace, or the Bauer-Grunwald or Cipriani's. I said that perhaps within a few years' time the American economy would recover and he said, no, he thought the grand luxury hotel business was permanently finished. I asked him what his business was and he said it was to do with advising companies how to form mergers with other companies, especially in England. (I seem to have met quite a few people floating around lately who have this enviable intermediary task.) At dinner, I didn't notice that he drank very much, but he became less coherent. Now he said that a lot of people in Venice said he belonged to the C.I.A. (a thought which had crossed my own mind, as an episode in a story about someone who whatever he did and wherever he went always found he was being supported by the C.I.A.). He started making half-mystical pronouncements, followed fortunately by the remark which absolved me from having to reply: 'You understand better than I do what I'm trying to say.'

At one point Philippe de Rothschild leading – or rather being led by – a large golden retriever burst through the bar on his way to the upper storey restaurant. I got up to greet him and when I returned to our table, our host apologized to me for inviting us when I might have been with other friends. I said we were very grateful to him and that in fact I would have missed seeing Philippe and being told by him that Pauline was also coming to the restaurant, if he had not invited us here – as I thought they had already left Venice.

The evening became more dreamlike when a voice at the table next to ours said: 'Hullo Stephen,' and turned out to have emanated from an ex-student of mine at Sarah Lawrence College in 1947. This student had once told me when I asked him what he wanted to do in life: 'I want to be supported by a rich man,' and there next to him on the banquette, paying for Brad's dinner, was a gentleman with a great deal of white flesh and a small bristly ginger moustache who seemed evidence that at least one of my students had achieved his life's ambition.

As we were leaving Harry's Bar, I whispered to Brad that I had not the faintest idea who our hosts were. Brad leaned forward and said in his low, solemn, discreet American voice which had the timbre of a husky bassoon: 'Well, he's mad for you and she's mad for Matthew.'

Our hosts, before we realized what was happening to us, had thrust us into another gondola. 'I don't suppose you've been in a gondola on this trip,' he said, 'let's go for a little giro [tour].' We soon found ourselves moving rather rapidly past the Seguso on the Zattere, our pension. Matthew, who had been singing snatches of *Don Giovanni* exclaimed: 'Dad, it's past my bedtime, we should go home.' I was occupied in trying to empty my glass of wine into the sea (they had bought three bottles with which they were constantly refilling our plastic cups) when he said this. Our host said: 'Our house is only just round the corner. Come back with us and we'll put on a recording of *La Clemenza di Tito*. Besides, we want you to see our house.' It seemed too rude to refuse to go another few yards, so we went with them. We went upstairs into a barely furnished drawing room, and one of them put on the first record of the opera. Our host poured from a carafe what looked like neat gin or vodka into his tumbler. Suddenly I felt 'We must really go now,' so making our apologies, we fled. As soon as we got outside the front door we nearly fell down with laughing, feeling we had escaped something – but what? Discussing it the next day what we really felt was the desperation and boredom of our hosts: the qualities which are the vacuum at the centre of all social life and which lead to diverse conclusions. Brad had put it rather firmly into my mind that what they wanted was some kind of orgy. But it may have been an orgy of the spirit rather than of the body. They had in fact been generous, and it was mean to suppose that their generosity was not disinterested. But [what] is interested, what disinterested in such a situation? It is inseparable from any social relationship embarked on that you do expect some kind of result. And what is wrong about that? Perhaps the expectation might be too crude or too greedy, ultimately inconsiderate of what the guest entertained could sensitively be expected to give. [. . .]

There is, as so often, something 'Jamesian' about an episode such as this. Our hosts may have been a bit 'decadent', but they were not unserious. One further note about the man. He could see very little, had eyes that seemed to swivel against the lenses of his spectacles when he looked at me with his wavering gaze. He also mentioned his age – which was 45 – asking me my age at the same time – and saying – 'You look in perfect health. I'll be dead within 2 years.' He had a 'heart condition' someone told us.

* * *

Peggy said to me in the course of our conversation that Cubism and Surrealism are the outstanding achievements of the 20th Century. She does not have outstanding examples of Cubist works. The works of the Peggy Guggenheim Foundation in Venice vindicate above all Surrealism. The pictures in the Palazzo Guggenheim in Venice are a surprising success because they form a bridge between the imagination of the High Renaissance and that of the last explosion of Renaissance imagination, which was Surrealism. The bridge has a utilitarian purpose for those Americans brought up on 'modern art' who crowd to see the Guggenheim pictures as examples of the art with which they are familiar, before plunging into the deep waters of the Accademia or the Scuola San Rocco. But the hidden connection is between certain Surrealist works, particularly those by Ernst, Magritte, and the early Dalí and works like the allegories of Giovanni Bellini, in the Accademia. Of course, the Surrealists found precedents for their own work in these paintings, and those of Hieronymus Bosch in the Correr Gallery and Doge's Palace. But the precedence lies in the attitude to painting as a method rather than in the goal achieved. The method replaces the visual logic of more-or-less representational painting with that of poetry. In this, it is different from illustration in painting of literary vision. For instance, Blake's picture 'And pity like a naked, newborn babe / Striding the blast' although full of imaginative intensity, is illustration in that it follows the logic of picture-making, for which, indeed Shakespeare's metaphor [in *Macbeth*] provides an opportunity. The baby is a whole baby striding a real cloud. But a line such as 'My love is like a red, red rose' [by Robert Burns] is visual in its symbolism, but only in terms of poetry. If you tried to paint the visual content of the line you would have to paint a girl who was seen to be like a rose and who therefore was both girl and rose. This, as method, would be Surrealist, the introduction into the pictorial image of the literary image of the poem. It always seems to me strange that there is not more Surrealism in the history of painting – that throughout history painters stick so strictly to the logic of heads being stuck onto bodies onto which are stuck legs.

* * *

When I was a boy and used to go fishing sometimes my optic nerves seem to have become hypnotized by the little float moving with the water and occasionally bobbing under it when there was a bite from a fish, so that when I lay in bed after a day's fishing I would see the float and a surrounding patch of water move on a wall or the ceiling of my bedroom. In the same way there is something about the perpetual movement of sunlit water reflected on marble walls in Venice, which interposes itself as nerve-inflamed imagery on the landscape one sees after one has left. [. . .]

What I have not expressed here is that the holiday in Venice meant to me Matthew and to some extent meant to him me. We were both free from all consideration except one another and Venice. One result of this for me was that I looked at the things we both looked at with undistracted eyes. Part of the pleasure I share (I think) with him is a kind of detachment that can go with joyous affection. When we went together to the Correr Gallery, he sat himself down in a chair and did a drawing of Carpaccio's two courtesans. While he did this I went to look at the Giovanni Bellini Crucifixion and one or two other pictures in the same room, mostly to savour the pleasure of thinking of him immovably sitting there drawing three rooms away. John Julius Norwich and a Mr and Mrs Sainsbury (who were going to contribute to the 'Save Venice' Fund) walked past me and I had a foolish impulse to run after John Julius and say 'the foot you can see just beyond that doorway is my son's. He's sitting there drawing Ruskin's favourite picture.'[1] Our feeling partly was of recapturing past time, for instance, that time when he was twelve and we went to the Edinburgh Festival together for the opening of *Mary Stuart*: sharing a long narrow top storey room with three beds in it and a window too high to see out of. And just before the play began in some great hall (there was no curtain) he turned to me and said: 'Dad, there's nothing I can say to help you as I'm afraid I know nothing about the theatre. But if it's any comfort just remember that it can't possibly be as boring as *Hamlet*.'

When we were driving down from Edinburgh that time, I must have been driving very abstractedly with a gloomy absorption of face, because he said: 'Dad, don't look like that. I simply can't bear it.' He seemed always to want signs of affection. Even when he was sixteen, once, when we were looking at TV he said: 'Dad, put your arm round me.' And in Venice he would now suddenly put his arm round *me* or when I was walking the steps up the Accademia Bridge stand behind me and push me up them. In fact, in every way, he took me over, looked after me arranged everything.

July 1975, St Jerome

The Bayleys [John Bayley and Iris Murdoch] were ideal guests as usual, so thoughtful and always pleasant and amusing. Iris was reading Plato (on account of something she was 'working on'). John had new false teeth instead of the only three teeth of last year – this made catering easier. They create joke legends – that they are the couple looking after us. To them, the place is an enchantment and they fill it with their love – the black wasps flying in and out of the deep centres of the morning glory, the stretch on a viaduct of the agricultural water, the hidden valley, the secret copse etc etc. Every afternoon they walk down to the water and take their swim. Douglas Cooper in his

---

1 John Julius Norwich (b. 1929), British historian and television presenter.

castle – known as the Monster and therefore much tolerated in all his roles – is part of the legend.[1] We went over to lunch there. There was Renée Laporte, author of a book describing her love affair with Picasso at the age of seventeen, and her tall, perfectly demure and self-possessed, exquisitely polite and exquisite-looking son, Fabrice, aged 12.[2]

12 August 1975, St Jerome

Dined with Douglas Cooper. There were two youngish Americans there – purchasers of works of art for some museum or foundation – whose names we didn't get. One had features once boyish and handsome but now too plumped out. He was an ex-movie star – Michael W.; the other one more conventionally handsome, an impressive sculpted looking head with fitted into it well-fixed American teeth, greying hair [. . .] Douglas seemed a bit restless and, under everything, lonely. He seems to get like that at this time of year. His vindictive remarks about Peter Watson, Don Bachardy etc lacked conviction. His politics seem to have changed since the death of Picasso. He is now very anti-Communist. He said he thought that after the death of Franco there would be a revolution in Cataluña joining forces with the Portuguese Communists. He said he thought that within ten years the whole of Europe would be Communist.

He described his last meeting with [Bernard] Berenson, nine days (he said) before B.B.'s death. They had a conversation in which B.B. kept on making remarks, and then said Douglas: 'I saw him, I saw him with my own eyes, leave himself, go away, over there, while he was sitting in his chair. We talked about Caravaggio. Then we talked about someone and his wife who were visiting Florence. Every sentence B.B. said was in a different language, English, Italian, French or German mostly and I tried to make up sentences in the language he had last spoken in. When I told him —— and wife were seeing me in

---

1 Douglas Cooper (1911–1984), British art collector and critic whose Château de Castille in Provence was a place of pilgrimage for anyone interested in cubist art. In the 1950s, Cooper was frequently visited by Picasso.

2 Spender refers to the French writer and filmmaker Geneviève Laporte (b. 1926) and to her book *Si tard le soir le soleil brille* (1973), published in English as *Sunshine at Midnight* (1974).

Florence, he faded away, then opened his eyes and said "Etwas so dumm [something so stupid]," and faded away again.'

Michael W. said that his father had died in his arms. 'He was talking to me, he said something. This sentence left his mouth like one of those demons leaving a sinner from his mouth in a medieval painting. I saw it go. Then suddenly there was this heavy limp and inanimate meat in my arms.'

Michael W. talked about Santa Monica where he lived close to Christopher Isherwood. He told the following anecdote. A great friend of Christopher, who had been an extremely beautiful young man, had been killed in a terrible car accident. Christopher had gone to the 'funeral home' where the mortician was making up the destroyed face trying to give it a tolerable appearance for the moment when the boy's parents arrived to see their dead son. Of course the mortician had no idea what the boy looked like. Christopher and he started drinking to keep their courage up. They got very plastered. Suddenly Christopher said 'Let me have a try' and he took some of the mortician's melted wax and started covering with it the cracks in the boy's face laughing wildly and trying to produce out of the flesh and wax a sculpture of the face he had known.

I noticed that when Douglas reclines in his chair and his stomach is horizontal it assumes an independent personality from his face – as though it too were a face that laughed, frowned, shrugged, burped, agreed and disagreed violently.

23 August 1975, St Jerome

On the 13th Noel and Gabrielle Annan came to stay for eight days, on the first three of which they brought their daughter Lucy. [. . .] Natasha made terrific efforts for them and from this point of view the visit was a bit exhausting but in fact they were extremely helpful and very nice guests. Noel would get up before anyone else and rush out to Mouriès to buy croissants, Gaby insisted on washing up, they used extremely little water (owing to the drought we had almost none in the well), they bought wine, took us out to dinner one night, and got things for the house. We all got on very well, though while feeling I knew them better at the end of the visit, I didn't feel that anything happened which was more than to confirm what I knew of them already. Noel was really *en vacances* [on holiday], did very little work, read about a novel or other book a day (*Great Expectations, Jude the Obscure* among them). He was relaxed in manner, behaviour, and most strikingly in attire – or the lack of it. Being addicted to sun-bathing he wore almost nothing; only just that kind of very short shorts or loin cloth which marks the line between 'naked' and 'stark-naked'. The loin cloth was the colour of raw silk. His head was barely protected by a kind of jockey's cap of bright purple with a very pronounced peak. He lay on a chaise-longue exposed almost completely to the sun and read avariciously in the manner of one who seizing on a book with mental teeth knows exactly what pages contain the juice or marrow which he devours, while the remaining pages seem to lie scattered round him like discarded husks or bits of the leaves of an artichaut [artichoke]. As a result of sun-exposure Noel's skin – shiny on his head and stomach – was a deep orange, a dark background to the brilliant bathing-shorts and purple cap.

Noel is an organizational man and this makes me nervous with him. I find myself searching in my mind for subjects important enough to discuss. In fact I was often rather silent at meals on account of this and Natasha thought that our guests must have been bored with us – which is true, I dare say. However it is also true that I am not his intellectual equal and may have bored him for this reason, and that it is unjust to say he is only concerned with public and important matters. He has the interest of someone who is truthful and has independent views. He is also interested in people of whom he is a good judge and he is always prepared to sacrifice the discretion which might be expected of a man in his position in the interest of telling the truth. He gives a private and personal view of public people, which is always interesting. He is self-critical, perhaps deeply so. He said once 'Let there be no doubt about it[,] any kind of creative work or real literary task is immensely harder than directing, organizing or doing public work.' This seemed rather astonishing coming from a man who is a scholar and also perhaps the living writer most capable of writing what is called 'trenchant' prose. Noel also keeps alive his intense interest in homosexuality which goes back to his Cambridge days and which forms quite a part of his often uninhibited conversation. He is a character in an unwritten novel by E. M. Forster and I sometimes feel he is conscious of playing such a role.

A terrific storm most of the night. About four inches of rain fell while Natasha was going to Marignane Airport to fetch Lizzie (whose plane was 2½ hours late). [. . .] Philippe de Rothschild appeared. With him his daughter Philippine. He is staying with an old friend Mme Delbée who has a so-called chateau near Fontvieille.[1] This is reduced now to one large square stone 17th or 18th century building with a cramped driveway and little terrace overlooking a garden almost completely filled with box hedges cut into a formal pattern, also crushed into a very small space and with just beyond them a tall screen of cypresses and poplars.

Philippe and Philippine said that every room in Mme Delbée's house was crammed with innumerable objects. When Philippe was shown his room he immediately swept large numbers of these off chairs and tables. Having cleared a space he noticed with relief that there was a huge cupboard in his room. He opened it to discover that it was crammed with all the household linen. Feeling immensely bored by this most bourgeois of women, he telephoned a friend and asked what he should do in her house. The friend replied 'Whatever else you do, don't move a single one of her objects.'

We had invited Douglas Cooper to dinner, for the return of the Wollheims here on Saturday (August 23). They sent a wire on Friday – 'Dimanche' [Sunday] – from Portofino, where they were staying with the Berlins. So as Philippe is so bored and longing to be asked out, we asked him. He said he would have to bring his hostess – for whom he shows surprising considerateness. When we mentioned Douglas, he said: 'that terrible man,' and recalled that Douglas, bludgeoning his way into Mouton when Philippe and Pauline were away, declaring that he was a close friend of theirs, was literally thrown out by the butler, who said 'anyone could say that.' However, we thought Douglas was not to know that any of us knew about this, so Philippe said he would come.

On Saturday our guests arrived close on one another's heels. I just had time to whisper to Douglas who his fellow guests were to be.

---

1 Suzy Delbée-Masurel was the widow of the French interior designer and collector Pierre Delbée, who had been president of the prestigious Parisian firm Maison Jansen.

Mme Delbée had brought a basket containing cheeses and a very superior almond cake cooked by her cook, which had to be heated. The first part of the evening was a bit subdued. But then the conversation got onto the Royal family. Douglas declared he was a Republican, all the Royals were cretins – the Queen Mother in particular was not even royal but a fat Scottish bourgeois. Lizzie stood up for Prince Charles, who had been her fellow house guest at some weekend party. She said he was modest, witty, friendly, helped with the washing up etc. Douglas brushed all this aside saying the Prince of Wales was a repeat performance of the previous Prince of Wales, Edward VIII, a Nazi. I said this was really nonsense. Mrs Delbée looked at her plate, too proud to speak out of her personal acquaintance with her guest of more prosperous days, the Queen Mother. Douglas also said he had passed two hours with the Queen Mother, because, to oblige his friend Charles de Noailles, he had shown her his collection.[1] (Mme D. later told Philippe this was quite untrue: it had been carefully arranged that the Queen Mother saw the collection when D[ouglas] was away.) Douglas now was galloping ahead attacking the royal equerries and everyone who had anything to do with the family. He moved on to other European royalties and said the only decent and intelligent one – a brilliant man – was Leopold of the Belgians. I asked: 'Do you mean the one who killed a million people in the Belgian Congo, or the one who betrayed his allies in 1940?'[2] D. said that Leopold was quite right to stay with his people in their darkest hour, etc, etc. Philippe asked: 'What about his relations with the Nazis?' D. said that they were very limited. Philippe said: 'All I ask is that you don't tell that to a Belgian Jew.' Then he said resoundingly 'Now we shall speak no more on this subject.' Douglas stopped short. Natasha introduced a new subject. The temperature sank from fury to cordial mutual dislike. Philippe and Douglas had a conversation of two testy old gentlemen each of whom corrects the other's every statement, employing those phrases which

---

1 Charles de Noailles (1891–1981), French patron of modern art.

2 Leopold III (1901–1983) was King of Belgium from 1934. When Belgium was invaded in May 1940 the government fled to France and then London. King Leopold, then commander in chief of the army, refused to follow the government and was taken prisoner by the Germans, who held him in Austria until 1945.

can sound rather like rusty swords in a French dialogue. 'Je regrette mais je ne suis pas d'accord.' 'M'excusez mais je ne suis pas de votre avis.'[1] The evening ended early and when I saw Douglas off the scene there were no ecstatic embraces as there had been when the Wollheims brought [their son] Bruno.

26 August 1975, St Jerome

Philippe called and explained that his hostess would be out fetching a guest from the airport this evening – so would we all dine? [. . .] Throughout this meal, Philippe acted as though he were the top sommelier of the greatest restaurant in Paris, taking a busman's holiday in the provinces and quite unable to resist telling the local sommeliers, that having a waiter constantly watching a table and filling up the guests' glasses was officious annoyance, that a wine bottle could perfectly well stand up vertically on the table and not be placed horizontally in a wicker cradle, that when the bottle is uncorked the inside of the neck of the bottle should be wiped with a napkin in some way of which Philippe had the clue and could provide lessons but which was caricatured by the waiters present. He also insisted that the second bottle of the claret was corked. We all heaved a sigh of relief when a third bottle, abjectly produced, he pronounced to be excellent. Lizzie and Natasha were irritated by all this and thought that the waiters would have gladly murdered Philippe. I expect this is true but I found it rather charming and felt that the staff was more amused than annoyed. At any rate, the totally silent bourgeois family seated at the next table was hypnotized. [. . .] We really enjoyed the evening – but were very tired. Lizzie made me a big speech to the effect that Matthew and she were agreed I could write *anything* about them in my diary. She is quietly excited about starting her training at Theatre Presentation next week. Does her meditation and also sits playing her guitar and singing, quietly – I was going to write – and quietly is really the word – with a sweet absorption and seriousness.

---

1 'I'm afraid that I don't agree.' 'Excuse me, but I'm not of your opinion.'

6 November 1975, New York

On November 5th [. . .] went to Philadelphia speaking at Temple University and Tyler (?) Art School. They managed to get me to speak five times in two days for the price of two lectures. Then I stayed for the weekend with Henry McIlhenny.[1] This was two days of luxe and calme, but no volupté because he had an elderly Irish neighbour, a very nice and voluble lady, as my fellow guest.[2] I delighted in Henry. He is so sane and witty and so completely in control of himself and his life, so contentedly and unapologetically the rich man, treating every day of his life as though he himself were a guest at a banquet provided: and at the same time he is so benevolent and hospitable where and when he wants to be, and too wide-eyed and sharp to be cheated or exploited.

At 3.30 in N.Y. met Matthew, Maro and Cosima at Metropolitan Museum. At six went to party given by Liz Hardwick for us all. There were all my friends – Bob Silvers, Barbara Epstein, Bob Craft, Vera Stravinsky, Cleve and Francine Gray, Bill Mazzocco, Everett Fahy, John Ashbery.[3] Also, some young people, particularly Helen Wilson – Edmund [Wilson]'s daughter, etc. Jo Buttinger came, and no one talked to him. He sat in a chair as though he were in a waiting room, an important visitor, waiting among a crowd of irrelevant socialites occupied with trivialities, to visit the Prime Minister. For him, the P.M. was Bob Silvers, to whom he was going to announce that he, Jo, had several new articles of a post-obit kind, about Vietnam, to offer the *N.Y.R.* [*New York Review of Books*] From time to time he got up and asked me when Bob would be there. Bob did arrive at eight, I introduced them, Bob said amiably, 'Of course, Mr B., you wrote us that excellent article about Vietnam.' 'Yes, and I

---

1 Henry McIlhenny (1910–1986), American art collector and philanthropist, friend of Spender's since the 1940s.

2 Spender is quoting Charles Baudelaire's *L'Invitation au voyage* (1857): 'Là, tout n'est qu'ordre et beauté, / Luxe, calme et volupté' (There all is order and beauty, / Luxury, peace, and pleasure').

3 Cleve Gray (1918–2004), American abstract expressionist painter married to the American writer Francine du Plessix Gray (b. 1931). Robert (Bill) Mazzocco (b. 1933), American critic, frequent contributor to the *New York Review of Books*. Everett Fahy, American art critic and curator, director of the Frick Museum since 1973.

have three more to give you,' Jo said. Bob said, 'Excellent. But we'd have to talk about it some other time,' and walked away. I was surprised, and, I fear, not unpleased by his brusqueness. I remarked on it later to Barbara Epstein. She said: 'Oh he has to be like that. He's learned it from bitter experience of people coming up to him even in the street and offering things.' [. . .]

After the party, I gave dinner for twelve at a very grand restaurant in 67th Street (Café des Artistes? Bill $146, but Bob Silvers with his extraordinary generosity, paid for the wine.) Jo sat next to Maro and immediately, always business-like, got down to making a pass at her. He said he would give a year of his life to spend a night with her. Went on the subject of years added that he was 72 but still a magnificent stud. Said he longed to contemplate the space between her chin and her knees. Maro said her breasts were nothing to write home about as she had borne two children and her tits were pretty droopy. He said that men – some old Austrian saying went – were divided between those who liked the legs and those who liked the face. In her case he, although primarily a leg-liker, was prepared to like both. Maro reported all this to me very juicily, immediately after the meal. I felt annoyed with Jo, thinking why did he have to act like Philippe de Rothschild who after all is a born, and not made, millionaire. A thought that does me little credit really. What aroused it perhaps was Maro telling me that Jo also said that there was he, a pauper, the son of a peasant, and that he and not Stephen had married the millionairess Muriel, etc. Jo's subjects of conversation are Vietnam, his health, his sleeping or not sleeping, what he dreamed last night (uninteresting). Very little else. Yet he is really a good man, who having left Austria where he was leader of the underground Socialist Party, has made a great deal of his life, educated himself, made himself a very adequate writer, collected libraries of great interest about Vietnam, the Nazis, the Jews and given them to great institutions (the last one to Harvard. He showed me photos of this) and he is kind. Muriel must have suffered, been humiliated sometimes, bored a lot of the time, but her deepest feeling must be love and appreciation of his very real qualities.

15 November 1975, New York

Natasha [. . .] rang from London and said she was terribly upset. She has been sent by Frank MacShane his biography of Raymond Chandler.[1] The last part of it is about his time in London when Natasha, Jocelyn Rickards, Alison Hooper formed a kind of team of gracious ladies who were looking after Raymond. Raymond who was alcoholic and often in a stupor of booze was especially attached to Natasha – I suppose in love with her. She concerned herself greatly with him, and they went abroad on two or three trips: to Tunis and to California, as far as I can remember. It was quite obvious that her role in this was a role of mercy. Which does not mean that she did not like him. He was an interesting, Walter Mittyish, self-revealing character. Matthew who was ten or twelve at the time described him yesterday to me as a sweet man. My own attitude was to have complete confidence in Natasha's relationship with Chandler which was entirely based on her devoting herself to saving him from despair and, in fact, from killing himself. This was the motivation of all these ladies who had frequent consultations with one another about Chandler. There was no jealousy, envy, or self-interest as between them – which would not have been the case if any of them had been fortune-hunting, present-hunting, or had any kind of design on him.

Raymond and I got on very well whenever we met. However he harboured deep resentments of me, partly on Natasha's account, but mostly I suppose on his own. I knew this but was detached about it because I regarded him as what he was – an invalid.

Raymond was a compulsive writer whose compulsiveness took the form at the end of his life of writing short character sketches (of which he sent many to Natasha) and letters. The last chapter of his biography seems to consist largely of letters written to various correspondents and expressing his fantasies and delusions about Natasha. I have only Natasha's account of these at present but I want to write down my *reactions* to news of this last chapter *before* I see it, as they may calm me when I have to read it. The reason for preparing in myself a calm attitude is that Natasha, in London, is utterly shattered, has had to give up her teaching, and stays in bed.

---

1 Frank MacShane, *The Life of Raymond Chandler* (London: Cape, 1976).

She is worried because accusations are being made of a dead man and she is put in the position of having to reply to them. These accusations are a) that she was having an affair with Raymond; b) that she received gifts from him; c) that she deserted him at the end of his life so that he died forsaken and unhappy.

I think that the answer all these charges is that her attitude to him was based entirely on compassion. It is not true that she had any kind of affair with him and because it is untrue she feels the force of his accusation, as though she has to prove she is not guilty. Myself I feel that she can well afford to disdain the charge altogether. *Honi soit qui mal y pense* [Shame be to him who thinks evil of it]. Even if it were true, it would be completely irrelevant, given the fact that her motivation was compassion. Let people think what they like. Out of her truth which is her compassion she can well afford to despise those who choose to believe a lie.

The same applies to whatever gifts Raymond gave her. One gives gifts because it was one pleasure to do so as well as giving pleasure to the person who accepts them (this can often be a more limited pleasure than that of the giver). The situation in which this would not apply is a) when the recipient solicits gifts b) when the donor gives them to obtain favours from the recipient or – worse – out of a kind of malice or desire to humiliate her by putting her in the position of one who desires and receives favours.

No one who knows anything about Natasha can imagine for one moment that she has ever solicited a gift from any one. She is entirely a giver. I might add, under the pressure of accusations that my wife and I ever tried to obtain gifts or favours from people, that this is true of me also and that even by the sordid standard of many values. Natasha and I have given more than we have received from Raymond or anyone else. What is odious is that Raymond should ever have raised these kind of considerations. All I can think – and do certainly think – is that when Raymond did make any particular gift to Natasha – he did so in the spirit of a real gift – for the pleasure of giving and of having the gift received. I can only think that what I call the malicious side of his giving came as a kind of afterthought, or was an effect of his illness.

21 November 1975, New York

Friday. Rang Natasha. She seems better about the Chandler business which will I think be settled without too much upset, though it is bound to remain very unpleasant. Her real horror is that Chandler insinuates that she was his 'mistress' – whatever that implies. I pointed out that this is not important today because even if it were true no one would mind. She said 'But I do happen to mind.' Then I asked her to suppose that the relationship with Chandler had happened not with her but with some other lady who in fact had been Chandler's mistress. If she read about it, would it make in her mind the slightest difference to her understanding the compassionate motives of such a person, assuming they were compassionate? Natasha saw the point of this, but it did not alter the importance she attached to her not having been Chandler's mistress.

30 November 1975, New York

Party given for Matthew and Maro and me by John Ashbery. Maro was tired after the very prolonged N.Y. luncheon and did not go. [. . .] Larry Rivers was at the party, very much himself, and with no signs of his drug addiction.[1] So was Clarice Rivers, though they are now separated. Clarice pointed out to me a young man, told me she was terribly in love with him but he did not respond to her, asked my advice what to do about it and so on.

Muriel Buttinger arrived at about 7.30 with the idea that Matthew, she and I should dine together. However it was evidently impossible to break up the party at this stage as John did not want us to go. She had some conversation with Bill Mazzocco, which she enjoyed, and some with me. I didn't have the sense to drag Matthew away from Bob Silvers with whom he was having a long conversation about politics. I think she was sad that Matthew did not talk to her. She left before the end of the party (I took her down to get a taxi). At nine, Bill Mazzocco, Susannah, Matthew and I went to a restaurant called 'Elaine' where we dined.

---

1 Larry Rivers (1923–2002), American artist who had stayed with the Spenders at Red Brick Cottage at Bruern in the early 1960s. He was addicted to heroin.

1 December 1975, New York

At 6 a.m. breakfast with the Buttingers who were setting off for the Virgin Isles. Jo told me about his publishers, Simon & Schuster, [who] had written to say his new book on Vietnam was excellent, but unfortunately they could not publish it as no one in America was interested in Vietnam. He wanted me to read the typescript. I said I would do so as soon as I possibly could. He was embarrassed and said I should have it sent me in London.

I have the feeling that M[uriel] has aged quite a lot, is rather deaf, worried, not happy – that after all their life together Jo has cut her off from knowing people like Barbara Epstein, Elizabeth Lowell and others, who would be very close to her were it not for the awful barrier of Jo's egoism and total self-preoccupation.

3 December 1975, New York

Lizzie rang me from London about Natasha. Says she has done almost nothing since getting the MacShane chapter of his book on Raymond Chandler, except stay in bed, which is covered with sheets of paper, writing her account of her relationship with R. How awful this is. My family are made to suffer – Natasha – and as a result Lizzie also – for what is clearly my doing. If I had not neglected Natasha for various young men in whom I was interested, she would never have confided in Chandler – at any rate she would have had nothing to confide that would have given him the occasion to write these letters, for which she suffers. It is no use saying that there are worse things in the world happening to people than what these letters do to her. The point is they make her re-live, re-suffer situations which are now presented to her as damnations.

Rang David Plante who was very sweet. Said the Chandler business was objectively a molehill turned into a mountain but understood that this was not the point. The point is that Natasha does mind, mind in an ultimate kind of way . . . I rang Natasha's doctor, Dr Herbert, who was rather reassuring. Rang Natasha who was a bit annoyed that Lizzie had rung me and that I had rung the doctor. [. . .] We have somehow struck the bottom of the reality of our lives and the only hope of improvement is that which we can construct on our not forgetting this. I feel really that I should not – in some way do not – sleep at all. My conscience – bad conscience – is awake all the time. But what a vulgar phrase – 'bad conscience'.

25 December 1975, London

Christmas Day and therefore, ten days since I left America, which seems incredible. [. . .] With Europe looming ahead of me, it struck me how completely different an evening of American hospitality at the home of friends is from an English one. But I cannot analyse the difference. I think that in London, perhaps England altogether, there is more a merging into the warmth of mutuality, so that a dinner party can seem really a very inside occasion. In America there is undoubted warmth, a lot of trouble can be taken, but everyone remains more outside everyone else. Communication between hosts and guests, guests and guests is like those round-robin letters, cyclostyled, which Americans send to relations friends and acquaintances, giving all the family news at the end of the year. (These must be considerably falsified by the way to be sent out. Most American family news seems to be the bad news of one generation about the other.) Anyway I felt America to be very foreign.

Spender gave up his teaching job at UCL in late 1975. He and Natasha took a three-week winter break in Spain, December 1975– January 1976, their first trip to Spain post-Franco, during whose rule they had not visited the country. They stayed with Janetta Parladé (née Woolley) and her husband Jaime Parladé, a Spanish diplomat. After this, Spender began an arduous lecturing tour in the US.

4 January 1976, Malaga

Marriage is ultimately an agreement – or conspiracy – between two people to treat – each of them – the other as having the right to be loved absolutely. If there is not this understanding, there is no marriage. If there is this understanding, all the things which are supposed to go with marriage – children, sex etc – are secondary to it. There is a deep even if perhaps frustrated bond. For this reason, whereas marriage between two people of opposite sex who are physically attached to one another may fail if there is no such bond of understanding – marriage between two people of the same sex may be immensely binding.

13 January 1976, London

We returned home on our Charter Flight. How remote Spain seems already – the orange trees with their deep leaves and golden fruit in Seville, the vast cathedral, the semi-circular Victorian Plaza de España, red-brown brick, the strip of canal bisecting its imaginary completed circle, and crossed by several miniature bridges, all the winding streets opening onto little squares, revealing balconied houses painted in Venetian reds and emerald greens, the Gardens of the Alcazar. Ronda, Arcos, Cordoba. I did not much care for the Cathedral of Cordoba, the outer parts Moorish with arches built over arches, superimposed on one another, many parallel lines of such arches like miniature aqueducts, and on each side connecting with the high walls surrounding the Christian part of the Cathedral which seems a centre hollowed out of all this Moorish [structure] and the bridge and arch-work either side with one end from floor to ceiling in an immense altar-piece, with the texture one so often finds in Spain of material being used to the same effect of producing an immensely wrought embossed decorated highly polished surface whether it be marble, silver, gold, or leather.

Although all this became cut off, separated made the other side of a curtain run down or a screen drawn across the moment we landed on our charter flight at Luton airport, I feel it has become part of me in a way in which many days or weeks torn out of context of grey routine and set in brightness, haven't done. Where Italy or France impress one with a history which recedes into the past, history in Spain seems a past that forces itself on one as a still present problem. Art and even landscape are still locked in past conflicts and combinations.

17 March 1976, New York

I visited Philippe de Rothschild a week after Pauline's death.[1] He told me about their last day at the hotel in Santa Barbara [California]. She had been exceptionally happy (having had a miserable winter following on an operation for cancer of the breast last October). She had spent the morning and afternoon making long telephone calls to friends and had got very late for the walk they planned to make on the beach. He said he had made a slight scene (one can imagine this) about her losing the sunshine of the afternoon through her lateness. She said: 'Don't worry. I'll come out without putting on my make-up. That will save time.' So she came out almost at once. They had a pleasant relaxed stroll on the shore. They talked about plans for the future. She said exceptionally nice things 'I feel we have been through a difficult time but now are reconciled and drawing closer together etc.' They went back to the hotel. He waited for her by the swimming pool while she went to the hotel lobby. People came running out after him to come at once. She had fallen down in the lobby, longways, striking her head against the porter's desk and bruising her face. She was unconscious and did not regain consciousness though her heart continued beating for some hours in the hospital.

When I met Philippe we began by having a quite long conversation about the contemporary theatre. Then he went back to the subject of Pauline and himself without Pauline. He cannot bear to go to Mouton, to the flat at the Albany, anywhere which carries so much the mark of her style. He asked me what he should do and I said 'Perhaps stay in America.' His daughter Philippine is too much absorbed in her own intensely active life to help him. His grandchildren are too young. 'I can see my way through till the vendange this year but after October there is nothing but the abyss.' I said that by October things would look quite different from how they looked less than a week after Pauline's death.

---

1 Pauline de Rothschild had died of a heart attack in the lobby of the Biltmore Hotel in Santa Barbara, California, on 8 March 1976.

19 March 1976, New York

Was driven back to N.Y. by the painter Robert Motherwell, who had the air of being a highly successful prince of art with a wide culture, great politeness.[1] Although extremely exhausted after a court case which took him a car journey of 800 miles (his limousine was driven by an assistant) he kept up informative conversation for the whole two hours of the journey. Told me he had learned his art as the result of the flight from Europe to New York of the French Surrealists during the war. His own education was with a Surrealist called [Kurt] Seligman. He thought that after the war there had been a complete collapse of European art and all that were left were a few 'decadents', like Francis Bacon and [Jean] Dubuffet. He talked about Arshile Gorky.[2] Said he had never got on very well with him but immensely admired his talent. He said Gorky was technically greatly gifted the most brilliant of his generation. With his exotic appearance he was a dandy immensely attractive to some women. He was willing to exploit his attractiveness. A remark Gorky once made to him: 'I always like people who are in power.' Described the tragic end of his life – cancer followed by a car accident in which he broke his neck, followed by suicide – Magouche having gone off with the Chilean artist of extraordinary talent in the eyes of them all and admired by Gorky – [Roberto] Matta.[3]

Motherwell talked about the squareness, officialism, of Henry Moore. Said he thought it was the peculiar temptation of the English artist, to become attached to an English society which had standards nothing to do with art. The American artists had no such society, outside the values of art, to which to become attached. The successful American artists were the supreme American elite with no reason to become detached from their art-world. He himself lived in Litch-

---

1 Robert Motherwell (1915–1991), American abstract expressionist painter.

2 For Arshile Gorky, Armenian-born American painter and father of Maro Spender, see biographical appendix.

3 Roberto Matta Echaurren (1911–2002), surrealist artist born in Chile, came to New York in 1940 where he exercised a strong influence on several American artists, including Gorky. The scandal of his affair with Gorky's wife severely compromised his position in New York and in Paris, but his career continued productively in Cuba, South America and Italy.

field, Connecticut, a town of presidents and vice-presidents of corporations but he had never gone into any of their houses. They doubtless regarded him as a local eccentric who lived in the barn down the road (more likely they regard him as a commercially successful neighbour whose money they respect and whom they hold in awe, I thought). Motherwell thought the mood of America in the Bicentennial year was serious, concerned.[1]

I said to him that he and I were survivors. He seemed a bit worried at this. Said that in old age he regretted not having the body of his youth. (I said how much more fun I would have had with mine if I had been young among the young today.) Talked of his young wife – an East German. Said he had had five operations last year, is now OK. Does not drink. He took me to my door in New York and as I got out of the car I said I was afraid I had taken him half an hour out of his way. He said: 'It would have been worth going two hours out of my way.' I had the impression of a grand seigneur of the arts, polite, intelligent, tired, a bit sad, nostalgic for his youth.

23 March 1976, Purdue University, Indiana

Where was it they told me they gave a Faculty Party for Auden? He came padding into the room looked round blankly said 'Oh' – and then, 'Well, I have to go to bed. Good night.'

2 April 1976, Gainesville, Florida

Students at a writing course. If you suggest to them that they should read, most of them are affronted. They think that they belong to a superior race of those who do not read – they write. The relation of writer to reader is of master to servant. The idea of their reading is like suggesting to the master that he become the servant. Nearly all say they want to write because they consider writing to be a useful adjunct to that supreme aim of living which is to express themselves. One says she hopes that a writing course will free her of what she considers her excessive dependence on dictionaries and thesauruses. [. . .]

---

1 In 1976 America staged a series of events celebrating the bicentennial of the creation of America as an independent republic in 1776.

Like every period of my life which I look back on [my time at Gainsville] seems largely wasted. When I'm living it, I seem to be working a lot – writing all day. I did in fact complete – if that is the word – a passage of about thirty lines which I had been working at for months. 'Complete' seems the wrong word, because what I really mean is that after several months working on this I suddenly discovered what I wanted to write and the form in which I wanted to write it.

The passage in question was a long speech in a play [in] which I intend to have several long speeches, although I approach the long speech with nervousness.

But one of the real achievements of English post-War drama, in the work of [John] Osborne [Harold] Pinter and [Tom] Stoppard, [Peter] Shaffer, and of course [Samuel] Beckett, is the long speech. [. . .] There are really two idioms for the long speech in the current theatre – the lunatic and the lecturer, sometimes a mixture of both. The role of the lunatic is to release the material of the unconscious to the audience – the lobotomy, the Anger, the apocalyptic vision of the horses. The role of the Lecturer is to apply some modern apparatus of psychoanalytical explanation to the unconscious material. All this is clearest in *Equus* [by Peter Shaffer], that play being the crudest application of the interlocking unconscious outpouring into psychoanalytical clarifying – like a jug of blood being poured into a basin of water.

These remarks apply least to Samuel Beckett in whose plays the psychoanalytical lecture under any form is lacking. The reason for this is that Beckett's plays are poetry derived, like T. S. Eliot's *The Waste Land*, from that immense volcanic mass of poetry – *Ulysses*. One characteristic of poetry is that it fuses the unconscious outpouring material with the analytic explanatory material. The explanation of what obscure poetry is about may be itself very obscure but it is there. A play that is poetry does not require a psychoanalyst lecturer to stand around explaining what is being said. The role of Reilly in *The Cocktail Party* [by T. S. Eliot] is really that of priest got up as psychoanalyst – not psychoanalyst got up as priest. Reilly's poetic 'message' is religious and ritualistic, given to an audience which respects psychoanalysis more than religion. [. . .]

At his best Beckett employs a concrete language dense with imagery and at the same time providing its own explanation of what on the most conscious level it is 'about' – the unconscious and the conscious elements inseparable – which is poetry and this, I have suggested, derives from the molten lava of *Ulysses*. Beckett is the only living poet of the theatre, and it is interesting that his poetry comes from the poetic-prose novel, not from line-verse printed and spoken by line, regular-if-frequently-broken-down verse.

Eliot's achievement in 'putting poetry onto the stage' is remarkable – but nevertheless it has about it the aroma of a duty to poetry fulfilled by getting the West End theatre to take it. [. . .] The poetry in Yeats' and Eliot's drama often leaves one with the feeling that the stage is being used to do poetry, a needy spinster, a good turn. The situations are contrived in order that we may have the poetry. *St Joan* [by George Bernard Shaw] and *Equus* are examples of the opposite happening. The situation needs poetry and we get purple rhetorical prose. Sometimes as in most of Osborne's plays, this is dramatically convincing because Osborne's heroes or anti-heroes are empty rhetoricians, life-like because in real life there are many windbags. Tom Stoppard's George [a character in *Jumpers*], is an exercise in rendering the philosophy of A. J. Ayer as expounded conversationally by its inventor to a rhetorical parody. This makes poetry unnecessary. Yet I can't help feeling that if Stoppard really sets out to be an Aristophanes guying the intellectual and political fashions and figures of our time something more poetic is required.

My point is that the theatre needs poetry even more than poetry needs the theatre. The amount of bogus poetry in the long monologues indicates that real poetry is needed – and the language of *Happy Days* indicates (more even than anything else by Beckett) the kind of poetry required. I should say that this is imagistic language which projects the character speaking it, has the rhythm or cadence of natural speech and intensifies rather than escapes from the situation. It is not character or situation for the sake of escaping into flights of poetry. No rules of regularity and metre can be laid down – except perhaps that it should not be Shakespearean (*The Ascent of F6* [by Auden and Isherwood] is ruined for me by Ransom's flights into the rhetoric of *King Lear*). In fact, I should say that poetry should intensify the reality, if not the realism, of the drama. [. . .]

In basing a new play on *Trial of A Judge* – I am trying to observe the principle that the language relates always to three things. 1) situation. 2) action. 3) character of the person speaking. There is nothing else. If a character speaks poetry this is because verse form and imagery provide the utmost concentration of reference to these three things.[1]

29 July 1976, St Jerome

I neglect this journal because every moment for writing that I am not writing my play seems wasted. But reading through essays I have written over the past forty years, I think: 'You should never have written anything but poetry, stories, plays (perhaps) and journals or autobiography.' In writing criticism I was always trying to relate my own ideas to those of other critics I respected. Well perhaps that is not altogether bad: what is bad is not to start out from a position which is entirely one's own, based on one's own immediate response to a work, and not with that response tailored before one has written it down by other critics or, – rather – by the idea of other critics – their ghosts, schoolmasters in one's mind their schoolroom.

D. H. Lawrence is not the infallible critic other critics – out of a desire to connect their lifelessness with his life – sometimes maintain him to be, but he does always start out from his own response. If you read him on Melville or Whitman, you feel that he has only read *Moby Dick* or *Leaves of Grass* – and is entirely alone in his responding to it – he has never read any criticism about them at all. He is hit or miss. But his hits are more in the bull's eye than those of anyone else, for that reason.

* * *

Being alive, contemporary among contemporaries, we suppose that our relations with living people are different in kind from those which we have with the dead. We are impressed by the fact that people who are living have bodies like ourselves and this makes us think

---

1 This new version of *Trial of a Judge*, on which Spender worked intermittently until his death, was provisionally called *The Corporal*. Several full texts survive in the Spender archive, but the work was never produced on stage or published.

that the essential difference between relationships with the dead and with the living is that the dead are disembodied, the living bodied. [. . .]

I am merely pointing out that most of our communication with the living is of the disembodied kind undistinguishable from our relationships with the dead. I must qualify this however by limiting this communication to that with people who during their lives *do* communicate. In this respect there is a great difference between the authors, the creators and even today (thanks to records, movie films etc) some performers and one who goes through life without establishing such records of himself. The nanny whom we had when we were children, the servants who looked after us. Jules Renard writes in his journal: 'La récompense des grands hommes, c'est que, longtemps après leur mort, on n'est pas bien sûr qu'ils soient morts.'[1]

15 October 1976, Mount Vernon, Ohio

I have been at this place for nearly two weeks. Time has gone by quickly yet it seems much longer. [. . .]

It seems incredible that only two weeks ago Natasha and I were at Mouton for a week with Raymond Mortimer as fellow-guest. Other guests arrived for a day or two – Niko Henderson, the British Ambassador and his wife, and Louis Aragon.[2]

I had not seen Aragon for ten years, when I had dinner with him in Paris at Pauline de Rothschild's apartment, together with Elsa Triolet, Lili Brik (Elsa's sister and purportedly once mistress of [Vladimir] Mayakovsky) and Lili Brik's husband a professor.[3] Then, Aragon was still bristling, aggressive, 'prétentieux'. I had sat next to him at dinner and he had told me that he'd never been so insulted in

---

1 'The reward of great men is that long after their deaths one is not quite sure whether they are in fact dead.' The journals of the French author Pierre Jules Renard (1864–1910) had been published in 1925 and evidently made a strong impression on the young Spender.

2 Louis Aragon (1897–1982), French poet who founded the surrealist movement with André Breton.

3 Elsa Triolet (1896–1970), Russian-born French writer who married Aragon in 1928 and influenced him to join the Communist Party.

his life as when Ezra Pound (he said) had written to him asking whether he would publish Aragon's letters to him written in the 'twenties (it could not have been Pound who wrote – just some professor). I asked him why this was such an insult. He said Pound was a terrible Fascist. I said – yes but he was a poet and was also a man of letters who had treated other writers – poets and novelists – with extraordinary generosity. Aragon got up from the table and started shouting at me. Elsa told him he was being foolish and pulled him down.

The ten-years-later Aragon at Mouton three weeks ago was utterly changed. The thread that connects the youthful revolutionary with the great man had been cut and he was now a 'vieux monsieur' [old man]. His face had somehow become at once softer in expression and narrower in its features, so that he had the look of a 'colonel' returned from Algeria. He had grown exceedingly deaf, a fact he only acknowledged by occasionally, in his 'vieillard' [old man] manner, cupping his ears with both hands.

He was extremely elegant, wearing beautifully cut suits of what looked like soft wool and, when he went outdoors, large elegant hats. Rather maliciously I shouted to him my admiration for one of his suits and asked him where he got it from. He answered: 'Like all my clothes – except my hats which are from Dior (?) – it is designed by [Yves] St Laurent.'

Almost as soon as we met, he started explaining to me how disillusioned he was about Communism. He said he was only prevented from expressing his disgust by the fact that his sister-in-law (Lili Brik) lived in Moscow.[1]

In spring 1979, Spender was engaged to teach a semester at Vandebilt University in Tennessee.

5 January 1979, Nashville, Tennessee

This morning it is snowing. [. . .] I sit here watching the snow that seems not quite like the snow in England. During the last few days

---

1 Aragon used his sister-in-law Lili Brik as an excuse not to denounce the communists, because outspoken criticism would put her in danger of persecution from the state.

over New Year in England it has been exceptionally cold. A cold spell in England is totally unanticipated: a blow struck from a clouded-over heaven by a god with a javelin, unfair, causing shrieking disasters – three drowned in pond on Hampstead Heath rashly trying to walk on the ice – you cannot even trust the ice to freeze properly in an English winter. However, the pipes in – or rather outside – our house froze – throwing us as it seemed on the mercy of totally unreliable plumbers – whose inefficiency is evidenced by the very fact that the pipes of London houses do freeze. London airport, it was revealed, only possesses one snow plough. I just rang Nashville airport and they seemed quite astonished that I thought it might be closed just because six times as much snow is falling here as in London. Anyway the American snow gives one a dense, broad, opaque vision of the continent of America bright at the Californian edge, but frozen above, in Portland and Seattle, with the Mid-West one immense muffling hairy blanket of endlessly soft-falling icy snow.

I think of the last few weeks in London – of concentric circles of people, work (by which I mean my own work) and the outside world uncontrollable by us which controls our world.

People to me more and more means a span of at least fifty years, at one end of which are the children, and at the other the old. Between these are the young who have ceased to be children – Matthew, Maro, Lizzie, David [Plante] and Nikos [Stangos] for example. Beyond the perimeter of the old are the dead with whom one feels an increasing intimacy.

One's own immediate contemporaries – at any rate those of them whom one has known all one's life – become the special band, the crew of voyagers, who have lived through so much and who carry on just the same; but in the very high-up territory we have reached some of us fall abruptly off precipices, some of us – more distressingly – are shut away in the almost incommunicable chambers of the dying. But on the whole we carry on, going to parties, meeting each other frequently, travelling, working, joking, feeling how extraordinarily little we have changed. However there are changes, some of them external – wrinkles, white hair, false teeth, defective eyesight etc – some of them – though due to the same physical causes – seem internal, because mental, and therefore of a different order. The most obvious of these is loss of memory, which is like something going on inside you in your mind, as distinct from what goes on outside, the wrinkles and white hair.

But although remaining so much the same, one is very conscious of being at the edge of irremediable detrimental changes which people ten or fifteen years – or even five years younger – are not aware of. I seem to myself a very different person from myself even five years ago. Because five years ago, though conscious some of the time of my age, a lot of the time I was not conscious of it at all. If I bought a diary for 1975 I felt that I would be the same person at the end of it – December 31 – as I was at the beginning – January 1st. Now I can just about feel I'll be the same at the end of 1979 – but to look at a diary for this year haunts me with the idea of another diary – for ten years perhaps – at the end of which I shall be, in one or another way, finished.

We went to visit my Uncle George Schuster, at Nether Worton.[1] He is now 97. He and my Aunt Gwen were sitting together in an oak-panelled room, formerly, I think, their dining room, not their large drawing room which is beyond it. She was in an upright chair, smiling receiving us graciously, always the hostess. The only thing is that she did not know who we were or who anyone was. She just made polite noises. And when we were leaving she said not to us but to her nurse hovering in the background, 'It has been so delightful to see you. I do hope you will come again.'

Uncle George, in a reclining chair, was very arthritic. His mind was active but imprisoned by his body. He was delighted to see us and asked me, as he has always done whenever I have met him over the past thirty years, 'Tell me what you think about the state of the world.' I did what I have always done over the past thirty years – pass the question back to him – after I had mumbled a few common-places – 'Tell me what you think of the state of the world.' He told me that he thought it was very depressing and that for England the only hope would be that which was impossible to hope for – a national government. He had from his point of view, a perfectly realistic view of the situation. He said he had just finished his autobiog-

---

1 For George Schuster, see biographical appendix. The Milner Commission was sent to Egypt by the British government in November 1919 to resolve the uprisings against the British Protectorate in Egypt.

raphy and said quite modestly that he had been involved in several interesting things in his life – the First War, the Milner Commission, Financial Minister of the Indian Government [. . .]

Then he said: 'Here am I, scarcely able to move, my sight gone within the last year, unable to read. I'd hoped to spend the end of my life reading [Edward] Gibbon and other great masterpieces.' He had some kind of reading machine but complained that the available books read on it were not what he wanted to read. Here I was able to be helpful in suggesting that he could get cassettes of Shakespeare etc and that he could also get volunteers to read on cassettes for him.

When we said goodbye he said we could not possibly have any idea of what our visit meant to him, cut off from most human contact as he was.

All this gives me a feeling like that of Keats's about the chambers of life – though I don't see them quite in the way that K. did.[1] But it is as though people's lives are compartmentalized into boxes like different sections on a stage in which one sees – for example – all the rooms of a house. One of the impressions of my particular stage of old age is this sense of simultaneity: thus my uncle is in my mind the son of whom my grandmother was so proud when he excelled at Charterhouse, when he rode to hounds at Exmoor, when he was a staff officer in the war.

10 January 1979, Nashville

Read [Bernard] Bergonzi's book on the Thirties.[2] In it he adopts the method of exploring themes – the Audenesque, futuristic words like 'history', 'frontier' etc. It does not seem to be a very good way of discussing the Thirties, partly because it seems so arbitrary, partly because it leaves so much out. It seems as though the Thirties started up and started with these themes and gives very little idea of where

---

1 In a letter to J. H. Reynolds of 3 May 1818, Keats compared human life to 'a large Mansion of Many Apartments' where the inhabitant moves from the 'infant or thoughtless Chamber' to the 'Chamber of Maiden-Thought', which is intoxicating in its light and pleasure until 'the "burden of the Mystery"' reveals itself and doors all around 'are set open – but all dark – all leading to dark passages'.

2 Bernard Bergonzi, *Reading the Thirties* (1978).

in past literature they came from. We are told that Auden, Day Lewis, Isherwood, myself etc all went to public schools but not what we read. The Great War is considered part of our background, but there is no mention of Wilfred Owen, the many influences that went into Auden – such as Owen, [T. S.] Eliot, Robert Bridges, Laura Riding, Groddeck, Homer Lane – even, as I recently discovered, Gertrude Stein, are not considered.[1] All the same, he is very interesting about Graham Greene and I enjoyed what he wrote about Edward Upward. He is good on MacNeice.

11 January 1979, Nashville

I thought about form and music and poetry [. . .] the role of memory in music is different from that in most poetry. Playing records it struck me that in music (classical music at any rate) quite apart from the question of whether one knows it by heart one has a kind of anticipatory memory. Even after one has heard a work a very few times, one always knows what is going to come next in a symphony or quartet of Beethoven or Mozart – even I think with Stravinsky. Perhaps one knows the next few bars following on any preceding bar because of the rules of composition, one is always a bit ahead, like the conductor. But I do not understand why the whole work including surprises of development, changes of key etc is somehow contained in one's memory. With poetry – at any rate with Shakespeare – it seems quite different. Reading *King Lear* recently I kept on being shocked by awareness of how little I remembered.

13 January 1979, Nashville

Still here after ten days without anyone in Nashville having invited me even for a drink, except the lady along the corridor who gave me a general invitation to breakfast each day and did give me breakfast

---

1 Laura Riding (1901–1991), American poet and novelist. Georg Groddeck (1866–1934), Swiss psychoanalyst whose views on the psychosomatic origins of illness were adopted by Auden. Homer Lane (1875–1925), American educator, pioneer of liberal teaching techniques and school organization. Auden and Isherwood were introduced to his theories by the psychoanalyst John Layard (1891–1974), when resident in Berlin in the early 1930s.

yesterday. [. . .] A thing about the room I now have is that it has a kind of grating near the ceiling through which voices in the room next door come magnified. This happens mostly at 10 a.m. and 5.30 pm. At 10 a.m. the voice talks about the day and says things like 'Wheaties? Mustard? Toilet paper? Are you sure you got them all?' [. . .]

The TV with its awful jokes, songs, canned laughter and interspaced commercials now is on and I can't work till it stops. It's singing one of those dreadful Nashville country songs now – like Soviet art.

I tried to visualize the man talking in the next room but I could not do so. The sentences I heard were profoundly depressing. They seem to spring up like brown water from some pipe underground, especially in cities, where people talk with an undisguised brutality which is the ugly side of intimacy. There is a kind of basic unkindness, lack of charity here, and I recognize something of myself in it wondering whether this kind of callousness towards others is not peculiarly American. It links up with something Frank Kermode wrote me that in this country the really nice people (and they are extraordinarily nice) have an air of being dazed and lost as though they did not know how they got here.

This brings me to B [Bryan Obst] – who – to my surprise – telephoned me twice from Florida yesterday.[1] He had also written me a postcard to the department and had left me a telephone message there. He talked for a long time modulating always between his seriousness and his funniness so amusing so gentle and sympathetic and interesting. He is in a trailer he has rented which, he said, is 'a hundred times better than the shack he had before', teaching school in a remote town in Southern Florida. I worried about him spending so much making two calls and asked him if he would keep a bill so I could pay for this pleasure. He said: 'It's my pleasure.' He made me laugh and then I laughed more because it gives us pleasure to make each other laugh. It's one of our values. He is growing a beard. I laughed. He was so much himself it was as though he was in the room. We know each other's nuances. On his postcard he had written, in his very clear handwriting: 'I hope that the people you are

---

1 For Bryan Obst, see biographical appendix.

with are being helpful to you.' He told me he had written that knowing that in every department there is someone like Jim Goldsmith who reads all the postcards, and hoping it would influence him. I laughed and said 'When I read the postcard I knew that is why you had done it.'

14 January 1979, Nashville

More of what they call here in the news bulletins 'precipitation' – in this case, snow. A vague sun filtering through it. I dreamed what seemed a long dream about Cecil Day Lewis. (Funny how much I dream here about the dead: the other night I dreamed about Harold Nicolson.) It was a great pleasure to be with him as in fact it had always been when he was alive – joy, though I never felt that I knew him and was somehow vaguely suspicious of him. In my dream I wanted very much to play him a recording of a pianist (Clifford Curzon?) playing the Eroica Variations. I could anticipate the pleasure this would give him. The only thing – I could not find the record though I had just been playing it before I saw him. Also there was no plug at the end of the line connecting the gramophone with the wall-plug. It was just a frayed end with two wires sticking out. When I woke, I remembered in the winter of 1945 when I was teaching at Blundell's playing Cecil recordings of Haydn quartets when he came to stay with me once. He burst out laughing with pleasure at the Scherzo of one quartet. Some of the boys teased me after Cecil's visit. A boy called Sprigge said 'We wish you were like him, sir.'

15 January 1979, Nashville

Mrs Lerman – the lady along the corridor, whose apartment I'm going to rent – invited me to drink. Then I asked her to dine at Bishop's the restaurant where they make lots of omelettes.

B[ryan] rang and told me about his teaching in S. Florida. He gave a course on fossils trying to draw attention to the extreme oldness of some species fossilized and to the comparative recentness of man on the earth. 'The awkward thing is,' he said, 'that at some point I had to mention Evolution. When I did that the children let out shrieks and howled at me. Evolution is still a dirty word on the Bible Belt.'

He consulted other teachers – his colleagues – and all said he should not mention Evolution. 'But most of them, I discovered, are Bible Belters themselves.' He was so clear and obviously so interested in interesting the kids, I suggested he should write a text book. 'What happens,' he said, 'is that the educational committee meet with the directors of the school and lay down the lines of courses. Then some teachers rush away and write text books along these lines. Then, when the courses start, lo and behold their text books appear at just that moment and are used for the courses.'

In January 1979, England was in the middle of a so-called winter of discontent. The widespread strikes and rampant inflation led to the downfall of Labour Prime Minister James Callaghan's administration after a vote of no confidence in March 1979, resulting in the election of Margaret Thatcher's Conservative government.

18 January 1979, Nashville

Writing this while on the radio Richard Lewis tenor sings Vaughan Williams, [George] Butterworth, [Herbert] Howells etc. Funny how these English songs are like beer and water.

Suddenly I'm very worried about England. The truck strike on the news [suggested] that England was grinding to a halt no imports no exports etc. Mr Callaghan's warning that the truckers had one more chance before he called out the troops. I had lunch with Donald Davie etc, who was not at all like the idea I had formed of him.[1] A pale, but heavy (with a prominent stomach) bespectacled man, obviously very intelligent quite humorous. [. . .] Davie seemed to think Nashville might be a good place for retirement. He asked me about England. Wasn't it really impossible after living in America to go back to this country that was always being plagued with strikes, seized up. I said it was depressing but that London still seemed the most wonderful place in the world. One's friends, the theatre. I said that when I was

---

1 Donald Davie (1922–1995), British poet associated with The Movement in the 1950s, currently a distinguished professor of literature at Vanderbilt. He and his wife Doreen would become close friends of the Spenders during this academic stint.

young and lived in Hampstead I always wanted – compulsively – to go to the centre of town – Piccadilly Circus Trafalgar Square the hub of Empire with the pigeons wheeling round – but he would be too young to have had that feeling. He said he had it during the war when he used to go to London. I spoke of the proletarianization of the West End and how I really couldn't quite accept it – though it was what I wanted when I was young. He said that coming from the lower middle class he had never wanted a still lower class to take over. [. . .]

I have thoughts about Trades Unions – or, rather, I have a kind of poetic vision of them though I don't know whether to trust it.

If Callaghan is unable to settle the strike, his will be the second government (previously Heath's) to have been broken by strikers. More and more it seems that the chief function of any English government is to resist the Unions. It is easy to regard a British government as a knight on a horse armed only with a spear having to tilt at a foaming dragon – the T.U.C. (and perhaps not even them – the little dragons of strikers goading on their own union with strikes against them, like letting off fireworks behind their tails).[1] [. . .]

Trades Union Leaders, who appear frequently on British TV, nearly always assume the look of characters in a Greek tragedy. Asked by interviewers why they are causing the public great inconvenience and distress, they always explain that they are victims of ineluctable fate. It is not their fault they are pushed by the forces behind them. Apart from Clive Jenkins, who has the air of sticking his tongue out at the public[,] they look utterly miserable.[2] (Of course they would not look like this if they were members of an opposition which having made life impossible for the government could take over power.)

21 January 1979, Nashville

[Went] out to dinner [. . .] with Bob Hunter and his wife [Ann].[3] [. . .] Bob Hunter was a room mate at Harvard of John Ashbery. He has

---

1 TUC, Trades Unions Congress.

2 Clive Jenkins (1926–1999), head of the TUC and a principal thorn in James Callaghan's flesh.

3 Robert Hunter, Professor of English at Southern Methodist University, in Dallas, Texas.

pleasant spread out strongly lined features in a rather bun-like face. His wife is rather earnest and high-minded, a bit starved-looking. They also had a daughter – 16 or 17 extremely *belle laide* in fact very attractive.¹ She did not say one word but seemed to take in everything and whenever I looked at her I felt she was very aware of my interest. [. . .] The Hunters have a very agreeable house and a lot of small carefully acquired paintings of uncertain origin – he thought one was a [Thomas] Rowlandson another a [Edward] Lear etc – but very good indeed. He obviously has an eye and there is nothing ugly on his walls. Their guest was a very ancient medievalist lady, aged eighty-six, whom Mrs Loomis had rather ominously described to me as 'the youngest person I know' and one saw the point of the description. She obviously has perfect memory, indeed total recall. She buzzes about the country, enormous distances, in her car or on buses, taking everything in, insatiably. She was at Vanderbilt as a student with Allen Tate whom she evidently considers rather wicked – which is Allen's own exciting view of himself. She discussed with candour whether when they were undergraduates she and Allen had been lovers. I gather whatever they were they hadn't had sex though she seemed to suspect Allen of numbering her among his sexual scalps. They talked a great deal – too much really – about Allen. The medievalist has known him longer than anyone else has done. Apparently Allen's wife Helen loathes him utterly and completely. She keeps people away from seeing him, and also has taken the telephone away from his bedside through which he used to converse with his friends. She tells everyone that Allen doesn't really have emphysema and that it is quite unnecessary for him to keep to his bed. She thinks that the lionizing of Allen by those who visit – or are turned away from visiting – him is based on his having a fraudulent reputation. But she is no lover of literature. She brings up the two little boys to think all this about their father. They described to me a very scarifying scene in which when they last (all three of them, I think) visited Allen, Allen said 'Now I want Helen to come in and tell you what she thinks about me' – which she did. Allen then told them that the situation he was now in was punishment for his past sins.

---

1 The French phrase 'belle laide' means simultaneously beautiful and ugly.

22 January 1979, Nashville

Finished my review of David Jones.[1] [. . .] In my review, I praised
D.J.'s book but raised towards the end the question whether he wasn't
a First War neurotic and invalid [. . .] people like D.J. tend to think
that since no one can exist within the old 'natural' normal conditions
of the culture, everyone is conditioned by the 'utile' civilization. This
I think is simply untrue. And this is not because I believe in something
called the 'individual' (whom D.J. would anyway regard as symptomatic of the civilization) but because I think that many people are not
conditioned by the civilization, even if they are not able to get back
into the culture. The reason why they aren't conditioned by it is
because they ask questions about life and are serious. If one thinks in
a general way about the world in which we live, it is very easy to suppose that all the young, for example, must be spiritually and mentally
the products of the civilization. But in fact they aren't because the
scene it provides does not satisfy their sense of their own vitality or
answer their questions about life. It may seem miraculous that this is
so, but teachers are always coming up against this kind of miracle.
Most of the children reflect the 'scene' – drugs, sex etc – which the
'utile' now presents, but some of them simply ignore it – or it does not
affect them – and read books and have a real sense of literature or
love learning or are really interested in science. This happens because
it is part of human nature that it should happen. The Happy Few
exist and recognize one another. In the past they were the people who,
in the dark ages, went into the monasteries. Why should they have
done so? Because they really liked religion, poetry, music, art and
those things which always seem on the point of disappearing but
never do quite disappear, because it is natural that some people should
be serious. Beyond the social conditioning and the utile or non-utile
values there is life itself. Consciousness of life makes one serious and
also lifts one out of one's time into other times, into all history. This
does not answer D.J. but it to some extent is a challenge to his insistent nostalgic depressiveness, to his feeling that to care about the lost
values and the lost culture dooms one to live in the diaspora.

---

1 Spender was reviewing Jones's second collection of essays, *The Dying Gaul*,
published posthumously by Faber in 1978.

26 January 1979, Nashville

Got my pay cheque today. Thought I would celebrate by taking myself to a good restaurant. Julian's was full so I went to l'Auberge which has quite a nice atmosphere and a staff very willing to help but a meal which collapses with the entrée. A bottle of Alsatian wine quite good. Walked home, thought about so many things. One of them was how some weeks ago in London I walked along Long Acre from Covent Garden, where I had seen *Götterdämmerung* – alone as I thought, along the street I farted. It was much louder after five hours of Wagner than I had dreamed it could possibly be. Some boys and girls, rather charming, whom I had scarcely noticed, overheard me, or it, and started cheering. In the darkness I was more amused than embarrassed. Then a self-important thought came in my mind. Supposing that they knew this old man walking along Long Acre and farting was Stephen Spender – what would they think? Anyway for some reason a bit difficult for me to analyse, it *would* be embarrassing. Then I saw how an incident like this divides people one knows into categories – those who would laugh[,] those who would be shocked (shocked anyway at my writing this down). I don't think F. R. Leavis would have been amused. But Forster, Auden, Isherwood, [Cyril] Connnolly, [Joe] Ackerley, Matthew (my son) would be. [. . .]

[I rang] Muriel Buttinger. She said Jo was breaking up very rapidly. He had lost his memory, so that he might ask her the same question five times in the hour. He could not enjoy reading because he forgot what had preceded it before he got to the end of a page. She said she found the total dependence of Jo on her very trying as she could not really bear to have no time completely alone. Jo had just been staying with people in N.Y. (for two days) so she had had these two days alone. She was counting (she had told me before this) on being alone at the beginning of March.

Some memories of Wystan, as they come to me. He admired (when an Oxford undergrad) Wyndham Lewis's *The Lion and the Fox*.[1] Not quite consistently with this, he thought that Shakespeare's characters should not be thought of as having a history or personality

---

1 Lewis's 1927 study of Shakespeare's heroes divided them into two broad categories, the brave and the cunning.

apart from that which existed in the lines. To talk about Ophelia's relation with Hamlet before the play started was wrong – because Hamlet and Ophelia only existed within the context of the poetry. They were the poetry, the lines, everything outside the lines was a delusion of the spectator or reader.

3 February 1979, Nashville

Took the Davies [Donald and Doreen] to dinner at Julian seemingly the best restaurant in Nashville. It really is quite good, by any standard. The meal cost $130 which I didn't regret as I asked them very consciously meaning to give the best that Nashville has to offer. Also it is hospitality past and future returned (they are giving a large party for me on Feb 15). But the real reason is I like being lavish (in E. M. Forster's *A Room with A View* the character named after my cousin Emily Spender is called Miss Lavish).[1] I think the idea of the expensive ceremonious meal goes back in my life to Cyril Connolly in the mid-Thirties. But one of the things we talked about (*I* talked about) was Stravinsky-Bob-Vera, and how they treated life as a banquet – a tradition in their case going back to Liszt and Wagner. We thought it didn't apply quite to the Romantics – not in England at all events. They fed on bread and tears (all except Byron – and sometimes Shelley).[2] I said someone ought to write a book relating the two generations (Wordsworth's, Blake's / Shelley's, Keats's, Byron's) to their economic and class background.

17 February 1979, Nashville

On February 7th I went to visit Allen Tate in hospital. When I came to the room – with only two patients where he was – the nurses told me it was impossible to see him. There was a notice Absolutely No Visitors on the door. I told a nurse that I had received a note that Allen wanted to see me. She went off and came back with a doctor

---

1 Emily Spender (1841–1922), a novelist and staunch suffragist, was actually Spender's great aunt. As he says, she is generally taken to be the original of Miss Lavish.

2 Spender alludes to Psalm 80: 'Thou hast *fed* them with bread of tears.'

who asked my name. Then he went into the room and came out a moment later to say that Allen wanted to see me. Allen was lying in bed, extremely emaciated with one thin arm outstretched. The skin along the length of the bone seemed like white tape. The first question he asked was whether I had received his Collected Poems. Not quite remembering, I said 'yes' and then felt embarrassed lest if I said I had enjoyed them he would then ask me which I liked most and I might stumble in answering (I don't really like his poems – they seem to me terribly self-conscious and what Lawrence calls 'would-be'). He then asked me about MacNeice and how his reputation was doing. I said I thought students were very admiring of Louis. [. . .] Then he said: 'You know Helen, my wife, is very much younger than I am.[1] She has acquired an extraordinary jealousy of my friends. She doesn't want me to see any of them.' He said this with his kind of detachment in which in the past he has told me other things, combining clarity with a faint amusement. (He would talk about the Church in the same way.) He asked about Natasha. Altogether our conversation was very normal like it has always been, showing his interest in literary news, gossip, reputations. I was in the position that I thought I might be tiring him, also felt he wanted me to stay, also, ignobly, wanted to get away as soon as possible. When, after 15 minutes I said I had to go I felt guilty. That I was using the convention that visits of this kind are not meant to 'tire' the visited to satisfy my own cowardly desire to escape. I really despise this modern convention. If I had exhausted Allen or even killed him with shock by saying something outrageous, it would not have mattered. I realized that he had only a few days left to live anyway.[2] Outside, I thought there was something wrong even about the feeling of awe one has when visiting the sick and dying. I thought that if I were in his condition I would want my friends to keep away if visiting put this kind of awed strain on them. I would like them to feel that visiting me on my death bed was like being with me at any other time. Looking at them from my pillow, I would not feel that they were extraordinary or that they had to act up in any way or even feel anything special. I think that the

---

1 Tate had married Helen Heinz, a former student of his (and former nun), in 1966, having divorced his first wife.

2 Allen Tate would die on 9 February 1979.

people I would want least to see are those I most love if they were to undergo this sense of reverence, and were unable to be natural about it. The people I love I would just want to look at – if this did not hurt them. As when I hear the voice of a friend who is 3,000 miles away, on the telephone I feel that however much I enjoy this conversation, I would rather have them present and palpable in the room beside me, sitting in a chair and saying nothing. Hearing a loved voice one knows how precious it is to see a loved face, let one's eyes travel over it, to read the things the voice has left unsaid.

Friday February 9 went to Gainesville. On the Saturday Tony Lombardy rang me and told me Allen had died.[1] I said I was glad, as he had absolutely nothing to live for. B[ryan] met me at the airport, and we embraced. Everything about him seemed to say that nothing had changed and that in meeting again we harvested every moment of affection we had ever had together. It seems extraordinary that at his age he should be completely conscious of this and that our few weeks across three years together seem for him as well as for me to have been put outside all the very long periods of separation as though they have ripened as one full time – the time we are together. We went to the camera shop, where to my amazement the Rolleiflex which had been waiting there for two years, had been repaired. Then we went to a little restaurant where we dined after my arrival a year ago, and ate some fish. Then we went to the room at the Gainesville Hilton which always seems the same room with a balcony overlooking the lake which has trees all round it and a path fronting the edge in the hotel grounds and many birds, mostly gulls and cormorants at this time of year. Various people in the hotel and even in the street seemed to know me and some of them came up to say so. B made what I call a 'Bryanish' remark. He said: 'Everyone here seems to know you, from the lowest dishwasher to the highest ("most exalted", he says he said) desk-boy.' (As a matter of fact he made this remark a day later. There is a point to this.)

After lunch and putting my things in the hotel we drove fifty miles to B's trailer (which is 30 miles from his school) near the Sewanee River, and we took his miniature collie, Spot, for a walk. The country

---

1 Anthony Lombardy (b. 1954), American poet, one of Spender's star students at the University of Florida in 1976.

is flat with fields of stubbly grass, yellowish at this time of year, and firs, larch trees sometimes woods of them sometimes forming a screen of trees along the roadside. Through these driving past one has a flickering glimpse of cows in the fields, with the light brilliant on their flanks, as though seen through posts. Under the wide skies these glowing fields – burnished – reflect back the light like mirrors. There are a few little towns, shopping areas, filling stations, churches. B lives in a trailer, surprisingly large and comfortable really, bedroom living room and kitchen, a sofa and two or three chairs like a cabin. We drove to a camping area giving on to woods along the Sewanee River. Mango trees were swampy, very dense jungle-like. One tree, stripped of branches, a big S-shaped silver gleaming trunk rising up from the ground like modernist sculpture. Walking away from the river we almost lost sense of direction among the very dense trees. After feeding Spot we drove the 40 miles to Gainesville and dined at a Chinese restaurant. Saturday morning we bought cheese and wine for Joy Anderson's party that evening, and a barbecue party at B's trailer Sunday. I worked Saturday morning and B went out so as not to interrupt me, but otherwise we were only separated for an hour or so the whole weekend.

He said: 'You're different. You grin and show your teeth.' I did not tell him this was because Lizzie had made the dentist provide me with a new set because she thought the previous rather fang-like one made me look like Dracula – she said. Bryan too had changed. He has a beard now, just a fringe round his chin, leaving a small space below the mouth, thus emphasizing its lines, and the sensitive nostrils. With his pale green-grey shining eyes and dark-brown hair, he looks more than ever like a portrait of a young Frenchman by Manet: sensitive, alertly sensual, a firm and clear-cut but not very strong face, a hovering undeterminedness. He has grown a bit narcissistic – the result beards always seem to have – frequently looks at himself in the mirror. How unlike the days when he resented my photographing him and when I asked him why, said 'When they're developed you'll realize how homely I look.' I told him he was getting narcissistic. He said 'Yes.'

He told me that he felt very bad times were coming to America so he had rather changed his mind about being simply a zoologist and thought he would probably try to become a medical student. But for

50% of students chosen to study medicine there are another 50% equally qualified not chosen. He is never optimistic about his chances and seems lacking in confidence which is why I never realized he was a brilliant student.

We stopped at a filling station to get gas and there was a rather attractive-looking girl with blond hair falling forwards over a face with retroussé nose and slightly pouting lips. She was Christine, the girlfriend of Tom. B sees a lot of both of them and is rather fascinated by the nineteen-year-old Christine. He asked me what I thought of her appearance. I said I thought she was attractive. 'Do you think she is pretty?' he asked. I said yes. He said 'That's what I can't make up my mind about.' [. . .]

B's purpose this weekend was to show me his life – which I certainly wanted to see. To show me his trailer, the school where he teaches (but we missed out on this), his friends. [. . .] B also, as he told me, wanted to show me off to his friends. He has this candid wish, just as three years ago he took me to his home at Jacksonville to show me to his parents (his mother said 'my son loves you very dearly') and also brought his brother and girlfriend to see me. These encounters are very risky and make him very nervous, in fact they are a form of living dangerously.

On Saturday evening there was the party at Joy Anderson. Dick and Betty Eberhart, the Greens, and various other members of the department. B brought Tom and Christine. Jim Goldsmith also came. B, T, C and I formed a group rather separate from the rest – the young – while we formed another group of the old. B, T, C and I drank a lot and soon started misbehaving, I flirting outrageously with T, and C with B. B was very elated, and played back at her banter which was entirely of a sexual kind. She was not able to keep off this approach for one moment, even telling me that she 'liked tall men'. At first I was rather amused by this, because B looked so amazingly amused and vivid – I love his laughter. But, afterwards I began to get irritated because their act took up much too much of the space in the room. B came over and sat with the 'grown-ups' who were having a conversation about politics. Every single one of them seemed delighted to see America humiliated in various parts of the world.

9 March 1979, New York

A gap of nearly a month between the last entry and this, a month during which I've been to London and celebrated my 70th birthday.

The events of the evening at Joy's party have receded now. Yet they somehow marked a stage in our relationship. What happened was that, being drunk myself, and saying it was nearly midnight, I got up and said: 'I have to go home. Will someone find a taxi?' B was stunned. He said: 'You can't do this to me, Stephen. You know I'll take you back.' He said to J, 'May I speak to S alone a moment?' and we went into a side room. I said: 'But you can go home with Christine.' He said, 'You know I have no intention of doing so.' 'That's why I thought I'd get a taxi.' 'Well if you thought that you could have taken me aside quietly and told me so, instead of shouting for a taxi. You don't realize what you're doing to me.' I suddenly felt as if something irreparable had happened. What I had really done was blindly hit out against the trust there was between us. Bryan took me back to the Hilton. On the way he said, 'I realize now that I was terribly stupid.' His stupidity consisted of his introducing me to his friends, showing me his life, and showing me to them. What I remembered was the feelings I'd had three years ago when he'd lost the turquoise ring in my apartment. I was alone and started hunting for it. As I did so I realized how gentle and perceptive he'd always been with me. Incidents I still can't forget – at St Augustine, at Tallahassee, visiting his parents, his coming in at the end of classes to drive me back to my apartment, his grief and silence when we ran over the armadillo, the way he would act up to try and make me laugh then when I'd done so would burst into crowing triumphant laughter himself. So that sometimes we were just laughing at nothing but the joy of each other laughing – all that came back to me. However, he refused to make a thing of the scene which within two days had become 'that thing we shouldn't be self-indulgent about' because on the way to the airport when I left, I started telling him how I felt about it. He said he understood but if I thought about it, when I was alone, I must remember that I was being self-indulgent. In fact we seemed closer together this weekend than we'd ever been.

In this way he has of making things memorable, he said: 'We were only an hour apart this weekend. It was a weekend of firsts.' 'What firsts?' I asked. 'The first time we've gone shopping together, the first time you've been to my trailer and I've given a party for you and introduced you to my friends, the first time we've taken Spot for a walk together in the woods . . . .' He went on like this improvising firsts and I realized that what he was really doing was burying the one unhappy first which he knew I was still worrying about, under all these happy ones. We divide my knowing him into the pre- and post-moustache phases, pre-and post-Spot, and now pre- and post-beard. At the end, we were closer than we've ever been. Later he wrote something about our obsession with each other, our compulsive relationship. Judging by what I saw of his friends, I think that on his side there is a loneliness a lack of anyone to talk to except me, which these relationships make him realize – by comparing them with ours. This will probably go on until he leaves his present environment and meets people with whom he can really talk. One immense change is that he does talk so much now when we are together.

On the way to the airport, when I raised 'the subject we should not be self-indulgent about' I asked him when it was he realized that everything was OK between us. He said 'Oh, when I made that remark the next morning about how everyone in Gainesville from the lowest dish-washer to the highest desk-boy recognized you, and you laughed so much. Then I knew everything was OK.'

Nashville seems very faint compared with my life outside Nashville, especially as I sit here in the Buttinger apartment, looking out over N.Y.

London. Travelled February 23rd. The journey was very long because the TWA plane had to go to some outpost of America to get extra gas. There is a shortage of aviation fuel in N.Y.

I was very knocked out by this long journey and can't remember too much about Feb 24–27. Matthew and Maro came to London – also all Maro's Gorky and Phillips relations, because Magouche's marriage to Xan Fielding took place March 7 (but Matthew and Maro did not wait for this).[1] From the point of view of seeing Matthew the time was much too divided and distracted. Natasha

---

1 Magouche Phillips had married Alexander (Xan) Fielding (1918–1991), a soldier, writer and translator.

was very philosophic about this, though it must have brought back memories of Magouche's take-over of Matthew when he was sixteen and first in love with Maro.

I did quite a lot of work – the first week on my play, the second on an article 'Defence of Name Dropping' for the *Observer*, reviews for *N.Y. Times Book Review*, the *Observer* (Brecht's Journals), *Sunday Telegraph* (book about Fire Service). But the two weeks were dominated by social gatherings. My 70th birthday [28 February] at the Royal College of Art was really a great success wonderfully arranged by Natasha. About a hundred people came. Family – Humphrey, Christine, Philip, Jason Spender, Nancy Spender, Matthew, Maro and Maro's mother and sisters, Lizzie. Friends – the Berlins, the Glenconners, the Wollheims, the Gowings, Angus Wilson and Tony [Garrett], the Martyn Becketts, Anne Fleming (escorted by Pat Trevor-Roper), Lucian Freud, Dominique de Grunne, the Snowdons, Cyrus Ghani, Bill Coldstream, John and Myfanwy Piper, David and Nikos, Keith Milow, James Fox, Gareth Evans (with Antonia Phillips), the Longfords.[1] The rooms which consist of a large lounge, with bar, and a dining room large enough to seat everyone, proved excellent once they were full of people. Everyone could talk without being drowned in conversation. Philippe [de Rothschild] had provided Cadet Mouton claret which seems much better when it comes from him than from a shop. The food served up by the common room was excellent as was the service. The party would simply have been a noisy crush if we'd had it anywhere else, I think. The impression made was that everyone was fond of everyone else and delighted to meet. It was one of those reunions in which a lot of people present realize how long they've known each other, how little perhaps they've seen of one another, how glad they now are to do so. Natasha had arranged that

---

1 Martyn Beckett (1919–2001), British architect. Lawrence Gowing (1918–1991), British artist and curator; a member of the Euston Road School in the 1930s. Patrick Trevor-Roper (1916–2004) was Spender's occulist and an old friend. Dominique de Grunne (1913–2007), Belgian Roman Catholic priest who had met Spender in a Swiss hotel lounge while he was engaged in tutoring the sons of King Leopold III of Belgium during the king's exile in Switzerland. Cyrus Ghani, Iranian lawyer and scholar. Keith Milow (b. 1945), British artist. James Fox (b. 1942), journalist currently working on *White Mischief*, a book deriving from research initiated by Cyril Connolly. Gareth Evans (1946–1980), British philosopher of language who was shortly to marry Antonia Phillips.

four students from the R.C.M. [Royal College of Music] play a fanfare (from a Gabrielli piece) when the cake was brought in. During dinner I sat at a table with Isaiah, Aline and Cyrus Ghani. I kept on getting up nervously to see whether people at other tables had enough to drink so did not take in the conversation.

The Royal College people opened seventy bottles of Mouton Cadet. In addition to this there was champagne so we had twenty bottles of the claret left over and gave a drinks party on Sunday (March 4) to finish it. This was very nice also. Kingsley Amis, Elizabeth Jane Howard, Bill and Hetta Empson and their son Mogador and his wife, Matthew and Maro came. I took photographs. Bill Empson was beaming obviously very glad to get a knighthood.[1]

Before this, on Saturday we drove to Oxford, called on Stuart and Renée Hampshire in the morning then had lunch with the Berlins (Stuart also came). In the afternoon we drove to have dinner with the Pipers at Henley. He is working on stained glass windows for a new Cambridge College – Robinson College of which he showed us some designs.

I remember nothing of about what was said on Saturday. What I do remember very well was visiting Clifford Curzon at his wonderful house at Highgate overlooking the Heath on the following Wednesday for drinks. We had not seen Clifford for two or three years. I had not written him about the death of Lucille, his wife but Natasha had done so, because he spoke of this and apologized for not having answered.[2] He was in a rather nervous, yet very welcoming, gleaming and ardent condition. A lot of his conversation was a kind of talking aloud to himself in which he showed a charming and engaging candour. He said that when one hadn't seen friends for a long time, one wondered what reason one had ever had *for* seeing them. Now we sat in front of him, drinking sherry and eating macaroons. He seemed to recollect he did have good reason for seeing us. He apologized for not having written to thank Natasha for her wonderfully sympathetic letter, but it was very difficult to describe what it was like to accompany someone on that final journey, day after day, night after

---

1 As Spender notes, William Empson received a belated knighthood in 1979, aged 73.
2 Lucille Curzon had died in 1977.

night. But he gathered Natasha knew something about it from looking after her dying mother.

He went on talking about the past and said that he and I had been in Berlin at the same time though we had never met. We had common friends in Roger Sessions and Christopher Isherwood.[1] He said that the only occasion in his life in which he had actually fainted was with Christopher: who had taken him to some very smoke-filled *Bierhalle* (perhaps at Aschinger?) and then had proceeded to tell him about various forms of sexual perversion (I suppose got from Magnus Hirschfeld).[2] Suddenly he found himself lying on the floor and people unbuttoning his shirt collar.

He asked Natasha whether she found anything to admire in any living pianists. She tactfully brought him on to the subject of Schnabel.[3] He said that when Schnabel played he had made you forget the instrument and enter into a world of pure sound. [. . .] I left feeling very touched by Clifford. After all, he did tell one everything. Maybe a puritanical worker who respects in other people only work, but yet is a visionary of music, a totally dedicated artist and a highly perceptive and intelligent man. I wish I had known him better.

11 March 1979, New York

Went to Buttinger apartment. Dined with Bob Silvers, Grace Dudley.[4] Guests were Elizabeth Hardwick, Barbara Epstein, Bill Mazzocco, John Ashbery, David K. Very beautiful apartment in 550 Park Avenue. Grace looks statuesque, Junoesque. I sat next to her; we talked about the Dalmatian coast, Cartat, Mlini, Dubrovnik. There was some political talk, Bob saying that all the major conflicts in the world today were between Communist powers. Vietnam–Cambodia–China,

---

1 Roger Sessions (1896–1985), American composer.

2 Magnus Hirschfeld (1868–1935), German-Jewish doctor, sex researcher and gay rights advocate who was an important influence for Auden, Isherwood and Spender in Berlin in the 1930s.

3 Artur Schnabel (1882–1951), Austrian pianist.

4 Bob Silvers was living with Grace, Countess of Dudley, widow of the third Earl of Dudley.

China–Russia, South and North Yemen. Discussion of the origins of the First World War.

Bob Silvers said that the whole modern situation in which we lived, the collapse of the old regime began with the First World War, leading through the Russian Revolution. He didn't accept Marxist explanations of the origins of the war. Bill Mazzocco took a rather Marxist line. Even if – as Bob had argued – the war wasn't due to the breakdown of Capitalism – a major factor was imperialist rivalry, between the old colonial Empires and the latecomers – imperialist Germany. I said I agreed with this, but there was a strong fin-de-siècle psychology inclining to war. Feeling that Europe was decadent exhausted in need of re-birth. The war had been programmed by the imagination in a lot of pre-war literature. [. . .] Saturday. Bill Mazzocco and I lunched, at the Fleur du Lys, then we went for a walk in Central Park. [. . .] I told Bill I was keeping this Journal. 'Do you fictionalize it?' he asked. 'What do you mean?' 'Do you in describing, say, the party last night, take some person, or a fragment of dialogue, as the centre round which you make a kind of story?' I said my journal always seemed to me an effort of catching up with time, loaded with people and events, rushing past and I barely had the leisure to do more than write things down in order to keep up. We talked about casual sex. He said that he could see the point of people saying that total release of all their sexual inhibitions [was] the most important thing in life. He didn't agree though with those who said that all values would break down in a totally permissive society. He thought that if everything were permitted most people would impose their own restrictions on themselves simply by getting bored. [. . .]

Seated on a rock above where we were walking were two young people. From below their athletic bodies with the clothes almost drained of colour by the diffused black-and-white of the slightly misty, palely sun-lit afternoon, they looked a bit god-like, a boy and girl exhibited as youth. They stood up, revealing that they were wearing rucksacks. They were both boys.

As we watched the skaters (who skated surprisingly badly) I said, 'The kind of sex you're talking about is magic, the transformation scene. People who are living their routine lives in their routine world, wearing their routine clothes, go into a room and become the disporting nudes in a painting. To them everything is permitted.'

(Actually I didn't say this, but something much more clumsily put.) 'Having achieved the transformation in which they discover themselves as pleasure incarnate, it must be difficult to relate it to their routine lives.' (I did not say that either, but I did say: 'The definition of a vice is that it is an activity more interesting to the person who has it than anything else in his life.') I said that when I was young I was brought up in such an atmosphere of anything to do with sex being unmentionable that it was as though all the clothes of all the people in the world were a curtain. Behind this curtain were all their naked bodies – though some naked bodies, those of the old, for example, were not only unmentionable, they were unthinkable. Respectable elderly people must do things involving their nakedness like going to the lavatory etc, but I felt sure they did it without ever the use of the unmentionable parts of themselves becoming formulated as thoughts.

* * *

I have to speak on the Dick Cavett Show on Tuesday.[1] From some exploratory questions telephoned, it seems they may ask me about my religious views. I thought I would simply say I had none. By this I would mean I don't subscribe to any official religion, nor have I formulated for myself any private or personal religion. But simply to be negative about religion doesn't really cover my case, so in case I am asked I should write a few notes here.

I regard Christianity as poetic myth – whether or not it contains an increment of historic truth – which expresses very important truths about life. To me the most important part of its message is that humanity can only be saved by love, and inseparable from this is the fact that it will not be so saved on account of the innate selfishness of the individual, the group, the nation – quite apart from the fact that Christianity is not the universal religion. The crucifixion therefore expresses the truth that the truth is perpetually sacrificed.

Apart from this, I consider Christianity takes a too limited view of human potentiality. Despite the great achievements of Christian art, there is really no room for art in the Gospels.

I cannot accept dogmatic religion because dogma – though I see

---

1 American talk show, at this date going out late at night on ABC.

the necessity of it for some people – insists on treating poetic truth as literal truth. I see the arguments for doing so but I can't do so.

I believe that all living consists of systematizing sense impressions which we treat as real but which may well be illusions. The colours we see the sounds we hear the things we touch we apprehend through the medium of our senses. We can only think of them in terms of our senses, and our senses are subjective to us. We create the pattern of what we call reality. All life is lived fiction.

This being so, nevertheless we do believe that certain things are good beyond dispute. Love, and Truth. Truth is the extreme obligation imposed on us because even if there were no other values we believed in, it is impossible to imagine that we would not feel that as conscious sentient beings, the luminous points of awareness in which the universe itself becomes self-aware, it is our duty to attain the utmost consciousness.

Finally I agree with the passage in Proust in which the narrator says that we lead this life as though the obligation of another life were imposed upon us – another life the aims of which are truth and beauty so that a painter[,] so little eager for fame in his time that we are scarcely certain in the attribution of his name to his pictures, can devote unending time to painting the exact yellow of a wall in a picture of his native city.[1]

---

1 Spender refers to the passage in Proust where the writer Bergotte sees Vermeer's *View of Delft* in an exhibition and admires 'a little patch of yellow wall' and reflects that this is how he should have written his own books: 'My last books are too dry, I ought to have gone over them with a few layers of colour, made my language precious in itself, like this little patch of yellow wall.' The narrator reflects that 'all that we can say is that everything is arranged in this life as though we entered it carrying a burden of obligations contracted in a former life; there is no reason inherent in the conditions of life on this earth that can make us consider ourselves obliged to do good, to be kind and thoughtful, even to be polite, nor for the atheist artist to consider himself obliged to begin over again a score of times a piece of work the admiration aroused by which will matter little to his worm-eaten body, like the patch of yellow wall painted with so much skill and refinement by an artist destined to be for ever unknown and barely identified under the name Vermeer'. (*The Captive*, translated by C. K. Scott Moncrieff and Terence Kilmartin (London: Vintage, 2000), p. 208.)

In March, Spender went on a short holiday to New Orleans with Bryan Obst.

23 March 1979, New Orleans

The touristic centre of New Orleans is the French Section: about ten streets crossing ten other streets. The main street – Bourbon – is very crowded and also except at certain hours when it is shut off jammed with traffic. There are a lot of bars and shows much advertising their nudity. Dear old American ladies queue up in lines in order to go into a strip show. The whole thing is commercialized to such an extent that even the most exotic entertainment – all crammed into this small area which is the most French in America and architecturally one of the most curious – seems captive, tamed, like the booths of a funfair or circus. Nevertheless the dancing in some of the discos is exciting. The floor gets very crowded with people, each of whom is mainly occupied in doing his or her 'thing' curiously self-absorbed; but occasionally roused enough – with head bent and pumping arms – to react to the approach of another dancer in a ritualistic way, impersonal almost as in a fish tank a prawn might vaguely shift position as if to acknowledge the presence of another prawn. The dancing is not as exciting as it was when I saw it four years ago when many dancers seemed virtuosi. Today it is more like a spontaneous expression by individual dancers of their rhythm. The music seems to have got still noisier. The tunes are secondary to the percussive rhythms which are so loud that accompanied by the flashes of the strobe lighting, one has the impression of being inside the cylinder of a machine in which pistons are pounding and there are explosions caused by ignition. The strobe flashes can produce effects like lightning in which a scene of people raising fists at the sky or shaking legs can instantaneously be cut out – silhouetted for the instant of a vivid flash. When these are repeated over a few minutes with the flashing and the silhouetting every second, accompanied by the percussive band and the shrieking singers the effect is of a jerky film sequence, or of very rapid and frequent lightning illuminating jack-in-the-box figures jumping from darkness.

24 March 1979, New Orleans

Almost the first person I met in the street yesterday afternoon after arriving was Allen Ginsberg who seemed tremendously pleased at the meeting. He told me he was attending some symposium on meditation at Tulane College, also giving a reading to some group. The results of meeting him were fairly electrifying. Firstly, I was invited to lunch with the sister of Peggy Guggenheim, a Mrs McKinley.[1] She also invited B[ryan]. We all met up with Allen Ginsberg and his friend of very long standing – Peter Orlovsky who looks like a portrait by Géricault of one of the lunatics of the French Revolution – though in a rather passive phase.[2] We went in a taxi to the Garden Quarter part of N[ew] O[rleans] where Mrs McKinley lives (perhaps it was because Peggy lives in Venice that I kept on thinking of Venice all this weekend). Mrs M. has a charming spacious house, full of paintings by her husband (one of three or four) who was a painter, and various other painters equally Twenties-ish in their watery surrealism, combined with a look of being illustrations in a book of fashions. There was also some more primitive art, either by children or by Haitians. Mrs M. had a grand air of vagueness, large soft fleshiness, untidy hair, wandering blue eyes, a soft voice which uttered sentences that all seemed sections of some great rambling, free-associating autobiographical interior monologue. She knew everyone I almost knew – the figures of the Twenties. She talked of husbands who painted or didn't paint, who were killed in the war or some accident, or who survived to be divorced, also children who seemed to have been conceived, born and brought up within the surround of some great tapestry which is her life. The luncheon arrangements were odd. There were two little tables placed at the end of her sofa on which she reclined throughout lunch because, she explained, after some operation, the doctor had told her she must eat lying down. This rather excited Ginsberg – 'Do you mean the food has to pass horizontally?' etc. I found it more and more difficult as lunch went on to understand what Mrs M. was saying. I couldn't bring myself to say

---

1 Hazel Guggenheim McKinley (1903–1995), American artist, art collector and dealer.

2 Peter Orlovsky (b. 1933), American poet, long-term partner of Allen Ginsburg until 1987.

anything to Orlovsky. Bryan entered into conversation with Allen but as a scientist he was irritated with Allen's brand of mysticism. Later he said to me 'Of course I see that meditation is an aid to thinking, but there are other ways of doing this – just thinking, for example.' [. . .]

After lunch Ginsberg asked me whether I had ever heard his music for Blake's Songs. I said No but Auden had told me they were good. G. said rather sharply 'Did he? Are you sure of that?' I said 'Yes,' remembering that A. had actually said they were better than he expected. G. unpacking a bag which contained a keyboard harmonium said 'Well, he refused to hear them. As soon as I started to sing one, he said, "Won't you please stop? Hearing people sing songs they've composed embarrasses me terribly. I can't bear it."' After this Allen sang us 'Little Lamb who made Thee?', 'Tyger, Tyger' and at least six more. They were a bit like hymn tunes, but they retained something of the language, making one attend to it. Auden was right.

After this the cook-waiter changed roles once again and became chauffeur, driving us to our hotels. As we drove back Ginsberg started questioning him. We had heard at lunch from Mrs M. that the waiter had been a seminarist. G. asked him about this. He answered that he had trained to be a priest. 'Does that mean you believe in God?' asked Allen. 'Oh yes, I do believe,' answered the youth rather smugly. Ginsberg then went into an explanation of his own religion which did not seem necessarily to involve believing in God. I remarked that in some religions ritual was more important than believing in God. Ginsberg said the basis of his religion was meditation, [neither] ritual, nor belief. After more of this, they started asking the waiter-chauffeur where to go in the evening. At this he underwent a further change from religious into someone with the manner of a Drag Queen. 'Oh,' he cried with a joyousness which was like the swoop of a solo instrument from the solemn Adagio of a slow movement to a Vivace finale. 'You must go to Jules. Not just to the front room but the back room. And most of all to the Men's Room where *everything* is permitted.' He went on in this vein.

29 March 1979, New Orleans

Literary conference at Vanderbilt. The speakers coming from outside were Helen Vendler, critic, Wallace Stegner, novelist and Robert Pinsky, poet.[1] Helen Vendler, stoutish, pale rather transparent complexion, rimless spectacles which look like pince-nez seems like a governess in a Russian play. Of course I found her immediately attractive was longing to appear the good boy to her, at the same time to confess all my sins. Wallace Stegner with cropped white hair, square, solid appearance was a sympathetic figure. Unfortunately the extract he read from his new novel was very soporific made the more so by the monotonous reading on Wednesday. Of the two readers, Pinsky was far the livelier; in fact he gave a very good reading of his poems. Their merit is an accuracy of observation which can be breathtaking and at times (as in a long passage which was a rendering of a poem by Horace) movingly beautiful. Unfortunately the material – familial feelings mostly – is prosaic. The excellence of the reading emphasized this.

31 March 1979, New Orleans (midnight)

Was rung today by a highly eccentric rich lady calling herself Mildred Mountjoy (she is a friend of Mrs Lerman). She asked me to dinner and, out of curiosity, I accepted. She turned up at 6.30 and drove me to her immense sumptuously furnished but rather disordered-looking mansion. She prattled en route about her preoccupation with the Life Beyond (she is – almost – a medium), her friendship with various young-middle-aged Englishmen (bisexual – for who, unless bisexual, would care for an old lady like me?), all the cities she visited, Paris, London, Rome, Venice, and soon – she hopes – Jerusalem. She showed signs of considerable snobbishness. Whatever her age, she is quite pretty, fresh-complexioned with bobbed hair, retroussé nose,

---

1 Helen Vendler (b. 1933), American literary critic who has published on Keats, Shakespeare and Emily Dickinson, among others. Wallace Stegner (1909–1993), novelist, environmentalist and professor, who had founded the Creative Writing Program at Stanford University in 1964. Robert Pinsky (b. 1940), poet who had won the Wallace Stegner Felllowship in Creative Writing at Stanford in 1964.

pleasant features. When we got to her home we found her husband – a large, flabby man, like a huge flatfish – extending from an armchair his legs over a table. The TV was blazing away – one moment about atomic leakage in Pennsylvania – the next proclaiming the merits of a detergent – then showing us Mrs Thatcher receiving the news that a Conservative MP had been shot by the I.R.A., and wagging a finger while saying, 'No, no we must never give way.'[1] The husband did not move from his chair nor turn off the TV for some moments, at the end of which he said to me in sonorous tones: 'Greatly as I appreciate the idea of it poetry has never come my way and now I do not anticipate that it ever will do so.' He expanded a bit on this theme – how he had ignored poetry at school – though he suspected it was a phase some people went through at that period of their lives and then passed beyond, etc.

We went in to dinner which was laid out with gold knives, forks, spoons, and for each of us a golden goblet. Mildred Mountjoy and her husband talked at cross purposes throughout the meal – florid examples of marital non-communication. Husband returned to subject of poetry, comparing it – or, rather, asking, how could it be compared – with curative activities, which he said preoccupied him. 'At hospital,' he asked, 'ten minutes after a patient has expired under the knife and we ask ourselves whether we couldn't have done anything whereby the patient would still be living – where does poetry come in?' I saw him now as the Healer – one of those referred to in *The Fall of Hyperion* – and said that a poet called Keats who had himself – in the horrible condition of operating theatres in 1818 [–] been a medical student had concerned himself with this question – felt that the healer was superior to the poet – and the poet only justified in being

---

1 Airey Neave (1916–1979), Shadow Northern Ireland Secretary, was killed by an IRA bomb, leaving Westminster, on 30 March. Neave had been a close advisor to Margaret Thatcher, who was at this date head of the Conservative Party and would become Prime Minister later in the year. The Provisional IRA (Irish Republican Army) had formed in 1969, after splitting from the Marxist wing of the Irish Republican Party, who were willing to cooperate with the predominantly Unionist government in bargaining for increased civil rights for the Catholics of Northern Ireland, Throughout the 1970s, the Provisional IRA instrumented sporadic violence and bombing campaigns against the British-run Northern Irish state, in a bid to increase pressure on Britain to withdraw from Northern Ireland and implement the collapse of the Unionist state.

a poet if he could absorb into his imagination, and thus transcend, the real suffering of humanity. Like a sop to Cerberus this seemed to silence him for a time. I followed up with questions about architecture (his wife had told me he was – or had been – an architect). We got onto a discussion of architecture in Chicago – [Louis] Sullivan – Frank Lloyd Wright.[1] I mentioned that Wright had wanted to build a skyscraper a half mile high on the lake front. 'A mile high,' my host corrected and then launched into a very long disquisition into the difficulties of building a building a mile high. It would have 500 storeys; an elevator would take ten minutes to get to the 500th floor and would therefore have to have seats in it (and – for Americans – amusements like TV or short movies); it would require enormous voltage to illuminate the top floor; problems of wiring would be immense; the top of the building would have to consist of a pipe at least thirty feet in diameter; if someone went to the Rest Room on the 500th floor, by the time his load reached the bottom floor it would have attained the velocity of gravity unless a system of brakes was introduced to prevent its doing so. There was much much more than this. He went on and on as though he were providing his firm's inventory of all the skyscraper's requirements. I quite enjoyed all this – while his wife went on twittering about 'Spiritism' at her end of the table (at one point he broke off sharply to ask her how she distinguished between 'Spiritualism' and 'Spiritism'. He did not wait for her answer). After coffee we went into the drawing room. He started up again with renewed force about poetry. 'Now tell me. Whatever would make someone decide to be a poet? Would he wake up one morning and say "I am going to be a poet"? Would he say when all his contemporaries were deciding to go into the professions "My profession is going to be poetry"? Would he say "The most useful thing I can do in the world is to be a poet"?' Suddenly I felt completely fed up with this insolent baiting, got up and said as abruptly and emphatically as I could manage: 'I have to leave.' Then as I left the room, noticing that he seemed completely to disregard this, I said

---

1 Louis Sullivan (1856–1924), architect and a prominent member of the Chicago School of Architecture. His designs put an emphasis on both functionality and form. Sullivan mentored Frank Lloyd Wright (1867–1959), a fellow architect. Under the guidance of Sullivan, Wright formed the Prairie School, which placed emphasis on organic design.

loudly: 'I hope we never meet again.' Oddly he seemed to take this as though it were the kind of thing that had often been said to him before. Nor did Mildred Cowan [*sic*] seem particularly disconcerted. She ran out of the room after me and drove me back to this morgue I live in, absolutely overwhelming me with the kindest offers as she did so. She said she'd already left her husband twice and saw as little of him as possible, could she drive me to the airport tomorrow and fetch Natasha, well, if I didn't want that, could she telephone us Monday and take us anywhere we pleased then or at any other time. I didn't regret my rudeness to her husband. Anyway, perhaps all I was doing was to behave as madly as my host and hostess.

11 April 1979, Kentucky, 5 a.m.

My lecture. This was better than the one I gave at Indianapolis but I had the same sensation of not being in touch with the audience, of feeling and looking frightfully unhappy. [. . .] After lecture one of those faculty parties with a few students. This was boring apart from a conversation with one man who seemed to have lived through the Thirties in America, and who told me how excited he had been about the Russian Revolution and, later, Trotsky's history of it. He asked me about attacks by [George] Watson in *Encounter* and someone else in *Commentary* on the Thirties generation for being deeply implicated in the violence of the time, backing Communist violence etc.[1] I said I couldn't really read these attacks because I remembered how we felt at the time. It was always possible to take isolated statements to say we backed violence. But in a war or revolutionary situation all this means is that – unless you are pacifist – you back your own side. E.g. to back Israel or for that matter Islam today is to back violence – whether or not one likes the idea. Similar quotations could be made from Yeats, Pound, Wyndham Lewis or Eliot to show they backed violence. But these were no more men of violence than were we. Someone asked me whether I really liked Wystan? This was a disconcerting question because it seemed to imply that I had drawn a picture of him which was unsympathetic. Thinking it over, I can see that

---

1 George Watson, 'The Idea of Liberalism', *Encounter*, November 1978. Spender did not generally read the magazine he had left ten years earlier.

I may have partly done so. I described him seeing his friends one by one in his rooms at hours he had fixed and interviewing, cross-examining them. Laying down the law about the poets of whom he approved, the way poetry should be written, the personality of the poet, being very dogmatic about everything. I did insist that he was not a 'leader' or authoritarian and that he brought a touch of absurdity to his pronouncements which made them seem jokes. He did not wish to be taken altogether seriously. But this would mean nothing to a member of the audience without a sense of humour. In fact to the American who thinks that when one is serious one should be serious, and when funny un-serious, this would make Auden seem even more unsympathetic. But during sleepless patches of the night I asked myself a question I certainly didn't ask at the time – did I really like Wystan? To attempt to answer the question I have to recall what Wystan thought of me. He thought I was a wild romantic, rather 'mad' (using that word rather loosely). To him I was I suppose a kind of Dostoyevskian Holy Fool. I was so tall, he once told me, because I wanted to reach heaven ('the heaven-reachers') I wanted really to be a saint.[1] References to me in *Paid on Both Sides* and the original version of *The Orators* bear this out.[2] He was so contemptuous of my pamphlet *Nine Experiments* (which certainly was very bad) that when this was reported back to me (of course, by Gabriel Carritt) I destroyed every copy of it I could retrieve from friends.[3] On the other

---

1 cf. *The Temple* ('English Prelude'): Simon Wilmot (Auden) to Paul Schoner (Spender), of Schoner and his lover: 'You're both Heaven Reachers. That is why you are so tall. You want to get away from your balls.'

2 Auden's *Paid on Both Sides: A Charade* (1930) includes a character called Stephen (the actor doubles with the lesser character The Doctor's Boy). Stephen appears briefly at the beginning of the charade and George, another character, calls for him to be put to bed because he is 'tight'. The 1932 version of *The Orators* was dedicated to Stephen Spender: 'To Stephen Spender: Private faces in public places / Are wiser and nicer / Than public faces in private places'. Spender is also mentioned in Ode I of the Six Odes: 'Out of the reeds like a fowl jumped the undressed German, / And Stephen signalled from the sand dunes like a wooden madman / "Destroy this temple".'

3 *Nine Experiments* was a selection of Spender's own poetry and was one of two pamphlets printed by Spender on a hand press in 1928, while he was still a student at Oxford. The other, more successful, pamphlet was the first publication of Auden's early poetry.

hand, there was something about my utter vulnerability and open-ness which he respected. When I first knew him and told him about my plans for writing (which included writing novels etc) he said: 'We must save you for poetry' and I was instantly member of an elite which was headed by Auden and Isherwood, but included Day Lewis, Rex Warner and very few others. He said 'You will be a poet because you will always be humiliated,' and he felt that I had a kind of truth ('blurting out the truth' – Isherwood). I imagine he laughed at me a lot behind my back. He also regarded me as a bit paranoid (which I was, and am). So to measure my account of Auden I have to consider myself as a somewhat battered observer. To be totally honest now, I should ask whether Auden was not a bit envious of me because I had a large penis. He was certainly affected by this and mentioned it mockingly on many occasions. He explained my attraction for cer-tain women as due to this. 'How could they possibly know?' I asked once. He looked down his nose with his sly boyish expression and said 'They do.' The lady who asked me whether I liked Auden said I had made him sound a bit inhuman. This does ring a bell because I do remember thinking of him as *sui generis* not at all like other peo-ple and of an inhuman cleverness. I did not think of him as having human feelings and I felt about his early poetry a lack of a personal 'I' at the centre of it. If you appealed to Auden for sympathy or help he would be attentive, kind even generous, but like a benevolent doc-tor or psychoanalyst, whose task it was to provide a diagnosis and prescribe treatment, not of a friend who empathized entered into your situation as though it were his own. He seemed also to me to have this detached 'clinical' attitude towards himself, and this is borne out by some early poems. A poem called 'The Letter' is about the poet (who is walking through a showery countryside) sheltering behind a wall and reading a letter from someone with whom he is in love.[1] The contents of the letter are summoned up in a line, 'Speaking

---

1 'From the very first coming down' was one of the 1928 poems first printed by Spender:

> Shall see, shall pass, as we have seen
> The swallow on the tile, Spring's green
> Preliminary shiver, passed
> A solitary truck, the last
> Of shunting in the Autumn. But now

of much but not to come.' The reader scarcely feels the emotion here implied because the poet is so busy using this situation as a centre around which he arranges his poetry.

24 April 1979, Nashville

Natasha has been and gone. The visit was really a disaster, almost unqualified, and this was partly quite blatantly my fault, partly more subtly my fault, due to my being what I am. Natasha was anyway in one of those moods when the fact that I was in the midst of working and coping with people here made her feel excluded, as she does nearly always with Matthew, and often though not always with Lizzie. *But* I did the awful thing which was to telephone B[ryan] when she was in the apartment, saying very loving things to him. The telephone was actually two rooms away from our bedroom in which she was lying down. I completely failed to realize that the air-conditioning pipe or passage conveys all sound from one bedroom to the other in this apartment. When I went into the bedroom and she was crying I did not realize that she had overheard my side of our conversation. She was crying and when I asked her why she said 'It's always the same. I come to be with you and I find you have made your own life and are completely absorbed in it, and in love with someone.' (I'm not sure whether she said the last few words, but that was what she meant.) I tried to explain that B was a student I was concerned with. That was not the point, she objected. The point was not the person but the situation which she always came back to. I said: 'Remember I am seventy.' 'What has that to do with it?' she asked. I somehow feel that it does have something to do with it, but I could not explain except in terms of dotage. Yet if dotage is indeed part of it, the fact is that B is nevertheless different from anyone else, the polar opposite of youth gently answering the call of my dotage. I

    To interrupt the homely brow,
    Thought warmed to evening through and through
    Your letter comes, speaking as you,
    Speaking of much but not to come.

(quoted thus from *The English Auden*, ed. Mendelson (1977), as 'VII' of 'Poems 1927–1931'.)

certainly feel the force of N and her sense of a situation. She said nothing about the fact that she had overheard the telephone conversation and I believed it was impossible she could have done so and that her behaviour was somehow due to an intuitive realization of what I had done. The incomprehensible result of my not knowing (her not telling me) was that I repeated the offence a week later in the course of an overheard conversation to Christopher who asked me 'How is Bryan?' and I told him quite lyrically how happy I had been in this relationship. And it is a relationship of between a week and ten days in a year – that is all I see of B and yet it spoils everything for N and that, I see, is destroying the relationship with B.

Natasha went to Charleston and Savannah with Doreen Davie. She really did enjoy this, I think. I had arranged all these days to try and please her – but of course I know that is nothing in her scale of feelings. Someone wants something she does not get, and what else is there but the occasional distraction from incessant remembering of what she wants. While she was in Charleston and Savannah I went to Indianapolis – a desolate desolating place.

14 May 1979, New York

These three days at Gainesville seem to have gone as soon as they started, are already like a dent almost in memory. Yet they were entirely happy, without a shadow on them. B[ryan] met me on Wednesday at 6:31. We went to Hilton Hotel deposited my things there. Then we had dinner at the Fox (something or other) Restaurant. Two years ago this was excellent and expensive now it is merely expensive. My impression that evening of B is that he was tired and rather unwell. I thought perhaps the disappointment of not getting into graduate school had upset him more than I'd realized or than he would tell me. We did not talk about this. I did not want to start our short time together with discussion of career business. We went to the movie *Manhattan* (B had already been to this as he had also to *The Deer Hunter* which we went to the following night).[1]

Manhattan, a marvellous movie really, above all for the very

---

1 *Manhattan* (directed by Woody Allen, 1979); *The Deer Hunter* (directed by Michael Cimino, 1978).

closely observed dialogue, the beautiful acting, the stunning photography. The sentimental story-line perhaps a bit weak. We went back to the hotel and slept almost as soon as we got into our beds. Next morning (Thursday) B got up at six to drive the forty miles to his school. His car has the troubles his last car also had: that the radiator gets over-hot, this time because it leaks. He has to refill the radiator every twenty-five miles or so. I worked at Venice Essay all the morning. Took Joy out to lunch. [. . .]

At three Tony Lombardy came to the hotel. He looked very well. Is earning money by doing haulage of some kind – loading and unloading trucks. Had new poems with him but says he is not writing much. Is going during the summer to learn Ancient Greek at some intensive course in Manhattan. We lay side by side on *chaise longues* by the pool of the Hilton. In order to prove that my play really existed I showed him the 120 typed up pages. He began reading bits of it. From time to time he commented on the style suggesting things. He is an extremely meticulous critic, a very close student of language.

B joined us, returning from school at 6:30 or so. He looked surprisingly better than he had done the previous evening. We all had dinner, at a Chinese restaurant. B and T got on very well which made me happy, because for many reasons one might expect them to dislike each other (B is slightly jealous of T). Tony talked amusingly about his political ambitions when he was a student. Looking at him, one would immediately think of him as someone – with his good looks, his dark eyes with their smiling but slightly withholding expression – as wearing a dinner jacket or tails and being that year's Rhodes Scholar who becomes President of the Oxford Union. But he is loading, or unloading trucks, and writing poetry. B and I both felt that some kind of veil had fallen from him and that he showed an affection which he had never quite done before. He lingered with us and we all had dinner at a Chinese restaurant. Then he left to drive back all the way to Orlando. B and I went to *The Deer Hunter*.

Friday morning we started out a bit late for all sorts of chores. We tried above all to get the car's overheating radio fixed but the garagist said he could not guarantee to get it done on Friday – today – and then there was no work over the weekend. So we drove to B's trailer, stopping to fill up with water from time to time en route. Usually having to deal with machines oppresses B and one feels how he resents everything mechanical. But today it did not interrupt his flow of conversation. When he talks he does so very clearly. For example, he summed up for me articles he'd been reading about how to compensate for loss of memory, which he thought might interest me. We discussed his graduate school possibilities – that he might go to New Mexico somewhere – a college only – I think – where he could study tropical birds or whether he would go on teaching, as the headmaster had asked him to do. At first he had been very much against this, but now perhaps he thought he might stay on till the end of the year (obviously he is a very good teacher, and far more involved in the school than he himself realizes). Then he fantasized. 'Of course I see it all laid out. I go on teaching in order to pay the rent and because I have to get a new car. Then at the end of the year there are other payments. I can't find anything else to do so I go on teaching. Then perhaps in order to continue even in that, I have to take a teacher's diploma. So when I'm forty here I'll be still teaching school.' He said this in order to analyse the situation he *wouldn't* fall into. But there was fear in his voice and he was really saying what, with variations, thousands of young Americans today (even if they do graduate work) are thinking about their future. He said his parents have already accepted the idea that if he doesn't go to graduate school, he will spend much more time with them in Jacksonville. The fact is that ever since his schooldays he has distinguished himself from his family, passing every examination easily. They and he have accepted this almost as a matter of course. But now what faces him is the prospect of perhaps simply being one of the family – his father a machinist in a coffee factory, his mother manageress of a condominium, his brother a mixture of garagist, pawn-broker and ne'er do well who lives at home so as to save himself the money which he spends on girls. We talked a bit about his family which comes, on his father's side, from Milwaukee, and then from Danzig. They are anti-Polish and anti-Semitic. Bryan said he thought there might be Polish blood somewhere. That when at school he had been regarded by the other boys as Jewish. He also mentioned for the first time in our three years' friendship his acne. We were eating a cherry and brandy chocolate. He said he didn't much like chocolate. That when at school when his acne erupted badly, this was always blamed by his family onto something he had done – eaten chocolate for example. I said: 'You must have suffered a lot on account of your acne.' 'I did,' he said.

'Realizing that when I first knew you was one reason I loved you,' I said. 'Why?' he asked. But I could not really explain.

We went to the trailer, fetched Spot, drove to a spring, which was in a public park. The weather was thundery, and the few people bathing in the spring were hastily dressing and departed almost at once on our arrival. The park was completely deserted. The trees and grass were that kind of livid green against dramatically black and white cloudscape which comes with thundery weather. We walked along the duckboard along the side of a creek leading from the spring towards the open water. I took a lot of photographs out of my passion to record this moment which almost destroys the moment. After a bit, B said gently: 'Haven't you taken enough?' I apologized. 'I know it's an awful bore for you.' He said: 'No I was thinking of you. I was afraid you put yourself outside the time we're in by taking pictures of it.' I said, if not then later that day: 'How is it possible you can be so perceptive and intelligent and affectionate.' He hesitated a moment and then said lightly: 'I expect it's because I looked at TV so much when I was a child.'

He started talking about a bird there was here, the yellowiest bird anywhere, he said, a bird which seemed made of gold. Then he stood still and started whistling – very softly – like whistling under his breath. Birds appeared from everywhere. He seemed himself like one of them whistling to them and them to him. He talked about living in the trailer and how beautiful the country was there, and mentioned the names of all the animals. I suddenly felt that perhaps despite the considerable hardness and loneliness of his life – he might be happier in the trailer than he realized. Not that he considers himself unhappy. He just has very real reasons for some anxiety.

When we returned to the spring there was a great patch of yellow floating leaves – clusters of which drifted off from the mass – in eddies and circles – which covered about half of the transparent blue water below which long weeds were pulled by the current into dynamic moving lines like whip-lash. Shadowy shapes of fish darted above and below the weeds.

We both felt this was one of our happiest times. It had made our three days. That evening bearing wine and cheese we went to a party at Joy's. There was no one really interesting there. A birthday party for children was being run in tandem with the grown-up party. As soon as we'd unpacked the Stilton and Brie we'd bought and put them on a table, these seven children made a dash for them, covering biscuits with messes of cheese. The grown-up party consisted of one line sentences of disconnected conversation like that in *Manhattan*. I wish I could remember even one of the lines. Dinner consisted of a large fish called Sheep's Head, eaten using knees as tables. After eating, Joy said 'Come out onto the porch'. We went out; she stumbled on the boards which were wet. We picked her up and put her on her bed where she remained the rest of the evening. She had fractured her shoulder. She was extremely brave about this and seemed almost to take it for granted.

Next morning we went to the airport. B said 'Before we leave let's take a stroll by the lake.' I realized he wanted this because we had always done so. Once during the weekend we went to a restaurant and he walked straight to a table where we sat. 'This is where we were two years ago,' he said. At the airport before I boarded the plane, he said, 'Let's sit and talk for a little on this bench,' pointing to a place in the airport lounge – and I realized it was where we had sat and talked three months ago. But there was not time now. The flight was called. I think he was nearly in tears. I realized that, whereas he had had to teach Thursday, he had nothing to do Saturday and Sunday and we could (had I not made long-standing arrangements in New York) have passed it together. Somehow Saturday was ours by rights.

He says I tend to make more of things than there is in them really. And perhaps this is an example. But even if I make too much of them, these are things. This Saturday was like an empty hole, a slate that should have been filled by us. The difference between us is that he would accept this, but think it self-indulgent to suffer on that account. I have that feeling of a void that is irreparable. But voids do get filled up.

On the aeroplane I had more than ever the feeling that I had got out of the plane only to say goodbye. And yet this very feeling is what gives our meetings their timelessness. Thinking about each other, remembering every little thing, which becomes symbolic, always being happy and in holiday mood when we meet, considering the perfection of our affection for one another the norm – rather than the exception – that is our whole relationship. And in its very unreality it reflects the real situation – that I am 70 and he is 22. This only permits of days that are miraculous, not of long times together.

[489]

25 May 1979, New York

On Monday Camilla [McGrath] gave a luncheon to which I invited Bill Mazzocco. Anita Loos dressed very elegantly and wearing bangles and large round gold-rimmed spectacles was there.[1] She told me she is writing a book about Hollywood – the great period when Stravinsky, Aldous Huxley, Charlie Chaplin, Christopher Isherwood were all there. She is 89, I believe. The same night I gave the dinner I seem to give annually at the Coffee Club. Bob Silvers, Barbara Epstein, the Russells, Susan Sontag, Anne Moynihan, Mark Lancaster.[2] Neither the ambiance nor the meal seemed to me up to what they had been in past years. Nor did I think the evening went very well. Susan had just flown from Japan, and, naturally enough, was tired. As she has made a sensational recovery from cancer, her not being up to scratch slightly depressed everyone. I talked a bit about photography and movies with her. Her views are very forceful and she seems to have made up her mind about most things and already expressed her views in her books or articles. So I was hardly surprised when she told me that all movies today (*Manhattan* and *The Deerhunter*) are garbage – Well, I could not really contest this.

3 June 1979, London

Went to Much Hadham to Henry Moore's. He and Irina were alone. He was extremely lively, rubicund, a bit shrunk perhaps. He is 80. She, as usual, remained mostly in the background, but sometimes talked as it were [in] parallel and not across him, with Natasha, about her great interest, flowers. Everything with the Moores has expanded. The garden seemed fuller of trees, hedgerows, a herbaceous border, a goldfish pond, two small greenhouses, one for orchids. Perhaps some of these things were there before but they had grown. Henry's side of things had grown still more. There is the

---

1 Anita Loos (1888–1981), the American screenwriter responsible for *Gentlemen Prefer Blondes* (1928) and *The Women* (1939).

2 In 1975, John Russell had married the art historian and lecturer Rosamond Bernier. Susan Sontag (1933–2004), American writer and philosopher. Mark Lancaster (b. 1938), British artist, former assistant to artist Jasper Johns, at this date resident in New York.

Henry Moore Foundation in a house next to where he lives, on his property, three storeys of it, containing files, archives, drawings in folders and some framed on walls; photographs, books.

Henry has become an institution and he thrives on it, radiating happiness which Irina reflects. He is eighty, and, since we talked quite a bit about the dead and the decrepit – Herbert Read, Gregory, Philip Hendy, Kenneth Clark, – it is strange that a life so visibly at the end should so obviously illustrate a happy ending.[1] He talked much more than usual – about his childhood and what a marvellous man his father was – had read the whole of Shakespeare, played classical music on the gramophone, wanted Henry to learn the violin (H. hated this. When he failed his entrance exam to the secondary school he said: 'Dad, I failed because I have to do so many violin lessons, I can't study'). He and Irina talked about the incredible amount of work H.'s mother – a miner's wife – with seven children, had to do. How his father could get angry if everything was not right. He obviously feels that his father in different circumstances would have been famous. Was a friend of —— Smith the miners' leader.

H. talked about the war, how he was the youngest soldier in his regiment – only 18. The first night the other soldiers – for the fun – gave him all their rum and made him drunk. How he wanted to be a hero, win a medal. At first little happened in the way of fighting, then at Cambrai aeroplanes flew over. He asked the commander for permission to fire at them. Stood in a field doing so – of course hit nothing – 'It was as though the wall of this house flew over and you had to hit one brick in it.' On another occasion he went out with a sergeant and lay in a hole on look-out. The sergeant got dead drunk but got a medal. Henry's heroism went unrecognized.

He said a theory about his work which struck me as true for me of mine. 'I go by pleasing and not pleasing.' That is to say when he works he knows instinctively what he does right and what wrong, and proceeds on the basis of correcting what is wrong. He showed us the H.M. Foundation and gave me one of the portfolios of etchings 'The Reclining Figure' for which I wrote an introductory poem 'Sculptor and Statues'. Showed us the studio which contains

---

1 Eric Craven Gregory (1897–1959), Yorkshire patron of arts, early supporter of Henry Moore.

maquettes and various works from the past which are being dealt with for some reason or other and works in progress. His age shows in a kind of sagging of the forms in the sculpture a blurring of the line in drawings, etchings, lithos etc. He is also repetitious. But when he has a new idea, as in working a bronze of 3 figures which are modelled from the small Cezanne of 3 women in a landscape which he owns, he still seems completely in control of what he is doing. Also in perfectly straightforward drawings of hands, animals, trees.

After this little tour we went back to his sitting room. He got rather tipsy on three whiskeys. He talked a lot again. About how his great early aesthetic experiences had not been of sculpture, but of literature. The first novels he read were by [Walter] Scott. He had not cared much about Dickens. Later had read Tolstoy, Flaubert, Stendhal. Could not imagine anything greater in the world than Shakespeare. Could anything be put better than the vignettes of different stages of life in the seven ages of man? 'Mewling and puking in his mother's arms,' he said and 'as slow as a snail unwillingly to school' – could anything be better?[1] 'This wonderful world' – in spite of all its disadvantages how beautiful to be alive – what happiness!

I mentioned that the first Moore I had seen was shown to me by Michael Sadler the Master of Univ[ersity College, Oxford] – when I was an Oxford undergraduate. He said – 'Yes' when he was an art student and Sadler was Chancellor of Leeds University he had invited Henry and two other students to see his collection. Henry remembered a Gauguin. It was among his earliest glimpses of modern art. Later, Sadler had bought one or two pieces from Henry. Still later one day he received a letter from Sadler saying he wanted to tell Moore that he had always on his mantelpiece a sculpture of his, and how he looked at it every day and wanted to tell Moore how grateful he was for this pleasure. Two days later Moore read in the newspaper that Sadler had died. 'What spiritual greatness to have thought at that time of thanking me,' Henry said.

'I always had energy,' he said, 'tremendous energy. I would never stop doing things. Only recently have I felt less energy sometimes.'

---

1 'At first the infant, / Mewling and puking in the nurse's arms. / And then the whining school boy [...] creeping like snail / Unwillingly to school', *As You Like It*, II, vii.

9 June 1979, London

Went to Aldeburgh Friday and Saturday to stay with Charles and Lettie Gifford in their large solidly built house looking over a ragged slope of long grass, gorse and broom running down to the estuary: always at this time of year with two or three yachts on it. We have gone here every June for a weekend for about 15 years, attending concerts etc at the Festival.[1] Until Ben's death two years ago it was presided over by Benjamin Britten and Peter Pears. The festival has really always been dedicated to Ben B. – and now he is dead it is dedicated to his spirit. The public seems the same as it always was, now twenty years older and some thinning out through deaths.

One annual feature is the luncheon given by Lord and Lady Glad-wyn.[2] [. . .] On Saturday we went to the Gladwyns' party, beginning with drinks in their beautiful garden and concluding with a luncheon that spread out into three rooms.

I was put next to Diana Cooper. She has aged like all of us, and she is immensely conscious of it. 'I am very very old, but my spirit is the same' she said looking at me with her beautiful wide cornflower blue eyes in which tragedy seems at every moment cancelled out by laughter. Her eyes have a steadying look above her precarious tottering body, in her face with skin like whitewash on a crumbling wall where the paint does not quite conceal the cracks – and under some traditional eternally chic hat – wide-brimmed straw – of an ancestry of hats appearing in paintings by Reynolds and Gainsborough. One adores her as one might a Greek goddess (for that is her genre – Greek goddess photographed by Cecil Beaton) when she gives one a long look that seems to express things from a well of centuries past – and winds up with her saying 'I'm still here! My spirit is the same!' She knows all about mortality, graves, prisons, scandals, sex. When we were in the garden, having drinks, she said: 'Two days ago I made a gaffe but not as bad as the one I made some weeks ago. I'll tell you about the first one now, and the second one at luncheon, since you're

---

1 Benjamin Britten had founded the Aldeburgh Festival in the village of Snape in 1948 with the singer Peter Pears and the librettist Eric Crozier. Britten lived in the Suffolk village until his death in 1976.

2 Gladwyn Jebb (1900–1996), British civil servant and the first Acting Secretary-General of the United Nations, 1945–6.

sitting next to me.' The first one was at the party for Sir Robert Mayer's hundredth birthday.[1] A woman came up and started talking to her. 'I hadn't the faintest idea who it was. Then I saw two enormous diamonds on her dress, and I realized it was the Queen. So I put on a lot of ma'ams and said – "I'm so sorry I didn't recognize you ma'am. But you see I don't recognize you when you're not wearing your crown." The Queen explained: "I thought it was Sir Robert Mayer's show. So I'm not wearing it."'

The gaffe she told at lunch was not so amusing and took a long time to tell. What happened was that she was staying at some grand place and the whole party was to go over to some castle where the Queen Mother was staying. The night before this happened she felt very ill – 'I think I had a mini stroke' she said. So ill that she excused herself from lunch the next day. Then she slept a long time. When she woke it was broad daylight and she thought it was morning. She got up and put on daytime clothes. Everyone was waiting downstairs to go in a fleet of cars to the castle. She noticed that one or two women were in long dress and thought 'how silly of them – for luncheon.' 'No-one said a word to me. Not a word.' Then when they got to the castle, she realized it was a dinner party and everyone was dressed for the evening except for her in her daytime clothes.

I said: 'Your memory has always been marvellous. When you were in Paris you once invited me together with Julian Huxley, my then boss at UNESCO, to a party where there were about twenty people. Afterwards you said to me "your Professor Huxley is rather common"' – 'Not common,' she interrupted, ' I wouldn't have said "common".' 'Well "vulgar",' I corrected. – 'Perhaps.' – 'I asked "Why was he vulgar?" You said: "because he recited this rhyme," and you repeated word for word, 6 or 8 lines.' 'I remember that party,' she said. 'The thing is that Evelyn Waugh was there. I adored Evelyn but he had a very unkind side to him. He would keep on *tormenting* Julian Huxley. Though he was perfectly aware he was head of UNESCO, he insisted on treating him as though he were still head of

---

1 Robert Mayer (1879–1985), German-born businessman, patron of British musicians and founder of a famous series of concerts organized for school children.

the zoo.[1] "How are the giraffes?" he kept on asking. "I do hope you have a responsible attitude towards the elephants.'"

Adam MacMillan, grandson of Harold MacMillan, was on her left. A very animated intelligent youth. He gave a very lively account of how Harold M. had instructed him in public speaking. 'What were the rules?' I asked. 'Well, one was that you always make your gestures precede the sentence you are saying. If you are saying "the policy of that man, the Prime Minister, has resulted in the defeats falling upon this country" when you say "that man" – you don't point at him. You point at him before you begin the sentence. Also you must always raise your voice at the end of a sentence, not let it drop.'

On Saturday going shopping, we encountered Marion Thorpe, looking absolutely in possession of herself, shopping.[2] She asked us to drinks on Sunday at noon. We accepted. It would have been difficult to refuse. Anyway I'm afraid I felt devoured by curiosity as to how the Thorpes would seem the Sunday of the week on which he will be sentenced or acquitted for conspiracy to murder Norman Scott.

There were only three other guests – two couples – one Mr Taplin head of the N.Y. Metropolitan Opera and his wife, the other Sir Eric Penn.[3]

The Thorpes said nothing about the trial whatever, but talked a lot about plans. During the summer they intend to make a trip through France and Italy, visiting old friends on the way – they may come to see us in France. He talked about grouse shooting in the autumn.

---

1 Evelyn Waugh (1903–1966), British novelist, best known for satires such as *Decline and Fall* (1928) and *A Handful of Dust* (1934) and for his elegiac account of the lost world of the English aristocracy, *Brideshead Revisited* (1945). Julian Huxley had been in charge of London Zoo between 1935 and 1942.

2 The concert pianist Marion Thorpe was now the wife of Jeremy Thorpe (b. 1929), British politician and leader of the Liberal Party from 1967 to 1976. He lost his seat in parliament when he was accused of conspiring to murder the former male model Norman Scott. In 1971 Scott claimed that he had had a two-year homosexual relationship with Thorpe in the 1960s. Four years later Scott was the victim of an assassination attempt that he claimed was instigated by Thorpe. The trial began in May 1979 and Thorpe was acquitted on 22 June.

3 Frank Taplin (1915–2003), American industrialist and philanthropist, president of the board of directors of the Metropolitan Opera 1977–84 and vice-president of the American Friends of the Aldeburgh Festival. Sir Eric Penn was the former Comptroller of the Royal Household.

They think of buying a bit of land between them and the house next door on the dunes at Aldeburgh, so as to grow trees to protect their view. Rupert, Jeremy's son, who was with a school friend, wandered off somewhere along the coast, Jeremy got in his car and drove after them. Jeremy never talks much to me, but from where I was sitting talking nothings with the ladies, I heard him talking about some matter of Winston Churchill's policy with Penn. The atmosphere seemed slightly doomed and nervous. One felt immensely sympathetic with the T[horpe]s whatever he has done. They said they were coming next weekend to Aldeburgh. When we left Jeremy shook my hand more warmly than he has done before and looking me in the eye said: 'We mustn't let a year pass before we meet again.' I said to Marion who accompanied us as far as her garden gate: 'I do hope things go well next week.' She laughed and said 'I do hope so' and made a face of the kind the French call a 'moue' [pout].

At the luncheon at Gladwyns' Diana [Cooper] had also talked about the two occasions on which she'd been burgled by armed robbers. On the first occasion they were masked, and tied her and Iris Tree to their chairs, while they searched the house. 'I don't mind that kind of thing in the least,' said Diana. On the second occasion they were not masked. She said to them: 'There is nothing whatsoever to steal here, your friends have been here already. Haven't they told you that it's all gone?'

5 July 1979, St Jerome

June 18th went [. . .] to *The Rake's Progress* at Covent Garden. This was an extremely spirited, exuberant production. Robert Craft who, with Vera Stravinsky, was in the stalls, said he thought Tom Rakewell was the best he had ever seen.[1] The music is dynamic above all with very powerful rhythms in the orchestra. The libretto begins starkly with Tom setting out on his downward career. The relationships though are stereotypes of characters in Hogarth prints: the faithful lover Anne, her father who distrusts Tom, Nick the devil etc. Christian stereotypes of a very theological kind with acted out

---

1 The 1979 production of *The Rake's Progress* was a quasi-Victorian staging conducted by Colin Davis. The part of Tom Rakewell was sung by Robert Tear.

incomprehensible symbolism of the 'bread machine' and the Bearded Lady are imposed on the very straightforward (if sophisticated as observation of social manners) almost Salvation Army morality of Hogarth's warnings to young bucks. The parts of the *Rake* that are moving are the beginning with Tom, Anne and Anne's father, the sale of Tom's goods, the mad-house and the death. But the story is obstructed by the impedimenta of Auden and Kallman's symbolism, campiness and ideas about the kind of opera they would have liked to write (e.g. the Bearded Lady singing a trill which is stifled by a tea cosy being thrust over her head and then resumed later when the tea cosy is removed). A pity really that the essentially simplistic morality did not retain its pure continuity of narrative line, the sophistication being in the style as in Hogarth. Had this happened the *Rake* would be in the repertoire with *Bohème* or *Madame Butterfly*.

Possibly Strav felt dissatisfied with the libretto when he asked Dylan Thomas to write one for him – and not Auden and Kallman to do another – which brought down the curses of Auden and Kallman on him. Wystan sometimes joked about the fact that Dylan paid the price of usurping the librettist role in dying before getting down to the libretto. [. . .]

June 20th. We had lunch at the Ritz with Isaiah and Aline Berlin whose other guests were Bob Craft and Vera Stravinsky. Whenever Vera sees me now she starts explaining to me why she has not sent me a copy of a book which, at her suggestion that she should give me a present as a reward for writing the introduction to a catalogue of an exhibition of her paintings, I had asked for. It is of illustrations and text about Stravinsky, throughout his life. She looks at me with her enormous eyes in her large white face which seems surrounded by layers first of hair then of a cape made perhaps of silk perhaps of fur and says, 'What you asked me to do is so difficult. To send that book. First, I have to go to a shop and buy a copy. Then I have to get wrapping paper and cardboard. It needs cardboard so it does not get damaged. And string. I shall need string. Oh, I know. I shall get Barbara Epstein to do it for me. But where will she send it? Where are you? What is your address?' She laughs, looking at me in an exaggeratedly helpless way. I tell her to forget about it. 'Oh but I can't. I think about it all the time.' She laughs with that tremendous charm she must have had all her life.

13 July 1979, St Jerome

I rang Peggy Ashcroft [about Spender's play *The Corporal* – which she had been looking at for him] [. . .] She said she was thrilled by it, especially after Act II (the beginning she found a bit slow, which caused me to lie awake last night mentally rewriting it). She wanted my agent Peggy Ramsay to send it to Trevor Nunn at the Royal Shakespeare.[1] There was lots to say about the play which she couldn't say on the expensive telephone.

This morning my agent Peggy Ramsay telephoned. She said – as Peggy A. had done – that it was obviously a serious and important work. Discussing possibilities of production, she said that the National [Theatre] was in a terrible way. [. . .] I mentioned I had sent it to Pinter and Stoppard. She said Pinter was a very good idea, really liked reading things, admired poetry; Stoppard had become caught up in his recent successes and cared for little else. He had become hard, had no wish to help others. (This is hers not my impression of Stoppard. He has been very helpful over Writers & Scholars.) [. . .] When Joan Littlewood was here I showed her *The Corporal* (all except the last two scenes).[2] She became quite excited, had excellent ideas for a production.

But Joan and Philippe. I want to write about them. They seem such an extraordinary couple. Some years ago, Joan and her paramour of 30 years, Gerry Raffles, were together in Vienne walking in the street when Gerry dropped dead. Like that. They were only on a visit to Vienne but Joan has lived in Vienne ever since. Gerry died at approximately the same time as Philippe's wife Pauline. Philippe knew Joan through John Wells. He heard from John that Joan was miserably unhappy in Vienne. He drove from Mouton to Vienne and brought her to Mouton. At Mouton she was a stormy guest, always saying exactly what she felt on every subject. Sometimes she would leave abruptly without informing Philippe or anyone else where she was

---

1 Peggy Ramsay (1908–1991), theatrical agent. Trevor Nunn (b. 1940), British theatre director, Director of the Royal Shakespeare Company, 1968–86.

2 Joan Littlewood (1914–2002), British theatre director responsible for developing the left-wing Theatre Workshop in 1945 and the originator of *Oh! What a Lovely War* (1963). Littlewood moved to France in the late 1970s and became the companion of Philippe de Rothschild.

going. She told Philippe to his face that he was an old reprobate etc, in good moods addressing him as 'Gov'. She came to stay here a few days ago and was very funny about Philippe's relations with his daughter Philippine admitting that Philippine makes life intolerable for him, but also saying: 'Still you have to take into account that she was brought up seeing her father going around with all these Birds.' She also says she thinks Philippe is fundamentally gay: 'You don't go around with all that many birds unless you really want to get away from each one of them.' But she said on another occasion that he so adored women any woman could get anything out of him.

Joan is very small, lithe, lively, impertinent-looking, wearing a beret – an effect as though she were wearing kilts, which she doesn't wear. She looks like the mascot of some very virile troop of Highlanders whom she keeps perpetually amused. She seems largely occupied in trying to get the mayor of Vienne to put up some kind of memorial – a garden within a garden – to Gerry in a park there. We stopped at Vienne on our way from London and she and Natasha disappeared for about an hour while N. saw the site and advised her about plants. When she talks about the theatre she reveals the bitterly disappointed side of her nature. No-one is any good, they are all corrupt. Anyone off the streets could be a better actor than the best of them. One does not dare to mention names for fear of derision. But when she talks about producing a play, suggests a movement on the stage, she suddenly becomes a different person: can make a bowing sweeping movement of extraordinary grace as though her beret had become an Elizabethan courtier's hat with a wonderful plume in it. After reading *The Corporal* she kept on coming out with ideas for it: 'First of all abolish all those BLACKOUTS between scenes. Play it as one continuous action without breaks. No scenes. Two or three screens on which photographs can be projected which puts the action into the context of the Thirties. When it's at its most violent, project photography of poignantly beautiful scenery by way of contrast'.

7 August 1979, Corfu

[Last week] we drove to Salisbury, where I had my hair cut, then to the Sterns' house near Tisbury where we stayed two nights.

There was a great deal of talk at the Sterns, mostly about Wystan concerning whom the Sterns have many theories, some illuminating, some, I think, wrong.

Jimmy Stern is 75 or so. Rather frail-looking, bearded, gentle but also a bit testy and self-protecting (hostile to most of the surrounding world) – he looks strikingly like my grandfather E. J. Schuster. We come from strikingly similar backgrounds, though his seems a little grander than mine [. . .] We both had grandfathers coming from banking families in Frankfurt. His family were also wine merchants who put a magnum of wine in their living room window. Our Frankfurt relations certainly must have known each other. I would love to have talked to my grandmother about the Sterns. [. . .]

About Wystan. Jimmy's theory is that he was not queer. He attributes his queerness to the influence of Christopher who knew Wystan from prep school days and who demanded his loyalty to the homosexual tribe. Apart from Christopher, the other destroyer of Wystan's happiness was Chester – a totally selfish and self-interested neurotic, consumed with ambition and utterly depraved, who used Wystan to achieve his own ends. Tanya backs up this by her own theory that Wystan was very masochistic and that his sexual preoccupation (which she calls 'gobbling') is clinical evidence of this.

Of course, it can be said of any homosexual that he wouldn't do so, if he hadn't been influenced by someone else to do it. But Auden did not see Isherwood between the time when they both left prep school and they both went to their universities. There is no evidence that Christopher influenced W. to this effect at prep school. And at Gresham's [School] Wystan fell in love with Robert Medley and was much attracted by other boys.[1] Doubtless the re-meeting of Christopher led quickly to the mutual revelation that each was homosexual and this was the equivalent of a mutual *Blutsbrüderschaft* [blood brotherhood]. Each would know that for the other to become 'normal' would be the equivalent of betrayal. When, soon after he left Oxford, W. became engaged to a nurse, it was Christopher who persuaded him to break off the engagement. But before that he had explained to me and others that he regarded normal sex as an act of will – something which he would be able to make himself like, a self-

---

1 Robert Medley (1905–1994), British artist associated in the late 1930s with the Group Theatre, which staged plays by Spender, Auden and Isherwood.

imposed cure – of which he was capable as of all his other willed actions. Moreover, it was Wystan who 'discovered' Berlin by going there in 1929, staying at Magnus Hirschfeld's Sexual Institute, going to male brothels, taking up with Gerhart Meyer, befriending Layard and extracting from him the ideas of Homer Lane, etc.[1] Also, his friendship with Fronny Turville-Petre.[2]

Christopher and Wystan were a club of two. This does not make Christopher the dominating character who stopped W. becoming normal, though it is possible that without Christopher's influence, W. would have made his life fit into the pattern of imposed normality. Perhaps this would have been a success. Wystan's idea of the marital relationship which he wished to share with another man could have been realized by a real family with children. He would have made an excellent father and in his homosexual relationships he regarded himself as the boy's parent. (He was Gerhart Meyer's 'father', Chester Kallman's 'mother'.)

Wystan who believed so much in discipline, fitting life and work into extraneous patterns etc, nevertheless believed that he was inalterably homosexual. In 1946 he had an affair with a girl, Rhoda Klonsky, which he gave up because he could not enjoy sex with her (or with any other woman).

The women he knew best – Elizabeth Mayer, Ursula Niebuhr, Hannah Arendt – were to him priestesses, like Moneta in Keats' revised version of *Hyperion*, *The Fall of Hyperion*.[3] He became the confidant

---

1 Gerhart Meyer was a Hamburg sailor with whom Auden had an affair in Berlin. The British psychologist John Layard was one of Hirschfeld's followers in Berlin in the 1930s and had previously been psychoanalysed by the American psychologist Homer Lane. Lane was then arrested and charged with immorality for having sexual relations with female patients.

2 Francis Turville-Petre (1901–1941), British archaeologist staying at Hirschfeld's Institute in the 1930s. Turville-Petre was the model for the central character in Auden's and Isherwood's *The Dog Beneath the Skin* (1935).

3 Elizabeth Mayer (1884–1970), German-born American translator and editor who was the dedicatee of Auden's *New Year Letter* (1941). Ursula Niebuhr (née Kessel-Compton) (1908–1997), British Anglican theologian. Hannah Arendt (1906–1975), German-Jewish political theorist. Moneta, Roman goddess of memory and money and another epithet for Juno, the wife of Jupiter. In his unfinished poem, *The Fall of Hyperion*, Keats represents Moneta as a priestess and uses her to explore the philosophical and artistic implications of poetry.

of other women who used him as lay psychoanalyst to whom they poured out their secrets. Jimmy and Tania seemed to think that he had a compulsion to thrust himself into the lives of certain married couples whose love life was not going well, extracting from the wives their most intimate secrets, probing wounds, and driving them to desperate courses. There may be examples of his marriage-breaking, but I feel that the breakdown must have been less his fault than the result of the wish of the woman to use a vicarious intimacy with him as the instrument for breaking up the marriage. Wystan was the born father confessor whatever dogmatic church he happened to belong to at various periods of his life. In this he was like John Layard, John Thompson, and I suppose the predecessor of all three, Homer Lane. Part of his attraction for those women was that, as a result of their confabulations with him, each became convinced – with her – at all events – he was not 'really queer', but merely the member of a sect all bound to queerdom – and of course, Christopher played the role of villainous high priest of the sect, a kind of Sarastro [in *The Magic Flute*], whilst Chester was seal incarnate of the vow to men. The truth – but no, one can't discover the truth – but what is nearer to the truth than the idea of each of these ladies that Auden really loved her – is perhaps that this father confessor used women disciples who confessed their problems to him in part as substitute mothers to whom he confessed and which verged always on intimacy which – but for the insuperable obstacle – might have ended in marriage. In his 1929 Journal describing a conversation with 'Margaret' (Gardiner, I suppose) who prods him about his feelings for women, he reports himself saying: 'What I hate is the fucking.' I did not tell the Sterns of the existence of this diary and I think I was right not to do so, because I suppose them – perhaps for reasons to do with their own marriage – to have compounded their own myth about Auden, and one should not disturb this. Tania said that on one occasion Auden made a conditional proposal to her: 'If anything happened to Jimmy, would you marry me?' According to Thekla Clark he proposed to her, on condition that they adopted Chester.[1] Towards the end

---

1 Thekla Clark (b. 1927) met Auden on Ischia in 1951. She remained a lifelong friend with whom he stayed whenever he visited Italy. Twenty years after his death she published *Wystan and Chester, A Personal Memoir of W. H. Auden and Chester Kallman* (1996).

of life he proposed to Hannah Arendt that he share her apartment, and I dare say that marriage was a consideration (though certainly the understanding would be that everything of A[uden]'s must be left to C[hester]).[1]

An interesting idea of Jimmy's is that Auden lacked what J. calls a 'Menschenkenntnis' [knowledge about other people]. I think this may (in a way) be so, if it is true that you don't really know people, if you hold up between them and yourself a graph upon a transparent screen contained in your mind, upon which symptoms and character-istics are charted.

> Lay your sleeping head my love,
> Human on my faithless arm.[2]

These lines are quoted as a declaration of passionate love, yet what they portray are fever on a fever chart which on a particular occasion attains a peak of experience in the poet's feelings which he recognizes as human love. The poet's arm is 'faithless' – uncommitted to repetition of the symptoms, and the beloved is asleep, pathetically contributing to the symptoms which – as the poem asseverates are of a temporary nature – though undeniably real, and in harmony with parallel ecstatic human phenomena at the moment. How different from:

> Let me not to the marriage of true minds
> Admit impediment. Love is not love
> That alters when its alteration finds
> Or bends with the remover to remove.[3]

In all Auden's love poems the lover is removed from the beloved, being more fully conscious, more responsible, more guilt-ridden than that object. A consequence of this is that the poet at once knows his lovers and friends more completely than they know him, because of his very intelligent powers of analysis, and less well because he never

---

1 According to Thekla Clark, Arendt was considering this proposal when Wystan turned away towards the drinks cabinet. Seeing a large rip in the back of his trousers dampened her faith in his domestic habits.

2 Spender is quoting Auden's 'Lay your sleeping head, my love' (1937).

3 Spender is slightly misquoting Shakespeare's Sonnet 116.

lapses into that mutuality which is shared knowledge of each by the other. There is something arbitrary, on Auden's side, about even his closest relationships. A famous example is his choice of Isherwood as the friend who would decide for him finally and indisputably what were the good and what the bad lines in his poetry. An intelligent choice, of course, because it set up the standard of Isherwood's empathizing intuitive judgement against A.'s intellect but at the same time, however good a judge, Isherwood must have been fallible, and to set himself up as infallible was to make him a figure in Auden's systematization. One might say it was not altogether fair to Isherwood, just as one would certainly say it was unfair to Chester Kallman to set him up as the infallibly beloved. This could only show how very fallible Chester was in his behaviour to Wystan. Jimmy would say I suppose that Wystan's attitude to Chester showed his lack of Menschenkenntnis – yet he did know everything about Chester, and suffered greatly through doing so. I think it really showed that he had cast Chester for a role which Chester failed to carry out, because he could not consider or treat him as an equal. He once told me that Chester was far cleverer than he (Wystan) was. I looked astonished, and he said: 'Intellectually of course, I am cleverer than he is, but emotionally, intuitively, he is infinitely cleverer than I am.' In all relationships one has to be the superior of the other in some respect, and vice versa, but this makes the one who holds this view always the analyser and spectator never the sharer.

11 August 1979, Corfu

This beautiful place.[1] The little bay with its rocky beach and the cave shaped like a tip-tilted needle cathedral window, and studded inside with the lozenge-shaped different coloured slabs of stone, ferns and grass tufted on ledges. Just beyond it is the headland with two paws of rock thrust into the bright transparent blue water. It seems like the restful end of life, dreaming its way into poetry, Calypso's cave, the *Odyssey*, Byron's Cantos about Haidee and her piratical father and Don Juan.

---

1 Spender was staying at Rovinia, the holiday house of Elizabeth and Christopher Glenconner.

Harold Pinter, Antonia Fraser, her brother Tom Pakenham and three of his children – a daughter – Natasha – and two sons – came to lunch here Wednesday.[1] They all went down to bathe with the Glenconners, except Natasha (*my* Natasha) and Harold. He said he had read my play, which he described as 'passionate phantasmagoria'. He considered it should be produced and wanted to know whether I wanted him to show it, in its present state, to the National Theatre, saying also that my idea that the N.T. was so bankrupted by strikes it could not undertake such a performance was inexact. He said the play was extremely powerful with brilliant scenes, such as that of the trial. Like Peggy Ashcroft, Joan Littlewood, and Lizzie's friend Dick [Sylbert], he thought the excitement began with the Second Act.[2] Kolya was marvellous, the Corporal brilliant, but Herder was too abstract, as were his speeches and the argumentation that takes up much of Act One. I asked him whether he would read Act One again and discuss it in detail with me when I got back to London, and he said he would do this.

22 August 1979, Lake District

We drove from London to Newby Bridge in the Lake District. Stayed the night at the Swan Hotel, with a beautiful view of the river. On Thursday, we set out in search of the Farmhouse, where my family had stayed in the summer of 1915 – or 1916 – I suppose in order to get away from Sheringham on which Zeppelins dropped occasional bombs (this means it was 1915 rather than 1916 in which case I was only 6).[3] I have extremely vivid memories of those weeks in the Lake District, of walks through rain-showers which suddenly cleared: the woods gave off an exhalation of pine-scent: drops of rain hung on the curled ends of fern and bracken; large black slugs, which delighted

---

1 Tom Pakenham (b. 1933), historian, son of Frank Pakenham, Lord Longford.

2 Richard (Dick) Sylbert (1928–2002), film production designer. He worked on the film *Reds* (d. Warren Beatty, 1981), in which Lizzie Spender had a part.

3 This formative episode, at Skelgill Farm, August–September 1917, is described at length in *World Within World* (chapter 2).

me, crawled along the paths. Sometimes we came to caves along the roadside in which I would find stone or slate encrusted with crystals. It was a landscape of jewels, the greatest of them being the bright Derwentwater below us. I remember rowing and trawling on the lake and my father catching a pike, and our eating it afterwards. But the deepest memory of all was lying in my bedroom which overlooked a garden or lawn and hearing my father read poems of Wordsworth to my mother, where they sat outdoors in deckchairs.

24 August 1979, Yester House, East Lothian

Gian Carlo [Menotti], Chip and Chip's sister Sheila here. [. . .] Gian Carlo went to the Soviet Union and was asked to spend a morning listening to the work of young Soviet composers. They were all compositions in the manner of [Pierre] Boulez or [Edgard] Varèse, dry, percussive, heavily rhythmic, totally devoid of feeling. He went outside after this, very depressed, and saw an immense church. 'Let me go into this,' he asked his guide, who did all he could to prevent him doing so. He insisted however, entered an absolutely packed church, with many young as well as old people, and heard a splendid choir singing liturgical music. He immediately burst into tears.

30 August 1979, London

A tremendous relief to be home. Excess of travel this summer really disoriented me. The four days at Yester I did not go out at all, abandoning myself to my cold and trying to keep warm in this immense house of several drawing rooms, a ballroom, a great dining room, the huge well of a marble staircase under a glass dome which broke last winter, water flooding the carpets etc. The rooms which G.-C. and Chip have furnished are quite in the style of interiors photographed in *Country Life*. But one can never forget that there is not enough furnishing, not enough heating, not enough servants – and the final hollowness – not enough money; with Gian Carlo at the centre, heroic but exhausted and disillusioned working to provide the money on which all this should run. It is like an oil crisis reflected in everything – food, drink, service, furniture and heat. G.-C. said to me on the last day when we walked through the immense walled orchard and kitchen garden: 'After all, I'm happy having all this when I consider that every penny of the money that pays for it comes out of my music.' A remark at once touching, pathetic, and vulgar. He went on to say: 'Of course, it's all for Chip. As far as I'm concerned I'd be happy living in a hotel bedroom.'

The wonder is that one doesn't hate Chip, the spoiled prince exskating champion, snatched ten years or so ago from his ice rinks by Gian Carlo, and now his adopted son, Chip Menotti. There is something confiding, appealing, affectionate, genuine about him, and he has the wild vague glamour of an actor who in appearance at all events would do very well as Ludwig II, or that Austrian prince who committed suicide with his mistress in a hunting lodge. He is completely out of a fairy story, a kind of Jamesian prince high-living in Europe who remains an American. But one hates him when he takes the line with G.-C. – 'I'm creative too. I'm not going to do the housekeeping or train the servants. I'm going to have my own Festival of Theatre here.'[1] He says things which make one wish G.-C. would get up and say 'Goodbye' – and go to a hotel room.

In September 1979, Stephen and Matthew Spender went on another of their 'honeymoon' holidays to Venice.

21 September 1979, Venice

At midnight on Saturday – just when I'd given up hope of seeing him, Joseph Brodsky telephoned. We met on Sunday in the piazza at a rather awkward moment: a luscious looking lady sitting alone at the table next to ours drew our attention by taking a photograph of a group of children in the piazza. She showed professional skill in arranging the group. We watched this going on. Then Matthew and she struck up a conversation. (Matthew talks to everyone in Italy and has an idea that if he makes an Italian laugh, relations are established. This does not always work.) Soon the lady and M. were

---

1 Menotti sponsored an annual music festival at Spoleto. His attempts at Yester to collaborate with the nearby Edinburgh Festival were unsuccessful, and a source of sadness to him.

engaged in a fairly intense conversation. Later, M. explained that this was about the fact that she worked for an extreme left-wing magazine, and was somehow involved in taking sides with supporters of the group corresponding to Baader-Meinhof in Italy.[1] All this made me rather nervous because I had visions of M. introducing our visitor to Brodsky, our having to take her to lunch with us. In fact when B. suddenly appeared, M. did not immediately detach himself from the lady. However, at last he did so, and the three of us left Florian's to go to a restaurant of Joseph's choice. J. seemed happy that he had broken a journey from Rome to New York in the evening to be with us. He talked about restaurants in Venice and about Venice itself the place he seems to love next to Leningrad. He had compared Venice and Leningrad in an autobiographical essay in the *N.Y.* [*New Yorker*] and we talked of this. I said I liked the article. He smiled and asked: 'Do you think I qualify as an English writer?' The answer to this could only be 'a very distinguished one'. I said I had seen Gogol's *The Inspector General* [*The Government Inspector*] a few days ago at the London Old Vic and that it was played throughout as fortissimo roaring farce. He said that was how it was played in Russia also – but Gogol had meant it to be serious and did not see himself as a funny writer. He went on about Gogol – that he was split between wanting to be a religious, a saint, and wanting to be a writer. He said that all writers have this division in them. This struck me as true, but I find it difficult to express. I remember now a conversation before the war at dinner with Elizabeth Bowen when I said that a writer cannot be a saint. A writer has to have experiences – love, pleasure among them. For the sake of his art he cannot renounce them. For the sake of his religion a saint has to do so. At the same time a writer is concerned with truth, goodness. He is moral in that art for the sake of which he may be amoral in his life.

When the ladies had left the room, Alan Cameron, Elizabeth's husband, took me to task. 'I do not agree with your saying a writer cannot be a saint. Elizabeth is a saint,' he said. He was a huge red-hued man with a near-walrus moustache. His eyes had a glazed look perhaps because of the drink, perhaps because he was having a diabetic

---

1 The Brigate Rosse (Red Brigade), which in 1978 kidnapped and murdered the former Prime Minister of Italy, Aldo Moro.

attack. He started talking about a railway station in the midst of the country, a rural junction near where Elizabeth and he had a house. 'They have painted the railings. It was all new paint,' he said. 'I can't express myself but that is what I mean about Elizabeth being a saint.' I did not understand, yet his words recalled some scene in one of Elizabeth's stories or novels.

27 September 1979, New York

My last evening [in London], we dined with Lizzie and Dick Sylbert and Dick's son Mark at Lizzie's flat. Dick had been to Finland and brought back with him some special kind of smoked salmon which he was very keen to share with us. His son seemed intelligent, sensitive, shy. He studies art at the Cooper Union, N.Y. Dick held forth informedly about Finland and its architecture. He is extremely polite to us, genuinely fond of Lizzie. But now I come again to that exposed and vulnerable area of my mind which is my caring for my children – longing for them to be happy, wishing that they don't let time go by as mine has so that they wake up one day to find that it has passed and what ought to have happened simply hasn't happened.

In October 1979, Spender taught at Lynchburg College, Virginia. That year, America was facing what seemed to be a financial crisis. By October, inflation had moved up to a double-digit pace and many were predicting recession and rising unemployment. On 6 October, in an effort to prevent the situation escalating out of control, Paul Volcker, the new chairman of the US Federal Reserve, set a limit preventing the further expansion of the supply of dollars by the government. Spender's dismal predictions turned out to be unwarranted, although there was a brief recession and rise in unemployment in the early 1980s.

10 October 1979, Lynchburg, Virginia

The worst day in history on the American stock market. This is disturbing partly because it brings reminders of 1930. Partly though for reasons which go beyond this, which I've felt always, and of which economic crises are only the symptoms. We live in totally economic societies. That is to say the conditions in which we live are entirely dependent on an economy over which we have no control. But this economy if translated into human action and behaviour, is entirely frivolous: the gambling of operators and traders on the Stock Market, and beyond that the purchasing of commodities by people who do not need them. For the margin which keeps the economy buoyant is the unnecessary not the necessary – luxuries, useless things, not vital needs, useful ones. At one end the Stock Market at the other the commercials, advertising which makes people buy things they don't need. In a capitalist system what is solemnly called collapse of the economy is in human terms, collapse of the frivolity: people, because they panic, no longer buying un-necessities. And if this happens on a large enough scale, the young will become unemployable.

15 October 1979, Durham, North Carolina

Had a lovely weekend [with Reynolds Price], talking, gossip etc.[1] Reynolds said he had recently read all of Auden's poems and mine also. He said Auden had written several absolutely wonderful poems but that my poems had a dimension of humanity which his lacked. He also said that A. was perhaps really the greatest poet of the 20th century, greater than Yeats. I said A. was incomparably the greatest talent of his generation, and that I felt that after my early poems I had somehow lost my way in my poetry. R. said: 'I think the difficulty is that you haven't been able to deal with the problem of your homosexuality in your writing.' This is probably true. It gives so much to think about. One thing is that I don't think I could have made much of the homosexual theme without sentimentality and also a lack of contact with the ordinary life of family marriage which – without it – would have led to unreality.

20 October 1979, Nashville, Tennessee

During the weekend [staying with Bob and Ann Hunter] I reviewed Richard Percival Graves' biography of Housman. I also read

---

1 At this date Price was a Professor at Duke University, North Carolina.

Nicholas Blake's (C. Day Lewis) crime story *Death of A Traveller*.[1] This is the second N. Blake I've read in a week (*Thou Shell of Death* was the other). Cecil told me Nigel Strangeways, his investigator, is a portrait of Wystan – but in fact N.S. has only the faintest resemblance to W. He is on the other hand, in speech, learning, sense of humour, attitude to women, love of poetry, the mixture of affection and cynicism, sly secretiveness, convivial readiness to play a neighbourly or comradely or colleague's role, amazingly like Cecil himself. Cecil had a very conscious sense of his intellectual superiority, malice as well as affection towards others, a razor-like killing contempt – especially for women, whom he loved. He worked off the murderous side of him in the secretly autobiographical passages of his crime stories. In a straight novel and even in his autobiography, he can never depict character as well as he does in the crime stories, because in them he regards each character as potentially the murderer (or murderess) or the murdered. *Death of A Traveller* is really about the killing egotism of the poet who could amiably strangle everyone round him for the sake of his getting on with his poem, charm them even into suicide to protect his isolation. There is deep love of poetry in it, even liking for murderers and murdered, and a flickering whip-lash or snake-tongue sense of humour.

24 October 1979, Lynchburg, Virginia

Yesterday morning had to take a class on 17th century poetry for Miss [Dora Jean] Ashe. Had not had time to prepare this. Last night a girl from my class having invited me to a supper and get-together of her mates, at which they'd given me a strange mixture of sour cream and squashed cucumber, I could not sleep at all. I must have had slight food poisoning. So when while I was in my bath Miss Ashe's nervous knock roused me from immersion in water and stupor I suddenly realized I did not have a word in my head. Then one of those things happened which can make the exigencies of teaching provide one with revelations. It suddenly occurred to me that Hamlet as courtier, wit and personality foreshadows metaphysical poetry. If Hamlet were a poet, he would have been John Donne: 'to take arms

---

1 Spender refers to *Head of a Traveller* (1949).

against a sea of troubles, and by assailing [*sic*] end them' is the beginning of an Epistle by Donne in which the guns would have been cannon, battering rams, assault instruments, would all have fitted into an elaborate metaphysical machinery. Then I remembered the opening dialogue between H., Rosencrantz and Guildenstern in which the dress and physical parts of fortune who is a whore are played on. I think this went well.

8 November 1979, Philadelphia

I bought two weeks' editions of the *New York Times Book Review*. [. . .] A review of Volume V of Virginia Woolf's letters which contained the following quotation:

(1933) 'He [Stephen Spender]. . . talks incessantly and will pan out in ten years a prodigious bore. But he's a nice poetic youth: big nosed, bright eyed, like a giant thrush. . . He is writing about Henry James and has tea alone with Ottoline and is married to a Sergeant of the Guards. They have set up a new quarter in Maida Vale; I propose to call them the Lilies of the Valley. There's William Plomer, with his policeman . . ., then Stephen, then Auden and Joe Ackerley, all lodged in Maida Vale, and wearing different coloured lilies.'

O blessed Virginia, if you look down on me from any height where you now live, help me in my old age not to be a bore. Boredom was taking tea with Ottoline [Morrell]. Boredom was writing about Henry James and writing volume after volume of literary journalism about authors, politics – things I did not really have the mental grasp to master. Boredom was being like my father and my uncle, public figures. It's impossible not to write these lines without the sense of a reader looking over my shoulder. Am I not putting the best possible face on V.'s remarks? But what I write is true. I'm struggling at the end to get out of the valley of hectoring youth, journalistic middle age, imposture, money-making, public relations, bad writing, mental confusion.

To deal with mental confusion am reading that beautifully clear book on Spinoza by Stuart Hampshire.[1]

---

1 Stuart Hampshire, *Spinoza and the Idea of Freedom* (1960).

Virginia was never boring. She was cruel in her perceptions and the cruelty was partly the price of not being boring. Insane at intervals herself, one worries how she can have written [. . .] to Ottoline as she does about Vivienne Eliot whom she describes as 'malodorous'.

Last night went with Henry McIlhenny to a party given by some people called Lloyd who have a spacious house in which there are a few beautiful pictures – notably a [Piet] Mondrian. Walter Annenberg and his wife were there.[1] The Annenbergs talked to me as if he was still American ambassador in London, asking me to let him know if there was any way in which he could help me. He is large, bull-necked, vital, expansive – talking about the action Americans should take in Iran – a cordon of ships thrown round it to prevent exports and imports, Iranian students in America all to be sent home.[2] The reason America's name is becoming mud, he said, is because we have a jackass for a President [Jimmy Carter]. Another ex-Ambassador there – also ex-Secretary of Defense – was a man called Thomas Gates – sunburned, swarthy, a wooden face slashed over with a swathe of boot-black polished hair.[3] At first I thought Gates was of the same views about everything as Annenberg. Then someone told me he had been Ambassador in China, so I went over and asked him about this. He said the Chinese system was entirely different from Russian communism. The Chinese had no aims for expansion. Militarily and economically they were very weak and it would take them thirty years to catch up with the West. He loved China. He regarded Chinese communism as principled idealistic based on a passion for social justice and complete egalitarianism –

1 Walter Annenberg (1908–2002), American businessman, philanthropist and diplomat, US Ambassador to Great Britain, 1969–74.

2 February 1979 had seen the return of the exiled Iranian Ayatollah Khomeini, who had been forced to leave his country when he opposed the Shah Mohammed Reza Pahlevi's Westernizing 'White Revolution' in 1963. Westernizing involved reforms in health, education and land reform, and the implementation of legislation advancing women's rights. The Shah wanted to create a more secular state, which was unpopular with the religious hierarchy. Now the Shah himself had departed, following the outbreak of revolution and near civil war, and Khomeini returned to rapturous greetings.

3 Thomas Gates (1906–1983), US Secretary of Defense, 1959–1961.

whereas the Russian was based on bureaucratic privilege. He said he thought that communism was the only possible form of government for China. I said: 'Would you say the same for India?' He said, 'yes probably.' I laughed: 'You seem to be a capitalist in Washington and a communist in Peking.' 'That's so,' he said, 'our system is right for us, theirs for them.'

11 November 1979, Philadelphia

To revert to Virginia Woolf. Reading her letters and journals, I find this justification – that in her remarks that are cruel and treacherous (e.g. about Vita Sackville-West) to correspondents, what she is really doing is being candid about her own candour. She is more concerned – in her Journal certainly – with showing herself (the fifty-year-old Virginia, who will read what the twenty-year-old Virginia showed herself to be) as what she is at a particular moment than in being mean. There are layers of one's own truth which are deeply undermining of the lives of others: she was not afraid to show these – because they were the truth about herself.

Reading about Spinoza, I remember Matthew when he was about nine, asking 'When I bend my knees, does God bend?' Spinoza would have said yes.

Stuart emphasizes in his book that Spinoza regarded the images of the imagination as a very low form of mental activity obstructing the deductive arguments of pure reason whereby the truth about reality could be attained. At the same time his philosophy of God being nature, the wholeness of which every other existence is the part, is itself a metaphor, and if one is a poet reading him one is conscious of a vast scheme, an abstract construction, like the vision of the universe in the *Divine Comedy*, into which particular examples drawn from the minds and bodies of individuals, the stars, mountains and oceans, animals and flowers, primitive language and civilized intercourse etc would fit. So Systematized philosophies like Plato, Berkeley, Spinoza are initially visions, even if after their conception the philosopher has drained them of illustrational figures, which would obstruct the abstract processes of pure reason.

Another memory: Auden saying when we were undergraduates that philosophy was something to study late in life.

With old age I see myself more as object and less as subject. Perhaps this is because I look back on most of my life and see it as having happened, irremediable, as though it were the life of another person. It is clear to me that I am much more like my father whom I reacted against than I had realized. What characterized him was incomplete activities enclosed by optimistic rhetoric. Writing journalistic books about subjects he hadn't really studied and hoping that feelings, intuitions, sympathies, would carry him through: *Men and Mansions, Byron and Greece* etc.[1] I have done this: though what makes me different from him is my utter self-distrust. Still that hasn't been sufficient to stop me. Moreover it creates its own confusion. The feeling that any reading before an audience makes me despise what I am reading just because the audience listens, even likes it. Although it is distressing not to be attended to, the total silence of an audience which is really listening also distresses me.

19 November 1979, London

I went for the weekend of the 16th to Philadelphia, then on Monday to New York, then returned Wednesday night to London. [. . .] On November 12 I dined with Everett Fahy and his friend. Charming. Another Director of the Frick was there. On the 13th, I talked with students of Halpern at Columbia.[2] They asked questions which were good and the afternoon went well. I think conversations of this kind are what I really do best in the way of teaching. After that there were drinks with a select few of them in a very noisy pub. After that dinner in an equally noisy restaurant. Drue Heinz was the hostess, and very nice.[3] Harold Pinter was one of the nine guests. He was friendly. Practically everything he said related to Antonia [Fraser] whom, he told us, showed symptoms of E.S.P. Recently in the middle of the night she had woken him by repeating in her sleep the name of someone. The next morning, the first name he read in the newspaper was of that person. He told us another slightly embarrassed and

---

1 Harold Spender's *Men and Mansions* and *Byron and Greece* were published by Thornton Butterworth and John Murray respectively in 1924.

2 Presumably the poet Daniel Halpern (b. 1945).

3 Drue Heinz, American philanthropist and patron of the arts.

embarrassing story again illustrating Antonia's psychic powers which woke him in the middle of the night. 'I don't mean she never lets me sleep,' he added rather awkwardly, blushing. There was something charming about this naiveté – not very English, more like a character in Tolstoy. I felt he only wanted to talk about Antonia. He kept bringing her into the conversation.

Had breakfast with Ed Mendelson one of these days at New York. He brought his enormous typescript of his book *Early Auden*. I told him how I had used Hamlet's conversation with Rosencrantz and Guildenstern as an introduction to Metaphysical poetry. 'I do the same thing at Harvard,' he said. 'Do you think everyone uses it? Have I just stumbled on something very obvious?' I asked. 'No. No one else. Just you and I,' he answered.

23 November 1979, London

We had lunch at the Albany with Philippe de R[othschild]. This was for the Queen Mother. The other guests were Miriam Rothschild, Christopher Fry, Cecil Beaton, and the Q.M.'s Lady in waiting, Lady Fermoy.[1] Cecil who has had a stroke, paralysing one side of him did not realize perhaps that he would have to walk up two flights of stairs to Philippe's sitting room, another flight for luncheon. He was heroic about this tremendous effort. He had A. his chauffeur (or assistant) and Philippe's French houseboy helped him. He did not show exhaustion, but (as it were with the unparalysed side of him – though his face was hardly affected) was his sociable, friendly charming self. To make him laugh I reminded him of the time when we had *fou rire* [the giggles] at Mouton because I rather peremptorily asked Philippe to produce his gardener, famous for his beauty. Cecil leaned against a wall unable to stand for laughing. Afterwards he sent us a drawing he had made of the gardener. We stood around and talked a bit, then noises from the corridor and front door foretold the Q.M. She came in looking somewhat like a figure from a chess set of rather squashed squat pieces. This effect was emphasized by the hoop-like

---

1 Christopher Fry (1907–2005), British playwright best known for *The Lady's Not for Burning* (1948). Ruth Roche, Baroness Fermoy (1908–1993), appointed Woman of the Bedchamber by the Queen Mother in 1960.

hat she wore, the hooped skirt and other shapes which suggested rotundities. She shook hands with us all. What was irresistible was that she seemed the most at ease guest in the world, and also one of the freshest as though she had just come in from a marvellous outing to meet old friends whom it was bliss to see. Philippe had been explaining to her in the corridor that he had placed her on his left at the meal, because as she was Q.M. of England and he was French, he considered that in England he was her guest. She took his explanation with great humour. Philippe did his best act of unofficial host who served wonderful wine and food. She took up a wine glass filled with one of the Moutons sniffed in it and said: 'Oh what utter bliss. It's like being in heaven.' When partridges (perfectly roasted) were served, Philippe took one out of the dish by its claws and plumped it down in her plate. She giggled like a young girl. She talked to Cecil a lot of the time – as to an old friend whom she was refreshed by seeing and about whose welfare she was greatly concerned. I was mostly occupied with talking either to Lady Fermoy on my left or Miriam Rothschild (right). At one point I asked the Q.M. whether she remembered the concerts at the National Gallery during the war. She remembered them as absolutely wonderful: reminisced about how a bomb had gone off nearby in the middle of a Beethoven Sonata played by Myra Hess.[1] She said what a wonderful time the war had been – perhaps the happiest of our lives. 'Everyone was so . . . so . . . so I don't know what . . . so friendly with everyone else. The whole country was like one family.' Later, I said that when I was given the gold medal by the Queen she had asked me whether people wrote letters nowadays, and remarked that when she was on one of her tours she always wrote every day a kind of journal-letter for her mother. 'Oh yes, she does,' she said, 'and then I give it back to her after she comes home.' She said Prince Charles was a great letter writer.

I thought Philippe sailed a bit close to the wind when he said that Joan Littlewood had not come to lunch because of her, the Q.M.: 'She refused to meet you.' 'Oh, but that's very unfair. What a pity! After all, she might have liked me,' said the Q.M.

---

1 Myra Hess (1890–1965), British pianist who organized a series of lunchtime concerts at the National Gallery during the Second World War, boosting the morale of wartime Londoners.

Miriam Rothschild, who is writing a memoir, produced a photo-graph of a group of sportsmen standing in front of the house at Tring, and asked her whether she could identify them. 'Well I'll have to find my specs,' she said, and fished them out of her bag, put them on, roared with laughter at the posed group of sportsmen taken in 1903 and said she couldn't identify the ones Miriam R. wanted to know about. 'But I tell you what, I'll take them to Aunt Alice. Princess Alice. She's ninety-five, she may well recognize some of the faces. She'll be very pleased anyway to see them.'

There was a little talk about the theatre and things going on. She was very glad to hear that there was a success – *Amadeus* by Peter Shaffer – at the National, 'which seems to be doing so badly.' She only made one reference which seemed to reflect received ideas of Buckingham Palace. She said, 'That poor Shah [of Iran]. His people seem so ungrateful to him.'

We had lunched (on the 21st) with Michael and Judy Astor at the Connaught. Despite his having had cancer of the throat he seemed very well and told amusing stories. But I kept noting with apprehen-sion the bulge on the side of his face and part of the neck.[1]

That evening people came to drinks here before we went on to the Royal Free Hospital for a recital (to raise funds for the Body Scanner) by Peggy Ashcroft (she was not in good voice, having flu). After this, we went to the Annans at their new house. They were particularly friendly. Hugh Thomas and Derwent May were there.[2] I was greatly impressed by Hugh Thomas's immense head, his bulging impersonal eyes which never smile while his mouth attempts a welcoming look which is almost a grimace. I think he wants very much to be on terms of mutually friendly intellectual respect. We talked about Spain, Venezuela, the Middle East etc. Derwent May tried to intervene with some post-prandial near-witticisms – Hugh T. turned on him with a look of contempt which seemed shaken from his leonine curly Welsh locks and said: 'Why won't you listen to what I am saying. I am being serious.' I have a lot of respect for him.

There has been so much since I got home – these social events.

---

1 Michael Astor would, in fact, die on 28 February 1980, a few months later.
2 Hugh Thomas (b. 1931), British historian. Derwent May (b. 1930), British novelist and journalist.

Muriel Buttinger staying from November 18th–20th. Very nice, immensely relieved to be away from her husband Jo, whom she loves, but who has become almost completely senile – which tries her extremely – because when she is at home he is constantly asking her the same question over and over – can never leave her alone – is always coming into the room – but she has her hideouts. Then there is radio-therapy a ritual of every weekday morning I have at the Royal Free Hospital. In a way, I enjoy such rituals (I remember diathermy twenty years ago), they are like going to Communion.[1] Glimpses of the temptation of illness. From being a subject, and active, to becoming total object and passive, a flabby stretched out mass of flesh, on a trolley, into which someone jabs a needle. I wonder there are not far more sick people. How do the immensely active doctors at such a hospital – and the nurses – resist the temptation to become totally passive patients –

On 4 November 1979, a group of Iranian terrorists took over the American Embassy in Tehran in support of Iran's revolution and held 53 American diplomats hostage.

24 November 1979, London

At the Writers & Scholars' luncheon, Lord Longford came up to me and shouted the word 'Marx!' at me. I somehow guessed that this referred to Anthony Blunt.[2] What he wanted me to do, he explained, was write a book about the position of the Marxists today. I said I could not do this. Afterwards I thought though that one might edit a book of essays by divers hands, a kind of *The God that Failed* of the 1980's. This might take the post-dated moral bankrupting of the Thirties as its starting point. Anthony Blunt in his statement said that he had been loyal to his 'political conscience' instead of to his country. This did not seem to me quite to state the choice: which was not

---

1 Spender was having radiotherapy for prostate cancer. Twenty years before he had had diathermy for varicose veins.

2 On 16 November, Margaret Thatcher had publicly revealed the distinguished art historian, Sir Anthony Blunt (1907–1983), to have been the fourth 'Cambridge Spy'. He was stripped of his knighthood.

for a vague abstraction (political conscience) over patria but for the horizontal world of the whole of humanity viewed as one in the classless substratum of the oppressed and the proletariat as against the vertical segmented patria of England. The question this gives rise to is whether there is any international concept of humanity (the world) today which is represented by any political party or creed. [. . .]

Drove to Oxford, had lunch with the Berlins. [. . .] A lot of conversation about Anthony Blunt. Isaiah raised the question – what would one do if one discovered – in time of war for example that a close friend was an enemy agent? He said he didn't know what he would do – whether he'd denounce him. After lunch Lady D., Natasha, Aline and I played Scrabble. At tea time, Isaiah who'd gone meanwhile to All Souls, returned. We talked about the Middle East. He said there was no possibility of America and Russia ever joining to impose a settlement on the Middle East. The Russians had too much to gain from letting America mess things up in the Middle East. They had oil of their own and if there were shortages could impose terrific restrictions on their own people. They would let the Americans blunder confident that sooner or later the Middle East would fall like rotten fruit into their laps. The Americans were somehow too crude in their methods to effect any aim such as rescue of their hostages in Teheran. They made dinosaur-like movements. The Israelis could, perhaps, effect such an operation neatly.

Talked about Virginia Woolf's remarks about Isaiah and me in her letters. Isaiah said that writing that I would 'pan out to be a prodigious bore' was not very nice. But there were other remarks about my charm etc, I found. Also nice letters to me. In her remarks about Isaiah she always emphasizes his Jewishness – calls him 'a violent Jew'. When she first met him she seemed to view him as all influential Jewish mentality 'a fire brand'. Isaiah said that her letters increased one's sense of her cleverness but left one feeling that she was not as nice as one had thought previously. I said I thought that after all it was an honour to be mentioned by her at all. 'That's what we have to say to ourselves. That's the line we have to take,' said Isaiah.

28 November 1979, London

At the Royal Free Hospital where I go every morning for radio-therapy, the past few mornings I've found myself sitting next to Bill Coldstream, who accompanies his 86-year-old sister. He is 74 I suppose. He said to me today, 'I never feel old. I think every day that perhaps tomorrow I will stop being young and get down to work that is serious.'

12 December 1979, London

Friday evening [. . .] I had Patrick Woodcock, Keith Walker and a friend of his called John Thompson to dinner.[1] Keith W. and J.T. arrived first and Keith cooked the pheasants – some recipe with brandy. He arrived at six and unfortunately immediately began drinking. We had quite a pleasant dinner, everyone getting on well. But as soon as dinner was over and we went upstairs, Keith Walker fell asleep. As he formed a quarter of our party, this was painfully obvious. Also, it seemed difficult to bring the evening to an end. One did not like to wake him up and say, 'Good night, the party's over.' However at 12.30 he woke with a start, said 'I've behaved disgracefully,' and went to sleep again. His friend was sweet and firm with him, woke him again, took him home.

Saturday went to Oxford to attend the banquet at New College. I was the guest of Dick Ellmann.[2] I lunched with Stuart Hampshire. We talked about Goronwy [Rees], Burgess, Blunt etc. Also the same subject when I went to see Isaiah afterwards. During the war, several friends of mine were in Intelligence; including Isaiah and Stuart. They are all fascinated by the complications of people living in a world of lies – spies who betray spies. Francis Haskell, whom Isaiah and I

---

1 Patrick Woodcock (1920–2002), London doctor friend of Spender and Isherwood. John Thompson was a former student in the UCL English Department, and was currently working as a sub-editor at the *London Review of Books*, a journal set up when the *Times Literary Supplement* (with the whole other stable of *Times* newspapers) was on strike in 1979. He is not to be confused with John Thompson the psychiatrist.

2 Richard Ellmann (1918–1987), American literary scholar and biographer of James Joyce, Oscar Wilde and W. B. Yeats, was currently Goldsmith's Professor of English literature at Oxford University.

called on after lunch is a friend, protégé, and also now part protector of Blunt.[1] To complicate matters still further he has a Soviet wife who is permitted to visit her family in Russia. Belongs to a group of people who are passionate about art, culture, etc, and who consider that we in the West, are rather frivolous about things. Ultimately Mrs Haskell defends the Soviet Union. At Oxford they think that in order to be in such a privileged position she must do some sort of genteel spying: enough to make conversation about spies in front of her embarrassing. She is snub-nosed, plump, with old-style bobbed hair, immensely excited by works of art. Francis met her in the art gallery at Leningrad where she worked.

20 December 1979, London

Dined last night with Mervyn Stockwood, Bishop of Southwark at his annual Christmas dinner.[2] [. . .] I sat between Lady Sharples and [the Archbishop of] Canterbury.[3] Lady Sharples talked about speeches she made in the House of Lords, her children (anyway a daughter). She asked about Lizzie and I said she was having an affair with Dick Sylbert, and that marriage seemed unlikely as he was twenty-four years older than her, quite apart from his having tried marriage three times before and having several children. 'Those are no reasons at all,' she said in an enlightened tone of voice as though I were an old buffer who was expressing disapproval in my description, and she went on to say that her daughter – I think it was her daughter – lived with – or was married to – a much older man. [. . .]

I managed to disengage myself a bit from Lady Sharples and had some pleasant talk with the Archbishop Coggan (Canterbury) who said they were going to live at Sissinghurst. I said I knew Nigel Nicolson who lived there. 'Oh yes,' he said, 'the author of that strange book about his parents' marriage. What a business!' I said 'Nigel and his brother Ben thought it was the ideal marriage.' He said, quite twinkling: 'You mean his father having his boy friends and his mother

---

1 Francis Haskell (1928–2000), British art historian.

2 Mervyn Stockwood (1913–1995), Anglican Bishop of Southwark, 1959–80.

3 Lady Sharples (b. 1924) Tory peer. The current Archbishop of Canterbury was Donald Coggan (1909–2000).

her girl friends.' 'Yes,' I said. He laughed, really amused. I told him my idea about thinking of tunes and having friends as a formula for happiness.[1] He said: 'How strange your saying that. I was thinking something of the sort this very day.' 'I suppose you'd put religion where I put music,' I said. 'Well, yes. But I was thinking how much of one's happiness one owes to friends and, of course, to one's wife,' he said gleaming benignly at Lady Coggan. We talked about the Pope. 'Yes it seemed such a wonderfully hopeful thing, his travels to America, and seeming to open the Church to the world,' he said. 'But now he seems to be turning into a kind of Stalin with his opposition to birth control and so on. If one travels to India and places like that, and sees all the poverty one asks oneself what other pleasure do the people have except what goes into producing children, so how can one ask them to deprive themselves of that?' He seemed a really kind and nice man.

21 December 1979, Avane

We got to San Sano about 11 where Maro gave us an excellent dinner. Saturday, a gale and very cold. Matthew making a large doll's house from some planks of walnut he bought some years ago. It is to serve also as a children's cupboard. An ex-schoolteacher, now working in a bank, and her lover, studying economics at St Antony's, Oxford came to dinner. After dinner, Matthew put on the film he made during the summer. (We had a repeat of this today.) I read Elizabeth Bowen's *The Death of the Heart*. She is brilliant in the part that describes her sixteen-year-old heroine Portia's visit to a seaside resort, staying in the sea-front house of her sister-in-law Anna's governess. All the members of this family and their 'gang' are flashingly described, and the portrait of the man Eddy who makes love to Portia must be based on Goronwy Rees, who had a love affair with

---

1 On 12 December Spender had noted in his journal his gratitude for his principal resources: the accompaniment through his life of 'tunes going through one's head' which he knew by heart but could not quite identify and the consciousness of 'the beautiful character of one's friends'. The two came together in Bryan: 'I have been thinking of B's, playing my reels of him living in his trailer, loving the animals in the woods, listening to "tunes he tries to identify" which – in his case – are the songs of birds, and teaching school.'

Elizabeth and then left her, for Goronwy is drawn in venom. Portia's sister-in-law Anna is probably ironic self-portraiture. Anne's husband Thomas seems based on Elizabeth's equally opaque husband Alan, and St Quentin has the characteristics of William Plomer. The novel alternates between brilliant satiric observation and heavy seriousness. The attempt to narrate a love affair of Anna with a man called Pidgeon in the past, as a kind of parallel to the Portia–Eddy affair (and to Anna's own relations to Eddy) seems too evidently done to make the novel appear to have a solidity which it could do without. Even the scene in a woody dell in which Elizabeth tries to give depth to Eddy's character, and give him a tragic dimension fails, because it scarcely needs emphasizing that Eddy's way of taking himself seriously is what is most frivolous about him. One suspects that E[lizabeth] attempts to make him tragic because she has an eye on the real Eddy – Goronwy – who is going to read this. She also generalizes about love, life, situations etc sometimes with success but sometimes with an effect only of sententiousness, and her description of scenery, though evocative seems at the same time to be blurred. There is a muffled quality about her descriptions and generalizings which brings back vividly to mind a day a year or so before her death when I drove her from Oxford where she had been staying with the Berlins. It was one of those days in which sun struggles with mist, gilding and whitening the landscape and making it difficult to see because details are blurred by the mist and outlines made too definite by the sun. The whole hour and a half of the journey, Elizabeth talked, a long flow of anecdotes and comment, which owing to the weakness of her smoker's throat was, for the most part, just below the threshold of my hearing. The sound of her voice was as muffled to my hearing as the mist-swathed sun-filtering landscape was to my seeing, and I had a sense of everything being, as though the car I was driving was a crayon or chalk marking a line across a landscape which was made of paper. Usually she smoked all the time. But perhaps the stage her illness had reached prevented her doing so that day.

She could say unforgettable things and remarks of that kind sometimes occur in her novels but which sometimes strike a bull's eye, sometimes are all round the target. She described Jean, the first Mrs Cyril Connolly, as 'a great soft crook'; she said of Alan, her husband, that in talking with him there were 'mined areas'.

26 December 1979, Avane

We drove to lunch with Bill Weaver at his house near Arezzo.[1] He showed us the new house he has built into which he's going to move. To get there, we went through what I consider the real Tuscan landscape with its hills with long curves, fields that look flat, rather shiny as though they had been shorn and polished, interrupted by the exclamation marks of cypresses, black and occasionally very tall, sometimes standing above, sometimes clustered in groups around farmhouses which consist of separate blocks for living and storing, barns. [. . .]

Bill Weaver who was a genial and bright looking amico di [friend of] Chester Kallman – with all that that implies – five years ago has not at all lost his pudginess and amiability, though he now has an air of respectability gathered to himself together with several pounds weight. He made a good meal and good conversation: said he was writing a life of Eleonora Duse.[2] She was addicted, he said, to compulsive letter writing: two or three letters a day to people living under the same roof. He was rather dreading discovering hundreds more letters from Duse to lovers and admirers, since her letters were entirely about other letters. 'Beloved one! I wrote you three letters yesterday afternoon! Have you received these witnesses of my adoration? Did you get the telegram I sent yesterday afternoon?'

29 December 1979, Mouton

Our week with Matthew and Maro was beautiful, touching, without a resentful or hostile between-in-laws word. The weather was bad throughout, their house in winter dark, cavernous. In fact it is an assemblage of caverns, the connected caverns of kitchen and drawing room separated by curtains from the fire-lit hall which serves – with the kitchen – in winter as living room, and upstairs cavernous, pine-wood beamed bedrooms, clustering round the stairwell, and the huge bathroom, which seems the nucleus of activity in the upper part of

---

1 William Weaver (b. 1923), American translator and writer best known for his translations of Italian writers such as Umberto Eco and Italo Calvino.

2 Eleonora Duse (1858–1924), Italian actress.

the house. Small windows, red flagstones, stone stairs, a house that makes a very strong impression on one's memory. Seen from outside it lies in the landscape like some large spread-winged bird, with its central tower the chest, neck and blunted head, on its own hill which is a raised plateau in the middle of a valley of ochre-leaved oak trees, shrub, vineyards. Here M and M lead their very busy lives, looking after the children, getting them off to school in term-time[,] amusing them during the holidays, entertaining their friends. Matthew looks after the garden, farms his vegetables, vines, olives (Maro said what a relief it is when the olive harvest fails and there is not so much picking to do). One has the impression of children, parents, visitors, running through the hollow house as through some railway terminal. People going to the country to live quiet lives in which they can pursue their vocations develop routines (especially if they have families) which seem just as absorbing and distracting as town. Matthew, seasonably, was carpentering a wonderful three-storey American colonial-style clap-board doll's house-cum-toy-cupboard for the children. With all this activity I wondered whether to ask Matthew about his painting but finally did so. His development is slow (slowed-up) circuitous but nevertheless real, and he seems now on the verge of a breakthrough in several directions – landscape in which he is at last beginning to use elements of abstraction (in the manner of early Miró) with those of saturation in the countryside surrounding him; fantasy of a very Italianate Bellini-ish kind; and portraiture (but here he risks competing with Maro).

31 December 1979, Mouton

Philippe who has a cold and looked tired and depressed, cheered up at dinner. I remarked that he looked much better. 'I do,' he said. 'Sad as it is to say so, I feel better because Philippine is gone. Everything gets better when she goes, including the food. When she is here she rings the cook, alters the menus, upsets everything.' Then he said: 'Everything is much better now, except the news.' 'What news?' 'The Americans have announced that unless the Russians leave Afghanistan, they will occupy Pakistan. Moreover they've announced that they'll take action unless the hostages in the Embassy at Teheran are released within two weeks.'

After that, I did not sleep much, but woke at intervals which were abysses. I tried to read the ill-written scarifying *The Third World War*, which Sidgwick and Jackson sent me.[1] I noted that the author or authors (the book was published 1978) assume that in 1985 (the date of the Third World War according to their calculation) Iran under the Shah is the only stable country in the Middle East: and that Afghanistan is not on the map they provide. The Third World War is something I find I cannot read about, does not interest me, it is simply the most noisome possible tomb of everything. Some introductory information and statistics they provide do interest and in a way are more horrifying than their war. E.g. that in 1977 there were 'four billion people in the world of whom two-thirds (or 2.7 billion) lived in countries with a median income below $300 a head, while one third lived in countries with median incomes above $3,000 a head'. The very mention of these figures is like volcanic fire of the lives of the dispossessed under the thin crust of the millions of the prospering possessors. The impoverished billions are, of course, increasing, the prosperous ones decreasing.

I was brought up to have primitive Christian ideas which I got from the New Testament and non-conformist religion long before I had political views. Therefore I've always been conscious of the pressure of those who are starved of the means of realizing their own minds and senses, against the minority who enjoy the arts of civilization. Also that the pressure of those claims which come from deprivation and suffering which are terribly underlying realities, shallows [*sic*] the civilization, makes it the product of advantageous social conditions, empty of that reality – poverty – hunger – which must be on the margin of consciousness of the civilized happy few, but is not their experience. The oppressed live lives of living death buried under reality, the civilized lead curiously unreal lives.

Of course, I've never done anything much to deal with this situation. Yet I remain haunted by childish fantasies connected with it. One fantasy, based on the life of Jesus, that if I realized this in feeling and action, I would save the world – by witnessing to the truth which

---

1 John Hackett's *The Third World War: August 1985* (1978) is a fictional account of a war that breaks out between NATO and the Warsaw Pact forces. It was published by Sidgwick & Jackson.

is of the New testament – acting according to its realization, persuading others through incontrovertible witness. Another fantasy, that failing in this I would be judged after death by divine forces for my failure to live according to and bear witness to the truth that could save.

So here I am at Mouton, after a dinner of delicious wines and foods thinking these thoughts, and finding myself unable to sleep, reading prose as delectable as that food and wine – the essays of Max Beerbohm. There are things of his I have read as many times as any prose I love – 'No. 2 the Pines' and his parody of late Henry James *A Mote in the Middle Distance.*[1] [. . .]

After luncheon, we joined several of the household in visiting Pauline's grave in the cemetery of Pauillac. This is a depressing place like an enclosed asphalt playground stuffed with graves, with their cement headstones. However they are well cared for: flowers many of plastic but many also fresh on almost every grave. Caring for their dead, Guy told me, is a great preoccupation of people here.[2] The Mouton staff – men and women – had covered Pauline's grave with flowers. Philippe who talked all the time in his ordinary tone of voice delivered some kind of an address to the staff whom he called 'mes enfants' [my children]. He told them that this was only the temporary resting place of Pauline. Her remains would be removed to a site at Mouton – where exactly was still undecided. As we left, Guy – who seems to have known Pauline longer than Philippe or any of us (since before 1939) said to me in a ferocious voice – 'Exactly the same things, word for word, as he said last year. And as we left last year, he remarked to me – "You have no idea how expensive it is going to be!" – That ugly little cement grave –' he went on.

The Spenders saw in the New Year of 1980 at Mouton with the widowed Philippe de Rothschild and his new partner, Joan Littlewood. The decade began anxiously. Spender mourned the absence of

---

1 Max Beerbohm (1872–1956), British essayist, novelist and parodist. 'No. 2. The Pines' (1914) is about A. C. Swinburne and his companion Theodore Watts-Duncan. The James parody is called '*The Mote in the Middle Distance* by Henry James' (1906).

2 Guy Dumur (1921–1991), French critic and journalist for the *Nouvel Observateur.*

Pauline de Rothschild and worried about the political unrest unfurling in the world around him.

1 January 1980, Mouton

The New Year's Eve party a shadow of what it used to be twenty years ago (to think that we first came here in 1956) when Pauline was living. It consisted of Philippe, Richard Lippold and his friend Gianni, Fleur Cowles (newly arrived) and her husband Mr Meyer, Joan Littlewood, Guy Dumur, us.[1] It was preceded by the news which was of that gloomy, end-of-civilization kind which has been the background music to the little society to which I belong throughout my life. I found it difficult to shake off hideous thoughts about this game of musical chairs we live through. Lucky to have died before 1914, unlucky to be one of our grandchildren in 1980. At the edges of our Mediterranean world, the Khomeini Ayatollah in Iran, Russian tanks (and we saw them on TV) in Afghanistan.[2] President Carter outside the centres of these powers, a pale, feebly grinning, innocuous boy who has not been invited to some party of bloods and bullies.

We began dinner much too early for midnight – at about ten. It consisted of mussel soup, foie gras cooked in some kind of sauce, chocolate ice cream. Very good wines, the third of which was a Mouton of 1879. Dinner conversation pleasant but rather brutally crossed by a violent altercation between Guy and Philippe about the causes of anti-Semitism. By the time I was sufficiently interrupted from quiet interlocution with Gianni my table neighbour about Bologna, Philippe was shouting and banging the table with his fist, Guy was white and hissing, half-withdrawing. 'I tell you' shouted Philippe 'there was not the slightest trace of Christianity in the anti-Semitism of Hitler.' Guy had evidently been saying that the basis of anti-Semitism was Christianity and that this was an ever-present element

---

1 Richard Lippold (1915–2002), American sculptor. The American artist Fleur Fenton Cowles (b. 1910) had married her third husband Tom Montague Meyer, an industrialist, in 1955.

2 In April 1978, the Soviet-inclined socialist People's Democratic Party of Afghanistan had overthrown the regime in Afghanistan in the Great Saur Revolution. After a year of political turbulence the Soviet army entered Kabul in December 1979 and installed a pro-Moscow government.

in all anti-Semitism. Philippe was insisting that anti-Semitism was racist, of the same nature as hatred of Blacks by Whites, Whites by Blacks. Somehow, I felt for Philippe in his desire to remove from Hitler's detestable prejudices the faintest justification for it in traditional religious attitudes. To provide a kind of buffer argument, an alternative to their irreconcilably opposite points of view, I said that the cause of anti-Semitism was not that the Jews were seriously considered the crucifiers of Christ (at any rate not since the 14th century) but that they were an alien community bound together by race and religion within another community which resented its failure to assimilate them. 'All the same they are hated for not being Christian' said Guy 'as the enemies of the Christian religion.' 'If you say that,' I said 'I will tell you who Auden said were the murderers of Christ.' 'Who then?' asked Guy. 'The French.' 'Why?' 'Because the person who delivered Christ to his crucifixion was Pontius Pilate, the Roman governor, and the French are inheritors of the spirit of Roman rationality.'

The preposterous Audenism killed the conversation. Later, when we left the table, Guy produced a parcel for Philippe, containing Peter Quennell's illustrated book on romanticism, Philippe became all sweetness and conciliation.[1] Someone turned on TV. There was a last round-up of the apocalyptic news before the New Year. Philippe said: 'Let's go into the salon and drink champagne.' Joan Littlewood said: 'Why do you have to break the party up? Let's stay here. They'll announce the New Year on TV.' Which they did, before we moved into the great salon. I thought Joan's interruption unfortunate because I suddenly remembered what New Years have been like when Pauline was alive. The door had been flung open. Servants had entered the salon, carrying candles and flowers. All round the edges of the salon there were pots of flowering lilac to celebrate Pauline's birthday which was New Year. There were presents from everyone to everyone. A gong was struck.

When the mistress of a great house dies and the master is left alone there is a void, an absence which shows in a hundred negative things in corners of the house and the garden, in a laxness of standards, less

---

1 Peter Quennell, *Romantic England, Writing and Painting 1717–1851* (1970).

well-chosen menus, decline in the cooking, a kind of fraying at the edges of a hole which has been made by her vanishing. It shows certainly in the eyes of the servants [. . .], in the mixture of sentimentality towards her and malice towards her successors which shows in their constant expressions of regret for her, in an action like that of the servants going to the cemetery on her anniversary to lay flowers before Philippe, the master[,] had thought of doing so.

On 14 January 1980, back in London, Spender had what he described as 'a rather sensational accident'. 'Running out to buy some food for an unexpected guest, I fell off the slippery pavement (it was a rainy evening) outside Finchley Road station and broke the ligaments of both knees.' Spender was taken to the Royal Free Hospital in Hampstead where he underwent two operations. He stayed there for nearly three months.

The accident. Notes on tape. January 1980
Suddenly all your arrangements which had been leading in a certain direction at the moment of the accident   an accident can seem the very opposite of
    is the reversal of your plans which had been leading upwards towards a moment that was the accident
    suddenly then
    everything which had been a future towards which the past had been leading is reversed in the sense that the accident doesn't seem an accident at all so much as a correction of gigantic misapprehensions in which you've been living until that moment.
    suddenly the next minute is not going to be like the next minute the next hour the next hour
    a sense then in which it seems more revelation merely you have been misinterpreting everything which led up to this thinking it led to a series you suddenly discover an entirely different series.
my accident happened in a pretty typical way I suppose.
a change of plans led to inviting a guest to dinner at a very late moment with the idea that he could drive me on to a party to celebrate the thirtieth birthday of another friend
so my wife who was tired would not have to go to the party

I went to a row of shops with the idea of buying avocado.

Avocado all unripe so I went a further few hundred yards to John Barnes to get smoked salmon.

What seems strange is that the road seemed particularly dark although outside the underground station.

It was raining, quite a lot of traffic, how it happened I can't recall but I think I must have slipped with my heel off the pavement

doing that was followed by a cracking whip-like sensation and I fell to the ground

I did not feel particularly alarmed, something serious about my situation caused me immediately to [be] surrounded by people who took me across the road to the shelter of Finchley Road Station. When they tried to lift me by my arms and legs I suffered almost unendurable sensation. However the moment they got me in the shelter of Finchley Road Station and I could stretch my legs I felt quite at ease and in a calm state of mind. Two or three people lingered suggesting ways in which they could help me. One called for an ambulance. While waiting for this, another man appeared who was a New Zealander. He started asking me where I lived and told me about the pleasures of Christmas in New Zealand.

Although I felt calm I also felt I had behaved with extraordinary stupidity. I thought of all the numbers of ways in which I could have crossed the road with more precaution and in which this moment which was plunging me immediately in such a future need never have occurred. There was something irremediable about my stupidity which I felt even more than stupid. The crew of the ambulance arrived, made the same mistakes in carrying me into the ambulance but then having got there allowed me to lie down again where I felt again quite at ease. The ambulance people asked me questions which seemed partly to arise from a desire for information partly out of desire to show off since questions about my medical condition were bound to be asked by more efficient authorities when I arrived at the hospital. When we got to the hospital I was put to rest under a rug etc and asked more questions then left. Shortly after, Natasha arrived. We were taken up to the casualty ward and I was first examined by a surgeon. The surgeon looked at my right knee which was enormously swollen and said 'Well we've rarely had the privilege to look at swelling so complete before – have we?' I was all the time aware of my left knee being equally wrong with my right knee and I think I tried to point it out at the time.

I don't remember very much about the ward except it belonged to the strange world of hospital.

The R.F.H. [Royal Free Hospital] is a twelve-storey glass and concrete structure built up against the flattest elevation of Hampstead Heath.

Walking or being rolled along its various corridors one feels that one is in a vast modernistic stage set arranged so that scenery and characters can be transformed frequently – this specially true of the orthopaedic ward on the eighth storey. Here you see victims of accidents, young athletes and the aged and decrepit being shunted along on their trolleys.

The wards are mostly designed for four patients but can contain more. The ward I first went to contained apart from me one young man who glanced up with faint curiosity when I came in. He had a book – Holmes's Life of Shelley.¹ [. . .]

Whatever time of day it was changed rapidly to night. The casualties of the orthopaedic ward seemed a series of corridors with people being shuttled all the time from operating ward or brought back from them and put into their beds. This activity had an extraordinary normality about it. I hadn't been there ten minutes before I thought of being taken to the Operating Theatre, the most ordinary procedure possible.

But at night one could think of the ward of the whole twelve-storey hospital as a series of photo montages or cinematographic Jacob's ladders of people drawn from every class brought together by crises of their lives and enacting their very physical but also, in a sense, metaphysical – living or dying drama. I thought for a bit with embarrassment of my own death and what seemed peculiarly [sic] about the idea of my dying is that of all those there I was one of the very few who if I died would be thrown out upon the discussion heap of Journalism. I had a flash of my whole life's achievement and it seemed to me a succession of botched beginnings, of tasks inadequately done, perhaps a very few real achievements. These of which there were a dozen jewels on a refuse dump of failures; filth.

---

1 Richard Holmes, *Shelley: The Pursuit* (1974).

I thought how I had been planning rather carefully to create a selected version of my work which would separate the worthwhile from the junk. How I had been feeling I should dedicate the next five years to this. Perhaps the meaning of the accident was that although I have this intention I was not seriously carrying it out, I was still continuing to live the life of a journalist.

When blows of this sort come as it were from out of the night I always think of the figure of Auden as though he had said: 'He has to have some more definite signal which will really commit him to the path which he has still not properly set himself on.' Thinking these thoughts my next thought there was something wrong about them even in connection with death if death for me meant a tawdry begrimed botched reputation. What would that mean to all these other people in the wards assuming that they would not have names and careers evaluated in obituaries. Why should I think my death was different from theirs. Simply because it enjoyed a far-flung notoriety – notices in columns of other writers, some friends some enemies? It was part of the vulgarity which grows with public life.

4 February 1980, London

Francis Bacon visited me. Luckily no other visitor was there and I saw him alone. After a little conversation I mentioned that nothing I was going through – the discomfort of having both legs in plaster – compared with the real suffering of certain friends of mine – which they were enduring at this very moment – Renée Hampshire in the last stages of cancer.[1] Francis started talking about his sister who has multiple sclerosis. He told me how two or three days ago another bone of her body cracked. He said that physically she was completely helpless – only her mind and memory remained intact. He said in that voice of his which is always ironic – so that when he talks one always has the sense of the most tragic things being farcical in the sight of some Hardy-esque God surveying humanity – 'Every time I see her she remembers more and more, which doesn't help matters much because she and I (she is South African) never did get on, in fact, there were few things I could ever bear about her.' Francis pays

---

1 Renée Hampshire would die later in 1980.

£10,000 a year on her medical bills, etc. I asked him whether he didn't get any tax relief on this. He said 'Yes, £100 per annum.' While he was talking he seemed to shed light on his painting. I remembered a wholly distorted figure, like a head of remarkable ugliness on a sphinx-like torso, and with arms and legs so minimal they might have been holders of little wheels – which was in a painting of Francis the Dufferins used to have – which I found almost unbearably ugly, and criticized in my own mind as emotionally too cynical. Now it seemed to me that this image related to his sister and that it must be one that accompanies him every day. This throws light on his painting. [. . .]

Early on in my illness, I was disgusted by food and refused it almost entirely. Nikos [Stangos] used to shout at me: 'You must eat. You must eat. You're behaving as if you want to die!' He visited me almost every day it seemed while David Plante was with his family in America. Later, David and he both came about once a week, I suppose. James Joll and John Golding came, radiating sympathy and friendliness.[1] Stuart Hampshire, always rather elated, wonderful. I wrote to him two days ago saying it occurred to me that his visits were partly a gift from Renée who, though dying, must have pressed him to come and see me. Isaiah Berlin: conversation of one who regarded my illness as quite incidental – just went on talking as he might have at Headington House [the Berlins' house in Oxford] or in the Royal Box at the Opera – about Anthony Blunt, Stuart, Oxford etc. My brother Humphrey, agitated, anxious, protective, horrified that I, of all people, should be stricken. [. . .] Rosamond Lehmann, concerned with Sean Day-Lewis's biography of Cecil – but very warm and affectionate.[2] Peggy Ashcroft, who also had been at the same hospital for her knees. Juliette Huxley (who lives across the road from the hospital) nearly every afternoon, bright, perky. We exchanged reminiscences about her life with Julian, which she is

---

1 James Joll (1918–1994), British historian. The art historian John Golding (b. 1929), a specialist in cubism and himself a painter, was his partner.

2 Sean Day-Lewis's biography of his father Cecil Day Lewis, *An English Literary Life*, had come out earlier in the year, with its account of Day Lewis's liaison with Rosamond Lehmann. In the preface to his biography, Sean Day-Lewis acknowledged his dual desire to lionize and destroy his father.

writing about.[1] Francis Huxley.[2] Frank and Anita Kermode.[3] Jim West and Mary McCarthy: I asked Mary for a copy of her last novel, then was humiliated by finding I couldn't read it, partly because a side effect of this illness is that you have a considerable loss of sight. Later, I read one or two books for review – Peggy Guggenheim's memoirs.[4]

In fact as long as I could see I read all the time but can remember now almost nothing of what I read.

Other visitors – for the record. Clifford Curzon who, rather like Isaiah, carried on with the conversation of the outside world. Philip Spender – pale and tense – rather worried, I feel, about *Index*.[5] Lizzie, very often, bringing me prunes she'd stewed, chicken she'd boiled and two or three times a carry-in Chinese dinner. Once I couldn't talk to her for a few minutes because I suddenly started crying thinking about Michael Astor – like Renée, dying of cancer. (They both died before I left hospital.) Dick Sylbert – with Lizzie: always smiling, intelligent, helpful, talkative – but somehow something there is wrong. Cyrus Ghani – but much more surprising – Parviz – Lizzie's Iranian ex-Ambassador.[6] Karl Miller, wearing a great coat with leather lapels, which made him look like a rather gloomy hussar of some Death Watch Regiment, saying 'I'm sure it's horrible for you to be visited in hospital.' Dick Ellmann; Rivers Scott, literary editor of *Now* whom I hardly knew before this, and got to like. My sister Christine, terribly flustered when she ran once into Clifford Curzon.

---

1 Juliette Huxley's autobiography, *Leaves of the Tulip Tree*, was published in 1986.

2 Francis Huxley (b. 1923), British anthropologist, son of Julian and Juliette Huxley.

3 Anita van Vactor (b. 1929), literary critic and second wife of Frank Kermode.

4 Guggenheim had died in December 1979. Her autobiography, *Out of this Century: Confessions of an Art Addict*, was published posthumously in 1980.

5 Philip Spender (b. 1943), Spender's nephew, was at this time managing director of *Index on Censorship*, the magazine founded at Spender's initiative in 1972.

6 Parviz C. Radji (b. 1936), Iranian Ambassador in London, 1976–9, with whom Lizzie had had a relationship.

Then Matthew came for a week. He came every day and stayed for hours with great cheerfulness of duty till it nearly broke my heart and I said: 'I'm sure there must be people you want to see now that you've only a week in London.' He said 'No I just want to be with you.' But later did make visits to friends and to art galleries. In fact, he arranged an exhibition.

Natasha came every single day and was wonderful, though desperately tired a lot of the time.

At eight visitors would have to go, the strip lighting in my room went on – an intense glare, and one faced that white-vaulted sensation of a hospital at night.

I thought of B[ryan] a lot.

Most of my thoughts were of a summing up kind. I thought of my life – of my work. Everything I had done – or nearly everything – seemed, from the point of view of work, a failure, perhaps not of an exceptional kind but the *Journalier*, Journalistic kind: that of a person who does not use his talents – by this I mean more even – does not use them enough even to discover how much talent he has. I blame myself not so much for failure – but for not having pressed ideas of work original work to the point of proof where they either failed or succeeded. What I blame myself for in a sense is that I didn't have enough failures – but that I so often put aside the things I most deeply wanted to do – the things that were my own thing from inside myself – and did things which were proposed from the outside.

In mid-April, with the approval of his doctor and accompanied by Natasha, Spender taught a writing course in Louisville, Kentucky. The course consisted in listening to students' poems and commenting on them. The Spenders lived close to the classroom, to which he travelled in a wheelchair. Given the fragile state of his health, he tried to keep clear of most activities relating to 'poetry, pottery (easily confused, the two of them)'. They returned to London in July.

12 July 1980, Salisbury

On Sunday before I went to Salisbury Christopher [Isherwood] and Don [Bachardy] came to dinner with Lizzie, who had a friend – a rather glamorous girl – with her. They first of all came to Loudoun Road, and we had champagne. They were both in extremely good form – Christopher seemingly scarcely altered from when I first knew him – if anything, sharper, clearer, more completely in command of everything. Donny, being now clean-shaved, and having shed whiskers, moustache etc which have in the intervals of time occasionally obtruded on him, looked years younger. Their attachment to each other is wonderful. On Christopher's side it is a vast inclusiveness of Don in everything. On Don's it is an absorption into his own, quite independent personality, of Christopher's way of speaking, his voice, his enunciation, his phrasing. I felt strangely touched by the way in which, when C. talks, Don's eyes are never off him, his mouth half-open in a laugh or some deeply sensuous enjoyment of Christopher's continuous turn.

C. got very drunk. This makes him ever more emphatic, noisy, uproarious – with a great many exclamations – 'Oh yes!' 'Gee!' 'Oh yeah!' He has acquired an American accent – like chips with everything he says. Especially a flattening of his vowels and a few expletives – and occasionally, he speaks of Americans as 'us' ('We're real proud of our Senators,' he said about the Senate Committee inquiring into Watergate, at that time)[.][1] At the end of the evening, he uttered a cry and, flopping back his arms like flippers, advanced them and gave each one of us an all-inclusive embrace, followed by a resounding kiss on the cheek.

---

1 The Watergate Scandal (1972–4) was a landmark American political scandal that demonstrated the power of the press as an opposing force to the American presidency. The scandal arose after five burglars were arrested at the Democratic National Committee offices in the Watergate complex, Washington. Carl Bernstein and Bob Woodward, two journalists at the *Washington Post*, investigated the incident, uncovering links between the Nixon re-election campaign and those involved in the burglary. Tape recordings subsequently revealed Nixon's attempts to influence the police investigation of the crime. As a result of the controversy, forty government officials were either indicted or jailed and Nixon stepped down as President on 8 August 1974 under the threat of impeachment.

I had given him a copy of the proof of my essay on his *My Guru and His Disciple* which I had written for the *New York Review*.[1] I had taken great pains over this review – but it had turned into a general essay on Isherwood with a very interesting thesis – I think – but too developed for a review of this particular book – not sufficiently developed for a general essay. In France I rewrote it cutting down the general discussion and giving much more space to the book. When I read the proofs I was disappointed, realizing that it was the kind of piece one should put aside for three months and then rewrite. So I gave it to Christopher with trepidation. Next morning I rang him at his hotel, where he was having a fearful hangover. He was polite about the review – but, as though he was searching for reasons not to be annoyed about it – 'It was perfect' – 'Yes, you did say it was my best book' – whereas, if the review had been the essay of which I still dream, he would have said: 'It is the best thing ever written about me.'

During the next days I relived all the more agonizing passages of my relations with Christopher. The tone of the review was defensive about Isherwood and his religion as though his religious views were extremely vulnerable (which qua the religion, I think they are) and I had to point out that what the reader must look for in this book was the portrait of the Guru as Xtopher himself. But in fact all the reviewers said this, most of them leaving out the caveat about Christopher's views on Hinduism (all except Christopher Ricks who said he would have wished to see a review of the book by T. S. Eliot). I thought that Christopher's icy tones were meant to convey to me that I had in some way betrayed him. He had once told me (re. a less than enthusiastic review I wrote of his last book) that one should only give rave reviews to one's friends' books. I found myself carrying on a dialogue with him in which I said: 'After all, no one has used his friends more extensively for copy than you, and you have often been critical of them. Myself, I am only interested in the opinions of my friends about my work: and I do not expect them to be uncritical. Besides the only books I ever want to write about are those by my friends' – etc.

1 'Issyvoo's Conversion', *New York Review of Books*, 14 August 1980. Isherwood's 1980 *My Guru and His Disciple* is a portrait of the Hindu priest, Swami Prabhavananda, who had provided Isherwood with spiritual guidance for thirty years.

I re-lived all this disquiet for several days. Then, just before we left for America, Christopher and Don both rang from Santa Monica. They were completely friendly. I felt immense alleviation and happiness. How is all this?

In July 1980, Spender and other literary dignitaries travelled to New Mexico for the 50th anniversary of D. H. Lawrence's death. Lawrence's ashes were interred near the Kiowa ranch near Taos, New Mexico, which he and his wife had acquired in 1924 in exchange for the manuscript of Sons and Lovers. *The couple had only lived there together for two years before returning to Italy, but after Lawrence's death in 1930, Frieda returned to New Mexico and remained there until her own death in 1956. Spender himself had previously stayed at the ranch in 1948, while writing* World Within World.

31 July 1980, Newport, Rhode Island

We flew on July 15. Very long journey, with change of planes from London to Santa Fe. Margaret Drabble was with us.[1] We liked her very much. Were met by a disoriented raggle-taggle-bearded professor and a young woman who seemed stoned or drunk – but was probably just herself doing her thing (this included nearly killing Margaret Drabble while driving her to the motel). We had lost our luggage but this turned up the following morning. Al Alvarez, with wife and two children, very well organized and with their own car, were at the hotel. The following day Al and I gave a joint reading at Albuquerque. A youngish man who was an attorney in the offices of the city of Albuquerque drove us to Santa Fe. There we were taken to the house of our host and hostess, a Mr Mudd and a Miss (or Mrs) Bell who seem to be living experimentally together, with a view to marriage.[2] [. . .]

We drove to Lawrence's ranch now taken over by the University of New Mexico, where there was to be a ceremony at the shrine in which were Lawrence's ashes: and outside it a slab under which

---

1 Margaret Drabble (b. 1939), British novelist.

2 Harvey Mudd, namesake and descendant of the wealthy industrialist, Harvey Seeley Mudd (1888–1955).

Frieda was buried. The ranch had changed so much since I was there in 1948 that it was scarcely recognizable. Built up to be a tourist centre, a show place, and with the trees so grown that they shut out most of the wide view I had of the landscape below the sacred mountain. We were almost the first to arrive, apart from some girls dressed entirely in white, who were practising a kind of dance of sylphs outside the shrine. Harvey Mudd and I took photographs with my camera (he was trained as a photographer at some period in his life when he was in the U.S. Army). The white-attired sylphs, swaying, ran up to the shrine and then bent over, bending their right knees and raising and pointing their left legs so that I could see right up the skirts of the one nearest me. They kept on practising this, to the accompaniment of drum taps, until it began to grow dark. We learned that the bus-load of participants in the conference coming from Santa Fe had broken down. Finally they arrived, and together with them two movie stars direct from Hollywood, to give readings of Lawrence's poetry and prose, looking incredibly crushable and artificial. As soon as they started reading, in the semi-darkness, the rain came pelting down. I thought how Frieda would have roared with laughter at all this (but she would have been quite pleased) and of the malicious pleasure [Dorothy] Brett would have taken in it. [. . .]

Next day Harvey Mudd very kindly drove us to Albuquerque airport, from which we flew to Orono, Maine, via Boston. Quite a tiring journey. We were met by Carroll Terrell (Terry) whom I had already met in October.[1] He took us out to dinner at a quite good restaurant only a half-mile from the University Motel where I had stayed in October. I had partly prepared myself for lecturing on Pound, and had been reading books by him and about him in all my spare time recently. But in fact all I was expected to do was lecture each morning for 40 minutes or so about Eliot, Yeats, Auden, and (on the last morning) myself, to a group of students. Enrolment, according to Terry, was disappointing. In the afternoons I had to comment on students' work. It was all quite easy. One of the students was a mad nun who, after a poem had been read, would make comments such as 'I like that poem, it has so many Ws in it.' At one of my morning talks she asked the question: 'Is the name of Shelley a

---

1 Carroll F. Terrell (1917–2003), American literary scholar and publisher.

cryptogram?' She was a rubbery-looking woman, like a heap of motor tyres piled on top of one another and held together by a knitted woollen dress. On Thursday, when Terry gave a party for the students and us beside the pool in his garden she suddenly got up and flung herself backwards into the pool. She got out, with dripping clothes which she never changed. [. . .]

On Sunday, Terry drove us to Castine [Maine] where we lunched with Jim West and Mary McCarthy. Castine is one of those beautiful New England places that strike me as all white wooden screens of houses and church spires, amid bright green lawns, against bright blue sky and sea – an atmosphere of neighbourliness and cleanliness however many the ancient drunks, the divorcing tragic young, etc. Mary and Jim West have one of the most beautiful houses there – a very large, pale yellow clapper-boarded [*sic*] house with a hallway extending from front to back, and a double staircase with stairs descending to the back and front and meeting on a landing on the first floor. The furniture is all perfect, on the walls there are beautiful coloured prints of flowers and birds. The house incredibly clean. At the back of the house there is a lawn the size of a small park, surrounded by trees. The Wests had invited Elizabeth Hardwick, and we brought with us Carroll Terrell who had driven us. Mary was in pain from shingles: to make matters worse, Jim had broken a leg: and to top all (partly also explaining all), Mary is involved in a frightful law suit with Lillian Hellman. At a Dick Cavett TV interview, Mary – asked what she thought about L.H. – replied 'every word she writes is a lie, including the "ands" and the "buts".'[1] While we were talking about this, it suddenly occurred to me that perhaps Lennie Bernstein would, if asked to do so, persuade L.H. to drop the case, which Jim told me, was already costing the Wests $25,000.[2] Mary seemed quite pleased at the idea of my intervening. Later, I rang Lennie. He was

---

1 Lillian Hellman (1905–1984), American playwright. In February Hellman had filed a $2.2 million dollar lawsuit for slander against McCarthy for her statement on *The Dick Cavett Show* in January. The long, highly public feud between the two women formed the basis for Nora Ephron's 2002 musical *Imaginary Friends*.

2 Leonard Bernstein (1918–1990), American conductor and composer. Hellman and Bernstein were friendly neighbours at their summer homes on Martha's Vineyard and had collaborated on the operetta *Candide* in 1956.

very well-disposed. He said he had already asked L.H. why she didn't drop it, and she had answered 'Because I am angry.' 'She is a very angry lady,' said Lenny, 'not just about this but all the years I've known her she's been angry about something or other.' He said he would think over whether he would speak to her again about this or not – he had already asked her once. Whether he did so or not, on the following week when we dined with Elizabeth Hardwick, the Wests had heard nothing. Things seem going badly with them now. She talks as brilliantly amusingly and bravely as ever – only equalled by Liz Hardwick who accompanies Mary's Eastern seaboard accent with her almost operatic Kentucky one rich in 'oh's and 'ah's and exclamations – but her pale face, and the rather anguished expression in her eyes, seem struggling bravely to keep up with her words. Jim is large and calm, talking in his measured tones, but candidly and attentively anxious.

4 August 1980, New York

On Monday, July 29th we went for three days to stay with Alan Pryce-Jones at Newport [Rhode Island].[1] He has a kind of compound of three or four houses in a previously run-down now run-up area of that once very rich, then rather forsaken, now touristically revived town. He is a tremendous charmer and despite his mundanity, snobbishness etc, his caddishness, he has a kind of transparency. One looks through to him not into depths but into endless funds of good nature. He has one of those faces that seem to sweep back from the nose, the hair like a wave swept back from the scudding bow of a yacht. His conversation for the most part is an endless succession of anecdotes about his louche wicked working mostly very rich neighbours with all their Ruthless tragedies. Nobody can be funnier at describing the life-history of his German housekeeper, an ardent Nazi, the rape of her daughter, her relations with the six black children of some neighbours called the Raspberries, the sermon made by the local rector praising the exemplary life of a millionaire who had not been sober for the past twenty years, before his sniggering rela-

---

1 Alan Pryce-Jones (1908–2000), British writer and critic, editor of the *Times Literary Supplement*, 1948–59. His current partner was Larry Hudson.

tives. I am his utterly captivated audience when he tells these stories, my only grievance being when he takes us out to dinner with a group of people exactly corresponding to his descriptions, and I am left sitting between two bores, while beyond earshot, at the far end of the table, he is regaling others with his anecdotes. One of the strange things about him is that, being so un-boring himself, he lives contentedly among people who are so boring. Perhaps this is because he can always provide self-entertainment, or perhaps it is due to his endless good nature. [. . .]

[Larry Hudson] was really affectionate and happy with Natasha and me, at the end of our stay driving us the four-hour journey into N.Y. It seemed awful to let him leave us at the front door of Richard Sennett (who had invited us to dine) so I got Dick to invite him to dinner.[1] [. . .] The evening at Dick Sennett's was enjoyable. We also stayed the night with him. He has a fairly large maisonette with library-cum-sitting room on the first floor and below that entrance hall dining room, kitchen. A Steinway on the first floor, spinet in the dining room. He is an excellent cook. Larry and I helped him lay places at a large table downstairs. He seemed very uncertain as to how to place ten people. Susan Sontag, David Rieff, a Cuban poet who is supposed to be very good but who only talked banalities, in the style of Neruda, and Alan Marks, a pianist, were our fellow guests.[2] Susan and Natasha got together making contingency plans for a possible journey to America by Sonia Orwell. Susan was very excited said she felt like taking a plane to London immediately to save Sonia from English doctors treating her advanced cancer. On their missions of mercy they are like characters in T. S. Eliot's *The Cocktail Party*. Talk about Jimmy and Billy Carter.[3] David Rieff is now about six feet five, extremely hirsute, bespectacled with locks of hair falling down to his shoulders. As, a bit smirking, he talked about

---

1 Richard Sennett (b. 1943) is a sociologist whose field concerns social relationships in cities. He holds numerous academic posts and is the founding director of the New York Institute of the Humanities.

2 Alan Marks (1949–1995), American pianist.

3 In 1979 the American President Carter's brother Billy had registered as a foreign agent of the Libyan government and received a $220,000 loan. In the lead-up to the presidential election in October 1980 Billy became the centre of a storm of allegations about influence-peddling dubbed 'Billygate' in the press.

policy, I was suddenly reminded of him as a seven or eight-year-old child, small and rather exquisitely formed, like a tame parakeet accompanying Susan on her journeys and making pronouncements in the same slightly ogling way about the war in Vietnam. After dinner, Natasha and Alan played Schubert duets. They were inspired doing so, played them with tremendous zest and sensibility, both with the same feeling for those tunes of haunting melancholy which recur like horns heard through a dark forest, sounding colours like those in a painting of Uccello. Alan Marks and also Dick Sennett very appreciative of Natasha's intense musicality. Marks himself is rather fascinating, with mouth a bit open, always, snub nose, mobile eyes and features, small lithe body, he has a bit the look of Nijinsky – more that of a dancer than a pianist. He plays with padding hands like cat's or panther's paws, cruelly caressing to the piano. After the duets we got him to play Chopin, which he did extremely well. His manner is flatteringly affectionate. Dick told me that after we had gone to bed, Alan stayed until 4 a.m. flirting and kissing, but evading bed on the grounds that a female Russian dancer (whom he hated) was awaiting him.

5 August 1980, New York

For the weekend we stayed with the Buttingers, Muriel and Jo. As Muriel explained when driving us from the Princeton bus stop to Pennington, Jo is in a rapidly deteriorating mental condition, but is in much improved health physically. He no longer recognizes people or remembers anything about them. When told my name, he did not recall our having known one another for forty years but only that the name itself suggested associations. Looking at me with great baby eyes he said in his grave voice of a senile President of a small Republic greeting an official visitor: 'With a name like that, you must be dangerous' and he extended his right hand. [. . .] He remarks to Natasha looking at her dress 'The flowers on your dress are beautiful. But what is underneath must be still more beautiful.' He has got very over-weight but does not care about this, interrupting the conversation to demand more nuts, cheese, biscuits, another drink, whatever is being served. [. . .]

On Sunday Natasha went for a drive with Jo, and I was left alone with Muriel. She wanted to ask me questions about my life, work etc, which I tried to answer. Then she said: 'I want to ask you the question which now I ask all my old friends. What do you think of life?' I answered that I thought people were divided into those who wanted satisfactions of fame, of wealth, of love, of recognition, and those who simply enjoyed things that were given – beauty, for instance. That the latter had an immense advantage – unless they were very poor, ill, or in some other way deprived, they simply enjoyed life with their senses. Thus although I felt that I had failed in some important respects – in sex and in work – I still loved life and could say I was happy. And in a negative way, I counted my blessings and considered myself far luckier than most of the world's population. She said that on the whole she agreed with this. When she was young she had felt guilty about being wealthy and often thought she would be happier if she had been brought up in much less privileged circumstances. But later she had been grateful that she had money, because she certainly had been able to help people who were victims in Austria and other parts of Europe during the '30s. Now she was glad that she had money because whatever happened to her (and she might not live long, having high blood pressure, a weak heart etc), Jo would be well taken care of. She then went on to say that she had at times been made very unhappy by Jo's infidelities and deceptions. Finally, she had had a showdown with him and said that she would let him go his way, but she would also go hers – she would have affairs and if she wanted to marry someone else she would do so. [. . .]

She said she often thought about our relationship. She seemed to think she had made too much of my relationship with Tony [Hyndman] being an obstacle to mine with her. I said this was not so – that she had been extremely patient, and in fact had never once complained about Tony. I added that I should have ditched Tony there and then – but that if there had not been him there would have been someone else. He was the visible manifestation of something which was the deepest thing in my nature – my loyalty to the 'queer' world, the gay. She seemed not so certain as she had been at the time that my being what I was made our relationship impossible.

While she was speaking, I remembered a night at her little wooden house near Sulz Stangau in the Wiener Wald. She and Tony and I slept out of doors in the meadow that surrounded this 'Blockhaus' near the edge of the wood. Muriel slept between Tony and me. I lay awake absorbing with all my senses the blaze of the stars, the scent of the meadow. The woman beside me seemed the breathing flesh of all this. I felt for her hand and realized that she was also awake, thinking of me. Then I began to explore with my hand her thighs and the rest of her body. Tony was healthily asleep but all the time I was aware of him and that what seemed the most natural thing in the world for me at that moment, was also treachery to someone who trusted me completely and whom I had got into a position where he could not manage without me. Beyond this was the fear of what my friends would say.

The attachment to Tony was as though I were tied to him by cord. Looking back now it seems strange that Muriel and I did not simply get up and walk away into the woods, and leave him sleeping. But the idea never occurred to me. Later, when we did have an affair, there was always this feeling that Tony would collapse without me (in fact he did do so, but that is not the point. The point is that there was my guilt towards another person which was a kind of absolute – more pressing than any feeling for Muriel, more pressing than my responsibility towards my own self-development – which after all is a very great responsibility). In the long run, I did, of course, ditch Tony – but I never lost my loyalty to a commitment which he represented. I know what Christopher Isherwood means when he writes unforgivingly of his 'queer' friends who get married.

But recently the idea of making love with a woman in the woods has seemed to me very important. It was the situation, amid nature, in which doing so seemed natural. I feel that if Muriel and I had walked away to another part of the forest there would have been no inhibitions. Perhaps even I would have become freed of Tony. And somehow making love in rooms and beds was always unsatisfactory, with women. I connect this with a very early memory. When I was seven or eight, for some reason one night I slept in bed with a nursemaid called Marion. She was quite young, I think – seventeen or so – and had always attracted me. I was aware that she was very pretty. I did not sleep with her in a wood but in bed – yet my memory is of her wearing a gauzy nightdress that somehow resembled a meadow, of the scent of flowers and of my at once falling and being gently supported, through nature – night, stars, forest, grass, flowers.

8 August 1980, London

On Wednesday (Aug 6) we flew back to London by British Airways. Have had jet lag but spent most of yesterday correcting and cutting 'Letters to Christopher Isherwood and Two Journals'.

On Tues evening in New York we dined together with Susan Sontag, David Rieff, and Susan's Italian boyfriend. Susan talked again about Joseph Brodsky – said she had received a letter from him which contained things worse even than those [he] had said in the Chinese restaurant some months ago, defending the Shah [of Iran]. He has things both ways, she said. He hated conditions in the Soviet Union, and yet said that American writers were unreal in their work, because they had no experience of imprisonment and torture. Susan said that she was giving up writing essays and only wanted to write stories – if she could master the technique – and she seemed modest about this. [. . .]

More notes about America. Muriel in her reflections on life said that the greatest unhappiness to her was her conviction that there was going to be a nuclear war. As a rational person she could not believe this to be other than inevitable and it darkened her whole view of life for herself and her grandchildren. She always kept by her enough Seconal tablets to kill her. She hoped that if she had a fatal illness it would not take a form which deprived her of the will power to do this. If there were a nuclear war she would have to wait until she was certain that it could not be stopped and that there was nothing she could do to help those near to her – and that might be too late also.

When we were with Susan [Sontag], I said we had been to stay with the Buttingers and started to describe our weekend. Susan said 'Oh, now, I realize who you're talking about. I do remember meeting her once. It struck me then that she was extremely boring, and made me wonder why it is that people who do good are so boring.' [. . .] I can't write this without wondering about the concept of what is and what is not boring. People who easily dismiss others as boring are usually judging by the standards of some small self-admiring group of friends who speak a witty special language of personalities and gossip, and, if they go outside this can translate their wider interests into the terminology of this special language. That is what members of Bloomsbury did so well, and to belong to such a clique adds distinctly to one's enjoyment of life. Nevertheless, it has its disadvantages: almost every member of such a group anxiously asks himself: 'Am I boring the others?' and this imposes on him a kind of snobbery, which is that of the idea of the requirements of the clique in the minds of its members. Insiders can be pushed out because life involves them in complications of work, family or unhappiness which makes them bores.

Muriel is not in herself the least a bore and in the old days she could be sociable and amusing in a way that made her become friends with people like Goronwy Rees and Freddie Ayer. But she married a man whose only interest was in politics: firstly in the heroic politics of anti-Fascism and Refugees, but later, to a great extent, in the fading image of himself as a political leader. [. . .] Muriel's social life became boring because she was married to him and society for her became largely confined to the company of other political exiles and refugees. But her work as a psychoanalyst and as a school and prison visitor was only 'boring' in the sense that cliquish people cannot bear to hear about what is intensely serious and interesting unless it is made 'amusing' for them, or expressed in their kind of intellectuals' jargon.

Auden made the distinction between being boring and being a bore. God was boring but not a bore. Beethoven's posthumous Quartets a bore but not boring. In Proust, Mme Verdurin's circle came to regard Dr Cottard as a bore: but when we discover that he is the most distinguished diagnostician of his time we realize that he is not at all boring. According to this classification Muriel is a bore (to Susan Sontag) but not boring, married to Jo [who] is a bore and also boring.

15 August 1980, London

It's really taken a week to recover from jet lag – and perhaps going from the extreme heat of America to wet cool London. We haven't done much. The Ghikas, Nikos and Barbara, and the Hutchinsons – June and Jeremy – came to dinner on Tuesday, the night before the H[utchinson]s moved into their new house in Blenheim Road.[1] A

---

1 Jeremy Hutchinson (b. 1915), British lawyer married to Peggy Ashcroft until 1966, and then to June Osborn, widow of the pianist Franz Osborn who taught Natasha in 1940–41. Nikos, brother of Barbara Ghika.

very happy reunion. On Wednesday, Dick Sylbert took Lizzie, Natasha and me out to dinner at Langan's a restaurant off Piccadilly frequented by smart members of the pop, record and movie world. Sean Connery was there, and urged on by Dick came over and talked, reminiscing about the time when I stayed with the Flemings on Golden Eye – (twenty years ago?) and Ian was supervising the making of the first (I think) James Bond movie.¹ Connery was very amiable. These film stars stand over you, gleaming and beaming, as though they are giving every inch of themselves – every hair on Connery's beard and chest – for twenty minutes or so. At another table there was a dinner party given by some people called Bailey. Among their guests were Mick Jagger and Ossie Clark.² As we went out somehow Dick and Lizzie got us tangled with them. Natasha and I mistook Mick for Chris Jagger, but he took this in good part. He was very smiling and amiable. He seemed a rather shrunken version of his sprawling voluptuous public personality.

17 August 1980, London

We went to Blake's Hotel in Kensington to have tea with Sonia Orwell, who has cancer: first a tumour on the brain which has been removed, now on the lung. In spite of this she chain-smoked. Her body was thin but her face round, a bit puffy. She said this was because she was taking pills which made her face swell. In fact she looked well, her mind was completely clear and she gossiped pleasantly about the Moynihans.³ [. . .]

Peggy Ashcroft came to dinner – just her alone with us. She is greatly recovered from having her knees operated on and is rehearsing many hours a day at the National Theatre, a play of Lillian

---

1 Sean Connery (b. 1930), Scottish actor who starred in seven Bond films. Spender refers to Ian Fleming's Jamaican estate, Goldeneye.

2 Mick Jagger (b. 1943), lead singer in the Rolling Stones. Raymond 'Ossie' Clark (1942–1996), British fashion designer and trend setter of the 'Swinging Sixties'.

3 Sonia Orwell would, in fact, die in December 1980. Rodrigo Moynihan (1910–1990), British painter who studied at the Slade, was an official War Artist during the Second World War and subsequently a teacher at the Royal College of Art; husband of Anne Moynihan (née Dunn).

Hellman called *Watch on the Rhine*.[1] She said 'Some days it seems wonderful some days terrible. Rehearsals are like that.' Pre-first night performances start Friday. Then on Sunday they go for a week to the Edinburgh Festival. [. . .] She seemed worried about politics: Maggie Thatcher, the American election.

18 August 1980, London

Ian Hamilton, hatchet faced, looking as though cast for the role of Third Murderer in a performance of *Macbeth*, lively and amusing though not trustworthy[,] came to interview me for the biography he is writing about Robert Lowell.[2] I could remember – what was least useful to him – R.L.'s appearance, far better than anything he did or said. His way of holding his head down and forward and looking up at you with penetrating eyes under the dome of a magnificent forehead, balding and with locks of somewhat greasy-looking white hair falling to his shoulders. His look claimed all your attention. His smile pressed his benevolence down on you. The movement of his hands was like that of some conductor who moulds a phrase of music in the air. His misfortune was that somehow he seemed to be bringing pressure on you to sympathize with him. He gave me a sense of claustrophobia like that produced by a schoolmaster who wants to force his lesson upon you. Once when I was at Brandeis University during the summer, he visited me, and tried to persuade me to come to Boston with him and stay the night. I was panic-stricken at the thought of having to sit up with him till the small hours while he read his poetry to me or made pronouncements – pronouncements which were also a bit questioning – demanding – imploring – pressing one to agree or disagree. Once in N.Y. he wanted us to meet in his attic room looking over skyscrapers and water towers while we showed our poems to each other and mutually criticized them. What an excellent and generous idea, but the only time I did so I was embarrassed by finding

---

1 Ashcroft played Fanny Farrelly in Hellman's play, which was well reviewed.

2 Ian Hamilton (1938–2001), British literary critic whose biography of Robert Lowell was published in 1982. Hamilton wrote a somewhat sour appreciation, 'Spender's Lives', for the *New Yorker* in February 1994, drawing on some of the material gathered at this interview.

the suggestions he made to me for my poems meaningless (though very kindly intended) and my not being able to understand at such a reading his poems. And always feeling this terrific pressure.

Once I was at dinner with the Lowells (Elizabeth Hardwick and he) when the I. A. Richardses were there. At a certain moment in the evening Cal said to Richards that he had written some sonnets the subjects of which had been suggested to him by remarks made to him by Richards about China. He read about eleven sonnets – at which point, noticing a pent-up expression on Richards's face I tried to transmit to Cal the thought that perhaps Richards should now be called upon by his host to read some poems. But Cal – who never knew quite when to stop – was merely reminded by my nudging him of two or three other sonnets he might read. 'Oh, here's another that I think will interest you –' he said to R. At this R. who had gone a purple colour and was uttering turkey-cock noises, exploded. 'If you imagine,' he said, 'that any ideas about China contained in those sonnets were got from me, you are vastly mistaken. Moreover,' he went on, 'I notice in the poems you have just read a lamentable falling off in your work, Cal, which I have observed in other of your recent productions.' At this Ivor and Dorothea Richards left the apartment on a trajectory which seemed continuous with Richards's initial explosion. Much to my surprise, Cal took this perfectly calmly.

On another occasion in N.Y., I was in a taxi with Lowell, and Grey Gowrie (Earl).[1] Suddenly, Cal leaned over, and with all the force of his attentiveness tapped the taxi driver on the shoulder. 'Driver,' he said, 'I thought you might like to know that sitting in your cab beside me is Lord Gowrie the only surviving direct descendant of the ancient Kings of Ireland.'

20 August 1980, London

Lunch at John Bayley's and Iris Murdoch's. Noel and Gaby Annan were there also two German professors and their respective wives. We never got their names. One professor said he had travelled in

---

1 Grey Gowrie (b. 1939), Conservative peer and politician, academic and poet. He had been a colleague of Spender's at UCL in the early 1970s and had become close to Lowell while teaching at Harvard.

India with me at a conference arranged by Indira Ghandi to enhance her father's memory.[1] Iris is very taken up with a) her sick mother b) writing. She said she was trying to write philosophy but had got in a muddle.

24 August 1980, London

We went to see my Uncle George and Aunt Gwen [Schuster]. If anything, George seemed better than last time we saw him, now that he is 100. He talked firstly about his health – how his sight is much worse today than previously (John [George's son] says he often gets up, saying this). He [George] said that Gwen, sitting opposite him day after day, has not communicated with him for two years, but that in this last fortnight some kind of change has occurred in her and she was now attempting to do so. He said that a secretary of Prince Charles had been to consult him about Atlantic College.[2] 'He agreed with every word I said.' Prince Charles had sent him a signed photograph. (Natasha said afterwards that the secret of longevity was egotism. To some extent – the incapacity of the total egoist to accept death – this must be true.)

5 September 1980, St Jerome

A strange nightmare. That I was made Pope. I sat in a large waiting room preparatory to my having to make my first sermon before about a million people. I had about two hours to prepare it. From numerous flunkeys, autograph hunters etc who kept on interrupting me while I tried to put my thoughts in order, I asked for paper on which I could write notes. They only brought me torn up sheets of newspaper, covered with newsprint and impossible almost to write on. I scrawled a few notes between lines of typography and in looking at them, my handwriting was illegible. I had a faint hope,

1 Indira Gandhi (1917–1984), Prime Minister of the Republic of India, 1966–77 and 1980–84. Her father Jawaharlal Nehru was the first Prime Minister of India, from 1947 to 1964.

2 Atlantic World Colleges were founded by Spender's uncle, George Schuster, with Prince Charles as President.

undermined by past experience of how this does not work, that when it came to making my sermon, my illegible handwriting might stimulate me to inspired improvization. My sermon was intended to bring the full weight of starvation, preparations for atomic war etc into the consciousness of people so that they would change the world. If I had armed myself with only a few telling examples or statistics I could do this. But I knew my sermon would be a humiliating failure, then I thought that after all it could be very short. Everyone would be grateful if I spoke, say, for five or ten minutes: delivered some brief, tremendously moving exhortation. But I knew I would not do this. Now I started thinking of ways of getting out of being Pope. After all, I was married and in every way totally unqualified for exalted sacred office. I convinced myself that in fact it was inconceivable that I should be Pope, and proved by pure argument that this must be a dream. Then, having done this, I woke up.

Comments:

1. Thinking that perhaps the [car] accident we had last week was only a dream and I should wake up.
2. The fact that I have not yet written a line of my Henry James Lecture.
3. The only recurrent dreams I have are of situations of having to perform in public and being unprepared.
4. Illegibility of notes owing to my bad eyesight.
5. The poem I am writing about Auden's funeral, of which the ending is only a cloudy vision at present which I have not been able to articulate as workable machinery of metaphor.
6. The pope: Polish: concern with great issues of Third World: my own feelings about Poland: material about Poland in Iris Murdoch's *Nuns and Soldiers* which I was reading till 2 a.m.[1]

7 September 1980, St Jerome

I finished reading Iris's *Nuns and Soldiers*. She is extremely gifted yet doesn't seem quite a novelist. She can do certain things very well –

---

1 John Paul II, Pope since 1978, was by birth the Pole Karol Wojtyła (1920–2005).

passages of dialogue between cliff-hanging characters – here Daisy and Tim. Also set pieces of adventure-story type fiction such as the description of Tim being swept down the canal into and out of an underground tunnel through which it flows near here.[1] [. . .] She can describe very well the surface behaviour of characters – particularly sleazy ones, and yet seem[s] to have no very firm grip on their reality. She also goes in extensively for describing her effects – long passages in which she tells us not only the history of her characters but how intensely they are feeling. This surely should emerge from the action not be thrown at the reader. Perhaps she is trying to put across a view of life – 'people do behave in this arbitrary way – the only pattern is that which is imposed, there is no real underlying pattern' etc. But if this is so she hasn't really invented a form for conveying it. There are good observations about people in her novels, and some things (such as the adventure story bits) are brilliantly done. I feel that not having invented an adequate form for conveying her view of people and life, she has got into the rut of an inadequate pattern, based on a game with arbitrary rules, or the pavane. And this is a great pity.

Writing 'Auden's Funeral' gives me ideas for how I could complete other poems of which I have the sketches I wrote in hospital and of which I have drafts in notebooks etc. I realize that I have so many notes that I could be working on poems every day. In a sense they are all one poem, one oeuvre. I have the sense in writing one poem of chipping away at a corner of one big work.[2]

9 September 1980, St Jerome

Yesterday we went over to lunch at St Estève with Rodrigo Moynihan, his stepson Francis Wishart, and Francis's fiancée, who looks a bit like a crop-haired boy in a Blue Period Picasso – a boy who plays a guitar – which is what she does.[3] They were all, in their different

---

1 Murdoch's novel *Nuns and Soldiers* (1980) was dedicated to the Spenders and uses some of the landscape surrounding Mas St Jerome.

2 This sequence of poems, conceived on Auden's death and burial in 1973, was published in its final version in *Collected Poems* (1985).

3 Francis Wishart (b. 1951), painter, partly resident in Provence, the child of Anne Dunn's first marriage to the painter Michael Wishart (1928–1996).

ways, utterly charming, as they have been every time we have seen any members of that household ever since we got here – 15 years ago. Rodrigo a bit distraught, though: having to go immediately to London. Talk about Sonia [Orwell]. Rodrigo told how she had had a relapse, and had gone back from the Blake Hotel to hospital. Although she had collapsed completely, coming into the ward one recognized her at once by the distraught exasperated expression on her face. She was in tears. She continued to smoke, her face flat on the pillow, but a cigarette like a chimney stack giving off smoke, from her mouth.

Then two days later she was sitting up in bed staging a comeback. When we saw her in hospital on our journey out of London here, she was quite chatty, talking with some show of gaiety about Cressida Connolly – whose only trouble is – said Sonia – that she can't stick to anything – so she needs money, etc.[1]

10 September 1980, St Jerome

[A]s we were driving home, Natasha said something to me about Lizzie going to Los Angeles in October. She suggested Lizzie and I might fly to New York together – which is, in itself, quite a good idea. But all my anxieties about Lizzie struck me as though we were in a boat that had struck a rock. I thought of her being taken up by people in L.A. and then being dropped by them – being offered jobs which either never will be followed up or which come to nothing. I thought of her being very excited, stimulated, then very unhappy. I went to bed still trying to escape the unbearable sadness of my own thoughts about Lizzie. The fact is – however much one accepts the idea that most people are unhappy and frustrated – but sees too that most of them will put up with it – survive – one doesn't have reserves of philosophical – or cynical – indifference to one's children. Their unhappiness seems unbearable. It is worse than one's own unhappiness, because one is responsible for, or doomed to, oneself, and one is not self-pitying. At the same time this not being able to bear the children's unhappiness – and its becoming one's own worst unhappi-

---

1 Cyril Connolly's daughter, the novelist Cressida Connolly, was the goddaughter of Sonia Orwell.

ness – exerts blackmail on them: 'Be happy for dad's sake, because the one thing he can't bear is for Lizzie to be unhappy.' [. . .]

I have worked through the stage of despair about 'Auden's Funeral'. What I have written is articulate without being articulated. The stuff is there but not the movement which is clogged and hampered. The point is to write it as though one was there – at the grave-side, dropping the clod of earth on the coffin lid – thinking of Wystan in that box – his grinning – his thinking he had scored over us – his companions – got ahead in a game. While grinning to himself at us – he is also sufficiently still of this world to be sharing the joke with us – like a child in a game of hide-and-seek. But he has stolen a march on us. We are left alone on a star (a planet?) growing old as we walk back along the path we came this morning to the graveyard – walk back to the village. There in the village inn on benches we toast his ghost. Each of us becomes totemistic, a local habitation for his spirit to enter at the last feast. This one becomes a ventriloquist's doll through whom the voice of W. speaks recounting anecdotes. Then Chester puts Wagner – Siegfried's Funeral March – on the record-player. That music like a bier [on] which the corpse of Siegfried is borne. Underneath it we feel Auden's spirit carried out – the loss to us of one who made his life an instrument for expressing experiences in language, where each of us loses his loneliness, and becomes part of a spiritual community.

That is the idea – I want to write an elegy, which is like the person and the mourners.

21 September 1980, St Jerome

The weather changing here from the northern Mistral to the southern Sirocco which is moist and hot and seems quite unnatural to this place of crystal clarity, yew trees like black spiral tops twisted in the wind, Cannes de Provence [cane/reeds] shining like spun glass.

We went to luncheon at Tony Daniels. He has a house in a bosky country of hills looking over a not very level plain. The Duchess of Montesquieu, Daphne Fielding and her octogenarian Arizonian paramour Kittridge (a very amiable and intelligent man who has lost nothing of his quickness or his faculties in old age – a broad-faced ruddy Southerner with a thatch of white hair like a hat) were there.[1] Daphne had broken a leg and was walking with a stick, so we chummed up on the subject of legs. We last saw her perhaps five years ago when she lived in a house not far away, and was married to Xan Fielding. Somehow he got her down, perhaps because they were both trying desperately to earn money, he by translating, she by writing a book about Gladys, Duchess of Marlborough (a Vanderbilt). The house and they both seemed unhappy. Then on one occasion, Xan had to drive Magouche (Maro's mother) from London and Magouche and Xan fell in love en route, and later ran off together to Spain where they are now living.

This seemed very sad for Daphne, but then she found her American and they fell in love and have been going around together as happy as children ever since. Owing to her broken leg – or because she is now happy – she has stopped drinking – or only drinks red wine mixed with water. She is very tough and warm and bright-looking, like a mixture of aristocrat and barmaid. [. . .] I liked her immensely. I like people who see that life is a play one has to act out as writer of one's own part[,] also as spectator of all that happens to one – that the worst events – anyway as they affect oneself – are tragic farce.

23 September 1980, Mouton

On Monday Peter Abrahams, his wife, a baby sitter[,] a baby and a dog all arrived.[2] We were in the middle of two crises:

1. the garage at Avignon who swore they would have the car ready by Tuesday, now said they would *perhaps* have it ready by Friday.
2. water. [. . .]

The Abrahamses couldn't have been nicer about everything. Regard-

---

1 Ben Kittridge (d. 1981) had been in love with Daphne Fielding (1904–1997) prior to her first marriage in 1926 to Viscount Weymouth, later the Marquess of Bath.

2 Peter Abrahams (b. 1947), American crime-thriller writer. Abrahams and family were renting Mas St Jerome from the Spenders.

ing the car, they said anyhow they had been quite prepared for us to stay a week after their arrival: with regard to the water they said there was the garden hose they could use, and also another hose which is from rain water in a cistern at the back of the house. They were perfectly used to things like this.

Peter Abrahams is very striking looking; swarthy, black-haired; black eyes, a very penetrating glance, a seductive and pleasant smile, a very lively way of talking. His wife is rather thin, with short curly hair, an intelligent expression – a somewhat bird-like face. The baby very happy crawling about the floor, as active as a lizard in Iris Murdoch's novel. [. . .]

Peter Abrahams who has worked for C.B.S. in Canada, but who now has an astonishing and apparently very recent independence said that he'd written a novel which was just appearing (published by Macmillans New York) in America. He said he had no ideas about publishing novels, but did have some kind of idea about what made them popular reading. So he put ingredients of the eminently saleable into the book, and then sent it to an agent – now his agent – (a man of immense girth, he said). Rather to his surprise, the agent, instead of sending it to one publisher after another, had copies made of it and sent them all at the same time to ten publishers who then had the privilege of bidding against each other for it. The result is that he comes to France[,] buys a wonderful car with rotating flanges, with little buttons which you press, on either side of the steering wheel and a miniature chart on his dashboard, which lights with a red flash if anything in the car is functioning badly, two bicycles with ten gears each etc and his wonderful smile on his face. I liked him so much that I felt a bit sad that in his art, he had quite such aims. I reflected that I simply can't take pleasure in writing if I am doing so with the thought of money: that I can write the unpublishable – this account, for example – with great facility and ease, whereas anything I write for a market, I always have to write six or seven times. I don't mean that I want to be like him, or him to be like me, but I would like such a lively and aware person to be writing with an eye on the novel – the truth – and not on the market. Better then not view him as a writer at all – in any sense in which I understand the term – and be happy in the thoughts of his baby, car and dog, and his very great amiability to us. [. . .]

We decided to go by train to Mouton on Wednesday, and Natasha phoned to tell Philippe this. He at once said: 'Oh get on an aeroplane and the firm will pay your fares.' This really was a surprise. The Abrahamses as accommodating as ever said they would not only drive us to Marignane Airport, but they would take our hired car back to its garage. They then took us to Marignane, themselves then proceeding to buy a crib for the baby.

So the result of a disaster which seemed to make it certain we would arrive days late at Mouton, we actually arrived a day earlier.

24 September 1980, Mouton

Beth Chatto, the horticulturist[,] arrived just before lunch.[1] Meanwhile Joan Littlewood had been making a terrific scene with Philippe – and he had completely lost his temper with her [. . .] I felt furious with Joan who sometimes acts as though she were a dwarf – Mime – in the Ring. But this evening after my walk in the vineyards I felt differently. She was with Raoul the old man responsible for all the vineyards and wine. He was describing to us how he'd got up early in the morning and seen – across the vineyards – the moon rising. Now that's the most beautiful thing in the world 'la Nature'. 'Everything else is destruction, war, pollution, cruelty, terror,' he said. Joan listened to all this with the most wide-eyed appreciation. 'M. le Baron n'apprécie pas la nature,' went on Raoul – 'he has never seen the moon rise. Now Mme la Baronne she saw everything. She used to get up in the middle of the night and walk in the vineyards. She knew nature. C'était une femme extraordinaire. Le Baron a eu de la chance en se mariant avec une telle femme.'[2] I marvelled at the legend of Pauline, La Baronne, among the servants. But I can well believe that she had a very understanding relation with them. She talked to each separately and with sympathy. But one hardly sees her as a nature lover. A woman who lay awake all night reading books into which she inserted scraps of paper, sometimes with comments on them; who took two hours to dress and arrange herself in her extraordinary get

---

1 Beth Chatto (b. 1923), British garden designer and writer.

2 'She was an extraordinary woman. The Baron was lucky in marrying such a woman.'

up of hosepipe trousers, strange cloaks and hair in long plaits, like some elongated, gawky girl in a fairy story, who lunched at four p.m. and dined at ten p.m., who wrote long letters to John Huston, some Russian prince – and I don't know who else – which were full of novelistic-romantic passion; who thought the Soviet Union was the ideal place to live, wrote a book saying so and almost did a deal with the Russians to let Philippe and her have a palace there; agreed with characters like Mme Furtseva, the Russian Minister of Culture that censorship was inevitable in a country like Russia which needed discipline; confided in Glenway Westcott about her unhappiness in her relations with Philippe; had some concept of the duty or dignity of woman which made her without one scrap of sympathy with Peggy Bernier, when Peggy and Georges broke up, because Peggy complained too much and because Pauline thought that a woman with a grievance should stifle it and never make it known; who, towards the end of her life, left Mouton and Paris and was only happy living in the Ritz Carlton Hotel in Boston.[1] There is such a mixture of sympathetic and repellent here, but little that seems 'natural'.

Among her best qualities was her wonderful taste as a designer. Since 1945 she really made Mouton what it is: a place of original faultless taste of great long lines and strong colours where horizontal forms are always emphasized (there are no rooms with very high ceilings in Grand Mouton), each room has its own consistent style, all the objects in it are displayed for what they are, and the vineyards on the great flat plane outside, like a green ocean in spring summer and autumn, like a brown bare spread out Dutch landscape in the winter, reflect through the large porthole windows of the great salon. [. . .] She also obviously had great gifts of friendship.

I can never really work at Mouton, apart from writing this and a few letters etc. But I read a lot from Pauline's very random and ill-arranged library. I've been reading a life of Henry VIII, by J. J. Scarisbrick.[2] Reading history in old age can easily become a passion, something that one seizes on. It gives one an odd sense of déja vu; also of discovering at the end of the journey on some island upon

---

1 Pauline de Rothschild was in Boston for consultation with doctors about her cancer.

2 J. J. Scarisbrick, *Henry VIII* (1968).

which one has done servitude the documents which explain everything about its past and therefore why one has been put there. [. . .]
When I was young I couldn't read history because I had absolutely no
grasp of the motivations of rulers. I thought the world was run by
people older than myself whose behaviour resulted from ideas and
beliefs. Alter the ideas, and there would be a different world. A bit
later I thought that societies were divided into rich and poor, haves
and have-nots. Let lovers of justice take away their riches from the
rich and give them to the poor, and let them themselves while still
loving the justice which had motivated revolution retain their new
and just power, and the world would be a place of happy and enlightened equals called human beings. I did not see that the world is run
everywhere by a special race of monsters – those who understand the
reality of having power. I did not realize that even if a social system
is changed these will take over within the different outward appearances of the new order.

30 September 1980, London

Gordon McDougall from the Oxford Playhouse came to see me
about the version of the Oedipus plays (including *Antigone*) it is suggested I should do for them (I am mad to do it. And I spent the last
day at Mouton reading the Jebb version which is very good).[1] [. . .]

This evening I dined with Maud Russell – Richard and Day Wollheim were there, also Nikos.[2] It was a delightful dinner of only five
of us and all of us knowing one another well. [. . .] Richard got talking about his war experiences. He described how at the end of the

---

1 Gordon McDougall (b. 1941), British theatre director, director of the
Oxford Playhouse, 1974–84. Spender's translation of Sophocles' three Oedipus
plays, compressed to be performed in one evening, was put on at the Oxford
Playhouse in February 1983. Choruses from *Antigone* and *Oedipus at Colonus*
are printed in the 2004 *Collected Poems*. Spender was reading R. C. Jebb's
1893 translation of the plays of Sophocles.

2 Maud Russell (1892–1982), society hostess and patroness of the arts.
After buying Mottisfont Abbey in 1934 with her husband, the banker Gilbert
Russell, Maud commissioned Rex Whistler to produce a tromp l'oeil mural
in her home along with several watercolours in 1938. She helped finance
Boris Anrep's intricate mosaic floor in the National Gallery (1928–52), which
featured her as Folly, patron of the arts.

war he was an officer in the British Occupying Army at the time when the occupying forces were not allowed to have any social life with the Germans.[1] Especially, the solders were not allowed to communicate with German girls. After a time, it occurred to the authorities that the English soldiers were getting very frustrated. So then someone had the idea that there were girls at Belsen who did not come under this ban. So a party of emaciated girls were brought along to the English quarters and given a party. They were like terrified animals, all gathered into a corner of the room, not knowing what was going to happen to them. The soldiers went over to them and tried to make friends. All the girls could do was point with scratching fingers at the sole identification they had, the numbers tattooed (or branded?) on their wrists. Nikos said it was incredible how all through history whole societies apparently could become dehumanized. Since the War things as terrible – Cambodia, the Khmer Rouge with [the] massacre of tens of thousands of people – have happened. I said we could sit at table eating a meal and watching people starving or being tortured on TV. Nikos said he was actually eating when he watched some programme describing how parties of spectators were invited to see victims being murdered. I said: 'We are all in favour of black freedom in Africa etc. – we can't be anything else – and yet if the white regimes go in South Africa and Rhodesia, there will be dictatorships like Amin's and massacres like those in Southeast Asia.'[2] Rather to my surprise the others agreed with me about this. I asked Richard, 'Can you look with hope to any political party in the world today?' He said: 'Not really' but then added rather to my surprise that he was in favour of 'nations'. [. . .] I said the kind of thing that I still felt hopeful about was the Willy Brandt report with recommendations that the rich nations should make a sacrificial effort to aid the Third World Nations.[3]

---

1 These recollections were published posthumously in Wollheim's memoir *Germs* (2004).

2 Idi Amin (1925–2003), President and military dictator of Uganda 1971–9.

3 The 1980 'Brandt Report' was produced by the Independent Commission on International Development, chaired by the former West German Chancellor Willy Brandt. It insisted that developed countries were morally and pragmatically advised to tackle poverty in the developing world, if humanity was going to survive the 'immense risks threatening mankind'.

2 October 1980, London

Together with Laurie Lee and P. J. Kavanagh gave a poetry reading at St Paul's Church, Hammersmith Broadway.[1] [. . .] it's strange how intense my horror is of engagements such as readings, a few hours before them. I arrived too early and walked in the Hammersmith neighbourhood a bit – past the end of Brook Green, where Inez and I used to live. It has not changed much and brought back so many memories. One might it seems pass from present to past like opening a door and going from one room into another – then realizes the threshold is forty-five years wide. [. . .]

Paddy [Kavanagh] and Laurie are both unredeemed Georgian poets – in Laurie's case this cider is lightly laced with brandy of Dylan Thomas. Chatting up the audience Laurie commented that one of his poems was written between two bus stops and that the fare was at that time a penny, today would be 50p. (I wondered how much he was paid for publishing the poem.) Paddy held up his book to the audience to show the shape of the poems on the page. He read a long sympathetic poem of childhood reminiscences about his father, the war-time comedian Ted Kavanagh, a succession of anecdotes adding up to no total, lacking in economy and – for that matter – language. Laurie has a distinct feeling for words but no thoughts about them. When I got into that pit of light engulfed in darkness – the stage – I suddenly felt reassured, and read into a responsive silence (the audience was attentive). I think my poems were better than those of Paddy and Laurie – but that is not saying much: if they had been worse they'd have been nothing. But most poetry is the poet's self-delusion which he can – if he puts on a fair show – make the audience share. Since it is self-delusion it is very difficult for the poet to know its worth – all he can say is that the hallucination holds. True poetry is the external truth transformed in the poetry. It's the truth which reaches outside the enclosed poetry to the outside of nature, the human condition. Why one admires poets like Frost and Edward Thomas is because one sees so clearly that lines and images have an inside which turns back into their interior darkness, an outside which

---

1 P. J. Kavanagh (b.1931), British poet.

turns out towards nature and human beings. One doesn't tire of seeing them do this. I don't have confidence that I do it.

After the reading I felt I should take advantage of being with colleagues and persuaded Laurie and Paddy that we should eat together. We went to a Greek restaurant in the Fulham Road. Later, I wished I had been alone with Paddy who is interesting as a person. Laurie turns conversation into his stagy countryman's patter and baloney – the slightly boozy, tweedy pub-and-haystack poet. There were some pretences of discussing something then the subject – if a real one – was dropped. Laurie flattered me in his meaningless way, which might be caressing, might be mocking, but is neither – just automatic. My silver hair, my being handsomer now than when young. Paddy said he was making a study of Ivor Gurney.[1] I wish we could have gone on about that.

3 October 1980, London

Lunch in Soho with Nikos and Harry Fainlight, who is clinically mad but much better than for a very long time. With lustrous curly black hair pressed to the sides of his skull and coming down almost to his shoulders – white thin intense features – a good forehead, a nose that looks as if it has been carved into its distinctive hook, small bird-black eyes – he is someone whose glance does not let you escape his analysis.

I asked him where lines he had quoted in a letter to me came from. They were:

> Those who opposed the walls of our advancing sea
> Are crushed to pebbles. Their minds faded and failed,
> O failed and faded like pebbles before our enormous tide.

He looked – in his sideward way – at Nikos and said: 'Now isn't that extraordinary. He doesn't know his own lines.'

Then I remembered they came from *Trial of a Judge*.[2] Harry said:

---

1 Ivor Gurney (1890–1937), First World War poet and composer. Kavanagh's collection of Gurney's poetry was published in 1982.

2 From the Black Troop Leader's speech in Act V of *Trial of a Judge* (1938): 'Those who opposed the walls of our advancing sea / Are crushed to pebbles. Their minds faded and failed, / O failed and faded like flowers before our enormous tide.'

'Well, you see, that's what happened. Minds are crushed before the advancing tide which is like an electric field sending out rays which burn up everything that intercepts its path.' He said that 'they' – the advancing forces – especially wished to destroy poets, because poetry was a source of energy that resisted them.

I asked him where he lived now. He said he had a cottage in the depths of the Welsh countryside. Nikos said: 'You're so much better there, Harry, better than you've been for years.' 'Yes,' he said, 'but even there the forces follow me.' 'What forces?' 'Well, the form they take is that the complete silence – which is what I need in order to work – is all the time being invaded by aeroplanes directed by rays.' 'I understand what you mean,' said Nikos, 'but this happens every-where. You must accept that it does. You mustn't allow yourself to think like that or you'll be completely unable to do anything.' 'Oh I know I have paranoia,' said Harry, 'and I do try to correct it. I used to think that the noise was directed specially at me by people sitting at some centre with maps in front of them, but now I realize it is just the forces directed against all civilizations. But nothing is done against it. No one protests. No one resists.' [. . .]

I got up and said I had to catch a train to Oxford – and arrived at Paddington 1½ hour early and caught a previous train – the 3 p.m. instead of the 3.50.

Called on the Ellmanns and spent an hour with Mary (Dick whom I had not been able to forewarn had gone to the station to meet the 3.50). Mary seemed much calmer, clearer happier and physically bet-ter than I have seen her since her illness. We talked about being in hospital. I said the worst part, far the worst – when I had both legs in plaster – was all the business about bed pans. 'Yes,' she said, 'and when I first had my attack, I was incontinent. It was absolutely dread-ful. I had to call out for the nurse because I couldn't wait. And it made her so angry.' This proud, intelligent woman, so humiliated. Dick arrived and was also tremendously warm and affectionate. Asked me to promise to come as his guest at the annual banquet at New College – to meet at any time, whenever we could. He had helpful suggestions about my lecture in New York next month.[1]

---

1 The Ellmanns would move to Emory University in Atlanta later in 1980,

In October 1980, Spender went on another month-long trip to America, reading and teaching. He visited friends in New York and was there for election day and Reagan's victory on 4 November. On 9 November, he stayed in Tulsa for four days as the guest of David Plante, before going on to Los Angeles.

9 November 1980, Los Angeles, California

To go back to New York, Tuesday Nov 4 election day. I lunched with Nin Ryan at her East Side apartment.[1] Monroe Wheeler was there and an Australian professor now at Princeton who outlined the subject of a book he was writing, and a Swedish lady of the house of Bonner, and Marietta Tree.[2] It was nice.

Afterwards, I went to 920 Fifth Avenue to visit Vera Stravinsky who, I had been told, was in a bad way. Her nurse-companion took me into her large drawing room, lined with books most of which seemed enormous, and full of large sofas and armchairs. An effect of untidy opulence. Vera was sitting in an armchair at a table on which there were I think some painting things. 'Here is Stephen,' said her assistant. Vera looked up at me, in an unrecognizing way but seemed to realize I was a friend and not a stranger. Her face, beautiful, soft and round, with the enormous brilliant eyes and the sumptuous Titian-like hair, seemed to have shrunken – skin, red and white, drawn back like a scarf over the bone, wrinkled, heavily painted. She still smiled in her indulgent melancholy way. 'I don't know what this room is,' she said. 'I am sure these are not my things. Anyway I don't want them. One ought not to have any things. One should give them all away.' She wondered where we were. The nurse companion suggested New York. 'No, I don't think we are in New York,' she said, 'and it's not Paris either. I have been to so many places. I know so

---

largely because of the medical facilities. Mary Ellmann would in fact outlive her husband by two years, dying in 1989.

1 Nin Ryan (1901–1995), American patron of the arts, daughter of the banker and philanthropist Otto Kahn.

2 Monroe Wheeler (1899–1988), American curator, long-term partner of Glenway Wescott. Marietta Tree (1917–1991), American socialite and left-wing campaigner, formerly wife of the conservative billionaire Ronald Tree.

many languages. Let's see' – as though she were playing a game – 'how many languages do I know? – English, French, German, Italian –'

'Russian,' I put in.

'No I don't know Russian. No one anywhere knows any Russian any more. It is not spoken,' she said firmly.

At this point, I stupidly allowed tears to trickle down my face. If she had noticed – which fortunately she didn't – this would have been fatal. For once having indulged myself in this way, I couldn't stop and was quietly crying for the rest of the meeting. There was plenty to cry about – if one thought about the wonderful festive life, like an endless succession of gifts brought in on concert platforms, gondolas, cars, trays and tables – music, conversation, good company, fame, wit, laughter, rage, passion, wine, fruits – of the life of Igor Stravinsky, Vera and Bob Craft. So recent it seemed when after the first night of *The Rake's Progress* at the Fenice [11 September 1951], walking through the Piazza, people at café tables stood up and started clapping Stravinsky – or visiting them in Hamburg or Paris or in their Hollywood apartment. There was a life lit by Igor's glinting humours. I remembered how once somewhere – perhaps in London – being in a hotel room with them – perhaps at the Savoy – they were discussing going on a trip to Africa. 'I love the idea of Africa,' Igor said to me. 'There are animals like this' and suddenly he took up his walking stick, dropped on all fours onto the floor and placed the stick over the back of his head so that the handle curved over his forehead like the horn of a rhinoceros.

The nurse brought in a large framed photograph of a ballerina of a pure boy-like beauty. 'Do you recognize this?' she asked. 'No,' said Vera. 'That is you,' she said. 'That is me?' cried Vera, quite in her old enraptured voice and with smiling, upward-turning eyes like those of a girl in a painting by Greuze. 'No I do not believe it. It is too beautiful.' I said something to the effect that it was her and it was beautiful and she was beautiful. She smiled, half flattered, half uncomprehending. I left soon after this.

Another reason for crying, I thought, as I walked down Fifth avenue, is that the whole scene was theatrical. Even things Vera said – her 'Where am I?' 'What is this place?' 'I speak these languages,' above all 'No one speaks Russian any longer' – were the kind of things a librettist might have picked up, for an opera by Verdi or Puccini. I cried as one does in the last act of *Bohème* or in the movies, easily irresistibly. The tableau of pathos is supremely that in which one sees the life before one frozen into the gestures in which it will be hurried away into the vast lumber-rooms and galleries of past history. Stravinsky and Vera and their American lover, worshipper, and amanuensis Bob Craft – who remains in the world like Horatio at the end of *Hamlet* to record the scene – wheeled off to join the other festive princes of the art of music – Liszt, Wagner, Mozart. [. . .]

Last week joined Rosamond and John Russell and Jacqueline Onassis and her daughter Caroline Kennedy for dinner.[1] I had not seen Jacqueline for twenty years or so (at tea with Joe Alsop) (before J.F.K. became President)[2] [. . .] I sat next to J.O. at dinner. Her face is a box-like enamelled mask, square almost, with large dark slits for eyes and a mouth a bit like the opening in a pillar box. Yet she is beautiful like some totemistic piece of sculpture. She talks in a way that suggests she is marvelling at everything. She was beautifully polite and seemed to want to talk seriously. Caroline said that the poem of mine ('I think continually [of those who were truly great]') had been suggested by Professor [Robert] Coles at Harvard to John Kennedy Junior, as the one he should read at the opening of the Kennedy Library. J.K. Junior was himself not interested in poetry, only in politics. I asked how many young Kennedys were prospective politicians. 'Sixteen boys,' she said, 'and they are very annoyed with me because I am the only one who has political office,' she laughed, adding that she was a town councillor, or something of the kind. I asked why they were all going into politics, all so ambitious. 'It's not that they're ambitious so much,' she replied, 'as that it would never occur to any of them to go into anything else.' 'Perhaps they should form a third party of all the Kennedys,' I said. I asked Jacqueline O. what she considered her greatest achievement in life. 'Oh,' she said,

---

1 Jacqueline Kennedy Onassis (1929–1994), the wife first of American president John F. Kennedy, 1953–63, and then of Greek shipping magnate Aristotle Onassis, 1968–75. Caroline Bouvier Kennedy (b. 1957), American writer and lawyer.

2 The Spenders had met Jacqueline Kennedy in Washington DC at a tea given by the American journalist Joe Alsop (1910–1989) in the year of John F. Kennedy's presidential campaign (1960).

'I think it is that after going through a rather difficult time, I consider myself comparatively sane. I am proud of that.' We went on like this, having real conversation or keeping up the pretence of having one – at any rate playing a game of good manners which I enjoyed. [. . .]

[Dick Sennett] took me out to dinner one night, at a very noisy French Restaurant, with Michel Foucault.[1] According to him, the previous day Foucault had gone to the St Marks Baths (or St Mark's Place swimming bath)[,] had there had a blow job from a black, after which he had mingled with a crowd in Central Park, having given himself a shot of mescaline. He had a bad trip which made him completely blind for two hours, at the end of which he telephoned Sennett who fetched him in a taxi. The latter part of this story must have been true, because Foucault discussed it when we met. He said he was in agony, the four hours of utter misery seemed like ten hours.

Foucault I remember as having a chalk-white face, sparse black hair either side of a bald dome; the look of a waiter in a Mediterranean café, or perhaps of a detective – Poirot – stark but anonymous.[2] That's the impression left in my rather vague memory. He certainly was surprisingly unpretentious, and very willing to discuss anything, quite un-vain, and humorous.

Foucault said, in answer to some question at dinner, that he had not in his writings revealed his homosexuality because to do so would be to recognize some sort of obligation to reveal your private life which certain homosexuals felt, but which no one would feel imposed on heterosexuals. It therefore assumed an inequity which he would not recognize. Dick then made what sounded like a courageous declaration of principle. He said that he felt no obligation to come out of the closet now but that if under the moral crusade of a Reagan government homosexuals were persecuted, then he would proclaim himself. What was embarrassing about this was that it was so long drawn out as to seem the less convincing the more he said.[3] [. . .]

---

1 Michel Foucault (1926–1984), French philosopher best known for his work on the relationship between power, sexuality and knowledge, published as *The History of Sexuality* (1976–84).

2 Hercule Poirot, the detective who features in 33 of Agatha Christie's crime novels, is comically bald.

3 Ronald Reagan has been heavily criticized for his slow response to the Aids

I spent four days – Friday to Tuesday at Tulsa staying with David Plante. Tulsa – or what I saw of it – seemed quite surprising: rather elegant, stylish people, talking in mostly Southern accents, looking almost as if they came out of a movie, something between *Dallas* and *Oklahoma!* [. . .] D. is very popular with his students whom he teaches fiction writing. He fairly glows in the atmosphere of praise and thanksgiving. [. . .]

Germaine Greer also teaches at Tulsa sharing an office with David.[1] We went out to dinner with her (this was when for the second time in a week I lost my wallet through the same hole in my jacket pocket – and this time irretrievably – an imbecile thing to do). She radiates coarse vitality and has the look of a great overgrown girl who has won all the prizes and has never quite got round to tidying herself up. Nor does she want to. Lively descriptions of walking through Central Park and many men emerging from the dark and flashing their dicks at her. She says she is too hefty to be mugged.

David told me that she is dedicated to her students, and I can quite believe it. Earns $5,000 a week, appearing all over. If she has any complaints against the university, communicates it through interviews with the newspaper. Gets her way always. Is very amusing. Said to one student: 'That's the worst fucking story I ever read in my life.'

13 November 1980, Los Angeles

Lizzie met me at the airport and drove me, in the car that Dick Sylbert has rented for her, to his apartment. It is full of furniture, books, pictures, fishing tackle, rods and instruments for making artificial flies, and a great many photographs of Dick himself, handsome at all ages. Lizzie gave me fruit to put in the fridge of my suite at the Tropicana, a rather run-down motel with inhabitants and reputation corresponding to the Chelsea Hotel in New York. She took me there

---

epidemic in 1980s America. Aids was first reported in medical journals and the media in 1981, but Reagan did not address the issue publicly until October 1987, by which time 27,909 people had died of the disease.

1 Germaine Greer (b. 1939), Australian-born feminist writer and literary scholar.

and then went on to one of the interviews with agents and directors with which she fills her days.

B[ryan] turned up, looking the same as always (or rather, the same for the last two years, since he's grown his beard), smiling in the same welcoming expectant way as though he'd just walked into the room – any motel room where we've stayed together – after an absence of ten minutes. He still loves L.A. and defends it against all criticism. He likes the work he's doing, apart from the fact that he hates physiology. A good deal of his study consists of filling up gaps of things he neglected when he was an undergraduate.

Dick and Lizzie gave me a party which was really very nice. [. . .] On Thursday, Christopher Isherwood gave a dinner for me: David Hockney and his friend Gregory, Gore Vidal, the young director of an art gallery (whose name I did not catch), Edward Albee (who arrived very late), Bryan [Obst], Don Bachardy – of course – and myself.[1] Gore had just returned from a week's health cure which had completely changed his appearance. Thinner, he looked haggard, like some elderly disillusioned businessman – his cherubic self scarcely recognizable. David looked round-faced, pudgy, cheerful, the gold rims of his spectacles glinting. Edward Albee has long mustachios which look as if they are waxed. He looks like a melancholy drum major, and apparently has cause to be sad. His last play put on in New York flopped after three days.[2] Before Albee arrived, Gore said that not expecting to see Albee at the party, he was concerned whether he'd written anything particularly acid about him lately. After Albee arrived, Gore made rather a set at him – plastering hypothetical wounds, I suppose. Towards the end of the evening, Gore and Albee got together and sang a duet of hate against the theatre critic of the *New York Times* who can kill a play in three days. Albee's, and perhaps one of Gore's, I suppose, has suffered this demise – but I couldn't help thinking that the plays may have deserved to die just the same.

---

1 Gore Vidal (b. 1925), American novelist and liberal political activist. Edward Albee (b. 1928), American playwright best known for *Who's Afraid of Virginia Woolf* (1961).

2 *The Lady from Dubuque* opened on Broadway at the Morosco Theatre on 31 January 1980, with Irene Worth in the leading role. (Spender had worked with Worth, who had taken the title role in his version of Schiller's *Maria Stuart* in 1960.) Albee's play closed after twelve performances, not three.

Christopher was rather silent, and sometimes appeared not to hear what was said to him. The next day I asked David whether C. was a little deaf, or perhaps preoccupied – and if preoccupied was it with his being 75? David said: 'A little of both, and I think there's a third thing. He is much affected by the fact that Don is now the same age (48 or 49) as Christopher was when he first met Don, who was then 18.

After the dinner B drove me back to my hotel. I said: 'I feel a bit embarrassed for you on an occasion like that. It's as though I was responsible for your being inspected by many eyes.' 'I don't care in the least about that,' said B, 'because I don't feel I belong to that world, so I don't mind what they think. It is extremely unlikely that I will ever meet any of them again. I can't imagine myself living a life in which I went to parties like the two this week.' He said this without making any kind of judgement. I did not feel criticized. But I wondered whether Christopher noticed the reticence of B and felt it as criticism. C. is a great approver or disapprover of one's friends, and his perhaps faint jealousy of mine is a life-long affair. Why do I mind? Why do I want my friends to be approved of by him?

Someone also mentioned that Don had not sold any pictures in his show at New York. This seems a bitter blow. I think of the tremendous work Don's put into being independently (of C) an artist. He is a skilled but not very interesting one, yet in some large sense his comparative failure seems unfair – unfair of life. I told B. He said 'It shows that Don has immense courage to have gone on as he has done.'

I rang Christopher. He said polite things and mentioned that my Review of his last book [*My Guru and His Disciple*] in the *New York Review* was one of the best. He also said he was sorry we had not had any time alone together. I worry about this. I wonder whether there is anything he wants to discuss or to tell me. And in fact, lunching with Dick and Lizzie on Saturday before taking off to London, I drew them into a plot to drive me to see C on my way to the airport – for at least half an hour. But when I telephoned him to suggest this, there was no answer.

20 November 1980, London

Flew home from L.A. on night of November 15th. [. . .] In my mail there was a letter from George Plimpton enclosing letters from Martha Gellhorn and Laura Riding attacking remarks I had made in my interview with Stets in the *Paris Review* some months ago.[1] Laura Riding was indignant because I had said that Yeats, who loved gossip, was much amused by the Laura Riding/Robert Graves saga, including the story about Laura Riding throwing herself from a fourth-storey window. Martha Gellhorn was even more incensed by my describing a luncheon with Hemingway, her, Inez and me in a Paris brasserie in 1936 [*sic*], in which Hemingway had said Inez was 'yeller' because while Hemingway and Marty ate steak, she ordered sweetbread and only drank water, and remarked that Marty was like that when he first knew her, so he had taken her every morning to the morgue in Madrid to toughen her up. On the same occasion he had shown me photographs of murders in Spain which he thought I ought to see to overcome my squeamishness. Martha Gellhorn professed to believe that I had invented all this – it had simply never happened.[2]

I answered that it had happened. It took two days to deal with Gellhorn and Riding – not really a waste because there is nothing

---

1 George Plimpton (1927–2003), American writer and editor. Martha Gellhorn (1908–1998), American novelist and journalist and the third wife of Ernest Hemingway, 1940–45.

2 In the spring of 1980, Spender had stated in an interview in the *Paris Review* (volume 77) that he and his wife Inez had met Hemingway and Martha Gellhorn for lunch in Paris in 1937 and recounted details of his impressions of Hemingway and of walks they had been on together in Valencia (also recorded in chapter 4 of *World Within World*). In her riposte, which would be published in the *Paris Review* in the spring of 1981 (volume 79), Martha Gellhorn denied having met Spender for lunch in Paris and claimed that Spender did not have much contact with Hemingway himself. She objected to the level of intimacy Spender claimed he had with Hemingway, stating, 'I'd write Spender off as a silly juggins and wonder why he claimed an imaginary intimacy – for we never saw Spender in all that Spanish time.' Gellhorn took particular exception to Spender's implication that Hemingway went to Spain to 'test his own courage', rather than due to a genuine conviction about the Spanish cause. Spender replied in the same issue, insisting that the luncheon in Paris did take place in 1937. There was, as it happened, a photograph confirming the event. He did concede that he may have mistaken the location of the conversations with Hemingway.

much else I can do in my present jet-lagged state – also controversy is good for my prose. The 'situation' of being accused by Gellhorn of inventing a luncheon which took place forty-four years ago also fascinated me, suggesting possibilities for fiction.

Put it like this. There was a meal at a restaurant of four people. H., I., G. and S. H. and I. (Hemingway and Inez) are both dead. The only survivors are G. and S., Gellhorn and myself. G. denies that the occasion ever took place. She may genuinely think it did not because it is completely obliterated from her memory. To her, meeting I. and S. was completely unimportant – one tiny episode in the glamorous, mutually self-dramatizing life of Hemingway and herself carrying on like characters talking and fucking in a Hemingway novel. The reason that S. remembers is because meeting Hemingway was an important event in his life. I. and S. were spectators of the performance put on by H. and G. which was like a scene in a play – G. calling Hemingway 'Hem' and 'Hemingstein'; Hemingway acting up to his tough role before this butch bedmate. Preoccupied in their drama, H. and G. of course scarcely notice the spectators, from whom they are cut off by the proscenium arch of their flood-lit stage.

But what I remember is my re-enactment of the scene in my own mind for my pleasure. I don't really remember the original, I only remember these repeat performances going on in my brain. At least I think this is so. I search in my mind for some fragment of the original scene which is not part of the re-enacting. I don't remember anything 'new' about the luncheon itself, and I can't place the restaurant. It sounds like the Brasserie Lipp, but I don't see it in the Boulevard. The only thing I do remember is collateral – that about the same time Hemingway and I jointly gave a reading at Shakespeare & Co., Sylvia Beach's bookshop in the rue de l'Odéon. I have not thought about this for many years – though it is rather memorable – Hemingway ordering drinks and his reading a passage which I think I would recognize (its rapid violence made Inez laugh) if I re-read that book. Also James Joyce was there. Again, I cannot think of anyone today alive in that audience from whom I could obtain confirmation of it – but in fact there must be surviving witnesses, and there must be some record of the talks and readings at Shakespeare & Co. which someone is working on at this moment. It is part of historic time.

There is material for fiction in this situation: a story in which one

[575]

produced the documents – the passage in the interview – the denial by G. S., in the story, then goes searching for witnesses. He finds one – perhaps someone whom he told about the luncheon the very day it happened – perhaps even someone sitting at the next table – who produces a completely different version of what happened.

On Tuesday, we had a very lively dinner party. Paddy and Joan Leigh Fermor, John Wells and Teresa, Philippe de Rothschild.[1] The Leigh Fermors and John W. had spent the weekend at Anne Fleming's so the conversation was a continuation for them of the weekend. They raced along; Natasha and I managed to catch up after a time. Philippe was rather left out, though Natasha gave him special attention. He looked worn and tired and melancholy, a bit left out but resigned and rather sweet about it. He talked – before the race rushed ahead of him – with amused detachment about his cancer. I said – 'how can you take it all so calmly?' He said: 'Well when there was that pursuit in the mountains and the Nazis were a few yards from us – well that was an occasion to be frightened.'[2]

22 November 1980, London

They played the Schubert Octet on the wireless, and I stopped writing this and listened to it. Oboes, flutes, clarinets always bring to mind a day in 1929 when Erich Alport took me to visit friends of his – a young man called Lothar – and his wife Ilse – in the flat sandy pine forests among dunes near the sea not far from Hamburg. The small square modern concrete house had a large central room with a staircase along one side of it, leading to the bedroom on the upper floor. We lay on cushions in the dusk and someone put on the record player a movement from Mozart's Clarinet Quintet. The liquid voice of the solo instrument played through the semi-darkness of those hollow walls within the pine-filled forest, like a white waterfall through darkness. Then Lothar our host, a young man with a flap of

---

1 Teresa Gatacre would marry John Wells in 1982. She had been a student of Spender's at UCL.

2 Philippe de Rothschild narrowly escaped the Nazi invasion in 1940 to serve with the Free French forces headquartered in England. His first wife was captured and died in Ravensbruck concentration camp.

yellow hair falling down over his face through [which] his amber eyes resembled an animal's looking through iron bars, lit the fire and threw pine logs onto it. It blazed – the only bright thing in the dark, occasionally throwing out sparks. Then wearing a dress with a full skirt which extended the bulge of her pregnant body into a bow-like curve down to her feet, Ilse came out of the bedroom and stood looking down at us from on top of the stair-landing. Splashes of light reflected in her dress from the fire and made her bronzed young-German face with the shining smiling eyes seem one tongue of flame. Lothar sitting beside me said he could not bear to be home when his wife was having a baby, so he was going to leave early next day and bicycle to Holland. I imagined him in the grey dawn, leaning over handlebars, the tyres leaving tracks in the white sandy path, his eyes looking straight ahead, through the green flat country all the way to Amsterdam.

27 November 1980, London

We gave a dinner for Alan Pryce-Jones, who was with his friend Larry Hudson, Rosamond Lehmann, Claire Tomalin and V. S. Pritchett.[1] Pritchett at eighty was really my great impression of the evening. He arrived early so asked me about Vanderbilt, where he is going to teach. He is completely alert, smiling, attentive with an authentic light in his eyes. At the end of the evening when everyone else was gone we talked about the brilliant loquaciousness of Alan P.-J. Victor [Pritchett]'s theory is that there is a kind of pool of rhetoric story-telling fantasy in Wales which a great many Welshmen draw on. They all produce an unending stream of anecdote, wit, sentiment which derives from this shared source. Never particularly truthful, sometimes they are political sometimes poetical, sometimes devout, sometimes frivolous. But it is always the same flow.

He also had some theory about Americans which I have forgotten and with which I totally disagreed. V.S.P. is very English. There is something circumscribed yet inspired about him and conversation with him in Hampstead makes me think of the kind of talk that must

---

1 Claire Tomalin (b. 1933), British biographer and journalist.

have gone on between Hazlitt, Leigh Hunt, Benjamin Robert Haydon, Keats, in the 1810s.

Lucy Penna came to lunch with me alone one day this week.[1] I bought a lot of organic food – oatmeal biscuits, cheese, wholemeal bread, date and nut bars, from an organic food shop in St Johns Wood. Lucy said she hardly ever buys food from organic food shops because other shops are so good at that sort of stuff now and the vegetables in organic food stops look so dry and wizened and have so much clay attached to them. [. . .] Lucy told me her mother had said there was something in the atmosphere of England that seemed calamitous reminding her of the 1930s. This is certainly true, the winding down of everything, the unemployment, a government whose only idea is to economize etc. A difference is that with hindsight we can see where the '30s leaders went wrong. They should have gone in for expansionist instead of contractile policies. Perhaps the government is right that hotting up the economy will only lead to inflation. However, the lack of benefit of hindsight while in the midst of the slump *does* make it very like the '30s.

What is parallel, if not similar, is the feeling that the mainspring which keeps the whole economy going is breaking down and may collapse entirely. In the '30s this was trade, but today this is oil. I don't think that in the '30s there was the feeling there is today that recovery itself may be doomed, i.e. that any slight recovery made may be followed by a set back as the result of a rise in the price of oil, or the running out of oil supplies as a result, say, of the war in the Middle East. Then beyond everything else there loom vast uncontrolled perhaps uncontrollable problems – increasing population and increasing poverty of the third world, and beyond that even, the piling up of armaments which can more than destroy the world.

There is no self-sufficient locality. Everything is a target of everything outside itself.

I saw last night on TV part of the series about Oppenheimer. It seemed the most important part, being that in which experiments to explode the A-Bomb are complete and in which the Americans decide to use it. The onus of decision is put on Oppenheimer. There is a

---

1 Lucy Penna, daughter of Rex Warner and Barbara Hutchinson, before her marriage to Nicolas Ghika.

meeting of [Henry] Stimson and military heads attended by various scientists of whom the most important is Oppenheimer.[1] The military chief of staff explains the situation in the Far East supposing that the Americans decide to invade Japan (which they are all set to do). They are prepared for losses of half a million men. If the A Bomb is as effective as the scientists say the invasion will be unnecessary and the war brought to a rapid conclusion. There is the question though of whether an A Bomb might not be dropped on some barren island in whose neighbourhood the Japs could be invited so that they would see the overwhelming destruction into which – if they did not give up fighting – they were doomed. But Oppenheimer says they only have enough plutonium for two bombs. Besides, supposing this experiment were a failure – or supposing the Japs took it as a warning which they could forestall by preventing the bomb-carrying aircraft meeting its target. It is decided to drop the bomb. There is the experience with a bomb in the desert etc.

The dilemma is not quite as appears. At one moment one of the military reveals that in fact the Japanese are ready to negotiate. The real reason for dropping the bomb is to deliver a warning to Stalin. If that is so, the bomb should not be dropped. On the other hand, if dropping it really saved a half a million American lives, it seems justified.

Or that is how it seems to me. But really the whole thing is beyond argument. The capacity to destroy everything enters another dimension.

Human beings like Oppenheimer are no longer moral forces making moral decisions, they are instruments of a destructiveness inherent in the unleashed forces of nature. I am reminded of the theories of certain scientists in the nineteenth century who, anxious to justify the view of creation put forward in the Book of Genesis, adopted the view that there were several civilizations on Earth each of which had been totally wiped out by a universal catastrophe of nature (so that the Book of Genesis was true in the context of our Biblical civilization).

---

1 Henry Stimson (1867–1950), American politician, head of the US War Department, 1940–50, directly responsible for making the decision to bomb Hiroshima.

28 November 1980, Cambridge

Two undergraduates met me at the station, one of them a weedy youth wearing a kind of wreath round his head, and trailing garments. He looked a bit like Ophelia [. . .] [I]n a snowstorm joined Dadie Rylands, Frank and Anita Kermode, Helen Vendler and Natasha who'd driven from London at the Lodge of King's College. We took them out to lunch at some kind of University restaurant. Dadie who took my arm in case I should fall in the snow was all sweetness and concern and affection. I thought back over all the years I've known him – back to Ipsden staying with Rosamond and Wogan Philipps when I was there in 1930 or so.[1] Wogan did a painting of him with two heads like those of a King on a playing card. He painted it on wood put a nail through the middle which he hammered into a wall and had it swivel round. Then Dadie was the golden-haired blue-eyed boy favoured by Lytton Strachey. He had acted as the duchess in *The Duchess of Malfi* (Isherwood, as an undergraduate had seen him perform). He had written a charming book about Shakespeare, called, I think, *Words in Poetry*.[2] (I remember, I think, his discussion of 'perdurable' – or was it perdition?) Despite his acting – and his reading in a beautiful mellow voice – he had always the look of an eager spectator who sometimes chips in. His looking at Ros and Wog and then if they started to have a tiff – his way of shaking a finger and saying with satisfaction 'Now now, dears!' Wogan told me Dadie was broken-hearted when Lytton didn't leave him his library and I can well believe that Dadie loved Lytton as no one else did. Affection is his nature. And here he was guiding me across the ice (and I was thinking that if I did fall, I would be like a tower of bricks crushing this smiling frail delicate octogenarian). I thought how I had missed a life of friendship with him – because his clever mocking brittle manner made me think that affection – for someone as gauche as I have been all my life – was only an act. He talked of Anthony Blunt, how fond of him he'd always been, how shocked when he discovered that during their long relationship Anthony had

---

1 Wogan Philipps, 2nd Baron Milford (1902–1993), communist peer, married to Rosamond Lehmann, 1928–44.

2 *Words and Poetry* (1928).

[580]

been deceiving him when he accepted sympathy for the defection of Guy Burgess – as though that had been a great shock to him, Anthony. The luncheon was pleasant. Frank, the benign colleague. Helen Vendler said that in Cambridge she missed the material comforts of America. I said America was for me a place where if you turned a tap marked 'H', hot water really came out.

November 1980, London

Today I had lunch with Frank Auerbach.[1] First, I went to his studio in George Street, Camden Town. The floor looks as if it has been worn through to some surface of an old pathway below it of cobble stones. Actually it is made of paint fallen from canvases he has painted and has accumulated over the years in an abstraction that looks like a Tàpies.[2] The studio with its dark walls on which there are hung very few pictures – one a self-portrait by Mrs [Helen] Lessore, two early works by Leon Kossoff – has a skylight the beams from which make objects they fall on seem very contrasting.[3] While Frank talked to me one side of his face was in a darkness which seemed to have Venetian red in it, the other was lit white. I almost wished I had brought my camera and taken a photograph, which would have looked perhaps like one by the French photographer of Baudelaire.[4] With his dark hair – shorter than it used to be – dark eyes exceptionally white skin the bone structure of his jaws and his strong nose and sensuous mouth, more than like such a photograph he looks like a sculptor painted by Murillo. He has a weight and seriousness which are Central European, and his expression shifts rapidly from the serious to the smiling. He has a way of laughing which asks you to join in. Despite his virility and energy there is also

---

1 Frank Auerbach (b. 1931), German-born British painter.

2 Antoni Tàpies (b. 1923), Spanish 'tachiste' painter (a 'tache' being a splodge of paint).

3 Helen Lessore (1907–1994), British painter and early patron of Auerbach via the Beaux-Arts Gallery, which she directed; Leon Kossoff (b. 1926), British painter, also of the so-called 'School of London'.

4 Baudelaire was photographed by the renowned French photographer Félix Nadar (1820–1910) in the 1850s.

something a bit feminine about him, a quality of appealing for agreement.

He is the kind of person who makes me feel most humble when he seems most respectful. I did not interview him – because I thought that the reproduction of his pictures I have would speak better to me if I did not have a screen of his opinions about them between them and me. However, I did ask him about things which aroused my curiosity anyway. One thing that interests me very much with painters as well as poets is what sort of idea they have in their heads of it before they embark on a work. My own feeling is that I have a strong but vague idea of the work before I write; and that the actual writing is an effort to recall an impression. He said that for him his starting point was only a sketchy idea that he altered as he went on painting, discovering what was new. I asked him whether he thought that at the end the completed picture was only the realization of the original idea which had been vague in his mind when he first started. He said no, what he ended with was pure discovery. At most he would admit that the finished picture contained the ghost of the idea he had started with. We went to a Greek restaurant near Camden Town tube station. He insisted on taking me out to lunch, saying it was what he wanted[,] that he should do so – it pleased him. He said he didn't see Francis Bacon much – perhaps they had quarrelled? he asked himself – but answered he didn't think so. 'Friendships wear out,' he said. He accepted that. I suppose I do too, but it is the last thing I'd want to admit to myself. He didn't see much of Lucian [Freud], but he talked about him. He said he had now become rather like his father, had a totally Viennese respectable, comfortable apartment – a servant, I think – where he received visitors.

Frank strikes one as unworldly and perhaps it is part of the unworldliness, that he is totally without malice.

14 December 1980, London

Went to New College banquet, as the guest of Richard Ellmann. [. . .] At the banquet I sat between Freddie Ayer and Dick Ellmann. On Freddie's left was his guest, Mrs Lawson who looks like a post card in black-and-white of a film star of about 1925.[1] [. . .] The only conversation with [Freddie] is about himself, so I fired off questions about what he was doing and he fired back rapid replies. He had bought a house in York Street, near Baker Street, where he was going to co-habit with the lady on his left whom in two years' time he would marry. They had to wait two years for the divorce, the alternative to waiting being to have to enter into divorce proceedings which would be a waste of money. If you and your ex-wife remain separated for two years demonstrably never meeting, divorce follows automatically, he said, so this was the course they were embarking on (Mrs Lawson now flashed at me a gloss black and white print glittering smile. I thought that if you were seventy it would be worth updating your remarriage by a little expenditure on lawyers. Then, I reflected, there was no point in their being married anyway). Nicholas his son by Dee is going to live in the basement at York Street. He has stopped being punk and dyeing his hair saffron, and feels he needs further education. Freddie is writing a book which bores him very much (and which, he fears, may therefore bore his readers), which is a continuation of Bertrand Russell's popular *History of Western Philosophy*, which solved all Russell's financial problems.[2] Freddie said he sometimes felt now that he would like to stop working, put his feet up, and read. He asked me whether I found this sympathetic. I said I thought it was a noble aspiration – that it was a prevalent current heresy to think that everyone should be a writer and no one a reader – whereas the reader was just as essential to literature – as the writer etc etc – but I felt I had not begun to write yet. I was like Bill Coldstream who at the age of seventy-five tells me that whenever he takes up his paint brushes, he feels: 'Well one day perhaps this promising young painter will produce something worthwhile.'

'But do you really think you've produced nothing that will last? Don't you think that in your whole life you have produced twelve

---

1 Ayer would marry Vanessa Lawson, formerly the wife of Nigel Lawson, in 1982.

2 Ayer's book would become his *Philosophy in the Twentieth Century* (1982). Russell's *A History of Western Philosophy and its Connection with Political and Social Circumstances from the Earliest Times to the Present Day* had been published in 1945.

poems?' 'Well, perhaps twelve,' I said, mentally trying to count them on invisible fingers. But nothing that I am sure of, I thought but did not say, thinking this would be false modesty – or – worse, a cry from the abyss for sympathy. However, I was happy for Freddie that he'd shown this interest, and warmed towards him.

There were a few younger people at the banquet, but really it was a parade of the old. [. . .] There were nice faces – Herbert Hart and Christopher Cox, the sight of whom instantly transports all three of us back to a reading party fifty years ago at Crackington Haven in Devon.[1] [. . .] Herbert Hart has changed hardly at all, nor has Isaiah. Christopher Cox is visible beneath the dereliction of his architecture. When I say we haven't changed, I mean we have continually, some integral qualities of structure, expression and animation have as it were gone underground in us, and only superficially altered. But if one saw say a film of a picnic on the beach at Crackington, we would exclaim 'How could we have looked like that?' – seeing more the boys (of whom Pilkington – long dead – was the prettiest) rather than the backward projection into the past of our present selves.

15 December 1980, London

I saw more of Isaiah alone on Sunday than for many years. On Sunday morning we breakfasted then sat in his study for a bit. I asked him about Wittgenstein.[2] He said that all W.'s disciples denied indignantly that he was homosexual but he considered he certainly was though probably not pratiquant [practising]. Once in 1940 (I think) he (Isaiah) had gone to Cambridge to read a paper to a philosophy society. There were a lot of people there, some sitting on the floor. Suddenly he realized that a man with open-neck shirt and wearing a jacket with leather patches on the elbow must be W. Isaiah read his paper which he said went on much too long. At the end of it, after a pause Wittgenstein asked a question. Isaiah was terrified but answered

---

1 H. L. A. Hart (1907–1992), legal philosopher, Spender's contemporary at Oxford. Christopher Cox (1899–1982), a tutor at New College, Oxford in Spender's day.

2 Ludwig Wittgenstein (1889–1951), Austrian philosopher of logic and language, resident in Cambridge between 1911 and 1913 and, with gaps, between 1929 and 1947.

just as he would any other questioner, to the best of his ability. Then Wittgenstein went on questioning him for an hour. At the end of the meeting Shyah was surrounded by young philosophers congratulating him at having had a dialogue with the great man, as though he had won an award. He thought Wittgenstein must have thought he was sincere, confused but worth conversing with. He said the person W. most hated was Freddie Ayer: had once sent F.A. a postcard asking him never to mention, in any of his writings, W. again. Talked about the brother of W. a pianist who had lost an arm during the war for whom Ravel had written a concerto.[1] Isaiah said that what Wittgenstein stood for and cared about most was morality, but since he had no language for this it could never be discussed or explained.

I left Isaiah and sitting in my guest room overlooking the beautiful walled in garden with its tall burnt out-looking tree trunks, a few last leaves and the metallic looking grass reflecting a filtered golden sunlight, wrote this Journal.

Natasha and Day Wollheim – a smiling mouth but with scared liquid eyes from which tears about Richard [Wollheim] might at any moment fall – arrived having driven from London. Alfred Brendel, a tall scholarly very upright looking man with an expression on his face of extreme sensitiveness to things going on outside, a slow meticulous fastidious accent.[2] Friendly and really intelligent. His wife, blonde open air loquacious rather jolly Germanic, like an advertisement for things to do with snow in the mountains. Jerseys, skis, sticks, mineral water, toothpaste, shampoo, cigarettes – love – she might well be the tonic his sensitive slight desiccation needed. Serious – he is a bit dazed among us frivolous-toned descendants of Bloomsbury who rush on making a game of passing the ball of conversation from one to the other, feeling the cuff of rebuke if anyone tries to introduce the note of world-suffering into the conversation.

On 11 December 1980, Sonia Orwell died of a brain tumour.

---

1 Paul Wittgenstein (1887–1961), the philosopher's brother, lost his right arm in the First World War. Ravel's Piano Concerto for the left hand was written for him.

2 Alfred Brendel (b. 1931), Austrian pianist resident in London who, together with his wife Irene Semler, would become a good friend of the Spenders.

24 December 1980, London

On Thursday December 17, Sonia Orwell's funeral at a rather beautiful Roman Catholic Church in Cadogan Street, nineteenth-century Gothic, cold, grey, stony, unornamented, or almost so, the clarity of its columns and arches like those in a Dutch painting. Anne, Rodrigo and Dan Moynihan there, Diana Witherby, Janetta (who has gone under so many names), Bill Coldstream, darting in and darting out with a distracted air; Michael Pitt-Rivers looking grave.[1] Then a whole contingent of old ladies who looked like charwomen. The service in Latin – I thought the priest said 'At the request of Mrs Orwell' and had a mental glimpse of this being Sonia's last assertion of the correct and *comme il faut* shot down amongst us from the top of the Church tower. Of course I thought of her 'the Venus of Euston Road' in 1937 or 8 when I used to paint at the Euston Road art school. With a round Renoir face, limpid eyes, cupid mouth, fair hair, a bit pale perhaps, she had a look of someone always struggling to go beyond herself – to escape from her social class, the convent where she was educated, into some pagan aesthete world of artists and literary geniuses who would save her.

All the time I knew her, which was from her early twenties, people discussed whether she was sexually cold, virginal, Lesbian – what. Undoubtedly she had passionate loyalties – loyalty of some kind was her deepest nature and it transcended her disloyalty which was the expression of her frustration at none of the people who were objects of her passionate admiration quite responding – their always being faintly embarrassed by an enthusiasm that never quite hit the centre of the target. Stories illustrating this clung to her like burrs stuck on to her by Cyril Connolly. The most famous – told by Peter Quennell – and of which there are variants – being of how when staying with Richard Wyndham in the Thirties she was pursued by him – or some predatory guest of his – intent on raping her, and threw herself into

---

1 Diana Witherby, British poet. Spender refers to Janetta Woolley, whose name changed following the many marriages described by Spender in the next entry. Michael Pitt-Rivers was married to, though not living with, Sonia Orwell, 1958–65. The marriage was a chivalrous attempt on Sonia's part to help Pitt-Rivers reacquire social credibility after the scandal of his arrest for homosexual acts.

the duck pond – emerging from which, panting and muddy she exclaimed to Peter: 'It isn't his attempting to rape me which upset me so much as that he didn't understand what Cyril stood for.'[1]

But this is as much revealing of Peter Quennell as of her. And the point of the anecdote is lost if one takes it as meaning that she was completely naïve. She would have laughed at it. Her conversation consisted quite considerably of such anecdotes about other people and, I think, about herself. 'I was a bloody fool ever to believe in Cyril,' she might certainly have said.

15 January 1981, London

Christmas was very quiet. In fact Natasha and I spent Christmas Day quite alone, as Lizzie was staying with friends Ann and Gardner Brown [. . .] We just ate a capon, mince pies, and looked at TV and went on working. There were some very convivial parties over the season. One at the *Times* offices – the *T.L.S.* – given by John Gross. After this there was a party at Karl and Jane Miller's, an excellent buffet dinner, everyone getting drunk except Jonathan Miller who never drinks, and who throughout the evening was surrounded by shifting groups of people whom he entertained engagingly on various subjects – medicine, the theatre – at a level of discourse amusing but at a level more concentrated than that of others in the various rooms the party spilled through.[2] Downstairs Mark Boxer and Anna Ford, the extremely fashionable TV Announcer, lay making love.[3] Karl's son who is a painter had invited various young people who rushed about the house excitedly. It was enjoyable in that way all the parties we went to this Christmas were, because people were affectionate and excited. [. . .]

After the funeral service for Sonia on December 17, Janetta, Diana [Witherby], Dan Moynihan and I went to the Moynihans' house in

---

1 Richard Wyndham (1896–1948), British artist; the story relates to Sonia Brownell's (as she then was) working with Connolly in the early stages of setting up *Horizon*.

2 Karl Miller was currently editor of the *London Review of Books*.

3 Mark Boxer (1931–1988), British cartoonist and editor, contemporary of Karl Miller's at Cambridge. Anna Ford (b. 1943), journalist and television presenter.

Argyll Rd sitting there and chatting for about an hour before we were joined there by the contingent who had gone to the actual burial.[1] In the road outside the house, Janetta said: 'I dreamed about you all last night. It was absolutely delightful.' This remark instantly transported me to an evening in 1938 or 1939 when we had had dinner together then walked along Oxford Street as far as Selfridge's clock – or just opposite, on the other side of the road – where we separated. But we needn't have done, I would have asked her to go home with me, and I'm always conscious of this as a kind of turning point, an example of my timidity which had not so much a decisive effect on my life as an effect of perpetuating my indecisiveness.

I first met Janetta in 1938 (I think) when she turned up in London, wearing a trousered suit of dark velvet and carrying a shepherd's crook. She was a dream person, and I lay awake thinking about her – fantasizing as they say, because I was still married to Inez and I did not think of having anything to do with her. She was a secret thought which I mentioned to no one except Cyril – and then only after the breakdown of my marriage.

A year later – the time of the Selfridge clock face glowing its ugly amber – she was still very attractive, but she had become the Janetta I've known ever since: not the girl-boy shepherd-shepherdess but the mysterious elusive woman she's been ever since. To me she seemed to have aged; though what actually happened was that she had become ageless. After that there was the war when I married and she married Sinclair-Loutit.[2] She remained the same changeless within a great many changes – marriages, love affairs – Humphrey Slater (but he was before Sinclair-Loutit), Robert Kee, Derek Jackson, Jaime [Parladé] – her present husband, and her lover Andrew Devonshire – femme fatale (I suppose she must count as that, though I don't think husbands or lovers ever bore her any grudge).[3]

---

1 Danny Moynihan (b. 1959), painter, writer, filmmaker, son of Anne Moynihan.

2 Kenneth Sinclair-Loutit (1913–2004), British doctor who served on the Republican side in the Spanish Civil War while still a medical student.

3 Humphrey Slater (1906–1958), British painter and author. Derek Jackson (1906–1982), physicist, jump-jockey, himself married seven times and bisexual. Andrew Devonshire (1920–2004), 11th Duke of Devonshire.

In 1981, Spender was a visiting professor at the University of South Carolina.

18 January 1981, Columbia, South Carolina

Yesterday (Saturday) I read all day *Vanity Fair* [i.e. Thackeray's novel] and a volume of wonderful Essays on European Literature by Curtius.[1] *V.F.* is vivacious trash, most interesting as vivid journalism, with hypnotic dialogue. It is newsreel stuff really with an elaborate system of sentimentalized falsified values imposed on it making up the element of imaginative fiction. Although very readable, it isn't the kind of book that is compulsive reading (like Tolstoy or George Eliot) because one knows that nothing by which one can better live or more freely breathe is going to be told about life. It is morally as vain as its title. E. R. Curtius on the other hand is compulsive reading in being revelation – revelation firstly of the extraordinary character of Goethe, his intellect, his passion, his vision, his outer worldliness and his inner withdrawn-ness, his sense of awe and mystery, his grasp of present and past, and his power to relate to the two, his Byronically joyful mastery of form, which he controls and breaks through when expressing his vibrant ideas (ideas, of course which Byron never had). E.R.C. himself has great appreciation and is better the better and greater his subject matter. When he deals with Cocteau or [William] Goyen, he simply attributes to them, sentimentally, characteristics he has and which they haven't. [. . .]

We went to two plays with Matthew [in London, 3–9 December], *The Dresser* [by Ronald Harwood] and *Amadeus* [by Peter Shaffer] [. . .] The evening after we went to one of these plays, [. . .] Natasha and Matthew and I had late dinner at Bianchi. The music room of the restaurant was taken up by a large table at which were seated about a dozen people, among them Seamus Heaney and Ted Hughes and Melvyn Bragg.[2] When we went past their table, Heaney got up came

---

1 E. R. Curtius, *Europäische Literatur und lateinisches Mittelalter* (1948).

2 Seamus Heaney (b. 1939), Irish poet and winner of the Nobel Prize for Literature (1995). His *Selected Poems: 1965–1975* had been published by Faber in 1980. Melvyn Bragg (b. 1939), British author and broadcaster, who had been presenting *The South Bank Show* since 1978.

over to me and thanked me for having nominated his *Selected Poems* as among the three best books of the year. He said he had not written to me, because he thought to do so might be to cross some boundary which divides silent gratitude from sycophancy. I said he was quite right not to have written. I also shook hands with Ted Hughes. When we sat at our table in the next room another poet came over. He was Charles Causley.[1] He said that on the way from Cornwall he'd been reading my *Letters to Christopher*, and was much entertained by them.[2] Still later the waiter arrived with a bottle of champagne from the next table. I put these things down because I felt far more pleased than I did by the embarrassment of public recognition – like getting the C.B.E.[3] This was a gesture from fellow poets. Instead of feeling worse than neglected – doomed whatever I write – to be ignored – I suddenly felt the will to write something worthy of the attention of colleagues – to finish poems – to get out of my state of writing poems as an activity which does not imply finishing, far less publishing them, because it is so solitary.

The political situation in America at this time was volatile. The Republican candidate Ronald Reagan had been elected US President in November 1980 after a heated contest with incumbent Democrat Jimmy Carter. He was aided in his campaign by Carter's involvement in the Iran hostage crisis. The hostages were released on 20 January 1981, minutes after Reagan was sworn in as President.

21 January 1981, Columbia, South Carolina

Had yesterday a streaming cold. Reagan inaugurated as President, the hostages left Iran. I took my classes. Everyone I meet is polite amiable and helpful here, but very much of a level. The institutional life, but better than being in hospital last year. Impression of moving along a straight road on a day of white mist reducing everything to solid oblong forms, the element through which I move, being time. At night dreams about the dead. Last night Day Lewis. Read Curtius

1 Charles Causley (1917–2003), British poet.

2 Spender's *Letters to Christopher: Stephen Spender's Letters to Christopher Isherwood* had been published in 1980.

3 Spender had received a CBE in 1962.

on European history, Thackeray. Worlds through which far more powerful, sonorous, colourful, vivid forces move than this one which is threatened at every moment with what amounts to an appalling end by traffic accident, the introduction by machinery of fire and metal into soft flesh.

In May 1981, Spender went to China with David Hockney and his assistant Gregory Evans. Together they produced China Diary, *with text by Spender and paintings, drawings and photographs by Hockney. According to Hockney it was 'just a little personal trip' they had made together and the book was 'a bit bitty – like life – patched up in some way, as if made by three schoolboys on a tour of a continent for the first time'. Nonetheless, the book, for which Spender received £10,000, was the best paid of his career.*

   In 1981, China was governed by Deng Xiaoping, who had manoeuvered himself to the top in the power struggle following the death of the communist dictator Mao Zedong in 1976. For the ten years prior to his death, Mao Zedong had been attempting to reinvigorate the Communist Party and attack bourgeois values with a Great Proletarian Cultural Revolution, calling on the young to form Red Guard groups and mobilize against the bourgeoisie. On his accession to power, Deng Xiaoping immediately embarked on a course of economic and social reform, opening China to the rest of the world and de-collectivizing the countryside.

19 May 1981, Hong Kong

While we were sitting in the transit lounge at Tokyo airport, David did a drawing of me looking saturated with exhaustion like a sponge with water. After living with myself for over seventy years I have, I suppose, a kind of serial image of myself though it is unlikely that one will recognize oneself in the final emanation of the series. The general impression I made in David's drawing was of bulbous obesity: bulbous cheeks, chins, limbs and fingers. Later drawings in wash or crayon confirmed an overall redness rendered sheep-like by the whitest of woollen hair. The eyes are veined pink by eye-strain. With the retina of one eye distorting lines it sees – or doesn't see – into curves, and with knees creaking after an accident two years ago in which I severed the ligaments of both knees and had them sewn up – and with my considerable height and overall largeness I must have looked very much the odd man out compared with my two younger companions. It is obvious though that all three of us must have looked comical to the Chinese and this should be remembered because those observed are themselves observers of the observers and sometimes cannot prevent themselves laughing at them. We looked a bit absurd, especially me with my big feet.

Spender spent the flight reading Mao Zedong's speeches. He found that, according to the Chinese dictator:

State power is to be abolished like sin but not just yet, dear Lord – never just yet. But the longer the state is dictatorial, the more difficult will it be to abolish tyranny. There is not anywhere a dictatorship under which some class of public servants is trained to run the government when the state withers away. There was, I thought, the Cultural Revolution in China but, although this resulted for a time in near anarchy, its purpose was not to destroy the centralized power of the state. From Mao Tse-tung's point of view, its purpose was, in the name of continual revolution, to reinstate the authority of Chairman Mao, who had been set aside as a mere figurehead by his colleagues and who had lost his basis of power.

Thoughts like these pursued me all the time we were in China even in my sleep, I think, for sometimes they took the form of nightmares. They were typical thoughts of someone of my generation. It seemed appropriate that they should start in the aeroplane because they were floating – *flottant* as the French say. They corresponded though to something that I felt to be floating in China itself where the current of life seems today liquescent, with all the fixed ideas of communism, Maoism, pragmatism, individualism, in a state of flux, all floated over by the balloon-like portraits of Chairman Mao on walls.

David, being of his generation and 44 as against my 72, does not have the same tendency to think along lines laid down by the history of power politics in this century. He used, he told me when we talked about this, at one time to vote Labour but today party politics don't interest him. This may be due in part to the fact that, from the point of view of an English painter who divides his life between Los

Angeles and London, party politics seem parochial. He looks at life, he says, from the point of view of the imagination. The imagination is to him a kind of ultimate force directing – or which should direct – everything. Often he exclaims 'Everything is imagination', as though this thought were some touchstone in his mind. Science is there to provide the technological means whereby the imagined can be made real.

Once I mentioned to David that some French professor – a structuralist, I think – had said that we in the West could not possibly ever understand the Chinese because their whole way of thinking and patterns of behaviour conditioning them were outside the context of our way of thinking and the patterns of behaviour conditioning us. David was indignant: 'I could not believe that for one moment,' he said. 'To do so is to deny our common humanity.'

I suppose that one would have to describe David as an optimist, though myself I do not care for that word. It seems to indicate some kind of moral myopia, the opposite of the kind called pessimistic. It would be more to the point to say that he thinks it a virtue – almost a moral imperative – to regard life as a *donnée*, a condition given, to be enjoyed. He resents people doing life down. At any rate, he thinks that there's something to be got out of it for most people.

On our travels David and I were, I think, corrective to each other because I am able to point out to him that he should not expect everyone in the world to have his capacity for enjoyment; and he corrects in me the tendency to be got down or over-impressed by the sheer weight of seemingly insuperable obstacles and insoluble problems, to live as it were under a dark vague cloud of uncomprehended and, I suspect, incomprehensible statistics. He had a glimpse of the insoluble negations of the world, which I seem mentally to inhabit much of the time, when he went to India. On our travels he said that, however bad things may be in China, they are worse in India.

David likes Los Angeles because he regards it as being in a perpetual state of transformation. Los Angeles tomorrow will not be the Los Angeles you dislike today, he says to friends who complain about L.A. On our trip he sometimes said that he thought America was nearer to communism than China with its bureaucrats, its stratification of the population into about thirty different classes, its top rulers moving around in cars looking like hearses and with side windows through which it is as difficult to see the top people as it is to see harems in the smoke-glass limousines of Arab sheiks. In China today officials live in apartments more hidden from the public gaze than those of any Emperor and his retinue in the Forbidden City.

21 May 1981, Peking

As soon as we got through customs, which we seemed to do like lightning, we were met by our two guides, Mr Lin Hua – who for the next three weeks was to be Virgil to our threesome Dante – and Miss Li [. . .] David did a schematic drawing of the drive from the airport along a straight road with straight rows of trees on either side. Beyond the trees, of which there were sometimes as many as six rows, there were fields – all very flat and very green. The road finally became an avenue with blocks of high tenement buildings either side. I asked our local guide what these were: 'Housing for the people,' she said, and added that had it not been for the subversive activities of the Gang of Four, there would be many more such tenements.[1]

This was the first time we heard mention of Those who are Guilty for Everything that is Wrong – the thought of them caused the gentle Miss Li's voice to tremble and her face to redden. It was like the harsh vibrations on the drums in the orchestra accompanying a Chinese opera when the dragon-villain appears.

I asked what people were housed in the tenements, and she explained that occupiers were decided on according to priorities. I remarked on the great number of cyclists in the streets as we approached the city. 'Three million of the nine million inhabitants of Peking have bicycles,' she told us with a bright smile.

At breakfast the next morning David and Gregory worried about this. How did the six million people without bicycles get along? 'Well, some would be too young, others too old to need bicycles,' I said, 'and in a family one bicycle might conveniently be used by two people.' David later discovered, by going to bicycle shops, that a

---

1 The Gang of Four: the name given to the group of four radical members of the Communist Party who took a prominent role in the final years of the Cultural Revolution. The group was comprised of Jiang Qing (Mao Zedong's fourth wife), Zhang Chunqiao, Yao Wenyuan, and Wang Hongwen. After a power struggle in 1976, after Mao's death, they were arrested and put on trial.

bicycle cost 150 yuan and that the average monthly wage of a worker was 100 yuan. He also pointed out that all bicycles were padlocked, which seemed to contradict what we had been told by Miss Li, that no one in China ever stole. Not that we had any expectation that all the Chinese would be saints. It was only our being told how perfectly honest they were that drew attention to the matter. And, of course, nothing was stolen from any of us at any time there – the property of foreign visitors is meticulously guarded. It was curious to read in the newspapers when we got home that in the spring of 1981 China was said to be in the middle of a crime wave.

As we saw it then, driving in from the airport, Peking seemed to consist of vast grey dusty vague areas with broken walls that merge into houses, roads that seem to lead into roads being laid down (they are tearing up sections of the city to extend the underground railway). We had an impressionless impression which gave us the feeling that we were minute dots or crosses on an aerial photograph of a partly bombed out city which, in some areas, was undergoing reconstruction. We scarcely had time to put our things down in the hall of the Peking Hotel, before we were rushed off again in our minibus to meet the British Council Representative and his wife, Mr and Mrs Keith Hunter, at the Kau Ru Ji restaurant with tables outside on a balcony overlooking a part of the lake, Shi Sha Hai, the main expanse of which could be seen further off. With boys and girls dressed mainly in blue and walking by the lakeside and looking out across the water, the scene was like some pastel of working-class Parisians on the banks of the Seine done in the early part of the century; except that the boys and girls did not embrace or hold hands. Or that is how I saw it.

24 May 1981, Peking

Being alone without our two official guides each evening, at dinner, we exchanged impressions. Most of these altered daily, though we all three always agreed that the most obvious thing about China was that it had changed completely from what it had been early in the century. Everyone can see that it is no longer the China of coolies and rickshaws; women with bound feet; opium; war lords; civil war; Japanese occupation; exploitation by foreign imperialists [. . .]. It is a country where people can for the most part respect themselves and where they have at least the minimum standard of living which is necessary for self-respect. We realized though that in places we were not shown and which we would never see, there was still great poverty. Our guides did not exactly tell us this but they did not deny it either.

All the same, China did not give us any feeling of certainty about its future. There were too many unresolved conflicts for certainty: between left and right, the old and the younger generation, country and town.

David said he thought it was difficult, if not impossible, for China to attain communism because it had never been through the phase of industrialization under capitalism. Hence Mao Tse-tung tried to make it break through, in the Great Leap Forward, into communism without heavy industrialization, relying on the millions of the Chinese people to perform this miracle with their bare hands.[1] Today, they were trying to increase industrialization through the encouragement – within limits – of free enterprise; but that might undermine the principle of communism.

Things about China made us think of school: the organization of everyone into groups, like classes, which were indoctrinated with the assumptions of the school: the certainty of the authorities that each member of the school must be fitted into the school's requirements, according to its curriculum. [. . .]

We discussed Mr Lin, our guide. He was a man of the world who had travelled to some extent, having worked in some capacity as a Chinese representative in Reykjavik for some years, and travelled to Denmark. He made it clear that he was a convinced communist. He was both proud and pleased to be an official. He never said anything that left the slightest doubt as to his political convictions, and he conveyed points of Chinese policy clearly, though not dogmatically. He translated for me a long article from the Peking newspaper show-

---

1 In an attempt to dissociate himself from the Russian brand of communism and to catch up with the Western economy, Mao announced that China should make a 'great leap forward' into modernization in 1958. Mao wanted to use China's vast population to collectivize and industrialize farming. The regime was cruelly instituted and poorly implemented, resulting in a famine between 1960 and 1961.

ing that – within the limitations of Marxist-Leninist-Maoist thought – the party was taking an increasingly liberal attitude towards writers. [. . .]

Although we were shown only the places open to tourists, we were not stopped from photographing whatever we saw, which included some very poor people, peasants pushing or pulling carts loaded down with very heavy objects, back streets which were slums and houses in villages little better than hovels.

David said that one thing lacking in Chinese life was vicarious pleasure. No one enjoys simply the spectacle of others better off than himself making a show of their good fortune. The now elderly heads of government, in order not to excite envy, I suppose, look like undertakers trudging to their own graves, or being driven towards them in limousines like hearses.

The negative aspect of vicarious pleasure is envy. One looks at those better off and wishes they were worse off. One does this, I think, when it is impossible to see any connection between the conditions of one's own life and the lives of the more fortunate. The spectacle of another's enjoyment merely draws attention to one's own wretchedness. Envy can arise from a sense of social injustice and therefore expresses a yearning for justice. There are circumstances in which the conditions of a whole society might be based on the satisfaction of the envy of one social class for another.

Reading the newspapers, sometimes one has the impression that in China there is a licensed, institutionalized envy carried to ludicrous lengths. One reads about some official who, entertaining more exalted officials, goes to a good restaurant and orders an excellent meal, using the excuse of providing entertainment for superiors to satisfy his own greed. He is denounced and, in the bureaucratic equivalent of the game of Snakes and Ladders, descends to the tail of a snake. Necessary divisions in allotted tasks are interpreted as incipient class divisions. Managers of factories excite envy so they are made to work on the shop floor. Townspeople have advantages not shared by country people so they are sent into the country to do agricultural work (especially if they belong to that most easily envied class, the intellectuals). The Cultural Revolution was the most ferocious expression of the view that the high must be made low and the low made high: teachers must scrub floors and take lessons from their pupils. Envy is no longer of the poor for the rich, but of the stupid for the clever.

In March 1983, Stephen and Matthew Spender went on another Venetian 'honeymoon'.

25 March 1983, Venice

Matthew gave me this book this morning in Venice – and to Natasha a photograph album. It is a good sign I must take up my journal again, abandoned for almost a year, owing to pressure of work.

27 March 1983, Venice

It was a wonderful day sunlit, everything in pale colours. The buildings across the lagoon were coral and yellow with touches of a darker brown like amber, and very white stones and pillars and pediments and towers. Soft shadows like pools of transparent ink. The sky was a pale blue, the water greenish-turquoise with waves like horizontal flame, moving across it. From the Giudecca to the buildings at the edge of the harbour from the mouth of the Grand Canal to the Maritime Museum looked like a strip of brocade richly stitched and embroidered, pale-coloured, fading in places, and with key-hole shaped window-openings stamped all along its length stretched against a sky, white-puffed with patches of cloud in its azure, in places. There was a coldness in the air which seemed itself to spread a glassy sheen through which buildings shone clear. We looked at the Palladian Church of the Redeemer on the front of the Giudecca, then we got a traghetto to the Rezzonico palace, where M. and I had gone two years ago, with its scenes of Venetian life in the 18th century, beautiful picture of the dress and manners of society people then. One picture is of a banquet with about fifty men one side of the table and women in brocade and velvets and satins, the men be-medalled, the women be-ribbonned, with faces turned to the painter exactly as to a camera, each of them, I suppose, a portrait in miniature by the artist. The food and drink were also meticulously portrayed. 'I can never look at a picture like that without thinking, they're all of them dead,' I said to Matthew. I was thinking of FitzGerald who apparently thought this when he read history.[1] They're all dust, the dirt in our fingernails. Looking at scene after scene from that Venetian life which seem so poignant with death, I thought also – 'They didn't have anaesthetics.' But I said to Matthew 'It looks as if they enjoyed life in those days.' He said, 'it was before Beethoven. Life would have been intolerable before Beethoven. I wouldn't want to have lived before 1830.'

3 April 1983, St Jerome

Care-taking for us at St Jerome are two American girls, from Minnesota. They are quite sweet and rather attractive, but terribly boring. They seem to know nothing, have no initiative. One of them has been living here for four months, companioning our tenant Mrs Ipsen. Neither she nor Mrs I. seems to have met anyone here all that time. The two girls are both vegetarians, sit opposite each other eating leaves, munching and murmuring in low squeaks like two little rabbits. It is cold. I feel depressed. What I feel to have been the disgrace of my *Oedipus Plays* at Oxford has, like the cold grey weather, got into my bones.[2] Ashamed also to have these feelings, which only show that I allow the image of myself in the eyes and minds of newspaper critics to depress me. The penalty of publishing is that one projects a personality which, in the form of published works, one throws to the wolves – and then allows the mangled version of this which may have been chewed over, to seem, even for oneself, one's real personality – which it may be. But of course to refuse to publish – given that one has the work to show – is cowardice because it means one dare not run the risk of self-disgrace. But what about the judgement of people who love me? Why do I feel they are either deceived about my work, or that they conceal from me their real

---

1 Spender is apparently thinking of the 26th stanza of FitzGerald's *Rubáiyát of Omar Khayyám* (1859):

> Why, all the Saints and Sages who discuss'd
> Of the Two Worlds so wisely – they are thrust
> Like foolish Prophets forth; their Words to Scorn
> Are scatter'd, and their Mouths are stopt with Dust.

2 The *Oedipus Plays* had been performed at the Oxford Playhouse in February.

feelings so that their tolerance feeds the unkind – to me, I mean – judgement of those whom I take to be disinterested outsiders? And under it all, there is the feeling that I have never done my best.

Perhaps though the feeling 'if I had produced masterpieces – or a masterpiece – I would be happy in my old age' is itself a delusion. Others do not need to have produced masterpieces – known themselves to be geniuses – in order to be happy. And those who have done so are not the happier for it. It is the romantic in me that thinks that the artefact created is a mirror image if not [of] the real self of the person who created it – his immortality. I confuse the immortality of the work with sense of the creator of it feeling that he is immortal. But this is a childish error. The person who makes a work that is immortal may have sacrificed the fullest realization in his life of his own personal existence in order to do so. Auden, for example. Probably the feeling that he had completed his oeuvre gave him more satisfaction than most poets. He would sit in a chair reading his own books with a look of happiness on his face. A smug look – a bit senile. But outside whatever happiness this gave him, he seemed far from happy. Not disappointed with himself – he tasted a far deeper kind of disappointment, with the world. From quite far back he lost all spontaneity (I once said this to Chester K[allman] – and he said 'yes, that's it! he's lost all spontaneity'). He did not want to go out to anything – a play a concert a film (perhaps an opera). He liked – within limits – to be with old friends – because they reminded him of his own past. He hated old places – Oxford, for example – because they reminded him of how that past had changed. He enjoyed reading his poems doubtless for the same reason as he liked seeing old friends – they were his past. But even if he could think the poems were immortal (as that gave him some satisfaction) that was not his immortality – any more than the moon is a hunk of the earth chipped off and flown into space – as we were told when I was young, that is the earth's immortality.

10 April 1983, London

Dined last night with Francis Bacon. I felt a bit apprehensive about this – almost hoping he would cancel – as David [Plante] and Nikos [Stangos] whom he'd invited could not come – and his friend John was ill – and we were alone and I have the feeling he finds it a strain to be alone with me (perhaps it is I who find it so to be alone with him).[1] I climbed up the very steep stairs, with a rope one side as banister, to his room next his little studio where he paints those huge pictures. He was quite relaxed and very amiable asking me about my American tour, and *Index* etc. He said he'd just given a picture to Amnesty International – they sold it in Dublin. He suggested there was perhaps some kind of duplication between the work of Amnesty and that of *Index*. He said he'd been to the Lawrence Gowing exhibition and it was better than he thought it was going to be. David Plante had told me that Francis detested Gowing, so I was surprised at his tolerance about him and his work. He didn't, of course, go so far as to say he liked it. After drinking champagne we went to Wheelers. There in the bar we met Bruce, brother of Oliver and Jeffrey Bernard.[2] A vast hard-drinking man he seemed absorbed in some very intelligent kind of depression and had only bad news of Jeff and Oliver. They are truthful and intelligent people and it is sad that none of them has gone further. Francis asked him to join us and go on drinking while we ate (he himself would not eat). Bruce somehow served as a useful third between Francis and me. I was grateful to him. The whole evening was charming. I got very drunk and was amused at my weaving walk as I walked part of the way home.

In the spring of 1983, Spender went on a fund-raising trip to America for Index on Censorship, *the human rights journal initiated by the Spenders in 1971. Spender was accompanied by Lois Sieff, a director of Writers and Scholars International. According to Spender himself, 'I was completely inexperienced in fund-raising, and my journal becomes concerned with my amateurish attempts to do so. A few hundred dollars were raised by speaking and handing out leaflets at cocktail parties in Washington and Chicago. But we would hardly have done more than cover our expenses had it not been for the*

---

1 John Edwards (1950–2003), Francis Bacon's companion since 1976 and, after the artist's death in 1992, his heir.

2 Jeffrey Bernard (1932–1997), British journalist famous for his 'Low Life' column in *The Spectator*. Oliver Bernard (b. 1925), British poet and translator. Bruce Bernard (1928–2000), British photographer, art critic and picture editor for the *Guardian*.

enterprise and generosity of Anne Cox Chambers in Atlanta, who organized a reading given by Joseph Brodsky and myself at the Historical Society in that city, the benefit of which went to Index.'

12 April 1983, New York

Woke up this morning unhappy about my mission for *Index*. Lizzie had said to me two days ago that Marietta Tree had said to her: 'Who wants to support *Index*? It contains nothing but gloomy news about repression, and who would want to read it?'[1] I see her point. Lois [Sieff] told me at drinks before our dinner that some other possible sponsor had said much the same to her, adding that the name INDEX should be changed. He suggested an equally doomed name – CENSORED with a large X half crossing it out. I woke this morning with the name VOICE in my head, and, at the moment, find that very good – good for its obviousness and, imagining the cover, think the image of Munch's picture THE CRY should be in it. Why not, SHOUT or THE SHOUT?[2]

14 April 1983, New York

Telephoned Christopher [Isherwood] who was delighted to be called and wanted to go on talking for hours. We did, in fact, talk for half an hour. Discussed loss of memory in old age. I said I sometimes started telling a story[,] could remember the name of the person I was telling it about[,] but suddenly just as I was about to say it – forgot his name. 'Oh yes,' said Christopher. 'I'm perfectly familiar with that situation. I start a conversation in which I am intending to tell such an anecdote, by saying "Do you know that bird we see in the garden every morning while we're having breakfast?" and then gradually work round to what I mean to tell.' Later he asked for my telephone number, and, writing it down, at his end, in Santa Monica, he said, 'A horrible old wizened claw writes crooked letters.' I said – 'All the same that's exactly the kind of thing you'd say if it was fifty years ago

---

1 Marietta Tree (1927–1991), New York socialite and philanthropist.

2 The title of Edvard Munch's famous painting is more often translated as 'The Scream'.

and I was telephoning you in Berlin.' 'Yes,' he said – 'what could be more untrue than that remark someone made – "If things are not getting better, they're getting worse"?' 'Who said that?' I asked. 'Oh some awful old nineteenth-century bore. Gladstone perhaps. What a shit.' After we put down receivers I thought 'Perhaps it was Tolstoy. Perhaps Kierkegaard. Perhaps Lenin.'

Dinner at the Russian Tea Room with Bill Mazzocco. He talked quite a lot about politics and questioned me about the Thirties. Said they were difficult to understand. How could people then be anti-fascist and at the same time support disarmament? I said it was un-realistic but we tried to believe in the myth of Collective Security. I said after all it was not dissimilar from the attitude of people today who support nuclear disarmament in the face of Russian nuclear forces. He said it was dissimilar because today what was involved was total destruction of the world. I said, well in those days we did imagine that cities would be totally destroyed by the new bombs of that time. Still, I admitted there was a difference. [. . .]

[This] afternoon Lois and I went to see a lady called Miss Floyd (no – something else) at Richman Oil. [. . .] Miss Floyd (Fluellin? Flail?) listened with the utmost attention while Lois explained about *Index* to her, then she said in very considering tones 'The thing is to get these things started. What you want is to interest a few people and then get them to talk to a few other people. After a time suddenly everything comes together. Now how much money would you be wanting?'

Lois hesitated, then she said – 'We were thinking of something in the neighbourhood of $100,000.'

Miss F. seemed to think this quite reasonable. 'Well if you man-aged to provide entertainment for 1,000 people and each person paid $100, you'd get your 100,000. Or if you get people each to provide ten thousand. You might get a lot more than that. It depends who you ask. I could ask Alexandra Schlesinger about Norman Mailer.'[1]

I said I had seen Alexandra only yesterday – at drinks with Joe Alsop. She warmed perceptibly – 'Well Alexandra's about my best friend.' – I thought, well Americans are really wonderful – not just

1 In 1971 Arthur Schlesinger had married Alexandra Emmet Allan. Norman Mailer (1923–2007), Pulitzer Prize-winning American writer.

that they give money – but that they are capable of such seriousness in asking their friends. It's really more the time-giving than the money-giving which seems admirable. She asked what people in what places – Dallas – Houston – L.A. – we would approach. I mentioned Anne Chambers. 'Oh, do you mean Anne Cox Chambers, well that would be wonderful.'[1] I seemed to have put on a light in her face. There was also she said Mr Anderson who was flying to New York tonight to see her and would be lunching tomorrow – could either of us see him? Lois couldn't. I said I'd put off my engagement to lunch with the Institute of Humanities and would see him at luncheon at the Pierre Hotel.

22 April 1983, Boston

Television programme about *China Diary*. My interviewer, enthusiastic about the book was so pleased with our interview which was live on their breakfast A.M. programme, that she asked me to go on after the ads, and to extend the programme. All the interviewers have been extremely pleasant and have taken the trouble to read the book – much better than the English ones. [. . .]

I was interrupted writing this by John Fairchild coming into my room.[2] He started talking about the rich and said he didn't know any rich person who was happy. He said that to be happy you had to work. Americans, he thought, were affected by what he called 'creeping laziness'. They – especially the young – did not see why they should work. His son was married to a psychiatrist who worked extremely hard. He had given up his job and did nothing. He did not realize that of which John was sure – that he was extremely unhappy.

I said I thought Philippe [de] Rothschild was happy and certainly worked very hard. John said he could not bear to think about Philippe, he had made Pauline so miserable. At the end of Pauline's life he had visited her in the Ritz-Carlton – in her room there – surrounded by all her books – and she said she was happier in this room

---

1 For Anne Cox Chambers, see biographical appendix.

2 John Fairchild (b. 1927), celebrated as publisher of the mass circulation magazine *Woman's Wear Daily*, now retired. He and his wife Jill were friends from Provence and now hosted Spender on this fund-raising trip.

than she had been anywhere for years. She hated Mouton, she hated everywhere else she lived, she had even come to dislike Philippe. And yet, but for her Philippe would never have been able to make Mouton what it was or, indeed, to do anything. [. . .]

I lunched with Muriel [Buttinger], going first to her apartment and then conducting her to the restaurant near the Lincoln Center. She is really not at all strong after a back injury – slipped disk – which laid her up for some weeks. She also has cataract – yet she is going on Wednesday to Paris to be with her ninety-year-old friend Hannah Benzion who is ill. She'll take her out of Paris to a hotel in the country, she told me – and seemed happy at the prospect. She told me some woman was applying for support from her Foundation for a project which seemed to duplicate *Index*, and she thought all of us should get together.

24 April 1983, New York

Tremendous downpour and gale during the night and continuing till about 11 a.m. New York, much more than London, can seem a rocky outpost in the Atlantic – like Land's End – or the Giant's Causeway – all these quadrilinear skyscrapers lashed by the elements, water pouring down their sides. I thought I would have to abandon going out to lunch with Dick Sennett. But Jill [Fairchild] called me a taxi on some private call system they have. The driver was Russian from Leningrad – looking a bit like a Russian doll. Dick Sennett made sorrel soup and provided some mussels which were quite frightful. I don't know whether this was the cooking or the shellfish. He just boiled them I think, and that was that. Rubbery and bright chrome-yellow they frightened me and having eaten about six I managed to shove them aside. I think that even he was a bit afraid of them. He was rather calm and not boastful or exaggerating. We exchanged impressions about fund-raising Washington. He said the awful thing about those people is that they never stopped flattering each other. They were doomed to do so. This struck me as true. [. . .]

[Patrick Merla] explained arrangements about celebrations for tenth anniversary of Wystan's death, October 18th, 1983.[1] I signed a

---

1 Patrick Merla, American literary agent and editor prominent in gay publishing.

document saying I would participate in this. Joseph Brodsky arrived with another large squashy man – evidently a scholar – Joseph very warm. A lot of questions. 'Stephen, now there is a question I must ask you. When did T. S. Eliot first get to read the poems of Thomas Hardy?' He suggested Eliot was influenced in his modernism by Hardy who wrote poetry about modern themes, unlike most of his contemporaries. I said Eliot disliked H.'s poetry, thought it amateurish (so did H. who didn't really consider himself a pro comparable with Tennyson, Browning, Swinburne). The point about 'Modernism' is that it was extremely self-conscious, not just traditional carry-on poetry which happened to be about a modern subject matter. Also it was influenced by French continental models – whereas Hardy was totally English. There was something of 1880s French-influenced Symbolist poetry in Eliot and Pound. We asked about modernism in Russia, Joseph was not very forthcoming because he wanted to discuss his theories about modern English poetry. He produced a few quips of the outrageous kind: e.g. 'I don't like Ezra Pound's poetry but do like his politics.' Very Brodsky. [. . .]

Susan Sontag and David Rieff appeared. Susan very sweet and cosy really. We talked again about the Auden memorial service. A plaque is to be put up at 77 St Marks Place etc.[1]

28 April 1983, New York

Lunch with Richard Wollheim. Called for him first at his apartment, 157 East 57th which seems rather nice for New York – (New Yorkers have to be extremely rich to live in what by English standards are pleasant apartments or houses). Anyway the room was illuminated by the sight of beautiful Day [his wife] and her beautiful baby. While glad that I should admire baby, they showed the anxiety of elderly parents who have produced a miracle late in life, lest my presence might curdle the milk or stop Emilia dropping off contentedly to sleep, the moment feeding time was over. Actually, I almost seemed to wake her irremediably up, and she started staring and smiling and

---

1 The apartment where Auden lived from 1952. The bronze plaque was installed in 1983 and stolen, or lost, in 1997, during a renovation of the building.

waving her arms at me vigorously. Richard and I went out to lunch, Richard saying as soon as we got into the street in his voice that can seem slightly nasal on such occasions – 'I'm afraid I haven't given much thought to the difficult question of where we should eat. In this district where every shop turns out, on inspection, to be some kind of boutique, it is difficult to come to a decision.' We put our noses into a boutique, which was somehow also a salad bar full of old ladies seated at small square tables, and with whatever volume knob that controls the sound made by old ladies, turned on to loudest – and decided we would not be able to talk here. We left the shop, ran into John Richardson and the Queen Mother's cousin, a bankrupt, dissolute Bowes Lyon, had a few moments' conversation in which one or two indiscretions of mine may have done us all permanent injury, and walked on.[1]

We found a restaurant frequented by John Richardson who liked some of the spécialités. Richard talked about being at Columbia and living in New York. He said it was different from the impression one got by just visiting. I wondered – I supposed – he was referring to that strange feeling one can have here of both being made a lot of and neglected – which I've had when teaching at American universities. He said 'You said the apartment we live in is nice. Well that is a first impression. If you live there, you find many things you object to – that repel you.' I understood what he meant. Thinking about his house in London, I thought one would have to be very well off in New York to overcome this feeling of repulsion – if one lived here. Richard said that, living here, everything cost three times as much as in England. Then also there was taxation – being subject to American taxes. I knew something about this, having lived here – 35 years ago. He said Columbia University was very depressed, very run down, even physically. The windows were so thick with grime that you could not look out of them. He went a bit into his financial situation. He had, from London, half his salary, as a pension. Then he had a very good salary here. But they had to economize, they never

---

1 John Richardson (b. 1924), British art historian and biographer of Picasso, earlier a partner of Douglas Cooper. The Queen Mother's Bowes-Lyon cousin was the Earl of Strathmore (1928–1987), a notoriously dissolute figure on the international scene.

went to restaurants, they had very little social life, partly owing to baby.

He talked about the Kermodes, saying that [. . .] Frank was very accident prone.[1] He had the habit, for example, of applying for jobs 24 hours after entry was closed. I began to feel that I must really pay for the lunch. And I think this was a right decision. (Richard said Day and he never went to restaurants.) At some point, I said I was – or had been – the opposite of Frank's accident-prone-ness. Somehow something had always 'turned up'. I had no pension[,] no unearned money to speak of – but things happened – like earning £10,000 from the China book. (I thought I must pay for this luncheon – Richard has invited 35 people for his birthday – and I produced my American Express card, threw it down like a trump on the table.)

The message I went away with was 'living in New York is very different from visiting'.

After the 1948 Arab–Israeli war, Lebanon had become home to a large number of Palestinian refugees, leading to tensions with Israel, and bombings of Beirut in 1968. In 1969, Yasser Arafat, the leader of the PLO, formalized his involvement with Lebanon's Palestinian resistance movement through the signing of a declaration with Lebanon's Army Commander-in-Chief, Emile Bustani, in Cairo. The political situation was aggravated after the number of Palestinians in Lebanon increased following King Hussein of Jordan's bid to quash Palestinian forces in the 'Black September' of 1970, resulting in the mass emigration of many Palestinians to neighbouring Lebanon. This precipitated later Israeli attacks on Lebanon.

In 1975, civil war erupted in Lebanon between the Christian and Muslim Lebanese and the Palestinian refugee population, with Syrian troops later entering the country to restore peace and subdue the Palestinians. In March 1978, Israel launched a major reprisal attack on the southern area of Lebanon which was sanctioned by the Prime Minister of Israel, Menachem Begin and by Ariel Sharon, Israel's Defence Secretary. The United Nations intervened, demanding that Israeli troops withdraw. In 1982, Israel launched another attack on Lebanon following a Palestinian assassination attempt on Shlomo

---

1 Like Wollheim, Kermode was currently a professor at Columbia.

Argov, the Israeli ambassador to Britain. Begin's avowed aim was to rid the Lebanon–Israel border of Palestinian forces, although there had been no direct attacks on Israeli territory by Palestine for the preceding year. Arafat and his supporters fled to Tunisia and in September 1982 Lebanon's President-elect Bachir Gemayal was assassinated. International peace-keeping forces entered Lebanon and in May 1983 Israel and Lebanon signed an agreement on Israeli withdrawal. The 1982 Israeli attack on Lebanon was heavily criticized by the international community, resulting in between thirty and forty thousand Palestinian and Lebanese deaths, with a hundred thousand seriously wounded, and half a million made homeless. In February 1983, Ariel Sharon would resign as Defence Secretary following an inquiry into the massacre of Palestinian refugees in Beirut and in October 1983 Begin would resign as Prime Minister.

29 April 1983, New York

Dinner at a Chinese restaurant with Barbara Epstein, Dominique Nabokov, Elizabeth Lowell.[1] Dominique is admirable, indomitable, interesting, but she has the bourgeois French woman's habit of destroying conversation between even four people by immediately bisecting it into two conversations *à deux*. If I asked Barbara a question, while Barbara was answering, D. would immediately shout another question across the table to Liz. If I said something to Liz, within a second she would start a diagonal conversation with Barbara. By talking directly to Dominique I managed to elicit from her that she is photographing for *Vogue* and doing well. She said, with all her candour, that she would like to marry again, but that all the men she had affairs with proved, after a few weeks, too dull. She has drunk of Honey Dew, the fatal curse of having lived with a man so crazy, amusing, egotistic and demanding – Nicolas Nabokov – that after him anyone else seems boring (women who had affairs with Cyril Connolly used to say 'After Cyril, everyone is boring').[2]

---

1 Dominique Nabokov, American photographer who was the fourth wife of Nicolas Nabokov.

2 'For he on Honey-dew has fed / And drunk the milk of Paradise.' The last two lines of 'Kubla Khan' by Samuel Taylor Coleridge.

Barbara – in so far as I could hear what she was saying while Dominique was shouting across the table at Liz, said she thought the Wollheims – apart from their joy in the baby – which nevertheless did not really bring them together – were unhappy. The supposed benefits of New York – salary of $60,000 etc – did not really work out. Their two- or three-roomed apartment – one of which rooms was entirely taken up by the baby – was a wretched exchange for their London house – taxation was enormous – they were shut off from their friends. They had very little New York social life, anyway, on account of the baby. It would have been better, she said, if Richard had come here alone and earned some dollars which he could take back to England. As it was, everything was swallowed up in expenses. I was very glad I paid for yesterday's lunch, I thought, listening to this. New York did indeed seem a dreadful trap, once one saw Richard as harassed, distracted and unhappy (and he did seem all these things yesterday, though there were still several glittering prospects ahead of him – the book of his Harvard lectures, the Mellon lectures to be given (I wonder how R. will take to Washington, Washington to R.), etc). The real obstruction to happiness was that the baby had not brought them together. I thought how many of one's friends' lives seem to become fiction as we all grow older – simply because things happen – there is a story – and also a pattern – a plot. *Plus ça change plus c'est la même chose* is the ultimate reality of every fiction.

I thought how two people, to all seeming happily married – suddenly are brought to the verge of separation – by the wife's discovery that her husband is still in love with the woman whom before the marriage, he left in order to marry her, and that he has had various other affairs of less import throughout their marriage. Her disillusionment, her rage, her outpourings to all their friends. Then while they are still together (for financial reasons, though contemplating separation) she becomes – after all these years – pregnant. At the age of 43 (he is 63) she bears him the child whom they both *worship*, and they are brought together, as it were at opposite sides of the cradle of this quite exceptionally beautiful and radiant baby. Each worships the child separately. Only intermittently do they even share their feelings of love for her. Like nearly every story of our lives it seems an anecdote someone at a dinner party might have told Henry James

– which will blossom into a novel. Perhaps the child's story – *What Maisie Knew*.

Murray Kempton appeared – a lean grey keen man – sat at our table and talked about Israel.[1] He said Israel had incurred ultimate irrecoverable moral disaster. Dominique immediately set up a stream of counter-chatter, shouting across the table to Elizabeth: 'Oh, do let us go to Israel. When can we go? I will take my ca–me–ra and do photographs for *Vogue*.' Then turning to Murray Kempton: 'Is it not a wonderful country?' 'The most wonderful country I have ever been to,' said M.K., disconcertingly. He went on to say how much he liked Begin, who could be utterly charming. From the way in which he'd been talking this was like saying 'Hitler is utterly charming', but he then went on to say [Ariel] Sharon and some general were utter thugs 'as bad as the worst of ours'. [. . .]

When I got into a taxi at the end of all this, the driver commented: 'You look very tired.' I remember how when we were last in Israel, a general drove us to the frontier somewhere and told us of an incident the previous night in which two Arabs had been killed. Later on an Israeli said to me: 'Would you like to see last night's bag?' referring to the dead Arabs. I refused of course but had unutterable feelings which ever since I've felt I ought to have uttered.

3 May 1983, New York

Went to Keith Milow's studio in Chelsea. Saw his new work – apocalyptic end of the world pictures in very dark colours contrasting with whites and vermilion. The general structure based on the light falling through the top of a dome – the Pantheon. They are probably his best work, but gave me thoughts about arbitrary choice of subjects and style by many living painters. As though they are simply searching for something new to do without inner vision or impulsion. The most hopeful thing was when Keith said that having got an idea for a series of pictures, he worked through it in them, that usually the first picture turned out to be the best, that he could not do the same picture twice over. We had dinner at a restaurant called Grace, which had a very good Greenwich Village atmosphere and also good food.

---

1 Murray Kempton (1917–1997), left-wing American journalist.

Leaving the table for a moment and coming back, I experienced something like an optical illusion — or so I thought. Keith's face which earlier on had seemed very much as I have always seen it though of course fuller and less youthful – but still with the same gleaming cat-like eyes, cheeky nose, full mouth, ears cocked out each side and matted hair – an amusing face, a beau laid – suddenly looked leathery, creased, sneering, cynical: and it did not really change from this the rest of the evening. It was the disappointed rather disgusted face of a middle-aged man. I expect the same ageing had happened to my face in Keith's eyes the other side of the table. [. . .]

Tuesday, lunch with David Rieff at a restaurant called Les Pleiades. He fidgeted a lot seemed a bit distrait, then towards the end of the meal said 'After this I have to go to hospital for a minor operation.' He went at 1.30 and I waited till two when a car arrived to take me to the Fairchilds where Jill joined me and we were driven to the Botanical Gardens. [. . .]

The Botanical Gardens was tatty and slightly absurd, especially in the part devoted to the English garden with an absurd slice of lichen-green thatch and two windows of a cottage at one end. Jill was very dismayed and funny about it. She said some of her very sui generis things in the course of the afternoon e.g. that she was never able to listen to Horowitz and that Proust seemed to her as great as Shakespeare. We talked about a lot of things. She keeps on coming back to 'the young' and their difficult lives, and all the tragedies we know of the drug scene, etc.

5 May 1983, New York

Read and wrote. Letters. This diary. Went to the Mayflower Hotel and picked up David [Hockney] who was in the lobby being photographed by some Japanese fan. We took a taxi to the Century Club. In the taxi David told me straight away his latest ideas about photography as an extension of Cubism. He said it was no coincidence that black and white movies began at the same time as Cubism and that no one had ever remarked on this before. I have forgotten what followed on from this. Doubtless it will be published before long. He told me that about two months ago, he had been in New York, visiting the sick bed of his friend Jo, a male model. Jo had died of the mysterious sexual disease Aids. David visited him three times daily in hospital. He was completely emaciated had lost all his hair and could hardly speak. Visitors had to wear masks and rubber gloves. 'You could not kiss him,' said David. 'He was resigned to the idea of dying at the end. He said he did not regret his life but felt he had wasted a lot of time.' I asked David whether Jo had had a lot of sex. 'Yes, more than any one I've ever known. He was completely promiscuous. He'd go with people five or six times a day. He'd had every single sexual disease.' All this seemed inexplicable, baffling, upsetting.

We lunched with Henry Geldzahler and his friend Raymond at the Century Club.[1] In their – and my – company David became almost silent. Geldzahler made some conversational opening to him and David only murmured an inaudible reply. Henry said, 'Your attention span seems to be diminishing even further than before, David.' I said, in an aside, to Henry – 'Sometimes David does not hear what one says.' David made some facetious comment to show he had heard. Owing to David's refusal to make any real effort – in effect to treat us as though we were scarcely there – the meal was boring and a bit embarrassing, though Henry tried very hard, I thought.

After returning briefly to London, Spender went to Canterbury for a celebration of T. S. Eliot and then on another trip to Venice, this time for a PEN Club gathering.

9 May 1983, Venice

Yesterday we went to the University of Canterbury for a celebration in honour of T. S. Eliot. First there was the showing of a film about him. Interviews with people, also selections from *Murder in the Cathedral*, *The Family Reunion*, *Sweeney Agonistes*. These were extremely good, I thought, bringing out the desolation on which his religion was really based. Reminiscences, chiefly by Hope Mirrlees of Vivienne his first wife.[2] Tom reading his poetry. Although his declared

---

1 Henry Geldzahler (1935–1994), Belgian-born American art curator.

2 Hope Mirrlees (1887–1978), Bloomsbury poet and translator, friend of Virginia Woolf and T. S. Eliot, literary executor of Ottoline Morrell.

aim in his writing was to be impersonal, the impression I had was above all of his personality, and the asceticism[,] the dedication, the straining for belief, the union of the physical man with some mystical self invisibly striving towards God, regretting the society (here mostly Bloomsbury) in which he lived in order to exist in his poetry.

The speeches and papers read were a bit of a caricature. There was Mr Chiari talking about the 'universality' that Eliot achieved in his writing, a Frenchman who in fact rather caricatured Eliot's position which is marvellous in Eliot, not so when vulgarized.[1] There was an absurd man called Tomlin – very popular with the audience – who gave examples of Eliot's wit and humour – for the most part, far less witty or genuinely funny than the despised Cyril Connolly.[2] [. . .]

There was a good speech by Denis Donoghue and something by me about the effect of *The Waste Land* on 'our' generation.[3] I could see why Eliot liked Tomlin, the bland clubman British Council type. Valerie [Eliot] sat there with her ice-sugar pink complexion and her surround of marzipan hair, sugary and supremely edible, but also discreet, knowing, sensible, really humorous – more so than Tom – and intelligent, loving, lovable, and utterly devoted, someone, in spite of the superfice of absurdity to admire – a goddess in a temple more Hindu than Christian perhaps. I would burn incense to her. The deepest thing in Tom Eliot was perhaps a kind of loving irony. I was a terrible fool with him, and certainly provoked the irony, but Valerie somehow reassures me that he also sent in my direction some love. It is nice of her to feel that I deserve some love – and I suspect she knows all the reasons for the irony. Forgiveness.

Then I came to Venice with a lot of PEN Club ladies most of them like desiccated pressed flowers. But Mary McCarthy and Jim West here also [. . .]

The morning after my return to London, a letter from the P.M.'s office saying she [Margaret Thatcher] was recommending me to the

---

1 Joseph Chiari (b. 1911), French poet and critic who described his friendship with Eliot in a memoir published by the Enitharmon Press in 1982. Chiari met Eliot in 1943 when Charles de Gaulle appointed him as French cultural attaché to Scotland.

2 E. W. F. Tomlin (1913–1988), British essayist.

3 Denis Donoghue (b.1928), Irish literary critic.

Queen for a knighthood. Although I've all too often said I would never accept this, when I got the letter I realized at once that I would do so, both for myself and for Natasha. There are those whom I respect for despising such things – they are the best. But there are many – including those in America and elsewhere who pay fees – and whom I am greatly dependent on – who don't despise them, and in their eyes, this will be the equivalent of five or ten years taken off my age. Also there comes a time when one craves for recognition – not to be always at the mercy of the spite, malice, contempt – and perhaps even the just dismissal – of one's rivals. I feel pegged up in some way, given a shot in the arm. I've always felt some saving angel does guard me from the worst – sometimes thinking it a good sometimes a bad angel. Probably it's an in-between angel not wholly good or bad. Apart from all other considerations, it would be priggish cruelty to deny Natasha the ladyship. One thought in her direction would remove all hesitation, feeling that I should refuse out of a quite authentic self-righteousness. Many of those I most respect have refused honours, and that they have done so is their supreme honour.

13 May 1983, Venice

Last night Mary, Jim, the [François] Bondys and I skipped an official invitation to some palazzo (it was not a palazzo at all, the Polish delegate told me later, but an apartment so small that the PEN could scarcely crowd into it) and went to Torcello, arriving there about 7 or 7.30. Before this I've always been there in the middle of the day and been slightly bored by these scattered buildings of brick and grey stone – a few monuments – among the parched fields and little vineyards, reached at the end of a canal path leading to a small quay. But in the evening it was all magical and enchanting, mysterious. Every detail stood out, the Byzantine capitals on top of round columns, each of them different, a sarcophagus with straight clear chiselled lettering, a bishop's stone throne lying in the courtyard, behind railings or an iron fence in a courtyard, some out of place statuary on pagan subjects, a nymph, a grape-bunch crowned Bacchus, a red brick wall vermilion in contrast to the surrounding stone, a pathway leading through a small vineyard to a section of canal with no path along it, like khaki-coloured glass. There were a few roses and some other flowers. Colours in the dimming light pressed onto one's sight, and little cluster of houses along the side of the canal seen from the yard in front of the restaurant were a deep cleft of magenta cut against hedges, and, beyond them, fields. We had an excellent dinner at the restaurant which is a branch of Harry's Bar, and walked back in the now complete darkness along the canal path to the quay for the vaporetto. Below deck, sitting on benches we watched two pairs of lovers, enfolded in each other, limbs like over-lapping angles of boards, heads boring like drills into each other's shoulders or knees. They must be very much in love, I thought, to get, on benches, into such uncomfortable positions. Occasionally, one or the other did shift, as though suffering from cramp or pins and needles. [. . .]

Read Muriel's book *Code Name 'Mary'*, about her life in Austria during the Thirties.[1] [. . .] Overflowing with kindness, sympathy, generosity as Muriel is, humorous, not at all puritanical, quite sensual, open, and fun loving, she yet seems to inhabit a pale transparent gelatinous world, like a lot of X-ray negatives, stuck up on a wall all round her. Not to have been bored to death by her pompous self-important husband Jo, born to be president of some tiny central European welfare state, seems a failing.

15 May 1983, London

I have now finished Muriel's book and think I have been unfair to Jo. In fact, extremely unfair, as one is if one judges people by complaints made about infidelities by wives (or husbands). I have inherited a tendency to think that addiction or vice is the final truth about someone, so when one evening Muriel complained to me about Jo the playboy millionaire photographed together with floozy nightclub partner on flaps of matchboxes, I thought this was the truth.

---

1 Lillian Hellman's memoir *Pentimento* describes her friendship with 'Julia', a member of the anti-fascist underground. After publication Hellman hinted that 'Julia' was herself. Muriel Gardiner recognized details of her own past in the book and was angry to see her life appropriated by Hellman, so she wrote her own memoir of her pre-war activity in the Viennese underground. *Code Name 'Mary'* established Gardiner's claim to be the 'real' Julia. Hellman always insisted that she had not heard of Gardiner prior to the publication of *Pentimento*.

Actually, Jo was a hero of the Austrian socialist underground who, when he left Austria, stayed in France working on Rescue Committees to help refugees, was then interned by the French at the outbreak of war in circumstances wretched enough to suffice as punishment for a lifetime. Having got to America, they both continued to do rescue work. Probably his American life with all the opportunities of escape into comfort it offered was the greatest test of his character, but, re-creating himself, he acted with great determination, writing a book about the Austrian socialists (unreadable unfortunately) and assembling on the basis of the material studied in that book, a library about socialism, anti-Semitism and the Nazis; later making a whole other library (now given to Harvard University) about Vietnam and writing a three-volume book which is considered the authoritative work on the history of that part of Indo-China. His weaknesses were sexual vanity, an enormous sense of his own achievement and being boring to a degree which must have limited the circle of the Buttingers' friends to the circle of victims, refugee politicians and a few fellow-workers. But perhaps that was enough anyway.

16 May 1983, London

Lunch with Lizzie. She was very sweet. I was also astonished how intelligent she was, talking about Muriel's book. She said that Muriel was the most compassionate person who acted upon her compassion. She did not quite agree with me that it was this complete dedication to people who needed her and a few who worked with her [that] explained her complete lack of the aesthetic in her life – was a consequence of it, which also meant that she didn't have any social life like we had. Lizzie said M. was quite pleasure-loving – give her a couple of martinis and she became a different person. I thought, yes, she does become released and talkative laughing (she insists a lot on laughter in her book) but only in the manner of an alumna of Wellesley College or a student or social worker – very open, of course, very sympathetic to everyone's point of view – but only as an extension of her general tolerance of manners and styles foreign to her. I could not see how she could be anything else but this, she was too deeply serious in a social service sort of way to be anything else. If she and I had got married it would have been quite alien to her for me to interest myself in the arts – or she would have regarded it as an eccentricity which she respected. Lizzie admitted that there was a side of M. which was practical and materialistic – the meat-packer's daughter – but she thought it was Jo who had prevented her from developing any aesthetic side of her nature. [. . .]

After this I went to the London Library and got Lillian Hellman's book, *Pentimento* containing the story 'Julia' which I read. I can't think why she has any reputation as a writer of prose. The actual writing seems to be done with some crude blunt instrument. She impersonates the manners of the group of writers acting tough in which she moves, but never gets beyond this in her writing. The hero-ism of Julia is partly a device for flattering herself whom she portrays as Julia's dearest friend, in fact lover. Some of the events described and the general idea of a rich American girl who lives in Vienna and becomes a member of the anti-Fascist socialist underground are pre-sumably stolen from Muriel's life but the character – in so far as she exists – has little resemblance to Muriel. Muriel herself, I feel, cashes in rather, on the resemblance; though she may well be annoyed at (and also proud of) her actions being recognized, while the fact that she did them, is denied.

17 May 1983, London

We arrived late for the memorial service at a Church in High Hol-born to Clifford Curzon.[1] A tall beautiful interior with enormous 19th and early 20th century stained-glass windows, very bad acous-tics. It could scarcely have been more impersonal. A concert consist-ing of Mozart (Adagio from the B minor K. 54 Piano Sonata, played by Nina Milkina), 'Wie Lieblich sind deine Wohnungen' from Brahms' *Deutsches Requiem*, Schubert's piano duo Fantasia Op. 108, Mozart motet 'Ave Verum Corpus', the Scherzo from Dvořák's Piano Quintet in A Major, and Liszt's transcription of the Liebestod from *Tristan* (the singer Linda Esther Gray who was supposed to do this, being ill). There was also a reading of a long and interesting interview or dictated statement by Clifford about piano playing. A couple of prayers, but no personal tribute to Clifford. The whole

---

1 Clifford Curzon had died on 1 September 1982.

thing was as bleak as the unseasonal cold very rainy day in the streets outside. I kept on remembering irrelevant things about Clifford. How I first heard of him from a young Italian count, Alberto della Marmora an attractive and interesting dilettante in the early Thirties. Later when I asked about Alberto, Clifford, characteristically, said he wasn't serious; just as when many years later, Matthew, who was Clifford's godson, went to live in Italy, Clifford explained to me that he would now drop him – because – one had to make a choice – and he had chosen to live in Paradise. Clifford worshipped at a piano-shaped altar of work, and there was very little else he valued in life. He must in some ways have had a very strongly repressed side to his nature. He told me that Christopher Isherwood had once taken him to a bar (presumably a gay one) in Berlin in the Thirties, and he had fainted. He was amused at the memory of this, but it seemed a very vivid rather terrifying memory. When one met him, though one always had a sense of time having been cut out or cut into – he was always warm and friendly, an excellent talker. Meeting him in New York once, he told me that pianos on which he played all over America either had gremlins or were damaged by agents of rival pianists. After the death of [Artur] Schnabel, the playing of all living pianists seemed to him simply meaningless. Talking about X. or Y. he had a lost bewildered expression – but where is the music, where is the vision, he wondered?

His wife Lucille seemed, under a superficial impression she gave of coldness, an extremely kind, affectionate considerate person, who kept herself almost studiously in the background. When they could have no children they determined to adopt – but they could only have the best. They set their hearts on the sons of Cebotari a famous soprano, who were Austrians.[1] They had considerable legal difficulties in adopting them because the father, who had Nazi sympathies, did not want his sons to go into a household which he considered to be Jewish (Natasha is uncertain about all this, but we both remember how long the adoption process took and how concerned they were about it). (As I write these lines an old lady walking along the pavement plucks a rose from our garden, I rap the window and wonder

---

1 Maria Cebotari (1910–1949).

whether I should rush out and shout at her then think – well why shouldn't she have a rose?)

Clifford's soul went into his music – and if he really wanted to express himself, he sat down and played. He had the highest standards in everything and with his beautiful house, garden, pictures furniture – seemed the best possible product – redeemed and purified by work – of a very high remote remnant of civilization. Often the great musicians seem like this. They are the orchids of culture, hot-house flowers of the European nineteenth century – Wagner and Liszt, Diaghilev, Stravinsky.

22 May 1983, London

Time. I live in the present, grappling with it, trying to pour the work into the moment, yet all the time, even at this late stage of life, I think about that mysterious unfolding thing, the future. I don't think enough of what I will do to it, in it, but of what it will bring. I am still even interested in the newspapers, daily maps of world campaigns which will reshape territories. Yet what is the real interest? The past is simply the sum of all the futures that have ceased to be news. We know too that the future is simply the part we don't happen to know about, but will assuredly happen, simply become the past. The unknown excites our interest because it is unknown but as soon as it is known it will lose that excitement, and it is certain to be known and to lose it. The interest of today's newspaper, the excitement of tomorrow's, the boredom of yesterday's.

When I think about dying I only have one question in mind – will my unknown work be written? If I think 'well it would be the same to have died twenty – thirty – years ago, as ten years hence,' I think, 'yes, but if I had died twenty or thirty years ago, I would not have achieved my ambition to write the great immortal work, which I also will not have done if I die tomorrow – and which I am beginning to think I will not have done ten years hence.' [. . .]

Kenneth Clark died.[1] It is strange to have known two families who have bought castles – the Nicolsons, Sissinghurst, the Clarks[,] Saltwood. Bought them when they were ruins, rebuilt them, filled them

---

1 Clark had died on 21 May 1983.

with objects, cultivated their gardens – and then died. It all falls into the length of time it takes to tell it – an after-dinner anecdote over nuts and wine.

17 June 1983, London

Lunch with Tony Harrison at the Gay Hussar.[1] He was very good. We discussed *Oedipus* a bit.[2] He said he had the impression it was at a stage when by rewriting I might transform it. All the slogging had been done; it now needed to be liberated. As this is exactly what I have determined to do, here and now, in France, I was pleased. [. . .]

He talked about rhythm. He said he found it necessary to have an absolutely regular beating very pronounced rhythm like a metronome. I want a rhythm which moves as it were zig-zag across a stretch of about 10 lines like a line plotted across a graph (going across the squares on the graph paper which make up the regularity).

18 June 1983, London

Rosamond Russell came to dinner. There were also David [Plante] and Nikos [Stangos] and the Lawrence Gowings. Sir L. Gowing said to me: 'Thank you for accepting a knighthood.'[3] The dinner was pleasant but a failure I felt from R.R.'s point of view. She is exceedingly nice and generous and kind but what she likes is intense conversation in which each tells the other what he/she is doing. She is very good at telling about her and John like someone delivering an enthusiastic handout. They are the greatest success possible. She tells you this not to boast but really to give you/me pleasure. Then she looks at me with penetrating eyes and a smile of immense encouragement and faith in my propensities and says 'And what are *you* doing? Are you writing poetry?' And I fall flat on my face. I am never doing

---

1 Tony Harrison (b. 1937), British poet and playwright.

2 Spender's *Oedipus* plays.

3 At this time Gowing was principal of the Slade School of Art at UCL. He had been knighted the year before. Spender's left-wing friends, including his son Matthew, advised him against accepting the award from Thatcher's administration.

anything. And I feel here like Tony Harrison. I do not want to be asked Am I writing poetry? by people who are not in the least interested in poetry (but who *is* interested? – Tony would ask) and who yet feel it is tremendously important and that your life is worth nothing without it. It is as though you were issuing paper money which was on the gold standard – except that the gold was not gold – it was helium. The helium standard.

27 June 1983, St Jerome

We took the Southampton–Havre Thorsen night ferry to Le Havre then drove to Paris, where we arrived at about 10. Went to the Café Flore where Matthew and independently of him our tenant from St Jerome, Mrs Ipsen, met us. Matthew looking beautiful and at his gentlest and sweetest had travelled all night by train from Siena, and after being with us for the day was going to go by night train to Munich. He said that he likes travelling by night and does not consider going to Munich from Siena via Paris much of a break in his journey. Anyway he likes the Italian bit because six Italians in a carriage start talking to [one] another within ten minutes as though they had been friends all their lives. In the compartment next to Matthew's there were 5 nuns and one man – the most harmless and diminutive little man you ever saw, said Matthew – the nuns brought him into this compartment and asked could their little man be changed for the woman whom they had as it was not proper for nuns to sleep in a railway compartment with a man. Their woman said she was perfectly comfortable in the berth she had found for herself and did not change. 'That meant the nuns could not take their wimples off,' said M. and had to sit up all night. 'Of course, there were a lot of ribald jokes in our compartment, two or three male occupants suggesting to the lady that they change clothes with her and spend the night in the next compartment in drag.' [. . .]

When – a few days back – I told Matthew about my being knighted – telephoning him in Italy from London – he could not speak for about half a minute. A choking silence. Then he said: 'Couldn't you have refused?' He was very upset. I wrote explaining why I had accepted – i.e. giving all the practical reasons – there are really no others. He wrote back saying he understood the family and career

[622]

ones (giving me a boost at this late stage in life when I still have to support us). What he really hates is the whole English establishment. He could not take my explaining – England is like school all one's life. My friends are all in the sixth form – or monitors – now. Sir Isaiah [Berlin], Sir Stuart [Hampshire], Sir Alfred (Ayer), Sir Lawrence (Gowing), Sir Laurens (van der Post), Sir Angus (Wilson) – it is pleasing to be promoted.[1] Lizzie says Matthew's reaction is humourless and a bit mean – 'He doesn't realize how funny dad is about it.' But in fact I feel that M.'s reaction is not selfish and egotistical. It shows in its way a deep concern about my true reputation.

[We went to the] Manet exhibition [where there] were various people we knew. One was Claude Roy, my companion a lot during '*les évènements*' in 1968, where he was a sympathetic observer of the goings-on of the young.[2] He was with his wife, who seemed extremely nice, and another lady. He looked pale and tense. I asked him how he was. 'Pas si mal. J'ai eu un coup de cancer.'[3] So that was it – *is* it. Then a young man came up to me and said he had been with [John] Rewald in Ménerbes two days ago.[4] I have no idea who the young man was, so asked – Is Rewald still writing his famous demolition of Douglas Cooper?[5] Oh yes, of course, he replied. But Douglas is here somewhere in this gallery. And there at the end of the room, scarcely recognizable, so thin and shrivelled, was Douglas Cooper. However, he acted up to being a quite vigorous ghost of his old self. 'I hear you've been exalted', he greeted me. 'Well let's hope the poetry gets

---

1 Laurens Jan van der Post (1906–1996), Afrikaner writer whose first novel *In a Province* was published by Virginia Woolf at the Hogarth Press in 1934. He fought heroically on the British side in the Second World War and in later years he became a journalist, broadcaster and political advisor with close links to Prince Charles, Margaret Thatcher and Nelson Mandela.

2 Claude Roy (1915–1997), French poet and essayist. See Spender's *The Year of the Young Rebels* (1969).

3 'Not so bad. I have had a spot of cancer.'

4 John Rewald (1912–1994), German-born American art historian.

5 In 1944, Cooper had written a dismissive review of Rewald's book on Seurat, only to include passages suspiciously similar to Rewald's in his own book on Seurat, two years later. Cooper was forced to admit culpability, and relations between the two men remained rancorous until Cooper's death in 1984.

better' – a wish I could not quarrel with – because it's exactly my own devout prayer (injunction?). We congratulated him on the Cubist exhibition which he organized at the Tate. 'Well it was a great success,' he said, 'everyone liked it and it looked *extremely* well. The only thing that nearly *destroyed* me was having to spend six weeks in England. It nearly killed me. I can't think what keeps those people going, they're so boring and frigid. The French Ambassador gave a dinner for me – and my *dear* the people he invited – Lady Icicle Avon, Sir Niko Henderson and that Elgin marble his Greek wife.' I am making some of this up because I've forgotten. Perhaps Matthew will remember, because with arms folded, very tall, head looking down at the shrunken Douglas, a broad grin on his face, he was delighted at this attack on England – the two expatriates had got together. [. . .]

I must today review Cyril Connolly's *Journal*, then a book of letters of Middleton Murry.[1] [. . .] David Pryce-Jones's introduction to Cyril's *Journal*, and his postscript after it, is chatty and perceptive. He scores a great many points and succeeds in describing what might be called the 'mechanics' of Cyril's self-excusing career. Cyril was one of those who regard their psychological make-up as a machine controlling his behaviour and for which he is not responsible. Even the sense of guilt is part of the machinery.

He makes one judgement I question. This is that Cyril was an egoist. Or perhaps he does not quite say this. Well, yes, he does: 'Egoism alone remained constant, and the Journal throughout reveals the ingenuity and contrivance with which he managed to explain it away to himself. Blame was for other people.'

D.P.-J. later employs the word 'self-centred' which is true of Cyril. But the distinction between self-centredness and egoism explains, I think, a lot about Cyril's character. Cyril was self-centred, selfish, inconsiderate of other people and appalling – to an extent I had not quite realized until I read this book – in his readiness to take money

---

1 *Cyril Connolly: Journal and Memoir* was edited posthumously by the British historian David Pryce-Jones (b. 1936), the son of Alan Pryce-Jones. The British writer and editor John Middleton Murry (1889–1957) is best known as the husband and editor of the short-story writer Katherine Mansfield and as the editor of the *Athenaeum* and *Adelphi* in the 1920s. *The Letters of John Middleton Murry to Katherine Mansfield* (1983) were edited by C. A. Hankin and published by Constable.

from people worse off than himself. But he was not, as I understand the term, egoistic. An egoist is a person who has a fixed view of his own importance, is always using the pronoun 'I' to put forward himself as example. Egoism is not just a form of self-deception (Cyril one might say made a private industry of self-deception, but this was largely because he could never completely deceive himself) it is an opaque self-blindness, a large granule of insoluble stupidity in a probably successful and quite possibly intelligent person. Politicians, businessmen and philosophers, and some artists, can be egoists, but in being so they have fixed positions which is the last thing Cyril had. [. . .]

The point about C.C.'s self-absorption is that having realized, with some surprise, that he actually existed as a unique personality (a moment he recorded in *Enemies of Promise*) – he then spent his life trying to define who he was by appealing to other people to approve (or equally and conversely) to disapprove of him. [Add to this] he inhabited a Humanist version of the Divine Comedy in which he was always trying to discover whether he was *une âme damnée* [a damned soul] or, by an occasional wild chance, in paradise. [. . .]

The reader of his *Journal* comparing the genuine lyricism and love of beauty of some passages with the amounts of chic living in others will be aware of vulgarity. The only way to take Connolly is to accept the best together with the worst and see him as a confessional writer quite often off the track, often deceiving and self-deceiving, but sometimes wonderfully truthful because even if deceiving and self-deceiving he is never concealing anything. The famous apothegm about there being 'inside every fat man' – [. . . a thin man trying to get out.]

Well after I had written these notes, on Sunday, Terry Kilmartin rang and made it clear that I had to mail copy by express Monday morning.[1] Meanwhile we were due for dinner Sunday night at the Fairchilds. We arrived late, as we thought, because half-way there we imagined we had forgotten to lock up the house – the key was not in

---

1 Terence Kilmartin (1922–1991), journalist and translator, at this point literary editor of the *Observer*, later perhaps better known for his revision of the C. K. Scott Moncrieff translation of Proust's *Remembrance of Things Past* (1981). He and his family had a second home close to that of the Spenders in Provence.

N.'s bag. We drove all the way back, found the house was locked up. All the time the key was in my pocket. In old age we seem patient with each other when one or the other commits a *bêtise* [error] like this. We got back into the car without a word. [. . .]

This morning I started working. My plans are 1) to rewrite *Oedipus Trilogy* 2) to put together a new volume of Collected Poems. This involves completely rewriting about a dozen poems. My justification for this is that my C.P. are really a single *oeuvre* which I started writing about 50 years ago, some parts of which are incomplete sketches that can only be completed satisfactorily in the light of the whole *oeuvre*. I know very well which these are. They are failed attempts to do things which I muddled at the time. But the idea of what I was trying to do exists botched in them – and in some cases – not all – I feel 'I can still do it. I can clear away the weeds and undergrowth and release the idea I had at the time.' I started work on two poems today – and will, I think, succeed with them. Apart from these two ('Alas for the Sad Standards' and 'Abrupt and Charming Mover') I've rewritten, partly by introducing into them references to the historical material from which they derive, a poem called 'Perhaps', and another about Van Der Lubbe.¹ I intend to rewrite 'For T.A.R.H.' somehow ending with a reference to Tony's death which it seems to indicate.² I've put into the early poems a translation of Rilke's 'Herr, es ist Zeit', about Autumn, and also Lorca's sonnet 'Adam', both made by me in the '30s. 'Abrupt and Charming Mover' and 'Alas for the Sad Standards' are really new poems based on failed old ones.

5 July 1983, St Jerome

Read Middleton Murry letters and started review this morning. Will try to finish this evening. [. . .] Also sent telegram to the man in California who wants to take this house in September. I read Anthony Powell's new novel.³ It is clever and amusing but in the end fails I

---

1 The Dutch communist Marinus van der Lubbe (1909–1934) was the scapegoat executed for setting fire to the German Reichstag building in 1933.

2 'T.A.R.H.' is Thomas Arthur Rowett (Tony) Hyndman, who had died in 1972.

3 *O, How the Wheel Becomes It!* (1983).

think to decide quite what the tone should be. The satire on B.B.C. interviewers is a bit too close to the real thing, and at the same time, one feels that though sharp about it he is not really contemporary with that world. Here one feels the effort of the old man trying to be up to date. [. . .]

I am trying to screw myself up to read the *Oedipus* and see if I can transform it. Must fight the feeling that I'm under some obligation to do this. It might be better to get on with poems. There is also the commitment to write more autobiography.

Not really a very good day but I go to bed feeling quite elated. Not much work done but somehow have been in touch with beautiful things all the time. Read till 1 am last night Ivor Gurney's poems which are above all else exciting in their truth. Wrote the review on Middleton Murry's letters and mailed it to *The Listener*. It is too long and I suppose Derwent May will cut it just as Terry Kilmartin will have to cut my review of Cyril Connolly's *Journal*. But I think these reviews – Kleist for the *N.Y.R.*, Cyril for the *Observer*, Gurney's war letters for *The Tablet* and this about Murry – all say quite original things, and really are 'pieces'.

Gurney's poems are deeply moving and although not really accomplished still point to a kind of poetry which no-one – not even Gurney himself – has written. Firstly they are by someone who believes in the greatest art and the highest values. In music this is Bach, Schubert, Beethoven primarily. The point about these composers' ideas that they believed in and discovered the actual lines and rhythms for an ideal of beauty: and they hardly ever wavered from this. Undoubtedly in their own lives they worked and loved for this. They were aware of course that their lives could not be lived all the time on this level. But a purified sanctified part of their lives went into their art.

This division of his life by the artist into that which goes into his art where it achieves an existence almost separate from him and the life which is just everything – the body and all its motions on a par with all other bodies in the world – has a very dubious continuity in our age. All this century the 'moderns' have been on the verge of renouncing the ideal or idealized life and putting in, with a good deal of cynicism, everything. But again and again one sees that they have not done this, they have gone back to the ideal – literally gone back like Picasso in his classical style paintings and engravings – or they have projected it forward as in the noble purification of the world within an abstract reconstruction of it, which is cubism.

Gurney is the poet who happened also to be a composer who found himself a private soldier in the trenches on the western Front. What he does essentially is rediscover the ideals of the art he loves and wants himself to create in the souls of the men in the trenches; and, also in the destroyed landscape and skyscape of France, the landscape of Gloucestershire which he so loved. He was a bit mad already when he went to war, and the war sealed him for the rest of his life in his madness. His poems only show madness in technical imperfections which themselves become a kind of technique for expressing fragmentation. They retain always both ideal and earthiness, the quality of the sapphire in the mud. There is everything to learn from him.

10 July 1983, St Jerome

We've had a very social day. We were invited to lunch at Lacoste Art School by Bernard Pfreim the head of it.[1] [. . .] There were about 16 people invited for lunch ten of whom were trustees of the Art School. They were having a trustees' meeting in the working room while Anne Moynihan, Francis Wishart, Natasha and I sat having drinks in the sitting room. Through the arches in this open space planning arrangement we could have heard every word of what was being said in the committee, but for the fact that we were carrying on a conversation of our own. This was mostly about families and relations between generations. Francis was telling us how a month or so ago he had spent a day in Paris visiting the Manet exhibition with Matthew, Maro, Antonia Phillips and Martin Amis and how delightful it had been.[2] They had all lunched together at the Coupole Restaurant. Maro had talked a bit about how she had attacked me last year in Avane. Francis said how much he liked Maro, but how strange was her passion for insulting people and telling them home truths. He

---

1 Bernard Pfreim (1916–1996), American artist and teacher who had founded the Lacoste School of Arts in 1970.

2 Antonia Phillips would marry the British writer Martin Amis (b. 1949) in 1984.

said he thought that in my case it was partly because Maro thought she was protecting Matthew from my influence on him, or, perhaps, from the idea he had of me. Well, this may be so. Francis launched out into talking about how wives feel they have to protect their husbands from the influence of the husband's family. One realized very soon that, in part, by talking about us, he was talking *through us* to Anne about his own marriage. It was a pleasant conversation which I felt was also about deeply serious things, and was quite important to Francis. [. . .] The Fairchilds – with whom we had dinner at their house last night – appeared [. . .] A doctor and his wife were guests and during dinner talk turned to the subject of sleep. I said that during very hot weather if I lay down and started reading I had the sensation not of falling asleep but 'passing out', fainting perhaps for a few seconds or between sentences I was reading (two poems in the Greek Anthology). I thought Rory Cameron who falls asleep abruptly after or during a meal, and who 2 years ago had a bad accident, perhaps did the same thing.[1] The doctor (one of those benevolent disinfected looking medics – supremely a type for American advertisements – whose face seems modelled to fit their gold-rimmed spectacles) said this was falling asleep though there was a rare form of epilepsy in which patients lost consciousness for short intervals of time. Jill [Fairchild] said she had insomnia. She lay awake thinking about things, often terrible thoughts, she read, but then worried she was keeping John awake. The doctor's wife said there were little twinklet [*sic*] lights for only one of the double or twin-bedded couple. Jill said that she was afraid turning over a page of a book would wake John. John said nothing would wake him but that one thing kept Jill awake was him snoring – and he did a lively imitation of this. Jill laughed and said it wasn't that which kept her awake but her thoughts, and the lack of any technique for getting off the lines on which they ran. Someone mentioned counting sheep. Natasha said something about setting oneself a problem or trying to remember the names of all the states in America. The doctor said something to the effect that the

---

1 Roderick ('Rory') Cameron (1914–1985), American writer and connoisseur, lived with his mother in the Villa Fiorentina at Cap St Hospice on the French Riviera and later near Ménerbes at 'Les Quatre Sources', within neighbourly range of the Spenders at Mas St Jerome.

thing was to objectify the subjective train of thought by attaching one's thinking to something unsubjective outside of it. This conversation made N. feel very sleepy, and I could see that she was nodding off. [. . .]

When one is old the growing up of the young to maturity (if there is such a thing) and their assuming adult roles has something phantasmal about it. One feels that they are play acting and that when they have left the party, the office or their spouse, they will take off their masks and stage clothes, and become the children again.

At the party, John Fairchild who alternates hard-working facetiousness with making serious pronouncements ('the prosperity of Italy is unbelievable,' he said during luncheon, having just come back from Milan) said in his facetious tone: 'In Paris, I was told there had been a terrible attack on you in the *Spectator*' (referring to Auberon Waugh's remarks that I was 'abject', 'pitiful', had only written one line that was memorable and made a career out of knowing people far better than myself) then he went on to say rather superfluously, I thought, that there were always such attacks, one should ignore them, forget them, take no notice. 'In that case,' I felt like saying, 'why did you mention it?' – but realized he was trying both to tease me and give me the comfort of his public-worldly wisdom at the same time. The fact is though that W.'s hideous remarks provide a kind of leitmotif to my days now. They get under one's skin. The peculiarity of the word as secret weapon is that it acts on the recipient – when it is poisonous – as a spell cast by one of those voodoo witch doctors, which enters the blood and kills them. How Cyril Connolly would have understood this.

To continue these thoughts, which are useful, I think. People tell one in these cases that the attackers are negligible, contemptible, no-ones; that they are envious, spiteful, and care nothing of the truth. All that may be so. But apart from the fact that the poison that kills, like a vaccine, usually contains some minute concentrate of an extract of the victim's body, the character of the attacker is not relevant. It is no comfort to be told that the flea which gives you bubonic plague, or the mosquito, is only a flea or a mosquito, that Auberon Waugh is only a faint dilute of satiric malice inherited from a father of genius. [i.e. Evelyn Waugh] [. . .]

Undoubtedly though the best counter to such a poison is to use the adrenalin to produce one's best work. That answers everything, puts all attackers in their place.

14 July 1983, St Jerome

Still terribly hot. The heat is like a transformation of everything into itself, just heat. It insists on nothing but heat, drying up the earth, withering the flowers, cooking the apricots on the trees. It dries the air in one's lungs, like a vacuum taking the air out of them instead of letting it rush in. It seems to announce that it is here to stay, and will not be gainsaid. 'This is what Provence is about,' it declares, 'the heat and the mistral. Everything is just picture postcard tourism.' Natasha has been working throughout it at domestic things. Apart from cooking meals for us, having to deal with all the apricots – making them into jam, chutney, curd and cheese. Then there is the garden. I help by watering which really takes about two hours a day. She made beautiful blue curtains for the guest room.

We went at the rather late hour of 8.30 p.m., together with – in a separate car – Anne Chambers and Rory Cameron, to the exhibition of Picasso works which opens today at Nîmes. I did not want to go, was hoping they would cancel. When we got there, there was a very large crowd of the bourgeois of Nîmes. The damp hot air reeked with garlic. Though some very fantastic people, looking like Roman portraits of the time of Petronius, among them. I had expected little of this show, knowing how token such exhibitions can be. Actually it gave me a complete reappraisal of my idea of Picasso's genius. 'Genius' is really the word, because what characterizes him is the complete transformation at every moment of the lifetime of an extraordinary temperament of everything he sees, touches, fucks. Fantastic as his productivity is, one feels that what he actually produced, even if he were turning out a painting every hour of every day, is only a fraction of a far greater sum, because it is of the very nature of his work that every impression he has at every moment turns into a Picasso. Just as a creating life he stretches to the infinite, like spermatozoa. [. . .]

Picasso supplied an enormous need: a machinery of the imagination which without halt turned all the appearances of the modern world into visual toys, like one of Rilke's angels in the *Duino Elegies*

– forever transforming earthly things into heavenly ones. Looking at his pictures of women, one sees reflected there, the extraordinary attraction women must have felt for him – his pictures of them are like pictures of distorting mirrors which reflect him; mirrors concealing their activity behind grotesque frames in the shape of hats, and dresses: frames which are in fact the setting of modern fashion in which today's women caricature themselves.

22 July 1983, St Jerome

All these days I've been working at the *Oedipus Trilogy*. One result of writing verse a lot of each morning, and some of the afternoon, is that other poems keep writing their shadows in my mind. There are so many ideas, some of which I write down as notes, to others of which I say, as to unwanted guests: 'Go away!' (And there is always the *financial* necessity of journalism fretting too.) But one idea was so insistent that I've sketched it out – or am sketching it – at length, and will complete it. This arises from the passage in Gisa Soloweitschik's letter to me about her brother dying in Dachau.[1] Suddenly the sense that this information *annihilated* all the other news in the letter crystallized my feelings about the concentration camps. I saw that they were not just part of the history of the war but something quite different. Hearing that Grunia had died at Dachau was different in kind from hearing that he'd been killed during the German invasion of France. The concentration camps were Black Holes in history into which people, like stars or worlds disappearing into Black Holes, became as though they never existed.

Natasha and I went to Avignon to buy a 'sprinkler' for watering the garden, and during the drive the whole scenario of the poem, beginning with me meeting Gisa at Samedan, skiing, continuing through Christopher and my visits to the Soloweitschiks every Sunday in Berlin when they gave us a large luncheon – a tremendous blow-out – stuffing our pockets with fruit and cake when we left – all viewed in the perspective provided by the letter received over 50 years later – unwound itself before me, and during the next two days I've written about 100 lines.

---

1 For Gisa Soloweitschik see Gisa Drouin, note 1, p. 48.

26 July 1983, St Jerome

I made myself read my father's autobiographical *The Fire of Life*. I have been refusing to read it ever since it was published soon after his death – in 1927, I suppose. (There is no date given.) I was afraid to meet my father because I regard his rhetoric, his clichés, not just of journalist style, but of thought, his high-mindedness, his lack of any real grasp of reality in life, as insuperable deficiencies of him in myself. His book – which is not really a book at all, but rather disconnected reminiscences of life as seen in the most public way, from the reporter's desk, fully justifies these fears. I have all these characteristics though also a kind of built-in other side of my personality – the Schusters – which sees through them.[1] I haven't overcome them, I am a person whose belief in his existence depends on his having a public, and who takes this public view of his public self as the truth about him. On the other hand, the Schuster side of me despises all this. (No. Not utterly. The Schusters adore success.)

Given the quota of psychological obtuseness in his character, his total lack of penetration in what lies behind the externals of people's behaviour, my father comes across as a well-meaning, decent, public-spirited, enthusiastic, buoyant man. One scarcely feels that there is a private side of his personality which is suppressed – it simply isn't there. His affections go into camaraderie – rather than real friendship – kindness to those in need wherever he meets them – mountain climbing, natural scenery, the give-and-take ups-and-downs, ding-dong, public quarrels and private fellowship of the House of Commons. (The sum of these adjectives adds up, with him, to a philosophy

---

1 Harold Spender married Violet Schuster (Stephen's mother) in 1904. Violet came from a successful banking family, while Harold's career in left-wing journalism was erratic. His first job was at the *Echo* in 1888, and he later worked at the *Pall Mall Gazette*, *Westminster Gazette*, *Daily Chronicle*, the *Manchester Guardian* and the *Daily News*. His career was repeatedly compromised by political ideals: he left the *Echo* after his involvement in the 1899 East End Dockers strike and the *Daily Chronicle* over its Boer War stance. Harold had a special affinity with the East End. In the 1890s he lived at Toynbee Hall, a Whitechapel philanthropic centre, before settling in Stepney Green and in 1899 he unsuccessfully stood for election in the Bromley and Bow by-election. At the end of his career, Harold worked as a University Extension Lecturer, lecturing in provincial towns but never quite maintaining public success.

of life.) One of the few themes at all developed in the book is the idea of a Third Estate (parliament) and a Fourth Estate (journalism) which runs England. All the conflicts in society outside these are ultimately resolved by parliamentary votes. Parties support or oppose social reforms in order to win debates in parliament. Well, that is not quite fair, although his account of Third or Fourth Estate often make[s] it sound like that. The deepest thing in the book is his feeling about poverty, his respect for the poor, his understanding of Labour, which is really greater than that of many self-styled socialist[s], though he was never a socialist but always a Liberal. He accepts without at all examining it, the status quo. With all his sympathy for the poor East Enders (among whom he spent six years of his life) and his criticism of the rich, he thinks the furthest justification of Canon Barnett and Toynbee Hall slumming is that it stops revolution. Of course this may well be true, but he does not think out the root reasons for any position, he simply accepts the sentiment that 'best is British'. His writing is that of a fairly literate lecturer who, although he early on had an excellent education (a double first at Oxford) has become half-educated through lecturing the half-educated, and through the intoxication of his own style which is a Temperance beverage. Defending his friend Lloyd George against critics of him for his treachery and wheeler-dealing etc, he produces the argument that George is so high-principled that he occasionally sacrifices friends and allies to his noble principles – and the awful thing is that he him-self seems the only person deceived when he writes this.[1]

There is an old-fashioned journalist's – leader-writer's – determina-tion to end every argument on an up-beat with a simplified solution. One of the things he is interesting about is newspapers themselves. He gives a very good picture of the difficulties of the reporter and

---

1 For Harold Spender's complicated relationship with Lloyd George, whom he idolised, and whom in later life he conceived to have ruthlessly betrayed him, see John Sutherland, *Stephen Spender, The Authorized Biography* (London: Penguin, 2005) p. 60. Spender published a biography of Lloyd George in 1920 (*The Prime Minister*, Hodder & Stoughton), but then at the end of his career he was spurned by Lloyd George after he fed (apparently false) information about him to a New York paper. Lloyd George sent a letter of condolence to the Spender family after Harold Spender's death but no representative from the Liberal Party went to the funeral.

interviewer having to return to the newspaper office with his material, at the turn of the century. He sees well the consequences of the newspaper proprietors – the Harmsworths – who were making millions out of selling newspapers, instead of putting their millions made by other means (George Cadbury) into them.[1] He is extremely interesting about the almost total censorship of news during the First World War. But in describing any and every development, he always has to be optimistic. There are bad patches in public as in private life but in the end everything is for the best, there is always progress. On and on and up and up. This faith – true or false – is numbing because it prevents any really deep examination or criticism of anything.

31 July 1983, St Jerome

Still the same heat. It has not been under 90° Fahrenheit for a month. We have the Hugh Thomases staying – Hugh, Vanessa, and their oldest daughter Isabella, aged 17. They are remarkably interesting guests. We all dined with Anne Chambers last night. Rory Cameron and John Fairchild, Rodrigo and Anne Moynihan and Francis Wishart there.

What really takes up my thoughts is having read Mary Berenson's *Letters and Journals* (ed. Barbara Strachey).[2] I feel I have experienced

---

1 Alfred Harmsworth, Lord Northcliffe (1865–1922) and Harold Harmsworth, Lord Rothermere (1868–1940), British brothers and newspaper magnates. Through their combined efforts, the brothers built up a newspaper empire together before the First World War which was collectively known as the Amalgamated Press. The collective was made up of a number of titles and included *The Times* (acquired 1908), the *Daily Mail* (founded 1896), and the *Daily Mirror* (founded 1903). George Cadbury (1839–1922), factory owner, philanthropist and newspaper proprietor. George Cadbury inherited his father's failing chocolate business in 1861 and, with his brother Richard Cadbury (1835–1899), transformed its fortunes, expanding it to the production of ground cocoa. George Cadbury invested his fortune in the Quaker cause and became a proprietor of the *Daily News* in 1902. Harold Spender was made Co-Editor of the *Daily News* in 1901. The paper was Lloyd George's voice piece and it was Lloyd George who persuaded Cadbury to give Spender the job. Harold Spender found the paper's anti-war stance appealing but he found the job itself stifling and left in 1904.

2 Mary Berenson (1864–1945), art critic, married to Bernard Berenson from 1900. The book Spender refers to was published in 1983.

a whole life with the Berensons – the rhapsodic early days of their pre-marriage, her collaboration with him in art dealing, the pleasure she took in the piracy of smuggling pictures out of Italy, the risks and lawsuits: then his love affairs or passions for very glamorous ladies, and her crushes on various young men, their assistants and apprentices at I Tatti [the Berenson villa]. Geoffrey Scott.[1] I feel this lady always much taller and larger than B.B. physically turned – and saw herself turning – into a massive piece of furniture like a wardrobe. At the same time, she retained her intelligence – so useful to B.B. – and also all her feelings poured out on her husband, various young men and finally her grandchildren. At the end she abdicated in her relationship with B.B. – passed her trust on to Nicky Mariano (who I met in 1933 or 4) who was a wonderful person into whose loving kindness the affection under the recriminations of cruelty (on BB's side) of the tragic marriage became transcended (during Mary's dying and after her death).[2] Her thoughts at the end of her life when she was all alone and in terrible pain record the triumph of past memories over lived unhappiness and final solitude. She is left with nothing except the vivid past and scarcely wants to impinge on present consciousness [. . .]

The Thomases were agreeable guests. She seems affectionate and patient – very real. He is curious with a rather leonine head of an intelligent animal, a luscious mane of black and grey hair. A disconcerting way of turning his face directly on or at yours, meeting your face with what seem completely unseeing eyes. A rather indolent arrogance of manner which does not reveal anything about his inner life. I suspect a streak of cruelty, which is known to his family, and which Vanessa tries to cover up. Talking about Berenson I said how he flew into violent rages with Mary. Vanessa said something to the effect – that a wife ought to be able to cope with that. Later on when there was again talk about B.B.'s iniquities, Hugh said, 'You have to bear in mind that a man can have a very bad character but also do

---

1 Geoffrey Scott was a young classics scholar, brought to I Tatti to work in the library. Mary Berenson had a nervous breakdown when her affair with him broke up in 1918.

2 After the death of his wife Mary, Bernard Berenson took his assistant Nicky Mariano (Scott's replacement) as his companion. She described the relationship herself in her 1966 memoir *Forty Years with Berenson*.

very good work.' Isabella looked up rather sharply and said: 'Do you really think that?' He looked at her with his bleared heavy glance, as though he was on the verge of saying something very much to the point, and then looked away again.

Quite a lot of talk about English politics in the evening. We agreed that [Denis] Healey was [a] very intelligent able man (with a passion for music) and that Labour would have done much better in the election if he had been Labour leader.[1] But he was also a bully boy and could never quite conceal his contempt for other people. We talked about parliamentary rhetoric and what a disaster Foot was. He said that Foot was worried about his own appearance. He talked a bit about Mrs T[hatcher] – compared her with de Gaulle – thought she had perhaps restored the confidence of the English in themselves. He was rather sympathetic to the Alliance – said that Labour might easily sink to third place in the next election. Thinks nothing of Neil Kinnock (whom Vanessa finds very beautiful).[2] I said I thought it was a misfortune that when Mrs T. dismissed a cabinet minister he instantly became a non-person ([Ian] Gilmour, [Francis] Pym, [Peter] Carrington, Norman St John-Stevas). He gave his languid bleared look and said in his slightly drawling way, 'Oh, I should have thought they could look after themselves.' He is rather fascinating, after all. I should like to know him better. He talks quite modestly about his books. Has written a historic novel about a cabin boy.[3] He did not seem very confident about it – said his publishers 'seemed fairly pleased'.

Two days ago Iris Murdoch telephoned that they will not be able to come this year, because her mother, who is senile, has now become violent. The male nurse who looks after her, refuses to go on doing so. It is impossible in less than 3 weeks to get her into any mental

---

1 Denis Healey (b. 1917) had served in various senior cabinet posts in Labour Party administrations. He stood for election as Harold Wilson's successor in 1976, and as James Callaghan's successor in 1980; losing closely both times, on the second occasion to Michael Foot, in whose hands Labour had suffered its worst defeat for fifty years at the General Election in June 1983. Foot resigned shortly after the election.

2 Neil Kinnock (b. 1943), British politician, who would become leader of the Labour Party in October.

3 *Havannah* (1985).

hospital. So John and Iris have to have her with them, and to look after her. This must be a nightmare for Iris, and I do not see how she will be able to manage.

7 August 1983, St Jerome

Dreamed a lot about dying. I was going to have some operation which I thought I would not recover from. I did not mind in the least. I woke up thinking that all dying amounts to is shedding the burdens of practicalities which make up most of life. I thought how N[atasha], who hates practical things, seems always to get herself tied up in them – this house, the difficulties it involves of getting people to work for us – plough the olive fields, collect the olives – and people to occupy this house when we aren't there. Even dying, I thought, is a practicality for one's survivors. Dying ties the corpse up in as much tape as an Egyptian mummy. Forms to fill in. Death duties. Relations having to look after other relations. Executors. What to do with all the papers. Then, in my case, I suppose, the things people will write and say about my failure to do all that was expected of me. How painful this will be for Natasha and Lizzie. Dying is like creating a vacuum which the living have to rush to fill in – dying a bit themselves in the process.

13 August 1983, St Jerome

Angus Wilson sent me his book of critical essays.[1] They make enter-taining reading. Criticism as an autobiography of his own taste – leading to self-criticism and revising his opinions is interesting, though his ego tends to stand between the reader and whatever writer A. Wilson is writing about. In one piece he has a long parody of Virginia Woolf: in a later one he revises his opinion of her – says he had missed out the fact that she is – in *Mrs Dalloway* – a great master of narrative style. He condemns the early parody as crude – but does not see the point: that it is impossible. Virginia is an extraordinary example of a writer whose virtue exists from line to line in the actual

---

1 *Diversity and Depth in Fiction: Selected Critical Writings of Angus Wilson* (1983).

language she uses, which expresses a very fragmented sensibility of genius. Take away her words and write down what she was writing about – the middle-class feelings of a woman of the highest professional middle-class – a woman of great sensibility to the values, snobbery, selectivity of such a woman – and you get simply – such a woman – not Virginia Woolf, who was a wild mad wayward beautiful genius, enclosed in the circumstances – including dress and snobberies of such a woman. Her marriage was an ideal marriage because Leonard worshipped the spirit enclosed in the tree; and realized that he himself belonged to the forest – was a reforming, liberal gamekeeper or forestier. But in the middle of his forest one tree was his Daphne. The imitators of V.W. (among whom Angus includes himself, and also ranks Elizabeth Bowen) only take over, very intelligently, that which gets into V.W.'s writing and can be analysed into attitudes transferable to them in their writing. Who except for Angus himself would suppose that his central character in his novel *The Middle Age of Mrs Eliot* owes anything to Virginia Woolf?

22 August 1983, St Jerome

Lizzie left this afternoon after a five days stay which at this moment seems like five minutes. There is a heavy thunderstorm as I write this. But I suppose she is practically in London by now. We met her at the airport on Thursday and drove home via one of the big stores which have now become one of the features of Provence. We bought provisions for the luncheon party we gave for Jeremy Fry, the Snowdons and Sarah Armstrong-Jones and Jeremy's daughter on Friday.[1] Lizzie was very helpful about everything, and not tired when really we thought that after her office work she would want a rest. We went to the party for General Rogers at Anne Chambers' that evening.[2] [. . .]

During dinner, Natasha, who was seated at the general's table, asked him whether he had ever in his career had to take life and

---

1 Jeremy Fry (1924–2005), British engineer and patron of the arts. Sarah Armstrong-Jones (b. 1964), British artist, granddaughter of the Queen Mother.

2 Bernard W. Rogers (b. 1921), American general who served as Chief of Staff of the US Army, 1976–9, and then as NATO's Supreme Allied Commander, 1979–87.

death decisions. He said that was a question no-one had ever asked him before. In Korea and also in Vietnam he had had to make decisions involving 200 or 300 lives and doing so had always weighed on him terribly.

Jim, Anne's son, and also Lauren, his wife, were there. [. . .] I sat next to a countess-style Hungarian lady from Brussels, who talked about Arthur Koestler, and her various escapes from places to other places. Jim's wife Lauren was on my left, also a bit twenties-ish like a very frail, limpid, large-eyes and more innocent Bette Davis. She mentioned that her mother, who she described as being very short and always dressed in brown suits (that was my impression, via her, of her mother) was one of the top computer experts for space flights at Houston. She had monitored the Apollo.[1] I asked her whether this was nerve-wracking. She said: 'Yes, but luckily mother has quite a sense of humour.' She said vaguely she thought she had three step-fathers – she distinguished the present one as 'the man mother is now with'. She seemed to feel well-disposed to all these people, and a few wives of step-fathers, fluttering motherly figures (like the moths in Anne's garden as well). She was touching and charming I thought. Afterwards, Lizzie sat together with them on a sofa, the two, Jim and Lauren, looking so small beside Lizzie, who talked about her own theatre experiences, which the two received with 'ahs' and 'ohs' and occasional tid-bits from New York. I wondered about the level of seriousness of all three – or of each of the three. The thought crossed my mind that Jim and Lauren had the seriousness of money. And, of course it applies to all of *us* that we don't have this. And when one is with extremely rich people, though they may revere one, have the greatest respect for intellect, ask one to read poetry on the lawn (as Anne has asked me to do) next Saturday, or play one's piece (as Anne has asked Natasha to do) in a way one belongs to a world of light-some shadows for them, like moths, fluttering outside a light house window.

---

1 The Apollo Space Missions were conducted between 1967 and 1972, and involved both earth and lunar orbital missions and lunar missions. The crew of Apollo 1 was killed in a fire in a pre-launch test, and Apollo 13 did not reach its lunar target. The Apollo rockets were launched at Cape Canaveral in Florida and the ground control centre was in Houston.

28 August 1983, St Jerome

The great event of the summer took place last night – if you take the view that socially our summers here are becoming every year more and more like one of E. F. Benson's Lucia novels with Anne Chambers as Lucia.[1] Since we were to be performers at this party, we were asked to come early by Joanna, the black dancer whom Anne has adopted as her fourth child (Anne said to me that Joanna is such a good person that when she is with her every mean thought vanishes from her (Anne's) head). Joanna gave us a list of order of our contributions – Natasha first, then a girl who sang American/English ballads, then me, then Catharine Wishart, then Joanna herself, dancing on the lawn in a rabbit mask.[2] The weather was very uncertain, but, although it was not raining, against a great cloud bank above the house there appeared a perfect rainbow which Anne took, quite rightly, as a tribute to her and a sign that we were going to have a fine evening. Guests, as they arrived, reported coming through deluges, in Avignon, Tarascon, Gordes to get here. But tables were set outdoors on the terrace where there was also an upright piano. I sat next to a very intelligent and brave lady called Madeleine who looks after her terribly ill husband and obviously has an awful life, but always makes good conversation, never mincing matters; and, on my right, one of those vague brown, brown-dressed, chestnut-haired ladies who turn up at such parties. After we had finished dinner Anne made a gracious speech welcoming all of us who had made her summers here so agreeable. [. . .] After Natasha's three pieces which went down very well, a long-haired girl with a whining voice got up and accompanying herself on a reedy-sounding guitar sang some complaining ballads, one of them a wail about the lot of women, on Women's Lib lines. It did rain a few drops for my reading and we had to go inside, but Anne was delighted at this because one could hear words read

---

1 E. F. Benson (1867–1940) produced a series of six novels, known collectively as the Mapp and Lucia novels, between 1920 and 1939. The novels revolve around two characters: Miss Elizabeth Mapp, a long-term resident of Tilling, a small English country town, and Miss Emmeline Lucas (Lucia), a newcomer. The two compete for small social victories, Lucia outwitting Mapp, but triumphing only as a result of her remarkable selfishness and egotism.

2 Catharine Wishart, Francis Wishart's wife, is a guitarist.

better indoors. Then came Catharine and her guitar accompanying an exotic looking lady from Montmartre, dressed like a Spanish dancer, who did not speak a word of English, but who sang some Elizabethan songs in a voice like a saw. But Catharine's twanging with strong very well spaced powerful and separate notes was really effective and made me see the point of that much abused and rhythmically strummed on and battered instrument. After this we moved indoors. Francis told me that a pinched-faced pale intense young man, guest of Catharine and him, and husband perhaps of the Elizabethan songstress was in a state of agonized *crise de conscience*, because he was one of Francis's top left-wing young lawyers and he so thoroughly disapproved of the company he was in, particularly since he was très anti-Américain. I found myself casting furious glances at the young man who (I think) reciprocated with furious glances back at me. He did not speak to anyone outside his own 'groupuscule' I noticed. Since he had never been invited to the party, his behaviour seemed – well, very typical. Meanwhile the whole thing seemed to go to Catharine's head. She jerked about in the way she has, as though her limbs were pulled by wires, sat down at the piano and began to play jazz to an excited little group of *les jeunes* (mostly jeunes Sainsburys) who collected round her. I must say she has tremendous vitality of a slightly macabre kind, and is like a tigress on the keys, pouncing on a clutch of notes with fingers like claws and shaking frenetic music out of them. I did realize that one thing the rock world can do is to make – by comparison with its standards – the whole outside world of art – and perhaps even politics – seem extremely staid. The pale young lawyer did not take part in this – radiating his own kind of vibrations of disapproval – ice-cold rays, the opposite of Catharine's fiery ones. The rest of the party went on as though unaware of all this, though I am sure Emily (who has to go and visit the doctor in Lyons tomorrow) took it all in. I feel that Francis – rather pale, for his own personal reason – is being annexed by an alien world. He was affectionate in spite of this. I gave Anne the copy of my *Collected Poems* I had read from, inscribing it to her with the feeling that doing so I was protesting against the pale and pinched and mean young lawyer.

30 August 1983, St Jerome

We lunched with Rory yesterday. Anne Chambers, Catherine Fellows and her Costa Rican (?) friend were there.[1] Anne talked to me about Jim [her son] and his wife Lauren. [. . .] At lunch we talked a bit about Francis Wishart. A difficulty with these people is that the word 'left' is like the reddest of flashing lights to them. One enters a heavily mined area. I said that when I was the young lawyer's age I might have behaved much as he did. A tolerant smile, as though my saying this was like admitting I had once gone through a phase of alcoholism makes me say that I still sympathize with the left about many things. But this seems floundering. What I really mean is that as far as their aims are concerned I am completely for the left. What puts me against them is that their aims are subverted by their policies. I am not against Scargill's or Ken Livingstone's wanting a socially just society, but when I read (in *The Times* today) that Scargill has gone to Moscow and declared that the warmongers are Mr Reagan and Mrs T., and that the Russians stand for peace and disarmament – or Mr Livingstone saying that the British in Ireland are (or have been across their history) as bad as the Nazis, I am repelled by them.[2] The difference between my rich American friends and me is that they are against Socialism anyway. They would be as much against Dubček as against Stalin, fundamentally – their softness towards him being the reflection of their feeling that he can somehow be used against Socialism.[3] But I admire everything, as I understand it, that a man like Dubček stood for: his socialism combined with his complete awareness of the inhuman face of the socialized police state. What Anne Chambers believes in is the humanity of Anne Chambers and a few

---

1 Catherine Fellows, a painter and neighbour of Rory Cameron in Provence.

2 Arthur Scargill (b. 1938), the leader of the National Union of Miners, and Thatcher's arch enemy, would launch the miners' strike in 1984. Ken Livingstone (b. 1945) was currently head of the Greater London Council and another anti-Thatcher warrior. In December 1982, he had caused uproar by inviting Gerry Adams, the leader of Sinn Fein, the political branch of the Provisional IRA, to London. This was at the height of the Provisional IRA's bombing campaign.

3 Alexander Dubček had been leader of Czechoslovakia during the attempted Prague Spring reforms in 1969 and was a proponent of 'communism with a human face'.

people like her – Jimmy Carter perhaps.[1] I recognize that humanity but it is the humanity of the rich, and I am not in my heart on the side of the rich. By their standards we are poor, and I think we are better for being poor (given the fact that by any standards except those of the rich, we are not poor at all – we merely have to pay every bill through our own work, and my work is of a minimally paying kind). [. . .]

I wake up often with very disturbing thoughts, visions almost. I had one today about time, as vision rather than 'philosophy'. This is that time is simply one's way of looking at things. Just as we see colours that have no real existence in objects themselves but are conditioned by our sense organs, or as we see space as an arrangement of things near and far seen from the centre which is our own positioning in it, so we see time as before and after our place, our date, our moment in it. But actually there is no before and after except in our minds as our conditioned way of looking at things. [. . .]

But yesterday waking up I had disturbing thoughts of another order. I remembered that Cyril and Jean Connolly used to play a verbal game in which they acted the roles of friends of theirs who were 'queer'. The ones they particularly liked doing were Cuthbert Worsley and Tony Bower (I dare say they did 'Stephen' and my 'Tony' – Tony Hyndman – now I come to think of it).[2] The joke was that Cuthbert Worsley, in the manner of some men who have been trained as athletes, had a very very small penis. Cyril in the role of Tony Bower in bed with Cuthbert would pant and say hoarsely 'Bugger me, Cuthbert.' Cuthbert would say in his refined genteel voice: 'But I am buggering you, Tony.' Or Tony would 'feel' Cuthbert up and say hoarsely: 'Oh Cuthbert, I love your navel.' Cuthbert (acted by Jean) would say in a slightly offended tone of voice: 'But Tony, that's not my navel.'

---

1 Anne Cox Chambers was a supporter of Carter and was appointed US Ambassador to Belgium (1977–81) during his administration. She firmly supported the president's human-rights-centred foreign policies.

2 T. C. (Cuthbert) Worsley (1907–1977), British writer and theatre critic who went to Spain with Spender during the Spanish Civil War and recorded his experiences in *Fellow Travellers: A Memoir of the Thirties* (1971). Tony Bower had written pieces for Spender and Connolly in *Horizon* during the war and was later murdered by a boyfriend in New York.

All of them dead, and I wake up with these voices of Jean and Cyril acting out their rather cruel scene of Tony and Cuthbert in my ear. Of course, such a dialogue cannot but raise in one's mind the question whether Cyril may not have had some doubt about his own equipment. Only a few bones left somewhere – some were buried, some cremated – Tony Bower was murdered – at any rate the flesh by now all gone. How can memories of such obscenity cling around one's thoughts of the dead. How strange it is that I can even re-enact love scenes with the dead – especially when in fact the love remained unfulfilled – a proposition made but not followed up. Now I can go back to the times and place and body – now dust – and follow it up with that fleshly ghost to the sperm ejaculated in a towel or handkerchief.

31 August 1983, St Jerome

Lunch yesterday with Sascha Schneider.[1] With flowing locks of hair, face deeply lined, statuesque nose, scraggy neck, he is strikingly Central European, a cross between a great artist and a Zigeuner [gypsy] musician. [. . .] When we arrived, he was standing in his very shabby garden, wearing headphones, 'Don't you have these?' he shouted. 'They are telling me the news.' They had little stereos built into them. He at once asked us whether we had heard Backhaus playing the Diabelli Variations [by Beethoven] on a record from the 1950s last night – on France Musique – and what we thought of it.[2] Natasha said she thought that Backhaus rushed the whole thing as though he was in a panic. 'No no!' said Sascha, 'he was trying to say something, perhaps that he had been a Nazi during the war and he was not ashamed of it and he defied the whole world, or perhaps he was denying he had ever been a Nazi.' We none of us knew whether Backhaus had been a Nazi. I said we had to go in from the sun because of my doctor's orders. We moved into the kitchen where Sascha had prepared a very good cold meal, all bought at the local market in

---

1 Alexander Schneider (1908–1993), conductor-violinist, at this date director of the Schneider concerts at the New School, New York.

2 Wilhelm Backhaus (1884–1969), German pianist.

Tarascon at 7 a.m., he told us – prosciutto and melon, and figs, pâté de campagne, goat cheese, salad. [. . .]

Sascha [. . .] said the point of pianists like Backhaus's generation was that they were professional. They had mastered their techniques and having done so they gave a professional performance. Natasha said that professional or not, Backhaus (who was 70 at the time) played a lot of wrong notes besides playing too fast. This annoyed Sascha (who is 74). 'Every professional plays wrong notes. The point is the performance that the whole conception is professional. What have we now? Nothing. No feeling for the music. Technique. Technique only. Nothing but technique. Who has anything else today? Not one. Not one.' 'Oh but I think there are a few,' said N. 'Who? Who?' 'Well, there is [Alfred] Brendel.' 'Brendel, nothing but a technician who plays the score in front of him. If there were a squashed fly on the score he would play that.' We – or he rather – changed the subject by saying: 'Last time we met, you gave me excellent advice.' 'What was that?' 'You do not remember? I said that I was going to write my autobiography. You said: "Well remember if you write all the truth you will not be able to publish it in your lifetime. And if you don't publish it in your lifetime you will lose the pleasure of seeing people read it." Well I am offered $5,000 advance by my friend — — the publisher to write my biography. I say "Keep your money. I do not want your advance. I will write it. Then I will bring it to you, and if you like it then you may publish it." Well I write it, I say there is no-one today any good. They have wonderful technique but they cannot play music. I am fearless. I say what I think of everyone. I bring my manuscript to my friend the publisher and he does not want to publish it. He says, "Look Sascha, just because you are a great violinist, you do not have to be a great writer." Then he said: "What you need is a ghost to write the book for you. Now I know a young man who would do this. You have to work with him, tell him what you have to say, and he will write your biography for you."' Sascha then showed us a sheet of paper on one side of which was his own account of his projected biography, on the other side the ghost's reworking of this. Sascha's own account began by saying that Sascha Schneider was unique among instrumentalists in having played twice at the White House. I said 'But surely there were other musicians who played twice at the White House. Lennie Bernstein, Yehudi

Menuhin.' 'Leonard Bernstein is a conductor,' he roared. 'He is not an instrumentalist.' He had also played as a soloist by himself, with an orchestra, he had played in septets, sextets, quintets, quartets, trios and duos as well as being such a great soloist. He had played in Europe, America, South America, Australia and Japan. It went on like this. The ghost's account said that Schneider was one of the most distinguished performers of our time and that his biography was of more than general interest. Natasha said that she thought this ghost sounded rather banal and that S.'s own writing was more colourful. S. looked a bit vague and changed the subject back again to performers. He said, rather inconsistently, that there were wonderful young performers, Murray Perahia, 'he is like my son' (pronounced like 'song' without the 'g').[1] N. said Perahia was very fortunate in having benefited from the system of International Festivals with prizes for young artists. He had no success then won the prize in the Leeds Festival then had immediately engagements everywhere. At this Sascha got furious and started shouting: 'That is what is so terrible!' he said. 'Engagements everywhere! Every week, two or three engagements. Booked up with engagements for three years. Now Murray has hurt his right arm from so much playing everywhere. Perhaps he can soon play no more. He has hurt his right arm.' I said – well he didn't have to accept every engagement, did he? 'How can he refuse? He is under so much pressure' etc. Somehow the name of Peter Serkin came up, and Natasha said that in his case being the son of Rudolf Serkin had helped.[2] 'Not at all,' said S. 'It did not help at all. Everyone said you are the son of the great Rudolf Serkin who is such a marvellous pianist, how can you expect to be good? I know. He stayed with me here. We played duets – Mozart, Beethoven, Schubert, everything. I know the difficulties he has had. He is like my son. Now he has so many difficulties. Perhaps he will play no more.' [. . .]

We left him there alone in his house. I seemed to remember that some years ago there had been a woman around. In previous years

---

1 Murray Perahia (b. 1947), American pianist and conductor who had won the Leeds International Piano Competition in 1972 and collaborated with Rudolf Serkin at the Marlboro Festival, a Vermont-based music summer school.

2 Rudolf Serkin (1903–1991), Austrian-born pianist. A highly regarded talent, Rudolf Serkin led the piano department at the Curtis Institute. His son is Peter Serkin (b. 1947), an established classical pianist.

also he had organized a recital to which he invited people (you had to bring your own chair). I think that Peter Serkin played duets with him at one of these. Towards the end of lunch he turned the conversation to more neutral topics. But there was always the awful feeling that the only subject that really interested him was himself, his career, and that he also had terrible doubts about himself. We left feeling that he was a nice man but impossible to enjoy being with. To get away from him was like getting away from an enclosed space into the open air. The tragedians of daily life are the great egoists.

2 September 1983, St Jerome

Every other activity has been made insignificant by the overwhelming preoccupation with getting the house ready for the tenants, and ourselves ready for departure. (The tenants Mr and Mrs Houlgate from Santa Barbara, early middle-aged, with their twelve-year-old son have arrived, and seem in love with it all). Apart from this there was a tremendous storm which has washed away all the pebbles and gravel from the 'white garden' path, turning it into a muddy stream bed. We have been out every meal for the past two days, lunching once at Anne [Chambers]'s, dining one night alone at the Regalido, at Fontvieille, lunching yesterday at Dick Dumas' house at Les Imberlins and having a farewell dinner last night at Anne's – with Emily, Rory [Cameron], Gilbert as the other guests.[1] [. . .]

Bathrooms. On the way to the party (we went in Anne's car, Joanna drove) Anne said that when she was building her house, she was recommended a bathroom designer in Marseilles. He sent her a design for her bathroom. 'In the first place,' she said, 'there was an enormous bath, standing on four legs. Next the whole bath was surrounded by mirrors.' 'I can't possibly have this,' Anne said to the designer. 'Why, if I got into a bath like this, I would commit hara-kiri.' Afterwards she discovered he had designed a bath for Brigitte Bardot.

Anne said that the thing that interested her most in the world at the present time was the question of who would be the next presidential candidate for the Democratic Party. The trouble was, though,

---

1 Dick Dumas and Emily were friends of Anne Cox Chambers.

that she couldn't feel enthusiastic about *any* of them. [John] Glenn, she said, was coming on very well, had made remarkable progress over the past few months, and as for his wife, why everyone agreed she is just darling. [Walter] Mondale, she was not at all enthusiastic about.[1] Then there was another candidate called [Gary] Hart, whom many people thought well of but he had absolutely no base, and no money to speak of. I asked why wasn't she a candidate herself. She said that was an absolutely ludicrous idea, but Emily pressed her saying she didn't think it at all absurd. Anne said that quite apart from her own merits, it was unthinkable that 'as of here and now' there could be a woman President of the United States. This astonished us. After all, Mrs Thatcher? Indira Gandhi? Well, she thought that some years hence there might be a woman ('and, eventually, a black' chipped in Joanna) but not as of now. [. . .]

Conversation tended to peter out. I had mentioned Sascha Schneider's egoism, and put forward the idea that it would be amusing to invite, unbeknown to each of them, a party consisting of, say, six egomaniacs, each talking about nothing but him (or her) self and two observers. We discussed some varieties of egoists then had a feeling we'd run through all the possibilities, and fell silent. I wondered to myself how it is that in company where there is good conversation, one can pass from subject to subject without the feeling that one has run out of things to say about any particular topic. Somehow before one topic is exhausted the next one is dove-tailed into the continuity of the conversation.

One thing Emily told me was that Anne loved Provence because [the] social life was much more entertaining than in Atlanta. This made me wonder. Of course her social life isn't quite limited to Rory. There was the visit from General Rogers this summer and I dare say some other visitors we didn't meet. But Emily said firmly 'You have no idea how boring Atlanta is.'

---

1 The successful Democrat candidate would be Walter Mondale (b. 1928), who had served as Vice President under Carter, 1977–81. Reagan eventually won the 1985 election, capitalizing in his campaign on America's recovery from the recession of 1981 and on Mondale's own admission that he would raise taxes if elected.

10 September 1983, London

Horrible to think that it is already a week [since the Spenders' return from France]. We have both been extremely tired since that journey. I have done little except this journal. Nothing of Oedipus. Nothing that would earn money. This morning remembered Auden staying with me in Frognal [Spender's Hampstead childhood home] when he had left Oxford and was already out in the world, and saying that before he did anything else he must sit down and write a couple of reviews. He polished these off in a morning. One was about some sociological book for *The Criterion*. I wish I could organize my life like that. Two hours a day devoted to money-making. The rest to what I want to write.

With the house swathed in scaffolding we have scarcely been out. On Thursday our neighbours Jeremy and June Hutchinson came to dinner. He is warm, helpful, quite affectionate, very amusing, serious – most enjoyable to be with – but nevertheless there is something about him of the wall – a judicial wall, a wall that says 'this far and no further', a batsman wall which politely and coolly blocks all approaches. I doubt if he is really anyone's friend. He has a kind of habit of mockery in which he approaches others, parodying his own manner as counsel cross-questioning his victims in the witness box. He has this even with beautiful, pale, heroic, charitable June whenever she ventures an opinion about politics. We talked a bit about the shooting down of a South Korean aircraft by Soviet fighters.[1] 'Really!' he says – 'Really!' with an exclamation mark, 'Really?' with a question mark – both underlining the weakness of the argument of June or any of us. 'Really! You think that do you? Really? I'm most interested. Please do go on' – to Anne Moynihan when she attacked the policy of the Tate Gallery here some weeks ago. At the same time there is someone very decent, civilized and human in him who deplores his own manner. This is the helpful Jeremy who takes endless trouble and to whom we ourselves at various times of crisis owe a lot. This side of him is as unexpected as Diarmuid MacCarthy the doctor son of Desmond MacCarthy who sitting next to me at a

---

1 On 1 September Soviet fighters had shot down a South Korean airliner, KAL007, when it accidentally strayed into Soviet airspace. All 269 passengers and crew died.

Cranium Club dinner, suddenly took my hand, prodded the vein at the base of my thumb and said: 'You have a varicosity here. I don't think you have to do anything about it.'[1]

11 September 1983, London

We were woken by Lizzie telephoning from Athens to remind us that we are all going to Covent Garden on Sept 20 for the David Hockney triple bill.[2] She said her week in Greece had been magnificent.

Yesterday we drove to Oxford for the wedding of Quentin Spender to Elizabeth (née Manley) at St Andrew's Church, Old Headington. I went to this occasion in a rather sceptical frame of mind, and left moved and touched. The only discordant note is that Pauline, who wore a bright shocking pink and blue checker dress and a straw hat of a kind called a boater with a band around it of the same material (as the dress) – she looked as if she were leading boy/girl in a panto-mime – insisted on making a corner of the service (which being High Church was also a communion service) into a poetry reading.[3] She read [Philip] Sidney's 'My true love hath my heart and I have his', and Auden's early poem about not knowing a name for love.[4] She was hardly audible and interrupted by squalls from many babies who attended the ceremony. She read the Auden rather coyly, as though it were by A. A. Milne. But finally this, and more poems read even more feebly by a young actor, seemed – in the pathos perhaps of Pauline inserting her little claim to motherhood – to contribute to what was moving in the ceremony. This lay mostly in the enacted

---

1 Desmond MacCarthy (1877–1952), literary journalist and theatre critic. associate of the Bloomsbury group.

2 Hockney did a number of well-received stage designs in the early 1980s, for opera and theatre, including a Stravinsky triple bill. Spender wrote an appreciative essay for the printed exhibition catalogue, recording Hockney's theatrical work.

3 For Quentin Spender and his mother Pauline, see the Spender family in the biographical appendix.

4 Spender refers to Philip Sidney's sonnet 'My true love hath my heart and I have his' (from *The Countess of Pembroke's Arcadia*, 1580) and W. H. Auden's 'O Tell Me The Truth About Love' (1940): 'Some say love's a little boy, / And some say it's a bird.'

seriousness – solemnity even – of the responses given by Quentin and Elizabeth. The service was quite long drawn out and after the marriage vows, the couple were left kneeling in a kind of alcove beyond the altar, very still, almost like figures in wax, or, better, like figures in a medieval missal. They might have been young Elizabethans – especially Quentin with his crisp beard which usually I dislike and which takes away the natural distinction of his features (an effect, I am sure, not at all intended). At the reception – luncheon, champagne – at a hotel called Studley Priory, in pleasant Oxfordshire low-hilled emerald and blue countryside afterwards Quentin seemed to have stepped out of the missal back into his usual self when I greeted him, not introducing me to the bride who stood by his side, and asking curtly 'Where is Lizzie?' then giving his slightly contemptuous little laugh when I answered 'In Greece,' as if to say, 'Just what I expected.' I said it was her annual holiday in her job with Thames and Hudson [publishers] and he smiled with the cynicism of one who knows what work really is (as indeed, I suppose he does). But he stepped back into the role I found moving when he made a speech of thanks which went together with the wedding cake. He managed to make a catalogue of people to thank, light and amusing and really graceful.

15 September 1983, London

Last night the Dufferins, Lindy and Sheridan, and the Leigh Fermors, Paddy and Joan, to dinner. Paddy who has [had] various medical scares and treatments during the past 3 or 4 years looked healthy, spruce, combed and brushed after having gone to drinks with Diana Cooper. It was a loud and very happy reunion with friends we had not seen for ages, and it was 1 a.m. before they left. For a time, at dinner, I thought Lindy was going to monopolize the conversation with her obsessions – homosexuality and the rich. She goes, or sends spies (perhaps her husband) to a gay club called Bus Stop in Leicester Square where everyone is what she calls a clone. They all – and there seem to be about 3,000 of them, are short, squat ugly and togged up in leather. They make passionate love to one another, she said, gluttonously. I said I rather doubted whether they did this: citing bars in Los Angeles where young men go dressed in leather not for sex, not even for conversation (they are completely monosyllabic) but simply for display. She then got onto another subject that obsesses her – the rich. She made out they were always completely peculiar and per se, and they never thought about anything but money.

17 September 1983, London

Yesterday morning I went to Covent Garden – the opera – to see the rehearsal of David Hockney's designs for *Sortilèges*.[1] It looked quite different in Covent Garden from at the Metropolitan Opera in N.Y., where I had seen it a year or so ago. In the Met it was certainly very beautiful but although I had a seat in the stalls, one had a bit the feeling that it was an 'event' looked down at from a height. I had very strongly the feeling of its being staged and of its 3-dimensionality. Here it looked like a stain-glass window in which figures and colours changed constantly as in a kaleidoscope which one was looking at from the nave of a cathedral. The music also seemed to fill the whole theatre and come from every direction – so much so that I thought the orchestra and singers were using some kind of amplifier, but of course this was not so. [. . .] During a pause David came over and kissed me and said, 'We'll have lunch at Bertorelli across the road,' and Gregory [Evans] appeared and also kissed me and sat next to me. Even then, they seemed very changed, David quite different from the rather irritable brushing-off monologuizing David I had been with a few months ago in New York. He seemed then dispossessed of himself, out of tune with Henry Geldzahler and his friend Raymond when we were at the Century Club, not listening – physically deaf but also mentally deaf in some way. When we lunched after the rehearsal he didn't seem even physically deaf, and he seemed entirely at ease with others and himself. Gregory too was sensationally changed: thinner, younger-looking, fresh-complexioned, wide-eyed, short-haired, rather beautiful. They both seemed terribly glad to tell me all their news. Gregory said he had drunk no alcohol for a year. He also said that Ian had been thrown out by David in London.[2] He has a

---

1 Maurice Ravel's one-act opera to a libretto by Colette, *L'Enfant et les sortilèges* (1925).

2 Ian Falconer (b. 1959), American children's author and illustrator who had lived with David Hockney since 1982.

funny way of talking about the discomfiture of his rivals, curiously without malice but with distinct pleasure and a gurgling amusement.

Gregory and David said Christopher [Isherwood] and Don [Bachardy] were well, though Christopher getting very forgetful. 'If you ask him to dinner, he rings up a quarter of an hour after your call and asks what day you have asked him?' said David. He talked about Christopher as though he were just round the corner, and he talked to me as though we were always together and very close – whereas the last few times I have seen him he's talked as though there was a gulf between him and everyone else. It was a good feeling. David said that on Nov 22nd (after his Minneapolis show) he'd be through with all his commitments and he would start painting again – only painting – no more theatre. I believe this. The way he said it was with no looking through a chink to more photography or another opera.

18 September 1983, London

I'm reading the *Oxford Book of Dreams* – sent me for review by *The Listener*. [. . .] The fascination of dreams is that we think of them as a language: a language of vivid images which are symbols. In dreams the image coincides with the symbol. If their language is poetic it is symbolist poetry: and if poetry is dream then there is no such thing as imagist poetry.

Some of the poetry here supposedly about dreams does not really strike one as dream, but simply as romantic poetry. If Keats or Shelley writes in *Endymion* or *Alastor* – as they do of course – 'I dreamed' followed by a narration, the reader does not feel that what follows is any way different from what went before. The whole poem is dreaming. But it is waking dreaming, not real dreaming, though perhaps trance. Since real dreaming real dreams do exist they are in fact something different from romanticy [*sic*] wakeful dreaming. Freud sharply drew attention to the fact that dream was not the same thing as romantic poetic dreaming but was symptomatic of the repression of the unconscious by the conscious mind. The great achievement of Auden in his early poetry – which is largely about Freudian dreaming – is that he replaced the romantic symbol with the Freudian dream symbol which is also a symptom.

In October 1983, Spender went back to New York; this time he was teaching at the Brooklyn campus of CUNY.

19 October 1983, New York

I'm now in New York and have been for four days. Have done little except see people. Am still jet-lagged really, or at any rate, tired. Last night, there was at the Guggenheim Museum the reading of selections of poems of Auden read by several poets, the best of them Jimmy Merrill (who read from Epistle to Lord Byron), Joseph Brodsky, Derek Walcott, May Swenson, Richard Howard, all read.[1] [. . .] I went with Susan Sontag and David Rieff. We had drinks before the reading and were taken out afterwards by Richard Sennett to dine together with Joseph. Susan, David and I went ahead of the other two in a taxi to the restaurant. Susan complained about Joseph, said he was not a good character, was 'boorish'. One cause of her complaining was that she had been asked to talk about Auden on Thursday, when Christopher, Mrs [Ursula] Niehbur (a pain in the ass), Ed Mendelson and I – and also a bearded man called McClutch (I think) who evidently represents some sort of special interest (since he did not know Auden) will speak. Perhaps it's on account of McClutch (I must try to get his name right) that Susan feels she ought to have been asked. Her cause of annoyance was that she had asked Joseph to let her speak and he had said that 'only poets are speaking' – which is palpably untrue. This episode made me realize something about Susan which came as a bit of a shock: that she thinks of herself as a fund of information and opinion which should continually be tapped by some public or other. For her to be a member of the audience when others are speaking and not to be allowed to speak herself is like attending a banquet and being given nothing to eat.

Brodsky was the only poet who knew his Auden poem ('September 1939') by heart, and he said it rhythmically even though the rhythms didn't seem quite the English ones. After the meeting, before going to

---

1 James Merrill (1926–1995), Pulitzer Prize-winning American poet; the poem he read from is Auden's *Letter to Lord Byron* (1937). Derek Walcott (b. 1930), Nobel Prize-winning poet from St Lucia. May Swenson (1913–1989), American poet and playwright. Richard Howard (b. 1929), American poet, translator and academic.

dinner we stood on the pavement outside the Guggenheim Museum. He said to me: 'Aren't you cold without a coat?' I said I was perfectly warm, as in fact the evening was quite hot. Later, at dinner, he said he wouldn't eat as he had a cold. I touched his forehead. It was cold and clammy. I wonder if he is not ill.

Selma Warner my agent writes to me today in tones very unlike her usual friendly and charitable ones. 'Too bad that Mr Brodsky is trying to push into the scene. When he first came into this country, I went to see him at Auden's request who was trying to be of help to him and [I] was treated most discourteously. He at that time made scornful remarks about Auden – strange that he is now trying to ride along on Auden's fame.'

Susan, I think, who is so hostile to Joseph said that there was an element of self-promotion about his promotion of Auden (she also remarked that the poets in the remarks they made before reading their Auden extracts were exceptionally unself-promoting); and also that an article on Auden by Joseph in *Vanity Fair* was really the record of his love for Auden. And I think that is true. Auden is a kind of god for J. He has paid for this week of celebrations, I understand (out of that part of the money he has from the MacArthur award which he is asked to spend on charity).[1] If he spoke scornfully to Mrs W[arner] about A. he probably did so just to shock and annoy a 'dear old lady', who happened to be A.'s literary agent. Brodsky has that kind of infectiously excitable candour and extremism of opinions he utters. He also likes to shock. But he is fundamentally honest, and generous. Hence his attitude to Auden, and also to Derek Walcott. He can say extremely perceptive things which show great critical sense, but he has no sense of critical restraint. I enjoy his company, but am quite glad to get away from him. I don't care very much whether he disapproves or approves of me. I appreciate his friendship but would not worry if he became my enemy. And if he did I'd go on liking what I like about him, and feeling reserved about the rest. [. . .]

I had lunch at the Century Club with Harold Taylor. Since we last met, in the spring, he had had, in June an operation for a cancerous growth in his throat. He had never been ill in his life before this, so it

---

1 Brodsky had received a MacArthur 'Genius Award' in 1981.

had come as a shock to be sent to hospital and have tests and then surgery – an operation of seven hours. He described how the tumour had only been discovered because he had gone skiing and stretched a ligament for which he had hospital treatment and when asked about his medical history and present condition he had mentioned that he had a bad throat. Having known Harold ever since he was the youngest American college president, in 1946, of Sarah Lawrence College, I was overcome again by that feeling with old people I have known for many years, that I know their life stories like a novel which is now at p. 350. There will be a few more and then at the bottom of the page the words THE END.[1]

We talked about the Lillian Hellman–Mary McCarthy case and Lillian's recollection of a party given by N. and me at Sarah Lawrence, at which Mary had attacked Lillian for being a communist. But all the time I was thinking of the whole life of this man sitting opposite me on the other side of the table. Something happened 45 years or so ago. He was the bright young open-minded college president married to a snobbish suburban English wife whose attitude to him was perpetual astonishment, striding the campus with two joke dogs an enormous borzoi-like one and an extremely small long-haired silky haired miniature one. He greeted everyone with a few words in which he managed to encapsulate within an envelope of bright good-fellowliness an underlying hollow sententiousness. The funny thing is that although his sincerity of manner seemed embarrassingly false, he was a very sincere and dedicated spirit. One cause for embarrassment was that whereas his open cheery manner was all on the level of fact and could be frank to the point of being outrageous (once I asked him, concerning his wife, 'How is Muriel?' and he said in a voice which mixed the utter candour of youth with the sincerity concerned in equal portions – 'Well she's not quite such a pain in the ass as she used to be') his seriousness was only expressed in the most abstract terminology, drawn from the philosophy he studied with Dewey, I think after he had given up his earliest career as clarinettist in a jazz orchestra.[2] He was perfectly sincere in getting

---

1 Taylor in fact survived this medical episode to die, aged 78, in 1993.

2 John Dewey (1859–1952), American philosopher and educationist who evolved the theory that children learn best through doing.

to Sarah Lawrence a faculty of really distinguished people. Robert and Helen Lynd authors of the famous early sociological study called *Middletown*, Mary McCarthy, Robert Fitzgerald, Horace Gregory, Randall Jarrell, Sir Bernard Pares – and me.[1] When I was there in 1946, members of the Faculty were always uneasy and defensive when discussing the President. What made matters worse was that this was the beginning of the McCarthy era. Several members of the faculty, notably someone called Trinkus were secretly Communist Party members. Harold told me that he had discovered later on that there was a C.P. cell of about five members on the faculty two of whom he supported when they were summoned for hearings at Senator McCarthy's Un-American Activities Committee and who lied to him saying that they were not party members. Then two of his Faculty – Mary McCarthy and Randell Jarrell – wrote novels about him.[2] This is really his life story – a sensational beginning at Sarah Lawrence, then some staff row (no one quite knows what this was all about) followed by his resignation then a succession of advisory, committee, lecturing, teaching jobs which don't add up to anything. Now his cancer of the throat. He spoke with some difficulty, and ate with even greater, having to chew a great many times. Occasionally his talking and his eating were interrupted by fits of coughing. The meal was rather agonizing but I felt glad I had accepted his invitation. He wants to give a party for me before I leave, at which there will be music. I don't really want this though I feel curious about how it will be. He told me this was the first meal he'd gone to since his illness: and I felt that he has been extraordinarily loyal to his friendship for me (rather than mine for him – because I don't feel I've been a friend to him – or at best only of a very embarrassed kind).

In New York I feel as though I myself had had an operation and that some kind of automatic pilot has been planted in me, which is

---

1 Robert Lynd (1892–1970) and Helen Lynd (1896–1982), married sociologists who produced the famous early-twentieth-century sociological studies of Middletown, based on their findings in the City of Muncie, Indiana. Robert Fitzgerald (1910–1985), American lyric poet and translator of the classics. Horace Gregory (1898–1982), American poet and critic. Sir Bernard Pares (1867–1949), British academic and historian.

2 *The Groves of Academe* (1952) and *Pictures from an Institution* (1954).

composed partly of the traffic in N.Y. and partly an awareness of all the travel and obligations that lie ahead of me. In these circumstances all I can write is this diary – though tomorrow I must write some lecture notes.

I've seen quite a bit of Christopher and Don. They have been put into an apartment on the 15th floor of an ancient skyscraper (once the tallest in New York someone told me) One Fifth Avenue. It has an extensive very brown living room – with huge bits of brown wooden or sham-leather-covered furniture, brown walls, brown abstract paintings on the walls, a brown floor. Christopher looks at the floor and says 'It is amazingly clean. You can tell the people who own it must be millionaires because it is so clean, when everything else in N.Y. is so dirty.' Don looks at him with shining eyes an enormous grin, and occasionally hoots with laughter, his eyes even more shining. The thought occurs to me 'Don has been laughing at Christopher for thirty years' followed by the thought 'when Christopher dies, what will Don have to laugh at?' Somehow it is an appalling thought, worse than just thinking, how will Don face being alone. There's something so positive about someone attentively watching someone else's gestures and being immensely, unceasingly amazed. I said to them in the lift when we were going down to the Auden memorial banquet, 'Don's been laughing at Chris for thirty years.' Don laughed and said: 'Oh but I can assure you, sometimes it has been no laughing matter.'

The lunch was very crowded, noisy, almost impossible to hear anything said. I sat next to John Ashbery who was extremely nice. Christopher was on my right, and extremely silent – Don on his left. After a bit I changed places with John Ashbery, putting him next to Chris, explaining that I shouldn't monopolize Chris since I would be staying with him in L.A. next month. But C. didn't say much to John. He said that last night had done him in. He does look shrunken and frail. For some reason he cuts his hair very short now so that it seems to consist of sparse bristles, stubs of hair through which one sees the pink skin. With his body still squatter than when Auden wrote about its squatness, his round head, beaky nose, and bright eyes staring ahead of him – his rather wide mouth – he looks amusingly like a bird, a robin perhaps, which has lost the feathers on its head. He has a habit, when he stands up, of flapping his arms against his sides, as though they were wings, and in his uncommunicative moods, occasionally he lets out about half a bar of a tune being hummed inside his head, or, sometimes, a minute squawk. Joseph Brodsky sat at the next table. I leaned across and said I had to thank him that my fee was larger than I expected. He said: 'Oh that's nothing.' Later he said – apropos I forget of what – 'I think of you as being extremely self-effacing.'

After the banquet we were all driven to 77 St Mark's Place where quite large, and bronze, and with nice italic lettering, hammered into the wall was the plaque for Wystan. Some representative of the Mayor read out a very elegant proclamation inscribed on a sheet of what I suppose was parchment.

I drove with Maro who quite unexpectedly turned up at the ceremony, having discovered from N. that I am in New York and from the Institute of Humanities my immediate whereabouts – 77 St Mark's Place. She was cheerful but tired after flying yesterday from Rome.

Dinner given for me by the [Earl and Camilla] McGraths. Christopher and Don were there, also a very beautiful Miss Dumenil daughter of Mrs Dumenil of Texas and a great heiress. Keith Milow who was there became glued to her, hustling but perhaps also genuinely fascinated. They left the party together after everyone else had gone, Earl [McGrath] tells me. There were a lot of people there, most of whom I knew vaguely. I sat next to Camilla McGrath who is wonderfully firm and rooted and she talked uncomplainingly, with tolerant amusement about Earl who in his career seizes wrong opportunities and misses right ones. 'I hope you keep your fortune independent of his finances,' I said. 'Oh but I do' she said. 'It drives him mad, but what would be the sense of us both being ruined by his follies. Someone has to stay solid' – and that is what she is like a piece of sculpture hewn from the trunk of a tree – not smart or elegant but magnificent and with a kind of gleaming self-assertiveness. She complained rather bitterly about Gian Carlo [Menotti]; how he was such an old friend, how she had gladly provided a bourse [scholarship] for one of his students, how he had given a concert two days ago in New York and had never got in touch with them. She said Gian Carlo was the one of Sam [Barber] and Gian-Carlo who had always made the greatest protestations of friendship but Sam, sour and difficult, provided the real friendship and was the real talent.

Earl had told me that a few days ago when he was in L.A.,

Christopher got more sensationally drunk than he had ever seen anyone – and he did the same last night. He was paralytically drunk when he and Don left, flapping his arms, smiling, occasionally emitting a kind of grunt which was the overflow of some interior symphony, occasionally a bark which was meant for us all. Don stood by, perfectly calm, watching him with his appreciative smile, not saying a word, but obviously not at all alarmed and perfectly ready to take him home and put him to bed.

I must now write two lectures – damn.

In October 1983, the wives of Samuel Reed and John Fairchild organized another reading to fund-raise for Index, *this time at the Metropolitan Museum in New York. Now, in addition to Spender and Brodsky, Derek Walcott and John Ashbery also read poems. Spender also went on another lecture tour of America and visited Reynolds Price in North Carolina.*

30 October 1983, North Carolina

[. . .] this week is one which I am profoundly grateful to find is over [. . .] In the evening there was a banquet for all the grand and rich people in Atlanta who had contributed to make the reading by Brodsky, Derek Walcott and me [in New York] possible. They were extremely well dressed, the ladies particularly, a select few of them with huge diamonds and very cordial, though it was impossible to have any conversation except with Anne [Chambers] on whose right I sat. One of my legs had become completely lame – I should have mentioned – and felt as if it were made of wood. I really could hardly walk, and I felt a bit worried in case I had a blood clot or something and would embarrass Anne by having a stroke in her house. Somehow Anne with her amazing awareness and attention had taken this in – though I had said nothing – and made me sit down throughout the evening, not letting me rise to greet anyone. Emily was there, as cool and conspiratorially smiling as in France. I sat next to Mary Ellmann before and after dinner. She surveyed the scene with a wild eye I thought. Dick Ellmann also seemed a bit reserved about it, though cordial with me. (I so wish Anne really got to know the Ellmanns but fear Mary will dish this.) [. . .]

[. . .] we found that Derek Walcott had cancelled, as his flight from Boston had been cancelled. I was dreading that Joseph Brodsky would also do so and I would be left with the whole evening on my hands. In fact he turned up just as we were seated on the platform when Anne was in the middle of her excellent introductory remarks. In these she quoted from what Natasha had told her about Brodsky coming to London and staying with us at Loudoun Road after he had been with Auden in Vienna for a few days [in 1972]. She showed her extraordinary attention and very accurate memory. The reading went very well[;] in fact Joseph said afterwards he would always be glad to appear on a platform with me. He read poems in English then in Russian. Somehow if one has heard the English, with his kind of Russian rhythm and style of chanting imposed on it, then his reading of the poem in Russian adds to it even if one doesn't know a word of Russian. But the best part of the evening turned out to be the question and answer period – Joseph was absolutely at his best, taking great trouble and answering questions in a very detailed way. After this there was dinner at Anne['s] – Anne, her daughter Kathy and her boyfriend, Brodsky, I only – and Joseph talked about Russia and politics. He said a lot that was very interesting such as that in his view there was no prospect of any dissidents, racial minority or alternate party altering the nature of the Russian state and system. The succession could not lead to the emergence of some liberal leader in the way that hereditary succession could lead to the emergence of some liberal Czar. On the contrary it could only go from bad to worse – the tendency of the succession at present was towards a military dictatorship. Russia could only be looked on today as a power wishing to rule the whole world. His view was unrelievedly pessimistic.

On Friday morning a man and two rather attractive ladies came to the house to consult Brodsky and me as to what could be done to help a scholar called Mikhail Meilakh from Leningrad who is now being held in a K.G.B. investigation prison in Leningrad prior to trial for 'anti-Soviet agitation and propaganda'.[1] 'We understand that you

---

1 Mikhail Meilakh (b. 1945), Russian linguist, translator and literary scholar arrested in Leningrad by the KGB in 1983 for possession of such 'subversive' literature as novels by Nabokov. The case aroused considerable interest in America, and a protest article in the *New York Review of Books* by Lev Losoff (18 August 1983). He was released four years later.

are a friend of Mikhail Meilakh,' said the Amnesty man, 'and we'd like your opinion about the best way in which we can go about helping your friend.' Joseph said, rather surprisingly, in view of the charges made against Meilakh, 'I ought to make clear first of all. . . – I'll explain later why I do this – that in the Soviet Union there are two main categories of punishment – one imprisonment for criminal offences, second, imprisonment for political offences. It is much better to be imprisoned for criminal offences because when you get out of prison you may be able to work your way back into the society and your crime be more or less forgotten – but if you are imprisoned for political offences it can always be held against you and it's never forgotten and you can never really find your way back into the society. I tell you this because I think that Meilakh will be punished as a criminal.'

'But isn't he a scholar, a historian?' asked one of the ladies.

'Yes certainly he is a very fine scholar.'

'And he is a friend of yours?'

'Yes, indeed he is a friend of mine.'

'Why do you think he will be tried on a criminal charge?'

'Well to make this clear I have to tell you something of his background and history. In the first place I ought to say that his father [Boris] who is mentioned in the paper you've given me as a prominent Soviet literary figure and expert in Medieval French is the greatest scoundrel in the Soviet Union.' (I forget whether he went into details substantiating this.) Then he said: 'It is true that the son is a very fine scholar . . .' Brodsky said I think that his speciality was both Provençal and modern literature during the revolutionary period. He explained that for his work Meilakh depended on foreign sources. At first he used his contacts with foreign scholars living in Moscow and Leningrad, through whom he obtained material. Later, he had exhausted these, so through his contacts he started buying books from abroad. In order to get the money to do this he traded in exporting antiques – icons, dolls and other Russian rarities. He did very well in this and had, like his father who was one of the richest men in Russia, a high standard of living. Then he moved from this trade into dealing in narcotics. Mikhail Meilakh was arrogant and conceited, contemptuous of nearly everybody he worked with – not very much liked – and he became careless in his dealings. 'Oh, and I forgot to mention,' added Brodsky, 'that he is also a homosexual.' There was a pause filled by the Amnesty man asking: 'What have you left out?' 'I told you all this,' said Brodsky, 'to make clear why I think the proceedings against him will be criminal rather than political. Now my advice to you is to act [as] though you do not know any of the things I've told you.' And he went on to discuss with them whom they should write to in Moscow and Leningrad and what they should say in their letters.

Brodsky's message seemed to be that they should expect and, indeed, wish that Meilakh got a criminal sentence, rather than a political one: but his good will towards his friend was not evident. He talked about his criminality with gusto and seemed to be thoroughly enjoying himself. In fact, if it had not been that Meilakh's future was at stake I would have found Brodsky's attitude extremely amusing. He may in fact have been giving Amnesty good advice: know who your man is (I am telling you) and proceed cautiously with this knowledge in mind, but as though you know nothing about it.

I wondered whether there was not something very Russian about Brodsky's behaviour though: a kind of pleasure in demonstrating to the credulous supporters of a victim, that the victim was by no means innocent of crimes (even if the crimes were not those he was accused of – but in fact far worse), proving thereby Brodsky's superior knowledge. This, combined with protestations of friendship for the victim, made the more delectable by betraying him. One thought of some Russian dish, served up with sauces, and cooked according to some elaborate recipe. This reminded me of Nicolas Nabokov who certainly was not averse to betraying a friend, if he could demonstrate to another friend of that friend, that he knew the friend in question more profoundly and intimately than the other one who had been taken in by his superficial (i.e. good) qualities, did. But Brodsky had come all the way to Atlanta to give a reading for which he received no fee in order to oblige me (for he doesn't really care a fig about *Index*). He had arranged when I was in New York (for the Auden week which he had organized) that I got a fee three times that which I had expected, some of which perhaps came out of his own pocket ($1500 instead of $500). He had said after our reading together: 'I would always be glad to appear on any platform together with you,

Stephen.' All these pieces of his character seem to lie on a table in front of me and I can't put them together.

9 November 1983, Charleston, West Virginia

[Last week in San Francisco] I was taken to the airport by the member of the faculty who had also met me there. He was a bit flaccid, reserved, pale, interesting-looking. En route to the airport (unfortunately it only took ten minutes to get there) he told me that he had been a close friend of Tennessee Williams in Key West, and that Tennessee, whose sister and brother more or less gave up trying to look after him at the end of his life, would have liked him to help look after him, but much as he loved Tennessee (that he did so, was obvious from all he said) he realized that to be the constant companion of Tennessee would be utterly destructive to him.[1] He said that at the end of his life, Tennessee was in a constant state of mental depression, that he drank a lot and took an enormous quantity of pills which he shovelled into his mouth in handfuls. He said that all the capital of experience and impressions which went into Tennessee's work was already there when he was sixteen in New Orleans and that he spent his life drawing on them. When T. died he was worth (I think) ten million dollars. I had that sense of waste not just of talent but of capacity to enjoy success and money which seems to have destroyed so many American writers – Roethke, Jarrell, Lowell, Berryman, Tennessee. One can think of all sorts of reasons – more or less creditable for this – they are all unhappy Hamlets driven to extremes of unhappiness by the rotten state of Denmark (America) – but they are also surely very self-indulgent, ungrateful, arrogant and excessive. Auden's reaction to them is summed up in the remark he made on repeated occasions when he met Cal Lowell – to Cal and Elizabeth *ad nauseam* – 'gentlemen don't go mad.' There is certainly a sense in which they showed a lack of self-restraint which seems ungentlemanly – though they would have sneered, I suppose, at the idea of being a gentleman. But they were not frauds. If they measured

---

1 Tennessee Williams (1911–1983), Pulitzer Prize-winning American playwright who had died in February after choking on an eye-drop bottle cap in his hotel room in New York.

themselves as well-read, passionately dedicated, loving and creative makers of their art, against the commercialism, distractedness, vulgarity of the public and political, and pedantically intellectual life of their America – they did really represent the values and achievements they stood for. Perhaps some of the Gadarene swine were learned and intelligent animals who hurled themselves down the hill because they were disgusted by the world on top of it.[1]

8 July 1984, St Jerome

Alone here, because N went this morning to London in order to receive her fellowship or honorary degree on Monday and, later in the week, attend a banquet at the R.C.A. There is no doubt she had to go, although she was unhappy at having to leave on a beautiful morning and when she is making progress with the garden, and for me to be alone. [. . .] The trouble about being alone is that one is not alone but haunted. One's family being here prevents one from being haunted by them. Their physical presence acts as a kind of cork bottling up their full emotional significance. When N is here working in the garden, if I can't find her I think 'she's working in the garden. I know where she is.' I don't have to think about it. The moment she's gone away I'm haunted by a tremendously poignant ghostly her getting up at 6 A.M. to weed and water, buying plants to stick into our terribly bad soil, and each separate piece of gardening appears with its real significance as an act of love. This whole house is kept together by her emotions running through it like the force of gravity without which it would collapse.

20 September 1984, St Jerome

All the summer no line from Bryan who has been I know to Alaska and other places. He owed me a letter because he should have acknowledged one containing things from me. I began to have the

---

1 A biblical reference to Mark 5, verses 1–20; Matthew 8, verses 28–34 and Luke 8, verses 26–39. Spender alludes to the herd of pigs into which Jesus, preaching in the territory of the Gadarenes, cast the demons that had possessed a madman. As a result, the pigs ran down a steep cliff into the Sea of Galilee and were drowned.

kind of complicated feelings which go with a friend not writing. One knows that not getting a letter means nothing. Your friend may have been meaning to write, and then through delay and a sense of guilt felt it more and more difficult to do so. He may feel that a letter is an insult (whereas one knows that just his handwriting on a one-line postcard is reassuring), he may think he has written when he hasn't done so (I do this – I think out a letter then imagine later that I have written it). After three months I began to feel I had the right to be hurt. In my own mind I sketched reproachful letters. Then I thought I must not reproach him – after eight years being nearly 50 years younger than I, he has a perfect right to forget me, and I would ruin all that past if I wrote angrily – perhaps ending our relationship on that note. Besides he might really be hurt. Actually his whole career since we met has been a vindication of my belief in him. I know perfectly well that if he had been in any way dependent on me, I would have become bored with him. Anyway, finally I thought the only thing was to phone him and show I was a bit hurt. I did this. He said he had written and was distressed I hadn't got the letter. How long was I staying in France? He'd write again at once. Then we spoke of our summers and it was all calm and clear like we've always been. His letter arrived yesterday. As usual it begins "Dear S" – not dearest – in fact he is oddly like Matthew and Lizzie in being very undemonstrative. He is so gifted as a writer without his at all knowing it that I am dazzled by things he writes. His descriptions can be beautiful, absolutely straightforward and accurate scientific accounts and yet I am sure written to please me. Being a person who works with animals his way of showing affection is like an animal's, simply in certain beautiful appropriateness.

11 November 1984, Los Angeles

I am now in Los Angeles, having been to Beaumont Houston to give a reading [. . .] On Friday Mr Gwynne drove me back to the airport [from Houston]. I almost missed the plane which was jam-packed and where I was very lucky to get a seat where I could stretch my legs. I shared a taxi with a man going to Santa Monica and arrived at the Shangri-la Hotel where B[ryan] joined me in half an hour. We went to Christopher and Don's and had drinks there. Christopher seemed very spry. He said – 'Don't be afraid of being eighty'. Don showed us new pictures – male nudes he is doing. He seems to be moving towards something like German Expressionism. His method is to complete work in about an hour of frenzied dance-like activity which certainly gives his work rhythm. But he has no gift or use for contemplation and his colours and brush strokes are posterish.

We had dinner at a Japanese restaurant. After this went back to Chris and Don's for a night-cap. Then B drove me back to my hotel, coming up to my room to say goodnight. He said – 'I have the feeling that I'm doing well now and I want to say that nothing of what I'm doing would have happened without you. If I hadn't met you I'd be back in Florida, teaching school or being a vet or something.' I felt too that I owed an enormous amount to having met him. He said – 'I feel that our meeting was like an act of recognition between us, which we've never gone back on. I'm glad that things are as they are and that we don't go to supermarkets buying food together.' I felt this too.

Saturday morning woke at 7, thinking it was 9. Had breakfast and then walked to the Mall and bought a pen and changed my ticket to N.Y. tomorrow. I up-graded it because I simply cannot bear the idea of being cooped up tourist for nearly six cramped hours, and arriving at N.Y. utterly exhausted. Had lunch with B at the fish restaurant near the pier. It is his 28th birthday. I asked him to describe his life when he was in a ship near Alaska, then his life in Antarctica, then his deep-sea diving off the coast of California. [. . .] We walked back after luncheon to the Shangri-la – this hotel – I asked him about the risk of Aids and whether he thought about it. He said he thought about it a lot but if, as seemed the case, one could catch it through kissing another person, what could one do about it? There was a test now by which one could find out whether one was immune from it (have I got this right?) but what was the point of taking such a test unless one had already decided to give up sex if one was not immune. He had friends who had given up sex and they became unhappy and distressed.

I felt I could not possibly advise him about this, though he seemed to want to know what I thought. All I indicated was that one felt particularly anxious – apprehensive – today about people who seemed exceptionally gifted – the people we most needed – fearful that they were doomed. I was thinking of Reynolds Price, for whom B has a lot of sympathy, through hearing about him through me.

He went back to his work. I phoned Christopher [. . .] C said: We seem to meet always at these parties and not to talk alone together. So I wished at that moment that I had not made a date to meet Dagne for drinks, so I could jump into a taxi and see Chris.

B told me he was going to have his hair set and to change for the party which 20 of his friends and colleagues were giving for his birthday. He returned to pick me up at 7. He was transformed, his hair cut in punk style like a crest – this made him look like a very charming and lively cockatoo – leather jacket over a white shirt, black bow tie, leather trousers. He was laughing, swaggering a bit. [. . .] On our way to the party I started wishing I was not there. I wondered whether B was perhaps proud of his friendship with me, had boasted about knowing this famous me to his friends and [whether] I was brought here to show I really existed. I dreaded going into the restaurant where his friends seated at table were waiting for me to 'appear', as when I give a reading or lecture. As a matter of fact, when I did go in, no one raised his head to look at me, and the girl I sat next to on one side at the table, explained apologetically that she had not the faintest idea who I was, nor did she seem enlightened when I told her – What did I write? She seemed faintly put off when I admitted it was poetry, and did not pursue her inquiries. The girl on my left did know but what interested her was that I had known B so much longer than anyone else in the room. She was Beth, and I liked her enormously as I had thought I would. Beautiful in a rather intellectual thoughtful way with her black hair prematurely greying, swept back, searching eyes. We talked about B. A shock for me was to discover there was this kind of Bryan club. Bryan who was at a round table which had been drawn up close to the one at which I was sitting – there were about eighteen people in all – was flushed, excited, nervous, rather drunk (he gets drunk on two glasses of anything) trying to entertain the party. Three or four people had brought him presents. When he is flushed like that his forehead and cheeks look pock-marked. When I looked at him he did not look back at me but I felt he was aware of it and did not want me to look at him. I remembered the time in Gainesville eight years ago when at dinner in a restaurant he suddenly got up and said, 'Change places with me,' and put me in that chair that was next to a tank of tropical fish. 'Look at those,' he said. I felt divided between a sense of triumph that this person who had seemed so alone when I first knew him was now the toast of his colleagues, and a kind of regret. Beth said: 'B is nervous. He is afraid people are not enjoying themselves. He is over-sensitive.' And in fact he was the only person there trying to make this party which seemed to split up into little groups of three or four people – all of them a bit scruffy and dishevelled – entertaining in a general way. I told Beth that within five minutes of our first meeting in Gainesville, I had thought that Bryan was extremely perceptive and exceptionally sweet-natured. She said he was these things, he was also extremely well thought of as a biologist at U.C.L.A. The fact is that nearly everyone at the table reflected that kind of preoccupation and anxiety about the future which afflicts graduate students. The fuzzy-headed girl on my left told me she had had to go into a job in advertising: 'I hate it' she said, 'it is degrading. I hate everything to do with advertising.' The curly headed and curly-bearded young man on her left said rallyingly – 'Oh no, you like it really. You can't take me in.' She hissed at him like a cat and said: 'I hate anyone who says I like it,' and he subsided, crushed.

B evidently felt something was required of him to mark the occasion. He got up to his feet and said: 'I want to thank you all. When you come to California I've always understood you have to dig very hard to find gold and I've dug hard and found gold in my friends here. Everyone I most love is in this room.' Then he went round the two joined together tables, hugging every person in turn, beginning with me – or do I just think he began with me.

The food was populist Chinese, rather like what you get in the People's Republic. There seemed a lot of tripe of assorted kinds, stewed clams (very good sauce) roast duck etc. B's ex-lover Michael (the one who makes miniature models of houses) refused to eat any of this, which he clearly regarded as oriental garbage, and went off at the end of the party in search of a hamburger. I was left with B, his grizzle-bearded benign-looking friend Bob (a computer expert), and one or two others who wanted to see what they called The Sign. This was in a high building at the end of a parking lot not far from the restaurant. It is a vertical red-light strip, which if you look at it suddenly or turn your head back and forth when you look at it gives off a kind of aura which spells out the letters A.R.T. After that B, Bob and I left the others and the two B's drove me back to my hotel, B murmuring from time to time 'Oh, I feel so sick.' I was reminded of our trip to New Orleans. They put me down at the Shangri-la hotel. Next morning (yesterday) when I rang B from the airport he seemed extremely well and cheerful.

There are no surviving journals written by Spender between 1985 and 1990.

28 September 1990, London

Moravia has died.[1] I first met Alberto Moravia at an international conference of the PEN Club in the summer of 1957 in Tokyo. He looked greatly distinguished and famous but at the same time personal and sympathetic and, moreover, a bit alarming. He did not look in the least Jewish – more like an ancient Roman. His head seemed to ask to be sculpted in the classical Roman style, in marble. I hope there is a marble bust of him somewhere.

We think of Italians as effervescently happy, charming and delightful. But the Italian writers I have met on several occasions – Moravia, [Eugenio] Montale, [Ignazio] Silone, Elio Vittorini, [Nicola] Chiaromonte – have struck me as among the most melancholy people I have ever met in my life. With Moravia and Montale I began to guess at the causes of their melancholy. They felt themselves perhaps to belong spiritually to the Italy of the Renaissance or at least of the Risorgimento. They were spiritual exiles in the Italy of Fascism, the war and of *La Dolce Vita*.[2] Yet perhaps the foreigner's idea of the ever-effervescent Italian is a bit of a delusion anyway.

---

1 Alberto Moravia (1907–1990), Italian novelist best known for *Il Conformista* (1947), had died on 26 September.

2 Federico Fellini's 1960 film *La Dolce Vita* depicts the excesses of the glittery world of 1950s Italian celebrity culture.

1 January 1992, midnight, London

If I take this notebook, given me by Lizzie and write in it with the Waterman pen also given me by Lizzie, perhaps I'll be able to keep a diary in 1992.

At the age of 82, I feel tired and can only work effectively in the morning. Also am sleeping later sometimes getting up at 9.30 instead of 8.30. But there seems to be more pressure on me than I can remember having for many years. Pressure of things I want to write – poems – and my novel which I want to alter drastically – and of obligations – journalism – letters – business matters.[1] It seems a race to keep up with time shrinking every day – and running out in weeks and months rather than years.

There is also a wish to receive and enjoy and educate [myself] – the negative pressure of the outside world which is perhaps more important at this age than the positive one of work. I want to read, to listen to music to improve myself as apart from impressing myself upon the world. The two processes go together of course: but if one is 'working' – writing – there is always the feeling that everything else is categorized as 'not working'.

5 January 1992, London

Luncheon at the Annans. Other guests were John Golding, James Joll, Rupert Christiansen (author two years ago of a *terrible* review of my *Journals* in *The Spectator*), Jill Day Lewis, and a very intelligent and interesting Catalan – a poet.[2] [...] After lunch I found myself inextricably seated by the side of Jill who poured herself out about the projected publication of Cecil's Collected Poems.[3] She said that Cecil would feel deeply deeply hurt if he were alive at the lack of interest of *everyone* in his poetry. No one ever mentions him in the

---

1 Spender was writing *Miss Pangbourne*, a novel that would remain unfinished when he died in 1995. It was based on the housekeeper, Winifred Paine, who looked after the four young Spender children at the family house in Frognal when their parents died.

2 Spender's *Journals 1939–1983* had been published by Faber in 1985.

3 Cecil Day Lewis's *Complete Poems*, edited by Jill Balcon, would be published by Sinclair Stevenson in May 1992.

press except to be disparaging about him, and very few trouble even to be that. I told her that this happens to most poets after they are dead: but perhaps thirty years later they emerge again as part of their period, as happens, say, with poets in anthologies of periods or centuries. 'But Auden is not forgotten,' she said. 'Auden is another matter –' She told me her son Daniel, working in North Carolina, has been through fantastic training in order to star in a movie of Fenimore Cooper's *Last of the Mohicans*.[1] He has had to diet and take vigorous exercise month after month, living in a hut somewhere, in order to shed all fat while putting on a great deal of musculature.

9 January 1992, London

Over lunch yesterday I took Natasha's excellent essay about olive picking to David Plante for him to print out on his Amstrad (the printer of ours is broken).[2] He is having what he calls 'delicate negotiations' with Hamish Hamilton about his publishing future. Seeing his (their! Niko's and his!) flat so perfectly tidy with all their books and pictures a piece of sculpture like a stone altar piece in their sitting room for which they have recently acquired a beautiful sofa, I thought that the glue which enables them to fit together their different characters in a relationship is that they are, both of them, perfectly tidy.

12 January 1992, London

I was worried at having heard no word from either Reni or Adrian [Brendel] in acknowledgement to my Christmas gift of Vol. I of John Osborne's memoirs to Adrian.[3] I thought perhaps that Reni considered this a most unsuitable gift for a schoolboy (my own view was

---

1 *The Last of the Mohicans*, dir. Michael Mann (1992). Daniel Day-Lewis spent several months living off the land in the wilderness prior to making the film.

2 Natasha Spender's reminiscences of olive picking in Maussane would later be incorporated into her 1999 book, *An English Garden in Provence*.

3 Irene (Reni) Semler, Alfred Brendel's wife since 1975. Adrian Brendel (b. 1976), cellist son of Alfred and Irene Brendel. The first volume of John Osborne's memoirs, *A Better Class of Person* (1981) is dominated by an extended account of Osborne's difficult relationship with his barmaid mother.

that as an Austrian living in a very privileged milieu in England, it would do him good to read about the horrors of lower middle class England here described).

So I telephoned the Brendels and immediately got Alfred. He was very reassuring and said it was simply that (much to his own annoyance) his children were bad at answering letters. Then he said: 'I am going to Japan at 5 this afternoon. I have a strange suggestion. Would you like to come and hear me play two Beethoven sonatas at 2 p.m. or 2.30 at latest?' I was overwhelmed and said: 'Natasha will have to drive me. Can she come too?' 'Ah, but she is a pianist. That will make me nervous.' 'All right, I'll come alone.' 'No, she may come too.' We turned up at 2.15 and scarcely more than greeting us in his welcoming hugging manner with his broad smile accompanied by his deep comically despairing 'Oh' of a sigh, he took us immediately to his music room which has double doors leading into the sitting room where he could place us without seeing us at all. Then he played Opus 31 no. 2 and Opus 101. These works happen to be associated with earliest days at Oxford with N. soon after we were married: the unearthly voice from a tomb passage from the 1st movement of Opus 31 no. 2, the beautifully serene opening of Opus 101 which rather unexpectedly leads into a work in the manner of late Beethoven Quartets. It was wonderful to hear these as though from inside the piano. Brendel told Natasha that Czerny's notes to Opus 31 were very interesting.[1]

As we left he told us about his Japanese journey, which goes on for 3 weeks till the end of the month. 'I feel jet-lagged already,' he said with his woeful comic sigh. He has to play two concerts with the Berlin Philharmonic, Brahms Concerti 1 and 2 and to give two recitals. I went away thinking I would sooner be dead than have to undertake any corresponding such ordeal. A great performer combines in his person both master and slave – perhaps any great artist does.

---

1 The Austrian pianist and composer Carl Czerny (1791–1857) was a student of Beethoven who edited and wrote about Beethoven's sonatas.

15 January 1992, London

Last night to Nigel Nicolson's 75th birthday party at Grouchos – a very good party with George Weidenfeld, Lord and Lady Egremont, James and Alvilde Lees-Milne, the Frank Gileses and the Norwiches, Ed Victor, etc.[1] Excellent speeches by Weidenfeld, Nigel, and Nigel's daughter Juliet Nicolson. I sat between Alvilde and Kitty Giles. Alvilde began by complaining about the red wine which was Gigondas. I said that Gigondas had improved immeasurably as she would find if she tasted it. She had to admit that I was right. About the rack of lamb she asked rhetorically, 'How do they expect me to eat this, but I suppose I can't send it away!' She then went on to talk about Mick Jagger for whom she is designing a garden. I said that Rory Cameron until he got ill was doing interior decoration for M.J.'s house. 'Oh, Rory wanted to scrap half of the objects of M.J. Then he got impatient hanging around for Mick who never gets up before lunch. The thing is with these people, you have to accept their taste.' We got on so well that she was soon asking me whether we could come for a weekend to Badminton. I weakly said yes but I don't see how I could have said no.

By a merciful dispensation before the last course the placement was changed and now I was put between Lady Rupert Nevill and Rebecca Philipps, wife of Rosamond Lehmann's grandson Guy Philipps.[2] With Lady R.N. I talked about music. She was very pleasant and likes Beethoven Quartets. I longed to ask her about the Queen but didn't dare do so. R.P. seemed very bright and intelligent. She described Wogan Philipps (Rosamond's second husband with whom I travelled to Spain). He sounded much the same as he had always been. I told her about the article I had just written for *Index*. She enthused about this and said she would try to get it also for *The*

---

1 Lord and Lady Egremont, patrons of the arts and owners of Petworth House and Park in East Sussex. James Lees-Milne (1908–1997), British architectural conservationist and writer. In 1951, he had married Avilde Lees-Milne (née Chaplin) (1909–1994), a writer on gardens and a landscape designer. Frank Giles (b. 1919), British journalist, at this date literary editor of the *Sunday Times*. Ed Victor (b. 1939), literary agent responsible for representing Spender.

2 Lady Rupert Nevill (b. 1925), widow of Lord Rupert Nevill (1923–1982). Queen Elizabeth II (b. 1926) is the godmother to Lady Rupert Nevill's son.

Observer. She said that Graham-Yooll, editor of *Index*, was an extremely reticent man who never wanted to be drawn out of his office.[1]

23 January 1992, London

On both Monday and Tuesday went to parties at the Reform Club, Monday for the *Daily Telegraph*, Tuesday Desert Island Discs. Both parties attended by a lot of politicians. [. . .] Someone introduced me to Norman Lamont the Chancellor of the Exchequer whom I've always disliked on TV, but whom I found quite amiable when meeting him.[2] Denis Healey at both parties, always friendly, forthcoming, amusing: unlike Roy Jenkins who gets stuffier and stuffier. Ted Heath reproached me for not coming to visit him in Salisbury. Since Thatcher went he has become genial.[3]

The *D.T.* party much better than the D.I.D. one, because the *D.T.* people had quite a lot in common, and because the conservatives there were the liveliest and most intelligent of their tribe. At such gatherings one has the feeling that the minorities of the House of Commons are just for show, the act for which the performers are hired, where, behind scenes, all the participants are on good terms with one another, like members of the same club.

Peregrine Worsthorne was at the *D.T.* party.[4] I said I missed his editorials in the *Sunday Telegraph*. He said he had been writing there for

---

1 Andrew Graham-Yooll (b. 1944), British journalist and writer, born in Argentina. Graham-Yooll came to Britain in 1976, after being branded a communist by the government of Juan Carlos Ogania for his journalism in the *Buenos Aires Herald*. In 1989, he had become the editor of the *Index on Censorship*.

2 Norman Lamont (b. 1942), Conservative MP, at this date serving as Chancellor of the Exchequer.

3 Edward ('Ted') Heath had been British Prime Minister between 1970 and 1974 before the miners' crisis encouraged Heath to call a snap election which resulted in a Labour victory. In 1975, Margaret Thatcher, then Education and Science Secretary, ousted Heath as Conservative leader. Heath was relegated to the backbenches and a long political feud ensued. Thatcher resigned as prime minister in 1990.

4 Peregrine Worsthorne (b. 1923), British journalist, editor of the *Daily Telegraph*, 1986–9.

40 years and now he must stop – except, he added, that he was after all going on writing for them, because he needed the money. I mentioned Garvin and *The Observer*, who wrote editorials of interminable length over an interminable period of time.[1] He said that if one went on for so long one found oneself getting more and more extreme and sensational in what one wrote, because one was afraid of losing one's public and to be extreme was the only way of keeping it. [. . .]

To review for the *Sunday Times* I've been reading an anthology of pieces – stories, poems, journals etc – about the Second World War, edited by Mordechai Richler.[2] I am always amazed by the way in this century, society seems divided in two halves: those who have had to live and endure and suffer and be killed by historic events, and those who have remained outside them or on the sidelines. When I woke this morning it struck me that this division in our civilization was like that of some Oriental city – Cairo perhaps – into the City of the Living and the almost equally impressive City of the Dead. The two go on side by side, one city bustling with people, traffic, bazaars, the other [with] spirits, ghosts.

26 January 1992, London

Yesterday we drove to the Palumbos – Peter and Hayat's – house in the country.[3] A rather misty day with bursts of sunshine. Our fellow-guests were George Weidenfeld and his new lady friend Annabelle Whitestone. They intend to get married in August. George seemed absolutely transformed. He started reminiscing about how we had met at the end of the war and had discussed my editing a magazine he was to start, called *Contact*. I could not accept the job because I was going to America to teach at Sarah Lawrence College. How I told him there was a very brilliant man who I was sure would make a good editor. His name was Philip Toynbee. How Philip and he became close friends but owing to paper restrictions imposed by the

---

1 James Louis Garvin (1868–1947), editor of the *Observer*, 1908–42.

2 Mordechai Richler, *Writers on World War Two* (1991).

3 Peter Palumbo (b. 1935), collector of art and architecture, one-time owner of Mies van der Rohe's Farnsworth House. He was Chairman of the Arts Council, 1988–93.

Labour Govt. it was not possible to start a new magazine. However another young man called Harold Wilson who had just been taken up by Attlee, suggested a way out: that *Contact* should consist of a sequence of books or miscellanies each devoted principally to one topic – *Contact Books 1, 2, 3, 4* etc. How this arrangement had continued for 4 years. How George got to know Philip's friends from 'Out of Bounds' days, chief of them Giles Romilly.[1] Mention of Giles touched a very tender chord in me, how I had met him (and Gavin Ewart) through T. C. Worsley, how Giles had met Tony Hyndman and had an affair with him and later they both ran off to Spain.[2] No perhaps later, because I was at Medes with Helen Low and perhaps my brother Humphrey.[3] Gavin and Giles stayed at a kind of extension of the hotel leading their desultory charming life. Giles dressed up as an Austrian girl in a dirndl – memory of this led to memory of Giles after the war coming to London, having escaped near Munich from a prison camp at the end of the war disguised (or do I imagine this?) as a girl and wearing a dirndl. Giles' sad life, which George filled in with memories of his [Giles's] having kidnapped his two (?) children and taken them to America when his marriage broke up. The curious ineffectiveness of Giles contrasted with his brother Esmond. 'But can I write this in my autobiography?' asked George. 'Who will want to know about Giles Romilly?' 'You should certainly put it in, people will care because you describe it to them and create the character of Giles,' I said. Later I said, 'Put it in anyway. Put everything in for the time being. And when you have completed the book you may decide to take it out. But write it anyway.'

So there was this extraordinarily changed George W. I thought, I have missed knowing him all these years and it is my fault. I have

---

1 Giles Romilly (1916–1967), British journalist who served as a war correspondent in the Spanish Civil War and Second World War, when he was the first prisoner of war in Germany to be classified as 'Prominente' (politically significant). *Out of Bounds* was set up by public-school-educated brothers Giles and Esmond Romilly in 1934. The magazine's manifesto stated that it was 'against Reaction, Militarism and Fascism in the Public Schools'.

2 Gavin Ewart (1916–1995), British poet who contributed to *New Verse* alongside Auden and Spender in the 1930s.

3 Helen Low (née Gibb) was married to Oliver Low, the brother of Humphrey Spender's first wife Margaret.

sneered at his social life, thought he never cared enough about his writers unless they [were] famous names etc etc. Then I thought that I should not altogether blame myself. There was the George who, when we talked with him, always seemed to be looking past me to see whether there was not someone more important in the room, etc. It was he who had changed. Or perhaps we had both until now always looked sidelong *beyond* each other.

He was, throughout the two days' weekend[,] immensely and genuinely informative about Germany, Croatia, the Czechs and Slovaks, the new Europe. I attribute his change of character either to the fact that he has got rid of the perhaps false situation of his publishing, or to his new fiancée. [. . .]

This morning at noon people from all over the place started arriving for a large luncheon party. There was an interesting and intelligent American who, P[eter Palumbo] told me, was America's top interior decorator. Lady Nevill whom I had sat next to quite recently at Nigel Nicolson's 75th birthday party, the Duke and Duchess of York (Fergie).[1] Fergie is much quieter and pleasanter in private than one would gather from her press photographs. She talked almost from the moment she arrived about the brutal press coverage she had got for her recent visit to Palm Beach in Florida where she had been guest of a millionaire roué and also had attended a private party given at a club which turned out to exclude blacks from its membership. She had been asked, she explained, to go conditional on her receiving £100,000 for a charity in which she was interested. They would not have got the money if she had refused. I couldn't help rather sympathizing. The press is brutal exploitative, vile even. At the same time one feels she is rather badly advised 'unlike' as Peter said afterwards '[Diana] the Princess of Wales who never puts a step wrong.' 'The worst of all this is,' said Fergie, 'that it hurts the friend I care for most in this world, my mother-in-law,' a remark which, being made, one holds up for examination in some kind of mental forceps.

---

1 Sarah Ferguson (b. 1959) was then nearing the end of her marriage to Prince Andrew, the Duke of York.

29 January 1992, London

On TV last night one of those discussions about the state of the world, which do not get anywhere, but in which interesting things are said. Speakers: Conor Cruise O'Brien, Saul Bellow, Mario Vargas Llosa.[1] There were also clips from Toni Morrison, Gore Vidal and one or two others, speaking from their homes and interrupting the discussion like commercials.[2]

Conor Cruise said that after the collapse of Communism what he feared was emergent nationalism in a dozen different parts of the former Soviet Union and Eastern Europe. I can see he is really afraid of what would be in effect a return to the Europe of 1914. Saul Bellow talked about the fragmentation of the U.S. into groups representing their own immediate interests, inhibiting and in effect censoring each other [. . .]. Culture he thought was continuity and values, not the breaking up of the country into various interests each calling itself a culture. Rather surprisingly, everyone seemed to disagree with Saul – Gore Vidal saying he was a conservative representing a very small minority of academics who felt persecuted by Political Correctness. Conor said he had been studying Black Women's Rights literature and found it remarkably well reasoned. Toni Morrison cut in from the outside and put forward a very strong argument that the U.S. tradition was of an entirely White Culture, with its ruling class, its traditions all based on the assumption that the white race was superior and that the achievements of the Black, if admitted, were so because they passed standards set by the White.

As she talked, I couldn't help thinking of Isaiah saying he was convinced that the white race was doomed and that the future of the world lay with the coloured races. If this is so, does it mean that the greatest achievements which we consider to be of the white are submerged first by the process of deconstruction and secondly by the agreed on superiority of the Black or coloured (Morrison pointed out

---

1 Conor Cruise O'Brien (1917–2008), Irish politician, academic and writer. Saul Bellow (1915–2005), Nobel Prize-winning American novelist best known for *Herzog* (1964) and *Humboldt's Gift* (1975). Mario Vargas Llosa (b. 1936), Peruvian writer and politician.

2 Toni Morrison (b. 1931), Nobel Prize-winning American writer best known for *Beloved* (1987).

that characteristically the Whites assumed that antiquity – Greece and Rome – belonged to the Whites).

Trying to answer my question it strikes me that Morrison was so impressive to me because of her perfectly clear command of idiomatic and literary English; superior I couldn't help thinking to that of the other speakers on the programme. In having such a command of English – and not speaking, say, the language of Chicago slums where, it is sometimes claimed, their ungrammatical idiom is just as correct as that of white teachers of Eng. lit. – does she – albeit unconsciously – pay tribute to the superiority of 'white' English? And if, as a black, she considers that in so speaking such perfect English she has mastered a foreign language – what would be her original language which she is translating into the foreign one?

It seems to me that if there is a future literature written predominantly by coloured writers, it will for the most part not have come out of the language of the black ghettos – but have come out of absorbing and transforming to its own purposes the masterpieces of the white culture. Moreover these masterpieces will remain standards by which, for a long while, the new culture is judged – just as I judge Morrison's English by what I consider the highest standards of Eng. lit. today.

3 February 1992, London

We lunched with our neighbour Gwen Solomon whose husband the pianist Solomon died some years ago after thirty years of being crippled following on a stroke.[1] She lives in a large house of bare-looking rooms with big furniture and few ornaments. A powder-blue budgerigar was flying about the sitting room. She explained that her previous budgie had died. She had refused all offers from friends and relations to have another one ('What would happen to it when I die?') but then a friend had brought her this one and insisted that she have it. She refused though to let it have a mate. What would be the future of any little budgerigars?

She gave us steak and kidney pie, followed by tinned peaches.

---

1 Known in the musical industry by his first name, Solomon Cutner (1902–1988) was a British pianist who suffered a paralysing stroke in 1956.

Natasha got her talking quite interestedly about pianists. She said a great pianist had to have such superlative technique that he could forget about it. Clifford Curzon should never have attempted the Brahms piano concertos. [Artur] Schnabel was an exception to all rules because although his technique was inadequate he had such a vision of how the work ought to be interpreted according to the composer's intentions in the score that he carried all before him. Before Schnabel there were pianists who had studied the score once, in their youth, and then simply ignored it improvising their 'interpretations'.

She talked a lot about how much she wanted to die – she is 86. She could see no objection to committing suicide. The difficulty was to be sure that one would succeed.

16 February 1992, London

Philip Larkin's Poems.[1] They are curiously self-obsessed. He is forever telling the reader how cynical and bored he is. Hints that this is a) due to some peculiar misfortune, sexual or to do with love; b) that it is after all the fault of other people for not being worthy of him though; c) he is (judged by their miserable standards) not worthy of them either. No via media [middle way].

A curious generation. Thom Gunn is the opposite of Larkin in many ways.[2] He dresses up for the part which is to admire motorcyclists looking as like them as much as he can. One suspects though that secretly he despises them. His kind of hero worship is very deliberately set against my 'I think continually of those who were truly great', because my great are not his heroes.[3]

---

1 Larkin's *Collected Poems*, edited by Anthony Thwaite, were published in 1988, three years after the poet's death. Spender's thoughts on Larkin are inspired by the publication of his *Selected Letters* (ed. Thwaite) in February 1992.

2 Thom Gunn (1929–2004), Anglo-American poet who was associated with The Movement in the 1950s, although he later moved away from its concerns. Gunn became openly homosexual after moving to America in 1954.

3 Spender is thinking of Gunn's poem, 'Lines for a Book' and the couplet: 'I praise the overdogs, from Alexander / To those who would not play with Stephen Spender'. The direct reference is to Spender's poem 'My Parents Kept Me From Children Who Were Rough'.

3 March 1992, London

N. and I have health problems. She is undoubtedly very tired and weighed down by practical arrangements of our life, as well as obligations to people. Worries about finance. We both really have to work for money. She is trying to write travel pieces and sketches of characters we have known – e.g., an excellent one about Edith Sitwell. She tends to fall asleep after dinner, to sleep till 3 am, when she washes up, and perhaps does not sleep again. I also get very tired – Work in the morning, then sleep two or three hours after lunch. [. . .]

Well, the opening of Maro's exhibition a great success socially – don't know whether she sold anything – but that really does not concern her much. The grandchildren, Saskia and Cosima appeared, doing their great act of being their lively, smiling, enigmatic and perfectly controlled selves, each dressed for the part. Cosima, fresh from Paris, wore a large black hat, almost concealing her face and with the rim ornamented with artificial flowers. Her beautiful two, not very large, smiling eyes, which seem to watch one the whole time, are friendly and yet a bit mysterious or secretive. Saskia, her upper half in a kind of operatic breast plate, gold and with little bits of paste or glass studding it, her skirt very short and showing an awful lot of bottom. The expression on her face slightly dare-devil or impertinent, totally in command, yet with a feeling that she is fragile underneath. Matthew's family is riding very high – though in control of their powers – not arrogant or conceited. It is just that their powers are within their limits so considerable. All sorts of characters from their Avane life – visitors there, a tutor to their children, guests of the girls – turned up and were very lively, pretty people, most of them, and some of them, talented.

On Sunday we went to hospital to visit Dee Wells who has had her leg cut off below the knee.[1] Very lonely – her son Nick in Manchester with a girlfriend seems unable to get to London – her daughter editing a magazine called *Traveller* tied in New York. She is so brave and smiling but does not conceal her absolutely justified fear of the life

---

1 Dee Wells (1925–2003), London-based American journalist and writer who was married to A. J. Ayer in the 1960s and 1970s. She divorced him in 1982 and then remarried him shortly before his death in 1989. She would die, much later, in 2003.

ahead of her – alone in her London house and with an artificial leg the use of which it will take her some time to master.

The world seems full of horrors. Starvation, revolution, nationalism, insolvable economic problems all thrown at one through TV. Every day confronting me with a sense of the indecency of carrying on with one's own fairly high level life when the general misery pictured in all its ferocity gloom terror or penury unloads its images before one's eyes. The irony. Is it more indecent to turn the images off while one is eating one's quite decent meal or to keep them on?

21 March 1992, London

On Wednesday *Index* had a meeting in London of representatives of all its committees from abroad. These are mostly Dutch and Scandinavian though there is one from some African country and an Australian committee is about to be formed. To my surprise the mood of the meeting was very up-beat and *Index* is receiving a lot of support. The Ford Foundation seems to have guaranteed funds for the next four years, to be paid now. Pavel Litvinov was there – very friendly.[1] He came to Loudoun Road on Wednesday to be photographed with me for *Index*'s Archives.

In 1991, Bryan Obst had died of Aids. This is the first mention of Obst's death in Spender's journal.

24 March 1992, London

I have been thinking recently of Bob Dana, and then – not really surprisingly – because I always seem to hear from people if I start thinking about them – I got a letter from him together with his *Selected Poems* (much more distinguished than I had remembered them

---

1 Pavel Litvinov (b. 1940), Russian physicist and human rights activist who grew up among the Soviet elite but was then arrested after participating in the 1968 Red Square demonstration against the Soviet invasion of Czechoslovakia and moved to America after his release in 1974. It was the plight of Litvinov in 1968 which had inspired the creation of *Index on Censorship* (see biographical appendix).

to be).[1] In his letter he asked me whether I ever heard from 'the Gainsville lot', mentioning Bryan.

This set me off, until I finally took a sleeping pill, thinking of B. in the form of a letter I would write to him, saying B. probably had made no impression on him but in fact ever since I first met B. at a party given in the garden of Mrs Anderson's house, I had seen him and thought of him a great deal. How we seemed to have a shared consciousness which continued uninterrupted when we were away from one another (we did not in 15 years see each other [for] more than three months of meetings in all that time).

How we both remembered the same incidents, the things we said and had a mind of total recall so that if we met after five years it was as though we had been together all the time. How I had really changed his life after the time when he was teaching school children on the Sewanee River. I had written a letter of recommendation for him, copies of which he sent to universities, with the result that he got into the Biology Department of U.C.L.A. How well he did there, how he went to the South Atlantic and also to Alaska on scientific expeditions. How there was some underlying sadness about him, to do with the destruction of nature, especially of the birds. He wrote a paper on the subject of Terns in Florida, describing the way in which they were driven off the sea shore for nesting by racing cars along the beaches, and then took to resting on the tarred roofs of great depots, which, when the weather got hot, started melting. He used the word 'tragic' and I think he thought nature, the lives of animals, was tragic.

How incredibly perceptive he was, with a wonderful sensitivity to – and economy of – language which shows in every letter he ever wrote. There was such a sense of his presence – our presence together – that I can never even think about him without the sense that he is there, leaning over my shoulder while I am writing. When he was alive I felt this so, as far as he-and-I-with-me is concerned, his death does not make all that difference. I am very conscious, though, that it leaves a hole in the world for his friends at U.C.L.A. There is also that terrible sense of 'unfinished business' for survivors about those who die young. What an awful affliction for the parents, relations, lovers, friends of those killed in the war.

---

1 Robert Dana (1929–2010), American poet and literary critic.

14 May 1992, London

A big gap during which I was mostly in hospital. I went there to be operated on for hernia. A result of this op. (which turned out to be more serious than anticipated) was that I had to have an operation for prostate. I insisted, perhaps unwisely, on having this as soon as possible: unwisely because the sequence of the two ops. resulted in a weakening of the bladder muscles and my having to wear a sack for peeing into. I was in a panic that I might have to wear this for the rest of my life.

So I was more than three weeks in the Lindo Wing of Queen Mary's Hospital – a room with a high ceiling and long narrow windows that looked out on brick walls. This was one of several rooms along a corridor where one took walks from time to time.

[. . .] A lot of my friends visited me – particularly David Plante and Nikos Stangos: also Stuart Hampshire, Isaiah Berlin, David Sylvester, my brother Humphrey, David Hockney, Barry Humphries (who greatly impressed the nurses).[1] Lizzie coming to hospital before she went off to N.Y. and L.A. Matthew came over from Italy. Apart from his presence, one of the things that kept me going was the interest of his book being published and getting reviews.[2]

In my room when alone, I experienced mostly two obsessions. One was with time: the hammering of thought like ineffectual will against present time which does not go away: the idea that in a week or a month or a day my situation would be transformed but the difficulty [of] believing that this transformation could be effected simply by the passage of time – of believing in a future a tomorrow in which my circumstances would be transformed.

The second obsession was a feeling of shame about self-centredness of illness: a self-centredness which is perhaps excusable at the time, because it is a product of one's physical condition, but which, nevertheless, [ignores] the comparative situation of one's own sick body with that of other people's bodies far worse off. Dee Wells, for

---

1 David Sylvester (1924–2001), British art critic and curator. The Australian comedian and writer Barry Humphries (b. 1934) had married Spender's daughter Lizzie in 1990.

2 Matthew Spender had published *Within Tuscany*, his account of his Tuscan house (Viking, 1992).

instance, who had her leg amputated was far worse off than I. Reproach that one does not think enough about the ill.

These feelings were exaggerated – dramatized – by the doctors and several of my contemporaries while I was in hospital. Francis Bacon died after a heart attack in Madrid [on 28 April]. David Sylvester visited me and said: 'I want to tell you that your case is not the same as that of your exact contemporary, Francis. He had used up his life, you have not used up yours, in fact there are two or three things you still have to do in this world.' Two or three is exactly what I think I do have – a volume of poems and a novel *Miss Pangbourne*.

In hospital and looking at the news on TV, I thought a lot about the injustice, the gross and senseless contradictions of the world. On the one hand, hospitals, healing, marvellous surgery and drugs to heal and cure and diminish suffering; on the other the injustice, the misery caused partly by nature partly by society, and the sheer destructiveness of large parts of the world. A metaphor for the world at times seemed half of human effort being put into hospitals where flesh and blood and bone is healed and patched together by experts using marvellous technological means: the other half of the world occupied in using equally marvellous technology to blow flesh and blood and bone to bits, make thousands of people inaccessible to the marvellous machinery of healing. The civil war in Yugoslavia where people are killing each other for no reason at all except that different ethnic groups and people with different religions happen to cohabit the same areas is a kind of madness which makes one wish that the thugs and fanatics of nationalism and religion could be taken off to some open space and given the wherewithal to destroy one another.[1]

---

1 Following the Second World War, Yugoslavia was formed out of separate republics, which were nominally equal: Croatia, Montenegro, Serbia, Slovenia, Bosnia-Herzegovina, and Macedonia. In Serbia the two provinces of Kosovo and Vojvodina were given autonomous status. Initially, communism provided a strong enough force to keep the separate nation states united. Increasingly, however, ethnic tensions and unequal economic development encouraged nationalism to spread. By the early 1990s, Yugoslavia had broken up into separate nation states and in 1991 civil war broke out.

16 May 1992, London

On Wednesday Iris Murdoch came to visit us arriving at midday staying for lunch. She was affectionate, interested, informative as always, but did not seem altogether well. She becomes more and more conservative in her views, particularly in her views about Europe: not that I don't share many of her misgivings about England being extensively run by 'Brussels'. She cross-questioned Matthew about his novel at lunch.[1] What was the first sentence? Had he, before starting to write, worked out the plot? She said that she worked out in notebooks every detail of characterization, plot, structure, of a novel before she started out on it. [. . .]

Lizzie and Barry came to tea, having returned from L.A. They have made a bid for a house there. Lizzie described it room-by-room, views from every elevation, and the wonderful enclosed garden. She is evidently in love with it. I hope their bid succeeds.

Disneyland want to make a Dame Edna movie with Barry who also has several talk show engagements, filming for TV in London, etc., etc. The complexity of their engagements is mind-boggling, involving all their dealings with agents, accountants, lawyers, and managers. Lizzie, resenting all the 'rip off' which Barry is subject to[,] seems to have a grasp of all this. It has not so much changed her character as super-imposed on the gentle affectionate Lizzie the personality of someone who can understand very complicated deals, affairs and accounts and is determined that Barry should not be cheated.

5 September 1993, London

Three days ago a David Streitfeld from *The Washington Post* rang to say that a novelist called David Leavitt has written a novel (*While England Sleeps*) in which the last section, describing the narrator's going to Spain during the Spanish Civil War is taken entirely from my description of going to Spain to try to save Tony Hyndman after he had deserted from the International Brigade in *World Within World*.[2]

---

1 Matthew Spender's novel was completed but remains unpublished.

2 The American novelist David Leavitt (b. 1961) published *While England Sleeps* in 1993. Following a successful lawsuit instigated by the Spenders, in 1995 a revised version of the novel was published deleting a passage that

I have now read this very bad book and what he tells me is certainly true. I am asked by Mr Streitfield to react in some way. But I really have no reactions except distaste for the novel.

In September 1993, Spender, with other distinguished speakers, was attending a 'conversazione' at the Rockefeller Center, Bellagio, on Lake Como. The Spenders were guests of Drue Heinz on the other side of the lake.

10 September 1993, Lake Como

Drove what seemed the whole length of Lake Como to this villa. Our fellow guests were a very pleasant surprise: John and Iris Bayley, [Michael] Gearin-Tosh, Lord and Lady Carrington, a houseful and going it seems to spend ten days together.[1] I have a very bad night of pain with my arm. Gearin-Tosh is an expert on Browning and is also on Rochester, Charles II (etc). John told me he had written a play about Rochester. I discussed with him the concluding lines of the first book of [Browning's poem] *The Ring and the Book*, which I find extremely moving but very difficult to follow. Read them this morning with John Bayley who was brilliant at interpreting them.

22 September 1993, London

I did not work then at Como except to read Thom Gunn's *Collected Poems* and make notes for a review (in *The Spectator*). I cannot remember though that I have ever worked at Drue [Heinz]'s house. High up in its garden and below the precipitous hillside part of which is rock, its front of windows and terrace above the garden which

---

closely paralleled a passage in *World Within World*. For details of the lawsuit see John Sutherland, *Stephen Spender*, pp. 547–50.

1 Michael Gearin-Tosh (1940–2005), Australian-born Oxford literary academic who would famously develop the use of alternative medicine to combat his own cancer in the late 1990s. Peter Carrington (b. 1919), Conservative politician; Foreign Secretary at the time of the invasion of the Falkland Islands, presiding over the decision to send 28,000 British troops to defend the Falklands against Argentina; he resigned in 1982, taking ministerial responsibility for his failure to deter the invasion.

descends to a road between its railings and the edge of the lake, it seems to stare across the lake to mountains skirted by the town of Bellagio and various villas. One gets locked into this position: back on the steep hillside of house garden and rock cliff – fronting the lake on its far side, pinned down almost, looking and looking.

We also had particularly pleasant companions:

Owen and Ruth Chadwick
Iris and John Bayley (Dame Iris Murdoch)
Michael Gearin-Tosh
Lord and Lady Carrington
Paul and Marigold Johnson.[1] [. . .]

Carrington when he was there was wonderfully vigorous and amusing: forever striding up mountains, taking himself on expeditions across the lake, enjoying every moment of his holiday. Very open and pleasing to talk to. He had no hopes about Yugoslavia because, he said, we had no force or threat of force behind our arguing. All the heads of the former Yugoslavia were thugs who lied to their teeth, and [David] Owen could not really do anything except talk endlessly.[2] I was amazed how cheerful Carrington managed to be, telling stories at which he laughed uproariously. He seemed much the most energetic of the party – at any rate until the arrival of Paul Johnson.

Owen Chadwick looked a bit theological/donnish and I felt uneasy with him the first days. But he was so intelligent – without thrusting his views on us – and so understanding – that after a week I felt him irresistible. With him as with Auden I feel there is no real disagreement. I revere what they revere and yet I feel I must stand outside the institution of religion they support. To say 'I do not know' becomes

---

1 Owen Chadwick (b. 1916), British historian of Christianity. Paul Johnson (b. 1928), British Roman Catholic writer and journalist who had edited the *New Statesman*, 1965–70.

2 In 1991, Peter Carrington, in his role as EC Mediator, had warned against diplomatic recognition of separate Yugoslav states until a political settlement could be reached in which each nation accepted the political independence of the others. In August 1992, David Owen succeeded Carrington as EU co-chairman of the Conference for the Former Yugoslavia, along with Cyrus Vance, the former US Secretary of State, and was unable to alleviate the civil war between Bosnia and Serbia which lasted until 1995.

a principle, in itself a belief. To enter those doors of churches where people kneel a betrayal (to me, not necessarily to them) of the people who refuse to enter – even though the refusal may be the expression of a hatred of religion which I do not at all share. I suppose I love the noble atheists – Leonard and Virginia Woolf – and feel a deeper loyalty to them than to Eliot and Auden. Also, I only admire Auden and Eliot, and I suppose Chadwick, presuming that they do not accept as certainties the existence of God, life after death, etc which I am uncertain about. If I thought they were certain in their beliefs I would have less difficulty in not believing them. [. . .]

Iris and John very much themselves ensconced in the house where there is the library, absenting themselves from us all in order to go swimming, busy in their rooms writing, appearing punctually at meals, disappearing before anyone else after dinner. Iris who has become very out-size, murmured to me from time to time that she was hungry.

27 September 1993, London

We drove to Salisbury [and] found Ted Heath's house in the Close of Salisbury Cathedral. A plain clothes man at the gate said: 'Mr Heath will let you in,' and a moment later at the front door there was Ted Heath in some kind of yachting sweater on which something like a coat of arms was embroidered high up on one side and through the bottom half of which his stomach bulged exceedingly. He greeted us with a wide cordial gurgling smile and after we had emerged from the guest Ladies and Gents which he insisted on us visiting, we joined a group of important looking well-dressed guests, talking about music and gardens in a sitting room on the walls of which hung a great many pictures, most of them (apart from 3 Japanese prints) featuring ships in various nautical predicaments. We then went for a stroll in the garden which extended as far as the river, and contained two statues, a small orchard its trees bulging with rubicund immensely healthy apples, and Ted delivered a small lecture on the house, its antiquity, its abandonment, its being rebuilt, its suddenly becoming obtainable to him etc. After that we moved into the dining room gleaming with table chairs cutlery silver shelves of china and glass, paintings and prints by John Piper on the walls. I sat on Ted's left

[. . .]. Ted did not say much at first then was drawn into gardens by the lady on his right. I managed to draw him into politics by asking what he thought of Chris Patten in Hong Kong.[1] 'A disaster,' he said. The reason – that Patten lectured the Chinese on democracy just when we were leaving. 'The English always start giving lectures on democracy when they are on the point of leaving possessions which – until they reached that point – they have not ruled democratically – India – now Hong Kong.'

As the conversation was much about living abroad, I stupidly asked Ted whether he went abroad much. 'Well, tomorrow I go to Chicago then from Chicago to Beijing then . . .' he reeled off the names of about seven places. He talked about Pompidou's visit to England when he, Ted, was P.M., and said how much he liked Pompidou.[2] How he took Pompidou for a walk on the Downs, a walk which would have passed little noticed had it not been that Pompidou was surrounded by French secret police – in uniforms.

It was quite a pleasant afternoon really. Heath is rather admirable in overcoming his own shyness by entertaining so generously, perhaps a bit ostentatiously. His taste for yachting is very much on display in his house as is his quite decent taste in painting and, of course, there is the Steinway – its top covered with signed photographs of Great People in his drawing room. There is taste of a kind exemplified and fairly exemplary, but no personality. Ebullient noise and over friendliness – but no real warmth.

30 September 1993, London

Dinner last night at Grouchos, given by her publisher [at] Chatto, Carmen Callil, for Iris Murdoch.[3] Iris did look quite radiant. John Bayley also there and at his most agreeable. We had a long conversation, about what? I do not remember. Some of it about poetry. I sat

---

1 The Conservative politician Chris Patten (b. 1944) was the last British Governor of Hong Kong, 1992–7.

2 Georges Pompidou (1911–1974) was President of the French Republic, 1969–74.

3 Carmen Callil (b. 1938), Australian-born publisher, founded the Virago Press in 1972. She joined Chatto & Windus in a senior capacity in 1982.

between two ladies – Mrs Saatchi and a Norwegian lady.[1] Mrs S. was bright and had a strong Irish accent. The Norwegian lady very boring, but then finding her so was mean of me, because her husband a great friend of Iris had died a year ago. At the end of the evening I found myself sitting next to a youngish-looking man who talked about money. I said I could not think of a single member of my own Oxbridge generation who cared about making money – by which I meant any one to whom making money was an end in itself or was more important than fulfilling his or her vocation. My remarks were received politely, perhaps a bit incredulously, perhaps a bit scornfully. The person I was talking to was Mr Saatchi, Natasha told me afterwards.

The waitress filled our glasses to the rim. I feel tired this morning.

9 October 1993, London

Derek Hill and Frances Partridge came to dinner last night.[2] Not a very exciting evening; but there was a strange conversation early on about Desmond Shawe-Taylor, the music critic, and fellow inhabitant with Derek Hill of Crichel.[3]

Derek said he had gone to some concert or opera in the country somewhere expecting Desmond to join him there and Desmond had not appeared. A day later Desmond had turned up at Crichel covered with mud and very exhausted. He did not seem to know where he had been. Frances capped this with a story. She had been invited to go to the opera some Wednesday evening with Desmond, and cancelled an engagement to meet this date. When she arrived on the evening of their appointment there was no Desmond, but another friend who said: 'Why didn't you turn up last night? We were expecting you. Desmond had told us you were coming.' Derek and Frances

---

1 Josephine Hart (1942–2011), Irish-born novelist, wife of Maurice Saatchi and a close friend of Iris Murdoch. Maurice Saatchi (b. 1946), Iraqi-born Conservative peer and Advertising Executive.

2 Derek Hill (1916–2000), British painter.

3 Desmond Shawe-Taylor (1907–1995), chief music critic on the *Sunday Times*. Derek Hill had a studio in Long Crichel House, near Wimborne, where James Lees-Milne and Frances Partridge were frequent guests.

then embarked on a long conversation about Desmond: how deaf he was, how he would never take the blame for anything. If he spilled wine accidentally on the table, he would say it was the fault of the maid for distracting him at that moment. Derek also said that he complained a great deal and had a terrible habit of shouting at the top of his voice.

Taking all this in, I asked: 'Do you mean to say that when he gets lost in this way, he is driving a car?' 'Oh yes,' Derek said. 'Well surely it is very dangerous if he's driving alone at night without having the slightest idea where he is?' 'Oh yes, very dangerous.' 'But he might have a terrible accident. He might kill himself or kill someone else or kill both.' 'Oh yes, he might.' 'Well, ought not something be done about this? Oughtn't you tell the police?' At this they became completely vague and didn't answer. I have the feeling that like Desmond we were all lost and alone and driving round in circles. A conversation which is like traffic moving in a landscape on a foggy night.

In 1984, an operation for cancer of the neck left Spender's friend the writer Reynolds Price paraplegic. Price wrote an account of the event in A Whole New Life *(1994). The grievous handicap did not inhibit his career as a writer and teacher.*

10 October 1993, London

Yesterday William Price the brother of Reynolds Price took us out to lunch at the Italian Restaurant in Blenheim Terrace. We had drinks first at home. He has a rather shorthaired greying beard, lively eyes an alert expression. He talks a great deal about Reynolds, entirely in his praise: his wonderful recovery from his cancer, his total dedication to his work, his managing to travel all over America, his teaching at Duke, how at the beginning of each year's course, he asks the class whether any male student there will volunteer to take care of him the following year; how for several years now a different student has (really giving up a year of his life for Reynolds) and how perfectly this arrangement has worked out. Bill Price really seemed a character of gold.

11 October 1993, London

Went last night with Marguerite Littman to see *Vita and Virginia* by Eileen Atkins at the Ambassadors Theatre.[1] This was really a double bill diseuses [monologue] performance consisting entirely of letters between Vita and Virginia – most of them love letters. The performance was very restrained really, establishing its own conventions such as that when Vita stood far to one side of the stage she was in Teheran or Berlin *en poste* as wife of the diplomat, Harold [Nicolson].

Given that neither actress could really look like V. or V., they did pretty good imitations: though I think it was a mistake to dress Virginia as dowdily as her own self-mocking descriptions of her attire in her letters. Nor was Vita as smart as Virginia mockingly described her. In fact James Pope-Hennessy got it rather well when he described Vita as looking like a combination in one person of Lady-Chatterley-and-her-lover. In fact the actresses did not make anything of the fact that there is a gap between the V. of each in the other V.'s mocking letters and each real V.

13 October 1993, London

Last night our big dinner for the Seitzes (the American Ambassador and his wife), Isaiah and Aline Berlin, Anne Cox Chambers, Tony Harrison, Peter Ackroyd.[2] Very good introductions were made – Isaiah to Tony and to Peter and Peter and Tony to one another. Peter got very drunk and towards the end of the evening when all the other guests had left seemed quite enamoured of Tony Harrison. Peter was indeed already drunk at dinner. 'Very nice. Very intelligent and very drunk –' Isaiah said. I had forgotten how much I like Tony Harrison. He is one of those people who does not forget the past of a relationship and each time you meet him you feel you are adding a unit to an

---

1 Marguerite Littman, American-born editor of *Glamour Magazine*, resident in London. With her husband, the barrister Mark Littman, she was a collaborator with Spender on *Index on Censorship* and other charity work. Eileen Atkins (b. 1934), British actress with long-standing interest in adapting the works of Virginia Woolf for stage and screen.

2 Peter Ackroyd (b. 1949), British novelist, journalist and biographer.

already existing sum. Mrs Seitz is petite attractive serious without being heavy. She entered into a conversation with me about the disparity between the well-fed world we inhabit and the real world of horrors brought into our room by TV. Ought one to accept the obscenity of seeing natives starve to death on the TV screen while one is eating one's mutton chop or ought one, for the sake of decency even, shut one's consciousness out of such truth? I said that one would be annihilated or driven down into a kind of nothingness of horror if one did not shut things out. Images of TV in this respect are as though walking down the street one was aware of the condition of everyone concealed behind walls in it: that woman dying of cancer, that child in terrible pain. Living – and, indeed, civilization – implied a certain shutting out of other people's experiences in situations where one can do nothing or very little about these anyway. To be exposed to other people's sufferings in situations where one can do nothing about them – enter into no significant relation – just see them – means cultivating indifference to the thing actually seen – not to the things which we do not see.

But this argument runs into complacency, too.

Anyway the Ambassadress was quite serious about this conversation while feeling transparently that perhaps at a dinner party an Ambassadress should not be so serious. He [Seitz] was intelligent good-humoured candid. Peter Ackroyd fired off questions at him. Why was he leaving? What would he do next? Would he be Ambassador somewhere else? Did he like foreign affairs?

Isaiah said Jacob Rothschild now only liked billionaires.[1] I said we had met him the other day at the opening of John Craxton's exhibition, and he had not recognized me I had shrunk so in his estimation. Anne Chambers talked about her garden and seemed very happy to be with us. It was a good evening, that is to say slightly better even than we had expected and the time quite rushing by.

14 October 1993, London

Dinner at the American Embassy. Peter Ackroyd was there quite brisk but a bit touchy, I thought, when I teased him about last night.

---

1 For Jacob Rothschild, see biographical appendix.

He admitted how greatly he had taken to Tony Harrison. I said that one thing I loved about Tony was that wherever we met – even if there had been a space of years between that and our previous meeting – he seemed to take up our friendship at exactly the point where we had last met – so that friendship with him was cumulative – nothing had been lost or diminished over the intervening years – and the next meeting was pure addition to all the previous ones.

I sat next to Margaret Drabble – the nicest part of the evening I thought. We talked a lot about the life of Angus Wilson that she is writing. Was very nice about Angus's friend Tony – said what a wonderful person she thought him. On my left someone called Lady Waine told me she had been married twice and that she had a house near Ménerbes. She was supposed to get married a third time – on Nov. 19, I think she said. But after two previous marriages was having cold feet about this. She pointed out her prospective husband to me, and I could understand her reservations.

15 October 1993, London

Went to a party given by the Treuhafts – that is, Decca Mitford.[1] Margaret Gardiner, David Plante, Marina Warner's husband (whose name I forget). I was rather dreading this as I thought of Decca as combining Mitford smartness with Communist anti-Americanism. Actually she did not seem at all as I expected. For one thing, she seemed incredibly much older though I think we'd last seen her only two years ago. But now she was bowed she was wrinkled she stooped and had difficulty walking across the room. Not that she wasn't still very lively and bright. But the Mitford wittiness had suddenly become

---

1 Jessica (Decca) Mitford (1917–1996) was a British writer living in America and best known for *The American Way of Death* (1963), an exposé of the American funeral industry; she was one of the six Mitford sisters (Nancy, Pam, Diana, Unity, Jessica and Deborah ('Debo')) all of whom were known for their beauty, aristocratic style and extremist political sympathies. Decca had rethought her previous commitment to communist ideology, admitting in the late 1950s that certain aspects of Stalin's ideology were wrong, while Diana remained convinced by 1930s fascist ideology. Robert F. Treuhaft, (1912–2001), American lawyer and communist. He married Jessica Mitford in 1943, meeting when they were both on surveillance operations in Washington.

dead serious. She talked about Diana, her sister, and said she had not seen her for many years and had no intention of seeing her again – ever. (The Diana Mosley–Hitler connection had ceased to be funny.) She couldn't bear the way Diana seemed still to worship Hitler – said what an interesting amusing man he was, and how he had such beautiful hands.[1]

19 October 1993, London

Natasha went all day together with Tess Rothschild to visit various members of the Booth family.[2] I went on writing my story about Thorp.[3] Sam Sylvester rang to say he had arranged for us to go with him to meet counsel tomorrow about David Leavitt's novel the story of which is stolen from *World Within World*.[4] Had supper with the Alfred Brendels. The only other guest Lord Douro who looks like a beautifully formed model of some ancestor.[5] He talked about Spain said how wonderful the achievement there of a democracy – he now thought irreversible – in a country which had never had democracy before, the Republic not being really a democracy because it could not rule. Under his beautiful manners I feel there is someone who has deep reservations about the company in which he finds himself. What is his relationship with Reni [Brendel]? Alfred seemed perfectly at ease. They talked about their children and music, how wonderfully Adrian is doing as a cellist, and how one daughter has suddenly taken

---

1 Diana Mitford (1910–2003) had married the British fascist leader Oswald Mosley in 1936 at a wedding attended by Hitler and Goebbels.

2 Teresa Rothschild (b. 1915), widow of the scientist Victor Rothschild, who had died in 1990 (see biographical appendix).

3 Geoffrey Thorp was an inspirational teacher at University College School, London, who influenced Spender as a school child. For some time Spender had been working on a short story based on Thorp, 'Mr Branch', which was never published.

4 Sam Sylvester was the Spenders' lawyer, representing them in their plagiarism suit against Viking, the British publisher of David Leavitt's novel *While England Sleeps*.

5 Lord Douro (b. 1945), a descendant of the Duke of Wellington – the 'ancestor', presumably, Spender has in mind.

a great leap forward as a violinist. Marvellous hosts at their best when there are very few guests.

I worked all morning at my Thorp story. Afternoon read – or breezed through – the vast mass of correspondence of William Goyen. Obsessed with the image of himself as totally dedicated artist creating his own solitary world of totally dedicated art. Writes to nearly all his friends in the most exaggerated terms of love – as though he is his or her best friend. Making up tremendously to people who either admire him or are useful to him – outrageous really in his expressions of love and gratitude and admiration for [E. R.] Curtius – my dear beloved friend etc. It seems incredible that he could get away with so much flattery – writing to Curtius as though they were all but lovers. I really can't imagine anyone going further in this direction.

20 October 1993, London

I wrote yesterday an Introduction to the Collected Letters of William Goyen, which are being published by *Three-Quarterly* [*sic*] in Evanston, Illinois.[1] I agreed to do this out of some kind of feeling of guilt about Goyen who was a very close friend in the early '50s, but whom I took a sudden and great dislike to when we were on a two-day visit to Venice. He was gifted, intelligent, dedicated, and could never – all the time I knew him – earn his way, and he certainly lived for his art. But – as his letters show – he was gushing, a kind of performer or actor in all his relationships, and a terrible almost uncontrollable mischief-maker. In fact through the vein of his self-dedicated devotion to the ever-dramatized sense of himself as artist there runs an equally strong vein of something entirely false. This might not be so bad except that it affects all his relationships in which he is always playing the role of the totally affectionate totally dedicated friend. Sometimes there is also a vein of self-interest or self-promotion which is all too obvious. For instance he writes what are really love letters to Ernst Robert Curtius – an erudite greatly distinguished man but

---

1 Spender refers to the journal *TriQuarterly*, published by Northwestern University Press. *William Goyen: Selected Letters from a Writer's Life* was subsequently published with an afterword by Spender by the University of Texas Press in 1995.

liable to fall in love in an extremely sentimental way with a young genius (Curtius did so indeed with me in 1930, but I never accepted the role of his lover). Hardly ever meeting Curtius and therefore never having to pay out in gold the paper money of his stamped attention, he exploits Curtius for all his worth. Not that Curtius is not willing to be exploited. He falls for Goyen's writing becomes his translator into German advises him about his work and even sends him money.

I suppose I have written people I was in love with highly embarrassing love letters. But Goyen specializes in writing letters in which he is always dangling, through the intimacies expressed, the pretence that he has some kind of uniquely knowing relationship with whomever it is he happens to be writing [to]. The only thing to be said in his favour is that these letters are palpably insincere. He is being 'Bill' to his correspondent acting that role; and this does to some extent sanitize it.

Apparently he had some kind of love relationship with Katharine Ann Porter.[1] In some kind of transport of mutual deception they actually made love to one another. This gives him the privilege – while steering as clear as possible of the physical entanglement – of writing to her as though the two of them are the only ones who really understand each other. She plays this game too. But perhaps they both know it is a game. And perhaps a lot of people, entertained by what was really amusing unique, talented, about him entered his game even liked him greatly without being taken into him.

He could also turn on people viciously, especially if he felt they had not lived up to his expectations of benefits he would get out of them on the basis of their recognizing his genius. There are ferocious letters to publishers who are held to have neglected him: because his furthest idea of himself is as the utterly alone artist totally dedicated to his art, prepared to die for its sake, never understood by anyone, and mistreated by the world.

---

1 Katharine Ann Porter (1890–1980), Pulitzer Prize-winning American writer and political activist; another patron of Goyen in the early stages of his career.

21 October 1993, London

Hours in which I did not sleep [spent] lying awake fantasizing about my 'case' against *While England Sleeps*. Why are sleepless nights so rhetorical? so self-dramatizing? so demoralizing? Perhaps there is an outer skin where the globular sub-conscience [*sic*] becomes language and imagery – drama. The excitement. That place where the negative depression of being got down by a situation is transformed into positive reaction. Also alas the drama is silly. Out of one's senses. With morning light one comes back to one's senses.

I enjoy, up to a point, excitement. But when I wake up in the morning I wonder what is depressing me. Then it comes flooding back – reality, the situation slept on, that does not go away on waking.

In childhood – our-my-middle-class childhood – the day could be terrible, punishing. But one knew it would go away with night. Sleep was like a sponge which washed away the rows of yesterday so that one woke to a new clean day. That was health. Only in illness did one wake up tomorrow on yesterday re-played – 'I am still ill. I'll have to stay in bed' – today repeating yesterday.

29 October 1993, London

Saskia [Spender] arrived for dinner at about 8, Matthew about twenty minutes later. [. . .] Inevitably at dinner conversation got onto the subject of David Leavitt's book. Matthew feels that I should not be suing him for stealing my copyright material. Didn't Shakespeare steal copyright material? I pointed out a) that in writing plays based on legends romances and earlier plays Shakespeare was not stealing material which was in copyright and b) that I had said in an interview with the *Washington Post* that of course I would have no complaint if D.L. transformed the material, in the manner of a Tolstoy. But D.L. had not done this. M. who has not read D.L., but who knows him, and also knows that D.L. is a friend of James Pope-Hennessy, seemed unconvinced by this. I think partly he regards D.L. as someone whom the English literary establishment is ganging up against and therefore he takes his side. He feels above all we should not have taken a court action, but of course, knows nothing about the fact that for weeks all we asked of Viking was a satisfactory

[701]

acknowledgement or apology to be printed in the book, and that we resorted to action only when they refused to pronounce a satisfactory one. This is something to do with M.'s whole feeling about England.

M. was very interesting about the younger generation. He seemed to be saying that in writing about the past the young are completely indifferent to historic truth. Thus there is nothing wrong to them that in his novel L[eavitt] should describe Barcelona in 1936 as being full of traffic, bustling life etc as the tourist Barcelona he knew in 1981.

9 November 1993, London

I read (twice) the new Penguin vol. of poems by James Fenton.[1] Poems you read and re-read to discover whether you like them – which means I do like them. The same, I suppose, applies to my feelings about Thom Gunn's poems. In both Fenton and Gunn, I feel they stand a bit outside their subject (with Fenton the oppressed and the oppressors in Vietnam etc, with Gunn his motorcyclists in California). With Fenton this is because it is impossible to identify with human misery, the victims, the oppressors without entering into conditions which make the poetic life and the poetic work impossible. But it is a task for poets to do so. And if there are no poets who do so then poetry is a kind of luxury product (this is not right. Not what I mean).

With Gunn it is sexual snobbery, the poet seeking to identify with the brainless gods – motorcyclists, etc – he worships.

With Fenton one feels that on some level of the imagination identification is possible. Victims of this civilization are serious. Misery makes them so. In fact so serious is it that the poet can almost envy their misery thinking that if it were real to him and if entering into its reality he retained nevertheless the conditions which enabled him to write poetry, he would be the better poet for this.

Auden of course would not accept this argument, enter into this line of thought. The conditions which permitted him to write poetry were those of the bourgeois. If the poetry that resulted was bourgeois – and insensitive to the suffering of humanity – tant pis [so much the

---

1 James Fenton (b. 1949), British poet. The new book of poems was *Out of Danger.*

worse]. He would not pretend to enter into the misery which made bourgeois civilization possible.

13 November 1993, London

Of course the continued bore of this lawsuit. Wake up at 5 and for an hour or two go through it all rehearse my indignation.

Spent the morning writing notes about Christopher [Isherwood] and Sally Bowles and self in Berlin in the early 1930s. Then in the early evening went to Sadler's Wells where a group of performers are rehearsing for a musical version of *Cabaret*, and – at John Wells' invitation – I tried to give an idea of Christopher's and Jean [Ross]'s and my life in Berlin. Told them that Christopher and I could not have afforded to go to any of the bars described in the [Liza] Minelli movie *Cabaret*.[1]

The flirtatious sexy charm of young actors and actresses to someone old as myself. One or two of the boys (especially one) chiefly interested in our dealings with boys. Were they prostitutes? How much did one pay them? The answer was that there was an understood fee of 10 marks – but what they really wanted was a relationship – *Verhältnis* – perhaps be taken on a holiday with one but really a friendship. I think I managed to persuade them that [the] environment of Sally Bowles was poor – though there was a still poorer level of the unemployed and real misery below us.

After this John and I had a drink at a new and very dreary club near the Escargot Restaurant. Then we went to the Hungarian Restaurant Gay Hussar and were joined by Jane Horrocks the singer in the role of Sally and the producer, Sam Mendes.[2] Jane Horrocks off-stage speaks in a flinty Glaswegian [*sic*] accent, very difficult to follow. John says she is a brilliant actress and on stage can talk in any accent required in her role. I look forward to Sally Bowles in December.

---

1 The film *Cabaret* (1972), directed by Bob Fosse, is loosely based on the 1966 Broadway musical *Cabaret* by John Kander and Fred Ebb, which was adapted from Christopher Isherwood's *The Berlin Stories* (1946), and the play *I Am A Camera* (1951) by John Van Druton.

2 Jane Horrocks (b. 1964), British actress and singer, at this date the girlfriend of the British director Sam Mendes (b. 1965). In fact Horrocks is from Lancashire.

17 November 1993, London

Peter Porter interviewed me before a PEN Club audience. Talk about poetry. Peter as always intelligent – brilliant in fact – not as successful as he deserves to be – completely honourable and disinterested man of letters. In his poetry he is much influenced by Auden. It is almost as though he is carrying on a conversation with the witty accomplished intellectual Auden. But Auden of course was not just this. Kate —— (writer about Auden) was there.[1] Bright and agreeable, as always.

Peter said he had toured in Australia with D. Leavitt, who had never addressed a word to him thinking he was not important enough to address a word to and where Leavitt treated himself, and was treated, as the star of the tour.

21 November 1993, London

Last night we went to a party given by Professor and Mrs Schuchard, whom we knew at Emory University twelve (!?) years ago.[2] They are staying in a large inevitably bare apartment near Swiss Cottage. In their bare room with chairs drawn up against the walls and a table to one side beneath a window, they entertained a mostly academic and mostly male group of people to a kind of cold collation. I was pounced on by a small bearded busy-body of a man called Robin Austen, who told me that he was at the Duffield Festival in Yorkshire where Auden had gone for six days, two months before he died in Vienna. 'How was Auden?' I asked. 'Extremely disagreeable. He couldn't possibly have been more unpleasant.' He then told me how he spent hours driving Auden through the Yorkshire dales, which he supposed to be Auden's homeland – subject of many of his poems – which Auden would be delighted to revisit in Austen's delightful company, but, to his surprise, Auden was surly gruff uncommunicative.

On one occasion he took Auden out to a dinner which had been elaborately prepared for him by a hostess. Auden refused to touch

---

1 Katherine (Kate) Bucknell (b. 1957), American-born critic and novelist, editor of Auden's *Juvenilia* and Isherwood's diaries.

2 W. Ronald Schuchard, American academic based at Emory University, Atlanta, specialising in Irish literature and modernism.

the food and said that all he wanted to eat was a banana – an item that his hostess then had to get from a neighbour.

Austen also related how he had a great idea with which Auden should have been delighted. This was that Auden should make a small selection of his poems which he, Austen, would then print (or have printed) very beautifully, 'free of Faber and all other publication and vulgarity,' he said. He expected that Auden would fall in with this suggestion, delighted at the honour that was being done him. He was amazed that Auden did not respond at all. The idea that he Austen was being self-serving did not seem to have crossed his mind then or to do so now when he was telling me the story.

I pointed out to Mr Austen that many years ago when I was at the University of Connecticut, a very nice man (David Godine) had a private press on which he printed a small vol. of my poems for private distribution; and he had asked me to approach Auden with the idea that he should print a similar selection of his poems, giving Auden some of the copies.[1] 'But what would I do with them?' Auden asked when I did this. I said he could give them away to people. 'But who should I give them to?' asked Auden – a rather desolating desolated reply.

Hearing Mr Austen talk I could imagine very well Auden's situation. Ill (he must have been if he refused to eat dinner) lonely arriving at the Festival with the prospect of six interminable days before him, in which he was to make appearances, varied by being driven over Yorkshire moors by Mr Austen. Such a situation must have been like a visit to Hell with that kind of accompanying vision of an eternity spent like this which such occasions can bring. Sitting next to Mr Austen on a chaise longue for half an hour and being told this was enough to give me a sense of the horror of it. Poor Wystan, two months before he died.

(Especially sad when I remember how eager he was in 1928 that I should print the little volume on the hand press and how eager to distribute the gift among his friends. Incidentally, I suppose I should be grateful to Mr Austen because he had brought to the party for me a replica of this book printed at the Ilkley Literary Festival.)

This afternoon went to the Festival Hall to hear [Sviatoslav]

---

1 Spender's volume was an early version of *The Generous Days* (1971).

Richter play Bach preludes followed by Beethoven's Pathétique Sonata followed by Schubert's Fantasia sonata. The stage and hall dim-lit while Richter sat at the piano with one light illuminating the keys of the piano and the score from which he read the music. The Bach seemed rather subdued and not very interesting; in the Beethoven he came into his own and with the Schubert was magnificent. He took a lot of applause without once even for a moment smiling or seeming to recognize the existence of the audience – apart from his bowing to them. I said to Isaiah whom, with Aline, we joined afterwards that somehow the concert hall seemed inimical to this kind of performance which would be delightful in a drawing room among friends some in chairs or on sofas, some sitting on the floor. Isaiah said this was just how it had been in Russia where he [Richter] would play in their dachas to Pasternak, Akhmatova and their friends.

After the concert we went with Aline and Isaiah to a Café Restaurant called Richot in Piccadilly and had high tea. Isaiah said that Miriam Gross from the *Telegraph* had written asking him and some others to write each a short piece on what they regarded as the most influential book written since 1945. By 'influential' she meant which book had done most to change one's view of life. We thought that if the same question had been asked about 1920–1945 there would be a lot of answers – *Ulysses*, *The Waste Land*, Huxley's *Brave New World*, Keynes, Eddington, etc.[1] Post-1945 he could only think of anti-Communist books – Orwell, Solzhenitsyn etc, which troubled him. Stuart Hampshire suggested Rachel Carson on the environment [*Silent Spring*], but I thought this was opting out because everyone agrees about the environment. I suggested *Look Back in Anger* with the emergence of a new kind of lower middle class or working class vision of life. But the fact is that 1945–1985 was taken up with pro-Communist or anti-Communist positions (Isaiah suggested *The God that Failed* as a crucial book) and that this debate was really very sterile. The French

---

1 John Maynard Keynes (1883–1946), British economist. Keynes laid the foundations of modern macroeconomics with *The General Theory of Employment, Interest and Money* (1936), which argued that full employment is determined by effective demand and requires government spending on public works to stimulate this. Sir Arthur Stanley Eddington (1882–1944), British astrophysicist. In the interwar period, Eddington brought Einstein's Theory of Relativity to the English-speaking world.

intelligentsia had been almost uniformly Communist – Sartre etc, with only Camus opposing this.

24 November 1993, London

Last night a party at the Groucho Club for the publication of Mark Boxer's book of caricatures of famous people.[1] There was a young man there who looked like some dazzling pristine idealized version of Mark. I went up to him and, I think, before I could say anything, he said: 'Yes I am Mark's son.' 'Isn't he incredibly like him?' said a woman standing next to him and the youth said: 'Yes, that's what everyone says,' preening himself as it were posthumously.

Wedgwood Benn was there and I went up to him.[2] He immediately started asking me why the young did not support the causes we supported, and he said that one of the books that had influenced him in his youth was *Forward from Liberalism*.[3] 'A terribly bad book, I fear,' I said. 'How can you say that? It was one of the books that converted a generation.' 'It was so badly written and so ignorant.' He looked at me as though I was some kind of renegade. 'It isn't the opinions I object to so much as the writing,' I said. 'Why don't the young get excited about social injustices nowadays?' he asked and reeled off a list of injustices to show things were just as bad, if not worse, today than 60 years ago. 'Perhaps they need a book,' I said. 'Well, there's Marx. It's as true today as it was a hundred years ago.' 'Yes but it was published a hundred years ago. They need a new book by someone new.' 'Nonsense. Marx is as true today as he ever was.' It seemed impossible to persuade him that young people need voices of their own generation even if those voices [do not] say new things. Benn seemed to me to have the impenetrability of someone, some public figure, who does all the talking. I had a wild desire to take him

---

1 Mark Boxer had died in 1988. The book being celebrated was *The Collected and Recollected Mark* (1993).

2 Tony (Wedgwood) Benn (b. 1925), British socialist politician currently serving as the Labour MP for Chesterfield.

3 Spender's Marxist exegesis on literature *Forward from Liberalism* had been published by Victor Gollancz's Left Book Club in 1937.

aside, alone, away from the noise of the party, just to see if he could listen to anything. Perhaps he can, and does.

25 November 1993, London

Yesterday Matthew appeared having flown in from New York. [. . .] He said that when he first arrived in New York, he had the impression that sympathy among our colleagues and acquaintances was with Mr Leavitt about the novel [*While England Sleeps*]. But then some journalist who had done a lot of research, produced a devastating article exposing the 'theft' which appeared in *The Boston Globe* and he thought that now those in N.Y. sympathized with me. He was extremely objective about all this rather like a benevolent doctor or psychiatrist – well it is our sickness our neurosis.[1]

16 December 1993, London

We went to a large party at the American Embassy. It consisted mostly of politicians, among them Mrs Thatcher (surrounded by a gaggle of admirers – I wanted to go up to her just to see if she recognized me, but had no chance to do so).[2] Kinnock was there and I had a pleasant conversation with him. Really a nice man. How awful for him not to be P.M.[3] [. . .]

I have sent a dozen or so copies of *Dolphins* my new poems to friends and colleagues.[4] The fact is though that I have no confidence that to friends – or indeed to anyone except a few readers one does not know – poems are anything but an embarrassment. Well, David [Plante] and Nikos [Stangos] here (a Greek and an American) and Reynolds Price and Bill Mazzocco (two Americans) would be excep-

---

1 The position of Spender's son on the subject of Leavitt's book was that most books die, especially bad books, and that it would save his father many sleepless nights if he forgot about it.

2 Spender was curious whether Margaret Thatcher would recognize him because he had met her only a few days previously.

3 Neil Kinnock had resigned as Leader of the Labour Party after defeat in the general election of 1992.

4 *Dolphins*, Spender's last volume of poems, was published in January 1994.

tions. Also Harold Pinter. This is because I have no confidence that people like poetry (I am not sure whether I do myself). Doubtless they do like a few poems. These are by poets who break through the I-don't-like-poetry barrier – Yeats, Eliot, Auden, perhaps MacNeice. But I don't think I'm one of these. Anyway, I've sent them out: 'Go little book', etc.

Thinking about Ian Hamilton asking me about my ambitions and arising from that whether I expect to be remembered, famous. I have not paid the price in terms of my life, and perhaps also the lives of those around me which wins real fame. Probably I was right not to: because by paying it – as I have seen people do – I would not have proved sufficiently gifted to gain that fame any way. But the price people pay may be to sacrifice the greatest satisfactions in life. It may also mean sacrificing other people. I never forget how when Auden came to see us in London in April 1945, the first thing he said to me was: 'You have a son' (and later on when shown that son, he said: 'All babies look like Winston Churchill'). But Auden would have been a very good, and certainly an adoring, father: and if he had had a son would have been fulfilled as a man in a way in which he was not – condemned to live a bachelor life with – or, more often, without – Chester. Those who fulfil their potentiality in their work often sacrifice fulfilment in their lives for it – think of Beethoven. Clearly I have not even faced that choice.

21 December 1993, London

Matthew Evans and John Bodley took me to lunch at The Ivy.[1] This was a treat at which we also discussed business. The position with regard to *While England Slept* is that we see the rewritten version before agreeing to its publication – and that we won't accept a world settlement except on the condition of the rewritten and accepted (if it is accepted) version being the one published abroad.

John B. has the idea supported by Matthew [Evans] that I should edit an anthology of Thirties Writing with an Introduction by me. I

---

1 Both Evans and Bodley were senior editors at Faber; the occasion for the lunch was the imminent publication of *Dolphins*.

am interested in this but must start at once filling a notebook with ideas. [. . .]

Later on talked with Nicholas Mosley who, as always, was very friendly.[1] Although in every way a liberal, he seems to be fascinated by his father's – 'my old dad's' ideas. One of these was that if we had not made war with Germany and had let Hitler get away with whatever he wanted in Eastern Europe and Russia, then in the long run the Nazis would have stopped being so nasty and everything would have been all right. I pointed out that everything would have been all right perhaps from Mosley's point of view but Mosley called himself a British Fascist and from my point of view, it would not have been all right. Nicholas saw the point of this. I said the Nazis if left alone by us might perhaps have concentrated on Eastern Europe and Russia building immense highways there and cities run by Nazi Germans in which the Slavonic peoples provided slave labour. Nicholas seemed puzzled by this and when I referred to Speer seemed never to have read him.[2]

26 December 1993, London

In the last two days I have read two books one on the Billionaire Boys of Los Angeles, the other [Adam] Sisman's biography of Alan Taylor.[3] [. . .] During the early part of the war, i.e. in 1940–41, Natasha and I stayed with Alan and his wife Margaret in their house adjoining Magdalen College. While not ever becoming very close friends, we had, as paying guests, very good relations with them, and I have no memories except of their being kind to us. We realized I think that she was at this time madly in love with Robert Kee who was then a prisoner of war in Germany. Alan was friendly, dogmatic in all his views, very assertive, but good-humoured, extremely opin-

---

1 Nicholas Mosley (b. 1923), British novelist and the eldest son of Oswald Mosley.

2 Albert Speer (1905–1981), German architect who was given great power by Hitler and who intended totally to redesign the cities of the Third Reich.

3 The 'Billionaire Boys' was a gang of crooked young investors in the 1980s, whose crimes are chronicled in Sue Horton's *The Billionaire Boys Club* (1990). Adam Sisman's biography of the British historian A. J. P. (Alan) Taylor (1906–1990) would be published in January 1994.

ionated and very knowledgeable. She was sympathetic, a supporter of good causes, kind and generous. In the book Alan comes across as immensely energetic, powerfully intellectual, grossly maltreated by Dylan Thomas – to whom Maggie Taylor later translated her stifling and financially sacrificial affections.[1] Dylan is in all his dealings with the Taylors unspeakably awful really: playing up to while scarcely disguising his contempt for Maggie, grasping, treacherous, utterly inconsiderate in his behaviour to Alan Taylor, destructive to their family – and prepared to turn his own contempt for the woman whom he so exploited, into a continuous ribald performance for his cronies. His exploitation extended to getting at various times several houses out of her: but he didn't have the pretentiousness which in other such cases of 'genius' – Wagner – founded some style of living on these trophies gained, but transformed every place he was given into instant squalor where he cohabited with his even more squalid wife.

Sisman describes Alan as very stingy: but if he had been all that grasping surely he would have somehow prevented Maggie nearly ruining herself supporting Dylan Thomas. Surely when we were their paying guests and had meals with them we would have noticed the stinginess (we certainly did when earlier in the war we stayed with Clissold Tuely).[2]

---

1 Dylan Thomas stayed with Alan Taylor and his wife Margaret in April 1935 for a month in their house in Disley, near Manchester. Thomas needed somewhere to stay and earned his keep by painting the outside of the house. He and Taylor initially got along well, reading Rabelais together, with Thomas responding to the Taylors' efforts to curb his drinking. The relationship soured, however, when Dylan Thomas moved into the Taylors' summer house, 'The Studio' in the garden of their house in Oxford, with Caitlin and Dylan Thomas's children lodging in the main house. Margaret Taylor grew affectionate towards Thomas, becoming his patroness. She dealt with his tax, supplied him with cash and even paid his children's school fees. Alan Taylor was aware of the situation, but was unable to do anything. After Thomas's death he wrote of him, 'I have known no one of any great interest; and the few episodes I might record would give universal pain. How would the great like a picture of Dylan treating human beings as a boy pulls wings off a fly?' (Letter to David Higham, 23 March 1967).

2 The Spenders stayed at Clissold and Diana Tuely's house Underhill Farm, overlooking the Romney Marshes at Wittersham, Kent, in 1941. Diana Tuely's sister Margaret (née Low) was married to Humphrey Spender.

Sisman seems to suggest that the Taylors benefited from their p.g.'s [paying guests'] ration books. Maybe[,] we did not notice this.

What Sisman does portray is the way in which Taylor turned himself almost into a machine for producing journalism: writing articles or reviews in a matter of minutes. His opinions were ingredients of his journalism and lecturing. Though subject to alteration they were while held – anti-German, pro-Soviet, anti-European – almost automatic. His love of Beaverbrook above, really, everyone else in the world, including wives and family, was love of power determination grandeur – all the qualities concentrated in Beaverbrook – combined with delight in B.'s temperament and personality.[1] Sisman makes it clear that other admirers of Beaverbrook, like Michael Foot, refused to take gifts from B. Alan not only took gifts but also touted for more. But Alan surely would have felt – as M. Foot would have felt – that he had to prove to himself his own disinterestedness in the benefits to be reaped from a relationship by rejecting those benefits.

There is a kind of hollowness about Taylor: the hollowness of someone who only likes other people who have characteristics of power, success, professionalism, that are on display and demonstrable. His quarrels with other people are like the snapping of external connections or gratification in those people which have made him like them at all. All the same he had a kindness which was felt in relationships which were superficial as with many students and with Natasha and me. He seems to have loved music. Sisman mentions this but does not go into it at all deeply.

28 December 1993, London

I hate this dead period of the year which goes on in England till about Jan 5. Evading my real work, spent most of yesterday reading a paperback which consists of a collection of essays appearing in the T.L.S. about Imperial Russia (1902), the Soviet Union 1917 to 1990, and after. A lot of articles by E. H. Carr, so admired by A.J.P. Taylor, who later quarrelled with him and later on especially after his death articles attacking Carr (notably a brilliant one by [Leo] Labedz) and

---

1 William Maxwell (Max) Aitken, 1st Baron Beaverbrook (1879–1964), Canadian-British newspaper magnate and business tycoon.

letters defending him from these attacks.[1] Reviews of the Webbs on Russia.[2] What is indisputable is that no one foresaw the total collapse of the U.S.S.R. Some realized that in the long run it would break down but this would be a matter of years. With Isaiah I shared the wish that it would do so. For him it was (during the War when he was posted in Moscow and had nightmares that he would be re-claimed by the Soviet authorities as a Russian, and resolved, if that should happen, to kill himself) the most evil government in the World [. . .]

Perhaps what made it seem so enduring to outsiders was the symmetry between it and the U.S. The idea of two world powers counter-balancing each other. Reading, as I compulsively do, nearly every bit of news out of Russia, one has the impression of a vacuum. What has characterized the leaders who have had power since the collapse – Gorbachev and Yeltsin – is the impression they give of improvising in a void.[3] The remedy they have to offer – setting up capitalism – is dependent on the people having to endure years of penury, mass unemployment etc under an emergent class of profiteers, gangsters, for an indefinite period until capitalism gets to a stage when the capitalists will dare to impose order on their greed.

Meanwhile the internecine struggle between populations goes on in Yugoslavia producing thousands of victims shown every night on TV.

There comes into my head a not-self poem. I want to read a whole volume of translations of Russian poetry – because Russian poets of this century seem to me those most exposed to historic circumstances in which they've lived – under which they've suffered – of the poets

---

1 E. H. Carr (1892–1982), left-wing British historian, author of a pro-communist 14-volume history of the Soviet Union from 1917 to 1929.

2 Sidney and Beatrice Webb, prominent members of the Fabian society, whose books *Soviet Communism: A New Civilisation?* (1935) and *The Truth About Soviet Russia* (1942) were largely uncritical in their portrayal of Stalin's Russia.

3 Mikhail Gorbachev (b. 1931) had come to power in 1985 against a backdrop of a stagnant economy, crippled by defence spending and further damaged by a recent fall in oil prices. He instituted social, political and economic liberalizing reforms and a glasnost policy of free speech and political openness. Under his rule, communist regimes were deposed across Eastern Europe. In 1991, Gorbachev was succeeded by Boris Yeltsin (1937–2007) who ruled as President of the Russian Federation until 1999.

of our century. I remember, years ago, Robert Lowell saying to [Andrei] Voznesensky that as an American poet he envied – or could almost envy Russian poets – because although they could only work under terrible circumstances of persecution, thousands of Russians read their poetry.[1] We poets in the West have freedom – but only our fellow poets read us. In much of this Russian poetry the poet is a character[,] a personality at the centre of his experience of history but the events of that history are outside his personality. My own poetry seems limited to experiences which affect my personality as a poet, but does not reach out beyond what is personally experienced into the world of contemporary history lived in my time by people whose experiences – of war, imprisonment, destitution are beyond anything I have experienced – yet I am obsessively conscious of them.

'The world that is not' is a line with which the poem might possibly begin because to be comprehensible it has to lead into a description of that world – and even beyond that world.

1 January 1994, London

If you read individual poets in translation you get an impression certainly. I read a whole volume of [Anna] Akhmatova recently and I certainly got a strong idea of her personality in her poetry – increased perhaps by the fact that I met her when she was in London. And I have an impression of [Boris] Pasternak who wrote several letters to me when I was at *Encounter*. Also because I feel ashamed of the fact that when I went, with Muriel Buttinger, to Moscow ([. . .] just when Khrushchev had come to power) I did not visit P. (I also feel that he resented my not having done so). Perhaps wrongly, I am convinced that if I had hailed a taxi in Moscow and said to the driver 'Pasternak' he would have taken me to see him.

---

1 Andrei Voznesensky (1933–2010), iconic Russian poet of the post-Stalin era. He won the Soviet State Prize in 1978. His role as poet meant that he was free to travel and acted as an unofficial representative of the USSR. He published more than thirty literary works, some of them bestsellers selling in hundreds of thousands.

8 February 1994, London

On Wednesday Feb. 9 at something called the October Gallery there was a party all for poets, celebrating the appearance of the *Oxford Companion to Modern Poetry*, a volume edited in masterly fashion by Ian Hamilton. Several of the poets were kind and polite and touching to me as though greeting me for the first/last time. Some rather nasty snide lines by Yeats come to mind:

> Much did I rage when young,
> Being by the world oppressed,
> Which now with flattering tongue
> Speeds the parting guest.

(the 4th line must be misquoted).[1]

I remember walking through Christ Church Quad reciting these lines to myself and thinking of a variation which anticipated my own fame which came to a climax and then ended with reaction against me expressed in the line

> And then the rebelling dust

I forget the other three.

The poets were awarded a speech by Clive James – the least poetic but most televised poet in the room.[2] It was more amusing than any I – the oldest poet in the room – might have made, but nevertheless I felt miffed.

11 February 1994, London

Yesterday (February 10) I did an interview for Kaleidoscope (B.B.C.) with Peter Porter: rather a conversation piece than interview. As always with P.P. I felt 'here is a wonderfully intelligent gifted learned man, much neglected by the public, deserving of great rewards in any just society.' He turned his own witty conversation into questions to me and helped to make me rise above my form in a 40 minute

---

1 'Youth and Age' (1924); the last two lines should read: 'But now with flattering tongue / It speeds the parting guest'.

2 Clive James (b. 1939), Australian-born broadcaster, poet, journalist and memoirist, who lives in England.

broadcast which without him would have been very tiring. I was extremely grateful to him. At one point, after I had read a poem, I asked him to read one of his but he shrugged this off.

Then I went to Faber's where I had to sign copies of *Dolphins*. I was at once surrounded by three, I think[,] of Faber's young editors, two boys and a girl – and felt again this kind of loving attention which in them was beautiful, because they were, all three, beautiful in their youth. I thought 'this kind of caring attention to the old is almost like sex – measured as feeling almost identical with it – yet if the old person, breaking through what seems the frailest of barriers, treated it as sex – he would be obscene and horrible. So it is one of the experiences – relationships – in this world, this life, which is the most spiritual. It bestows too on them, the young, a kind of bodiless-ness which is made the more beautiful because they have bodies – as though the beauty in them which is their bodies, their sex, suddenly became translated into pure mind.' [. . .]

In old age vanity provides a sensation – a satisfaction – like resurrection.

25 February 1994, London

At present I really am overwhelmed by things connected with my birthday: we have undertaken and accepted too much. I long to get to France on April 1. Strangely enough, I want to write poetry – or, rather, I want to complete the poetry for which I have many notes. I would like to do a new volume within a year.

N. mentioned for the first time what she would or will do if I die. 1) Sell St Jerome. Much as she loves it she does not want to retire there alone or with a friend or help. I am sad with the feeling that for married people – or for people who live together like John Golding and James Joll – the end of life is inevitably solitude for one of them. They can share everything but parting.

I have to think about small speeches I must make at the Faber party and then, a week later, at an *Evening Standard* luncheon. I thought of making a speech at the Faber party, taking up my reputa-tion for being self- [blank space in manuscript]. I would begin by recalling how I once said to Wystan that, when I was a small boy at prep school I always had a very exact idea of all the boys I knew existing as it were in a solar system where some were larger or brighter[,] others smaller and dimmer – and how I, from my position in that system, had a very clear [word missing in manuscript] of my relation to those other people I knew. Auden said, 'How extraordinary. I always realized I was brighter than anyone else.' I would then go on to say I knew that several of my friends were cleverer in their degrees of intellect and achievement than I was; but I also knew that precisely because I was aware of this, I had a sense of truth greater than that of anyone else: and it was by this truth that I was a poet.

Instead I shall make a speech about being a Faber author.

1 March 1994, London

The dinner for 26 people given at The Ivy for my birthday [28 February]. Our hosts the Littmans and the Ed Victors. Guests Matthew, Maro, Saskia, Cosima; Barry, Lizzie; Isaiah and Aline Berlin; Michael Holroyd; John Bayley and Iris Murdoch; Stuart and Nancy Hampshire; John and Rosamond Russell (flown from New York); Anne Cox Chambers.[1] I sat between Rosamond and Anne, took my first spoonful of soup decided I did not want any more and went on talking to Anne who said: 'I think you're feeling ill,' at which I got up and went to the anteroom of the dining room where we were eating. Ed Victor then decided I must go to hospital and before I could protest I was hurried downstairs into the street and two strong ambulance men were making me lie down in a kind of stretcher. Downstairs in the lower part of the hospital I was very promptly and extensively examined for about two hours by two seemingly efficient and very friendly doctors who pronounced that I must stay in the hospital overnight – just what I most dreaded.[2] So there I was in a dimly lit room with an Arab doing gymnastic prayers in one bed, a man with a breathing mask in the bed next to him and next to me an almost motionless youth with sitting in front of him two policemen. There was the peculiar feeling of a hospital ward at night that all these

---

1 Michael Holroyd, British biographer (b. 1935).

2 Spender had suffered from a heart seizure; his pulse stopped for a minute and he was in fact carried downstairs by the ambulance men; Matthew Spender hosted the remainder of the party.

people lying in bed were in a state more of waiting watchfulness than of sleep. Then the curved girders which were rails for those curtains which were drawn when the patient needed the special attention of a nurse. I took two sleeping tablets and woke about 8 a.m. I did not have anything to read until midday when the visitors to the patient with the mask over his face gave me *The Times*.

12 March 1994, London

On Wednesday at Festival Hall, a discussion between Angelica Garnett, Valentine Cunningham and myself about the Thirties.[1] Angelica talked about a Bloomsbury childhood, her mother Vanessa, her brothers Julian and Quentin. She sounded very out of it all with her mother and Duncan painting away (though she also painted) and Julian and Quentin becoming involved in politics (the Spanish Civil War). She was very self-abnegating and one did feel that she personified in herself a strange lonely generation that had always been anything between five and fifteen years younger than her contemporaries and that this was sealed when she married Bunny Garnett, old enough to be her father. All the time she spoke I remembered being brought over from Rodmell by Leonard and Virginia Woolf, and playing croquet on the lawn at Charleston.[2] There Angelica was, standing apart, I seem to remember, the most beautiful girl I had ever seen. Now if I had at that time of my life had the will and energy of my wishes. But all my wishes did for me was to make me think their goals were unattainable. In any case Angelica was 8 years younger than my 24 years and that seemed a great deal since she was 16.

She has the air of having stood aside all these years and let life trample over her. There have been a lot of tragedies – a daughter, or daughters, committing suicide, and David Garnett proving a selfish old monster (what would I have proved, though?). It is curious to

---

1 Angelica Garnett (b. 1918), writer and artist associated with the Bloomsbury Group, illegitimate daughter of Vanessa Bell and Duncan Grant. She later married Grant's former lover David ('Bunny') Garnett. Valentine Cunningham (b. 1944), British literary scholar and Professor of English at Oxford University, author of *British Writers of the 1930s* (1988).

2 Rodmell was the Woolfs' house, and Charleston Farmhouse the Grants' house, both in Sussex.

[718]

think that her father (really, Duncan Grant) had a love affair with her husband (or is that not the case? It sounds very Bloomsbury).

We did not speak of all this. Matthew once told her 'my father fell in love with you when he saw you first' and he said she looked stunned with embarrassment.

She now lives in Foucalquier [. . .] where she knows friends of ours the chief of whom is Douglas Johnson the painter. She seems happier in Foucalquier than, I suppose, she has ever been. She once – perhaps 15 years ago – turned up at our house – Saint Jerome – with a young man her (then) Moroccan lover.

In April 1994, Spender spent a few days in Florence, celebrating the publication of his new collection of poetry, Dolphins, *and then visited Matthew in Tuscany.*

April 1994, St Jerome

Well, that was Italy. Florence and all those celebrations, followed by five days at 'Avane' – Natasha leaving for London on the second day from Pisa, where Matthew drove her and me. [. . .] Matthew seemed to drive from San Sano, near Siena, and back daily to join us. On the third day [. . .] he drove us to San Sano. I had not been there for six or seven years – last time we went there – left under rather bad circumstances. Maro had spent the time taunting me on various grounds – my egotism, my old age, my ugliness, etc., until we left, I vowing never to come back and be a sitting target for her. Barry and Lizzie had been there a few weeks ago, and things had gone very badly; Saskia and Cosima had been there, and what Lizzie and Barry found particularly offensive was the way the three women ganged up against Matthew, blaming him and teasing him continuously. Of course, it is very difficult to judge such family situations. Maro (and, sometimes, even Matthew) go in for teasing in a big way without seeming to take much thought about the effect on other people. But Barry and Lizzie's visit ended with a showdown between Matthew and Lizzie, in which Lizzie (according to Matthew) said that I had sworn never to go to 'Avane' again.

So my visit there had a symbolic importance. It proved that I would go there again. It healed wounds between Maro and us. It provided [. . .] an alternate happy ending. Everyone, especially Maro, was conscious of making a special effort. It was a great success.

8 May 1994, London

Went home [from France] for a week on account of celebrations for *Index* which has been entirely re-designed in a smaller format, and has a new Editor. The banquet was at Selfridges Hotel, and there were about 200 people. Speeches by Jon Snow, Salman Rushdie and myself.[1] Jon Snow was also a kind of master of ceremonies, which he did very well.

There were very good arrangements by which guests could sign on the spot subscription forms for *Index*. With all this the results seem to have been a bit disappointing. It is probably a bad time to raise money for anything, as the attacks on the government and its general shakiness, undermine confidence.

Following the banquet, on Wednesday we went to Oxford to attend a poetry reading given by Ted Hughes and Seamus Heaney at the Sheldonian. Half the money for this went to *Index*. We had to cadge a lift as our car is in France and we were driven by Bill Webb, formerly literary editor of *The Guardian*. He is an amiable intelligent man who gives the impression of being rather ineffective – in fact an impression so faint as hardly to exist at all. Bill Webb knew of some special route to Oxford which he went – with the result that we got held up in a traffic jam for two hours during which we certainly did not move more than ten miles. Conversation ran out. He put on LPs [*sic*] on the car radio consisting of very thin orchestral music by nephews of Bach and cousins of Handel.

We arrived at Oxford halfway through the speech introducing the poets – made by someone very distinguished. I don't know whom. Seamus read with assurance after making an introduction in which he referred to the fact that his term of office as Prof. of Poetry is

---

1 Jon Snow (b. 1947), British journalist and broadcaster. Salman Rushdie (b. 1947), British Indian novelist, at this point living under police protection because of the fatwa proclaimed against him in 1989 by the Ayatollah Khomeini, leader of Iran, as a result of Rushdie's irreverent treatment of the prophet Muhammad in his 1988 novel *The Satanic Verses*.

over.[1] He spoke with the kind of confidence of someone who not only knows he is well liked but that people have good reason to like him. Ripples of his popularity ran through the audience. And I am sure it is quite true. He combines being a man of immense good will and conscientiousness in his tasks beyond the call of duty, he is scholarly meticulous and he writes poems which are models of what we might call the late Georgian Yeatsian Irish peasant. Observation, style, force of recollection of humble origins, all achieve in him their fullest most scrupulous flowering.

The Irish brogue in fact prevented me following the reading very closely – but no one else seemed to have any problem with it. There followed Ted – an intermittent genius surely, and utterly *sui generis*. His poems are not easy to follow at a reading (or perhaps I was exhausted after the journey) but they come across in great flashes of passion and of insight – insight particularly into the animal side of humans and the dark side of animals. Oddly, both poets came across best when they were not reading their poems but extemporizing about the experiences from which these sprang – Seamus indeed on his childhood, and Ted in an absolutely gripping description of the life of the salmon, and his experiences salmon fishing in Alaska.

Behind Ted when he read was what seemed like a bare electric light bulb up to which, leaning back, he held the book from which he was reading: and the light from the bulb seemed to penetrate through one lens of his spectacles sending forth a ray visible to the audience from where I was sitting. Behind the rostrum from which each poet in turn spoke there was the highly ornate background and the Sheldonian like the elaborate plating of some armoured knight of old. Seamus's reading was slightly interrupted by shouting and cheering of undergraduates outside the hall, on some binge, I suppose, which penetrated within, provoking on his face while he went on reading, a slight smile of recognition. I felt some envy for Seamus and Ted thinking 'but I am from Oxford too and all this is connected with me. How nice it would be if they noticed me in the audience and asked me to come up and read two or three poems.' And I remembered from the Spanish Civil War sitting next to Manuel Altolaguirre, in

---

1 From 1989 to 1994 Seamus Heaney had been the Professor of Poetry at Oxford.

some hall where Rafael Alberti was reading, and my asking Manuel whether he liked the reading. 'No, I hate it,' he said. 'It is I who should be reading. Yo, yo [I, I] –' and he thumped himself on the chest.[1]

10 May 1994, St Jerome

Reynolds [Price] had sent me his new book which is a meticulous account of his having an operation for spinal cancer, which was followed by his gradually becoming paralysed from waist down.[2] It is, I think, a masterpiece. The whole book is penetrated with medical knowledge he has mastered, together with an exact memory of his own reactions and feelings and of every event over these ten years, together with his capacity to tell a story. Being written from the point of view of a patient who understands both the illness and the treatment he has received it is a book that will doubtless be read by doctors. It will also be read by people close to the sick who wish to understand the feelings of the sick. But for people like myself who seem never to have suffered serious pain, it is an enlargement of their knowledge and understanding of life – of what people endure.

I have known Reynolds for nearly forty years. Of course I have known he was ill, and I have visited him at his home in North Carolina since his illness: and have talked with friends of his who have looked after him there. But seeing him leading a very full life of writing and friends and even of travel and teaching and giving readings, I never realized how much pain he had, nor through how many crises he had passed.

His book is among other things a tribute to the people who have cared for him: though I doubt whether they would have shown such devotion to anyone else almost. He is someone who fascinates other people with his humour, his wit, his intelligence, his way of talking and, despite his illness, his looks. I think more than this: that there is something deeply religious about him which is wholly acceptable. He

---

1 Manuel Altolaguirre (1905–1959), Spanish poet, comrade of Spender's in the Civil War. Rafael Alberti Merello (1902–1999), Spanish poet, like Altolaguirre a member of the so-called 'Generation of '27'.

2 *A Whole New Life* (1994).

brings out in other people their best qualities. But it is a virtue of Americans, particularly his North Carolingians, that they respond in this way. The American use of the phrase 'it's a privilege' is relevant here. They say 'it's a privilege' to meet you – that is a form of politeness, but only Americans use it, and it draws upon very real depths of recognition.

24 May 1994, St Jerome

Yesterday, Monday, we gave a lunch party for Anne Moynihan, together with Michael Wishart, Angelica Garnett and Douglas Johnson who came over from Foucalquier. This is unfortunately two hours' drive each way which makes it difficult to go there. Douglas had brought a kind of lithograph like a poster which incorporated a poem of mine, *The Half of Life* or the *Café in the Park*, of which he wanted me to sign seventy copies, which I did. Unfortunately the print is rather disappointing: the first line almost obliterated by illustration, and for some reason, a postage-stamp-like drawing done after a Rembrandt self portrait at one side of the text. Doesn't make any sense really. It disquieted me about Douglas whom I wish to succeed, that he had taken apparently more trouble than thought about this. Perhaps he spends too much of each year in Ceylon. Also his utter inability to do anything but rearrange other artists' ideas, making them into his own clichés, is irritating.

We were extremely lucky in having a fine day yesterday (today it is raining) for the luncheon, as we had also done when the Hutchinsons came on Thursday. Michael Wishart who is waiting to hear the results of tests which will decide whether or not he is to have an operation for cancer, seemed remarkably calm, friendly, gentle.[1] I tried to draw him as much as I could into the conversation, because he seemed at times to lapse into a separate silence. Angelica seems very happy with her Foucalquier life – even to enjoy the winter there. I had been reading [Stendhal's] *Le Rouge et le Noir* and we talked about the nineteenth-century French novel – on the whole as consisting of works we had read when we were young, but would not wish to re-read now. No one wanted to read Balzac.

---

1 Michael Wishart would die of cancer in 1996.

I think I'd describe Julien [Sorel], hero of *Le Rouge et le Noir* as a very elaborated puppet with a great many strings attached which are capable of pulling him almost to life – perhaps when the reader least expects it. In order to turn it into a French novel, it has to have a tragic ending, but this is really forced onto Julien who, unless he was made to commit an arbitrary and completely unnecessary murder, qualifies eminently to be the hero of a success story. Stendhal is out to prove that in aristocratic and haut bourgeois French society after 1816 it is impossible for Julien, son of a provincial carpenter, to be accepted by the society and the haute bourgeoisie. What he really shows is that it is extremely difficult but not really impossible. Angelica said she could not really take Julien's love life with the wife of the bourgeois provincial in whose household he is tutor to the children or with the daughter of the Marquis de la Mole in Paris.

29 May 1994, St Jerome

Old age. I keep on forgetting to write about this. I get pain enough in my shoulders to make sleeping difficult. Memory really has blanks like the sensation of saying to yourself: here is a space. As long as I can remember the space I shall be able to fill it in afterwards. I am notably more tired than I ever used to be. Occasionally when being driven in the car, if there is strong light I get whiteouts – in which I just see whiteness with some dark scratches on it – or blackouts. Having both, I sometimes feel I'll never be able to get out of it and may die in it or on the loo. Sometimes a feeling of depression about time running out. How quickly the 25 years or so since we had the house have gone . . . but 25 years later?? Feeling that all my dead friends have walked through a door which through some kind of backwardness I have not walked through. In some ways rather like the feeling of belonging to some junior house of a public school, say, in which one will pass on to the upper house. A kind of envy for the dead. Worry about the awful mess of things I'll leave behind me which other people will have to tidy up.

20 June 1994, St Jerome

I read the life of Pasternak [. . .] a dutiful worthy book in which Pasternak is always courageous, standing up for the freedom of the writer against the conformists of the Writers' Union, braving Stalin.[1] His sex life sounds extremely complicated but it is very Russian in being a succession of relationships in which a serious concern for ex-wives and a lot of letter-writing remains. Although Pasternak was leader of his generation of Moscow writers, equalled only by Akhmatova since his youth almost, he never, even when he was internationally famous, attained a status in Russia where he could simply publish whatever he wrote wherever and whenever he liked. The bureaucrats of the Writers' Union treated him – as they did Akhmatova [Konstantin], Fedin the 'old hack' etc – all the others – as though they were contributors – sometimes accepted sometimes rejected – of a school magazine: knowing too that if the contributions were rejected they could not be published elsewhere.

One wonders about his translations of *Hamlet*, *Romeo and Juliet* etc into Russian. He seems to have felt that Shakespeare should be updated. But what would that mean in the Soviet Union?

Despite all the difficulties under which he laboured in Russia – and despite his contempt for the Soviet leaders – he seems to have felt that the greatest event of the Twentieth Century was the Russian Revolution. Perhaps – if one looks at it more from Asia than from Europe. But how combine a kind of pride in this achievement – as though it were the furthest development of civilization – with utter contempt for its leaders – and also with a passionate faith in the individualism of the artist – without which art is simply a brand of public relations of a ruling political party? I think that for him and his friends appalling as conditions in Russia were there was nothing outside Russia. And within Russia, even if persecuted and largely unpublished, they had their own little community, their civilization like that of Christians in pagan Rome: whereas beyond the persecuting Roman empire there was only paganism. Reading this book brings back to me Slonimsky's saying to me when I was in Warsaw where he was President of the Polish Writers' Union, when I asked him what he

---

1 Probably Peter Levi, *Boris Pasternak: A Biography* (1990).

thought of communism: 'My dear, the greatest failure of the Twentieth Century.'[1]

23 June 1994, St Jerome

John Bodley, of Faber, sent me the edition of Auden's juvenilia.[2] The cover consists of a photo I took of Auden in 1928, 1929 or 1930 – at latest 1930. Thanks to John's unobtrusive but unending care it looks absolutely straightforward – just the photograph and the lettering. It gave me great pleasure as, I am afraid, does the fact that I feature so largely in the book as the result of my having printed *Poems 1928* on my printing press designed for printing labels only.

Reading the juvenilia brings back the young Auden. A characteristic arbitrariness which distinguishes him from the Romantic idea of the poet. In his own account of the matter, going for a walk one day with his friend Robert Medley he decides to be a poet whilst Robert will be a painter. Therefore, he writes poems. Writing poems is an objective activity, like doing carpentry (only the material is language). Being a young artist he looks for examples of poets hammering together material drawn from observation, from experience, into poems. There is none of the feeling of the Romantic, of Keats, for example, that the material is his own soul, his ego even, as with Keats. Material is clearly 'nature': and there is the feeling that Auden's experience of nature put into his poems is not through digging a well into some source of an original experience in which the child was identical with the landscape surrounding him (in the manner of Wordsworth) but is the result of going for walks in which he makes mental notes of aspects of nature which will go into poetry, on the lines of various nature poets whom he admires, notably Thomas Hardy and Edward Thomas. There very little 'I' here and when there is an 'I' it is not a consciousness or sub-consciousness merging into the universe, it is a peg on which to hang a poem.

Being two years younger than Auden and having met him first

---

1 Spender worked with Anton Slonimsky when the two men were employed at the newly formed UNESCO, under Julian Huxley, in 1946.

2 Auden's *Juvenilia: Poems, 1922–1928*, gathered and edited by Katherine Bucknell, had just been published.

when we were undergraduates, I probably have an exaggerated idea of him as the objective creator without subjective uncertainties. He certainly seemed immensely self-confident: and it was my uncle J. A. Spender with his great experience of prominent men and women of his time, going back to the Great Victorians, who when he met the young Auden on the occasion of my first marriage said 'That is the most self-confident young man I have ever met.'[1]

In writing about Auden inventing himself as a poet, I have to remember that this feat is impossible unless one is already a poet or has the possibility to be one. There are many examples of writers thinking themselves poets when they have no poetry in them. That same uncle J.A.S. wishing to discourage me from writing poetry once showed me a whole volume of poetry by Ruskin, of which presumably, no one has ever read a line. So Auden was already a poet, or already had mysterious poetry in him when he decided by an act of the will, to become one.

Nothing is less Keatsian, further from Keats' idea of the poet 'continually in for, and filling, some other body –'.[2]

The young Auden reads a great deal of poetry, decides what poets are 'in' and who are 'out'. That is to say whom he can learn from, model his own poems on – and who he cannot use in this way and who therefore scarcely interest him. Models are Thomas Hardy, Edward Thomas and Robert Frost. They are examples of poets using material in their lives or that consists of objects observed and making poetry out of it. Go for long walks in the countryside and observe things which can become verbal objects in poems. The poems are not concerned with what the poet feels about these objects, they are

---

1 For J. A. Spender, see biographical appendix.

2 A thought that had manifesto status for Spender, over the whole of his long career as a poet: 'As to the poetical Character itself, [. . .] it is not itself – it has no self – it is every thing and nothing – It has no character – it enjoys light and shade; it lives in gusto, be it foul or fair, high or low, rich or poor, mean or elevated – [. . .] A Poet is the most unpoetical of any thing in existence; because he has no Identity – he is continually in for – and filling some other Body – The Sun, the Moon, the Sea and Men and Women who are creatures of impulse are poetical and have about them an unchangeable attribute – the poet has none; no identity [. . .]'. John Keats, letter to Richard Woodhouse, 27 October 1818.

verbal artefacts and what they 'say' is merely the string which ties them together into packets.

8 July 1994, Sissinghurst

The time of year we go for two weeks to Sissinghurst in Harold Nicolson's house in the garden which seems much more beautiful at this time of year than a few weeks later when we went there last year.[1] We arrived there after dark a week ago after going to Glyndebourne with Matthew to see *The Rake's Progress*. Matthew drove me from London to Glyndebourne. It was extremely hot. Early on Matthew could not find the way out of London and got in a very bad temper with himself and the other traffic on the road. When he does this he drives furiously and is quite liable to make a U-turn in a main road. In fact he did do this at least once. Later we got rather stuck in traffic for which I was grateful as it did not give him so much room to manoeuvre. What did worry me was that it was terribly hot and I began to worry that I might faint. What would poor M. do if I fainted? I imagined him having to draw the car up to one side of the road or perhaps on the pavement and then having to telephone a hospital. Fortunately I did not faint. We drove on and got quite effectively or efficiently to the bypass. From time to time Matthew held up the map against the windscreen while he was driving. A bit unnerving bringing me memories of how when I was young the Queen of the Belgians on the royal honeymoon did this and got killed.[2] Matthew always seems not to know his way and then surprises you by knowing it. He does have a very strong sense of direction and can say 'we are going too far West or East' or whatever, then hold up the map to the windscreen and correct our direction.

We got very early to Glyndebourne and treated ourselves to champagne in lemonade – about £10 a glass. We were very early [–] walked in the gardens. Then I sat down, Matthew left me and as

---

1 Following the deaths of Harold Nicolson and Vita Sackville-West the house and gardens had been bought by the National Trust, though the family retained a house in the grounds. Spender was the guest of Nigel Nicolson.

2 Queen Astrid, in 1935. Her husband, Leopold, was driving along a tricky Alpine road in Switzerland.

we discovered later booked a table in the restaurant[,] ordered our dinner and paid for it, refusing all my attempts to repay him.

We had very good seats in the beautiful new opera house. The performance was very good, David Hockney's scenery marvellous but I was in a mood when I found the libretto very irritating. The opera starts well with Tom Rakewell setting out to plunge himself in scenes of voluptuous debauchery as in Hogarth's engraving of *The Rake's Progress*. But there is nothing enjoyable about what follows – the Bread Machine (a kind of parody of the miracle of the loaves and fishes) and the love affair with the bearded lady. To my mind that evening it all seemed like Auden and Chester Kallman indulging themselves at the expense of Stravinsky who though pleased with Auden's poetry that went easily into his music did not have the slightest idea what the bread machine and the bearded lady signified. The opera recovers towards the end and becomes really moving with the lunatic asylum and the cemetery.

The opera gives one the feeling that Stravinsky and Auden/Kallman have passed an exacting test with surprisingly high marks – especially Stravinsky in his old age when he seemed only capable of producing very short works. Perhaps writing this opera opened a vein of inspiration because after Auden/Kallman he wanted to write an opera with libretto by Dylan Thomas (of course Robert Craft is the moving spirit behind all this). If Thomas had not died, he would have gone to Hollywood to work with Stravinsky: a prospect which so interested Auden/Kallman that ever after they attributed (seriously/not seriously) Dylan's death to the hex they put on him.

11 July 1994, Sissinghurst

I went to London a day and a night last Thursday, thinking that I should attend the British Academy Dinner in the City to which I had been invited. Another reason was to retrieve outdoor shoes and various other things I'd left in Loudoun Road. The Dinner was crowded with professors several of whom I knew but I was seated between two (physicists I think) whom I did not know but who were agreeable. It became extremely hot: so much so that I was seized with panic lest I might faint, so I excused myself to my neighbours and left, unobserved I think, before the pudding – and the speech which I had been rather dreading.

Before this I went for about twenty minutes to *The Spectator* party which was pleasant. But I did not really make anything of my visit to London except to retrieve a few things from Loudoun Road.

When I got back here Natasha had transferred all our belongings from this house to Nigel Nicolson's, where we were guests for two nights, because Mr and Mrs Seitz – the former American Ambassador and his wife – were put to lodge here for the weekend. We had to remove all trace of ourselves and keep it a dead secret from the Seitzes that we had been staying here – and in fact were still doing so. On Saturday night Nigel gave a dinner for about a dozen guests including Alan Clark and his wife, the Longfords, Michael Pakenham and his wife Mimi (American interior decorator), Guy and Rebecca Philipps, the Seitzes, Nigel's daughter and a friend.[1]

N. sat next to Alan Clark who told her that Hitler was right about everything except the Jews. The white races are doomed by the growing population and the expanding economies of the coloured races etc – China. [. . .] Alan Clark has a bulldog face, as though that of Jane, his mother, were cast in iron. But when he talks it relaxes into the genial rippling lines of a smiling conspiratorial host set on entertaining one.

For Sunday lunch Denis Healey and his wife, the Niko Hendersons, Frank and Kitty Giles, the Seitzes, John Ure and his wife – lunch on the lawn.[2] The Hendersons were very late. The morning seemed punctuated by calls from them reporting their ever-changing travel plans.

After lunch a discussion between Seitz, Healey, Nigel and myself about Bosnia. Seitz, now no longer Ambassador, and able to say what he thinks, said the U.S. and their allies should be prepared to send in 100,000 troops to impose what they considered a just settlement, and be prepared to police the area for an indefinite period in

---

1 Alan Clark (1928–1999), British Conservative MP, who had resigned from politics following Margaret Thatcher's fall from power in 1992. He would return as an MP in 1997. Michael Pakenham (b. 1943), British diplomat.

2 John Ure (b. 1931), Scottish-born diplomat and travel writer.

order to maintain the peace. He was contemptuous of our efforts so far.

N. and I stayed with Nigel over the weekend, the Seitzes taking over the cottage, all trace of our occupation of it having been removed. We returned here Sunday evening. On Monday Nigel and the Littmans came to lunch here. Nigel left while the Littmans and we were still sitting at table, and removed from the refrigerator all food and drink he had put there for the Seitzes.

17 July 1994, London

Dreamed last night that I went back to Oxford as a student. I felt rather guilty about taking a place there (perhaps from someone younger at my age). I spent the whole year studying two lines of German poetry (perhaps from the *Duineser Elegien*).

> Wer wenn ich schrie hörte mich aus
> Die Engelnen[1]

20 July 1994, London

David Plante came to tea. Says that after a very productive and happy holiday on the Greek island where he and Nikos have a house, back in England Nikos is bad-tempered with him. Perhaps he will take himself away somewhere for a week. His recent trip to America was a great success, his novel had good reviews is selling well etc.[2] He is disillusioned about his love affair with the *New Yorker*. In fact, dealing with the *N.Y.* is like dealing with a temperamental, demanding and rejecting, calling-up-and-dropping-down mistress. David's fortunes (which really were cause for concern among his friends a year ago) have leaped forward. He made £40,000 (?can this be right?) last year.

---

1 Misquoting Rainer Maria Rilke, First Duino Elegy, lines 1–2: 'Wer, wenn ich schriee, hörte mich denn aus der Engel / Ordungen?' ('and, if I cried, who among the ranks of the angels would hear me?')

2 *Annunciation* (1994).

26 July 1994, London

Reynolds Price and his carer Boh (?) who looks after him, came to dinner. We also invited David and Nikos. And two evenings ago we heard Reynolds, together with two other Southern writers, read stories by themselves at [the] Festival Hall (I could not understand their 'Southern'). Reynolds had cancer of the spine and was operated on ten years ago. He completely recovered from the cancer but was left paralysed from the waist down. After a bad two years, he accepted his wheel chair life of constant pain – treated it even as a bonanza – and as partly a joke – permitting him to devote himself entirely to his writing 'without interruption by having to go to the supermarket'. He was very fortunate to be a teacher at Duke University which, every year for ten years, has enabled him to have an assistant of his choice who, in fact, simply gives up a year of his life to Reynolds though, I suppose, that doing so is not without his learning quite a lot about literature. They seem always to love Reynolds who keeps his carer constantly entertained by his wit and affection.

January 1995, London

In November 1994 we went to New York in connection with the fact that the St Martin's Press were publishing a new edition of *World Within World* and also a volume of poems called *Dolphins*. I did not at all want to go on this trip and in fact had a strong premonition that if we did go on it something disastrous would happen. In fact it all went very well – reading at the Y.M.H.A. very well attended and another in a large bookshop and one over a dinner given me by the Poetry Society – a rather grand black tie affair I think at the Public Library.[1]

We also went to Boston being looked after by the friend of Matthew and Maro a very warm and energetic person who also gave us a party. The next evening I gave a reading at Brandeis. After this was taken to a restaurant to dine with some professors. Always the same great friendliness and cordiality.

In New York we stayed at the very luxurious apartment of Anne

---

1 YMHA, Young Men's Hebrew Association.

Cox Chambers who was hardly ever there. But she gave a grand dinner for us as did Drue Heinz. The Arthur Schlesingers were at both these parties as, I think, was Bob Silvers.

So everything went very well until our very last evening. We had arranged then to dine with Barbara Epstein with as our fellow guests Earl and Camilla McGrath. Natasha thought we should not go out our last evening because I was tired and as we had to leave early for the daytime flight New York to London the following morning.

However, we had arranged to dine at a restaurant on 57th Street and Park Avenue, with Barbara Epstein and Earl McGrath. I am, in general, very much against putting people off and cancelling engagements. Besides, we had scarcely seen Barbara and I very much wanted to do so.

It was a rainy evening and the only outdoor shoes I had were some rubbery ones which were – as I knew already – extremely slippery in the rain.

We got a taxi to the restaurant. When we arrived there I noticed that there was a pool of water on the sidewalk. Unfortunately I stepped straight into this, reached the curb and pavement and then fell over. I realized at once that I would not be able to get up without help.

The McGraths watched this scene from the restaurant. Earl at once came out and supported me. Then he shouted to a passer-by – or to several passers-by – 'Get a chair.' Some docile person went into the restaurant fetched a chair and planted it beside me. For quite a while I sat on this chair on the pavement with Natasha holding an umbrella over me and Earl entertaining me rather in the manner of a Shakespearean Fool. Passers-by occasionally recognized the McGraths as fellow socialites. They obviously thought that we were amusing ourselves – encouraged in this perhaps by the fact that Earl had fetched us glasses of wine from the restaurant. As a couple left, they turned round and said: 'Have a good time.'

While I was seated there drinking wine Barbara was ringing the nearest hospital which happened to be the best in the world for replacing hips. She spoke to a Doctor [Stanley] Mirsky who was her own doctor and a friend of hers. The doctor said 'Go outside and see if he is holding one leg out in front of him which he can't move.' She went outside and saw that I was doing exactly this. The doctor said: 'In that case we'll send an ambulance.'

My thoughts while I was sitting out there were that somehow we'd catch our plane. I imagined that I would be swathed in bandages – perhaps on crutches – an annoyance to the other passengers – but somehow we'd make it. Meanwhile Earl had shouted to four passers by: 'Help me get this man to the restaurant.' Docilely and silently (no one said a word to me) they did this and shoved me in a corner of the restaurant away from the diners there.

Eventually some men arrived with a stretcher and lifted me into the ambulance. I stopped thinking about returning to London. Now I became a completely passive patient simply awaiting whatever might happen to me. My memory at this point gets rather dim. I suppose I was put in some kind of Emergency Ward because I seem to remember someone else on a stretcher next to me.

My memories now become complete hallucination, I suppose because I was anaesthetized. I dreamed or imagined that I was in an enormous room full of shouting aggressive people some of whom seemed to be fighting with one another. They all seemed to be playing practical jokes and I thought they were going to attack me, though I did not feel frightened. Then I think just two were with me (the others had all withdrawn to the far end of the room). The two were, I knew, going to help me. At this point I completely blacked out and recovered consciousness to find myself in a ward with two or three other people. I was completely passive and submissive.

I do not know how much time passed before I found myself in a room with one other patient who I suppose, I soon realized was about to leave and go home. He was extremely active and ran round the room and into and along the corridor. He kept on saying to me: 'When they take those bandages off you, you'll be like I am now –' illustrating the point with a little skip or run. He also said that he'd had another accident a long time ago, which was exactly the same as this one.

The month or six weeks at the New York [Lenox Hill] hospital went by with me remaining in a state of passivity, just letting what happened happen, knowing that sooner or later I'd be back in London. I would not have been able to manage this, had it not been for Natasha who appeared every day and saw me through: relieved some of the time by Matthew. Fortunately M. did have another reason for coming to New York – interviewing relations, friends, survivors of Arshile Gorky, for

[734]

his book on G.[1] I think I was put on drugs which helped keep me in a state of tolerant passivity, as though time was an element to be patiently endured. Whatever efforts were required of me could be accepted in this light: as being wheeled out of the ward on one or two occasions, to be X-Rayed and to have a pacemaker inserted.[2]

I anticipated the flight as another exercise in passivity. I became a parcel which was put into a van which – with few interruptions – was driven to the airport. This all happened exactly as I imagined it would do. Fortunately the flight was not full so that in the First Class I could in my stretcher easily be laid across two first class seats in the reclining position. Natasha was with me and Matthew appeared intermittently in a place opposite me on the other side of the gangway.

At Heathrow the others were taken to check out the luggage etc, I was transmitted to a delivery place somewhere in the airport where there were elaborate arrangements for each human parcel to have a pee or whatever was necessary. A van or minibus delivered us all to Loudoun Road. There Matthew had converted my study into a kind of bed-sitter. Everything very manageable for me simply to sit and hobble and rest and endure 'getting better'.

Visitors nearly every day. What weighs on me, of course, is the subtle difference between meeting a friend because he is a friend and visiting him because he is sick or an invalid. Ideally I did not want anyone to visit me simply because I was 'sick'. In fact, I think people did just come as friends and there was very little sense of this becoming a hospital.

February 1995, London

[. . .] now I am in a kind of limbo – neither well enough for normal social intercourse, nor quite ill enough to be visited. We did though give a luncheon party yesterday – the Annans and Peter Parker and

---

1 *From a High Place*, Matthew Spender's biography of Arshile Gorky, was published by Knopf in 1999.

2 Spender's initial operation was a hip replacement, but while recovering from this he encountered heart problems which required the insertion of a pacemaker. (Joseph Brodsky came almost every day to cheer Spender up. The fact that Spender forgot about these visits is an indication of how far this accident affected his mind.)

his friend whose name I can't remember. Gabby Annan did not seem very well – she has something which makes her all the time in pain – but she did not show this and was very agreeable.

Peter P. very lively. He is writing a biography of Christopher Isherwood which will, I think, be very good.[1] He never met Isherwood – perhaps an advantage. Of course, he sees a lot of Don Bachardy and has access to all Don's material at Santa Monica to which he goes quite often – in fact is doing so in about ten days' time. The idea mentioned in passing that Christopher went to California, Auden to New York, dividing America between them. A kind of comic megalomania does characterize the 1930s where the poet-novelist-intellectuals played, at any rate among the young, such a leading role. Isherwood in Berlin becomes 'Isherwood's Berlin'.

10 February 1995, London

Read an article by Philip Hensher about Louis MacNeice in the *Spectator*, which contains the sentence, 'Spender, still among London's most desirable guests, has otherwise always been elevated by the company he keeps.'[2] [. . .] I feel that people are already writing obituaries, in which I am relegated to a position of inferiority to these friends. Well, that is not unjust. In fact, I don't want to be the writer of poems adding up to some total which is an *oeuvre*. I want a few of my poems to survive and perhaps some memory of myself also, as distinct from any group. In this article, C. Day Lewis comes out even worse than I do. 'Day Lewis seems destined to be remembered as the father of the distinguished actor.' Well, I've never cared much myself for Cecil's poems. What they are, though, is accomplished, and when I read some years ago his collected volume, I found much to admire [. . .] There will, in the twenty-first century, be anthologies of – histories of – twentieth century poetry and both Cecil's and my poems are part of that history. But having spent two days revising drafts of poems, I should revise others. My novel, though, seems to come first.

Lizzie, who is here in London for a few days, dined with us. Barry is unable to be here for more than a few hours – we hope to see him

---

1 Parker's biography of Isherwood would be published in 2004.

2 *The Spectator*, 11 February 1995.

later today. [. . .] Lizzie was remarkably cheerful, sweet, concerned – wanting to do all the cooking – to bring to us meals she has prepared – while being overwhelmed by circumstances and obligations of her own life – *their* life. Returning now to the subject of Auden and MacNeice and Cecil and me. I have been far the luckiest in my personal life, made up by Natasha, Matthew, Lizzie – by all of these.

13 February 1995, London

Thinking about dying. I very definitely do enjoy life and do not really feel less energetic than I was some years ago – but of course I *am* less energetic. Then although things remain enjoyable the fact that one is doing or experiencing them with ever diminishing faculties is distressing. Then only recently have I become conscious of myself as an old person or body – which means an outsider in the minds of other people. One suddenly becomes an object – old – in the minds of friends twenty or so years younger than oneself without any such dramatic change taking place in the way they look. Then there is death which I don't worry about except in that it is another more dramatic and final change which one will land on other people. One's death will be a disproportionately large event in the lives of those who are nearest to one. I just hope it doesn't upset them too much. From the point of view of one's family and friends, the trouble about death is that there is a corpse left. Every death is a kind of detective story with a corpse.

I've been writing this after midnight because I can't sleep. Also – a new thing – I dread and hate the night – the discomfort of being in bed. Nor can one – as I would like to do – treat oneself as awake – just because one is sleepless. Sleeplessness is a disturbing intermediary condition between sleeping and being awake.

26 Februrary 1995, London

Matthew, Maro, Saskia came to lunch. [. . .] Towards the end of lunch, while Natasha and I and Maro and Saskia sat at the dining room table having coffee, Matthew was on the floor by the door, which leads from dining room to kitchen – a tool bag open beside him while he repaired the door hinge. He said, 'If you gave this too much of a push, the whole house would fall down.' True indeed of this house into which we moved a few days before or after his being born – March 1945.

Every death has the scandal, excitement, annoyance, boredom, *ennui* of the fact that the survivors of the dead are left with a corpse, which has to be disposed of. The death of any and everyone who is married or cohabits with someone leaves that other person a corpse-laden loner.

I don't mind dying – but on the assumption that I predecease Natasha, some part of my mind is already in mourning for Natasha being left alone. She doubtless has similar feelings regarding me. The dead person who is mourned for mourns for the survivors.

2 March 1995, London

Together with Matthew we went, on Feb. 28 to the [Alfred] Brendel concert at the Festival Hall. Two Beethoven sonatas (I forget which) in the first half, followed by the Hammerklavier, taking up the whole of the second. This was in Brendel's manner, a driving performance. From opening to end he seems to thrust through (not rush through) the whole work releasing its compelling unity, its energy. The music takes one into another world, better than this one, and I thought that is what makes life worth living: to get beyond life among forms created by art that really are immortal.

Great performances linger in one's mind, but they rapidly become memories. Even if one had, as I would like to have, a recording of this performance, it would not be the same thing as hearing it played. In fact knowing that one could 'put it on' again and again prevents one ever giving a performance on a machine the same attention as one gives the live one. Not that I would not gladly have a recording of last night's Hammerklavier.

16 March 1995, London

In the afternoon while lying on my bed, I played, on C.D., the whole [Georg] Solti recording of *Fidelio*. What an extraordinary learning-how-to-write-an-opera-as-I-go-along work of genius it is: opening with a Mozart-like number to do with servants making preparations for things (as in *Figaro*), then moving into more echt-Beethoven numbers, culminating in the sublime vocal quartet. Then suddenly becoming very *mouvementé* [turbulent], with a black-noted wicked villain and a sublime ambiguously sexed heroine-posing-as-hero, Leonora. Then the visit to the prison like a journey to the dark centre of the earth – the universe even – where is to be found an imprisoned genius, now fettered and manacled, remembering in wonderful lyric song his past freedom when he was young like the springtime of the world. The magic of the word FREIHEIT [freedom] repeated frequently here and also as the light in the darkness – in the Prisoners' Chorus. Then the marvellous trumpet-call from outside, like a message from the sun – an eternal promise. Then the conflict between the forces of tyranny and freedom leading by way of a pulsating love duet into the final act with the imprisonment of the formerly imprisoning forces by the liberatory good ones, the chorus.

What an extraordinary work and really completely about human freedom. When one thinks that this was performed in Hitler's Germany before Nazi audiences, one can scarcely believe it even allowing for the ambiguity of music which makes a great symphonic work such as the Choral Symphony like a mighty steam engine which can be hitched to any train going in any direction – but, no not to Auschwitz or Buchenwald – I cannot believe that. [. . .]

During the night I think a great deal about friends who are dead: and realize indeed how few there are left surviving. I think of death as a kind of hurdle or test that has to be taken and can't help thinking of myself as only being alive because I am too cowardly to take that hurdle. At the same time, I am very aware that any idea that the dead survive in some after-life (where I might meet my friends again) seems fantasy. In these thoughts a lot of my dead friends seem very sexy.

17 March 1995, London

An article by John Bayley in the *London Review of Books* about a biography of Cyril Connolly by Clive Fisher.[1] Writing at a table in front of my glass-doored bookcase, I remember how ten years (say)

---

1 Two biographies of Connolly came out, almost simultaneously, in 1995: Clive Fisher, *Cyril Connolly*, and Jeremy Lewis, *Cyril Connolly: A Life*. Lewis had more cooperation from the estate.

ago on the shelf nearest me there was a copy of *Poems* (1928) by W. H. Auden printed by me on the handpress (for printing chemist's labels) when we were both undergraduates. Auden who was staying with us came back from having lunch with Cyril took up this book and said: 'Don't you think it would be a good idea for both of us to inscribe this for Cyril and give it to him?' I pointed out that it was the only copy I had of the book that I had printed of his poems when we were both undergraduates (well – he had left Oxford and I was in my last year). He said: 'There is a copy in my father's library and when my father dies I will give you that one.' So we inscribed the copy and gave it to Cyril. (Soon after, Cyril died, it was sold by his heirs to the University of Tulsa.) When Auden's father died it happened that Auden was again staying with us. I reminded him of his promise to replace the 1928 *Poems* which we had taken from my book case. A rather stubborn school-masterly look came on his face and he said abruptly: 'I remember nothing about it.' I reminded him of the circumstances relating to Cyril. He repeated: 'I remember nothing about it.' Then he added: 'Anyway the copy of the book in my father's library is lost.'

Reading now about Cyril, this story has come to the forefront of my mind. It's like a Cerberus barking away at me and I can only see the Cyril who exploited me, as he did many other people. The fact is though that he is not to be explained away as a scrounger who, when it came to books was also a conscienceless thief. He was a person of exceptional intelligence and sensibility who loved literature[,] who had real discrimination, who when he was editing *Horizon* cared about the writers he published and was interested in them as well as in their works.

He had good qualities the opposite of his bad ones. He was snobbish but he was also remarkably open to people who were obscure and undistinguished but whose characters or life-stories interested him. For instance, there was a shop assistant at Zwemmers with whom he would spend hours discussing things.[1] Cyril was a man of feeling and sensibility. Things that are notorious about him such as his having love affairs with two or three women at a time do not reveal cynicism or heartlessness – but, rather, the solipsism-egotism, perhaps of someone who had formed a psychological theory about himself

---

1 Art bookshop and dealer in the Charing Cross Road, London.

and considered that everyone concerned with him should agree that he had to perform this, even if doing so was sacrificial to them.

Regarding women the legend was that when he was a child in South Africa he had been left by his Mother with a woman who looked after him: therefore he re-lived this pattern in the reverse form that he always had to be with one woman and leaving another woman who willingly accepted her role as an element in a psychological pattern.

Self-indulgence of a kind in which all his friends and lovers were role-players in a pattern of which his need was the centre, was the key to his character. This does not mean that he was not fond of the people involved. He was genuinely affectionate and extremely vulnerable, easily hurt, very generous.

He was also for the most part good value for money: the friend or guest who always amused, or if he failed to do so (as sometimes happened) was nevertheless acting his part performing his role in his friends' or lovers' lives.

With his wit, his show of learning, his real love of literature, his good taste, also his vulgar taste (always wanting the most stylish cigar or motor car), he seemed to me a man of the Eighteenth Century. He once spent most of an afternoon with me discussing the name of the new car (nothing about it except the name) he wanted to buy. Should it not be a Scimitar?

18 March 1995, London

I am writing this with the Gold Pen awarded me yesterday at the PEN Club annual meeting.[1] This was held in the main assembly room of the Café Royal, a much more agreeable place than wherever we met last year. The meeting began at 10.30 a.m. with a discussion between Michael Holroyd and Margaret Drabble about description of characters in biography and in fiction.[2] They are both extremely intelligent, well read, serious, witty and attractive. It is not because I was given the prize that I found the whole occasion more enjoyable than previous ones. At lunch we were put at a table where among

1 Annual award, for 'a lifetime's distinguished service to Literature'.

2 Michael Holroyd was himself the winner of a Gold Pen in 2006.

other guests were Harold and Antonia Pinter and sitting just on my right the lively and clever Peter Parker, with his air of conspiratorial naughtiness who is writing the biography of Christopher Isherwood. We talked about this a bit. Christopher was not altogether a 'nice' character: domineering, unobtrusively making himself always the centre of any company he was in – and if he suspected people of not accepting him as such – which he might do even if he had never met them – he did not have the imperviousness to whatever impressions he made of Auden. I told Peter that thinking this about Christopher and remembering various things such as the catastrophic attempt of Christopher, Heinz, Tony Hyndman and myself to live together in Portugal in the winter of 1936/37 (was it 1935/36?).[1] I wondered sometimes whether I really like Christopher (or he me). The answer is that I decidedly do so. He and I were 'one of us', which included Auden and others – and there was no doubt about this. Such relationships – friendships – have a touch of eternity about them. 'We' are in a virtuous and all-forgiving and indulging way, 'the gang'.

20 March 1995, London

Slept badly with many interruptions till 4 a.m. when I took a sleeping pill. Woke or half-woke early and half-dreaming half-waking had fantasies about the bombing of Hamburg during the war. Really nothing cheerful the whole night through.

Yet we had a very pleasant day yesterday (a bit tiring though and perhaps too good or rich a lunch). We were guests of the Berlins, together with the poet James Fenton and his friend an American and, I think, connected with Harvard or Yale.[2] The friend is black – Fenton a largish slightly fleshy man reassuringly agreeable a good conversationalist. I forget what we talked about (perhaps I can recover some of this from Natasha). During the unpleasant watches

---

1 Spender alludes to the communal establishment he and Isherwood, and their respective partners Tony Hyndman and Heinz Neddermeyer, set up (unsuccessfully) in Cintra, Portugal, in late 1935–early 1936. The episode is described at length in chapter 12 of Isherwood's memoir *Christopher and his Kind* (1976).

2 Darryl Pinckney (b. 1953), American novelist.

of the night, I reflected that when I meet people for the first time I think 'Well perhaps this is the beginning of a long friendship.' But when they meet me, who am aged 86, they probably think 'Well I did meet him once before he died.' How stupid at my age to think 'If I send Fenton my book of poems of which Faber printed 50 copies for me to distribute among friends, I hope he will like them.' It is far too late to think about such things.

24 March 1995, London

The *T.L.S.* article by Robin Holloway entitled 'Stravinsky's Spiritual Son' discussing Robert Craft's *Chronicle of a Friendship*. Holloway writes: 'Throughout the book there is a sense of Craft as majordomo/naturalist/marriage-broker, who then rushes back to privacy to write up the result. Moreover, he has his cake and his bread crumbs, presenting cosmopolitan cultured exchange as desirably glamorous, yet at the same time indulging the pangs of diffidence and shame. Yet such snobbery (if this be the word) is an essential ingredient in the book's fascination. . .

'One page can focus the feeling. On it Stephen Spender writes to Craft that Francis Bacon "would be thrilled" to paint Stravinsky: "We see a lot of Chester and Wystan," he adds, "as their opera with [Hans Werner] Henze approaches Glyndebourne."'

I cannot remember how I got to know Stravinsky but do remember us – Natasha and me – being invited by the Stravinskys to lunch with them at their home in Hollywood. The occasion was – like every meal with them – festal – but I remember wondering whether there was not a reason for us being so beautifully entertained. After coffee this emerged. Strav asked me whether it was true that I knew some art dealers in London. On my admitting that I did, he then said that his wife, Vera Stravinsky, painted in gouache and that she would very much like to have an exhibition in London. I said I would speak to Rex Nan Kivell of the Redfern Gallery about this, and in fact did do so with the result, if I remember rightly, that they held an exhibition of Vera's work.[1]

---

1 Rex Nan Kivell (1898–1977), art dealer and collector. Spender's first encounter with Stravinsky, which he recalls here, took place in September 1951.

When the Stravinskys and Bob were in England we drove them to places or to see people they wished to visit. I remember three such trips – once to the theatre at Stratford-on-Avon (returning to London the same night), once to see David Jones, the painter, living in his cell-like room at Harrow, who impressed Stravinsky as being a holy man, a saint. Another time we went to see the Kenneth Clarks at their castle. En route Stravinsky had us stop at several pubs and have drinks (his name, he said, was becoming Stra-whiskey). When we arrived rather late at the Clarks, we were offered drinks. Vera said: 'Oh no, we would be completely drunk if we had anything more to drink.' K. Clark, looking at his wife, the alcoholic Jane, said: 'You couldn't possibly be more drunk than we already are in this house.'

After lunch, I went alone with Bob Craft [for] a walk round the battlements. I said to Bob, who was young then: 'Do you realize that if you are going on as you are now that, whether they are living or dead, your entire life is going to be taken over by the Stravinskys?' He looked round in a slightly scared way and said: 'Is this place bugged?' 'No.' 'Well, I never think of anything else.'

They were an amazing trinity – Igor, Vera and Bob. They entertained amused brought life and love and wit to one another. I once said to some friend of theirs and ours that I thought the young Bob was driving the octogenarian Igor to his grave. Our friend said that on the contrary he was driving him to stay alive.

At the end of S.'s life I saw Bob. He said: 'Stravinsky's just become a thing lying on a trolley that is wheeled between two row[s] of doctors each of whom jabs a needle into him.' I said wouldn't it be better for him to die. Bob said, 'It's I who insist on his being kept alive. I can't bear the idea of life without him.'

Nicky Nabokov told me that the real love affair was between Bob and Vera and that Stravinsky was torn with jealousy about it.

However that may be, for me it is the Trinity of them that exists – people who for the love of one another made life a non-stop celebration.

4 April 1995, London

On Sunday Ted Hughes came to lunch. I cannot remember anything of what he said – or rather I only remember the least important. How sympathetic he finds the Queen Mother (I agree with him about this)[,] how he feels obliged to write on occasion Laureate poems, how tremendously difficult he finds this.[1] However the point about his talk is its intelligence, the very wide range of subjects he covers, how amusing he can be: and how there seems always the underlying theme of Sylvia Plath. He said he had been writing a series of short autobiographical poems – had done about 40 of them? – then he realized his wife did not like the fact that they all went back to Sylvia – so he had given up for a time writing them . . . but I surmised it was more a matter of not publishing than of not writing.[2]

9 April 1995, London

In the *Sunday Times* today a columnist – Godfrey Smith – quotes an anecdote, going back to the war, of Cyril Connolly in a broadcast describing his friend S.S. as an 'indifferent poet with outstanding clumsiness of mind and a very bad ear.' S. was naturally miffed; but Cyril wrote to assure me that his remarks were 'only for India'! I remember this very well. Before Cyril wrote, I had decided to make my answer take the form of my not speaking to him for several days. It was in these circumstances that he wrote to me providing this explanation.

The columnist Godfrey Smith digs this up from the past and puts it on display as he frequently does with recollections of Cyril. It is a way of boasting that Cyril worked in the *Sunday Times* where G.S. got to know him. I wonder how well. I never heard C. mention G.S. But digging up this past G.S. keeps me awake long into the night.

23 April 1995, London

Together with James Fenton, Christopher Logue, Harold Pinter and John Burnside, gave a poetry reading at the Tricycle Theatre in Kilburn.[3] This was the first such thing I have done since America –

---

1 Hughes was Poet Laureate from 1984 until his death in 1998.

2 These poems, *Birthday Letters*, a sequence of poems describing Hughes's relationship with Sylvia Plath, were eventually published in the year of Hughes's death.

3 Christopher Logue (1926–2011), British poet, part of the modernist-inspired Poetry Revival in the 1960s and 1970s. John Burnside (b. 1955), Scottish poet and novelist.

since my accident in N.Y. My fellow readers were all very convivial. James Fenton is somehow formidable: completely determined to do things in his way and none other. Thus he reads as though the words he is reciting are accompaniment to a performance – which is a little war jig or tap dance all over the stage. All of us were good I think. Unfortunately the audience was small. A pity because those who didn't come missed something exceptionally interesting.

Harold Pinter praised my poems very highly to me and was, like Antonia, most friendly.

We went home, had supper, gave up on trying to listen to a murder story on TV and went to bed. I slept very badly and had those kinds of dreams which consist of one being very aware of the thoughts behind the dream, as though the dream were there to illustrate an argument.

For some reason I began by thinking it was impossible for an Englishman to write a novel about France. This merged into the opposite thought that many Englishmen had written novels about the French Revolution (e.g. Dickens). Then I started thinking about that French printer who had written several volumes about sex in France during the period of the Revolution.[1] He gives an extraordinary picture of working class French during this period, which they spent having a non-stop orgy. I thought more about the role of sex in some societies. Could it be seen as a key to the whole society – and without it no substitute? I was conscious of the non-Marxist nature of these thoughts.

Then I thought I would have no opinion or attitude towards such matters since I am 86 and have no sex in my life. Any attitude anyone has towards the world at my age is that of a person without sex, a kind of subjective impotence within the surrounding objective potency. These are terrible thoughts which can only end in one want-

---

1 It is likely that Spender is thinking of the notorious series of spoof biographies of the Cardinal Archbishop of Paris, Jean-Siferin Maury, believed to have been written collectively by Danton's ally, Camille Desmoulins and his sometime antagonist Jacques-René Hébert, who were both journalists rather than printers. In one of these biographies, Maury goes to hell and participates in lavishly described orgies with the working-class French. Desmoulins is one of the central characters in Hilary Mantel's novel *A Place of Greater Safety*, which had been published three years prior to this journal entry.

ing to die. I do not believe that writing or any other activity I am capable of can exist without sex. Therefore, I am in a state of panic that they no longer exist for me.

27 April 1995, London

Today – looked at from the perspective of 2 a.m. – two hours into tomorrow – has been a good day for work. One of the best for years.

The Poetry Book Club wrote, asking me to write an essay on what I think about the present state of poetry – 800 words. I have written a kind of definition and defence of poetry. Probably, I will consider the essay worthless, when I read it tomorrow – but writing it lifted me out of the depression I have been feeling about self and work and achievement recently.

I suddenly saw myself at the centre of the energy and imagination that are poetry, able to express this situation. I saw that within the poems of the true poets, there is a struggle between two energetic forces of meaning: 1) the paraphrasable prose meaning; 2) the poetry whose meaning goes beyond the prose into the magic of language itself – as in the line 'the icy precepts of respect'.[1] Writing this, I no longer felt myself limited by my own view of myself as a not first-rate mind in intelligence. I realized that one can go beyond one's own limitations by force of the vision of the problem in front of one, in this case the state of poetry. I don't think anyone else would have such a vision of poetry. Except perhaps Ted Hughes, whom I admire more and more.

2 May 1995

Lizzie left for Hong Kong. These past ten days, when they've been in England, she's been wonderfully helpful to us, coming in every day, almost, to see how she could help. While they are away she and Barry are lending me their secretary to help type my novel. I felt slightly envious of her for the air trip first class and she said, 'Yes, it was all wonderfully luxurious.' I could see she was looking forward to it.

---

1 Spender quotes from Shakespeare's *Timon of Athens*, IV iii.

Thank God, she enjoys such things as she has so much travelling to do.

I more or less collapsed – i.e. felt very faint and staggered – twice today. It is quite hot though not very. I worked hard partly at writing, partly at editing novel, all this morning. This afternoon I felt incredibly tired and collapsed onto a chaise longue. I have done so again this evening. It is a very unpleasant feeling of surrender and makes me miserably ashamed.

Reynolds Price sent me his new novel, which looks really interesting.[1]

Natasha helped me through today. Given that what I am going through are mild symptoms of an irreversible condition, which thousands of people of my age also have to endure, I should not complain. Well, I don't complain. What I really mean is, given all this, how little I care or have ever cared about other people going through the same distresses – of which I have scarcely even been conscious till they happened to me myself. Anyway, tonight at least I should sleep.

Stephen Spender died of heart failure on 16 July 1995.

---

1 *The Promise of Rest* (1996).

Biographical Appendix

Harold Spender (1864–1926) Spender's father was a liberal politician and supporter of the prime minister David Lloyd George, of whom he wrote a biography. His career as a politician came to an end in obscure circumstances and his wife, **Violet Hilda Schuster,** (1868–1922), died soon after. Harold Spender is described by his son in the early sections of *World Within World* as an empty, rhetorical, late Victorian figure – not altogether a fair portrait. Auden, who knew all the family, once said to Stephen, 'You killed him, my dear. You killed him by ignoring him.' (The 'you' is plural, referring to all four siblings.)

J. A. (John Alfred) Spender (1862–1942) Spender's paternal uncle was a journalist who edited the *Westminster Gazette* from 1896 to 1922. Following his brother's death in 1926, J. A. Spender made an effort to befriend his nephew, but he disapproved of Stephen's interest in poetry and was anxious that his nephew would 'settle down to being a dilettante on a small income'. He disapproved still further when Spender's poems were published. In 1939, he cut his nephew out of his will following the publication of Spender's poem 'The Ambitious Son', which inveighs against Harold's 'megaphone voice' and hair 'made of newspaper cutting'.

Michael Spender (1906–1945) Stephen's elder brother was a contemporary of Auden's at Gresham's, Holt. He then studied natural science and electrical engineering at Balliol. In 1928, he joined a Royal Geographical Society expedition to the Great Barrier Reef. In Germany, he subsequently for three years studied photogrammetry, the science of relating aerial photography to maps. A keen mountaineer, his participation in an Everest expedition in 1935 inspired the Auden and Isherwood play *The Ascent of F6* (1936). In the war he joined the Photographic Reconnaissance Unit. He was killed in an accident while still on active service.

Michael Spender's second son **Philip Spender (b. 1943)** is a public-sector fundraiser who for six years collaborated with his uncle on *Index on Censorship*. He is currently President of the Stephen Spender Trust.

Humphrey Spender (1910–2005) Stephen's younger brother was a photographer and painter, perhaps best known for his photographs of Bolton and Blackpool taken in the 1930s for Mass-Observation. In this period, Humphrey was a frequent presence in Stephen's life: in Berlin in 1932, where he studied architecture and became a friend of Isherwood, and in Sintra in 1936, where in a diary he commented on the often absurd behaviour of Tony Hyndman. The untimely death of his wife Margaret (Lolly) in 1945 was a source of great sorrow for the Spender family and inspired Stephen's sequence of poems, 'Elegy for Margaret'. After the war, Humphrey for many years taught textile design at the Royal College of Art.

Humphrey's second wife Pauline Wynn appears in the journals, together with their son **Quentin Spender (b. 1950)**, who is a child psychologist.

Natasha Spender née Litvin (1919–2010) Stephen's second wife was the daughter of Edwin Evans, a music critic who did much to promote new French music in England in the 1920s, and Rachel Litvin, an actress whose career was cut short by an illness which rendered her deaf. Natasha attended the Royal College of Music on a scholarship to study the piano. She first heard Spender lecture when she was seventeen. The pair met formally at a *Horizon* lunch party in 1940 and, united by a passion for music, they soon fell in love. Natasha had a successful career as a concert pianist in the 1940s and 1950s; then, in the 1960s, following an operation for cancer, she started a second career in the psychology of music. After Spender's death she was instrumental in producing his official biography and the definitive version of the *Collected Poems*.

Matthew Spender (b. 1945) Spender's son studied at Westminster and New College, Oxford, where he read history. After graduating he became an artist. In 1967 he married **Maro Gorky (b. 1943)**, herself a painter and the daughter of the Armenian-born American artist **Arshile Gorky (c. 1900–1948)**. Maro was brought up in Europe and England by her mother **Agnes Magruder (b. 1919)**, nicknamed 'Magouche'. Matthew and Maro moved to Italy in 1968 and have lived there ever since. Their daughters **Saskia** and **Cosima** were born in 1970 and 1972.

Lizzie Spender (b. 1950) Spender's daughter went to North London Collegiate Schools and studied acting at The Drama Centre, London. She has written TV screenplays and a book about her childhood, *The Wild Horse Diaries* (2007). In 1997 she married the Australian actor **Barry Humphries (b. 1934)**, who also appears in the journals.

*

Noel Annan (1916–2000) Spender and Annan met during the Second World War, when Annan was working as an intelligence officer for the British government. The two men shared an interest in the post-war situation of Germany and both were official visitors to the defeated nation in the immediate post-war period. Annan went on to become a writer and academic and he and Spender had a working relationship at University College London in the 1970s when Annan was Provost of the college.

Peggy Ashcroft (1907–1991) Near the end of the Second World War, the celebrated British actress invited Stephen and Natasha Spender to dinner to discuss the possibility of collaborating over a series of recitals of poetry and music. Natasha and Peggy quickly founded the Apollo Society, which was launched at an event at the Arts Theatre, Cambridge, presided over by Maynard Keynes. The pair came to see the recitals as their 'war work', hoping they would keep up morale around the country. They were often joined by poets such as Spender and Cecil Day Lewis reading their own work, and the Apollo Society staged the first performance of Eliot's *Four Quartets* at the end of the war.

Michael Astor (1916–1980) Spender met the British former Conservative MP in 1955 when the Spenders had rented a house near Burford for the summer and Astor and his then wife Barbara invited them to dinner at Bruern Abbey. After a pleasant summer of coming and going between the two establishments, Astor suggested that the Spenders 'might like to come and live in my garden'. For the next ten years they would have the 'Red Brick Cottage', a Queen Anne dower house in his grounds, as their second home. He was married to his second wife, **Pandora Clifford**, from 1961 to 1968.

W. H. Auden (1907–1973) Spender describes his first meeting (or rather 'appointment') with the fellow undergraduate and self-styled Great Poet in *World Within World*: 'He was seated in a darkened room with the curtains drawn, and a lamp on a table at his elbow, so that he could see me clearly and I could only see the light reflected on his pale face.' Spender gave the right answers to enough questions to be allowed to enter Auden's 'Gang' and thus began the fabled friendship that survived transitions from Oxford to London to Berlin and then became transatlantic with Auden's move to America in 1939.

Francis Bacon (1909–1992) Spender met the British painter in the 1930s. After the war the pair embarked on a course of late-night dining and discussion that would continue over the next five decades, Spender always longing to talk about painting, Bacon longing to talk about poetry. From the start Spender was a fervent believer in his friend's talent, purchasing an early painting, and Bacon gave Spender four sketches, which, exhibited after his death, would surprise art critics who were convinced that Bacon never drafted his paintings.

Jill Balcon see **Cecil Day Lewis**

Samuel Barber (1910–1981) The American composer Samuel Barber's success began at an early age. His *Adagio for Strings*, composed when he was twenty-eight and sent to Arturo Toscanini soon after, became one of the most performed classical pieces of all time. Spender met him in the early 1930s, possibly through the composer Roger Sessions, whom Spender had met in Berlin. In 1940, Barber set Spender's Spanish Civil War poem 'A Stopwatch and an Ordnance

Map' for male chorus. After the war the Spenders became regular visitors to 'Capricorn', the house Barber shared with the composer Gian Carlo Menotti at Mount Kisco, New York State.

John Bayley see **Iris Murdoch**

Isaiah Berlin (1909–1997) Spender and Berlin met at Oxford, brought together by a passion for music, which took them to Salzburg during Spender's last undergraduate summer. Berlin is the dedicatee of Spender's *World Within World*, where Spender states appreciatively that with Berlin he 'enjoyed a relationship as between equals', in contrast to his pupil–teacher relationship with Auden. Berlin himself recalled the Spender of his youth as 'irresistibly attractive to meet and to know' and found himself 'uniquely exhilarated by contact with him'. The liberal intellectual stayed on at Oxford after graduating, embarking on a distinguished career as a lecturer, broadcaster and philosopher.

Elizabeth Bowen (1899–1973) The Anglo-Irish novelist was already a distinguished literary figure when she was introduced to Spender by Isaiah Berlin in the 1930s. The two writers made instant friends and then became neighbours when the Spenders moved to St John's Wood, close to Bowen's Regent's Park house, which she would immortalize in *The Death of the Heart* (1938). During the war the four partied bravely in the face of the London Blitz, Bowen memorably taking them onto the terrace during a night of bombing in 1941 and announcing, 'I do ap-ap-apologise for the noise.' Bowen's place in the family was confirmed when she became the godmother of Lizzie Spender in 1950.

Joseph Brodsky (1940–1996) In 1965, Spender gave the Russian poet Anna Akhmatova some 'warm woollies' to take back to the Soviet Union and pass on to the then imprisoned Joseph Brodsky. He met the young poet for the first time in 1972, when Auden arranged for Brodsky to stay with the Spenders in Loudoun Road at the start of his exile. The Russian later recalled Spender on this occasion as a 'white-haired man with a gentle, almost apologetic smile on his face'. Spender was to assist Brodsky in his subsequent (Nobel-Prize winning) career in Britain and America, and Brodsky himself came to look on both Auden and the Spenders as his 'family'.

Sonia Brownell see Sonia Orwell

Joseph (Joe) Buttinger see Muriel Gardiner Buttinger

Anne Cox Chambers (b. 1919) The American media proprietor and Democratic Party sponsor was the Spenders' neighbour in France and became a constant companion during their French summers in the 1970s and 1980s.

Raymond Chandler (1888–1959) The Spenders met the American crime writer in 1955 at a lunch organized by Hamish Hamilton to introduce Chandler to the British intellectual elite. Chandler had moved to England following his wife Cissy's death in 1954. Natasha was struck by the alcoholic writer's moroseness and, hearing about his recent suicide attempt, decided to give a cheering dinner party for him to meet some British fans of his work. Attempting to stave off his depression, she and her friends organized what became a 'shuttle service', distracting the American with lunches, dinners and sightseeing. In the 1970s, Spender records in the journals Natasha's distress at allegations made in Frank MacShane's *The Life of Raymond Chandler* (1976) that Chandler and Natasha ended up having an affair.

Cyril Connolly (1903–1974) Spender and Connolly became close during the Second World War, when they were collaborating on *Horizon*. Connolly was a literary critic and journalist and was the author of *Enemies of Promise* (1938), a book that combined literary criticism with youthful autobiography. His marriage to Jean Bakewell had ended in 1939, and in 1950 he married Barbara Skelton. This tempestuous marriage lasted six years, during which time Spender witnessed (and recorded in the journals) a series of marital crises and reconciliations. In 1959, Connolly married Deirdre Craven.

Robert Craft see Igor Stravinsky

Ernst Robert Curtius (1886–1956) The German literary scholar (and first German translator of *The Waste Land*) became Spender's mentor while he was still at Oxford, introducing him to what Spender saw as 'an Apollonian Germany' of Goethe, Hölderlin and Schiller. After the young poet left Oxford, he went to Germany and was provided with a more successful education by Curtius. In the aftermath of the Second World War, Spender was keen to be given a commission to help with reconstruction in Germany, partly so that he could do what he could for his mentor. Spender found his former teacher living amidst the ruins, existing on a 'Tolstoyan diet' of potatoes and cabbage. He confronted the possibility that Curtius, like so many other Germans, had been too acquiescent during the Third Reich, and he posed this question in his *Rhineland Journal*, which was published in *Horizon* before he could send an advance copy to Germany for approval. Spender was astounded by Curtius's fury at what he saw as a conqueror taking advantage of a defeated victim and found the ensuing quarrel extremely painful. The pair were reconciled a year later when Curtius suffered a stroke and, believing he was dying, agreed to forgive his former student. They met for the next and last time in 1955, shortly before Curtius's death.

Clifford Curzon (1907–1982) The British pianist became Natasha Spender's teacher after he presented her with a prize for her playing at the age of twelve. Introduced by Natasha, he and Stephen Spender got on immediately and Curzon and his wife Lucille became godparents to Matthew and Lizzie Spender respectively. The two couples were friends throughout their lives although Curzon, who had dedicated his life to work, disapproved of Spender's peripatetic lifestyle.

Cecil Day Lewis (1904–1972) The British poet was part of the Auden coterie in the 1920s and became a great friend of Spender's in the 1930s. During the war he was a frequent reader at Natasha Spender's Apollo Society. After the failure of his first marriage, Day Lewis had a long and troubled love affair in the 1940s with Rosamond Lehmann. In 1951, he married the actress **Jill Balcon** (**b. 1925**), the mother of his children **Tamasin Day-Lewis** (**b. 1953**) and the actor and filmmaker **Daniel Day-Lewis** (**b. 1957**).

T. S. Eliot (1888–1965) An anonymous friend of Spender's sent the young poet's *Twenty Poems* to Eliot soon after their publication in 1929. Eliot published four of them in *The Criterion* in October 1930 and wrote to Spender that he 'liked the poems very much'. The two met for lunch; by 1931, Eliot had announced that Spender should drop the 'Mr' in his letters and invited him to be a regular reviewer for *The Criterion*. Spender's lifelong interest in establishing a literary magazine was undoubtedly influenced by Eliot's work at *The Criterion*. Immediately after the war Spender consulted Eliot about the foundation of a European-based literary and critical magazine but Eliot, knowing the financial difficulties, was sceptical. At the same time, Eliot acted as an intermediary between Spender and Ernst Robert Curtius in their dispute about Spender's reportage of the recent comments of Curtius on Germany. The friendship between the two poets continued until the end of Eliot's life.

***Encounter* and the Congress for Cultural Freedom** In June 1950, the American journalist **Melvin Lasky (1920–2004)**, editor in Berlin of *Der Monat*, headed the launch of the Congress for Cultural Freedom (CCF). Lasky had begun his career working on the *New Leader* of Sol Levitas, a companion of Trotsky during the Russian Revolution, and had now set himself up as a 'cold warrior', out to combat the influence of the communists in Berlin. The participants at the first Congress included Karl Jaspers, Ignazio Silone, Bertrand Russell, Alfred Ayer, Arthur Koestler and Tennessee Williams; they were generally anti-Stalinist left-wingers who wanted to undermine the prestige of Soviet culture and compete against the communists in the battle for hearts and minds in a post-war Europe harbouring anti-American sentiments. The CCF quickly received extensive funding the moved to Paris, where it was presided over by **Michael (Mike) Josselson (1908–1978)**, its Administrative Secretary and then Executive Director.

In 1953 Spender, recently featured in the anti-communist *The God that Failed*, received a request from the Paris committee of the CCF to co-edit a new magazine. The first number of *Encounter* (1953–90), edited by Spender and **Irving Kristol (1920–2009)**, appeared in October 1953. Kristol had started as a Trotskyite but like many of the people involved with the CCF he moved steadily to the right after the war. (As leading neo-conservative he was eventually given the Medal of Freedom by George W. Bush in 2002.) In 1958, Lasky replaced Kristol as co-editor of *Encounter*, and he remained with the magazine until it folded in 1991. Spender himself continued to co-edit *Encounter* with Lasky until 1966, when he decided to reduce his workload on the magazine by becoming a contributing editor. Under Spender's editorship *Encounter* thrived as one of the most successful periodicals in Britain, commissioning articles from major British, American and European writers, artists, philosophers and politicians across the political spectrum.

In 1966 an article in the *New York Times* alleged that the CCF received a secret subsidy from the American government. A year later it was revealed in the American magazine *Ramparts* that ever since its foundation *Encounter* had been funded by the CIA. Spender's outrage that he had been consistently kept in the dark by the CCF is recorded in the journals. He and his British co-editor Frank Kermode resigned as editors immediately.

Lucian Freud (b. 1922) In 1939 Spender went to Wales for a week's writing accompanied by two Bryanston boys he had recently been teaching, one of whom was Lucian Freud. Spender described the seventeen-year-old student as 'the most intelligent person I have met since I first knew Auden at Oxford'. The poet introduced the young painter to Peter Watson, who became one of his early patrons and, through Lucian, Stephen met his architect father **Ernst Freud** (1892–1970) and psychoanalyst aunt **Anna Freud** (1895–1982). When Spender became a fireman and was posted to the station in Maresfield Gardens in 1942, Ernst suggested that he and Natasha take the top floor of their house. The Spenders lived above the family for four years, letting Lucian take a room of their flat as his studio. In 1958, Freud painter Spender's portrait, but the friendship faded after 1970.

Muriel Gardiner Buttinger (1901–1985) Spender met the American in Croatia in 1934. He was holidaying with his then boyfriend Tony Hyndman and Gardiner was on her spring vacation from Vienna, where she was in analysis with Ruth Mack Brunswick. Both were passionately concerned with the political situation in Germany and Austria and Muriel's initial impression of Stephen as 'strikingly hand-some' and 'a little sad' was matched by his admiration of her 'black hair and eyes' and sense that she had 'suffered at some time'. The two became lovers and then lifelong friends. From 1934 to just after the

Anschluss in 1938, Gardiner helped save the lives of Jews and anti-fascists, working with the Austrian underground. She escaped first to Paris and then returned to America accompanied by her husband **Joseph Buttinger** (1906–1992), whom she had met when he was leading the Austrian Revolutionary Socialists.

Maro, Magouche and **Arshile Gorky** see **Matthew Spender**

Stuart Hampshire (1914–2004) Spender met the Oxford philosopher through Isaiah Berlin in 1936 and the pair quickly became good friends. Hampshire acted as a confidant during Spender's early love affairs, supported his later political causes and finally delivered the address at his funeral.

David Hockney (b. 1937) The poet and painter got to know each other in the 1960s, and Spender was a great admirer of Hockney's work. In 1981 the two collaborated on *China Diary*, an illustrated account of their trip to China. Looking at Hockney's portrait of himself in Tokyo airport, Spender found that 'the general impression I made in David's drawing was of bulbous obesity' and lamented that he must have looked 'very much the odd man out' compared with his younger companion.

Horizon magazine (1940–1949) In 1940, Spender, Cyril Connolly and **Peter Watson** (1908–1956) founded the literary magazine *Horizon*, which became the voice of liberal intellectual Britain for a decade during and after the Second World War. The magazine juxtaposed writers including Virginia Woolf and T. S. Eliot with artists such as John Piper, Henry Moore and Paul Nash and philosophers, critics and political commentators. Spender himself was an associate editor for the first year and published the early versions of *September Journal* and the *Rhineland Journal* in the magazine. Cyril Connolly remained the editor throughout the magazine's life. The art collector and benefactor Peter Watson financed the magazine, while also acting as patron to the Institute of Contemporary Arts and to artists such as Francis Bacon. He was a great friend of Spender's in the 1940s and 1950s and it is clear from the journals that his sudden death was the source of great sadness for the poet.

Ted Hughes (1930–1998) The Spenders met Hughes and his wife Sylvia Plath (1932–1963) at a dinner of T. S. Eliot's in 1960. They saw each other intermittently over the years but the friendship between the two men was at its peak in the 1980s, when Hughes was Spender's closest poet friend. After Spender's death, Hughes (now Poet Laureate) helped Natasha Spender to devise the literary programme for Spender's memorial service.

Barry Humphries see Lizzie Spender

Barbara Hutchinson see Victor Rothschild

Julian Huxley (1887–1975) When Huxley met Spender in the 1930s he was the Secretary of the Zoological Society of London and in the early years of the war the Spenders enjoyed visiting him at London Zoo. It was through the help of the biologist that Spender was interviewed by the Allied Control Commission for a post in occupied Germany. And six months later Huxley, now head of the newly formed UNESCO, invited Spender to be the organization's first head of literature. Huxley's involvement with UNESCO was to be short-lived, however. He was not re-elected for a second year as the American delegation, already influenced by McCarthyism, suspected him of being 'soft on commies'. In 1919, Huxley had married Juliette Baillot, whom he left briefly in 1929, after proposing an open marriage. Huxley suffered from severe depression throughout his life, which resulted in several breakdowns, alluded to in the journals.

Tony Hyndman (1911–1972). 'Jimmy Younger' in *World Within World*, Hyndman met Spender in 1933 when the young Welsh ex-soldier was living a precarious existence in London. Spender invited Hyndman to live with him, and after a summer spent touring Europe they moved into a flat in Maida Vale (causing Virginia Woolf to make a caustic remark about 'Lilies of the Vale'). During the Spanish Civil War, under Spender's influence, Hyndman joined the Republican side and soon found himself under arrest for insubordination. Spender's visits to Spain were undertaken at least partly to help Hyndman return safely to England. This achieved, the relationship began to fade. Hyndman went on to have affairs with many men in Spender's circle. Hyndman was seldom able to support himself, and his last years were spent in a home for reformed alcoholics in his native Wales. He planned an autobiography describing his relationship with Spender but this was never written.

Index on Censorship (founded 1972) On Friday 12 January 1968, the Spenders read *The Times* at breakfast and saw an appeal to 'the world press' from the Russian dissident scientist Pavel Litvinov, deploring the conduct of authorities at the Yuri Galanskov–Alexander Ginsburg trial in Moscow. As it was a Friday, the Spenders realized that there could be no response from Amnesty until Monday, by which time Litvinov would be arrested for his outspoken protest. By Monday they had mobilized the support of friends, including W. H. Auden, Julian Huxley, Henry Moore and Igor Stravinsky, and Litvinov was kept out of prison. He suggested that the Spenders might form 'an organization in England that would concern itself with making known the fate of victims of persecution and censorship – writers, scholars, artists, musicians'. And thus *Index on Censorship* was born, set up by David Astor, Edward Crankshaw, Stuart Hampshire, Michael Scammel and Spender.

Christopher Isherwood (1904–1986) Spender had heard a great deal about 'The Novelist of the Future' before Auden decided to introduce the two writers. The meeting took place in 1928 in Auden's rooms in Christ Church, where Spender found Isherwood playing the schoolmaster to an unusually humble Auden, criticizing his poetry. In his own autobiography Isherwood describes Spender bursting in upon them 'blushing, sniggering loudly, contriving to trip over the edge of the carpet – an immensely tall, shambling boy of nineteen, with a great scarlet poppy-face'. It was an unlikely beginning to a friendship that would continue into 1930s Berlin and London and then into post-war America, but the two writers quickly came to treat each other as equals.

Frank Kermode (1919–2010) Spender and the literary critic Frank Kermode became colleagues in 1966 when Kermode was persuaded to take on the position of co-editor of *Encounter*. This collaboration was short-lived, as both editors resigned the following year. However, they became colleagues once again in 1970 when Spender was appointed as a professor at University College London, where he would teach for the following seven years. Kermode himself was then Lord Northcliffe Professor of English at UCL and was using the college as a base from which to introduce French post-structuralist theory to British literary criticism. At the start of his time at UCL Kermode had published his influential *The Sense of An Ending: Studies in the Theory of Fiction* (1967). He would resign in 1982.

Arthur Koestler (1905–1983) Spender met the Hungarian writer when he was living in London during the Second World War, and the two writers were brought together by a shared commitment to social equality and to an ideal of European cooperation. Like Spender, Koestler was attracted to communism in the 1930s and unlike Spender the Hungarian spent seven years as a Party member. But by the late 1940s Koestler (now a naturalized British subject) was an outspoken anti-communist. In 1949, the two writers contributed to Richard Crossman's *The God That Failed*, a collection of essays in which 'six famous men tell how they changed their minds about Communism'. After the war Koestler lived briefly in France, where he formed part of the set gravitating around Jean-Paul Sartre and it was in France that he began his two-year marriage to **Mamaine Paget (1916–1954)**, with Spender attending the nuptials and recording them in the journal.

Irving Kristol see *Encounter*

Hansi Lambert (1900–1960) The widowed head of the Banque Lambert (and member of the Belgian branch of the Rothschild family), Hansi Lambert was the hostess of a distinguished pro-European intellectual salon in post-war Brussels. The Spenders first visited her house in the Avenue Marnix in 1946 and would be frequent visitors to the Lambert establishment over the next decade.

Melvin Lasky see *Encounter*

Rosamond Lehmann (1901–1990) Spender met the novelist, whom he described as 'one of the most beautiful women of her generation', as an undergraduate, and it was through her that he was introduced to Bloomsbury veterans such as Lytton Strachey in 1929. A year later Rosamond introduced Stephen to her younger brother **John Lehmann** (1907–1987). The two hit it off instantly, planning a new publishing house devoted to the Auden Gang in a conversation recalled by Rosamond as a chorus of 'I, I, I, I – like a flock of cawing crows'. Stephen declined John's suggestion that it might 'be splendid if we went to bed' but in 1931 Lehmann, now instated as assistant at the Hogarth Press, urged the Woolfs to take on Spender's novel *The Temple*. This plan came to nothing but Lehmann went on to publish Spender himself in his literary magazine *New Writing* (1936–46).

Joan Littlewood see **Philippe Rothschild**

Robert Lowell (1917–1977) During his spell teaching at Sarah Lawrence College in 1947, Spender was introduced to many of the key figures on the American literary scene. Lowell, currently the Consultant at the Library of Congress in this period, came to do a reading, and the two poets remained friends until Lowell's sudden death in 1977, seeing each other during Spender's frequent extended trips to America.

Mary McCarthy (1912–1989) Spender and McCarthy were colleagues at Sarah Lawrence College in 1947 and quickly became friends. McCarthy was already a successful novelist and political activist and the involvement of both writers in questions of literature and human rights would lead them to meet at several PEN events in the future. Spender was inadvertently responsible for exacerbating the feud between McCarthy and Lillian Hellman when he invited the two to be present at an undergraduate party. Hellman left in a huff, convinced that the event had been set up to 'red-bait me'.

Louis MacNeice (1907–1963) The Mac in 'MacSpaunday', Louis MacNeice was another undergraduate poet and close associate of Auden's. Spender and MacNeice were initially wary of each other. Introduced to the slightly younger poet, MacNeice felt that Spender 'was the nearest to the popular romantic conception of a poet – a towering angel not quite sure if he was fallen'. The two would co-edit *Oxford Poetry* in 1929 and continue to move in the same literary circles in London in the 1930s and 1940s.

Agnes Magruder see **Matthew Spender**

Gian Carlo Menotti (1911–2007) Samuel Barber met Menotti when both were studying at the Curtis Institute in Philadelphia, and their lives and careers proceeded in tandem thereafter. Menotti wrote the libretti for two of Barber's operas and revised a third. In 1958, Menotti founded the Spoleto music festival, which he directed for more than forty years. An offshoot in Charleston, Virginia, was also very successful. Spender took part in several poetry readings at Spoleto in the 1970s and Lizzie Spender became a close friend of Menotti's lover, the American actor and figure skater **Francis 'Chip' Phelan** (**b. 1938**). In 1974, Menotti and Chip bought Yester House at Gifford in Scotland, where the Spenders were occasional visitors.

Henry Moore (1898–1986) The English sculptor was one of several artists with studios in Belsize Park whom Spender visited in the 1930s. Moore made a series of portrait drawings of Spender soon after they met, a rare exception in the sculptor's work. With the onset of serious bombing of London during the war, Moore moved to Much Hadham in Hertfordshire. After the war, the Spenders became frequent visitors. In the 1950s, both men were involved in initiatives organized by UNESCO. In 1960, Spender asked Moore to make an anniversary cover for the hundredth number of *Encounter*. Spender wrote introductions to exhibitions of Moore's work and possessed several drawings and maquettes. Also mentioned in the journals is Moore's daughter **Mary Moore** (**b. 1946**).

Anne Moynihan (née Dunn) (b. 1929) The Spenders knew the English artist in London in the 1930s and 1940s but it was when she became their neighbour in France in the 1960s that they started seeing her regularly. In this period she was married to the Anglo-Spanish artist **Rodrigo Moynihan** (1910–1999) and between 1964 and 1968 they were co-editing *Art and Literature* together with John Ashbery and Sonia Orwell.

Iris Murdoch (1919–1999) The Spenders met the novelist and her husband the literary critic **John Bayley** (**b. 1925**) at a party in 1962. The couple quickly became annual visitors to Mas St Jerome, the

Spenders' house in Provence, swimming in the nearby rivers, streams and ditches. Murdoch's novel *Nuns and Soldiers* (1980) is dedicated to the Spenders and portrays the landscape of the Alpilles near Mas St Jerome.

Nicolas Nabokov (1903–1978) Spender met the composer through Isaiah Berlin in the 1930s. A distant cousin of the writer Vladimir Nabokov, Nicolas was an international figure, multi-lingual and passionately anti-Soviet. After the war he shared with Spender a preoccupation with forming a new European community. With the onset of the Cold War, Nabokov became the Secretary General of the Congress of Cultural Freedom. He was instrumental in supporting Spender's nomination as co-editor of *Encounter*. In 1952, Spender helped with the 'Festival of Twentieth-Century Masterpieces of Modern Arts', which Nabokov was directing for the CCF in Paris. In 1958, at Nabakov's request, Spender wrote the libretto for the opera *Rasputin's End*. Nabokov was better informed than Spender about the CIA's role in the CCF but did not reveal the fact. Knowing the complexity of his background, Spender did not hold it against him and they remained friends.

Bryan Obst (1956–1991) In 1976, the twenty-year-old biology student Bryan Obst attended one of Spender's poetry classes at the University of Florida. The two men became friends and then lovers, with Spender recording the intense joy he experienced with Bryan in his journals and helping Bryan to get his first academic appointment. In 1991, Obst died of Aids. Spender's first mention of Obst's death in the journals is in March 1992.

Sonia Orwell (née Brownell) (1918–1980) The effervescent young aspiring intellectual became part of Spender's circle in the 1930s. From 1940 she worked as an assistant at *Horizon*, where she was often left by Connolly to run the magazine while he lunched. It was in the offices of *Horizon* that she met the writer **George Orwell** (1903–1950) whom she married two months before his death. After Sonia Orwell's own death Spender recalled the 'Venus of the Euston Road', 'with a round Renoir face, limpid eyes, cupid mouth, fair hair, a bit pale, perhaps'.

Mamaine Paget see **Arthur Koestler**

PEN (The International Association of Poets, Playwrights, Essayists and Novelists) (founded 1921) PEN played a crucial role in enabling the cultural acclimatization of exiled European writers in Britain during the war and Spender was a keen supporter of the cause. After the war PEN combined forces with UNESCO in trying to establish a community of cooperative European writers and Spender regularly attended their yearly conferences. In 1976, he was elected as the president of the English branch of PEN.

Francis 'Chip' Phelan see **Gian Carlo Menotti**

David Plante (b. 1940) Together with his long-term partner Nikos Stangos, the American novelist David Plante was a close friend of Spender's. He was a key player in Spender's American social life in the 1970s and 1980s, providing enlivening conversation amidst strenuous lecture tours.

Sylvia Plath see **Ted Hughes**

Reynolds Price (b. 1933) In 1956 Price, then a gifted Rhodes scholar at Oxford writing a PhD on Milton, posted a letter to Spender mentioning that they had met once before and that the poet was 'the kindest-looking man I'd ever seen'. Spender was impressed by Price's novels and short stories and was supportive of his early publications. He visited Price several times at his home in Durham, North Carolina, and the two men remained friends over the next forty years. Spender particularly admired the resilience and courage of Price in facing spinal cancer and its ensuing disability. He remained one of the few people to whom Spender showed unpublished·work for advice and criticism.

Philippe de Rothschild (1902–1988) The Spenders became acquainted with the French racing-car-driver-cum-winegrower in the 1950s. They met through Hansi Lambert, whose late husband was also part of the Rothschild banking dynasty. Over the next decades the Spenders made yearly trips to Mouton, the house of Philippe and his second wife, the fashion designer and writer **Pauline de Rothschild** (née Potter) (1908–1976). After Pauline's death, the British theatre director **Joan Littlewood** (1914–2002) became Philippe's companion.

Victor Rothschild (1910–1990) Spender met the third Baron Rothschild in the 1930s and saw a lot of his then wife **Barbara Hutchinson (b. 1911)** during the Second World War. Rothschild was a communist sympathiser and has been accused of being the so-called 'Fifth Man' in Burgess's and Maclean's 'Cambridge Spy Ring'. Other English Rothschilds to appear in the journals are Victor's sister the zoologist **Miriam Rothschild (1908–2005)** and Victor's and Barbara's children **Sarah (b. 1934)** and **Jacob (b. 1936)**, the present Lord Rothschild. Barbara herself went on to marry Rex Warner and then Nicolas Ghika.

Sir George Schuster (1881–1982) Stephen's maternal uncle was an official of the last phase of the British Empire and the last person to be made a Knight of the Indian Civil Service. A financial expert and experienced bureaucrat, he formed part of the team that advised Mountbatten on the future independence of India. He subsequently took an active part in setting up Atlantic College in Wales, again with the help of Mountbatten. This school and its offshoots are dedicated to nurturing a sense of international cooperation and philanthropy via education at a formative age. Spender viewed his great-uncle with affection and respect, qualified by a feeling – which he may have inherited from his parents – that whereas the Schusters signified power and efficiency, the Spenders were artistic and well-meaning, but confused.

Edith Sitwell (1887–1964) The Spenders met the eccentric aristocratic poet in the early 1940s and she immediately took both under her wing. The two writers were brought together by a love of poetry and at the same time Edith befriended Natasha independently, concerned that she would be lonely while Stephen was on fire service duty. Natasha found that her own 'inexperience of the world of great literature brought out Edith's almost parental desire to protect and instruct' and that the two women enjoyed discussing the merits and foibles of their mutual acquaintances. In 1945, Edith became the godmother of

Matthew Spender and he was brought in a Moses basket to be cared for in her bedroom during literary lunches. Also mentioned in the journals are Sitwell's brothers the writer **Osbert Sitwell (1892–1969)** and the writer and art critic **Sacheverell Sitwell (1897–1988)**.

Nikos Stangos (1936–2004) Spender met the Greek poet in London in 1965. Stangos was serving in the London press office of the Greek embassy. Through Spender, Stangos was introduced to the London literary world, and he worked with Spender and David Hockney on an English edition of the poetry of C. P. Cavafy. The young poet went on to pursue a successful career in publishing, and during his time as editor at Penguin Books in the 1970s Stangos was responsible for publishing American poets such as John Ashbery in England for the first time. Later Spender translated Stangos's poetry and wrote a sonnet celebrating his friendship with the Greek poet and the profundity of their communication: 'When we talk, I imagine silence / Beyond the multiplying words.'

Igor Stravinsky (1882–1971) Spender was introduced to the celebrated Russian composer by Hansi Lambert in 1951. The Spenders were staying with Lambert in Venice for the first performance of the Auden–Stravinsky opera *The Rake's Progress* and they walked across town with Stravinsky and his wife Vera (1888–1982) after the performance. Stravinsky was keen to meet the artistic intelligentsia in England and Spender introduced him to David Jones and then in 1956 to Eliot. The Stravinskys were usually accompanied by the American conductor **Robert (Bob) Craft (b. 1923)** who collaborated with Stravinsky and organized the lives of the older couple.

Dylan Thomas (1914–1953) Spender got to know the young Welsh poet in the early 1930s and admired the energy of his poetry. In 1940, Spender became Thomas's patron when Thomas wrote pleadingly from Swansea complaining that he was buried 'in this worst of provincial towns', desperate for cash. Spender provided favourable reviews and raised a subscription for the alcoholic cadger in literary London, with T. S. Eliot declining to donate any funds on the grounds that Thomas would blow it all on drink. Thomas was a contributor to Natasha Spender's Apollo Society during the war and Spender remained an advocate of Thomas's cause, seeing the Welshman's early death in 1953 as catastrophic for post-war British poetry.

UNESCO (United Nations Education, Science and Cultural Organization) (founded 1945) Spender was invited to be the 'Literary Counsellor to the Section of Letters' for the newly formed organization by Julian Huxley, its first Director General, in 1945. He began by arranging a series of lectures by speakers such as J. B. Priestley and Anna Freud in 1946 and remained with the organization until summer 1947.

Edward Upward (1903–2009) A school friend of Isherwood's, the young novelist was quickly taken up by Auden. Spender first met Upward, then a school teacher, in 1931. In *World Within World* he recalled his 'miniature sensitive beauty of features'. Upward was one of the first card-carrying communists he had met and immediately after the meeting Spender remarked to John Lehmann that 'I think we have all become communists'. Upward was to remain truer to the new faith than Spender, although he was disillusioned by the brutal suppression of the Hungarian uprising in 1956.

Peter Watson see *Horizon* magazine

Virginia Woolf (1882–1941) In 1929, Spender announced to his grandmother that Virginia Woolf had seen his poems and had 'tried in vain to get a copy'. Quickly, Woolf became one of his mentors, advising him to carry on with fiction after Eliot had advised he confine himself to poetry. In 1933, they met for the first time and she recorded in her diary her impression of this 'nice poetic youth; big nosed, bright eyed, like a giant thrush'. She would later state her preference for Spender's 'large sensitive sincerity' over Auden's and Isherwood's 'contorted nerve-drawn brilliancy'; sincerity that appeared to her in a blacker mood as the product of 'a loose jointed mind'. After Woolf's suicide in 1941, Spender described her absence in the *Listener* as 'a light which has gone out'. Two years earlier he himself had made a pact with **Leonard Woolf (1880–1969)** to commit suicide in the case of a German invasion, since both men knew themselves to be on the Nazi blacklist.

Index

Beerbohm, Max, 528
Beethoven, Ludwig van: Brendel at Festival
    Hall, 738; Brendel plays for Spenders, 674;
    and *Cabaret*, 703; Diabelli Variations, 646;
    failure as man, 16, 709; *Fidelio*, 738–9;
    as greatest art, 627; hymns to peace, 6–7;
    and memory, 454; 9th Symphony, 739;
    Richter's *Pathétique*, 706; Stravinsky on,
    265; string quartets, 549, 675
Begin, Menachem, 611
Behrens, Tim, 380
Bell, Julian, 717
Bell, Quentin, 717
Bell, Vanessa, 388, 717
Bellini, Giovanni, 426, 427, 526
Bellow, Saul, 680
Belsen, 250, 563
Benn, Tony, 707–8
Bennett, Arnold, 321
Benson, E. F., 641
Benson, Theodora, 232
Benzion, Hannah, 605
Berenson, Bernard, 74–5, 429–30, 636
Berenson, Mary, *Letters and Journals*, 635–6
Bergonzi, Bernard, *Reading the Thirties*,
    453–4
Berlin: architecture, 207–9; Auden's
    'discovery' of, 501; feeling of commonality,
    301–2; Fuchs case play, 210; gay bars, 619;
    as Isherwood's, 736; political cabarets,
    211; Soloweitschiks' luncheons, 632;
    Wall, 299–300
Berlin, Aline, 335, 350, 375, 389, 391, 469,
    470, 497, 520, 695, 717
Berlin, Sir Isaiah 'Shyah', 287, 288, 335,
    379, 497, 717: on Ackroyd, 695;
    appearance, 584; on Auden, 375; avoids
    Connollys, 112–13; Clarissa Eden on,
    227; conversation with Jobst, 12–13;
    denouncing agent friend query, 520; on
    doomed white race, 680; and *Encounter*,
    140; in Intelligence, 521; Israel trip, 389,
    392; on Jacob Rothschild, 696; at Kennan
    luncheon, 200, 201; knighthood, 623;
    opposes Ayer on Nihilism, 144–5; picks
    influential book, 706; Richter plays for,
    706; on Romantics, 354; on Russians and
    art, 292; S on friendship with, 116; on S's
    Gauss seminar, 353–4; at S's 70th birthday,
    469, 470; Turgenev lecture, 375; on
    Vietnam, 350; visits S in hospital, 535, 686;
    on Wittgenstein, 584–5; on Woolf, 520
Bernal, J. D., 215–16, 219, 220–1
Bernard, Bruce, 601
Bernard, Jeffrey, 601
Bernard, Oliver, 601
Bernecker, Dietrich, 297, 298, 299
Bernier, Georges, 83, 561
Bernier, Peggy, 83, 84, 561
Berns, Walter, 65, 75

Bernstein, Leonard, 542–3, 646–7
Berryman, John, 665
Beth (Obst's friend), 669, 670
Betjeman, John, 368
Bettman, Gilbert, 135–6
Bevan, Aneurin, 156–7
Bevin, Ernest, 52, 61, 414
Bicycle Thieves (film), 64
Bigger Splash, A (documentary), 413
Blackett, Patrick, 261–2
Blackmur, R. P., 110
Blake, William, 427, 462, 477
Blakiston, Noel, 388
Blenheim Palace, 182
Blok, Alexander, *The Twelve*, 282
Blomfield (BBC employee), 107
Bloomsbury group, 548, 585, 614, 718–19
Blunt, Anthony, 519–20, 521–2, 535, 580–1
Bodley, John, 709–10, 726
Bologna, 253–4
Bomberg, David, 310
Bondy, François, 148, 193, 243, 615
Bonington, Richard Parkes, 143
Bonn, 23, 24, 36, 39, 43, 202–7; University,
    40–1, 42, 44–6, 52
Booth, Charles, 237
Borchert, Wolfgang, 178–9
Borges, Jorge Luis, 322
Bosch, Hieronymus, 426
Bosnia, 730–1
Boswell, James, 292, 322
Boulez, Pierre, 289, 334
Bowen, Elizabeth, 65, 508–9, 639; *The Death
    of the Heart*, 523–4
Bower, Tony, 644–5
Bowra, Sir Maurice, 164–5, 168–9, 242, 313
Boxer, Mark, 587; *The Collected and
    Recollected Mark*, 707
Boyle, Sir Edward, 313
Brad (S's former student), 425–6
Bragg, Melvyn, 589
Braine, John, 269
Brandolini, Countess Christiana, 421–2
Brandon, Henry, 341, 351, 352
Brandt Report, 563
Braque, Georges, 336
Brazil, 107–9, 110, 369
Breit, Harvey, 123
Brendel, Adrian, 673, 698
Brendel, Alfred, 585, 646, 674, 698–9
Brendel, Irene 'Reni', 673, 698–9
Brett, Dorothy, 111, 541
Bridges, Harry, 347
Bridges, Robert, 454
Brik, Lily, 267, 449, 450
British Council, 108, 595
Brittain, Victoria, 364
Britten, Benjamin, 117, 344, 493
Broadwater, Boden, 173
Broadwater, Mary, *see* McCarthy, Mary

Brodsky, Joseph: at Auden anniversary, 655–6, 660, 661; character, 656, 664–5; on Eliot and Pound, 606; on Gogol, 508; on Meilakh, 662–4; on Russian dissidents and leaders, 662; on Russian intellectuals, 361; Sontag on, 548; in and on Venice, 507, 508
Brogan, W. J., 200
Bronowski, Jacob, 180–1
Bronxville, 55
Brooke, Rupert, 213–14
Brown, Ann, 587
Brown, Gardner, 587
Browning, John, 344
Browning, Robert, 606; *The Ring and the Book*, 689
Bruce, David K. E., 372
Bruce, Evangeline, 372
Bruern, 307, 323–4
Bruller, Jean, 216
Bruner, Jerome, 340, 341
Brunswick, 11, 258
Brussels, 66–8, 165–6, 175–6, 177
Buchenwald, 103, 250, 739
Bucknell, Katherine, 704
Budapest, 326–34
Buenos Aires, 321–2
Bulganin, Nikolai, 226
Burgess, Guy, 521; Butler on, 279; Connolly censured by Berlin over, 112–13; defects, 581; meets S in Moscow, 267–71; photostat of Lehmann letter, 256
Burns, Robert, 427
Burnside, John, 745
Butler, R. A., 279
Butler, Samuel, 309
Butnera, Reuben, 97
Buttinger, Joseph: on Africa and the West, 260; ill-health, 461, 519, 545; makes pass at Maro, 436; pomposity of, and Muriel, 616; S's second thoughts on, 616–17; on Vietnam, 350, 435–6, 440
Buttinger, Muriel (M – –), 350, 436: at Ashbery party, 439; *Code Name 'Mary'*, 616–17; Foundation of, 605; on Joseph, 440, 461; Konenkov visit with S, 277; Lizzie on, 617–18; as not a 'bore', 549; on nuclear war, 548; S and Tony Hyndman, 546–7; stays with Spenders, 519
Button, John, 287
Byron, Lord, 282, 399, 462, 504, 589

Cabaret (film), 703
Cadbury, George, 635
Calder, John, 311
Calder-Marshall, Arthur, 206
Callaghan, James, 457, 458
Callil, Carmen, 692
Cambodia, 563
Cambridge, University of, 431, 470, 580–1, 584–5

Cameron, Alan, 508–9, 524
Cameron, Roderick 'Rory', 629, 631, 635, 648, 649, 675
Campagnolo, Umberto, 215, 218, 253–4
Campbell, Archie, 197–8
Campkin, Denis, 370
Camus, Albert, 70, 707
Canterbury, University of, 613–14
Capote, Truman, 354–5
Caravaggio, 429
Carlyle, Thomas, 314
Carpaccio, Vittore, 427
Carr, E. H., 712–13
Carr, Raymond, 323
Carrington, Lady, 689, 690
Carrington, Lord, 637, 689, 690
Carritt, Gabriel, 111–12, 413, 482
Carson, Rachel, *Silent Spring*, 706
Carter, Billy, 544
Carter, Jimmy, 513, 529, 544, 644
Caruso, Igor, 168
Causley, Charles, 590
Cavett, Dick, 473, 542
Ceylon, 148–9
Cézanne, Paul, 259
Chadwick, Owen, 690–1
Chadwick, Ruth, 690
Chagall, Eva, 275
Chagall, Marc, 274, 275
Chamberlain, Neville, 4, 38
Chambers, Anne Cox, 631, 635, 695, 696, 717; at Atlanta banquet, 661, 662; on Democratic candidates, 648–9; fund-raising for *Index*, 604; and humanity of the rich, 643–4; New York apartment, 732–3; parties in Provence, 639–42, 648
Chambers, James Cox, 640, 643
Chambers, Kathy Cox, 662
Chambers, Lauren, 640, 643
Chandler, Raymond: declines coffee and brandy, 162; farewell dinner, 232; MacShane biography, and Natasha, 437–9, 440; on Natasha as musician, 153; promised bequest to Natasha, 238
Chaplin, Charlie, 225–6, 227
Charles, Prince of Wales, 433, 517, 553
Charlie (AFS sub-officer), 27–8
Chatto, Beth, 560
Chekhov, Anton, 334
Chiari, Joseph, 614
Chiaromonte, Nicola, 243, 244
Chicago, 62–4, 335, 480, 681
China: bicycles in, 594–5; and children's stories, 215; Cultural Revolution, 592, 594, 597–8; Gates on communism in, 513–14; Hong Kong handover, 692; S visits with Hockney, 591–8; US aim in Vietnam, 352; Wei and *Encounter*, 154–5, 184, 185
Christiansen, Arthur, 255, 256–7
Christiansen, Rupert, 672

reading, 19, 68; as Apollonian, 21–2; denounces Nazis, 37; disgust at Germans, 48–9, 51; *Europäische Literatur und lateinisches Mittelalter*, 589; on European history, 590–1; first meeting with S, 17–19, 36; as Goethean egoist, 22–3; and Goyen, 699–700; in love with S, 700; on Occupation, 40; remains in Germany under Hitler, 37–8; sells books, 47; and S's Cologne robbery, 24; S's post-war visit, 202–7; as S's teacher, 36–7, 203–4; on Third Reich, 38, 40; translates S's poems, 19

Curtius, Ilse, 36–7, 202, 203

Curzon, Clifford, 456, 470–1, 536, 618–20, 682

Curzon, Lucille, 470–1, 619

Czechoslovakia, 25, 378

Czerny, Carl, 674

Dachau, 632

Daily Express, 255, 256–7, 309

Daily Telegraph, 676, 706

Dalí, Salvador, 426

Dam Busters, The (film), 157, 158

Dana, Robert, 684–5

Daniels, Tony, 557

Danquah, Paul, 293, 304

Dartmouth College, New Hampshire, 417

Datta, Sundrin, 200

Daumaerts (invalid in Paris), 83–4

Davenport, John, 185

Davidson, Michael, 407

Davie, Donald, 330, 457–8, 462

Davie, Doreen, 462, 485

Davis, Rhys, 330

Day Lewis, Cecil, 401, 454; in Auden group, 483; biography by son, 535; *Complete Poems*, 672–3; and Eliot, 367; Hensher on, 736; memorial service, 368; Nicholas Blake books, 511; S luckier than, 737; S's dreams of, 456, 590

Day Lewis, Jill, 361, 368, 672–3

Day-Lewis, Daniel, 673, 736

Day-Lewis, Sean, 535

Dayton, University of, 341–4

de la Mare, Walter, 322

Deakin, William, 200

Deer Hunter, The (film), 485, 486, 490

Delbanco, Gustav, 371–2

Delbée-Masurel, Suzy, 432, 433

Deutsch-Englische Society, 207

Devonshire, Andrew, 588

Dewey, Alvin, 354

Dewey, John, 657

d'Harnoncourt, René, 275

Diaghilev, Sergei, 620

Diana, Princess of Wales, 679

Dickey, James, 347

Donne, John, 363, 511–12

Donoghue, Denis, 614

Dos Passos, John, 126

Dostoevsky, Fyodor, 18, 19, 204, 281; 'A Gentle Creature', 68; *Notes from the Underground*, 68

Douglas, Lord Alfred, 314

Douglas, Norman, 109

Douglas, Sharman, 350

Douglas-Henry, Jim, 310

Douro, Arthur Wellesley, Marquess of, 698

Dover, Cedric, 155

Drabble, Margaret, 540, 697, 741

Driberg, Tom, 279, 291, 310

Drouin, Gisa, 48, 632

Dryden, John, 365, 371

Dubček, Alexander, 643

Dubuffet, Jean, 444

Dudley, Grace, Countess of, 471

Dufferin, Lindy, 652–3

Dufferin, Sheridan, 652

Dumas, Dick, 648

Dumenil, Mrs and Miss (of Texas), 660

Dumur, Guy, 528, 529–30

Dupee, F. W., 359

Durrell, Lawrence, 294, 320

Duse, Eleonora, 525

Dux, Dr, 105

Eberhart, Betty, 466

Eberhart, Dick, 466

Eddington, Sir Arthur Stanley, 706

Eden, Anthony, 271

Eden, Clarissa, 225, 226–7

Edinburgh, 319–21; Festival, 428; University, 370

Edward VIII, King, 433

Egremont, Max Wyndham, 2nd Baron, 675

Ehrenberg, Victor, 281

Ehrenburg, Ilya, 267

Einstein, Albert, 278

Eisenhower, Dwight D., 260

Eliot, George, 589

Eliot, T. S., 274, 345, 454, 539, 541; on addressing large crowd, 264–5; Aiken on, 357–8; on Auden, 173; book sales, 124; Canterbury celebration, 613–14; character, 614; Cummings's nickname for, 64; defends Wyndham Lewis, 295; dislikes Craft, 367; double negatives, 112; eliminates self in poetry, 195; and European nostalgia, 314; and Hardy, 606; indifferent to Day Lewis, 367; irony in, 316; Juliette Huxley on, 407; lectures in US, 141–2; at Lehmann luncheon, 121, 122, 123; on magazines, 170; meeting with Stravinsky, 262–4; poetry in his drama, 447; on Pound, 357; Rebecca West on, 320; and religion, 691; self-dramatizing of, 212; signs books, 285; Soviet writers on, 282; and Symbolism, 606; TV show on, 400; 'uninfluenced' by Santayana, 356–7; as unprolific, 152

Freud, Lucian, 469: on Auden, 248; Auden on, 240; Auerbach on, 582; Bacon on, 240; Craxton on, 89; Dean Street house, 181; effect of war on, 177; and S's 'invisible *ménage*', 181–2; typical girlfriends of, 173

Freud, Sigmund, 320, 654

Freudian psychology, 105

Frost, Robert, 138, 139, 357, 564–5, 727

Fry, Christopher, 516

Fry, Jeremy, 639

Fuchs, Klaus, 210

Furtseva, Ekaterina 'Mme', 561

Gainesville, 445–6, 464, 465, 468, 485, 669–70, 685

Gaitskell, Dora, 189, 310

Gaitskell, Hugh, 173, 189–90, 280, 310

Gallacher, William, 64

Gandhi, Indira, 649

Gardiner, Margaret, 308, 502, 698

Gardiner, Muriel, *see* Buttinger, Muriel

Garnett, Angelica, 718–19, 723, 724

Garnett, David 'Bunny', 718–19

Garnett, Edward, 320

Garrett, Jackie, 367

Garrett, Tony, 469

Garvin, James Louis, 677

Gascoyne, David, 88

Gates, Thomas, 513–14

Gattuso, Renato, 253

Gaudier-Brzeska, Henri, 275

Gauguin, Paul, 16, 413, 492

Gaulle, Charles de, 637

Gearin-Tosh, Michael, 689, 690

Geldzahler, Henry, 613, 653

Gellhorn, Martha, 574–5, 576

General Post Office Film Unit, 408

Germany

– POST-WAR: Allied Occupation, 40–2, 46, 51, 60, 177, 563; anti-Semitism, 209; border with East, 298, 299–300, 311; Calder on, 311; CIA in, East, 311; Curtius's prognosis, 204; dehumanisation of language, 302; destruction of Cologne, 33–6; guilt about Nazi period, 299; mechanical toys, 178; need for outstanding individuals, 51–3; paucity of people of good will, 50; Rapacki Plan, 300; rearmament, 300–1, 303; remnants of Nazism, 304; restoration of cities, 177–8, 179; reviving political life, 51; and unified Europe, 72

– THIRD REICH: atrocities, 250; and Beethoven, 739; concentration camps, 103, 250, 563, 632, 739; Curtius denounces Nazis, 37; dilemma of anti-Nazi Germans, 39; dupes of, 11–12; education in, 40, 44–6; English perception of Nazi idealism, 37–8; graffiti, 43; and Jews, 9–10, 11, 48, 102; Nicholas Mosley on, 710; Night

of the Long Knives, 38; opposition of intellectuals, 51; Philippe de Rothschild's escape, 576; resistance in Rhineland, 45–6; Ribbentrop–Molotov pact, 20–1, 25–6; secret weapons, 25; treatment of Poles, 49–50, 51

– WEIMAR REPUBLIC: absence of sin, 7; beginning of end, 10; friendship in, 8; S robbed in Cologne, 23–4; sense of peace in, 6, 7; S's reminiscences, 576–7; weakness and fatigue in, 13, 14

Ghandi, Indira, 553

Ghani, Cyrus, 469, 470, 536

Ghika, Barbara, 386, 549

Ghika, Nicolas, 293, 549

Giacometti, Alberto, 229, 335–6

Giacometti, Giovanni, 336

Gide, André, 205, 420

Gielgud, John, 186, 187–8

Gifford, Charles, 493

Gifford, Lettie, 493

Giles, Frank, 675, 730

Giles, Kitty, 675, 730

Gilmour, Ian, 637

Ginsberg, Allen, 353, 476–7

Giroux, Robert, 124

Gladwyn, Gladwyn Jebb, 1st Baron, 493

Glazer, Nathan, 153

Glenconner, Christopher Tennant, 2nd Baron, 154, 162, 163, 296, 313, 469, 505

Glenconner, Elizabeth, Lady, 154, 162, 240, 296, 310, 313, 469, 505

Glenn, John, 649

Glyndebourne, 728–9, 743

God that Failed, The (collection), 706

Godine, David, 705

Goebbels, Dr Joseph, 11–12, 39, 42

Goering, Hermann, 49

Goethe, J. W. von, 21, 22, 37, 589

Gogol, Nikolai, *The Government Inspector*, 508

Golding, John, 535, 672, 716

Goldsmith, Jim, 466

Gollancz, Victor, 111, 190

Gorbachev, Mikhail, 713

Gordon, Caroline, 62

Gorky, Arshile, 289, 444, 734–5

Gorky, Magouche, *see* Phillips, Magouche

Gorky, Maro, *see* Spender, Maro

Gosling, Ray, 292

Gowing, Sir Lawrence, 469, 601, 621, 623

Gowrie, Grey Ruthven, 2nd Earl of, 552

Goyen, William, 65–6, 589; *Selected Letters*, 699–700; *The White Rooster*, 75

Graham, Kay, 354

Graham-Yooll, Andrew, 676

Grange, Henry-Louis de La, 85

Grant, Duncan, 119, 388, 719

Grass, Günter, 330

Graves, Maurice, 336

550; as 'most wonderful place in world', 457–8; National Gallery, 258, 517; National Theatre, 315, 498, 505, 518, 550–1; Neal Street Restaurant, 371; Poetry Society, 365; Queen Mary's College, 249; Queen Mary's Hospital, 686–7; Ritz, 497; Royal College of Art, 469–70; Royal Free Hospital, 518, 519, 521, 532–7; Sadler's Wells, 133, 703; Savoy, 262, 364–5, 568; in Second World War, 4, 10, 26, 27; Slade, 289, 292; Stafford Hotel, 377, 399; Tate, 291, 624, 650; Tricycle Theatre, 745–6; White Tower Restaurant, 164; Zoo, 495; Zwemmers, 740

London Magazine, 170, 372

Longford, Elizabeth Harman Pakenham, Countess of, 111–12, 469, 730

Longford, Frank Pakenham, 7th Earl of, 111–12, 169, 190, 414, 469, 519, 730

Loos, Anita, 490

Lorca, Federico García, 243, 626

Los Angeles, 571–3, 593, 652–3

Lothar (Alport's friend), 576–7

Low, David, 65

Low, Helen, 678

Lowell, Elizabeth, *see* Hardwick, Elizabeth

Lowell, Robert, 349: on Auden, 359; Auden on, 665; 'Central Park', 345; character, 551–2; on English literature, 360; envies Russian poets, 714; isolation of, 415; and Jarrell's death, 340; mental health, 63, 344, 358–9, 419; on Pound and Wordsworth, 335; as self-absorbed, 360; on Vietnam, 345

Lübeck, 298

Ludwig, Margaret, 423

Luft, Friedrich, 299

Lukacs, Georg, 331–4, 378

Lushington, Stephen, 312

Lynchburg, 509

Lynd, Helen, 658

Lynd, Robert, 658

Maar, Dora, 293–4

Macaulay, Robie, 329

Macaulay, Rose, 91

MacCarthy, Diarmuid, 650–1

McCarthy, Mary, 172, 245, 287, 322; on *Encounter* editors, 244; Hellman lawsuit, 542–3, 657; and James West, 358; on national novel, 319–20; 'The Oasis', 55–6; PEN club in Venice, 614, 615; at Sarah Lawrence College, 658; visits S in hospital, 536

MacDonald, Dwight, 160, 193–4, 286–7, 329

McDougall, Gordon, 562

McGrath, Camilla, 334, 416, 490, 660, 733

McGrath, Earl, 334, 349, 416, 660–1, 733–4

McIlhenny, Henry, 435, 513

Mackenzie, Compton, 64

McKinley, Hazel Guggenheim, 476, 477

Maclean, Donald, 112–13, 256

Macmillan, Adam, 495

Macmillan, Harold, 269, 352, 382, 495

MacNeice, Hedli, 255

MacNeice, Louis, 122, 153, 184–5, 255: aloofness of, 348; American 'hatred' of, 64; Bergonzi on, 454; Hensher article, 736; S on, 463; S luckier than, 737; *The Strings are False*, 347–8

MacShane, Frank, 437

Madariaga, Don Salvador de, 322

Magritte, René, 426

Mahler, Gustav, *Songs of a Wayfarer*, 130–1

Mailer, Norman, 287, 603

Maine, University of, 541–2

Malevich, Kazimir, 274, 276

Malraux, André: Curtius on, 205; experience of communism, 70; on European Union, 81; gift to S, 83; on Koestler, 80; on Soviet Union and US, 81–2

Malraux, Clara, 395–6

Malraux, Madeleine, 81

Manhattan (film), 485–6, 488, 490

Mann, Thomas, 178; *Buddenbrooks*, 333

Mao Zedong, 592, 596

Marceau, Gabriel, *L'Oeuf*, 285–6

Margaret, Princess, 89, 171, 350, 351, 469

Mariano, Elisabetta 'Nicky', 74, 636

Marina, Princess, Duchess of Kent, 198

Marks, Alan, 544–5

Marmora, Count Alberto della, 619

Marshall (*Times* correspondent), 107

Marshall, Margaret, 55, 58

Marx, Karl, 707

Marxism: Campagnolo on, 218; Mazzocco's, 472; S on, 84; teaching in US, 126; *see also* communism

Mas St Jerome (S's house in Provence), 553–8, 599, 622, 631: selling, 716; tenants, 648; visitors to, 361–2, 428–34, 635–8, 639–40, 719, 723

Masani, Minochef Rustin, 200

Matson, Peter, 418

Matta, Roberto, 444

Maud, John, 413

Maussane, *see* Mas St Jerome

Maxy (Lizzie Spender's friend), 367, 372

May, Derwent, 518, 627

Mayer, Elizabeth, 501

Mayer, Sir Robert, 494

Mayne, Peter, 318

Mayou (*communisant*), 254

Mazzocco, Robert 'Bill', 435, 439, 471, 472–3, 490, 603, 708

Medley, Robert, 500, 726

Meilakh, Boris, 663

Meilakh, Mikhail, 662–4

Melitz, Dr, 97–8

painting and drawing: abstraction, 399–400; Bacon exhibition, 291, 293; Bacon and Pollock contrasted, 410; Berlin on Russians, 292; Cubism, 612, 624, 628; the dead in, 598–9; and *Encounter*, 283–4, 289, 290; and English landscape, 143; Hockney on modern art, 411; Hockney's uniqueness, 382; logic of Surrealism, 427; of mad expressionist, 19; Matthew Smith's views, 191–2; Modernism and idealism, 627–8; Moore's hierarchy, 336; Morandi's studio, 251–3; as most objective of arts, 17; Motherwell on US artists, 444–5; painters' education, and war, 177; Peggy Guggenheim on, 426; Piper on English, 296; Rembrandt in Brunswick, 11, 258; Rembrandt exhibition in Rotterdam, 257–9; in Soviet Union, 274–7; Sutherland as investment, 120; under communism, 330; see also *individual painters*
Pakenham, Frank, *see* Longford, 7th Earl of
Pakenham, Michael, 730
Pakenham, Mimi, 730
Pakenham, Tom, 505
Palestine, 393–4
Palmon, Joshua, 393–5
Palumbo, Hayat, 677
Palumbo, Peter, 677, 679
Pares, Sir Brendan, 658
Paris: Café de Flore, 83–4; CCF office, 137; German occupation, 48; Hemingway incident, 574–5; Hockney's studio, 410–11; Koestler's house, 78; 'les évènements', 623; Pauline de Rothschild's flat, 449–50; Stravinsky's 80th birthday, 289–90
Parker, Peter, 736, 742
Parladé, Jaime, 588
Partisan Review (magazine), 54, 63
Partridge, Frances, 313, 693–4
Pasmore, Victor, 399
Pasternak, Boris, 271, 706, 714, 725
Patten, Brian, 366
Patten, Chris, 692
Peak, Michael, 374–5
Pearn, Inez, *see* Spender, Inez
Pears, Peter, 493
Pearson, Norman Holmes, 402
Peking, 594–5
PEN Club: abstract discussions at, 299–300; congress in Buenos Aires, 321–2; Darina Silone's reminiscences, 70; London conference, 255; Porter interviews S, 704; S awarded gold pen, 741; S as president, 404; Tokyo conference, 671; UNESCO notice, 89–90; Venice trip, 614; Vienna meeting and party, 166, 167, 168
Penn, Sir Eric, 495, 496
Penna, Lucy, 578
Penrose, Roland, 155
Peters, A. D., 64

Pfreim, Bernard, 628
Philadelphia, 344, 435; Museum of Art, 58–9
Phillips, Antonia, 469, 628
Phillips, Guy, 730
Phillips, Magouche, 293, 309, 444, 468–9
Phillips, Rebecca, 675–6, 730
Phillips, William, 135
Phillips, Wogan, 580, 675
Picasso, Pablo: Bacon on, 293–4; Blue Period, 7; as centrifugal, 259; classical style, 627; as genius, 631; Matthew Spender's drawing, 288; Moore on, 336; paintings of women, 632
Picture Post, 88
Pilkington, Richard, 404
Pinsky, Robert, 478
Pinter, Antonia, *see* Fraser, Antonia
Pinter, Harold, 315, 376, 446, 709, 742; on Antonia Fraser, 515–16; on *The Corporal*, 505; Peggy Ramsay on, 498; on S's poems, 746
Piper, John, 295–6, 399, 469, 470, 691
Piper, Myfanwy, 469
Piranesi, Giovanni Battista, 245
Pitt-Rivers, Michael, 169, 194, 586
Plante, David, 375, 451, 469, 535, 601, 621, 732: *Annunciation*, 731; on Chandler and Natasha, 440; on Greer, 571; London flat, 673; and poetry, 708; in Provence, 362; on Stokes's death, 376; visits S in hospital, 686
Plath, Sylvia, 284–5, 745
Plimpton, George, 574
Plomer, William, 91, 121, 390, 512, 524
poetry: absurd UNESCO notice, 90; Auden on form, 338; Auden on impossibility of, 196; Auden's dogmatism, 482; and dreaming, 654; Elizabethan, 212; forgotten poets remembered, 673; German, backwardness of, 179; Indian, prolixity of, 149; and intellectuals, 173–4; and madness, 402–3; and memory, 454; Modernist, and Symbolism, 606; and necessity of escape, 152; poets in Brazil, 110; reviews more read than poems, 345; and science, 180–1; as self-delusion, 564; self-dramatizing of poets, 212; Shakespeare prefigures Metaphysical poets, 511–12, 516; twentieth century, as tiresome, 171; in theatre, 446–8; unhappy American poets, 665–6; use of 'I', 195; as unread in West, 714; Yevtushenko on, 289; see also *individual poets*
Poland, 4, 725; abstract art in, 330; Calder on, 311; Jewish emigration to Israel, 105–6; perception of Germans, 49–50, 51
Polevoy, *see* Kampov, Boris
Pollitt, Harry, 61, 64
Pollock, Jackson, 277, 410
Pompidou, Georges, 692
Pope, Alexander, 365, 371

with Buttinger, 436; on his daughter, 526;
escapes Nazis, 576; generosity, 560; and
Joan Littlewood, 498–9, 560; and Pauline's
death, 443; and Pauline's grave, 528, 531;
Pauline's unhappiness with, 561, 604–5;
and Queen Mother, 516, 517; at St Jerome,
432–4; as top sommelier, 434; translation
of Elizabethan poems, 363; in Venice,
424–5; wine for S's 70th birthday, 469;
see also Mouton Rothschild, Château
Rothschild, Philippine de, 432, 443, 526
Rothschild, Robert de, 363
Rothschild, Sarah, 182–3
Rothschild, Teresa, 698
Rotterdam, 257–9
Rougemont, Denis de, 148
Rousseau, Jean-Jacques, 82
Roy, Claude, 254, 623
Roy, Jamini, 251
Royal Shakespeare Company, 373, 498
Runciman, Steven, 171
Rushdie, Salman, 720
Rusk, Dean, 359
Ruskin, John, 313, 428, 727
Russell, Bertrand, 332, 583
Russell, John, 289, 490, 569, 621, 717
Russell, Maud, 562
Russell, Rosamond, 490, 569, 621, 717
Russia, *see* Soviet Union
Ryan, Nin, 567
Rylands, Dadie, 363, 580

Saatchi, Maurice, 693
Sacchetti, Giocondo, 196, 197
Sackville-West, Vita *see* Nicolson, Vita
Sadat, Anwar El, 412
Sadler, Sir Michael, 312, 413, 492
Sainsbury, Mr and Mrs, 428
St Jerome, *see* Mas St Jerome
St John-Stevas, Norman, 637
St Laurent, Yves, 411, 450
Salinger, J. D., 330
Saltwood Castle, 620–1, 744
Samuel, Mr (US academic), 135
Sansom, William, 122, 289
Santa Barbara, 443
Santa Monica, 430, 667–71, 736
Santayana, George, 356–7
Sarah Lawrence College, Yonkers, 425, 657,
658
Sargent, Sir Malcolm, 264
Sartre, Jean-Paul, 79–80, 215, 219–20, 332,
707
Scargill, Arthur, 643
Scarisbrick, J. J., *Henry VIII*, 561
Schiller, Friedrich, 21
Schlesinger, Alexandra, 603
Schlesinger, Arthur M., 140, 339, 733
Schlesinger, Marion, 339
Schnabel, Artur, 471, 619, 682

Schneider, Alexander 'Sascha', 645–8, 649
Schnurre, Wolfdietrich, 299
Schubert, Franz, 6, 576, 618, 627, 706
Schuchard, W. Ronald, 704
Schuster, E. J., 500
Schuster, Sir George (uncle), 452–3
Schuster, Gwen (aunt), 452, 553
Schuster, Violet Hilda (mother), 506
Schutz, Dr, 202
Schwarzenberg, Johannes von, 241
Schwarzenberg, Princess, 241
Scott, Geoffrey, 636
Scott, Norman, 495
Scott, Rivers, 536
Scott-Montagu, Lady Elizabeth, 194
sculpture: Konenkov's peasant style,
277–8; Moore on Giacometti, 229, 335–6;
Moore's experiments, 318–19; S's poem,
491
Sederowsky, Ben, 410, 411
Second World War: air-raid warnings, 10;
barrage balloons, 4; Blackout, 26, 27;
creativity in, 157; destruction of Cologne,
33–6; and English realism, 13–14; Italian
Resistance, 76; 1940 as miracle, 158; S's
day dreams about, 20–1; S's Intelligence
friends, 521; Wollheim on sex after, 563;
see also Germany
Seferis, George, 304
Seitz, Caroline, 696, 730, 731
Seitz, Raymond, 695, 696, 730–1
Selig, Richard, 182–3
Seligman, Kurt, 444
Sennett, Richard, 544–5, 570, 605, 655
Serkin, Peter, 647, 648
Serkin, Rudolf, 647
Sessions, Roger, 471
Sewanee, 140–1; river, 465
sex: affairs in 1930s as 'kitchen sink',
170–1, 183; birth control, 29; bisexuality
in Germany, 8; casual, 472–3; charm
of youth, 703, 716; as distinct from
relationships, 15–16; and German notion
of freedom, 14; and guilt, 180; as key to
society, 746; literature as pornographic,
402, 413; and love, 15–16; Macmillan
on 'sexual immorality', 382; in occupied
Germany, 563; and old age, 746–7; in
Russia, 725; Sally Coole's tastes, 108;
S's Hamburg life as 'pornography', 19;
S's penis, 483; syphilis in Brazil, 110; in
Wordsworth and Lawrence, 195; *see also*
homosexuality
Shaffer, Peter: *Amadeus*, 518, 589; *Equus*,
446, 447
Shakespeare, William: Auden on, 462;
Hamlet, 428, 511–12, 516; Jill Fairchild
on, 612; *King Lear*, 325, 447, 454; Lowell
on, 360; *Macbeth*, 185–7, 427, 551;
Matthew Spender on, 701; Moore on,

Spender, Matthew (son), 451, 461, 589, 717:
and Angelica Garnett, 719; at Ashbery
party, 439; on Chandler, 437; dead fish,
237–8; dormouse gift, 120; driving style,
728; engravings, 372; family squabble in
Avane, 719; first exhibition, 371; *From
a High Place*, 734–5; gift gaffe, 193; on
God, 514; house in Avane, 525–6; insight
about Lizzie, 159; on Jesus, 114; on
Leavitt plagiarism, 701–2, 708; on life
before Beethoven, 599; on Loudoun Rd
house, 737–8; makes doll's house, 523,
526; Maro 'protects', 629; in New York,
435; Oxford interviews, 323–4; as painter,
526; passes Connolly's test, 198–9; prints
of Cosima, 380; return to London, 371; S
teaches Latin, 153, on school, 288–9; 238;
smoking as child, 183–4; on sparks from
horses, 151; as S's greatest accomplishment,
128; and S's knighthood, 622–3; Swanage
trip, 145–6; in Torri del Benaco, 127–8,
183; trapped finger, 237; upset on leaving
Washington, 340; in Venice with S, 421–8,
507–9, 598–9; visits S in hospital, 537, 686;
Within Tuscany, 686
Spender, Michael (brother), 199
Spender, Natasha (wife), 173, 228, 232,
292, 297, 505, 576, 585, 589, 598, 628:
arranges S's 70th birthday, 469–70; aural
perception research, 341; on Backhaus,
645, 646; and Connolly's day-dream, 171;
and Curzon, 470, 471, 619; defends Craft,
367; on dreaming, 163; dressmaking, 380;
effect of her absence on S, 666; on event of
S's death, 716; Goyen's dream, 65; health
and illness, 152–3, 363, 374, 375; as
hostess, 430; on Jews, 116; and ladyship,
615; and Lizzie's unhappy childhood, 366;
on longevity, 553; and Matthew, 468–9;
olive-picking essay, 673; on Oppenheimer,
261; overhears S's Obst and Isherwood
calls, 484–5; piano playing, 81, 153, 545,
640, 641, 674, 682; promised bequests to,
238; questions Gen. Rogers, 639–40; at the
Sitwells, 316, 318; on sleep, 629; and
S's death, 638, 738; and S's hip injury, 733,
734, 735; upset by Chandler biography,
437–9, 440; visits Booths, 698; visits S in
hospital, 532, 537; writing for money, 683
Spender, Philip (nephew), 374, 536
Spender, Quentin (nephew), 651–2
Spender, Saskia (grandchild), 371, 379,
380–1, 683, 701, 719, 737
Spender, Sir Stephen
– HEALTH: breaks knee ligaments, 531–7,
566; fainting anxiety, 728, 729; hernia,
686; hip injury, 733–5; radiotherapy for
cancer, 519, 521; sleeplessness, 701, 737;
taken ill at Ivy, 717–18; whiteouts and
blackouts, 724

– MISCELLANEOUS REMARKS AND EVENTS:
on adults as children, 630; application
for translator job, 17; on attraction of
war, 19; on Auberon Waugh's review,
630–1; in Auden group, 483; Auden
prepares obituary, 308; on being repelled
by the Left, 643; on bequests, 238–9;
on capitalism and frivolity, 510; Ceylon
and India trip, 148–50; on children's
unhappiness, 556–7; China visit with
Hockney, 591–8; on cliques and 'the
boring', 548–9; on communicating with
the living, 448–9; Como 'conversazione',
689–91; curious hallucination, 234; day
dreams, 20; on death and the corpse,
737, 738; on death and friends, 232–3,
381, 383; on death and historical figures,
234–5; dream of Auden, 383; dream of
Peter Watson, 248–9; dreams of Day
Lewis, 456, 590; on dreams and vision,
163; on dying, 638, 737; East–West
intellectuals' meeting, 215–21, 281; at
European Cultural Association, 254–5;
on facets of others, 245; on fame, 709;
on famine and war on TV, 563, 684;
Gellhorn/Hemingway incident, 574–6; on
his generation and 'getting stuck', 308–9;
on Hell, 179–80; Hungarian trip, 326–32;
on global inequality, 527; on hallucinatory
love, 420; on hatred of traffic, 367–8; on
hospital visits, 462–4; on the 'individual',
460; intimidated by Annan, 431; Israel
trips, 96–106, 389–98; joins AFS, 27–32;
on love of publicity, 403; on marriage,
441–2; on meat-eating, 391; at Mermaid
Club, 246–7; on the moneyed, 640, 643–4,
693; Moscow tour, 267–78, 714; on oil,
578; on old age, 297, 451–2, 515, 626,
716, 724; on old couples and babies,
610–11; on pacifism, 5, 21, 603; on
partly liking Auden, 481–2; on party for
egoists, 649; PEN club in Venice, 614,
615–16; picks influential book, 706; Pope
nightmare, 553–4; post-war Curtius visit,
202–7; premature obituaries of S, 736;
prints Auden's poems, 705, 726; protests
UNESCO Israel boycott, 385; on reactions
to farting, 461; on reality and the senses,
474, 644; on reading history, 561–2;
reasons for happiness, 400; receives CBE,
295, 590; receives knighthood, 614–15,
621, 622–3; redemption through art, 188;
reviews life's achievements, 533–4, 537,
583–4; robbed in Cologne, 23–4; Rome
editors' meeting, 243–5; sails to Haifa,
94–6; saving the world fantasy, 527–7;
self-analysis, 85–8, 246; 70th birthday,
467, 469–70; on socialists' dilemma, 78;
Spain trip, 442; stays with the A. J. P.
Taylors, 710–12; on students' reading,